Wissenschaftliche Untersuchungen
zum Neuen Testament · 2. Reihe

Herausgeber / Editor
Jörg Frey (Zürich)

Mitherausgeber / Associate Editors
Markus Bockmuehl (Oxford) · James A. Kelhoffer (Uppsala)
Tobias Nicklas (Regensburg) · Janet Spittler (Charlottesville, VA)
J. Ross Wagner (Durham, NC)

597

Jacob A. Rodriguez

Combining Gospels in Early Christianity

The One, the Many, and the Fourfold

Mohr Siebeck

Jacob A. Rodriguez, born 1987; BA and MA at Wheaton College; DPhil at the University of Oxford; Assistant Professor of New Testament at Trinity School for Ministry, Ambridge. orcid.org/ 0000-0001-9761-8146

ISBN 978-3-16- 161471-2 / eISBN 978-3-16- 161973-1
DOI 10.1628/978-3-16- 161973-1

ISSN 0340-9570 / eISSN 2568-7484
(Wissenschaftliche Untersuchungen zum Neuen Testament, 2. Reihe)

The Deutsche Nationalbibliothek lists this publication in the Deutsche Nationalbibliographie; detailed bibliographic data are available at *https://dnb.de*.

© 2023 Mohr Siebeck Tübingen, Germany. www.mohrsiebeck.com

This book may not be reproduced, in whole or in part, in any form (beyond that permitted by copyright law) without the publisher's written permission. This applies particularly to reproductions, translations and storage and processing in electronic systems.

The book was printed on non-aging paper and bound by Gulde-Druck in Tübingen.

Printed in Germany.

for Tessa

τερπέσθην μύθοισι πρὸς ἀλλήλους ἐνέποντε

Preface

The present monograph is an edited version of my doctoral thesis, which I defended at Oxford University in September 2021. I am grateful to Prof. Jörg Frey for accepting my manuscript for publication in the WUNT II series, and for the helpful suggestions offered by the editorial team.

I would like to thank my *Doktorvater*, Prof. Markus Bockmuehl, for his tireless supervision and generous friendship throughout this project. His vast knowledge of Christian, Jewish, and Greco-Roman antiquity, his meticulous attention to detail, and his reverence for Sacred Scripture came through in every meeting; ὑπομνηματίζω αὐτὰ ἐν τῇ ἐμῇ καρδίᾳ (cf. *Hist. eccl.* 5.20.5–7). I am exceedingly grateful to my examiners, Prof. Simon Gathercole and Dr. Andrew Gregory, who engaged my thesis with robust, critical, and sympathetic advice; my thesis benefited greatly from their input, and any remaining shortcomings are entirely my own.

I am grateful to Dr. Peter Head, who gave invaluable feedback, entirely out of his own generosity and love for the subject matter. Prof. Jenn Strawbridge and Dr. Eric Eve also gave crucial input and regular encouragement. It is hard to do justice to the immense help that Jeremiah Coogan offered as a friend and colleague; not only was my content improved by his expertise, but my prose was regularly saved by his better grasp of the English language. Andrew T. Cowan has been a constant sounding board and dear friend. Daniel Schumann helped bring my German to fighting condition, without which I could not have handled the secondary literature. Shannon Parrott gave much-needed encouragement during the final stages of writing. Prof. Charles Hill, whose scholarship inspired much of my own thinking, encouraged me and shared resources throughout the writing and editing process. Ian Mills also was incredibly generous with sharing resources and insights.

I am deeply grateful to the Formation of Oxford Scholarship in Theology, Ethics, and Religion (FOSTER) Postgraduate Scholarship in New Testament, who funded my Oxford study and much of my living expenses. This current project would be impossible without their generosity. The subtitle for this project was inspired by Ronald A. Piper, "The One, the Four and the Many," in Markus Bockmuehl and Donald Hagner, eds., *The Written Gospel* (Cambridge: Cambridge University Press, 2005), 254–73.

VIII

For those who have mentored me into the life of scholarship as faith seeking understanding, thank you: Prof. Jon Laansma, Prof. Douglas Moo, Prof. Greg Beale, Prof. Jane Beal, Prof. Karen Jobes, Dr. Steve Bryan, and Dr. Tim Green. The community at St. Ebbe's, Oxford, has been a source of spiritual and practical support for many years. Vaughan Roberts, Ben Vane, Glenn and Lizzy Nesbitt, Penny Wearn, and the Overseas Partners Support Group deserve special thanks. Before embarking on DPhil studies in Oxford, I had the joy of living, learning, and serving in Ethiopia with SIM and the Episcopal Diocese of North Africa. My studies in Oxford are very much indebted to what I learned there. The Ethiopian calendar coordinates the four-year leap-year cycle with the four evangelists. It is therefore fitting that it was in the Ethiopian highlands that the idea for this project was born. Special thanks are given to my Ethiopian *wolajoch*, Woldeamlak and Wetete, my dear Ethiopian *wendemoch* Desalegn Kebede, Temesgen Sahle, Esayas Mario, Abeneazar Urga, Frew Tamirat, and many more than I could name here.

I am grateful to the clergy and parish council of the Church of the Resurrection, Washington, DC, who kindly offered me study leave in order to prepare my manuscript for publication.

The process of copyediting would have been impossible without the generous help of Markus Kirchner and Tobias Weiss at Mohr Siebeck. I owe many thanks to Hunter Brown for helping me solve several formatting problems in the final stages.

Deep gratitude is due to my parents, Marco and Roxanne, for modeling for me a love for Scripture, a diligent work ethic, and a longing for the new creation. The current project is the fruit of their labor as much as mine. My brother, Steven, has always been a constant encourager. My children, Oscar, Gabriel, and Lexie, constantly reminded me to find joy, even during the stresses of dissertating. Finally, I extend my deepest gratitude to Tessa, my wife. Words cannot express the depths of her companionship and support. In her the Ethiopian proverb comes true: "the man who is sent by his wife does not fear death." It is to her that I dedicate this project.

kiber le-Eyesus yihun

Ethiopian Feast of Lidet (Christmas), The Year of St. Luke
January 7th, 2023, Gregorian Calendar
Church of the Resurrection, Washington, DC

Table of Contents

Preface... VII

Abbreviations... XIV

Introduction: Focus and Method... 1

Chapter 1: The *Gospel according to Thomas*: Combining Gospels through Interpretive Rewriting................................... 17

1.1 Earliest Gospels: Setting the Patterns of Interpretive Rewriting............ 17

1.2 Combining Gospels in the Gospel according to Thomas...................... 19

    1.2.1 Identities and Mode – *GThomas'* Use of the Proto-Canonical
        Gospels.. 19
    1.2.2 Identities and Mode – Noncanonical Gospels in *GThomas*........... 29
    1.2.3 Summary of Gospel Sources in *GThomas*.............................. 37
    1.2.4 Integrity and Interactions of Gospel Materials in *GThomas*.......... 37
    1.2.5 Textual Authority in *GThomas*... 43

1.3 Summary and Conclusions.. 46

Chapter 2: The *Epistula Apostolorum*: Combining Gospels through Interpretive Rewriting..48

2.1 Prolegomena to the Epistula Apostolorum..................................... 48

2.2 Identities: Proto-canonical Gospels and Noncanonical Traditions..........54

2.3 Identities: Noncanonical Traditions in the Epistula Apostolorum...........56

2.4 Mode: Combining Gospel Excerpts in the Epistula Apostolorum........... 58

2.5 Integrity and Interactions of Gospels in the Epistula Apostolorum......... 60

X   *Table of Contents*

2.5.1 Sequencing, Stitching, and Creative Additions in the Gospel
    Epitome of *EpAp* 3.10–12.4... 60
2.5.2 Healing the Hemorrhaging Woman: *EpAp* 5.3–7...................... 61
2.5.3 Freeing the Demoniac: *EpAp* 5.10–12.................................. 63
2.5.4 Feeding the Five Thousand: *EpAp* 5.17–21........................... 63
2.5.5 Crucifixion and Burial: *EpAp* 9.1–5................................... 63
2.5.6 Summary of Integrity and Interactions of Gospels in *EpAp*........... 65

2.6 Textual Authority in the Epistula Apostolorum................................. 65
2.6.1 Minimizing the Authoritative Status of Prior Gospels in *EpAp*?...... 65
2.6.2 Four Gospels or More in *EpAp*?....................................... 65
2.6.3 Rewriting Liberally and Resolving Discrepancies in *GJohn* and
    GMatthew... 67
2.6.4 The Authority of Prior, Written Gospel Traditions in *EpAp*.......... 71
2.6.5 *EpAp* as Gospel Compendium, Consensus Document,
    and Apologia for a Nascent Biblical Canon............................... 74

2.7 Summary and Conclusions... 76

Chapter 3: Orchestrating the Gospel: Tatian's *Diatessaron* as a Gospel Combination...77

3.1 Identities... 78

3.1.1 Proto-Canonical Gospels in Tatian's *Diatessaron*.................... 78
3.1.2 Noncanonical Gospels in Tatian's *Diatessaron*...................... 84

3.2 Integrity and Interactions.. 94

3.2.1 Macro-Level Sequencing.. 94
3.2.2 Micro-Level Sequencing.. 98
3.2.3 Integrity and Interactions: Summary...................................100

3.3 Mode.. 101

3.4 Situating Tatian's Diatessaron *in Relation to Its Historical Context*...... 102

3.5 Authority.. 105

3.6 Summary and Conclusion.. 110

3.7 Excursus: The Longer Ending of Mark.. 111

Table of Contents XI

Chapter 4: Second-Order Discourse on Gospel Authors and Their Texts, Part 1: *GMark* to Justin Martyr............................ 115

4.1 The Beginnings of Multi-Author Discourse: Earliest Gospels.............. 116

4.2 Gospel Authorship in Papias and His Traditions............................. 121

    4.2.1 The Question of Papian Fragments..................................... 121
    4.2.2 Analyzing the Papian Fragments...................................... 125

4.3 Gospel Authors and Their Texts in New Testament Apocrypha............ 130

    4.3.1 Competitive Textuality.. 130
    4.3.2 Solo Performance.. 132
    4.3.3 Apostolic Collaboration.. 132

4.4 Justin Martyr.. 134

4.5 Summary and Conclusions... 140

Chapter 5: Second-Order Discourse on Gospel Authors and Their Texts, Part 2: Irenaeus, Clement, Heretics, and Celsus..... 142

5.1 Irenaeus... 142

    5.1.1 Identities and Mode of Gospel Combinations in Irenaeus'
         Writings.. 143
    5.1.2 Integrity of Gospels: The Persona of the Evangelist as the
         Means of Defining Unity and Difference............................. 148
    5.1.3 Gospel Interactions: Bibliographic Reading of the Gospel on
         Two Axes – Vertical and Horizontal................................. 149
    5.1.4 Authority.. 153
    5.1.5 Summary of Gospel Combinations in Irenaeus....................... 155

5.2 Clement of Alexandria... 156

    5.2.1 Clement and Noncanonical Gospels.................................... 158
    5.2.2 Identities and Mode of Gospel Combinations in Clement.......... 162
    5.2.3 Integrity of Gospels in Clement's Writings........................... 163
    5.2.4 Gospel Interactions.. 164
    5.2.5 Authority of Gospels in Combination................................. 169
    5.2.6 Summary of Gospel Combinations in Clement of Alexandria...... 170

5.3 "Heretics" and "Pagans" and the Emergence of the Fourfold Gospel... 170

5.4 Summary and Conclusions... 174

Chapter 6: Gospel Combinations in Early Christian Artifacts: Gregory Aland 0171 and P4+P64+67 176

6.1 Gospel Combinations in Gregory Aland 0171 176

6.1.1 Provenance and Physical Features 176
6.1.2 Paleography and Date 179
6.1.3 Scribal Collaboration 181
6.1.4 Identities and Mode 182
6.1.5 Integrity 183
6.1.6 Interactions: Scribal Harmonization 184
6.1.7 Authority 187
6.1.8 Summary of Gospel Combinations in Gregory Aland 0171 188

6.2 Gospel Combinations in P4+P64+67 188

6.2.1 Description and Provenance 188
6.2.2 Paleography and Date 189
6.2.3 Physical Features and Compositional Unity 190
6.2.4 Identities, Mode, and Integrity 194
6.2.5 Interactions 195
6.2.6 Authority 201
6.2.7 Summary of Gospel Combinations in P4+P64+67 202

6.3 Querying Canonical and Noncanonical Gospel Overlaps in Manuscripts 202

6.4 Summary and Conclusions 206

Chapter 7: Gospel Combinations in Early Christian Artifacts: P45 and P75 208

7.1 Gospel Combinations in P45 208

7.1.1 Provenance 209
7.1.2 Paleography and Date 209
7.1.3 Physical Features 210
7.1.4 Identities and Mode 213
7.1.5 Integrity 217
7.1.6 Interactions 218
7.1.7 Authority 221
7.1.8 Summary of Gospel Combinations in P45 222

7.2 Gospel Combinations in P75 222

Table of Contents XIII

7.2.1 Provenance... 222
7.2.2 Paleography and Date.. 223
7.2.3 Identities... 224
7.2.4 Mode: Scribal Habits and Textual Affinities as Clues to the
Gospel Codex Composition.. 225
7.2.5 Integrity.. 226
7.2.6 Interactions... 226
7.2.7 Authority.. 232
7.2.8 Summary of Gospel Combinations in P75.......................... 232

7.3 Summary and Conclusions on Artifactual Gospel Combinations........... 233

Summary and Conclusions... 235

Appendix 1: Synoptic Sequencing... 241

Appendix 2: Paleographical Analyses... 253

Bibliography.. 267

Index of References.. 295

Index of Modern Authors... 314

Index of Subjects................. 318

Abbreviations

Unless listed below, all abbreviations are according to *the SBL Handbook of Style: Second Edition* (Atlanta: Society of Biblical Literature, 2014).

Ancient Christian Gospels and Other Jesus Books

ApJas	*Apocryphon of James*
EpAp	*Epistula Apostolorum*
GEbionites / GEb	*Gospel of the Ebionites*
GEgyptians / GEgy	*Gospel according to the Egyptians*
GHebrews / GHeb	*Gospel according to the Hebrews*
GJudas	*Gospel of Judas*
GLuke / GLk	*Gospel according to Luke*
GMarcion	*Marcion's Gospel*
GMark / GMk	*Gospel according to Mark*
GMatthew / GMt	*Gospel according to Matthew*
GNazoraeans / GNaz	*Gospel of the Nazoraeans*
GPeter / GPet	*Gospel of Peter*
GPhilip	*Gospel of Philip*
GSavior	*Gospel of the Savior*
GThomas / GTh	*Gospel of Thomas*
IGThomas / IGTh	*Infancy Gospel of Thomas*
LEMark	*Longer Ending of Mark*
PJas	*Protevangelium of James*

Patristic Sources and Relevant Abbreviations

Aphrahat, *Dem.*	*Demonstrationes*
Did. Apost.	*Didascalia Apostolorum*
Ephrem, *CGos.*	*Commentary on the Gospel*
Ephrem, *Serm. Fid.*	*Sermones de Fide*

Other

LDAB	Leuven Database of Ancient Books
TM	Trismegistos Number

Introduction: Focus and Method

Birds of a feather flock together; but was this true of ancient Christian gospels?[1] Irenaeus, the late-second century theological ornithologist, claimed that the gospels according to Matthew, Mark, Luke, and John had wings of the same feather, and no other gospels flew within their flock. Scholarship is divided as to whether Irenaeus' taxonomy was a theological innovation, or whether Irenaeus was reflecting what was already commonplace. Many significant contributions have been made to this scholarly question, but there is still much more to be said.

The Focus of this Study

The focus of my study is to present an account of how and when the four proto-canonical gospels began to keep exclusive company with one another. At the end of the 20th century, Theo Heckel and Martin Hengel made strong cases that the four-gospel collection was early, inevitable, and based on intrinsic characteristics.[2] More recently, their arguments have been significantly challenged by Francis Watson, Chris Keith, and Matthew D. C. Larsen.[3] Foremost among these challenges is Francis Watson's thesis that all gospel writing until ca. 200 CE was a single process of interpretive rewriting, and that the canonical boundaries were a late second-century theological construction, rather than a natural outworking

---

[1] The term "ancient Christian gospels" is used here to describe gospels that were written and used by Jesus followers in antiquity. While recent scholarship has emphasized the diversity of early Christian identities, a strong case can be made for a network of family resemblances coalescing around the life and teachings of Jesus of Nazareth (cf. Lampe 2003; Behr 2013: 1–12; Markschies 2015: 335–45; Ayres 2017). I use this broad definition of "Christian" to encompass the proto-orthodox, Marcionites, Encratites, and Gnosticizing sects such as the Valentinians, and those residing on the overlap between Judaism and Christianity. This definition also allows for these identities to be "nested" (simultaneously held) by an individual or group in lived social patterns.

[2] Heckel 1999; Hengel 2008; in anglophone scholarship Stanton 2004, Hill 2010b, and Bird 2014 have developed their arguments. For a less maximalist approach, but still concluding that the four proto-canonical gospels gained pride of place early in the Christian movement, see Kelhoffer 2000, Schröter 2007; 2010; 2018a; 2019a; Markschies 2012; Bockmuehl 2017; Gathercole 2021.

[3] Watson 2013; 2018; 2019; Keith 2020; Larsen 2018b. For other arguments against an early fourfold gospel canon, see Campenhausen 1972, Koester 1990; 2005; Hahneman 1992; Petersen 2004; Lührmann 2004; Robinson 2004; and McDonald 2017b.

2 *Introduction: Focus and Method*

of properties intrinsic to the gospels. Indeed, Watson argues that the fourfold gospel "remained a work in progress well into the fourth century."[4] By demonstrating the thoroughgoing intertextual relationships among most gospels of the first two centuries, and by showing that the same patterns of literary composition and interpretive rewriting exist in both canonical and noncanonical gospels, Watson has effectively reshaped the entire debate regarding the how and when of the fourfold gospel.

Given the rich intertextual relationships bridging the canonical/noncanonical divide, we cannot simply ask, "how and when did the four become a fourfold collection?" There is a more fundamental question: "how and when did two or more gospels of any kind, proto-canonical or apocryphal, begin to keep company with one another?" It is within this broader phenomenon of gospel combinations that we will most likely find the origins of the fourfold gospel. Furthermore, recently published canonical and noncanonical gospel fragments,[5] and current advances in the interrelations of gospels,[6] the compositional techniques of Marcion and Tatian,[7] the scribal habits behind gospel manuscripts,[8] and the role of the materiality of the written gospel call for a fresh analysis of the fourfold gospel through the lens of gospel combinations.

In the present study, I will define a gospel combination as a collocation of two or more distinct, written gospel traditions in a single text, artifact, or conceptual category. No book-length study has yet examined the specific dynamics behind gospel combinations and interactions in the second-century process of reception.[9] This wide-angle account is the aim of the present monograph. I will seek to uncover which gospels tended to congregate in webs of relationships, both conceptually and artifactually. I will also investigate how gospels interacted with one another within these webs of relationships. The goal of my study is to identify the patterns, habits, and strategies of gospel combinations from the late first

---

[4] Watson 2013: 454.

[5] For a recent list, see Chapa 2016.

[6] E.g. Foster *et al.* 2011; Poirier and Peterson 2015; Watson and Parkhouse 2018; Heilmann and Klinghardt 2018; Schröter *et al.* 2019.

[7] On recent advances in Marcion studies, see Moll 2010; Beduhn 2013; Vinzent 2014; Roth 2015; Lieu 2015; Klinghardt 2015; on recent advances in Diatessaronic studies, see Watson 2016; Crawford 2013; 2016; 2017; 2018; and Crawford and Zola 2019.

[8] E.g. Kannaday 2004; Royse 2007; Jongkind 2007; Mugridge 2016; Pardee 2019.

[9] Several essays in the recent volumes edited by Watson and Parkhouse 2018, and Schröter *et al.* 2019, have given preliminary assessments of the interactions between gospels in the combinations found in *2 Clement* and Justin Martyr (Kloppenborg 2019), the *Epistula Apostolorum* (Watson 2018; 2019; 2020), the *Protoevangelium of James* (Goodacre 2018), Irenaeus (Mutschler 2019), and Tatian (Crawford 2018). However, no study has yet attempted to give a big-picture account of the dynamics of gospel combinations in the process leading up to the *tetraevangelium*.

Introduction: Focus and Method 3

century to the late second century, as Christianity gradually moved toward distinguishing a fourfold gospel canon.

From Interpretive Rewriting to Discrete Juxtaposition

My thesis will build upon Watson's premise that all gospel writing up to ca. 200 is in some way interpretive rewriting within a broad milieu of social memory.[10] There is a web of intertextual relationships between all gospels simply because they exist in the same ecosystem of social memory of Jesus tradition.[11] In this sense, it is no surprise that *GMatthew* and *GLuke* both develop *GMark*, *GThomas* seems to be "borrowing" from *GMatthew* and *GLuke*, *GEgerton* from *GJohn*, or P.Oxy. 840 from all four canonical gospels.[12] It is probable that these relationships existed through literary borrowing of some kind, even if this borrowing took place through secondary orality. This interconnectedness resulted from Christians remembering and retelling the same stories about Jesus even two centuries after they happened. From the early second century, gospels constituted a widespread and influential source for this communal recollection.

Given that interpretive rewriting characterized all gospel writing for our period of enquiry, another question we must ask is, "When and how did Christians begin to read gospels in parallel, as distinct versions of the same phenomenon, rather than merely rewriting prior versions?" To put it another way, when did Christians begin to categorize gospels and group two or more into the same family? When did gospel combinations shift from an act of composition (e.g. *GLuke* taking material from *GMark* and *GMatthew*) to an act of discrete juxtaposition

---

[10] While my thesis is greatly indebted to Watson's seminal thesis, I do not presuppose his contention that, because all gospel writing was interpretive rewriting, there is therefore no intrinsic distinction between the "canonical" and "noncanonical" gospels (cf. Watson 2013: 609–616); rather, I will query this contention in my study. The present monograph is an appreciative critique of Watson's trailblazing work on gospel writing and reception.

[11] For a recent history and appraisal of the "social memory" approach to the study of early Christianity, see Butticaz 2020 and Schröter 2018b, with their bibliographies. I use the term "social memory" to describe "the way in which a community adopts its past as history… the process of oral transmission, literary shaping and adaptation to new contexts of the Jesus tradition" (Schröter 2018b: 79), that is, the "multiple and selective narrative of the Nazarene" chronicled by Jesus-followers of antiquity (cf. Butticaz 2020: 310). This process of recollection was a communal rather than an individualistic phenomenon, extending across the entire spectrum of Jesus-following social networks, and evolving from the generation of the apostles (ca. 1–70 CE) to the generation of those who followed the apostles' disciples (ca. 130–200 CE); cf. Bockmuehl 2006; 2007. Gospel literature is like a variety of trees growing within this ecosystem of social memory, diverse yet interconnected. For a superb description of gospel writing as a subset of the larger phenomenon of communal memory, see Knust and Wasserman 2019: 49–95.

[12] It is possible that *GMark* contributed to this process of interpretive rewriting by combining a passion narrative with pre-existing sayings collections.

(e.g. a four-gospel codex)? At some point in early Christianity, recognition of the integrity of the textual "other" paved the way for a set of textual "others" to congregate rather than conflate or absorb one another. This emergence of the textual "other" and the mutual coexistence of a plurality of "others" runs against the view that gospel writing is merely the development of an amorphous, unfinished, and fluid textual tradition that is constantly mutating with each new rewriting.[13] To borrow an analogy from Paul Ricoeur, just as the self is defined in distinction from and in relation to the "other,"[14] so an individual gospel finds self-definition as a correlate of a collective body of other gospels, sharing the same conceptual or artifactual space. *GMark, GMatthew, GLuke, GJohn*, and dozens of gospels that were later declared noncanonical, did indeed crystallize into textual traditions that could be distinguished one from another, juxtaposed next to one another, set in competition with one another, or placed within a hermeneutically rich, mutually interpreting relationship. The present study will contribute to scholarly understanding of this textual crystallization.

Christians in the late first and second centuries combined gospels in a variety of ways. One way was to draw material from already existing gospel books and rework them into a fresh composition, contributing a substantial amount of special material. This is what is properly termed "interpretive rewriting". Another method was pericope interpolation –grafting a free-floating tradition into an already established gospel book (e.g. the *Pericope Adulterae*). Yet another way was gospel orchestration, where the composer adds little to no additional special material but rather combines and rearranges materials from two or more existing gospels into a meaningful sequence, oftentimes ironing out discrepancies.[15] Still

---

[13] Schäfer 1986 advocated this view of textuality for Rabbinic literature in his seminal 1986 article, and Eva Mroczek 2016 has applied this theory to ancient Jewish writings in general, with special reference to the Psalter and Ben Sira. Larsen 2018b has situated gospel writing into this narrative of open, unfinished, and fluid textuality. This narrative does not fully appreciate the early crystallization of textual traditions into distinct books, which I will address in my study.

[14] Ricoeur 1992.

[15] I have chosen to use the term "orchestration" rather than "harmony" here. Recently, scholars of Tatian's *Diatessaron* have suggested that we abandon the language of "harmony" when describing Tatian's composition and similar gospel-combining projects in early Christianity (Watson 2019a; Crawford 2013). The term "harmony" best describes a work whose main aim is to resolve the discrepancies between two or more gospels without compromising their claims of authenticity (I will continue to use "harmony" to describe this phenomenon). These scholars argue that this was not Tatian's main objective (if it even was an objective). Rather, Tatian sought to create his own *gospel*, albeit constructed from the building blocks of the proto-canonical gospels (and possibly other sources). In light of these concerns, I have chosen the term "orchestration" in order to preserve the sense that a composer was *coordinating* pre-existing gospel narratives rather than creating a gospel from new material, even if harmonization was not the composer's aim. I am grateful to Jeremiah Coogan for suggesting this term, which we have chosen to use in Coogan and Rodriguez 2023.

Introduction: Focus and Method 5

another way was scribal harmonization, where no new gospel text is created, but two or more discrete gospels intermingle in the minds and pens of the scribes who copy them. Finally, gospels could be combined by discrete juxtaposition, wherein two or more gospels preserve their own integrity while sharing the same conceptual or physical space. These five kinds of gospel combinations are laid out in Table 1.

Table 1 – The Characteristics of Gospel Combinations

Type	Characteristics	Special Material	Examples
Interpretive Rewriting	Prior material is combined and reworked into a fresh composition with its own integrity	New composition substantially contributes its own *Sondergut*	*GMatthew, GThomas*, P. Egerton 2, P.Oxy. 5.840
Pericope Interpolation	A free-floating tradition is situated into an already established gospel book	Special material juxtaposed next to already stable textual tradition	*Longer Ending of Mark, Pericope Adulterae*
Gospel Orchestration	Two or more written gospels are combined, original wording is mostly preserved, material is rearranged into a coherent sequence	New Composition contributes minimal *Sondergut* but bears its own mark on the sequencing and omissions	*Diatessaron,* P.Dura. 10
Discrete Juxtaposition	Two or more written gospels preserve their own integrity while sharing the same conceptual or physical space.	No new *Sondergut* added	Irenaeus' discussion of four gospels, physical juxtaposition of four gospels in P45.
Scribal Harmonization	Two or more established written gospels overlap in the mutual cross-pollination of wordings as scribes – intentionally or unintentionally – conformed the wording of one discrete gospel to that of another, indicating that both gospels shared the shame conceptual space in the expectations of the scribe.	No new *Sondergut* added	Harmonizing variants in GA 0171, P4+P64+67, P45, and P75

As one moves down the table from interpretive rewriting to scribal harmonization, gospels gradually begin to behave as discrete parallel entities rather than merely absorbing previous written traditions into fresh composition. This movement is not necessarily chronological. While gospel combinations, as interpretive

6 *Introduction: Focus and Method*

rewriting, are an early phenomenon (e.g., *GMatthew* combining *GMark* and Q, or *GLuke* combining *GMatthew* and *GMark*), gospel combinations as discrete juxtapositions could also have early origins. It is entirely possible that the Lukan evangelist had both *GMark* and *GMatthew* in front of him as he was drawing from both to write his fresh, re-interpretive gospel composition. Or, as Martin Hengel would argue, it is possible that the church in Rome had a *Bücherschrank* containing all four proto-canonical gospels by the first quarter of the second century.[16] In either of these cases, discrete juxtaposition of two or more gospel books could be an early phenomenon. Furthermore, interpretive rewriting occurred well into late antiquity with numerous Christian apocrypha.

It is therefore helpful to depict the different types of gospel combinations in a Venn diagram (Figure 1.1), to demonstrate that these various forms of gospel combinations are not chronologically sequenced but rather conceptually gradated based on the level of novel *Sondergut*. Moreover, the Venn diagram also shows how one form of gospel combination might involve the dynamics of another. For example, the interpretive rewriting known as *GLuke* might involve the discrete juxtaposition of *GMark* and *GMatthew* in the mind, if not the physical writing space, of *GLuke*.

The reason I am engaging these five dimensions of gospel combinations is to discover what kind of momentum may have led to the discrete fourfold juxtaposition that we see in the discourse of Irenaeus or the pages of P. Chester Beatty I. Perhaps the origins of fourfold discrete juxtaposition lie in the patterns of material combinations in interpretive rewriting. If the same patterns of gospel combining emerge in interpretive rewriting, gospel orchestration, scribal harmonization, and discrete juxtaposition, then we will be able to speak of momentum leading to the fourfold gospel collection. If these *patterns* exude a distinct consistency, we may even be able to speak of early Christian *habits* of gospel combinations. Finally, if early Christians speak explicitly about how and why they created such gospel combinations in the ways they did, we can speak of the *strategies* of early Christian gospel combinations.

---

[16] Hengel 2008: 197–237.

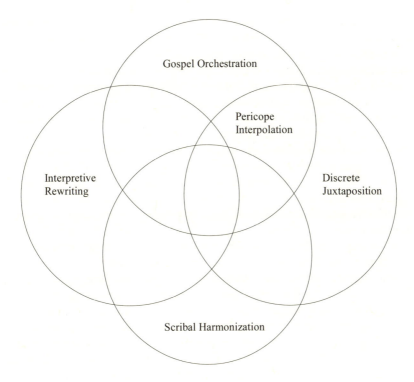

Figure 1 – The Interrelatedness of Gospel Combinations

The Method of this Study

In order to determine the patterns, habits, and strategies of gospel combinations in early Christianity, I will pose five diagnostic questions for investigating gospel combinations in the second century (and slightly later for artifactual combinations). These questions, summarized below in Table 2, pertain to 1) source identity, 2) mode, 3) integrity, 4) interactions, and 5) authority.

Table 2 – The Dynamics of Gospel Combinations

	Dynamic	Question
1	Source Identity	Which written gospels?
2	Mode	Secondary oral or written consultation?
3	Integrity	Discrete or conflated?
4	Interactions	Primary architecture or epiphenomena?
5	Authority	Authoritative status for written gospels in combination?
		Difference in authority between written gospels and the text combining them?

8 *Introduction: Focus and Method*

(1) The question of source identity. Which gospels tended to cluster in combinations? To answer this question, I will use the criterion of textual distinctiveness to identify the use of a gospel by a second-century author. In many cases, I will follow Helmut Koester's redactional criterion, which identifies a specific gospel by the unique redactional elements of that gospel author.[17] However, I will not apply Koester's now obsolete form-critical standards that argue for priority or posteriority based on relative primitivity. Instead, I will pay attention not only to redactional lexical choices, but also to the way these redactions are situated. For example, Koester's penchant for form-critical methods convinced him that *GThomas* was not dependent on the Synoptics.[18] But the recurring propensity of *GThomas* to tweak Markan *logia* exactly the same way as Matthean and Lukan redaction sufficiently demonstrates that *GMatthew* and *GLuke* can be identified as sources for *GThomas*, and are therefore in some sense combined in its composition.[19]

Koester's method has significant shortcomings.[20] Therefore, in some cases I will identify textual distinctiveness of a gospel based on frequently occurring lexemes and themes favored by the respective evangelist,[21] or narrative accounts distinct to that evangelist,[22] even if an exact redactional quotation is absent. I will also use the explicit exegesis of named gospel sources in later authors such as Theophilus of Antioch, Irenaeus, Clement of Alexandria, and Origen as *comparanda*. If a second-century text contains gospel material that resembles a particular gospel but neither names the source nor cites it word-for-word, and if a later second-century author handles the said gospel material in the same way while naming the suspected gospel as the source, then the case is fortified that the earlier second-century text is drawing from that gospel.[23]

---

[17] Koester 1957: 3.

[18] Koester 1990: 84–128.

[19] For fuller arguments, see Gathercole 2010; 2012a; 2014a; 2014b; Goodacre 2012; 2014; 2019. I will make this case in greater detail in Chapter 1 below.

[20] Significant critiques of Koester's method have been made by Kelhoffer 2004: 7–10; Hill 2010a: 235–42; Zelyck 2013: 14–20. Even scholars sympathetic to Koester's method have cautioned that the absence of redactional material does not necessitate the certainty of a written gospel's non-usage (cf. Köhler 1987: 2–5; Gregory and Tuckett 2005: 71–72; and Kloppenborg 2019: 46). Koester's strict method, while producing tidy results, imposes unnecessary standards on ancient Christians, who did not follow twentieth century redactional criteria in their citations but rather mimicked the flexible citational habits of the Greco-Roman philosophical and literary milieu (cf. Hill 2012, building on Blumenthal 1981, Whittaker 1998, and Inowlocki 2006).

[21] E.g. the clusters of Johannine language in Justin Martyr; see Section 4.4 below.

[22] E.g. *EpAp*'s reference to the Johannine miracle at Cana in Galilee (5.1), and the Matthean miracle of the coin in the fish's mouth (5.14-16); cf. Justin Martyr's reference to the Matthean account of the Magi in *Dial.* 78.1–2.

[23] This method has recently been proposed by Zelyck 2013: 13–24. Zelyck presents as an example the pairing of *GJn* 5:39 and 5:45 in P.Egerton 2 (omitting 5:40–44), which strongly

Introduction: Focus and Method 9

Two factors caution against strict adherence to Koester's redactional method: the geographical mobility of early Christian texts and the phenomenon of secondary orality. The trans-local nature of early Christian identity, and the speed at which Christians could traverse the Roman Empire in the first two centuries CE strongly suggest that gospels did not stay parochial, especially if their narrative impulse envisaged a global outreach.[24] A manuscript could be carried by messenger from Ephesus to Rome in less than twenty days.[25] It is therefore not wise to assume, for example, that a second-century author in Rome, who makes frequent use of Johannine lexemes but never explicitly quotes that gospel, had no access to *GJohn* on the basis that *GJohn* was originally published in Asia Minor.

Furthermore, rather than proving the absence of a gospel's influence, the lack of a direct quotation from a gospel could instead be the result of hearing the gospel text read out loud and reproducing the gospel material in a re-oralized form that does not cite it word-for-word.[26] Jürgen Becker makes the crucial observation that the Christian understanding of Scripture began with Jesus' secondary-oral interpretation of Torah, and the subsequent reception of written gospel material in the second century followed the same interplay between oral and textual authority.[27] The dynamic interplay between oral and textual authority via secondary orality in the early Jesus tradition is displayed in the ἠκούσατε ὅτι ἐρρέθη sayings in *GMatthew* 5.21–48, which occur right after Jesus declares

---

resembles Irenaeus' (*Haer.* 4.10.1), Origen's (*Comm. Jo.* 6.109), and Cyprian's (*Test.* 1.18) citations of the same Johannine sayings; cf. Zelyck 2013: 36–37.

[24] On the trans-local identity of the early Christian movement, see Tellbe 2009: 241–47. On the efficient travel of Christians in the Roman era, see Thompson 1998. Furthermore, since texts like *GMt* 28.19–20, *GLk* 24.47–48, and *GJn* 20.21 envisage a global mission, it seems likely that the tradents of these texts would distribute them widely.

[25] This calculation is taken from ORBIS: The Stanford Geospatial Network Model of the Roman World, www.orbis.standford.edu, accessed 4 April 2019.

[26] Since the ground-breaking and controversial work of Kelber 1983, who appropriated the term "secondary orality" from the media studies of Ong 1982, secondary orality has been increasingly emphasized in the study of second-century gospel reception (e.g. Byrskog 2000; Kruger 2005; Kirk 2007; Becker 2012; Gathercole 2012a; Watson 2013; Bockmuehl 2017). Goodacre 2012: 135–40 notes well how Kelber 1983: 197 has not used "secondary orality" in the same sense in which Ong coined the term but has re-appropriated it to mean the recycling of textual material into oral medium (e.g. hearing a gospel manuscript read out loud). Furthermore, Goodacre soundly critiques an unnuanced use of this term in the study of Christian origins, wherein "secondary" orality presupposes "primary" orality as inherently more primitive than the textualized form of Jesus tradition. Goodacre advocates a more nuanced model in which textuality and orality are always in mutual interaction in the development of the Jesus tradition in the early centuries CE. I use the term "secondary orality" in this more nuanced fashion to describe the process of written texts feeding back into the communal memory of Jesus through re-oralization without presupposing a sharp polarity between "orality" and "textuality".

[27] Becker 2012: esp. 1–24.

10   *Introduction: Focus and Method*

emphatically in *GMatthew* 5.18: ἰῶτα ἓν ἢ μία κεραία οὐ μὴ παρέλθῃ ἀπὸ τοῦ νόμου. Because secondary orality was central to the earliest Christian movement, we cannot assume that second-century authors, even when they resembled the parlance of a particular gospel, were not influenced by that gospel simply because they show no redactional elements or word-for-word citations.

(2) The question of mode: Does a particular gospel come to be combined with another gospel by consultation of a manuscript or by another means, such as secondary orality? In some cases, it can be demonstrated that the author of a gospel combination drew from written sources. For example, it is obvious that the gospel-combining scribe of P75 had physical exemplars of *GLuke* and *GJohn*. Similarly, the way that Tatian draws from all four proto-canonical gospels, while scarcely reduplicating any pericopes, makes it virtually certain that he was consulting physical manuscripts of the four gospels, perhaps even using a technological mechanism to annotate what material he had already used from each manuscript in front of him.[28]

Secondary orality, on the other hand, is practically impossible to identify with certainty. There are, however, clues that a particular author might be drawing on sources through hearing them rather than consulting a manuscript. For example, an author may depict instances of re-oralization of these gospel sources.[29] One can also detect secondary orality when a second-century author does not cite a gospel word-for-word but consistently shows thematic and lexical parallels across several pericopes from a particular gospel, and then combines this material with parallels that imitate other gospels, uniting them by a common theme. In such cases, the absence of a word-for-word citation on the one hand, and the confluence of material from diverse sectors of ancient Christianity on the other, makes it likely that the second-century author is drawing from the re-oralization of pericopes from several gospels, based on a common theme.[30] In most cases,

---

[28] Cf. Metzger 1977: 11-12. Barker 2016: 109–21 and Mattila 1995 hypothesize a scenario in which Tatian had four lectors seated around him, crossed-legged, reading to him from the relevant portions of each gospel as he sought to harmonize them in his Diatessaronic composition.

[29] E.g. Justin Martyr refers explicitly to re-oralization in *1 Apol.* 67, when, after the lector finishes the public reading of the apostolic memoirs, the presider over the congregation exhorts the congregation to the imitation of their teaching. *2 Clement* begins with the call to listen well (1.2), and it alludes to a re-oralization of Jesus traditions in 13.3–4. *Ad Diognetum* 12.1 also describes both the reading and hearing of "these truths," which probably refers to the Law, the Prophets, the gospel, and the tradition of the apostles mentioned in 11.6.

[30] Kruger 2005: 145–205; 2009: 156–58 makes this observation about P.Oxy. 840, which does not cite any gospel word-for-word, but it makes consistent parallels with unique material from *GLk* 11.37–52, *GMt* 23.1–39, *GJn* 7.1–52, *GJn* 13.1–30, and *GMk* 7.1–23. The only other alternatives are that the second-century author is drawing from diverse oral traditions, or from a lost harmony. These alternatives are unnecessarily complicated and, given the trans-local mobility of Christian texts in the first two centuries CE, the easier explanation is that the author is drawing from gospels through secondary orality.

Introduction: Focus and Method   11

however, it is best to apply R. H. Lightfoot's fabled advice to our adjudication of secondary orality and admit that "we do not know."[31] For our purposes, even though secondary orality can seldom be proven, it can still be used as a helpful category to sustain the plausibility that a given text makes use of two or more written gospels even while not showing redactional features.

(3) The question of source integrity: Does the author of a literary combination or the manufacturer of an artifactual combination respect the individuality of each gospel, or does he view the combination as a singular text? To answer this question, I will look for clues internal to the literary and artifactual sources. For example, a second-century author can refer to the source texts in the plural,[32] or a manuscript may contain gospel titles demarcating the distinction between the gospels combined in one codex.[33] On the other hand, a second-century author may conflate two or more gospel sources at the clausal level, treating his combination as a new, singular composition.[34] Similarly, there is at least one case of a gospel-orchestration manuscript that does not signal when one gospel source ends and another begins, but it combines them in a continuous manuscript.[35] Scribal harmonizations in codices containing two or more discrete gospels may yield important data regarding how early Christians negotiated the tension between the one gospel and multiple discrete witnesses of this gospel.[36] My analysis of the integrity or conflation of discrete gospels will interact critically with Larsen's provocative thesis that there is no clear evidence of Christian discourse about gospels as discrete, authored books before Irenaeus.[37]

(4) The question of source interactions: How do multiple gospels found in a combination interact with one another in that combination? For example, did some gospels play a primary, architectural role, and others a secondary, epiphenomenal role? This is apparent in some cases, such as Tatian's preference for the proto-canonical four as the primary architecture of his narrative, but his insertion of what we now consider noncanonical material into the established narrative framework of the fourfold gospel (although, as we shall see in Section 3.1.2, these insertions are questionable). In artifactual cases like the interpolation of the *Longer Ending of Mark* and the *Pericope Adulterae*, it is evident that the architecture of the gospel narrative is provided by the canonical texts of *GMark* and *GJohn*, while the appended Jesus traditions latch onto these already-structured gospel texts as epiphenomena.

---

[31] Mentioned by Gathercole 2012a: 221.

[32] E.g. Justin Martyr (*1 Apol.* 66.3; *Dial.* 103.8).

[33] E.g. P75; see below, Section 7.2.6.

[34] E.g. *1 Apol.* 15.14 (*GMt* 6.25–26 and *GLk* 12.22–24); 16.11 (*GMt* 7.22–23 and *GLk* 13.26–27).

[35] The Dura Europos Fragment (0212).

[36] Cf. Pardee 2019: 429–40.

[37] Larsen 2018b: esp. 79–120.

12 *Introduction: Focus and Method*

There might also be diversity in how gospels interact in the work in which they are combined. If a particular author conflates two gospels, does the same author also employ other patterns of gospel usage, such as discrete quotations of the individual gospels? If diversity in gospel usage is apparent, then it will caution us against making sweeping claims about the fluidity of written gospels in the second century. It should also caution us against concluding that a particular second-century author prefers gospel harmonizing over a collection of discrete gospels. Irenaeus, for example, can blend various gospel materials even at the clausal level.[38] Few, if any, would argue that he is a gospel harmonizer. On the other hand, Tatian, whose gospel orchestration is the most famous from antiquity, usually preserves the integrity of citations from *GMatthew*, *GLuke*, and *GJohn*. Five continuous verses from *GJohn* may precede an even larger continuous section from *GLuke*.[39] In some places, however, Tatian will blend sayings from *GMatthew*, *GMark*, and *GLuke*, down to the clausal level.[40] Thus, diversity in gospel usage might suggest that the apparent malleability of gospels in the second century – whether combined or used individually – is due more to the author's situation than to the status of the gospel itself. Alternatively, if a particular second-century author consistently conflates gospels into combinations and never cites them individually, this would suggest that he envisages gospel materials more as a pool of amorphous tradition than as discrete sources.

(5) Finally, the question of textual authority: Does the act of gospel combination demonstrate a regard for the gospels as authoritative and fixed, or as free and malleable, or somewhere in between?[41] Does the second-century gospel combination present itself as equal in authority to the gospels it is combining? Does it envisage itself as the same kind of gospel writing as *GMatthew*'s relationship to *GMark*, or *GLuke*'s relationship to *GMatthew* and *GMark*? These questions will be answered by investigating the discourse that second-century authors use to describe the gospel combinations, and the setting in which these

---

[38] E.g. *Haer.* 3.10.6 (combining *GMk* 1.2 and *GLk* 1.17), and *Haer.* 3.19.2 (combining *GMt* 16.16 and *GJn* 1.13); cf. *Haer.* 3.16.2 (combining *GMt* 1.18 and *GJn* 1.13–14).

[39] E.g. Ephrem's commentary (*CGos* 1.1–27), which exegetes *GJn* 1.1–5 as a unit, and then *GLk* 1.5–25.

[40] E.g. Tatian's harmonized version of the incident in Nazareth (*CGos* 11.23–25; Codex Fuldensis §78), combining phrases from *GMt* 13.54–58, *GMk* 6.2–6, and *GLk* 4.23–27.

[41] I define "textual authority" as the overall fixedness, finality, and identity-forming function of a text within a particular reading community. Texts considered to be Scripture, such as the Jewish Law and the Prophets, exhibited authority in this way among various groups of early Christians. At some point in early Christianity, similar authority was attributed to gospels as well. In the present study, I will identify points when gospels and gospel combinations exhibit fixedness, finality, and an identity-forming function, and I will also draw out the implications of when gospels are treated on the same level of authority as the Jewish Scriptures. The topics and definitions of "textual authority" and "Scripture" in antiquity is a vast subject, and I can only offer working definitions for the sake of the present study. For recent treatments of these terms within the context of early Judaism and Christianity, see Nicklas and Schröter 2020.

Introduction: Focus and Method

13

combinations are used. For example, does the second-century author refer to them as γραφή or with the verb γέγραπται? Are the gospel combinations juxtaposed with citations of Old Testament texts that were considered as authoritative Scripture for early Christians?

Investigating the *identities, mode, integrity, interactions,* and *authority* involved in gospel combinations will paint a picture in which gospels begin to cluster in the second century and will further the discussion about whether the formalized fourfold gospel collection of the late second century was a recognition of an earlier reality or a later theological construction.[42] In this way, my study will shed light on the somewhat obscure pathway leading to the fourfold gospel as the authoritative gospel combination in the third century CE. Undoubtedly these questions will yield a variety of results, depending on the sources to which they are posed. But this diversity of results will be fertile ground for identifying the patterns that gradually emerged in second-century Christian gospel combinations.

I will mostly apply the five methodological questions in the order listed above (see also Table 2), but in some cases the second-century sources will be structured in such a way that the methodological questions will flow in a different order. For the reader's convenience, I will structure each chapter according to the five dynamics of gospel combinations.[43] After I have applied my method to a selection of sources, spanning the second century (and in the case of the manuscripts, the third century), and covering a wide geographic distribution, then I will be in a position to draw conclusions on the big picture of how the fourfold gospel eventually became the gospel combination *par excellence*. Perhaps the most important contribution that my study will make to scholarship is to situate the late second-century articulation of the fourfold gospel against the broader backdrop of gospel-combination patterns of the second century. From this vantage point, we will be able to see more clearly whether Irenaeus is an

---

[42] Not every instance of gospel combination will demonstrate a strategy *per se*. Some gospel combinations may have more of an *ad hoc* character to them. Others may have an explicit strategy laid out by the author making the combination.

[43] Chapter 4 is the exception because of the plethora of sources I investigate from Papias to Justin. However, I summarize and offer a conclusion based on the five dynamics of gospel combination.

14 *Introduction: Focus and Method*

eccentric canonical innovator, a reliable tradent of widespread Christian practice, or something in between.

The Outline and Primary Data of this Study

The present study will systematically investigate gospel combinations in interpretive rewriting (Chapters 1–2), orchestration and pericope interpolation (Chapter 3), discrete juxtaposition in Christian discourse (Chapters 4–5), discrete juxtaposition in codices (Chapters 6–7), and scribal harmonization in codices (Chapters 6–7). I will provide a summary and conclusion at the end of this monograph. This outline corresponds broadly to the conceptual spectrum in Figure 1.1. I have chosen not to follow a strict chronological order in my sequence of chapters because the dating of two of my primary sources – *GThomas* and the *Epistula Apostolorum* – falls anywhere between Papias and Clement of Alexandria. I therefore resist drawing a chronological progression of gospel combinations that relies heavily on dating either of these two documents.[44] Rather, I have chosen to structure the present study based on the literary progression within which gospels emerge with their own distinguishable identity in relation to one another and in distinction from one another. This structure embodies my primary quest to discover the dynamics undergirding and leading to the fourfold gospel.

I will not be able to make an exhaustive analysis of second-century gospel combinations, but I will intentionally focus on sources that span a wide array of early Christian affinity groups to achieve as balanced a perspective as possible. My dataset includes provenances from Upper Egypt, Alexandria, Syria, Asia Minor, Rome, and Gaul, and it engages texts and writers that would later be described across the spectrum from orthodoxy to heterodoxy. Chapters 1–3 investigate texts that were either excluded from or ignored by canonical lists: *GThomas*, the *Epistula Apostolorum*, and the *Diatessaron*. Chapters 4–5 engage ancient Christian voices within proto-orthodoxy (Papias, Justin, Irenaeus, Clement, and the anonymous author of *LEMark*), those later deemed heterodox (Valentinus, Ptolemy, Heracleon, and Marcus), and a pagan source (Celsus).

Two broad categories of data will occupy the present study: literary and artifactual. The literary combinations will include *ad hoc* combinations found in early Christian Jesus books (e.g. *GThomas* and the *Epistula Apostolorum*), comprehensive combinations (e.g. Tatian's *Diatessaron*), and second-order Christian discourse on gospel writing (e.g. the discussions of gospel origins in the writings of Papias, Irenaeus, and Clement of Alexandria).[45]

---

[44] On the dates of these documents, see below, Sections 1.2 and 2.1.

[45] I borrow the term "second-order discourse" from social theory to describe the epistemological posture of "observing the observer" (cf. Luhmann 2013: 102). If gospel authors inscribe their observations of the Jesus tradition into narratives or sayings collections, then second-order observers (e.g. Papias, Irenaeus, and Clement) stand at one literary remove from this

Introduction: Focus and Method   15

The emergence of "New Philology" and the "Material Turn" in the humanities and social sciences has highlighted the importance of the materiality of the texts we are studying. Recognizing the semantic value of the physical features of artifacts is a positive development in the humanities in general, and in the study of early Christianity in particular. In some sense, every manuscript as a physical artifact is constitutive of the text it contains, with all its eccentricities and uniqueness.[46] It is to the detriment of scholarly enquiry to divorce the study of the text and the study of the artifact. Therefore, wherever possible, I will also engage gospels as material artifacts, paying special attention to what the physical aspects of the manuscripts and scribal features can tell us about what kinds of books these were, how they were used, and how gospels were combined within them.[47] The literary and artifactual evidence will work together to form a three-dimensional image of gospel combinations in Christian antiquity.

Two notes on terminology are in order. First, in a recent, co-edited volume, Francis Watson and Sarah Parkhouse have pioneered a new system of gospel abbreviations (e.g. *GMatthew*/*GMt*, *GThomas*/*GTh*, *GPeter*/*GPet*, etc.).[48] This is to indicate that all gospels of the first 200 years CE existed in the same ecosystem of social memory with intertextual links, and to avoid privileging the proto-canonical four in analysis and presentation of evidence. This abbreviation system, however, is not value-neutral and can influence the reader to presuppose that there is no intrinsic difference between gospels that were later declared to be canonical and those later declared to be noncanonical. I do not wish to presuppose this neutralization of the canonical/non-canonical divide. However, neither do I wish to privilege the four over against the others in my own method of examining the evidence.[49] Furthermore, the shared ecosystem of all ancient gospel writing is a heuristically fruitful starting point, and this abbreviation system proves to be more practical than other methods for referring to distinct textual traditions that were recognized by early Christians as gospels attributable to a particular author. It is for these methodological, heuristic, and practical reasons that I have chosen this abbreviation system.

---

textualization and offer commentary on it, often with regard to the authors and their books as discernible entities.

[46] Cf. Lundhaug and Ingebord Lied 2017.

[47] In the first two decades of the 21st century, scholars of early Christianity have increasingly taken into account the value of physical manuscripts in the analysis of ancient texts; in general, see Hurtado 2006a; 2007; 2011; 2012; Kraus and Nicklas 2006; Kraus 2007; Kraus and Nicklas 2010; Nongbri 2018; for ancient gospels in particular, see Kruger 2005; Tuckett 2007; Kraus *et al.* 2009; Foster 2010; Markschies 2010; Hill 2013; Chapa 2016; Charlesworth 2016; McDonald 2017: 173–264; Zelyck 2019; Larsen and Letteney 2019; Keith 2020.

[48] Watson and Parkhouse 2018.

[49] It is for this reason that I have chosen not to capitalize the word "gospel" when referring to Jesus books, since capitalizing "Gospels" might inadvertently privilege the four proto-canonical gospels in our description of written Jesus traditions circulating in the second century.

16 Introduction: Focus and Method

Second, for the sake of brevity, I have chosen to use the term "noncanonical" to describe ancient gospels that did not eventually make it into the canon of Christian Scripture.[50] The less anachronistic alternative, "gospels that later came to be deemed noncanonical" is cumbersome, and the present study requires a grammar by which to describe how – even early in the second century – some gospels clustered as a center of gravity while others remained at the periphery. Moreover, I use the term "noncanonical" without any intention of assuming the primacy of the fourfold gospel prior to Irenaeus. In an historical investigation, such primacy, if it is indeed argued, must only be asserted insofar as the evidence allows. On the other hand, the term "proto-canonical" is an economical way to describe gospels that were read throughout the second century but formally recognized as the church's exclusive Scripture in later centuries. Indeed, our present study will unpack the dynamics behind this development in early Christian gospel reading.

---

[50] When an ancient gospel portrays itself as a secret teaching, I use the term "apocryphal" to describe it.

Chapter 1

The *Gospel According to Thomas*: Combining Gospels through Interpretive Rewriting

In the previous chapter I laid out the roadmap and method for this study. I am tracing the momentum leading to the fourfold gospel in the late second century. In order to determine the pre-history of the fourfold gospel, we need to uncover the patterns of how gospels kept company with one another in the period before ca. 200 CE. In the present chapter, I will explore the dynamics of interpretive rewriting. Strictly speaking, interpretive rewriting involves combinations of materials drawn from gospels, not combinations of whole gospels. These combinations are invaluable in that they show us which gospels were the most popular, available, and influential textual pools of tradition. Moreover, they show us which gospels came together when early Christians authored Jesus books – whether they literally came together on authors' laps as they consulted their sources, or whether they came together in the minds of authors as they wrote about Jesus in a new composition.

1.1 Earliest Gospels: Setting the Patterns of Interpretive Rewriting

All gospel writing – both canonical and noncanonical – is part of the process of reception of the words and deeds of Jesus of Nazareth. One might call this process, especially up to 200 CE, gospel proliferation.[1] This proliferation involves the combination and expansion of previous traditions. Assuming Markan priority and the Q hypothesis, we can safely say that *GMatthew* and *GLuke* both develop the Markan narrative and combine it with sayings from the Q source. Alternatively, assuming *Markan* priority without Q, we can safely conclude that *GLuke* develops the Markan narrative and combines it with material from *GMatthew*, rearranging the Matthean sayings into a new sequence.[2] By way of expansion, *GMatthew* and *GLuke* develop *GMark* by inserting an infancy narrative, and *GMatthew*, *GLuke*, and *GJohn* develop *GMark* by inserting post-resurrection appearance narratives. James Barker has recently argued that *GJohn* expands upon

---

[1] I draw this term from Francis Watson 2013: 604 and James W. Barker 2019.

[2] Watson 2013: 117–216; one might conversely argue for Matthean posteriority and reworking of Lukan traditions; cf. MacEwan 2015 and Hengel 2008: 320–50.

18   *Chapter 1: The Gospel According to Thomas*

the Synoptics in a way that "interlocks" with them to such an extent that it is highly probable that he intends to supplement them.[3] Dynamics of expansion and combination are a feature of many ancient Jewish and Greco-Roman bodies of literature.[4] In gospel writing, these dynamics first appear within the earliest gospels, and they continue well into the second century.

Francis Watson has termed this development of the written gospel tradition "interpretive rewriting."[5] In each case of this phenomenon (*GLuke* rewriting *GMark* and *GMatthew*, *Thomas* rewriting *GMatthew* and *GLuke*, *GPeter* rewriting *GMark* and *GJohn*, etc.), previous gospel material is combined to form a fresh composition. Gospel material from specific gospels such as *GMatthew* and *GLuke* is not explicitly differentiated as such in the fresh composition. Strictly speaking, the prior material is not juxtaposed as discrete units from discrete sources. Rather, it is combined and often harmonized to form a new textual object. But it is combined nonetheless, and it is worthy of consideration in the present study.

Gospel combinations in interpretive rewriting exist on the opposite end of the spectrum from discrete juxtaposition, because they do not preserve the integrity of the written gospel materials they are combining, nor do they explicitly attribute them to a separate text. Present in the four proto-canonical gospels, these kinds of gospel combinations are the earliest extant examples of two or more gospels keeping company with one another.[6] Some have argued that this act of "combining" is actually a process of one written tradition swallowing up and replacing another in a competitive fashion.[7] Others have countered that this interpretive rewriting was not necessarily meant to supplant but rather to develop and supplement.[8] Although the present study gives only a cursory look into the interrelations of the proto-canonical gospels,[9] our conclusions about second-

---

[3] Barker 2015a.

[4] Barker 2019 finds fruitful *comparanda* for these dynamics in the Greek Epic Cycle, encomia for Cato the Younger, histories of the Jewish Revolt, Jewish biblical texts (e.g. Deuteronomy and Chronicles), *1 Enoch*, *Jubilees*, and Greek translations of the Hebrew Scriptures.

[5] Watson 2013: 286–88; 608–09.

[6] We could conceive of Luke literally "juxtaposing" scrolls of *GMark* and *GMatthew* in one room as two different lectors read from each of them as he composed his own gospel, but this would be no more than speculation; for an argument on this scenario (applied to Tatian's *Diatessaron*), see Mattila 1995. If we accept the literary interconnectedness of *GMark*, *GMatthew*, *GLuke*, and *GJohn*, the earliest extant examples of gospel combinations therefore are the four proto-canonical gospels themselves.

[7] E.g. Watson 2013; Larsen 2018b; Keith 2020.

[8] E.g. Allen 2018; Barker 2015a; 2019.

[9] The secondary literature on this topic is vast, but for a relatively recent appraisal of these relationships, see Bird 2014: 125–220, as well as the essays in the now classic volume by Dungan 1990 and various essays in the *Festschrift* for Christopher Tuckett (Foster *et al.* 2011). Heckel 1999: 32–218 offers a thoroughgoing theory of developing inter-gospel relationships between the writing of *GMark* and the writing of *GJohn*. The Farrer theory allows for more

1.2 Combining Gospels in the Gospel according to Thomas

century gospel reception will shed light onto the question of replacement versus supplementation. In the present chapter (and continuing through chapters 2–3), I will be primarily interested in how second-century authors combined materials from multiple gospels – from which gospels did they draw most extensively? I am likewise concerned with *how* this material was combined – what might these combinations tell us about how proto-canonical and noncanonical gospels were viewed in relation to one another when second-century authors combined their materials?

1.2 Combining Gospels in the *Gospel according to Thomas*

In the following section, I will apply my diagnostic questions to ascertain the patterns of gospel combinations as interpretive rewriting in the *Gospel according to Thomas*. GThomas can be reasonably dated anywhere between 135 and 200 CE,[10] so it is valuable to our reconstruction of second-century patterns of gospel combinations.

1.2.1 Identities and Mode – GThomas' Use of Proto-Canonical Gospels

a. The Case for the Influence of the Synoptic Gospels on GThomas

Since the discovery of the Oxyrhynchus fragments of *GThomas*, and especially since the publication of the Coptic translation,[11] scholars have engaged the question of whether *GThomas* is dependent on one or more of the canonical gospels. This is a fair question, given that approximately 50% of the sayings in *GThomas* have a parallel in the Synoptic tradition.[12] This represents a broad range of sayings found in the Triple Tradition, Double Tradition, Matthean redaction of *GMark*, Lukan redaction of *GMark*, and *Sondergut* from *GMatthew*, *GLuke*, and *GMark*.[13] In 1959, Robert Grant was the first to build a comprehensive case for *GThomas'* derivation from the Synoptics.[14] Around the same time, G. Quispel

---

interactions between proto-canonical gospels, and it has gained significant popularity in anglophone New Testament scholarship, e.g. Watson 2013, Abakuks 2014, Poirier and Peterson 2015, and Eve 2016.

[10] This is the most judicious date range, summarized and defended by Gathercole 2014: 112–24.

[11] The Oxyrhynchus fragments were published in Grenfell and Hunt 1898; 1904. The Coptic version, contained in Nag Hammadi Codex II, was first published in Guillaumont *et al.* 1959.

[12] Gathercole 2012a: 152–53 and Koester 1989b: 46–48 both count 67 out of 114 sayings in *GThomas* that have clear parallels in the Synoptics, though they differ slightly in which 67 these are. Aune 2002: 256 counts 63.

[13] Cf. Goodacre 2012: 21–22, building on Meier 1991: 137.

[14] Grant 1959.

20   *Chapter 1: The Gospel According to Thomas*

published a succession of articles in which he argued for Thomasine independence.[15] In the following fifty years, as scholars refined the method for determining whether there was any kind of literary dependence between *GThomas* and the Synoptics, the criterion of Synoptic redaction emerged as the gold standard. In 1960, H. K. McArthur was the first to employ this method in Thomasine studies,[16] and the method has reached a zenith of nuance in the recent work by Simon Gathercole and Mark Goodacre.[17]

Following in the footsteps of Christopher Tuckett's earlier work,[18] Simon Gathercole takes advantage of the 21st-century consensus of Markan priority and limits his dataset to include only cases where *GThomas* parallels Matthean or Lukan redaction of *GMark*. Thus, Gathercole's argument evades the counterargument that *GThomas* is merely drawing from the same Sayings Source (Q) or some hypothetical source responsible for Matthean or Lukan *Sondergut* (M or L).[19] Gathercole's argument also enjoys the relative demise of Form Criticism's "rules" of oral transmission that in the 20th-century frequently portrayed *GThomas* as collecting "earlier" forms of the sayings shared with the Synoptics.[20] With this strict redactional criterion, Gathercole identifies 11 cases where *GThomas* contains Matthean and Lukan redactional changes of *GMark* (see Table 3 below): *GThomas* 5.2, 13, 14.5, 31.1, 33.2–3, 44–45, 47.3–5, 65, 66, 99, and 104.

Mark Goodacre has a more expansive approach than Gathercole, including instances where *GThomas* shares terminology that is strikingly Matthean or Lukan. Thus, Goodacre considers *GThomas* 20 and 54, both including the distinctly Matthean term "kingdom of the heavens," as bearing Matthean redaction.[21] Goodacre also considers *GThomas* 57 to be carrying over *GMatthew*

---

[15] Quispel 1957; 1958–59; 1959; 1960; 1966; see also Cullmann 1960; Montefiore 1961.

[16] McArthur 1960: 286–87.

[17] Gathercole 2010; 2012a: 127–224; Goodacre 2012; see the earlier studies by Schrage 1964, Ménard 1975, and Snodgrass 1989–90.

[18] Tuckett 1988.

[19] These were the chief rebuttals from Schramm 1971, developed more fully in Koester 1990: 84-113, and continued still in Kloppenborg 2014a.

[20] Form-critical arguments have been made by Quispel 1966, Sieber 1965, Koester 1965; 1989b: 38–49; 1990: 84–113, Fallon and Cameron 1988, and Patterson 1993.

[21] Goodacre 2012: 66–69 points to *GTh* 20, 54, and 114 which contain the Coptic phrase ⲧⲙⲛ̄ⲧⲉⲣⲟ ⲛ̄ⲙ̄ⲡⲏⲩⲉ. In the cases of *GTh* 20 and 54, the Thomasine versions parallel the Matthean saying with this phrase, over against the Lukan parallels (*GLk* 13.18–19 and 6.20 respectively). Goodacre draws on Pennington 2007 and notes that it is nearly certain that the phrase ἡ βασιλεία τῶν οὐρανῶν belongs to Matthew's hand, since it does not appear in any literature that predates *GMatthew*. It does not appear in the Hebrew Bible, Qumran, the OT Apocrypha or Pseudepigrapha, and it is absent from the earliest Christian period (significantly, there are no instances in Pauline literature). Patterson 1993: 28 and Kloppenborg 2014a: 210–12 argue that *GThomas* uses this phrase to avoid talking about "God," and that the phrase is due to a later osmosis of a third-century "meme," but this does not appreciate the distinctly Matthean

1.2 Combining Gospels in the Gospel according to Thomas 21

13.24–30, which Goodacre sees as a Matthean expansion of *GMark* 4.26–29.[22] Goodacre also makes a case on redaction-critical grounds that the Parable of the Rich Fool (*GLk* 12.15–21) is the product of Luke's authorship, and that *GThomas'* use of this same parallel in *GThomas* 63 bears the essential Lukan marks of the parable (an example story, eschatological reversal, and interior monologue).[23] Similarly, Goodacre argues for signs of Lukan authorial action in *GThomas* 72 (cf. *GLk* 12.13–14)[24] and *GThomas* 79 (cf. *GLk* 11.27–28 // *GLk* 23.27–31).[25] Finally, Goodacre highlights the significance of verbatim agreement shared between *GThomas* and Synoptic parallels found in the Greek Oxyrhynchus fragments (*GTh* 3.1–3, 4.2–3, 5.2, 26, and 39.3) and in retroversion of the Coptic Nag Hammadi Codex II (*GTh* 14.5, 73, and 86).[26]

A cumulative Gathercole-Goodacre case runs as follows. Matthean or Lukan redaction of *GMark* is found in *GThomas* 5.2, 13, 14.5, 31.1, 33.2–3, 44–45, 47.3–5, 65, 66, 99, and 104. Distinct Matthean language or compositional markers are found in *GThomas* 20, 54, and 57. Distinct Lukan language or compositional markers are found in *GThomas* 63, 72, and 79. This evidence comprises a total of seventeen instances of Matthean and Lukan redactional fingerprints in the text of *GThomas* (see Tables 3 and 4 below). Of these seventeen instances, *GThomas* 5.2 and 14.5 can also be classified as in verbatim agreement with Synoptic parallels.

b. Counterarguments against Synoptic Redaction in GThomas

The Gathercole-Goodacre argument has not gone without criticism. Even the strongest rebuttals, however, have conceded that there are Synoptic redactional

---

texture to this phrase in its uses in the first and second centuries. Kloppenborg's point that ἡ βασιλεία τῶν οὐρανῶν is absent from the Greek Thomasine fragments is essentially an argument from silence, given that the fragments are indeed rather fragmentary (Kloppenborg's case would only be conclusive if *GTh* 20, 54, and 114 were extant in the Greek fragments).

[22] Goodacre 2012: 73–80.

[23] Goodacre 2012: 87–91.

[24] Goodacre 2012: 91–96.

[25] Goodacre 2012: 97–108.

[26] Goodacre 2012: 30–44. Goodacre highlights the Greek parallels from P.Oxy. 1, P.Oxy. 654, and P.Oxy. 655, containing strings of verbatim agreement as follows: *GTh* 3.1–3 // *GLk* 17.20–21 (seven-word verbatim agreement, with paleographical reconstruction), *GTh* 4.2–3 // *GMk* 10.31 // *GMt* 19.30 (seven-word verbatim agreement, with paleographical reconstruction), *GTh* 5.2 // *GLk* 8.17 (eight-word verbatim agreement, with paleographical reconstruction), *GTh* 26 // *GLk* 6.42 (thirteen-word verbatim agreement), and *GTh* 39.3 // *GMt* 10.16 (nine-word verbatim agreement, with paleographical reconstruction). Goodacre also highlights parallels based on the Greek retroversion from the Coptic, found in Greeven 1981 and Aland ed. 2001: 517–46. These retroverted parallels are *GTh* 14.5 // *GMt* 15.11 (roughly 14 out of 20 in agreement), *GTh* 73 // *GMt* 9.37–38 // *GLk* 10.2 (16 out of 18 words in agreement), and *GTh* 86 // *GMt* 8.20 // *GLk* 9.58 (roughly 21 out of 29 words in agreement).

22 *Chapter 1: The Gospel According to Thomas*

features in at least some of the seventeen examples proffered by Gathercole and Goodacre. Within their paradigm, the strongest cases for Synoptic influence on *GThomas* are found in *GThomas* 5.2, 14.5, 31.1, and 79.

John Kloppenborg, while giving a sophisticated response to the Gathercole-Goodacre hypothesis, either offers no response to these instances or concedes that they do indeed pass the test of demonstrating genuine Synoptic redaction of some sort (see Tables 3 and 4 below).[27] Kloppenborg leaves unaddressed the case that Goodacre and Gathercole make for *GThomas* 5.2 ("there is nothing hidden etc."), which shows the following verbatim agreement with *GLuke* 8.17: οὐ γάρ ἐστιν κρυπτόν ὃ οὐ φανερὸν γενήσεται,[28] even against its parallels in *GMark* 4.22 and *GMatthew* 10.26. Kloppenborg concedes that *GThomas* 14.5, 31.1, and 79 show Synoptic redaction. As for the other thirteen instances, Kloppenborg offers a brief response to ten of these, in some cases appealing to later influence on the Coptic translation of *GThomas*,[29] in other cases arguing against Matthean or Lukan authorial creativity,[30] and in still other cases seeking to neutralize the clear Synoptic redactional elements by appealing to Thomasine primitivity,[31] Thomasine dissimilarity,[32] or the influence of Q.[33]

Kloppenborg offers no response to Gathercole's arguments for Synoptic redaction in *GThomas* 47.3–5 (cf. *GLk* 5.36–39) and *GThomas* 104 (cf. *GLk* 5.33–35), as well as Goodacre's argument for *GThomas* 72 (cf. *GLk* 12.13–14).

---

[27] Kloppenborg 2014a.

[28] The verbatim agreement is reconstructed from P.Oxy. 654.29–31, which does have significant lacunae: [οὐ γάρ ἐσ]τιν κρυπτόν ὃ οὐ φανε[ρὸν γενήσεται]. However, the later Coptic translation reflects Lukan verbatim agreement: ⲙ̄ⲛ ⲗⲁⲁⲩ ⲅⲁⲣ ⲉϥϩⲏⲡ̀ ⲉϥⲛⲁⲟⲩⲱⲛϩ ⲉⲃⲟⲗ ⲁⲛ.

[29] Kloppenborg 2014a: 210–11 implies that ⲧⲙ̄ⲛ̄ⲧⲉⲣⲟ ⲛ̄ⲙ̄ⲡⲏⲩⲉ is the result of third-century Matthean influence.

[30] Kloppenborg 2014a: 212–13, 215–17, argues against Matthean creativity in *GMt* 13.24–30 // *GTh* 57, and he similarly argues against Lukan creativity in *GLk* 12.15–21 // *GTh* 63.

[31] Kloppenborg 2014a: 220–24. Kloppenborg argues, on the basis that *GTh* 65 represents first-century horticultural practices more accurately than the Synoptics, that the Thomasine version coheres more closely to the earliest strata of the parable of the vineyard owner than its alleged redactional parallel in *GLk* 20.9–16.

[32] Kloppenborg 2014a: 212 focuses on the differences between *GTh* 13 and *GMt* 16.17, which are indeed obvious. However, Kloppenborg does not appreciate the significance of Thomas *naming* Matthew, whose apostolic ministry was relatively insignificant in early Christianity, apart from his putative role as a gospel author, and how this naming of Matthew coincides with a dialogue that resembles *GMt* 16.17 by recognizing a single apostle as the special tradent of Jesus' true identity, and how both contexts introduce Peter attempting an answer to Jesus' question of his own identity.

[33] Kloppenborg 2014a: 208, 214. Kloppenborg considers *GTh* 33 to reflect agreement with *GMt* 5.15 and Q 12.3, rather than Lukan redaction of *GMk* 4.21 (cf. *GLk* 8.16 and 11.33), but it must be stressed that this is based on a hypothetical reconstruction of Q, which multiplies complexity beyond a simpler redactional solution.

1.2 Combining Gospels in the Gospel according to Thomas 23

Kloppenborg's rebuttal to the Gathercole-Goodacre hypothesis does not sufficiently address a constellation of coincidences that are most easily explained as Synoptic influence on *GThomas*. Kloppenborg attempts to minimize the gravity of Synoptic redaction on *GThomas* by arguing that Synoptic influence only affected a handful of Thomasine sayings. Kloppenborg argues rightly that *GThomas* was a complex, gnomological anthology that drew on an eclectic range of sources within the Jesus tradition.[34] But he takes this argument too far in claiming that the Synoptic tradition is just one, *minor* source among several. Extensive Synoptic influence in *GThomas* is fully compatible with the fact that other strands of Jesus tradition also shaped Thomasine composition. The presence of these other strands does little to invalidate the presence of Synoptic influence.

Furthermore, Kloppenborg does not fully appreciate that Gathercole and Goodacre have identified plausible Matthean and Lukan redactional features scattered across the 114 Thomasine *logia* (they are not relegated to an isolated cluster).

---

[34] Kloppenborg 2014a: 226–32. Kloppenborg's depiction of *GThomas* as a "school document" within a philosophical tradition, similar to Alcinous' early second century, Middle-Platonic epitome (the *Didaskalikos*), is a valuable insight that should lead to fruitful exploration in Thomasine studies, especially if one appreciates *GThomas* as a second-century, philosophical, Platonizing reception of the Jesus tradition (cf. Schröter 2019b).

Table 3: Synoptic Redaction in *GThomas* (Gathercole) with Kloppenborg's Responses

Markan Logion	*MattR*	*LukeR*	*GTh* Parallel	Topic / key phrases	Kloppenborg's Response
GMk 4.22	[*GMt* 10.26]	*GLk* 8.17 [*GLk* 12.2]	*GTh* 5.2	Nothing hidden that will not be revealed	Unaddressed
GMk 8.27–32	*GMt* 16.13–22	[*GLk* 9.18–22]	*GTh* 13	Jesus asks his disciples to name his identity	*GTh* is wholly different from *GMt* account, and mention of Matthew is not significant
GMk 7.15	*GMt* 15:11		*GTh* 14.5	Defilement through the mouth	Genuine Redaction
GMk 6.4	[*GMt* 13.57]	*GLk* 4.24	*GTh* 31.1	Prophet unwelcome in his own town	Genuine Redaction
GMk 4.21	[*GMt* 5.15]	*GLk* 8.16/11.33	*GTh* 33.2–3	Lamp under a bushel or on a lampstand	Dismisses on the basis of complicated Q influence.
GMk 3.28–29	*GMt* 12.31–32	[*GLk* 12.10] [*GLk* 6.44]	*GTh* 44–45	Blasphemy against the Spirit; speaking from the abundance of the heart	*GTh* 45 actually combines what looks like MattR to Q/Lk 6.44, so it is more complicated
GMk 2.21–22	[*GMt* 9.16–17]	*GLk* 5.36–39	*GTh* 47.3–5	Wine, wineskins, patch, and garments	Unaddressed
GMk 12.1–9	[*GMt* 21.33–46]	*GLk* 20.9–16	*GTh* 65	Vineyard owner, servants, and son	Dismissed on the basis of *GTh*'s greater realism than Synoptic parallels
GMk 12.10–11	[*GMt* 21.42]	*GLk* 20.17	*GTh* 66	Quotation of LXX Ps. 117.22–23	Dismissed on the basis of *GTh*'s interpretation of LXX Ps. 117
GMk 3.32–35	[*GMt* 12.47–50]	*GLk* 8.20–21	*GTh* 99	Identity of Jesus' mother and brothers	*GTh* has similarities to *GMk*, *GMt*, and *GEb*, so we cannot point to one redactional preference
GMk 2.18–20	[*GMt* 9.14–17]	*GLk* 5.33–35	*GTh* 104	Fasting and prayer around the bridegroom	Unaddressed

Table 4: Synoptic Redaction in *GThomas* (Goodacre) with Kloppenborg's Responses

Markan Logion	*MattR*	*LukeR* / Sundergut	*GTh* Parallel	Topic / key phrases	Kloppenborg's Response
GMk 4.22	[*GMt* 10.26]	*GLk* 8.17	*GTh* 5 (P.Oxy. 654.29–31)	Hidden and revealed	Unaddressed
GMk 7.14–15	*GMt* 15.10–11		*GTh* 14.5	Defilement through the mouth	Genuine Redaction
GMk 4.30–31	*GMt* 13.31	[*GLk* 13.18–19]	*GTh* 20	Th kingdom of heaven is like a mustard seed	Dismissed on the basis of later scribal harmonization in Coptic version and fragmentary nature of Greek *GTh*
GMk 6.4	[*GMt* 13.57]	*GLk* 4.24	*GTh* 31 (P.Oxy. 1.36–41)	Prophet unwelcome in his own town	Genuine Redaction
	GMt 5.3	[*GLk* 6.20]	*GTh* 54	Blessed are the poor	Dismissed for the same reasons as *GTh* 20
GMk 4.26–29	*GMt* 13.24–30		*GTh* 57	An enemy sabotaging a sower's good seed with bad seed	Dismissed on the basis of compositional procedure in *GMt* 13.24–30 and *GTh* 57
		GLk 12.15–21	*GTh* 63	The rich fool	Dismissed on the premise that *GLk* 12.15–21 is not a Lukan creation
		GLk 12.13–14	*GTh* 72	Who has made me into an arbiter?	Mentioned in passing but unaddressed
		GLk 11.27–28/23:27–31	*GTh* 79	Wombs that bear and breasts that nourish; hearing the word of the father and keeping it	Genuine Redaction

26 *Chapter 1: The Gospel According to Thomas*

This datum validates Gathercole's analogy that "a blood sample reflects the entire circulation."[35] Indeed, Gathercole and Goodacre have identified samples across Thomas' entire circulatory system.[36]

Kloppenborg also nods to the theory that *GThomas* is a layered text.[37] In this model, Synoptic influence could have entered *GThomas* in the last quarter of the second century and yielded the extant Greek fragments. Proponents of this model still maintain that the earliest layers of *GThomas* were independent of, and in many places prior to, the Synoptics. In response to this argument, Gathercole demonstrates that nearly all the cases of Matthean and Lukan redactional elements occur in Thomasine *logia* that proponents of the rolling corpus argue are the earliest layers of Thomasine composition. As stated above, Gathercole identifies redactional elements at *GThomas* 5, 13, 14, 31, 33, 44–45, 47, 65, 66, 99, and 104. April DeConick, John Dominic Crossan, William Arnal, and Armand Puig, all of whom argue for a rolling Thomasine corpus, locate ten of these eleven sayings as part of the earliest stratum of composition.[38] Therefore, if indeed *GThomas* is a rolling corpus (which is far from certain), it is probable that Synoptic redactional influence entered its composition at the earliest stages.

Critics of the Gathercole-Goodacre redactional hypothesis, and its earlier versions in the scholarship of McArthur, Schrage, and Tuckett, have also appealed to even later scribal assimilation, namely, that by the time the scribe in the fourth century was copying his or her Coptic manuscript in NHC II, *GMatthew* and *GLuke* were so influential that some of their redactional features slipped into *GThomas* at this later stage of transmission.[39] However, it is unlikely that the Matthean and Lukan redactional elements attested in Nag Hammadi Codex II are the result of later scribal assimilation with Synoptic material. The Coptic text of NHC II indicates that its scribe was less predisposed to Synoptic assimilation

---

[35] Gathercole 2012a: 213.

[36] The pervasiveness of Matthean and Lukan influence across the composition of *GThomas* invites speculation that *GMark* might also stand at only one remove from Thomasine composition. However, presupposing Markan priority, a rigorous methodology is lacking for identifying Markan distinctiveness in the text of *GThomas* beyond clear and consistent examples of Markan material, such as those found in Tatian's *Diatessaron* and, to a lesser extent, the *Epistula Apostolorum*; cf. Justin's single yet clear reference to a Markan locution (*GMk.* 3.17) in *Dial.* 106.3–4. For this reason, my conclusion is limited to *GMatthew*'s and *GLuke*'s influence on *GThomas*.

[37] Kloppenborg 2014a: 201, 224–26; cf. Wilson 1960: 231–50; Arnal 1995; DeConick 2006; Puig 2008: 133–78; Patterson 2014: 258–59.

[38] Gathercole 2012a: 221–23, lays out in his Table 9.1 the layering articulated by Crossan 1991, Arnal 1995, DeConick 2006, and Puig 2008. The only exception of Gathercole's redactional cases is *GTh* 13, which Arnal, DeConick, and Puig all place in their latest stratum (although Crossan places it in his earliest stratum).

[39] E.g. Patterson 1993: 93; Kloppenborg 2014a: 211.

1.2 Combining Gospels in the Gospel according to Thomas   27

than the Thomasine Greek fragments.[40] For example, Greek *GThomas* 4.2–3
(P.Oxy. 654) more closely aligns with its parallel in *GMark* 10.31, while the
Coptic version omits an entire phrase.[41] The clearest example of Coptic
GThomas resisting Synoptic assimilation is *GThomas* 36, where the Coptic version appears to be abbreviating a more primitive version of *GThomas* preserved
in the Greek of P.Oxy. 655. *GThomas* 36 in P.Oxy. 655 is longer and contains
parallels both to *GMatthew* 6.25 // *GLuke* 12.22 and to *GMatthew* 6.27 // *GLuke*
12.25, whereas the Coptic version omits the latter parallels entirely.

Insofar as the fragmentary evidence allows comparison between earlier (sec-
ond- and third-century) Greek *GThomas* and later Coptic *GThomas*, the trend
points in the opposite direction: *GThomas* was less assimilated to Synoptic material in its Coptic form than in its earlier Greek form. Therefore, it is unwise to
dismiss Synoptic parallels found in the Coptic text of *GThomas* as later assimi-
lations. They are more likely to reflect earlier stages of Thomasine composition.
Alternatively, the Coptic manuscript of *GThomas* might exhibit a tendency towards *decreasing* or even *eliminating* Synoptic influence from a second-century
version of *GThomas* that showed far more affinities with the Synoptics.

c. Mode of Proto-Canonical Gospel Reception in GThomas

Since none of the rebuttals provide sufficient counterevidence, it is safe to conclude that Gathercole's and Goodacre's judgments stand firm: *GThomas* combined elements of *GMatthew* and *GLuke* to form its own fresh, recontextualized
composition. *GThomas* is therefore a valuable witness for our study of gospel
combinations in the second century as an example of interpretive rewriting of at
least two earlier gospels. *GThomas* will be even more valuable for our study
when we consider how it integrates redactional material from *GMatthew* and
GLuke with traditions that eventually found their homes in noncanonical Jesus
books. For the purposes of this study, we will consider Gathercole and Goodacre's seventeen instances of Synoptic redaction as conclusive examples of
GThomas combining materials from *GMatthew* and *GLuke*.[42] Since these seventeen instances are scattered throughout the entire sequence of 114 *logia*, since
these instances occur at the allegedly earliest stages of Thomasine composition,
and since these instances encompass a variety of types of Jesus' sayings (e.g.
aphorisms, parables, responses), we can safely conclude that *GMatthew* and

---

[40] Cf. Goodacre 2012: 57–61; Marcovich 1969: 53–74. Goodacre makes the case that
GThomas 26 in NHC II shows less influence from the Synoptics than in P.Oxy. 1.1–4, but this
might be due to the Coptic translation technique. The other examples Goodacre proffers are
more convincing (highlighted in the present section).

[41] P.Oxy. 654.25–26 (*GTh* 4.2–3) has ὅτι πολλοὶ ἔσονται π[ρῶτοι ἔσχατοι καὶ] οἱ ἔσχατοι
πρῶτοι, but the Coptic does omits a translation of καὶ οἱ ἔσχατοι πρῶτοι.

[42] Gathercole: *GTh* 5.2, 13, 14.5, 31.1, 33.2–3, 44–45, 47.3–5, 65, 66, 99, and 104. Goodacre adds: *GTh* 20, 54, 57, 63, 72, and 79.

28   *Chapter 1: The Gospel According to Thomas*

GLuke exert significant influence on *GThomas*. In the subsequent section, we will see how this Synoptic influence far outweighs the influence of noncanonical traditions in *GThomas*.

The question remains, however, by what mode *GThomas* accessed these redactional elements stemming from *GMatthew* and *GLuke*. The cumulative weight of verbatim agreement, redactional parallels, and the distribution of these agreements and parallels across the 114 *logia* that constitute *GThomas*, strongly suggest these two proto-canonical gospels exerted their influence as on *GThomas* as textual objects. But what was the *mode* by which *GMatthew* and *GLuke* entered the bloodstream of *GThomas*?

A plausible scenario is what William Johnson has called "deft excerpting."[43] Excerpting was a feature of elite reading practices in the second century, whereby an intellectual would maintain an active stance towards the text he was reading and collect extracts from his reading. The intellectual could draw upon these notes when composing his own treatises and showcase his knowledge of canonical texts in numerous citations and allusions. For example, Pliny the Younger writes to Tacitus about his habit of notetaking while reading Livy: "I read as though at leisure, and made excerpts, just as I had been doing."[44] Similarly, Aulus Gellius mentions how he took notes as an aid to memory:

> After I read the book of an early writer, I tried afterwards… to call to mind and review the passages… for example, I record the following words I have been able to memorize from the first book of the *Annales* of Quintus Claudius, a book I read over the past two days…[45]

Intellectuals took notes as memory aids and they also composed synopses, compendia, and epitomes. Parthenius, writing in the first century BCE, speaks of his work Περὶ ἐρωτικῶν παθημάτων as a "little notebook" (ὑπομνηματίων) in which he collected short love stories derived from more refined, literary texts.[46] Galen, in the latter part of the second century, writes about the common practice of composing epitomes (ἐπιτομάς), synopses (συνόψεις), and summaries (ἐπιδρομάς).[47] Additionally, there are numerous examples of such documents in the extant papyri.[48] This practice flourished among intellectuals in the High Empire, as a

---

[43] Johnson 2010: 118; for a rich treatment of ancient excerpting, see Konstan 2011; cf. Most 1997.

[44] Pliny, *Ep.* 6.20: *et quasi per otium lego atque etiam ut coerperam excerpo*; text and translation Konstan 2011: 17–18.

[45] Aulus Gellius, *Attic Nights* 17.2.1–2; translation Johnson 2010: 119.

[46] Parthenius gives these comments in the prologue of his work. The text and translation of the prologue can be found in Rossum-Steenbeek 1998: xiii–vv.

[47] Galen, *Synopsis librorum suorum de pulsibus* 1; Kühn 9.431.4–6.

[48] For example, P.Oxy. 18.2192, a second-century CE letter, mentions the epitomes of Thersagoras' treatise on tragic myths (Rossum-Steenbeek 1998: 3n12). In the extant papyri, there are numerous hypotheses (e.g. P.Oxy. 27.2457; P.Oxy. 20.2256; P.Oxy. 56.3829; P.Mil.Vogl. 1.18), works of mythography (e.g. P.Oxy. 56.3830), catalogues (e.g. P.Haun. 1.7), and scholia

1.2 Combining Gospels in the Gospel according to Thomas 29

means of establishing a cultural identity around the most respected ancient philosophers and their schools.

John Kloppenborg has argued convincingly that *GThomas* is a gnomological anthology constructed around the memory of Jesus the "wise philosopher."[49] It is therefore plausible for the author of *GThomas* to engage in "deft excerpting," either by manually extracting excerpts from *GMatthew* and *GLuke*, or by working from *hypomnemata* containing excerpts from *GMatthew* and *GLuke*. The pervasiveness of Matthean and Lukan redaction in *GThomas* make it probable that such *hypomnemata* were excerpts from the Synoptic gospels rather than archetypal sayings sources or *testimonia* from which the Synoptic authors drew. Even if through the medium of *hypomnemata*, the textual distinctiveness of *GMatthew* and *GLuke* dominates *GThomas*' own composition, and the agencies of the authors of *GMatthew* and *GLuke* certainly exerted a ripple effect in *GThomas*. Enough redactional material is scattered across *GThomas* to allow us to speak of these two proto-canonical gospels keeping company with one another within the pages of *GThomas*, as Homer and Vergil kept company in Shakespeare's theater.

1.2.2 Identities and Mode – Noncanonical Gospels in GThomas

It is difficult to ascertain whether noncanonical gospels exerted any literary influence on *GThomas*. Noncanonical gospels do not exhibit the level of intertextual relationship that the Synoptics have with one another, and we cannot apply the same redactional criterion to determine whether *GThomas* is borrowing from a noncanonical gospel. Nevertheless, *GThomas* contains seven possible parallels with noncanonical *logia* (laid out in Table 5 below). It will be fruitful to determine the relationship between *GThomas* and the noncanonical gospels it resembles in these seven instances. After determining this relationship, we will be able to see more clearly whether *GMatthew* and *GLuke* keep company with any noncanonical gospels in the text of *GThomas*, and which of these gospels exert the most influence.

---

that summarize works of canonical Greek literature. For a comprehensive study of the forms and patterns of these summaries, see Rossum-Steenbeek 1998.

[49] Kloppenborg 2014a: 226–32; Jesus' is called a "wise philosopher" in *GTh* 13. The creation of gnomological anthologies was a central facet of literate education in the Hellenistic and Roman periods, and mastering this art was a sign of an accomplished *paideia*; cf. Morgan 1998: 90–119.

30 Chapter 1: The Gospel According to Thomas

Table 5: Parallel Apocryphal Traditions in *GThomas*

Apocryphal Gospel Parallel	Citation Location	*GTh* parallel	Topic (in *GTh* version)
GHeb §1 (Gregory 2017: 62)	Clement, *Strom.* 2.9.45.5; 5.14.96	*GTh* 2	Seeking, finding, reigning
GEgy	Clement, *Strom.* 3.13.93; *2 Clem.* 12.2	*GTh* 22	Two and one, outside and inside, male and female
GEgy Cf. *Dial. Sav.* 84–85 Cf. *AcTh* 14	Clement, *Strom.* 3.13.92	*GTh* 37	Stripping off clothes as children
GEgy; Cf. *Excerpts of Theodotus* 36.1–2	Clement, *Strom.* 3.9.64.1 (cf. 3.6.45.3); 3.9.66.1–2	*GTh* 61	Salome's question to Jesus
Unknown	Origen, *hom. Jer.* 3.3.104–105	*GTh* 82	He that is near me is near the fire; he that is far is far from the kingdom
GEb §5 (Gregory 2017: 241)	Epiphanius, *Pan.* 30.14.5; *2 Clem.* 9.11	*GTh* 99	These are my brothers and mother
GHeb §5 (Gregory 2017: 120)	Jerome, *Adv. Pelagianos* 3.2	*GTh* 104	What is the sin that I have done?

a. Parallels with the Gospel According to the Egyptians

GThomas 22, 37, and 61 contain constituent parts that the *Gospel according to the Egyptians* appears to have as a coherent whole in an episode where Jesus converses with Salome, as shown in Table 6a–b below. This narrative coherence is conspicuously absent in the Thomasine uses of the common *logia*. The Thomasine evangelist preferred to situate the sayings in different contexts. It is impossible to determine whether *GThomas* is dismembering a prior narrative unity found in *GEgy* (*GTh* thus showing dependence on *GEgy*), or *GEgy* is arranging Thomasine *logia* into a narrative coherence (*GEgy* dependent on *GTh*), or both are integrating common memory of Jesus into their compositions (independently drawing from the same tradition). It is unwise to argue for priority or posteriority strictly on the basis of narrative or dialogical coherence. There is nothing inherent to coherence that privileges it to priority or automatically positions it in posteriority.

Table 6a: GEgyptians and Parallels

GEgyptians fragments	Apocryphal Parallels[e]	GThomas Parallels[f]
GEgy 1: Τῇ Σαλώμῃ ὁ κύριος πυνθανομένῃ μέχρι πότε θάνατος ἰσχύσει; ... μέχρις ἂν εἶπεν ὑμεῖς αἱ γυναῖκες τίκτητε.[a]		*GTh* 67: ⲡⲉϫⲉ ⲥⲁⲗⲱⲙⲏ ⲛ̄ⲧⲁⲕ`ⲛⲓⲙ`ⲡ̄ⲣⲱⲙⲉ ϩⲱⲥ ⲉⲃⲟⲗ ϩⲛ̄ ⲟⲩⲁ ⲁⲕⲧⲉⲗⲟ ⲉϫⲙ̄ ⲡⲁϭⲗⲟϭ ⲁⲩⲱ ⲁⲕ`ⲟⲩⲱⲙ ⲉⲃⲟⲗ ϩⲛ̄ ⲧⲁⲧⲣⲁⲡⲉⲍⲁ   ⲡⲉϫⲉ ⲓ̄ⲥ̄ ⲛⲁⲥ ⲇⲉ ⲁⲛⲟⲕ` ⲡⲉ ⲡⲉⲧϣⲟⲟⲡ` ⲉⲃⲟⲗ ϩⲙ̄ ⲡⲉⲧ`ϣⲏϣ...
GEgy 2: ἦλθον καταλῦσαι τὰ ἔργα τῆς θηλείας...[b]		
GEgy 4: φαμένης γὰρ αὐτῆς καλῶς οὖν ἐποίησα μὴ τεκοῦσα... ἀμείβεται λέγων ὁ κύριος· πᾶσαν φάγε βοτάνην, τὴν δὲ πικρίαν ἔχουσαν μὴ φάγῃς.[c]	*Dial. Sav.* 84–85: ⲡⲉϫⲉⲡϫⲟⲉⲓⲥ... ⲛ̄ⲧⲱⲧⲛ̄ [ⲇⲉ] ϩⲱⲥ ϣⲏⲣⲉ ⲛ̄ⲧⲙⲏⲉ ⲉⲧⲉⲧⲛⲁ† [ϩⲓ]ⲱⲧⲧⲏⲟⲩⲧⲛ̄ ⲁⲛ ⲛ̄ⲛⲓϩⲃ̄ⲥⲱ ⲉⲧⲁϩⲟ [ⲟⲡ] ⲡⲣⲟⲥⲟⲩⲉⲓⲁϣ· ⲁⲗⲗⲁ †ϫⲱ ⲙ̄ⲙⲟⲥ [ⲛ]ⲏⲧⲛ ϫⲉⲧⲉⲛ̄ⲛⲁϣⲱⲡⲉ ⲙ̄ⲙⲁⲕⲁ[ⲣⲓ]ⲟⲥ· ϩⲟⲧⲁⲛ ⲉⲧⲉⲧⲛ̄ϣⲁⲛⲃⲉϣⲧⲏ[ⲛⲟ]ⲩ...	*GTh* 37: ⲡⲉϫⲉ ⲓ̄ⲥ̄ ϫⲉ ϩⲟⲧⲁⲛ ⲉⲧⲉⲧⲛ̄ϣⲁⲕⲉⲕ ⲧⲏⲩⲧⲛ̄ ⲉϩⲏⲩ ⲙ̄ⲡⲉⲧⲛ̄ϣⲓⲡⲉ ⲁⲩⲱ ⲛ̄ⲧⲉⲧⲛ̄ϥⲓ ⲛ̄ⲛⲉⲧⲛ̄ϣⲧⲏⲛ ⲛ̄ⲧⲉⲧⲛ̄ⲕⲁⲁⲩ ϩⲁ ⲡⲉⲥⲏⲧ` ⲛ̄ⲛⲉⲧⲛ̄ⲟⲩⲉⲣⲏⲧⲉ ⲛ̄ⲑⲉ ⲛ̄ⲛⲓⲕⲟⲩⲉⲓ ⲛ̄ϣⲏⲣⲉ ϣⲏⲙ` ⲛ̄ⲧⲉⲧⲛ̄ϫⲟⲡϫ̄ⲡ̄` ⲙ̄ⲙⲟⲟⲩ...
GEgy 5: ἔφη ὁ κύριος· ὅταν τὸ τῆς αἰσχύνης ἔνδυμα πατήσητε καὶ ὅταν γένηται τὰ δύο ἓν καὶ τὸ ἄρρεν μετὰ τῆς θηλείας οὔτε ἄρρεν οὔτε θῆλυ...[d]	*2 Clem.* 12.2: ἐπερωτηθεὶς γὰρ αὐτὸς ὁ κύριος... εἶπεν· Ὅταν ἔσται τα δύο ἕν, καὶ τὸ ἔξω ὡς τὸ ἔσω, καὶ τὸ ἄρσεν μετὰ τῆς θηλείας, οὔτε ἄρσεν οὔτε θῆλυ.	*GTh* 22: ⲡⲉϫⲉ ⲓ̄ⲏ̄ⲥ̄ ⲛⲁⲩ ϫⲉ ϩⲟⲧⲁⲛ ⲉⲧⲉⲧⲛ̄ϣⲁⲣ̄ ⲡⲥⲛⲁⲩ ⲟⲩⲁ ⲁⲩⲱ ⲉⲧⲉⲧⲛ̄ϣⲁⲣ̄ ⲡⲥⲁ ⲛϩⲟⲩⲛ ⲛ̄ⲑⲉ ⲙ̄ⲡⲥⲁ ⲙ̄ⲡⲓⲧⲛ̄ ⲁⲩⲱ ϣⲓⲛⲁ ⲉⲧⲉⲧⲛⲁⲉⲓⲣⲉ ⲙ̄ⲫⲟ`ⲟⲩⲧ` ⲙⲛ̄ ⲧⲥϩⲓⲙⲉ ⲙ̄ⲡⲓⲟⲩⲁ ⲟⲩⲱⲧ` ⲇⲉⲕⲁⲁⲥ ⲛⲉ ⲫⲟⲟⲩⲧ` ⲣ̄ ϩⲟⲟⲩⲧ` ⲛ̄ⲧⲉ ⲧⲥϩⲓⲙⲉ ⲣ̄ ⲥϩⲓⲙⲉ...

Notes: [a] *Strom.* 3.45.3 [b] *Strom.* 3.63.1 [c] *Strom.* 3.66.1–2 [d] *Strom.* 3.92.2–93.1 [e] Coptic text Emmel 1984. [f] Coptic *GTh* text Ehrman and Pleše 2011.

Table 6b: GEgyptians and Parallels in English Translation

GEgyptians fragments[a]	Apocryphal Parallels[b]	GThomas Parallels[c]
GEgy 1: When Salome asked, "How long will death prevail?" The Lord replied, "For as long as you women bear children..."		GTh 61: Salome said, "Who are you, O man? As if you are from someone, you have climbed onto my couch and eaten from my table." Jesus said to her, "I am the one who comes from what is whole"...
GEgy 2: "I have come to destroy the works of the female..."		
GEgy 4: [Salome] said, "Then I have done well not to bear children." ...The Lord responded, "Eat every herb, but not the one that is bitter."		
GEgy 5: The Lord replied, "When you trample on the garment of shame and when the two become one and the male with the female is neither male nor female...	Dial. Sav. 84–85: "The Lord said, '...But you, as children of truth, not with these transitory garments are you to clothe yourselves. Rather, I say to you that you will become blessed when you strip yourselves.'"	GTh 37: Jesus said, "When you strip naked without being ashamed and take your clothes and place them under your feet like little children and stamp on them..."
	2 Clem. 12.2: For the Lord himself... said: "When the two shall be one, and the outside like the inside, and the male with the female, neither male nor female..."	GTh 22: Jesus said... "When you make the two one, and make... the outside like the inside... and you make the male and the female be a single one, with the male no longer being male and the female no longer female..."

Notes: [a] Trans. Ehrman and Pleše 2011. [b] Dial. Sav. trans. Emmel 1984; 2 Clem. trans. Holmes 2007. [c] Trans. Ehrman and Pleše 2011.

1.2 Combining Gospels in the Gospel according to Thomas 33

Furthermore, the "two-one" *logion* is set within a short narrative context in all three extant parallels; in *GEgy* the context is a dialogue with Salome,[50] in *2 Clement* 12.2 the context is a dialogue about the kingdom, and in *GThomas* 22 the context is a situation regarding nursing infants and an ensuing conversation about the kingdom. That *GThomas*, *GEgy*, and *2 Clement* each situate this *logion* within a different situational context suggests not that *GThomas* is borrowing from *GEgy*, but rather that these *logia* within the Jesus tradition were malleable for fresh composition and were often situated into new episodic contexts. This is corroborated by the fact that the version in *GThomas* differs significantly from the version in either *GEgy* or *2 Clement*. Furthermore, given the uncertainty of dating for either *GThomas* or *GEgy*, we cannot rule out the possibility that the direction of influence moves from *GThomas* to *GEgy* rather than the other way around.

While we might safely conclude that *GThomas* is drawing from the same social memory as *GEgy*, it is unlikely that *GThomas* does so with direct or secondary-oral contact with *GEgy*. The assumed narrative context involving Salome in *GThomas* 61 does suggest that there is a narrative trope behind it, in the same way that *GThomas* 100 (the question of taxes to Caesar) presupposes the narrative context in *GMark* 12.13–17. The major differences between the saying in *GThomas* 61 and *GEgy*, however, make it highly unlikely that this narrative background is derived from *GEgy*.

b. Parallels with the Gospel according to the Hebrews

GThomas 104 inscribes another noncanonical *logion*, this one paralleled in a fragment that Jerome attributes to the *Gospel according to the Hebrews*:[51]

They said to Jesus, "Come, let us pray and fast today." Jesus said, "What sin have I committed, or how have I been defeated? But when the bridegroom comes out of the bridal chamber, then let them fast and pray."[52]

Interestingly, *GThomas* 104 connects this noncanonical saying with Lukan redaction at the clausal level, displayed in Table 7 below. Our question here regards whether *GThomas* is drawing from both *GLuke* and *GHebrews*. We can see that *GThomas* here mimics Luke's redaction of a Markan *logion* (*GMk* 2.18–20 > *GLk* 5.33–35 > *GTh* 104). *GMark* 2.18–20 and its Matthean parallel (*GMt* 9.14–

---

[50] Portions of this dialogue are preserved in Clement of Alexandria, *Strom.* 3.6–13; see below, Section 5.2.1.

[51] In *Pelag.* 3.2, Jerome says this *logion* is found "in the gospel according to the Hebrews" (*in euangelio iuxta Hebraeos*); Latin text taken from Moreschini 1990. Scholars are divided as to whether Jerome is referring to the *Gospel according to the Hebrews* or the *Gospel of the Nazareans* (or indeed whether this gospel is one and the same); cf. Klijn 1992; Edwards 2009; Luomanen 2012; Gregory 2017. See below, Section 3.1.2.

[52] Translation Gathercole 2014: 574.

34   *Chapter 1: The Gospel According to Thomas*

17) only make mention of fasting (νηστεύουσιν), but *GLuke* includes prayer (νηστεύουσιν… καὶ δεήσεις ποιοῦνται). *GThomas* 104 follows the Lukan redaction in mentioning both fasting and prayer, in that same order (ⲙⲁⲣⲟⲩⲛⲏ̄ⲥⲧⲉⲩⲉ ⲁⲩⲱ ⲙⲁⲣⲟⲩϣⲗⲏⲗ`). The parallel is corroborated by the Greek word for bridegroom and its Coptic cognate, both with the definite article (ὁ νυμφίος // ⲡⲛⲩⲙ́ⲫⲱⲛ).

The parallel with *GHebrews* is slightly more difficult to establish, but it is apparent nonetheless (see Table 7 below). Jerome's fragment of *GHebrews* – *quid peccavi* – is more succinct than Coptic *GThomas*' ⲟⲩ ⲅⲁⲣ` ⲡⲉ ⲡⲛⲟⲃⲉ ⲛ̄ⲧⲁⲉⲓⲁⲁϥ`.[53] However, if indeed Jerome translated this fragment from Hebrew (or an Aramaic dialect), as he claims in his *Commentary on Matthew* 12.13,[54] it is important to mention that he is often flexible in his translation of Semitic sources, and he can find more economic ways to recast Semitic idioms into Latin phrases.[55] The original wording of this *logion* in *GHebrews* might have paralleled more fully the syntax in Coptic *GThomas* 104, but of this we cannot be certain. Equally, the differences in Coptic *GThomas* 104 might be due to the syntactic options available to the Coptic translator. Thomasine dependence on *GHebrews* cannot be ruled out entirely, but the literary connection is slightly weaker than with the Lukan redaction. At any rate, *GThomas* is undoubtedly drawing on Jesus tradition not found in the proto-canonical gospels and uses it alongside Lukan material.

GThomas 2 shares a saying with Synoptic parallels but expands it in a way similar to *GHebrews*. *GThomas* 2 says,

Jesus said, "He who seeks should not stop seeking until he finds. And when he finds, he will be astonished, and when he is astonished, he will reign, and having reigned, he will rest."[56]

The collocation of seeking unceasingly, finding, marveling, and ruling is closely paralleled in *GHebrews*: "One who seeks will not stop seeking until he finds. When he finds, he will be astonished, and having been astonished, he will rule. And when he has ruled, he will rest."[57] The core of the seeking/finding *logion* is

---

[53] *Pelag.* 3.2.

[54] *Comm. Matt.* 12.13, *In euangelio quo utuntur Nazareni et Hebionitae, quod nuper in graecum de hebraeo sermone transtulimus…*); Latin text from Hurst and Adriaen 1969. In *Pelag.* 3.2, Jerome specifies that this gospel was written in Aramaic or Syriac but with Hebrew letters (*quod Chaldaico quidem Syroque sermone sed Hebraicis litteris scriptum est*). Jerome apparently also translated sayings from it into Latin in the fragments he preserves in his *Commentary on Matthew* and tractate *Against the Pelagians*.

[55] I am grateful to Michael Graves for this insight; see Graves 2007.

[56] Translation Gathercole 2014: 198. This is translated from the Greek of P.Oxy. 654, which is fragmentary.

[57] This *logion* is attributed to *GHebrews* by Clement of Alexandria in *Strom.* 2.9.45.5 and given in its full form in *Strom.* 5.14.96.3.

1.2 Combining Gospels in the Gospel according to Thomas   35

well-attested across early Christian literature,[58] so we cannot establish dependence between *GThomas* and *GHebrews* on this basis alone. Among these ancient variations to the seeking-finding saying, only *GThomas* and *GHebrews* include the theme of reigning. This suggests a stronger connection between the versions of the saying found in *GThomas* and *GHebrews*, and we cannot rule out the possibility that *GThomas* is drawing from *GHebrews*, but it is impossible to build a composite picture such as the relationship between *GThomas* and the Synoptics, since the text of *GHebrews* is so fragmentary. The most we can say is that *GThomas* and *GHebrews* overlap in their use of Jesus tradition that was later deemed noncanonical.

c. Parallels with the Gospel of the Ebionites *and an Anonymous Source*

GThomas 99 (on Jesus' mother and brothers) contains a noncanonical *logion*, which some argue agrees with the *Gospel of the Ebionites* over against its Synoptic parallels (it also shows up in an abbreviated version preserved in *2 Clem.* 9.11):

The disciples said to him, "Your brothers and your mother are standing outside." He said to them, "Those who are here who do the will of my Father – these are my brothers and my mother. It is they who will enter the kingdom of my Father."[59]

Because the saying is attested in all three Synoptic gospels (*GMt* 12.47–50 // *GMk* 3.32–35 // *GLk* 8.20–21), as well as *GThomas, GEbionites,*[60] and *2 Clement* 9.11, it is impossible to ascertain whether there is any dependence one way or the other. However, the "brothers and mother" saying is closest to *GLuke*'s redaction of this saying (*GLk* 8.20–21), with its omission of "behold" at the beginning of Jesus' response, and its omission of Jesus' rhetorical question, "who are my mother and my brothers." The rhetorical question is found in the parallels in *GMark* 3.33, *GMatthew* 12.48, and *GEbionites* (Epiphanius, *Pan.* 30.14.5). *2 Clement* 9.11 is the most abbreviated out of all the parallels, and it is impossible to determine its relationship to any of the other parallels other than its habitation in the same ecosystem of social memory.

The last remaining possible parallel with noncanonical gospel literature is a saying in *GThomas* 82: "The one who is near me is near the fire; and the one who is far from me is far from the kingdom." This saying is paralleled in the *Gospel of the Savior*, which is probably a later document than *GThomas*.[61] If

---

[58] *GMt* 7.7–8; *GLk* 11.9–10; *GTh* 2, 38, 92, 94; Tertullian, *Praescr.* 8.1–2; cf. *GMt* 13.45–46; *GJn* 1.37–41; 16.23–24; *2 Clem.* 5.5; *Thom. Cont.* 140.41–43, 145.10–16; *Ac. Thom.* 136; see a helpful discussion in Watson 2013: 356–70.

[59] Translation Gathercole 2014: 559.

[60] In Gregory's numbering, it is *GEb* §5 (*Pan.* 30.14.5); Gregory 2017: 241–44.

[61] While scholarship at the turn of the 21st century confidently placed *GSavior* in the mid to late second century (e.g. Hedrick and Mirecki 1999; DeConick 2001: 136–51; Frey 2002: 71–

36   *Chapter 1: The Gospel According to Thomas*

there is any literary dependence, *GSavior* is probably dependent on *GThomas*. This saying is also paralleled without reference to its source in Origen, Didymus, and (Pseudo-)Ephrem. Origen parallels this saying verbatim,[62] but he is probably quoting directly from *GThomas* in this instance,[63] although he shies away from explicitly attributing it to *GThomas*.[64] A century later, Didymus quotes the same saying nearly verbatim, but he is probably deriving it from Origen.[65] (Pseudo-)Ephrem's *Exposition of the Gospel* 83 gives a slightly different version of the saying, substituting "life" for "kingdom," and attributes it simply to "what our Savior-Redeemer said."[66] It is more likely that later authors drew from *GThomas* than that *GThomas* is drawing it from a separate noncanonical gospel.

Our analysis of the seven noncanonical parallels in *GThomas* has shown that none of these parallels exhibits the same kind of redactional correspondence as the Matthean and Lukan parallels. Therefore, we cannot say that *GThomas* is drawing from noncanonical Jesus books in the same way it draws from *GMatthew* and *GLuke*. It is safer to say that *GThomas* draws from traditions that were also inscribed in noncanonical Jesus books. The author of *GThomas* did not have the Eusebian categories for "canonical" and "noncanonical,"[67] but he nonetheless inhabited a literary world in which certain gospels captured the Christian imagination more than others and enjoyed a wide level of acceptance. Thus, *GMatthew* and *GLuke* saturated Thomasine composition while traditions that would later be

---

96; Plisch 2005: 64–84), more recent scholarship has placed *GSavior* more comfortably in the theological and social milieu of late antique Coptic Christianity (cf. Nagel 2003: 215–57; Hagen 2010: 339–71; Piovanelli 2012: 229–48). The novelistic character of *GSavior* is more typically a feature of gospel writing later than the *terminus ad quem* of *GThomas* (ca. 200 CE).

[62] *Hom. Jer.* 27.3.7: *qui iuxta me est, iuxta ignem est; qui longe est a me, longe est a regno*; this follows nearly verbatim the Coptic translation of *GThomas* 82: ⲡⲉϫⲉ ⲓ̄ⲥ̄ ϫⲉ ⲡⲉⲧϩⲏⲛ ⲉⲣⲟⲉⲓ ⲉϥϩⲏⲛ ⲉⲧⲥⲁⲧⲉ ⲁⲩⲱ ⲡⲉⲧⲟⲩⲏⲩ̀ ⲙ̄ⲙⲟⲉⲓ ϥⲟⲩⲏⲩ ⲛ̄ⲧⲙⲛ̄ⲧⲉⲣⲟ. The text of Jerome's Latin translation of Origen's homily is found in Husson and Nautin 1977: 324.

[63] Luijendijk 2011: 241–268 and Carlson 2014: 137–51 make the case convincingly that Origen was indeed citing from *GThomas* in *Hom. Jer.* 27.3.7 and *Orig. Hom. Jos.* 4.3, based on the verbatim agreement, the way Origen refers to the saying as coming from a written source, and the fact that Origen elsewhere admits to having read *GThomas* (*Hom. in Luc.* 1.2).

[64] This is likely due to the fact that Origen elsewhere repudiates gospels outside of the *tetraevangelium* (e.g. *Hom. in Luc* 1.2), explicitly mentioning *GThomas* as one of these unapproved gospels. Origen's relationship with *GThomas* is complex, however, in that he appears to use it as a supplement to the Four with the special Jesus tradition it preserves in *GTh* 82 (*Hom. Jer.* 27.3.7; *Orig. Hom. Jos.* 4.3); cf. Luijendijk 2011; Carlson 2014.

[65] Didymus (*In Psalmos* 88.8) introduces the saying as "therefore the Savior said" (διὸ φησιν ὁ Σωτήρ), and then relates a verbatim agreement with *GTh* 82: ὁ ἐγγύς μου ἐγγὺς τοῦ πυρός· ὁ δὲ μακράν ἀπ᾽ ἐμοῦ μακράν ἀπὸ τῆς βασιλείας. Greek text: PG 39.1488.

[66] Translation in Egan 1968: 62. The *Exposition of the Gospel* – not to be confused with the *Commentary on the Gospel* – is attributed to Ephrem, but the authorship is uncertain. It was originally written in Syriac but survives only in Armenian.

[67] For Eusebius, these terms are ὁμολογούμενα (accepted) and ἀντιλεγόμενα (disputed); *Hist. eccl.* 3.25.

1.2 Combining Gospels in the Gospel according to Thomas   37

recognized as noncanonical only seem to have influenced *GThomas* at a shallow level.

1.2.3 Summary of Gospel Sources in GThomas

On balance, we can conclude that *GThomas* combined material drawn from *GMatthew* and *GLuke*, as well as material elsewhere paralleled only in noncanonical gospels or free-floating tradition. We can say further that *GMatthew* and *GLuke* exerted significant influence on *GThomas*, and the signs of this influence are clear in the Synoptic redactional features that *GThomas* carries.

As for the noncanonical material in *GThomas*, the parallel gospel texts (*GEgy*, *GHeb*, and *GEb*) are fragmentary, and none of them are attested before Clement of Alexandria. It is therefore impossible to establish priority or posteriority between any two of these noncanonical gospels. Moreover, the paucity of early Christian quotations from these noncanonical gospels suggests that their distribution was neither quick nor widespread. It is therefore unwise to assert with much certainty that *GThomas* is drawing from noncanonical gospels in the same way or to the same extent that it draws from *GMatthew* and *GLuke*. It is abundantly clear, however, that *GThomas* does incorporate noncanonical Jesus tradition that also finds a home in other apocryphal gospels, and *GThomas* can easily combine this material with material drawn from *GMatthew* and *GLuke* – a phenomenon we will explore in the following section. At this juncture we can conclude that *GMatthew*, *GLuke*, and disparate noncanonical traditions keep company with one another in Thomas' composition.

1.2.4 Integrity and Interactions of Gospel Materials in GThomas

None of the gospels or sources from which *GThomas* draws provides an overarching structure to *GThomas'* sequence. *GThomas*, as a sayings collection, is arranged by catchword, thematic link, and sometimes the form of the saying.[68] While *GThomas* preserves sayings from *GMatthew* and *GLuke*, it does not preserve either of their narrative sequences. In *GThomas*, Jesus' teaching is not introduced by the baptism of John, nor does it progress towards a narrative of Jesus' passion and resurrection. Furthermore, the discernable Matthean and Lukan sayings are arranged out of their Matthean and Lukan order.[69] The narrative integrity of the gospel sources for *GThomas* is not preserved.

---

[68] Cf. Gathercole 2014: 128–36, with bibliography on 128n1.

[69] Sayings with Matthean redactional features are out of sequence in *GThomas*: *GTh* 13 (// *GMt* 16.13–22), *GTh* 14.5 (// *GMt* 15.11), *GTh* 20 (// *GMt* 13.31), *GTh* 44–45 (// *GMt* 12.31–32), *GTh* 54 (// *GMt* 5.3), *GTh* 57 (// *GMt* 13.24–30). Lukan sayings are likewise out of sequence: *GTh* 5.2 (// *GLk* 8.17), *GTh* 31.1 (// *GLk* 4.24), *GTh* 33.2–3 (// *GLk* 8.16/11.33), *GTh* 47.3–5 (// *GLk* 5.36–39), *GTh* 63 (// *GLk* 12.15–21), *GTh* 65 (// *GLk* 20.9–16), *GTh* 66 (*GLk* 20.17), *GTh* 72 (// *GLk* 12.13–14), *GTh* 79 (// *GLk* 11.27–28/23.27–31), *GTh* 99 (*GLk* 8.20–21), *GTh* 104 (*GLk* 5.33–35).

38   *Chapter 1: The Gospel According to Thomas*

On the other hand, *GThomas* often presupposes narrative details surrounding certain sayings. *GThomas* preserves sayings involving Mary (21, 114), Peter (13, 114), Matthew (13), James the Just (12), Salome (61), and John the Baptist (46-47), without introducing any of these characters, thus presupposing the narratives that shaped their identities in the early Christian imagination. The identities of characters from the proto-canonical gospels are assumed, rather than introduced. In other places, *GThomas* leaves out crucial narrative details to certain sayings – details that nevertheless must be presupposed.[70] The result is that several sayings in *GThomas* only make sense if one is familiar with the narrative contexts they presuppose. In this sense, some narrative residue of *GMatthew* and *GLuke* does exert itself into the composition of *GThomas*.[71]

There are several instances where Matthean redaction is conjoined with Lukan redaction, and in these instances, we can see how *GMatthew* and *GLuke* interact in *GThomas*. *GThomas* 54 combines the Lukan beatitude "blessed are the poor" (*GLk* 6.20) with the Matthean declaration, "for the kingdom of heaven is yours" (*GMt* 5.3). *GThomas* 55 combines the Lukan redaction "whoever does not hate his father and mother... his brothers and his sisters..." (*GLk* 14.26) with the Matthean "will not be worthy of me" (*GMt* 10.37).

Interestingly, *GThomas* 20 has features distinct to *GMatthew* 13.31–32, *GLuke* 17.18–19, and even *GMark* 4.31–32. These parallels are laid out below in Table 8. *GThomas* 20 introduces the parable of the mustard seed as an indirect question, phrased in the same way as the direct question in *GLuke* 17.18. It has the clear Matthean element, "kingdom of heaven," as well a parallel to *GMark*'s mention of the seed producing a "great branch."[72] *GThomas* here also includes a phrase paralleled in *GMark* and *GMatthew*, but not *GLuke* ("smallest of all seeds"), as well as a phrase paralleled in *GMatthew* and *GLuke*, but not *GMark* ("it is like"). It is unlikely that *GThomas* is intentionally blending all three Synoptic versions of this parable. Equally unlikely is the proposal that *GThomas* preserves a version of this saying earlier than all three Synoptics – this argument

---

[70] See especially *GTh* 100, which leaves out the important detail that Jesus shows his interlocutors the image of Caesar on the coin (*GMk* 12.15–16 // *GMt* 22.19–20 // *GLk* 20.24). The saying only makes sense with this detail. Also, *GTh* 104 begins with a third plural verb (ⲡⲉⲭⲁⲩ probably translating εἶπαν) with no clear antecedent subject. See also *GTh* 60, 61, 72, 79, 91, and 99, which all presuppose a fuller narrative framework but give minimal narrative referents; cf. Goodacre 2012.

[71] We know little of the narrative integrity of *GEgy*, and we have not been able to establish a literary relationship between *GEgy* and *GThomas*, so we cannot conclude that any of *GEgy*'s narrative integrity has seeped into *GThomas*.

[72] Watson 2013: 282 places the three Synoptic versions in parallel with the *GTh* 20, and he claims, on the basis of simplicity and coherence, that *GThomas* preserves a more primitive version. However, his column for the Thomasine version completely omits the phrase "[the soil] produces a great branch" (ⲱⲁϥⲧⲉⲩⲟ ⲉⲃⲟⲗ ⲛ̄ⲛⲟⲩⲛⲟϭ ⲛ̄ⲧⲁⲣ), and he therefore misses the parallel between *GThomas* and *GMark*.

1.2 Combining Gospels in the Gospel according to Thomas   39

is usually based on arbitrary rules of primitivity. We can, however, see that both *GMatthew* and *GLuke* abbreviate *GMark*'s version of the parable.[73] The tendency is to abbreviate this parable. *GThomas* 20 is shorter than both its Markan and Matthean parallels, and it is approximately the same length as its Lukan parallel.

The Thomasine version is probably a later reception of this saying than the Markan version, and, given Thomas' proclivity to carry over Matthean and Lukan redactional elements, it is likely that Thomas' handling of this saying is also influenced by Matthean and Lukan style, even if the author of *GThomas* did not intentionally include these elements. An important upshot from this example is that the Jesus tradition preserved in *GMatthew* and *GLuke* is somewhat malleable for the author of *GThomas*. He is not beholden to the textual fixedness of the Synoptic gospel sources from which he draws. Since *GThomas* can juxtapose elements from *GMatthew* and *GLuke* in the same saying, and at other times adhere more closely to either the Matthean or Lukan redaction, we can reasonably conclude that *GMatthew* and *GLuke* interact within *GThomas*' compositional procedure as malleable, mutually interpreting repositories of Jesus tradition.

GThomas also has several instances of combining canonical redactional material with noncanonical traditions. *GThomas* 104 juxtaposes material paralleled in *GHebrews* with Lukan redactional material from *GLuke* 5.33–35 (see Table 7 below). *GThomas* 114 integrates several distinct Thomasine themes with the Matthean phrase, "kingdom of heaven."[74] *GThomas* 61 begins with the distinctly Lukan phrase, "two will be resting on a couch,"[75] and then integrates this with Jesus' apocryphal discourse connected with his sharing an intimate couch with Salome, perhaps paralleled in *GEgy* (see Table 6 above). *GThomas* 22 is a complex saying that juxtaposes language that is paralleled across a variety of ancient Christian sources (both proto-canonical and noncanonical): "infants entering the kingdom,"[76] "two-one," "male-female," "outside-inside," dual body parts,[77] and the role of an image. Gathercole is right to comment that these elements are difficult to disentangle,[78] but there is enough evidence to provide another example of proto-canonical and noncanonical material keeping company in the same Thomasine saying. What these combinations demonstrate is that, for *GThomas*,

---

[73] On the Farrer hypothesis, Luke continues to abbreviate this parable even more than *GMatthew*.

[74] The abrupt inclusion of "kingdom of heaven" into a section that has already used the term "kingdom of the Father," among other factors, has led Davies 2005: 175 to conclude that *GTh* 114 is a later accretion. However, see Gathercole 2014: 608 for a convincing rebuttal, and Brankaer 2005: 151 for an argument that *GTh* 114 draws together several Thomasine themes.

[75] Cf. *GLk* 17.34 over against *GMt* 24.40.

[76] Cf. Triple Tradition: *GMk* 10.15 // *GMt* 18.3 // *GLk* 18.17.

[77] The "two-one" saying is paralleled in *GEgy* (Clement, *Strom.* 3.13.92) and *2 Clem.* 12.2; "outside-inside" and other binaries are paralleled in *Acts of Peter* 38, *Acts of Philip* 140, *GPhilip* 69, and *Acts of Thomas* 147.

[78] Gathercole 2014: 308.

40 *Chapter 1: The Gospel According to Thomas*

Jesus tradition preserved in proto-canonical gospels (*GMatthew* and *GLuke*), and Jesus tradition also inscribed in noncanonical gospels (e.g. *GHebrews* and *GEgyptians*) exist on a level playing field for the author of *GThomas*. There is no clear ideological superiority given to material that would later be deemed canonical.

Nevertheless, it is still clear that material from the Synoptic tradition exerts greater influence on *GThomas* than material also inscribed in noncanonical gospels. As stated above, over 60 sayings in *GThomas* overlap with Synoptic parallels, and 17 of these can be shown to bear redactional features or special material from *GMatthew* or *GLuke*. By contrast, material paralleled in noncanonical gospels only appears in 7 sayings in *GThomas*, and none of these bear the same level of resemblance as the Synoptic redactional similarities found in *GThomas*. Moreover, there is a certain gravitas in the way that *GThomas* receives the Synoptic tradition. *GThomas* does not rely on *agrapha* or apocryphal tradition to introduce major themes not previously discussed in early Christianity. In stark contrast with Gnostic or Gnosticizing literature found in the Nag Hammadi Corpus, *GThomas* includes no mythological figures, and it gives relatively little fresh material about traditional figures such as Peter or Mary. On the other hand, we have seen how extensively *GThomas* presupposes the Synoptic tradition for its own logical coherence. This suggests that at least *GMatthew* and *GLuke* compelled the imagination of the Thomasine evangelist more than apocryphal traditions, even in his process of composing an apocryphal gospel.[79]

---

[79] *GThomas*, in its prologue, claims to contain "the secret sayings which the living Jesus spoke" (the fragmentary Greek text of P.Oxy. 654.1–3 can plausibly be reconstructed as οἱ λόγοι οἱ ἀπόκρυφοι κτλ; cf. Gathercole 2014: 189). Since *GThomas* explicitly acknowledges the secretive nature of its sayings, it is entirely appropriate to call it an apocryphal gospel, even in its original context (cf. Nicklas 2014: 224).

1.2 Combining Gospels in the Gospel according to Thomas 41

Table 7: Composite Parallels in GThomas 104

GHebrews fragment[a]	GLuke Parallel	GThomas Parallel[b]
In euangelio iuxta Hebraeos… quo utuntur usque hodie Nazareni… narrat historia: Ecce mater Domini et fratres eius dicebant ei: Ioannes Baptista baptizat in remissionem peccatorum: eamus et baptizemur ab eo. <u>Dixit autem eis: Quid peccaui, ut uadam et baptizer ab eo?</u>	GLk 5.33-35: οἱ δὲ εἶπαν πρὸς αὐτόν· οἱ μαθηταὶ Ἰωάννου <u>νηστεύουσιν</u> πυκνὰ <u>καὶ δεήσεις</u> <u>ποιοῦνται</u> ὁμοίως καὶ οἱ τῶν φαρισαίων… ὁ δὲ Ἰησοῦς εἶπεν πρὸς αὐτούς… ἐλεύσονται δὲ ἡμέραι, καὶ ὅταν ἀπαρθῇ ἀπ᾽ αὐτῶν <u>ὁ νυμφίος, τότε</u> <u>νηστεύσουσιν</u> ἐν ἐκείναις ταῖς ἡμέραις.	GTh 104: ⲡⲉϫⲉ ⲛ̅[ⲓ̅]ⲥ̅ ϫⲉ ⲁⲙⲟⲩ ⲛ̅ⲧⲛ̅ϣⲗⲏⲗ̀ ⲙ̅ⲡⲟⲟⲩ ⲁⲩⲱ ⲛ̅ⲧⲛ̅ⲣ̅ⲛⲏⲥⲧⲉⲩⲉ ⲡⲉϫⲉ ⲓ̅ⲥ̅ ϫⲉ ⲟⲩ ⲅⲁⲣ̀ ⲡⲉ ⲡⲛⲟⲃⲉ ⲛ̅ⲧⲁⲉⲓⲁⲁϥ̀ ⲏ ⲛ̅ⲧⲁⲩϫⲣⲟ ⲉⲣⲟⲉⲓ ϩⲛ̅ ⲟⲩ ⲁⲗⲗⲁ ϩⲟⲧⲁⲛ ⲉⲣϣⲁⲛ ⲡⲛⲩⲙⲫⲟⲓⲥ ⲉⲓ ⲉⲃⲟⲗ ϩⲙ̅ ⲡⲛⲩⲙⲫⲱⲛ ⲧⲟⲧⲉ ⲙⲁⲣⲟⲩⲛⲏ̀ⲥⲧⲉⲩⲉ ⲁⲩⲱ ⲙⲁⲣⲟⲩϣⲗⲏⲗ̀
In the Gospel according to the Hebrews… the following story is found: "Behold, the mother of the Lord and his brothers were saying to him, 'John the Baptist is baptizing for the remission of sins. Let us go and be baptized by him.' But he replied to them, '<u>What sin have I committed</u> that I should go to be baptized by him?'"	GLk 5.33-35: They said to him, "John's disciples often <u>fast and pray</u>, and so do the disciples of the Pharisees…" Jesus answered, "…the time will come when <u>the bridegroom</u> will be taken from them; <u>then</u> in those days they will <u>fast</u>."	GTh 104: They said to Jesus, "Come, let us <u>pray</u> today and let us <u>fast</u>." Jesus said, "<u>What is the sin that I have committed</u>, or how have I been overcome? Rather, when <u>the bridegroom</u> comes out of the bridal chamber, <u>then</u> people should <u>fast and pray</u>."

Notes: [a] Jerome, *Pelag.* 3.2; Latin text from Moreschini 1990; trans. Ehrman and Pleše 2011. [b] Trans. Ehrman and Pleše 2011.

In summary, *GMatthew* and *GLuke* function as repositories of Jesus *logia* for *GThomas*, which detaches these *logia* from their narrative context and recontextualizes them into a fresh composition. Since the gospel narratives are not made explicit, *GThomas* has no need of harmonizing their sequences, and therefore *GMatthew* and *GLuke* do not properly "interact" at the level of narrative sequence. However, gospels do interact in *GThomas* on a presupposed Synoptic narrative background. This narrative background is reworked in the form of a gnomological anthology. The radically rearranged sequence of presentation is due to the genre of *GThomas* as a sayings collection. Matthean traditions, Lukan traditions, and apocryphal traditions are not set in competition but are treated as mutually interpreting.

Table 8: Synoptic Parallels in *GThomas* 20

GMk 4.30-32	GMt 13.31-22	GLk 13.18-19	GTh 20[a]
Καὶ ἔλεγεν· πῶς ὁμοιώσωμεν τὴν βασιλείαν τοῦ θεοῦ ἢ ἐν τίνι αὐτὴν παραβολῇ θῶμεν; ὡς κόκκῳ σινάπεως, ὃς ὅταν σπαρῇ ἐπὶ τῆς γῆς, μικρότερον ὂν πάντων τῶν σπερμάτων τῶν ἐπὶ τῆς γῆς, καὶ ὅταν σπαρῇ, ἀναβαίνει καὶ γίνεται μεῖζον πάντων λαχάνων καὶ ποιεῖ κλάδους μεγάλους, ὥστε δύνασθαι ὑπὸ τὴν σκιὰν αὐτοῦ τὰ πετεινὰ τοῦ οὐρανοῦ κατασκηνοῦν.	Ἄλλην παραβολὴν παρέθηκεν αὐτοῖς λέγων· ὁμοία ἐστὶν ἡ βασιλεία τῶν οὐρανῶν κόκκῳ σινάπεως, ὃν λαβὼν ἄνθρωπος ἔσπειρεν ἐν τῷ ἀγρῷ αὐτοῦ· ὃ μικρότερον μέν ἐστιν πάντων τῶν σπερμάτων, ὅταν δὲ αὐξηθῇ μεῖζον τῶν λαχάνων ἐστὶν καὶ γίνεται δένδρον, ὥστε ἐλθεῖν τὰ πετεινὰ τοῦ οὐρανοῦ καὶ κατασκηνοῦν ἐν τοῖς κλάδοις αὐτοῦ.	Ἔλεγεν οὖν· τίνι ὁμοία ἐστὶν ἡ βασιλεία τοῦ θεοῦ καὶ τίνι ὁμοιώσω αὐτήν; ὁμοία ἐστὶν κόκκῳ σινάπεως, ὃν λαβὼν ἄνθρωπος ἔβαλεν εἰς κῆπον ἑαυτοῦ, καὶ ηὔξησεν καὶ ἐγένετο εἰς δένδρον, καὶ τὰ πετεινὰ τοῦ οὐρανοῦ κατεσκήνωσεν ἐν τοῖς κλάδοις αὐτοῦ.	ⲡⲉϫⲉ ⲛ̅ⲙⲁⲑⲏⲧⲏⲥ ⲛ̅ⲓ̅ⲥ̅ ϫⲉ ϫⲟⲟⲥ ⲉⲣⲟⲛ ϫⲉ ⲧⲙⲛ̅ⲧⲉⲣⲟ ⲛ̅ⲙⲡⲏⲩⲉ ⲉⲥⲧⲛ̅ⲧⲱⲛ ⲉⲛⲓⲙ ⲡⲉϫⲁϥ ⲛⲁⲩ ϫⲉ ⲉⲥⲧⲛ̅ⲧⲱⲛ **ⲁⲩⲃ̅ⲗ̅ⲃⲓⲗⲉ ⲛ̅ϣ̅ⲗ̅ⲧⲁⲙ** <ⲥ>ⲥⲟⲃⲕ ⲡⲁⲣⲁ ⲛ̅ϭⲣⲟϭ ⲧⲏⲣⲟⲩ ϩⲟⲧⲁⲛ ⲇⲉ ⲉⲥϣⲁ(ⲛ)ϩⲉ ⲉϫⲙ̅ ⲡⲕⲁϩ ⲉⲧⲟⲩⲣ̅ ϩⲱⲃ ⲉⲣⲟϥ ϣⲁϥⲧⲉⲩⲟ ⲉⲃⲟⲗ ⲛ̅ⲛⲟⲩⲛⲟϭ ⲛ̅ⲧⲁⲣ ⲛ̅ϥϣⲱⲡⲉ ⲛ̅ⲥⲕⲉⲡⲏ **ⲛ̅ϩⲁⲗⲁⲧⲉ ⲛ̅ⲧⲡⲉ**
And he said: "How shall we liken the kingdom of God, or in what *parable* shall we place it? As a **grain of mustard**, which when it is sown on the ground, which is *the smallest of all seeds*... it makes great branches, so that the **birds of the air** are able to shelter under its shade."	He presented another *parable* to them, saying: "The kingdom of heaven is like a **grain of mustard**, which a man took and sowed in his land, which although *it is the smallest of all seeds*... becomes a tree, so that the **birds of the air** come and shelter in its branches."	Then he said, "What is the kingdom of God *like*, and to what shall I compare it? It is like a **grain of mustard**, which a man took and cast into his garden, and it grew and became a tree, and the **birds of the air** sheltered in its branches."	The Disciples said to Jesus, "Tell us what the kingdom of heaven is *like*." He said to them, "**It is like a grain of mustard**. It is *the smallest of all seeds*. But when it falls on worked soil, the soil produces a great branch and becomes a shelter for **birds of the air**."

Key to parallels: <u>*GMark* only</u>; <u>*GMatt* only</u>; <u>*GLuke* only</u>; *GMark and GMatt* (all italics); *GMatt and GLuke*; **all three Synoptics**. Notes: [a] Trans. Gathercole

1.2 Combining Gospels in the Gospel according to Thomas

However, Synoptic material has a much larger share at the table of Thomasine composition than material paralleled elsewhere, and this illustrates how *GMatthew* and *GLuke* far outweighed apocryphal traditions in their influence on the imagination of second-century gospel writers. How *GThomas* envisages its own authority in relation to these gospels will be discussed in the following section.

1.2.5 Textual Authority in GThomas

GThomas gives several indications that its revelatory authority surpasses that of the gospels it combines in its composition. In the prologue, Thomas begins his textualization of the Jesus tradition as follows: "These are the secret sayings which the living Jesus spoke, as Judas Thomas wrote them down."[80] At the outset, the implied author, Judas Thomas, sets himself up as *the* authoritative interpreter of the Jesus tradition, with his superior hermeneutical lens furnished in the secret sayings to which he alone has access.

This dynamic is also evident in *GThomas* 13, which parallels the "Who do people say that I am?" saying of the Triple Tradition.[81] In *GThomas* 13, Simon Peter and Matthew both give inadequate answers to Jesus' question. Thomas, the third to speak, gives an answer that, although corrected by Jesus, leads Jesus to usher Thomas into special revelation that establishes him on a higher level of authority than the other apostles. Simon Gathercole has made a strong case that in *GThomas* 13 "there is almost certainly a polemic, probably aimed at a wider church group for whom Peter was a foundational figure and Matthew's Gospel an/the authoritative portrait of Jesus," and that Thomas in this sense acts as a "separatist."[82] Thomas's separatism is corroborated in the way he redefines the Matthean term "kingdom of heaven,"[83] the way he calls the Jewish prophets dead in contrast to the Synoptics viewing them as living,[84] and especially in the way that Thomas disavows the Jewish Scriptures and the *praeparatio evangelica.*[85] These dynamics cut against the grain of all four proto-canonical gospels. Thus,

---

[80] Translation Gathercole 2014: 189.

[81] Cf. *GMk* 8.27–30 // *GMt* 16.13–20 // *GLk* 9.18–21.

[82] Gathercole 2014: 260–61.

[83] Though the author of *GThomas* borrows this Matthean phrase, he envisages the "kingdom" in a way that is "consistently non-eschatological, nonapocalyptic" (King 1987: 52; cf. Gathercole 2011; Kvalbein 2006); cf. *GTh* 3, 18–19, 22, 99, 113–114.

[84] *GTh* 52 is in direct contradiction with *GMk* 12.27, *GMt* 22.32, and *GLk* 20.38, not to mention *GMt* 12.6, *GJn* 5.39, and a whole host of other fulfillment passages in the proto-canonical gospels; cf. Bockmuehl 2017: 179.

[85] This dynamic is seen in Jesus' depiction of his revelation as unprecedented (*GTh* 17, 38), and his characterization of the prophets of Israel as dead in contrast with his own living witness (*GTh* 52); cf. Gathercole 2018a; Goodacre 2012: 187–90; Baarda 2003; Popkes 2006.

44 *Chapter 1: The Gospel According to Thomas*

we might say that *GThomas* evinces a competitive textuality that challenges the authority of its predecessors, even while drawing extensively from them.[86]

At this juncture, it is helpful to bring *GJohn* into the discussion for its points of comparison and contrast. By way of comparison, both *GJohn* and *GThomas* stand at one literary remove (or more) from the Synoptic gospels and engage with one or more of these gospels. Both "tamper" with the Synoptic tradition by infusing it with their own theological idiom.[87] Both presuppose narrative details from the Synoptic tradition without explicitly mentioning these details. One might even say that just as *GJohn* was written for readers of *GMark*, so *GThomas* was written for readers of *GMatthew* and *GLuke*.

On the other hand, *GJohn* and *GThomas* differ starkly in the ways they handle the Synoptic tradition. The most obvious difference is in the way *GJohn* and *GThomas* present the Jesus tradition they inherit. The former rewrites an entire narrative of Jesus' ministry, passion, and resurrection; the latter ignores or presupposes most of this narrative and gives instead a sayings collection of the living Jesus. Furthermore, *GJohn* shares with the Synoptics a veneration of the Jewish Scriptures,[88] and a catholicity in its proclamation of the crucified and risen Messiah.[89] *GJohn* adds an additional witness alongside the twelve disciples, without challenging, usurping, or undermining Peter's authority,[90] and without delegitimizing *GMark*, which it presupposes for its own narrative logic.[91] By contrast, *GThomas* denigrates the Jewish scriptures, fails to mention the crucifixion, and it undermines Petrine authority – its separatist inclinations are clear.[92]

---

[86] On competitive textuality in *GThomas*, see Keith 2020: 154–60. To my knowledge, Keith coined the phrase "competitive textuality" in Keith 2016: 321–37.

[87] There is currently a growing number of scholars that argue that the author of *GJohn* had access to, or at least was aware of the contents of one or more of the Synoptic gospels; cf. Hengel 1989: 75; Bauckham 1998: 147–71; Thyen 2005: 4; Brant 2011: 10; Bird 2014: 188–213; Barker 2015a; Keith 2016: 321–37; 2020: 131–54; cf. Windisch 1926.

[88] E.g. *GJn* 1.23; 3.14; 5.39; 12.38–41; 19.24; 20.9.

[89] E.g. *GJn* 1.41; 18.37; 19.3, 19–13; 20.30–31.

[90] While it is true that the author of *GJohn* presents himself as having privileged access to key events in Jesus' ministry (e.g. *GJn* 19.35–37), he does this in a way that is supplementary rather than in competition with Peter. Although the "disciple whom Jesus loved" arrives at the tomb first, it is still Peter who enters the tomb first (*GJn* 20.3–8). And while the final "colophon" of 21.24–25 establishes this disciple as an authoritative witness, this happens only after the reinstatement of Peter (21.15–19), a reinstatement that is exclusive to *GJohn* and that attributes to Peter the honorific status of martyr. Even if *GJn* 21 is a later postlude, it is written with flawless Johannine idiom (e.g. 21.7, 15–17, 20, 24–25), and in seamless continuity with the prior narrative (e.g. 21.14, 20), such that it resonates with the original author's narrative intention and could possibly be the product of the original author's close associates (cf. Heckel 1999: 128–43). For two recent, thorough, and convincing cases for the authenticity of *GJn* 21, see Porter 2015 and Hill 2017.

[91] On whether *GJohn* undermines previous gospels, see below, Section 4.1.

[92] Cf. Gathercole 2014: 163–67.

1.2 Combining Gospels in the Gospel according to Thomas
45

Although *GThomas* presupposes the revered, influential status of *GMatthew* and *GLuke* as narratives and repositories of Jesus tradition, it also exerts a new level of revelatory authority by functioning as a hermeneutical key to a higher, esoteric understanding of the living Jesus and his teachings. In contrast with *GJohn*'s exclusive tradition (e.g. *GJn* 13–17), *GThomas*' hermeneutical esotericism marginalizes and subverts central tenets in the Synoptic tradition. It cannot be said, therefore, that *GThomas* is engaged in the same kind of interpretive rewriting as *GMatthew*, *GLuke*, and *GJohn* in their relation to *GMark* and to one another. *GThomas* exhibits a symbiotic, dialectic relationship with *GMatthew* and *GLuke* by presupposing their influence while also subverting them with self-aware hermeneutical superiority.

Moreover, when one contrasts the narrative structure and kerygmatic illocution of the Synoptics with the lack of narrative sequence and the non-kerygmatic, esoteric features of *GThomas*, it is clear that the author of *GThomas* was *not* intending to write the same kind of Jesus book as *GMatthew* or *GLuke*. Rather, his aim was to mediate exclusive, special revelation that was unavailable in previous gospels. Thus, paradoxically, *GThomas* could serve a competitive function (offering exclusive revelation unavailable elsewhere) at the same time as a supplementary one (respecting the Synoptics as influential resources of the words and deeds of Jesus) *vis-à-vis GMatthew* and *GLuke*.[93] *GThomas* is a second-century text that combines portions from *GMatthew* and *GLuke*, subverts aspects of these gospels by offering superior revelatory authority, but nonetheless affirms their position in the reading practices of early Christianity.

---

[93] The papyrological record of *GThomas* corresponds to this dialectical relationship between *GThomas* and proto-canonical gospels. Hurtado 2008 and Charlesworth 2016: 122–27 argue that the unconventional features in all three papyrus fragments of *GThomas* (P.Oxy. 1, P.Oxy. 654, and P.Oxy. 655) indicate that these copies were intended for private and personal use, rather than public and liturgical use. Luijendijk 2011, on the other hand, argues that the *coronis*, *diaeresis*, and *paragraphus* in P.Oxy. 655 indicate that its exemplar was indeed a Thomasine manuscript intended for public reading, even if P.Oxy. 655 itself, as a bookroll, was a personal copy. Furthermore, Luijendijk suggests that P.Oxy. 1 might have belonged to the same Christian library as P.Oxy. 2 (*GMt* 1.1–17), based on the original archeological site of both papyri. The differing interpretations of Hurtado, Charlesworth, and Luijendijk yield two plausible scenarios. First, a copy of *GThomas* could have been read alongside a copy of *GMatthew*. Second, *GThomas* could have been read in private usage. Though the evidence is piecemeal, and conclusions must be made with due caution (see esp. concerns raised in Heilmann 2020), either of these scenarios would facilitate a reading of *GThomas* that takes place alongside a reading of the Synoptics while simultaneously offering an apocryphal, esoteric and even subversive hermeneutical key to the interpretation of the Synoptics.

46 *Chapter 1: The Gospel According to Thomas*

1.3 Summary and Conclusions

The *Gospel according to Thomas* is an early example of one particular kind of gospel combination. It is a fresh interpretive object shaped by creatively juxtaposing Matthean and Lukan *logia*, extracted from their narrative contexts and placed into a new theological context alongside noncanonical *logia*. Regarding *identity* and *mode*, *GThomas* combines portions of *GMatthew* and *GLuke* by means of excerpting – either directly from *GMatthew* and *GLuke* or from *hypomnemata* constructed from these gospels. Noncanonical sayings are not so easily attributed to Jesus books, and we must remain agnostic as to their mode of entering Thomasine composition. Transposed into a sayings collection, *GMatthew* and *GLuke* do not retain their narrative *integrity*, though at the clausal level they often retain redactional integrity. Neither *GMatthew* nor *GLuke* form a narrative structure of sequence in *GThomas*. *GLuke* enjoys more redactional representation than *GMatthew*, although *GMatthew* could probably boast its author's pedigree in *GThomas'* testimony (*GTh* 13).

On the one hand, *GMatthew*, *GLuke*, and noncanonical *logia* also inscribed in noncanonical gospels *interact* on a level playing field in *GThomas'* compositional procedure and can equally be juxtaposed. They are all sources for Jesus *logia* from which *GThomas* can draw freely, creatively juxtapose, and reinterpret, sometimes even subversively. On the other hand, the Double Tradition, the Triple Tradition, Special Matthew, and Special Luke exert a greater level of influence on *GThomas* than noncanonical traditions. Moreover, given the distinctiveness and frequent recurrence of redactional features, *GMatthew* and *GLuke* stand behind *GThomas'* composition as *books* rather than as free-floating oral traditions. We cannot say the same for the noncanonical *logia* that *GThomas* includes. In this sense, *GMatthew* and *GLuke* emerge in *GThomas* as the largest, most widely available, and most influential pool of written Jesus tradition from which *GThomas* draws. For *GThomas*, there does not appear to be a clear ideological distinction between the Synoptic textual tradition and what would later be deemed the noncanonical Jesus tradition. At the same time, by the sheer quantity of its usage of Synoptic material (a significant amount of which has been shown to bear Matthean and Lukan redaction), we can discern *GThomas'* tendency to draw predominantly from what would become the canonical gospels when combining material into a fresh composition.

GThomas acts as if it is relativizing the *authority* of the gospels it combines, and it credits itself with a superior revelatory authority than those preexisting gospels. But it does so in a way that nonetheless presupposes, affirms, and even depends upon the influential status of those prior gospels.

The implied *testimonium* to Matthew's authorship in *GThomas* 13, the redactional fingerprints of both *GMatthew* and *GLuke* scattered throughout *GThomas*, the instances of verbatim agreement between *GThomas* and these texts, and the way that *GThomas* presupposes the general Synoptic narrative, all give

1.3 Summary and Conclusions 47

GMatthew and *GLuke* a distinguishable shape as textual "others" in relation to *GThomas* and in relation to one another. This textual "otherness" can be recognized by the distinctiveness of the two Synoptic redactors' voices placed in close proximity. Whether or not the author of *GThomas* intentionally brought *GMatthew* and *GLuke* together in combination, these two proto-canonical gospels can be said to keep company with one another by virtue of their redactional influence on *GThomas* – a redactional influence that meets the criteria of textual distinctiveness and frequent recurrence.

My analysis demonstrates that no noncanonical gospels can claim this same status as a textual "other" in relation to *GThomas*, *GMatthew*, or *GLuke*, even in the several instances of noncanonical parallels in *GThomas*. In the setting of *GThomas'* second-century composition, *GMatthew* and *GLuke* keep company with one another, contributing significantly to the Jesus tradition that *GThomas* restages. Noncanonical traditions contribute as well, but they bear no distinct fingerprints of any gospel book. In *GThomas*, then, we have a witness to the tendency of *GMatthew* and *GLuke* to keep company with another as well-respected peers contributing to the second-century memory of Jesus of Nazareth, even if *GThomas* attempts to subvert their contribution by its own special witness to esoteric Jesus tradition.

Chapter 2

The *Epistula Apostolorum*: Combining Gospels through Interpretive Rewriting

In the previous chapter we saw how gospels interact in combination when their materials are reworked into a fresh composition. Due to the genre of *GThomas* (a gnomological anthology), the narrative integrity and sequence of the source gospels (*GMatthew* and *GLuke*) was not preserved. Themes and catchwords form the architecture rather than any evangelist's narrative sequence. In the present chapter, I will examine another case of gospel combination through interpretive rewriting, but one that does so with a noticeable narrative sequence, the *Epistula Apostolorum* (*EpAp*).

2.1 Prolegomena to the *Epistula Apostolorum*

EpAp is immensely valuable to the present enquiry because it clearly draws from *GMatthew*, *GJohn*, and *GLuke*, and probably from *GMark*. Over a century ago Carl Schmidt suggested that the author "possessed the four-gospel canon."[1] Charles Hill and Darrell Hannah take this argument a step further and claim that the fourfold gospel was practically fixed and authoritative for the author.[2] But *EpAp* 4.2–4 also cites a tradition later deemed by Irenaeus to be "apocryphal and spurious,"[3] but that was preserved in textual form in *Infancy Gospel of Thomas* 6.9. The presence of this *logion*, together with "the freedom in the usage of gospel material"[4] has led Manfred Hornschuh and Judith Hartenstein to conclude the opposite – that the fourfold gospel was not fixed for the author.[5] Francis Watson agrees with this assessment and finds the creative reworking of written gospel material in *EpAp* as a perfect fit into his paradigm of pre-200 CE gospel writing. For Watson, *EpAp* engages in "free adaption from earlier written traditions still regarded as fluid and malleable,"[6] and asserts its own authority rather than

---

[1] Schmidt 1919: 216: "daß unser Verfasser den Vier-Evangelienkanon besessen hat."

[2] Hill 2004: 368–71; Hannah 2008: 633.

[3] Irenaeus, *Haer.* 1.20.1: ἀποκρύφων καὶ νόθων γραφῶν; Greek text SC 264.288.

[4] Schmidt 1919: 373: "die Freiheit in der Verwendung des evangelischen Stoffes."

[5] Hartenstein 2000: 120: "läßt sich m.E. aber weder schließen, daß die EpAp den Kanon der vier Evangelien voraussetzt;" cf. Hornschuh 1965: 11–12; Müller 2012: 1064.

[6] Watson 2018: 206.

2.1 Prolegomena to the Epistula Apostolorum   49

upholding prior gospels as sacrosanct.[7] According to Watson, *EpAp* is part of the same amorphous process of gospel writing and re-writing as *GMark*, *GMatthew*, *GLuke*, and *GJohn* and should be considered as a "Gospel of the Eleven."[8] The validity of the fixed-canon or the fluid-canon view in *EpAp* remains to be seen.

Wherever the date of *EpAp* is placed,[9] its combination of gospel materials has massive implications for my study. If it can be reasonably dated to the first half of the second century, then it would be a significant witness either to an early habitus of proto-canonical gospel combination or to the malleability of gospel tradition in "the period c.75–150 CE, prior to the formation of the canonical collection."[10] On the other hand, if it is dated to the second half of the second century, then it would be relevant either as corroboration of Irenaeus' fourfold gospel combination or as a contrasting paradigm that would make Irenaeus seem more like a "lonely Lyonian"[11] than a representative of a mainstream conception of written gospel combinations in the 180s CE. Since the date is far from certain, my analysis below will deal as much as possible with internal data not contingent upon a specific dating. Wherever my method requires dating, I will work with a mid-second century date for heuristic purposes, and I will be cautious with conclusions based on that date.[12]

The *Epistula Apostolorum* can be divided into four major sections: an epistolary introduction, historical foundations for apostolic faith, a post-resurrection discourse, and the concluding ascension narrative (see Table 9 below).

---

[7] Watson 2018: 214. Watson's groundbreaking publications on *EpAp* (2018; 2019; 2020) have reinvigorated scholarship on this ancient text, and though at several points I come to different conclusions than Watson, I am greatly indebted to his rigorous methodology and foundational insights.

[8] Watson 2018: 193 appeals to Origen's mention of the "Gospel of the Twelve" (*Hom. in Luc.* 1.2) as a historical parallel which *EpAp* may resemble.

[9] Hornschuh 1965: 116 and Hill 1999 place it in the early second century; Watson 2018: 190 places it "no later than the mid-second century," but changes his view later (Watson 2020: 11) to "dating from *c.*170;" Müller 2012: 1065 and Hills 2008: 9 place it mid-second century; Schmidt 1919: 361–402 and Hartenstein 2000: 107 place it in the late-second century.

[10] Watson 2018: 190.

[11] I borrow this creative moniker from Charles Hill 2010b: 42.

[12] A mid-second century date for *EpAp* is not necessarily precluded by *EpAp*'s use of *LEMark*, which I will advocate below, since *LEMark* can be plausibly dated anywhere between 120 and 150 CE (Kelhoffer 2000: 175). Furthermore, a date slightly preceding 150 CE for *EpAp* is compelling, especially considering Jesus' prediction of the Parousia "when the hundredth and the twentieth part is fulfilled" (*EpAp* 17.2 in the Coptic; differing from the later variant "one hundred and fifty years" in the Ethiopic text), perhaps referring to 120 years after Jesus' resurrection discourse ca. 30 CE, which would place 150 CE as the *terminus ad quem*. Watson 2020: 7–11 argues for a ca. 170 CE date, based on the correspondence between the language of plagues in *EpAp* 34–37 and the historical realities of the Antonine plague in Asia Minor in 165–81 CE. However, one could make an equally compelling comparison between the language of earthquakes in *EpAp* 34–37 and the numerous earthquakes that struck Asia Minor in the 150s, 140s, or even 120s CE (cf. Hill 1999: 39–47).

50　　　　　　　　　*Chapter 2: The Epistula Apostolorum*

Table 9: Outline of *EpAp*

Section	Reference	
Epistolary Introduction	1.1–2.3	Greetings, warnings, main theme and exhortation
Historical foundations	3.1–13	Creedal foundations
	4.1–4	Jesus' childhood
	5.1–22	Jesus' earthly ministry
	6.1–8.2	Interlude: Reiterating warnings and exhortation
	9.1–12.4	Jesus' death and resurrection
Post-Resurrection Discourse	13.1–18.6	Jesus reveals his incarnation
	19.1–26.7	Jesus reveals the resurrection
	27.1–30.5	Jesus reveals his descent into Hades
	31.1–39.13	Jesus reveals and validates the ministry of Paul
	40.1–45.8	Jesus reveals the final judgment
	46.1–50.10	Jesus reveals the apostolic mission
Ascension Narrative	51.1–4	Jesus ascends into heaven

In the present chapter, I will focus much of the analysis on *EpAp* 3.10–12.4, which is part of a larger section, 1.1–12.4. This is the long introduction to the post-resurrection dialogue that constitutes the majority of *EpAp* (13.1–50.10). 51.1–4 is the narrative conclusion to *EpAp*. *EpAp* 1.1–12.4, as a broad introduction to the post-resurrection dialogue, naturally divides into the following sections:

EpAp 1–2: Epistolary Introduction

EpAp 3: Creedal and Biblical Foundations of Old and New Testaments, Introduction to
　　　Gospel Epitome

EpAp 4–5: Gospel Epitome Part 1: Miracle Catena from infancy to Galilean Ministry

EpAp 6: Summary and Exhortation

EpAp 7–8: Warnings against Heresy

EpAp 9–12: Gospel Epitome Part 2: Crucifixion, Burial, Resurrection, Appearances

EpAp 3.1–13 flows seamlessly in creedal fashion from patriarchs and prophets to apostles and disciples (3.9), from creation (3.1–8) to incarnation (3.10–13), from Old Testament revelation to the beginning of the gospel narrative. A discernable gospel narrative is introduced at 3.10–13 and carries on from 4.1 to 5.22. After a brief hiatus in *EpAp* 6–8, the gospel narrative continues from 9.1 to 12.4. *EpAp* 3.1–12.4 in many ways functions as the historical, biblical, theological, and creedal foundation for the apocalypse of 13.1–50.4. One might call *EpAp* 3.1–12.4 a summary of divine revelation prior to the apocalypse of 13.1–50.4. The gospel narrative, pieced together from 3.10–5.22 and 9.1–12.4, is an integral part of the biblical foundation laid out in 3.1–12.4. As part of this biblical

2.1 Prolegomena to the Epistula Apostolorum

foundation, the cluster of gospel materials found in *EpAp* 3.10–12.4 is a gospel epitome composed almost entirely of excerpts from the canonical gospels.

The epitome, as a literary category, was a common tool employed by intellectuals in antiquity. Authors often summarized epics, philosophical treatises, medical works, and historical writings into epitomes.[13] 2 Maccabees offers a helpful parallel in the form of a historical epitome. It combines a collective epistle directed to a wide audience with an epitome of an earlier historical writing (the five-volume work of Jason of Cyrene).[14] This epitome is meant to strengthen Jewish memory of the victorious Maccabean revolt against Antiochus IV, and in so doing strengthen Jews across Egypt in their commitment to the Deuteronomistic covenant.[15] The author of 2 Maccabees states his purpose in 2.23–31, showing the congenial relationship between his own epitome (ἐπιτομή) and abridgement (μετάφρασις), and the prior history of Jason of Cyrene. Similarly, the *Epistula Apostolorum* includes an epitome of the narrative of Jesus' life, from birth to resurrection, in order to strengthen this apostolic memory for believers worldwide and edify them in their faith.[16] The epitomizer of 2 Maccabees does not seek to undermine or make redundant the five-volume work of his predecessor. Rather, he summarizes the earlier historiography to facilitate memorization.[17] In the same way, I will argue in this chapter that the epitomizer of *EpAp* does not seek to supplant the gospels that preceded him, but rather to summarize them as an aid for memory. In the present chapter, I will focus mainly on this gospel epitome as an example of second-century gospel combination through interpretive rewriting, but I will also have in mind the other gospel citations and allusions throughout the rest of the *Epistula*.

---

[13] See, for example, Dionysius of Halicarnassus' *Epitome of the Treatise on the Formation of Names* (ΤΟΥ ΠΕΡΙ ΣΥΝΘΕΣΕΩΣ ΟΝΟΜΑΤΩΝ ΕΠΙΤΟΜΗ); Radermacher and Usener 1965: 145–94. See also the first or second century *Bibliotheca* of Pseudo-Apollodorus (LCL 121), which gives epitomes of a number of Greek myths. Plutarch gives an epitome of his biographies of Aristophanes and Menander (LCL 321). Galen frequently refers to making epitomes or synopses of medical books and philosophical treatises: e.g. *Ars. Medica* (Kühn 1.410.8); *De placitis Hippocratis et Platonis* (Kühn 5.466.12); *In Hippocratis de natura hominis librum commentaria* (Kühn 15.25.10–17). Galen also speaks of the use of epitomes in the synopsis of one of his own works, *Synopsis librorum suorum de pulsibus* (Kühn 9.431).

[14] 2 Maccabees opens with an epistle in 1.1–9, and an explanation of the epitomizing of Jason's five-volume work in 2.19–32, which introduces the epitome in chapters 3–15.

[15] The Deuteronomic intentions are shown in the opening epistle (2 Macc 1.1–5), which pronounces a blessing to the Jews of Egypt, that God may "remember his covenant with Abraham, Isaac, and Jacob" and "open" their "hearts" to his "law and commandments."

[16] *EpAp* 1.1–2.4

[17] 2 Macc 2.26: τοῖς δὲ φιλοφρονοῦσιν εἰς τὸ διὰ μνήμης ἀναλαβεῖν εὐκοπίαν: "ease for those who desire to undertake remembrance."

Table 10: Complete List of Gospel Parallels in *EpAp*

Gospel Source	Key phrase, Theme, or narrative	Parallel in *EpAp*	Redactional Features (Eusebian Canons)	Rating
GJohn 6.44; 8.16, 18; 12.49; 14.24; cf. 4.34; 5.23–24, 30, 37; 6.38–39; 7.16, 18; 7.28, 33; 8.26, 29; 9.4; 12.44–45; 13.20; 15.21; 16.5, 7; 20.21	"The Father who sent me"	12; 13; 17; 19; 21; 26; 28; 33; 36; 39 (x2); 43; 45; 51		AbC
GJohn 17.21–23	"I am in the Father and the Father is in me."	17; 19; 31		AbC
GJohn 1.14	"The Logos of God"	3; 14; 17; 31; 39		Pb
GJohn 1.14	"Logos became flesh"	3; 14; 39		AbC
GJohn 2.1–11	Water into wine at Cana	5		AbC
GJohn 20.19–29	Doubting Thomas	11		AbC
GJohn 13.34	"a new commandment"	18.5		Pb
GJohn 17.20ff	"glorified in those who believe"	19.6, 21		Pl
GMatt 17.24–27	Coin in the Fish	5.14–16		AbC
GMatt 18.15–17	Ecclesial discipline of the sinning brother	48.1–3		AbC
GMatt 23.8	"call no one father or teacher"	41.3–4		AbC
GMatt 25.1–13	Parable of the ten virgins	43–45		AbC
GLuke 1.26–38	Gabriel's annunciation to the Virgin Mary	14.1–5; cf. 3.10		Pl
GLuke 2.7	"Swaddling clothes"	3.12		AbC
GMatt 14.13–21 // *GMark* 6.30–44 // *GLuke* 9.10–17 // *GJohn* 6.1–13	Feeding of the five thousand	5.17–19	I, II, VI, X1 (*GMt* 14.21)	AbC

GMatt 14.22–33 // GMark 6.45–52 // GLuke 8.22–25 // GJohn 6.15–21; GMatt 8.23–27 // GMark 4.35–41	Walking on water, calming the waves	5.13		Pl
GMark 2.1–12 // GMatt 9.1–8 // GLuke 5.17–26 // GJohn 5.2–9	"he made the paralytic walk"	5.2		Ps
GMatthew 27.33, 38, 60–61, 28.1 // GMark 15.22, 27, 46–47, 16.1, 10 // GLuke 23.33, 54–55, 24.1 // GJohn 19.17–18, 40–41, 20.1, 5	Crucifixion, Burial, and Resurrection	9.1–5	I, II, IX, X2 (GMk 16.1, 10), X3 (GLuke 23.33; 24.1, 3), and X4 (GJohn 20.5)	AbC
GMatt 8.28–34 // GMark 5.1–20 // GLuke 8.26–39	Freeing of the demoniac	5.10–12	II, VIII, X1 (GMt 8.29)	AbC
GMatt 9.18–26 // GMark 5.21–43 // GLuke 8.49–56 // cf. GJohn 11.38–44	Raising the dead	5.2		Ps
GLuke 7.22 // GMatt 11.5 // cf. GMatt 4.24	"the blind see… the lepers are cleansed… the deaf hear… the dead are raised" "he expelled demons from the possessed"	5.2, 9		Ps
GLuke 3.17 // GMatt 3.12	Chaff thrown into the fire	49.8		Pl
GLuke 8.43–48 // GMatt 9.20–22 // GMark 5.25–34	Healing the bleeding woman	5.3–8	II, V, VIII, X2 (GMk 5.31), X3 (GLk 8.35)	AbC
GLuke 24.51 // Acts 1.9	Jesus' ascension	51.2–4		Ps
IGThomas 6.3–4	Jesus disputes with his teachers about "alpha" and "beta".	4.2–4		Ps

Key: Ps = Possible; Pl = Plausible; Pb = Probable; AbC = All but Certain. For Eusebian numbers, see Section 2.5.1

54   *Chapter 2: The Epistula Apostolorum*

2.2 Identities: Proto-Canonical Gospels and Noncanonical Traditions

The *Epistula Apostolorum* gives clear indications that its author drew from an eclectic range of gospel sources in his process of composition. A list of gospel parallels, both canonical and apocryphal, is provided in Table 10 above. As we shall see below, the consistent use of material found only in *GJohn* and *GMatthew*, and the meticulous way that the author stitched this material together, make it nearly certain that the author drew intentionally from *GJohn* and *GMatthew*. It is also plausible that the author was influenced by *GLuke* and *GMark*, and he includes a childhood narrative that was later deemed apocryphal.

In degree of influence, *GJohn* has pride of place. Not only does the author relate episodes from Johannine *Sondergut*,[18] but Johannine language also saturates his linguistic register to such an extent that we might even say that *EpAp* was written in large part in Johannine idiom. Several phrases have nearly verbatim parallels in *GJohn*. The phrase "the Father/one who sent me"[19] appears throughout *EpAp*.[20] The Johannine phrase, "I am in the Father and the Father is in me" appears in *EpAp* 17.4 and 17.8.[21] *EpAp* even speaks of the "word" that became flesh,"[22] and a "new commandment."[23]

GMatthew comes in close second. *EpAp* borrows several episodes and key phrases from Matthean *Sondergut*: the coin in the fish (*EpAp* 5.15–16),[24] the teaching on ecclesial discipline (*EpAp* 48.1–3),[25] the injunction not to call anyone

---

[18] The wine miracle at Cana in Galilee (*EpAp* 5.1 // *GJn* 2.1–11); doubting Thomas (*EpAp* 11.7 // *GJn* 20.19–29) – although with the Thomas episode, *EpAp* adds Andrew and Peter to the doubters.

[19] E.g. "my Father who sent me" in *EpAp* 26. Ethiopic: አቡየ ዘፈነወኒ; Coptic: ⲡⲁⲉⲓⲱⲧ ⲉⲧⲁⲅⲧⲉⲟⲩⲁⲉⲓ (ⲉⲧⲁⲅⲧⲉⲟⲩⲁⲉⲓ is a sub-Akhmimic dialect variation of what would be ⲉⲛⲧⲁⲩⲧⲁⲟⲩⲟⲓ in Sahidic). Compare Ethiopic *GJn* 12.49: አቡ ዘፈነወኒ, and Sahidic Coptic *GJn* 12.49 ⲡⲁⲓⲱⲧ ⲉⲛⲧⲁⲩⲧⲁⲟⲩⲟⲓ (Codex Qau has ⲡⲉⲓⲱⲧˋ ⲛ̄ⲧⲁⲩⲧⲉⲩⲁⲉⲓ). All of these are probably translating from the Greek *Vorlage* similar to the Johannine ὁ πέμψας με πάτηρ. For *EpAp*, all Coptic citations from Schmidt and Wajnberg 1919; all Ethiopic citations from Guerrier and Grébaut 1913.

[20] *EpAp* 13.3, 6; 17.3, 6; 19.5, 29; 21.1, 3; 26.2, 5; 28.4; 33.6; 36.6; 39.6; 43.7; 45.8; 51.1.

[21] *EpAp* 17.4: Ethiopic: አነ ባአቡ ወአቡ ብየ ("I am in my Father and my Father is in me"); Coptic: ⲁⲛⲁⲕ ⲧⲏⲣⲧ ϯϩⲛ̄ ⲡⲁⲉⲓⲱⲧ ⲁⲟⲩ [*sic.*] ⲡⲁⲉⲓⲱⲧ ϩⲟⲟⲡ ⲛ̄ϩⲏⲧ ("I am wholly in my Father, and my Father is in me").

[22] Ethiopic *EpAp* 3.10: ቃል ዘቦነ ሥጋ directly paralleling Ethiopic *GJn* 1.14: ቃል ሥጋ ኮነ, undoubtedly reflecting (whether directly or indirectly via Coptic, Syriac, or Arabic), the initial Greek ὁ λόγος σὰρξ ἐγένετο. See also *EpAp* 39.12, where the Coptic reads ⲁⲛⲁⲕ ⲡⲉ ⲡⲗⲟⲅⲟⲥ ⲁⲓ̈ϣⲱⲡⲉ ⲛ̄ⲥⲁⲣⲝ (I am the word; I became flesh) and parallels Greek *GJn* 1.14 even more closely than the Sahidic (ⲡⲱ̣ⲁ̣ⲝ̣ⲉ ⲁⲩⲥⲁⲣⲝ).

[23] *EpAp* 18.5.

[24] *GMt* 17.24–27.

[25] *GMt* 18.15–17.

2.2 Identities: Proto-Canonical Gospels and Noncanonical Traditions 55

"father" or "teacher" (*EpAp* 41.4–5),[26] and the parable of the ten virgins (*EpAp* 43, 45).[27]

GLuke is not as prominent, but the author of *EpAp* would be hard-pressed to find passages and phrases more distinctly Lukan than the ones he includes in his work: Gabriel's annunciation to Mary (*EpAp* 14.1, 5),[28] the "swaddling clothes" at Jesus' birth (*EpAp* 3.12),[29] and the declaration that the women at the tomb "did not find Jesus' body " (*EpAp* 9.5).[30] *EpAp* 51.1–4 also gives a version of the ascension narrative that might be drawn remotely from *GLuke* and Acts, but this is more difficult to establish.

In the case of *GMark*, the evidence is much more limited, but this should be expected because so much of *GMark* is swallowed up by *GMatthew* and *GLuke*; by definition it is more difficult to find distinct Markan redactional features than the other two Synoptics. It is therefore more remarkable when we do in fact find either Markan *Sondergut* or Markan redaction in a second-century Christian re-writing. This is what happens in *EpAp*. The first instance of Markan redaction is in the account of the man with the withered hand.[31] In the wording of *EpAp*, Jesus "extended" the man's hand (ⲡⲱⲣϣ · ⲛ̄ϭⲓϫ). This fits with the Matthean and Markan καὶ ἐξέτεινεν καὶ ἀπεκατεστάθη ("and he extended it and it was restored") against the Lukan ἀπεκατεστάθη ("it was restored").[32] The author of *EpAp* includes neither the Matthean phrase ὑγιὴς ὡς ἡ ἄλλη ("whole as the other [hand]") nor the Lukan detail that it was the man's right hand (ἡ δεξιά). The Markan version is therefore the closest parallel to the version in *EpAp*. The second instance of Markan redaction is a minor detail in the episode of the hemorrhaging woman.[33] Only in *GMark* do the disciples reply to Jesus after he asks, "who touched me?" The phrase in direct speech, τίς ὁ ἁψάμενός μου, is Lukan (*GLk* 8.45; cf. ἥψατό μού τις in 8.46),[34] but the response from the disciples is from *GMark* 5.31 (in *GLk* 8.45, only Peter responds). Third, in *EpAp* 9.1, Jesus is crucified between two brigands. The Coptic uses the loanword ⲗⲏⲥⲧⲏⲥ, which parallels the Greek lexeme λῃστής in *GMatthew* 27.38 and *GMark* 15.27, rather than κακοῦργοι ("evildoers") in *GLuke* 23.32–33 and *GPeter* 4.10, or simply "two others" (ἄλλους δύο) in *GJohn* 19.18. Here the author of *EpAp* does not describe the brigands' crucifixion with a passive verb, as in *GMatthew* 27.38 (σταυροῦνται). Thus, *GMark* provides the closer parallel. Finally, the author at

---

[26] *GMt* 23.8-9.

[27] *GMt* 25.1–12.

[28] *GLk* 1.26–38.

[29] *GLk* 2.7.

[30] *GLk* 24.3.

[31] *GMt* 12.9–14 // *GMk* 3.1–6 // *GLk* 6.6–11; cf. Hannah 2008: 623–24.

[32] *GMt* 12.13 and *GMk* 3.5 agree against *GLk* 6.10.

[33] *GMt* 9.20–22 // *GMk* 5.21–34 // *GLk* 8.43–48.

[34] *GMk* 5.30 says τίς μου ἥψατο τῶν ἱματίων. In *GMk* 5.31 τίς μου ἥψατο is given in the disciples' indirect speech.

56   *Chapter 2: The Epistula Apostolorum*

EpAp 9.4 incorporates a detail found in *GMark* 16.1 and *GLuke* 24.1 into his account of the women at the tomb. The intention of the women to anoint Jesus' body, expressed with the ἵνα clause, only appears in *GMark* 16.1 (ἵνα ἐλθοῦσαι ἀλείψωσιν αὐτόν), not in *GLuke* 24.1. *EpAp*, in both the Coptic and Ethiopic versions, express this clause of intention.[35] *EpAp* therefore parallels *GMark*. When these four instances are taken cumulatively, along with the number of occasions where either *GMatthew/GMark* or *GLuke/GMark* parallels are at hand,[36] as well as the author's probable awareness of the *Longer Ending of Mark*,[37] the case is strong that *EpAp* made use of *GMark*.

2.3 Identities: Noncanonical Traditions in the *Epistula Apostolorum*

The author of *EpAp* also includes two traditions that did not eventually make it into the canonical gospels. The first is the episode of Jesus' childhood alphabet lesson (*EpAp* 4.1–4):

He [Jesus] was taken to school by Joseph and Mary his mother. And his teacher taught him saying, "Say alpha." He answered and said to him, "First you tell me what beta is; then indeed you shall do what is true and real."[38]

It is impossible to establish whether the author is drawing from a written or oral source. The author could be inserting an *agraphon* into the gospel epitome of *EpAp* 3.10–12.4. Although this episode is also found in the *Infancy Gospel of Thomas*, it is difficult to establish that the author of *EpAp* is drawing from this source,[39] since *IGThomas* most likely was composed in the late second or early

---

[35] The Coptic manuscript reads: ⲁⲩⲝ̄ⲓ ⲛ̄ⲟⲩⲥⲁϭⲛⲉ ⲁⲩϣⲟⲩⲱϥ [ⲁⲝⲛ̄ ⲡ]ϥ̄ⲥⲱⲙⲁ ("they took ointment, they poured on his body") but, given the context, this is probably a scribal error for what should be ⲁⲩⲝ̄ⲓ ⲛ̄ⲟⲩⲥⲁϭⲛⲉ ⲁϣⲟⲩⲱϥ [ⲁⲝⲛ̄ ⲡ]ϥ̄ⲥⲱⲙⲁ ("they took ointment to pour on his body"); Watson 2020: 230; Hannah 2008: 617. The Ethiopic expresses the intention clearly: ⲱⲗⲉ ⲝ ⲝⲋⲕⲧ ⲕⲱ ⲝ ⲝⲋ-ⲙ ⲝ ⲱ-ⲕⲧ ⲝ ⲣⲟⲩ ("and they took ointment in order that they might pour it onto his flesh"); cf. Hannah 2008: 616–17.

[36] For these references, see Section 2.5 below, where Eusebian canons VI and VIII are identified.

[37] For these parallels, see below, Section 2.5.5.

[38] Translation Hills 2009: 24. The final phrase ⲱⲝⲅⲙⲏ ⲝ ⲝⲙⲅⲝ ⲝ ⲩⲋⲱ ⲝ ⲅⲕⲍ ⲝ ⲕⲧⲅⲕⲍ (lit: "and when truly wholly the work that was done") is probably corrupt in all manuscripts and makes little sense.

[39] Watson 2020: 95 attempts to strengthen the connection between *EpAp* 4 and *IGThomas* by a conjectural emendation: "and then I will trust you and say 'Alpha!'". "And then," is attested in a relatively weak manuscript (S, belonging to Family 2). The latter part of this emendation, "…you and say Alpha" is entirely conjectural and is not attested in any manuscript. Watson constructs this emendation based on the parallel in *IGThomas* 6.9.

2.3 Identities: Noncanonical Traditions in the Epistula Apostolorum 57

third century.[40] Furthermore, *IGThomas* has several early recensions, and it is impossible to determine if this episode existed in its earliest form.[41] This episode does, however, have a parallel in a second-century Marcosian text known to Irenaeus.[42] Irenaeus describes this source as a written source, and he mentions that it relates the story of Jesus speaking back to his teacher regarding the meaning of "Alpha" and "Beta."

Here we have the genuine possibility that the author of *EpAp* has combined an episode from an apocryphal gospel together with a series of episodes that stem from the proto-canonical gospels. Whatever the source behind the inclusion of this episode in *EpAp*, its inclusion is slightly different than the rest of the gospel material included in *EpAp* 3.10–12.4. The Synoptic material integrated into *EpAp* 3.10–12.4 from *GMatthew*, *GLuke*, and *GMark* is deeply interwoven. Some of the episodes in the miracle catena of *EpAp* 5 show redactional material from two or even all three Synoptic gospels. Similarly, even *GJohn* is interconnected with the Synoptics in *EpAp* 3.10–12.4 by the mention of Jesus walking on water, the feeding of the five thousand, and Peter's three denials. All four canonical gospels are deeply interconnected in the episodes the author of *EpAp* chooses to include in his epitome. The author of *EpAp* includes not only *Sondergut* from *GMatthew* and *GJohn*, but also Matthean material that overlaps with the other canonical gospels. Moreover, the author includes Johannine material from prologue to resurrection, Lukan material from nativity to resurrection, and Matthean and Markan material from throughout Jesus' ministry, passion, and resurrection. It appears that the author of *EpAp* intends to include a thumbnail sketch of each of the proto-canonical gospels.

Quite the contrary, the isolated nature of the infancy episode makes it probable that, whether the author of *EpAp* derived this episode from a Jesus book or an oral collection of *logia*, he did not intend to integrate its source *pars pro toto* into his gospel epitome of *EpAp* 3.10–12.4. The episodes from proto-canonical gospels in *EpAp* are interconnected in a way that the alphabet episode is not, and it is inserted more as an attempt to fill in the gaps left by the canonical gospels than as lynchpin to the author's portrayal of Jesus.[43] The isolated nature of the author's inclusion of the alphabet episode also sheds light on the nature of the source from which the author draws this episode. If it is a written source, then it is likely to be a short narrative about Jesus, probably relegated to an infancy narrative. On the other hand, the isolated nature of the episode also lends itself to the nature of

---

[40] On the date of *IGThomas*, see Burke 2008:132–34.

[41] On the recensions, see Burke 2004; Kaiser 2012.

[42] *Haer.* 1.20.1.

[43] In antiquity, *IGThomas* was a rolling corpus with multiple recensions that perhaps enabled this kind of amalgamation of its traditions alongside proto-canonical gospels; on the multiple recensions of *IGThomas*, see Burke 2004; 2008; 2010.

58 *Chapter 2: The Epistula Apostolorum*

agrapha, and it could be an oral tradition that has found its way into the composition of *EpAp*, the Marcosian apocryphon, and the *Infancy Gospel of Thomas*.

The second apocryphal tradition inserted into the narrative is a saying that the author alleges "is written in the prophet": "the footprint of a demonic phantom does not fasten upon the ground."[44] This *logion* has no exact parallel in any extant Jewish or Christian literature. Some scholars speculate that it comes from a lost Jewish apocryphal writing.[45] Others surmise that it is a scriptural citation invented by the author of *EpAp*.[46] There are indeed resonances with certain Jewish texts, and the saying can be situated within second-century disputes about the corporeality of Jesus' resurrection. Our present concern is whether this *logion* constitutes the use of another text that was combined with the proto-canonical gospels in the author's composition of a post-resurrection scene. This *logion* is referred to as belonging to a written source, and the author appears to envisage it as part of a prophetic corpus. It is therefore unlikely that the author of *EpAp* is drawing this *logion* from a gospel that would later be deemed a noncanonical *gospel*. It is more likely that the author is inventing a prophetic text (or quoting from a now lost Jewish apocalypse) which Jesus' resurrection fulfils.[47] This text – whether imagined or real – would function more like the Jewish Scriptures rather than a parallel gospel *vis-à-vis* the proto-canonical gospels that are summarized and combined in *EpAp*.

The author of *EpAp* draws heavily from *GMatthew* and *GJohn*, and substantially from *GLuke*. The author also draws minor details from *GMark*, and more significantly from material that *GMark* shares with *GMatthew*, *GLuke*, and even *GJohn*. The author's combination of these materials evokes a *pars pro toto* approach toward the proto-canonical gospels. The author's insertion of an apocryphal episode and an otherwise unattested *agraphon* are more epiphenomenal rather than central to his construction of a Jesus narrative.

2.4 Mode: Combining Gospel Excerpts in the *Epistula Apostolorum*

In what way did the author of *EpAp* combine these gospel materials and traditions? Is it right to imagine the author surrounded by assistants with (at least) four gospel bookrolls (or codices) opened on their laps? One might envisage Tatian composing his *Diatessaron* in this way. Or might the author of *EpAp* be

---

[44] *EpAp* 11.8.

[45] E.g. Hornschuh 1965: 78–79; cf. *Bel and the Dragon* 19–20, where the reality of human footsteps convicts claims of false gods.

[46] Watson 2018: 214; Hills 2008: 85–93.

[47] Cf. the use of a similar tradition in *Carmen Apologeticum* 564 and *Acts of John* 93, which featured in debates about Docetic Christology.

2.4 Mode: Combining Gospel Excerpts in the Epistula Apostolorum   59

utilizing a kind of synopsis table where gospel episodes are laid in parallel, similar to what some scholars envisage of Ammonius' project?[48]

The author, in *EpAp* 3.10–12.4, probably engages in the same "deft excerpting" that we encountered in the compositional process behind *GThomas*.[49] In light of ancient reading practices, it is plausible that the author of *EpAp* drew from excerpts that he had taken from all four canonical gospels. In *EpAp*, we do not have a comprehensive four-gospel orchestration such as the *Diatessaron*, so it is not as likely that the author is drawing material from several opened gospel bookrolls or codices. We do, however, have in *EpAp* 3.10–12.4 a summary of the birth, life, ministry, death, and resurrection of Jesus with an eclectic array of materials. This eclectic summary presupposes a thorough and thoughtful engagement with the primary texts, probably facilitated by excerpting. The author's excerpting is all the more likely when we consider the connection between excerpting and memory in the second century, as seen in the example of Aulus Gellius, cited above, in Section 1.2.1c. *EpAp* is fundamentally a treatise built on memory, as the apostolic author claims: "What we have heard and remembered we have written."[50] We can envisage the process of remembering the words and deeds of Jesus being aided by copious excerpts from the proto-canonical gospels.

Interestingly, the author of *EpAp* appears to have arranged the episodes into meaningful sequence. We will unpack this sequence in section 2.5.1 below, but it is important to note here that the mode of gospel combination employed by the author of *EpAp* facilitated both *vertical* and *horizontal* readings of the proto-canonical gospels (vertical reading appreciates the narrative sequence and horizontal reading appreciates parallels in multiple gospels).[51] The author's combination of redactional minutiae in Synoptic parallels and the author's progression in a Synoptic-Johannine hybrid sequence presuppose a dual-axis map by which to chart a narrative progression while simultaneously appreciating parallels across several gospels. This map could be merely a conceptual topography in the mind of the author, or it could be an example of sophisticated note-taking that resembled Ammonius' later project. We cannot know for certain.

The author of *EpAp* combined excerpts from all four proto-canonical gospels and from at least one other source and arranged these excerpts along a vertical narrative axis and with reference to horizontal parallels. The mode of combination probably involved the textual mechanisms of excerpting and epitomizing.

---

[48] Cf. Crawford 2019: 56–95. An alternative view is that Ammonius' project, described by Eusebius (*Ep. ad Carp.*, 3-14) was plausibly an edition of *GMatthew* with Synoptic and Johannine parallels annotated in the margins. See Coogan and Rodriguez 2023.

[49] Johnson 2010: 118; see above, Section 1.2.1c.

[50] *EpAp* 1.4; see also *EpAp* 14.3; 20.3 (Eth); 36.4.

[51] For an in-depth explanation and exploration of vertical vs. horizontal gospel reading, see Coogan and Rodriguez 2023.

60 *Chapter 2: The Epistula Apostolorum*

2.5 Integrity and Interactions of Gospels in the *Epistula Apostolorum*

How does the author of *EpAp* handle the gospel texts from which he draws, and how do these gospels interact within the pages of *EpAp*?

2.5.1 Sequencing, Stitching, and Creative Additions in the Gospel Epitome of EpAp *3.10-12.4*

We need first to appreciate where gospel allusions and citations are clustered in *EpAp*. The highest concentration is *EpAp* 3.10–12.4 (with a brief interlude in 6.1–8.2). This is structurally significant. The majority of *EpAp* is a post-resurrection apocalyptic discourse. The post-resurrection discourse in chapters 13–50 is built upon the theological groundwork laid in 1–12. The cluster of gospel allusions in 3.10–12.4 follow a broad canonical sequence: incarnation, birth, infancy, ministry, death, resurrection, post-resurrection appearance. *EpAp* 3.10–12.4 functions as a gospel epitome, coming on the heels of the summary of creedal and biblical faith in 3.1–9. The birth narrative in *EpAp* 3.10–13 overlaps with the creedal affirmations in 3.1–13. The Johannine narrative begins at *EpAp* 3.10 with "the Word who became flesh," and joins a Synoptic account of the Virgin birth in Bethlehem and a Lukan detail on the "swaddling clothes". Taken as a whole, *EpAp* 3.1–12.4 establishes the historical and creedal foundations of the following post-resurrection apocalyptic discourse.

Following a summary statement on the Son as co-creator with the Father in 3.1–8, and a summary of the Old Testament in 3.9 (in the phrase "patriarchs and prophets"), the gospel epitome in 3.10–12.4 contributes to the foundational, identity-forming history of the author's imagined Christian community.

We can discern dynamics of gospel interactions within the epitome when we lay out the sequence as in Table 11 below. First, *GJohn* frames the narrative sequence at the beginning and the end. The gospel narrative begins with "the Word who became flesh" in *EpAp* 3.10 and ends with a distinctly Johannine account of the resurrection appearances in 10.1–12.4, amplifying the Johannine theme of doubting disciples touching the risen Christ (adding Andrew and Peter to the Johannine Thomas). The beginning of Jesus' public ministry in the miracle catena in 5.1 is also set within Johannine terms, with the miracle at Cana in Galilee as the inauguration of Jesus' ministry (*GJn* 2.1–11),[52] and the end of the

---

[52] Watson 2020: 97–99 argues that *EpAp* 5.1 preserves the vestiges of an earlier, pre-Johannine version of the episode in Cana in which only Jesus' brothers, not his disciples, are present at the wedding. Watson argues this on the basis of the manuscript tradition of *GJn* 2.12 (P66, P75, ℵ, A, it^{abe}, cop^{ly}, K, Π, f^{13}), which, by Watson's reckoning, from the third to the ninth centuries, gradually introduces "the disciples… into a text from which they were previously absent, and subsequently promoted above Jesus' brothers…" (Watson 2020: 99). Watson's hypothesis is untenable when we consider that the manuscript tradition of *GJn* 2.2 and 2.11 is

2.5 Integrity and Interactions of Gospels in the Epistula Apostolorum   61

catena at *EpAp* 5.17–22 includes a Johannine twist to the feeding of the 5,000 – a spiritualizing explanation to the loaves. The sequence within the Johannine bookends of 3.10 and 12.1–4, however, is not guided strongly by one gospel.

Second, the broad patterns of Johannine and Synoptic sequencing in the gospel epitome are contrasted with intricate stitching together of multiple redactional features in four episodes: the healing of the hemorrhaging woman, the freeing of the demoniac, the feeding of the five thousand, and the crucifixion and burial. Francis Watson has pioneered the use of the Eusebian canons in analyzing the use of gospel materials in *EpAp*. I follow his markings in sections 3.5.2–4 below, and I apply them in a fresh analysis of the crucifixion and burial account in 3.5.5.[53] For the reader's convenience, I give the relevant Eusebian numbers with their corresponding meaning:

I = *GMatthew/GMark/GLuke/GJohn*; II = *GMatthew/GMark/GLuke*; V = *GMatthew/GLuke*; VI = *GMatthew/GMark*; VIII = *GLuke/GMark*; IX = *GLuke/GJohn*; X1 = *GMatthew* only; X2 = *GMark* only; X3 = *GLuke* only; X4 = *GJohn* only.

2.5.2 Healing the Hemorrhaging Woman: EpAp 5.3-7

In the first of these intricately stitched episodes, we see gospel material from the Eusebian categories II, V, VIII, X2, and X3, as well as creative tweaking by the author of *EpAp* (the author's changes and additions are given in *italics*). The passage has parallels in *GMatthew* 9.20–22, *GMark* 5.21–34, and *GLuke* 8.43–48:

[II]And a woman who suffered her periods twelve years touched [V]the hem of [II]his garment [VIII]and was immediately well. *And as we considered and wondered at the glorious things he had done,* [VIII]he said *to us,* "Who touched me?" [X2]And *we* said to him, [X3]"Lord, the press of the crowd *touched you!" And he answered and said to us, "I felt that power came forth upon me." Immediately* [VIII]that woman came *before him and answered him saying, "Lord, I touched you."* [II]And he *answered and* [II]said to her, [VIII]"Go, [II]your faith has made you well."[54]

The author allows *GLuke* and *GMark* to influence his retelling of this episode, as well as *GMatthew* and *GLuke* together, *GLuke* and *GMark* together, and all three Synoptics together. The author is essentially giving each Synoptic gospel a part in retelling this episode.

---

unanimous that Jesus' disciples were also invited to the wedding and were present at this miracle.

[53] By employing the Eusebian canons here, I do not imply that the author of *EpAp* was reasoning within the same, sophisticated textual geography of Eusebius' fourth-century apparatus. I only use the canons as a practical tool for identifying the relationships between gospel materials.

[54] Translation and Eusebian canons from Watson 2020: 100.

62   *Chapter 2: The Epistula Apostolorum*

Table 11: Gospel Parallels and Sequence in *EpAp* 3.10–12.4

EpAp	Episode	GMt	GMk	GLk	GJn	Others
3.10–11	The Word made flesh by the will of God				1.14	
3.10	In the womb of the Virgin by the Holy Spirit			1.27, 34–35		
3.12	Jesus wrapped in swaddling clothes in Bethlehem			2.7		
4.1–4	Jesus' Alphabet Lesson					*IGTh*
5.1	Wedding miracle in Cana				2.1–11	
5.2	Raising the dead	9.18–26 11.5	5.21–43	8.49–56 7.22	11.38–44	
5.2	Healing the Paralytic	9.1–8	2.1–12	5.17–26		
5.2	Withered hand	12.9–14	3.1–6	6.6–11		
5.3–8	Bleeding woman	9.20–22	5.25–34	8.43–48		
5.9	The deaf hear	11.5		7.21–22		
5.9	The blind see	11.5		7.21–22		
5.9	Demons are cast out	cf. 4.24				
5.9	Lepers are cleansed	11.5		7.21–22		
5.10–12	Legion is cast out	8.28–34	5.1–20	8.26–39		
5.13	Walking on the sea	14.22–33	6.45–52	8.22–25	6.15–21	
5.13	Calming the wind and waves	8.23–27	4.35–41			
5.14–16	Coin in the fish's mouth	17.24–27				
5.17–22	Feeding the 5,000	14.13–21	6.30–44	9.10–17	6.1–13	
9.1	Jesus crucified by Pontius Pilate between two brigands	27.38	15.38	[23.32–33]	[19.18]	
9.2	Jesus buried at the place called the Skull				cf. 19.17, 40–41	
9.3–5	Mary, Martha, and Mary Magdalene bring ointments, weeping, and do not find the body		16.1 16.10	24.1 24.1	20.1	
10.1–11.1	Jesus' appearance to Mary and Martha Mary's proclamation to the apostles				20.1–11	

2.5 Integrity and Interactions of Gospels in the Epistula Apostolorum 63

EpAp	Episode	GMt	GMk	GLk	GJn	Others
11.2– 12.4	Appearance to Doubting apostles				20.25– 29	

2.5.3 Freeing the Demoniac: EpAp 5.10–12

In the second episode, the author weaves a tapestry from Eusebian categories II, VIII, and X1, with a considerable amount of his own contribution. The passage has parallels in *GMatthew* 8.28–34, *GMark* 5.1–20, and *GLuke* 8.26–39.

And the demon [VIII]*Legion, who dwelt in a man,* [II]*met Jesus and cried out and said,* [X1]*"Before the day of our destruction have you come to drive us out?" And the Lord Jesus rebuked him and said to him, "Go out of this man and do nothing to him!" And he* [II]*went into the pigs and plunged them into the sea,* [VIII]*and they were drowned.*[55]

The author appears to favor the account where *GLuke* and *GMark* agree (VIII), as well as where all three Synoptics agree (II), and a special Matthean element (X1). In this episode as well, each of the Synoptics is given its say in the creative retelling.

2.5.4 Feeding the Five Thousand: EpAp 5.17–21

In the third episode, all four canonical gospels are brought into conversation with one another. We see the Eusebian categories I, II, VI, and X1, as well as a completely novel allegorical interpretation of the event, introduced by the author of *EpAp*. The passage has parallels in *GMatthew* 14.13–21, *GMark* 6.32–44, *GLuke* 9.10–17, and *GJohn* 6.1–13.

Then when we had no food except [I]*five loaves and two fishes, he commanded the men to recline. And their number was found to be* [X1]*five thousand besides women and children, and to these we brought pieces of bread.* [II]*And they were satisfied, and there was some left over, and we* [VI]*removed* [I]*twelve basketfuls of pieces. If we ask, "What do these five loaves mean?", they are an image of our faith as true Christians; that is, in the Father, ruler of the whole world, and in Jesus Christ and in the Holy Spirit and in the holy church and in the forgiveness of sins.*[56]

The author of *EpAp* maintains his consistent pattern of juxtaposing and arranging redactional details from multiple gospels – in this case, all four proto-canonical gospels – in order to craft a narrative mosaic of a familiar episode.

2.5.5 Crucifixion and Burial: EpAp 9.1–5

In the crucifixion and burial scenes, the author of *EpAp* takes more liberty in his creative retelling of these accounts, but he still shows use of material that falls into Eusebian categories I, II, IX, X2, X3, and X4. The parallel passages are

---

[55] Translation and Eusebian canons from Watson 2020: 101.

[56] Translation and Eusebian canons from Watson 2020: 103.

64   *Chapter 2: The Epistula Apostolorum*

GMatthew 27.33, 38, 60–61, 28.1, *GMark* 15.22, 27, 46–47, 16.1, 10, *GLuke* 23.33, 54–55, 24.1, and *GJohn* 19.17–18, 40–41, 20.1, 5.

This is he [of whom] we bear witness that he is the Lord, who was [I][crucif]ied *by Pontius Pilate [and A]rchelaus between* [II]two brigands, *[and] was buried in* [I]a place called [X3][the Skul]l. *[Three] women went there:* [II]Mary, *Martha,* and [I]Mary [Magd]alene. [X3]They took *ointment* [X2]in order *to pour [upon h]is body,* [X2]weeping and grieving *over [what] had happened. But when they* [X4]reached the to[mb] *and* [IX]looked inside [X3]they did not find the body.

This passage in *EpAp* is a complex mixture of several pieces of redactional minutiae. As mentioned above, the Coptic loanword ⲗⲏⲥⲧⲏⲥ is used here, paralleling *GMatthew* 27.38 and *GMark* 15.27, which use the lexeme ληστής to describe the men crucified alongside Jesus. Only in *GLuke* 24.1 do the women "take" (φέρουσαι) the ointment to the tomb. Only in *GMark* is their intention expressed (ἵνα... ἀλείψωσιν αὐτόν). *EpAp* 9.4 expresses the intention with slightly different wording, but the element of intention is probably Markan. The mention of "weeping and grieving"[57] parallels the phrase πενθοῦσιν καὶ κλαίουσιν found in *GMark* 16.10, although here it is transposed from the disciples to the women at the tomb.[58] In *GJohn* 20.5, it is the beloved disciple who "reached the tomb," and in *GLuke* 24.12//*GJohn* 20.5 a disciple "looked inside" the tomb (in the Lukan version it is Peter, and in the Johannine version it is the beloved disciple). Finally, *GLuke* 24.3 records the exact phrase "they did not find the body" (οὐχ εὗρον τὸ σῶμα).

What we have in the gospel epitome of *EpAp* 3.10–12.4 is a summary of the life of Jesus with Johannine bookends and a mostly Synoptic body. Within the mostly Synoptic body, there is an intricate intermingling of redactional features unique to each of the proto-canonical gospels. This is strikingly similar to the way Tatian composed his *Diatessaron*, as we will argue in Chapter 3. This method of gospel combination embodies an attitude of congenial interaction among *GJohn* and the Synoptic gospels.[59]

---

[57] Coptic: ⲉⲩⲣⲓⲙⲉ ⲁⲟⲩ ⲉⲩⲣ̄ⲗⲩⲡⲉⲓ; Ethiopic: ይበ,ይ : ወይ,ኃዘ.

[58] The author's knowledge of the *LEMark* is corroborated by Jesus' command in *EpAp* 30.3 to "go and preach" (cf. *LEMark* 16.15). Knowledge of *LEMark* does not necessitate the ca. 170 CE date that Watson 2020: 11 advocates, since *LEMark* could plausibly be dated anywhere between 120 and 150 CE (cf. Kelhoffer 2000: 175). On the other hand, if *LEMark* could be conclusively dated to the second half of the second century, this would indeed necessitate an even later date for *EpAp*.

[59] The author of *EpAp* also combines and reworks gospel materials in the extended post-resurrection dialogue in *EpAp* 13–50, but space does not permit us to analyze this in depth. However, we deal with this material below in section 2.6.3 insofar as it pertains to the measure of authority accorded to gospel books.

2.5.6 Summary of Integrity and Interactions of Gospels in EpAp

In the gospel epitome of *EpAp* 3.10–12.4, Synoptic and Johannine gospels interact congenially through the arrangement of an eclectic array of excerpts from each of these gospels. *GJohn* and *GMatthew* are the most influential pools of Jesus tradition from which the author of *EpAp* draws.

2.6 Textual Authority in the *Epistula Apostolorum*

2.6.1 Minimizing the Authoritative Status of Prior Gospels in EpAp?

How does *EpAp* relate to the gospel books from which it borrows? How does *EpAp* envisage its own authority *vis-à-vis* the gospel books it epitomizes in 3.10–12.4? Francis Watson has recently argued that *EpAp* does not represent a second-century adherence to a fourfold gospel canon, but it is itself an attempt to rewrite the gospel into a new, superior form.[60] Watson builds this case on three premises: 1) *EpAp*'s fluid use of both proto-canonical and apocryphal gospel traditions, 2) its apparent correcting of anomalies and inconsistencies in the proto-canonical gospel tradition, and 3) its liberal redaction of prior gospel tradition. However, as we shall see, *EpAp* has a special relationship with proto-canonical gospels, given that it draws almost exclusively from canonical material. Furthermore, the author of *EpAp* does not so much "correct" *GJohn* or *GMatthew*, rather, he is a faithful reader of these gospels who develops their themes in concert with one another and with other apostolic voices. Rather than "fixing" faulty texts, the author of *EpAp* is tuning these earlier gospels to the same scriptural key, exhibiting the beginnings of canonical hermeneutics within an already authoritative apostolic corpus.

2.6.2 Four Gospels or More in EpAp?

Watson sharply critiques Charles Hill and Darrell Hannah for arguing that *EpAp* represents a second-century adherence to the four-gospel canon.[61] He points to *EpAp*'s use of the apocryphal infancy tradition elsewhere found only in the *Infancy Gospel of Thomas*.[62] Watson makes the case that this episode, situated at *EpAp* 4.1–4, plays an integral role in the theological argument of the larger section (4.1–5.22), namely, to reinforce a Christological point – that Jesus is the Alpha and the Beta, corresponding to Jesus' divinity (in *EpAp* 3.1–2, 4–5) and

---

[60] Watson 2018; 2019; 2020.

[61] Watson 2018; 2019; 2020: 82n6 critiques Hill 2004: 366–74; 2010: 169–76 and Hannah 2008.

[62] One might also add the apocryphal account of Jesus taking the form of an angel to pass through the seven heavens to reach earth for his incarnation. Irenaeus knows this account as well, but he does not condemn it (*Epid.* 9, 84); cf. Hill 2010b: 173.

66 *Chapter 2: The Epistula Apostolorum*

his incarnation (in *EpAp* 3.13–15).[63] Watson also contrasts the apparently positive use of this infancy tradition with Irenaeus' explicit condemnation of that same tradition.[64] Watson interprets *EpAp*'s inclusion of the infancy tradition to mean that the author of *EpAp* is not bound by an authoritative collection of gospel books, much less a fourfold canon.

Watson is right to question whether *EpAp* endorses a closed, fourfold gospel canon. *EpAp* simply does not say this much, and perhaps Hill and Hannah push the evidence beyond what it allows. However, the inclusion of an apocryphal episode into a proto-canonical collection of gospels does not necessarily preclude the authoritative and exclusive status of that collection. As mentioned above, it is impossible to establish whether the author in *EpAp* 4.1–4 is drawing from a written or oral source, or whether the author is inserting an *agraphon* into his gospel epitome. The inclusion of noncanonical sayings and even episodes into an established gospel text finds many parallels: the *Longer Ending of Mark*, the *Pericope Adulterae*, *GJohn* 5.4, *GMatthew* 20.28 in D, and *GLuke* 6.4 in D. None of these insertions of *agrapha* undermine the cohesion of fourfold gospel canon. Rather, all of them are inserted into codices that contain all four canonical gospels.

Furthermore, we can identify a probable cause for the author of *EpAp* to insert an apocryphal tradition into a gospel epitome that was otherwise constructed from proto-canonical material. Epiphanius, the fourth-century heresiologist, offers a helpful *comparandum*. Although he holds to the exclusive, fourfold gospel canon,[65] he still considers the narrative of the boy Jesus saying "Alpha" to be useful for combating heretics who espouse a docetic or adoptionist view of Jesus in which "the Christ" descended upon Jesus in the form of a dove at his baptism.[66] According to Epiphanius, "it was necessary for him [Jesus] to have childhood signs, in order that other sects may not have reason to say that at the Jordan the Christ – namely, the dove – came into him."[67] Epiphanius goes on to relate a version of the childhood story in which Jesus does not say "Alpha" and "Beta" but rather, "I am the Alpha and the Omega," proving Jesus' eternal nature.[68] Interestingly, Epiphanius relates this story as happening *before* the first sign at Cana in Galilee,[69] resembling the way *EpAp* situates this story before the beginning of Jesus public ministry at Cana. We see a similar dynamic in the way

---

[63] Watson 2020: 96.

[64] Watson 2019b: 118–20; 2020: 93–97.

[65] For a robust study of Epiphanius' defence of the fourfold gospel, see Manor 2016: 143–60.

[66] The following discussion develops the argument from Hill 2010b: 175.

[67] Epiphanius, *Pan.* 51.20.3: ἔδει γὰρ καὶ παιδικὰ ἔχειν αὐτὸν σημεῖα, ἵνα μὴ πρόφασις γένηται ταῖς ἄλλαις αἱρέσεσι λέγειν ὅτι ἀπὸ τοῦ Ἰορδάνου ἦλθεν ὁ Χριστὸς εἰς αὐτόν. Translation my own.

[68] Epiphanius, *Pan.* 51.20.3–4.

[69] Epiphanius, *Pan.* 51.20.3–51.21.4.

2.6 Textual Authority in the Epistula Apostolorum

Clement of Alexandria can quote from an apocryphal gospel at the same time as upholding the fourfold gospel that was "handed down." He might quote from the *Gospel of the Egyptians* for rhetorical purposes, and he might even refer to it as ἡ γράφη,[70] but this does not diminish Clement's highest regard that he reserves exclusively for the canonical four (see below, Section 5.2.1). Origen refers to material from the *Gospel according to the Hebrews* and even the *Gospel according to Thomas*, but he too holds to the unique authority of the four.[71] Ephrem the Syrian, Didymus the Blind, and indeed Epiphanius carry this same exegetical tendency into the fourth century.[72] In short, ancient Christian authors can appeal to noncanonical traditions without compromising the unique status of the fourfold gospel.

As for the use of the apocryphal childhood tradition in *EpAp* 4.1–4, the apostolic author inserts this episode into his gospel epitome (3.10–12.4) in order to "fill in the gap" left by the collective account of *GJohn* and the Synoptics. The author was plausibly combating Cerinthus' teaching that Jesus was born by human means rather than by the Spirit through the Virgin, and that the Christ descended upon Jesus at his baptism.[73] By including the childhood episode in 4.1–4, the author of *EpAp* demonstrates the continuity of Jesus' divine status as the "Alpha" and the "Beta" – the "divine creator who is one with his Father in the work of creation" (*EpAp* 3.1–2, 4–5) and the "Word made flesh and born of Mary" (*EpAp* 3.13–15).[74]

2.6.3 Rewriting Liberally and Resolving Discrepancies in GJohn and GMatthew

Watson argues that the author of *EpAp* treats the texts of *GJohn* and *GMatthew* – the two gospels from which the author consistently draws – with liberal creativity rather than respect for sacrosanctity. The apostolic author freely reworks these written traditions rather than considers them fixed and unalterable. For example, the apostolic evangelist "redeploys" the "Johannine women" (Mary and Martha of Bethany; cf. *GJn* 11.1–12.11) to the resurrection and first appearance scene (*EpAp* 9.3–10.2), rather than having only Mary Magdalene at the

---

[70] *Strom.* 3.9.64.1; see discussion below in Section 5.2.1.

[71] For a congenial, possible citation of *GTh* 82 in Origen, see *Hom. Jer.* 27.3.7 and *Orig. Hom. Jos.* 4.3 (cf. Luijendijk 2011). For Origen's classic defense of the fourfold gospel, see the preface to *Hom. Luc.* For Origen's citations of *GHebrews*, see Gregory 2017: 32–33.

[72] For Didymus' use of *GHebrews*, see *Comm. Ps.* 184.8–10. For Didymus' four-gospel canon, see Ehrman 1983. For Ephrem's use of noncanonical traditions, see Crawford 2015c: 45. Ephrem depicts the fourfold gospel as four fountains flowing from the four corners of the world (*Serm. fid.* 2.39–40; CSCO 212: 8); cf. Crawford 2015c: 15.

[73] Cf. Irenaeus, *Haer.* 1.26.1.

[74] So Watson 2020: 96.

68   *Chapter 2: The Epistula Apostolorum*

empty tomb. The ointment of Mary referred to in *GJohn* 12.3 is transposed to the scene where the women visit the tomb.

What is more, according to Watson, the author of *EpAp* even resolves three Johannine anomalies by replacing alleged Johannine inconsistencies with more coherent proto-Johannine versions of the same traditions or augmenting certain Johannine themes to a more rhetorically effective prominence. First, in *GJohn* 20.2, Mary Magdalene says "*we* do not know where they have put him" (a first-person plural even though she is the only witness mentioned in the previous verse), but in 20.11 she uses the singular "*I* do not know where they have put him." *EpAp* 9.3–5 appears to resolve this tension by naming three female eye-witnesses at the tomb. Second, whereas the Johannine evangelist does not explain how Mary gets back to the tomb in *GJohn* 20.11 when she has exited the site in 20.2, *EpAp* 10.1–3 leaves all three women at the tomb when Jesus appears to them, *before* Mary goes and reports the news to the male disciples. Watson suggests that *EpAp* fixes these Johannine anomalies by reverting to proto-Johannine traditions – a tradition where several women visit the tomb rather than just the solitary Mary, and a tradition where Mary's encounter with the risen Christ happens before she informs the apostles.[75] In Watson's reconstruction of the proto-Johannine version of this episode, *GJohn* 20.11 immediately follows *GJohn* 20.1. The third Johannine anomaly that *EpAp* purportedly resolves is that the Johannine evangelist does not actually say that any of the disciples touched the risen Jesus with their hands, even though the narrative moves the reader to expect as much (e.g. *GJn* 20.24–29). *EpAp* 11.5–12.2 resolves this tension by having three apostolic eyewitnesses – Thomas, Andrew, and Peter – touch the risen Christ. *EpAp* plausibly augments the Johannine theme of touching the risen Jesus to meet the Jewish and early Christian standard that "every matter must be established on the testimony of two or three witnesses."[76]

For Watson, the resolution of Johannine anomalies implies that the author of *EpAp* "does not regard the earlier text [i.e. *GJohn*] as an infallible authority to which he must accommodate himself... it is his own text [i.e. *EpAp*] that lays claim to authority."[77] Watson's hypothesis needs to be queried on several levels. First, Watson frequently appeals to earlier versions of the traditions that are preserved in the canonical gospels as we now know them. Watson's reasoning is based primarily on the presupposed dictum that the earlier form is the more coherent form. In another context, Watson argues that P. Egerton 2 preserves a more coherent form of the narratives and dialogues assembled in *GJohn* 5.1–47, 7.21–30, 8.20–59, and 10.31–39.[78] Watson argues that the more coherent form

---

[75] Watson 2018: 210–15; 2020: 107–21.
[76] Deut 17.6; 19.15; *GMt* 18.16; 2 Cor 13.1; Heb 10.28–29.
[77] Watson 2018: 214.
[78] Watson 2013: 286–340.

2.6 Textual Authority in the Epistula Apostolorum

is probably the earlier form.[79] But coherence is frequently in the eye of the beholder, and there is no reason to assume that coherence necessarily correlates to an earlier form.

Moreover, each of the alleged anomalies in the Johannine narrative has an equally plausible explanation in terms of the Johannine evangelist's own intentions. In the first alleged anomaly, the Johannine evangelist does not say that Mary went to the tomb *alone*. In *GJohn* 20.1 and 20.11 he could simply be focalizing Mary as the central witness of the resurrection. Furthermore, the Johannine evangelist might be aware that his audience already knows the context of the versions they have heard in the communal readings of the Synoptic gospels. The first plural οὐκ οἴδαμεν in *GJohn* 20.2 is not so anomalous. In the second alleged anomaly, it is not abrupt for the Johannine evangelist to "teleport" Mary into the scene, weeping at the tomb in *GJohn* 20.11. The Johannine evangelist does this with other characters throughout his gospel. In *GJohn* 4.1, the evangelist has Jesus leaving Judea for Samaria, and he makes no mention of the disciples going with Jesus on this journey. But then in 4.8, he suddenly – in a parenthetical comment – makes the reader aware that they had gone into the city to buy food. He assumes that his reader understands that the disciples had traveled with Jesus to Samaria. Similarly, in *GJohn* 6.1 the evangelist only mentions *Jesus* crossing to the other side of the Sea of Galilee, but in 6.3 Jesus sits down with his disciples. John's narrative technique is even more salient when we consider that John is wont to highlight when Jesus *does not* travel in the company of his disciples (*GJn* 6.17, 22, 7.10). Again, in *GJohn* 12.1 Jesus comes to Bethany and reclines at the table with Martha, Lazarus, and Mary, and there is no mention of the disciples up to this point in the episode. But then Judas appears on the scene in *GJohn* 12.4, playing a focalized role in the episode. In light of John's propensity to introduce characters abruptly into the scene, it is no anomaly for Mary to be suddenly standing by the tomb, weeping in *GJohn* 20.11.

Finally, the fact that the Johannine evangelist does not mention any eyewitnesses touching Jesus would not leave an ancient reader unsatisfied. Quite plausibly, behind 1 John 1.1 is a reading community that understood the Johannine narrative to imply that the apostles did indeed touch the risen Jesus. Furthermore, *GJohn* 21 portrays Jesus in corporeal terms – preparing and serving bread and fish with his disciples, and perhaps even eating with them. *GJohn* 21 diminishes the alleged lack of corporeal touch of the resurrected Jesus – and it does so by affirming rather than undermining the account in *GJohn* 20 (see especially *GJn* 21.14). The author of *EpAp* follows and amplifies this same trajectory, to the point of depicting the actual point of touch between the disciples and the resurrected Jesus. In essence, the author of *EpAp* is not so much correcting Johannine anomalies. Rather, he is a faithful reader of all four proto-canonical gospels, and

---

[79] Watson 2013: esp. 290–325.

70   *Chapter 2: The Epistula Apostolorum*

he seeks to develop Johannine themes further and interweave these themes into a consensus account of the resurrection.

Watson also finds *EpAp* to be freewheeling in its handling of *GMatthew*. *EpAp* 41.3–7 and 42.2–4 appear to be directly subverting the Matthean Jesus' injunction, "do not call anyone 'teacher'… do not call anyone 'father'."[80] To the contrary, Jesus says in *EpAp*, "you will indeed be called fathers" (*EpAp* 42.2) and "you will be called teachers" (*EpAp* 42.4). Strikingly, this comes in response to the disciples recalling, in *EpAp* 41.4–5, the same Matthean locution mentioned above:

We said to him, "O Lord, is it not you who said to us, 'Do not call anyone father on earth, or teacher, for one is your Father and your teacher, who is in heaven'? And now do you tell us that we shall be fathers of many children and teachers and servants?"[81]

Jesus' reply in *EpAp* 41.6 begins with "You have spoken well" and affirms the disciples' call to be effective fathers and teachers. Watson interprets Jesus' reply to be critiquing the Matthean injunction against calling anyone "father" or "teacher."

But this is not necessarily the case. First, Jesus does not deny saying what is recorded in *GMatthew* 23.8–12; in fact, he says they have "spoken well" to remember such words. Second, even within *GMatthew*, there is a hermeneutical movement from Jesus' commands *before* his resurrection to Jesus' commands *after* his resurrection. In *GMatthew* 10.5–6, Jesus famously instructs his disciples not to go to the Gentiles (εἰς ὁδὸν ἐθνῶν ἀπέλθητε) or to a city of the Samaritans, but rather to go "to the lost sheep of the house of Israel." Jesus appears to be directly contradicting himself in *GMatthew* 28.19 when he commands the apostles to make disciples of "all the nations" (πάντα τὰ ἔθνη). This apparent discrepancy does not have to be the residue of conflicting, pre-Matthean sources, or even an incoherent evangelist. Rather, there is a natural flow of Jesus' ministry first to the Jews (pre-resurrection) and then to all nations (post-resurrection).[82] Indeed, Michael Bird has convincingly argued that the Gentile mission flows out of the prior, eschatological gathering of Israel in the person and ministry of Jesus of Nazareth.[83]

The author of *EpAp* seems to be aware of the tension between *GMatthew* 10.5 and 28.19 in his version of the Great Commission in *EpAp* 30.1: "He answered and said to us, "Go and preach to the twelve tribes of Israel, and to the Gentiles…" The apostolic author resolves the tension by combining elements from

---

[80] *GMt* 23.8–12; Watson 2020: 167–73.

[81] Translation Hills 2009: 69–70.

[82] See, among others, Foster 2004: 218–52.

[83] Bird 2006: esp. 26-57; cf. Lagrand 1999: 135–44. However, the dominant view in the 20th century was that Matthew was representing contradicting views: the later Gentile mission and the historical Jesus' exclusive ministry to Israel; cf. Harnack 1961 [1906]: 40; Jeremias 1971: 14.

2.6 Textual Authority in the Epistula Apostolorum

both commissions. Likewise, given that *EpAp* draws extensively from both Pauline and Johannine sources, it would seem that the author would find a tension between the injunction in *GMatthew* 23.8–12 and the Pauline theme of ministerial fatherhood (1 Cor 4.14–15) and the role of teacher in the church (e.g. 1 Cor 12.28; Eph 4.11). Similar themes of ministerial fatherhood are scattered throughout the Johannine corpus.[84] By having Jesus simultaneously affirm his prior Matthean statement (*EpAp* 41.6 // *GMatthew* 23.8–12) and move beyond it to a new era in which the apostles will become spiritual "fathers" (*EpAp* 41.7), the author of *EpAp* is not subverting the Matthean evangelist, but he is rather harmonizing *GMatthew*'s teachings with those of the Johannine evangelist and the apostle Paul. In short, he is resolving intra-apostolic tensions not by erasing discrepancies but by creatively interpreting them.

Watson is right to highlight the creativity displayed by the author of *EpAp* in his reworking of gospel materials. In this way, Watson has advanced the scholarly discussion on gospel writing in *EpAp*. However, the author's insertion of an apocryphal episode, his amplification of Johannine themes, and his resolution of gospel discrepancies do not necessarily undermine the authoritative status of the gospel texts that function as his primary sources of Jesus tradition. To answer the question of the textual authority of written gospels within *EpAp*, we need to explore its explicit statements of gospel writing.

2.6.4 The Authority of Prior, Written Gospel Tradition in EpAp

EpAp 1.1–5 speaks openly about an already existing written Jesus tradition.

The book of what Jesus Christ revealed through the council of the apostles, the disciples of Jesus Christ... so that you may be strong, and not falter, nor depart from the word of the gospel that you have heard. Just as we have heard and remembered, so we have written for the whole world. We greet you in joy.[85]

EpAp 1.3 states that Jesus revealed this apocalyptic discourse "so that you may be strong, and not falter, nor depart from what you have heard: the word of the gospel." *EpAp* 1.4 then clarifies: "just as we have heard and remembered so we have written for the whole world." Because "the word of the gospel" (ቃለ ፡ ወንጌል) stands in closest proximity to "just as we have heard... so we have written" (በከመ... ወጸሐፍነ), it is most judicious to interpret the hearing, remembering, and writing as a description of gospel writing.[86] Some translations begin 1.4 with the relative pronoun, "what we have heard... so we have written," thus separating the thought in 1.4 from 1.3,[87] but the Ethiopic conjunction በከመ is best translated

---

[84] 1 John 2.1, 12–14, 18, 28; 3.7; 5.21; 2 John 1, 4.

[85] Translations modified from Hills 2009: 21.

[86] Cf. Hill 2004: 370–71; Watson 2018: 194–96 agrees that this is describing gospel writing, but he argues that the gospel writing is referring to *EpAp* itself rather than prior gospels.

[87] E.g. Hills 2009: 21.

72 Chapter 2: The Epistula Apostolorum

"just as..." Francis Watson favors the textual variant in 1.5 አምኦናኅክሙ, "we entrust to you..." and links this with the relative pronoun at the beginning of 1.4.
The complete idea would thus be as follows: "what we have heard... we entrust
to you."[88] But this option both mistranslates በከመ,[89] and it favors the weaker textual variant አምኦናኅክሙ.[90] In short, the best translation of 1.4 exhibits the logical
flow: "just as we have heard... so we have written..." and this most naturally is a
description of "the word of the gospel" found in the previous clause in 1.3. But
what is this written "word of the gospel"? Is it any one of the four proto-canonical
gospels? Is it a combination of two or more? Is it an early instance of the fourfold
gospel? Or is it the *Epistula Apostolorum* itself?

The fact that ወጸሐፍነ ("so we have written") is in the perfect tense suggests
that "the word of the gospel" is something that was written prior to the composition of *EpAp*, unless, of course, this is an Ethiopic translation of the Greek epistolary aorist ἐγράψαμεν. We find the same verb in 1.4, 2.2, and 2.3. In 2.2 and
2.3 ጸሐፍነ is most likely an epistolary aorist, and the content of what is written
closely resembles the central focus of *EpAp*, namely, the fleshly encounter with
Christ after his resurrection. In 1.1–4, however, the post-resurrection apocalypse
related as the main content of *EpAp* is presented as a confirmation of the word
of the gospel that is already presupposed to have been heard. The confirmation
of the gospel (i.e. the content of *EpAp*) is therefore distinguished from the gospel
itself. It is this gospel that the apostles "have written" prior to their supposed
composition of *EpAp*. This interpretation of ጸሐፍነ is corroborated by 31.11,
where the risen Jesus refers to "everything that you have written about me" and
then specifies two locutions from *GJohn* as the content of this material already
written: "that I am the Word of the Father and that the Father is in me."[91] Again,
the perfect tense of ጸሐፍክሙ strongly suggests that what was written was written

---

[88] Watson 2018: 194; 2020: 44.

[89] Hills 2009: 21 cites *EpAp* 21.5, 30.2, and 30.3 as evidence for በከመ being used as a relative
pronoun ("what...") rather than the adverbial use ("just as..."), but these other references can
just as easily be translated in the adverbial use. The more standard lexical meaning of በከመ is
the adverbial use.

[90] Ethiopic Family 1 mss C K N O have አግኦናኅክሙ ("we greet you"). Family 2 mss L S, as
well as Family 1 ms B (which is occasionally corrupted by Family 2 readings), have አምኦናኅክሙ
("we entrust you"). The overall reliability of Family 1 manuscripts over Family 2, and the
greater number of witnesses, make አግኦናኅክሙ the stronger option; see Hannah 2021: 97–115,
esp. 99–100, 115; see also Hills 2009: 5–12.

[91] One might make the case that when Jesus says in *EpAp* 31.11 "everything you have written about me," he is referring to the writing of *EpAp* itself, especially since the locutions he
mentions ("that I am the Word of the Father etc.") echo *EpAp* 3.13; cf. 17.4, 8; 18.1; 25.3.
However, Jesus refers to *everything* that the apostles had written, which would include more
than these Johannine locutions, and it would encompass the multi-gospel epitome we see in
EpAp 3.10–12.4. As I argue below in Section 2.6.5, the epitome represents the gospels it summarizes, and Jesus' saying in *EpAp* 31.11 could plausibly be referring to the epitome and to the
gospels behind it.

2.6 Textual Authority in the Epistula Apostolorum

prior to the compositional time frame of *EpAp*. Since 31.11 is well over halfway through *EpAp*, it is clear that ጸሐፍክሙ· here is not an epistolary aorist.[92] Furthermore, the content of the apostolic writings about Christ are juxtaposed with "the Scriptures... that your fathers the prophets spoke," suggesting a bipartite structure of the prophets (writing in anticipation of Christ) and the apostles (writing about Christ in retrospect).

The above evidence suggests that *EpAp* presupposes and confirms a written gospel that strongly resembles at least *GJohn* and that it places on the same level of authority as the prophetic Jewish Scriptures. We can reasonably infer that *EpAp*'s concept of a prior, written gospel also encompasses the ministry and kerygmatic gospels from which it draws extensively: at least *GJohn*, *GMatthew*, and *GLuke* (and perhaps *GMark*). *EpAp* handles the gospel as much more of a textual object than any proto-canonical gospels do. While *GLuke* and *GJohn* may allude to prior gospels as textual objects (on which, see below, Section 4.1), *EpAp* takes this to another level by speaking of "the gospel that you have heard" and that "we have written for the whole world" (*EpAp* 1.4).

Another indication of the authoritative status of prior gospels in *EpAp* is the way that *EpAp* allegorizes the account of the feeding of the five thousand in *EpAp* 5.17–22 and the parable of the ten virgins in *EpAp* 43.16–17.[93] The use of allegory on culturally significant texts in Greco-Roman and Jewish antiquity was a marker of the texts' authoritative, scriptural, and canonical status.[94] Second-century Christians wrote allegorical commentary on *GJohn*, *GMatthew*, and *GLuke*, but never for apocryphal gospels.[95] Even *GMark*, though never given a proper

---

[92] Watson 2020: 254–55 interprets this verb to have a future perfect sense (i.e., "what you will have written"), but the Ethiopic perfect tense does not naturally support this interpretation.

[93] Allegorical interpretation is "metaphorical exegesis" that involves attributing non-literal, metaphorical meaning to specific details of a narrative (cf. Cancik-Lindemaier and Sigel 2002: 511–16), oftentimes transcending vertically outside of the coherence of the narrative and entering into a world of atemporal forms and concepts (cf. Frances M. Young 1997: 162). For an extensive analysis of early Christian allegorical exegesis and the extent and direction of metaphorical correspondence (e.g., vertical vs. horizontal, or platonic vs. eschatological), see Martens 2008.

[94] Christians followed in the footsteps of their Jewish forbears, especially Philo of Alexandria, who, by allegorizing the writings of Moses, inhabited the intellectual milieu of the Alexandrian bibliographers who demonstrated the sacredness of Homer's writing by allegorizing it; see Berthelot 2012: 155–74; Niehoff ed. 2012; Niehoff 2011; Young 1997.

[95] Heracleon (ca. 145-80 CE) wrote an allegorical commentary on *GJohn* (on which, see Berglund 2020) and plausibly also on *GLuke* (see Löhr 2003). Irenaeus' Valentinian interlocutors most likely had some kind of allegorical commentary on *GMatthew* (see Jorgensen 2015). Irenaeus even indicates that certain Marcosians and Valentinians also interpreted portions of *GMark* allegorically (*Haer.* 1.3.3; 1.20.2; 1.21.2). On early gospel commentaries, allegory, and the emergence of the gospels as Scripture, see Bockmuehl 2005.

74   *Chapter 2: The Epistula Apostolorum*

commentary in antiquity,[96] was interpreted allegorically by Clement of Alexandria and perhaps as early as Irenaeus' Valentinian interlocutors.[97] The fact that *EpAp* interprets gospel material allegorically demonstrates a progression towards exegetical distance from the gospels and a regard for these texts as authoritative Scripture. Whereas *GMatthew*, *GLuke*, and *GJohn* all rewrite *GMark*'s account of the feeding of the five thousand, none of them interpret the event allegorically.

To be sure, *GJohn* 6.48–58 shows a development in this written tradition when it relates Jesus' symbolic interpretation of the loaves as his own flesh. But this symbolic interpretation is not yet at the level of proper allegory that we see in *EpAp*'s interpretation of the five loaves as five early Christian articles of faith (the Father almighty, Jesus Christ, the Holy Spirit, the holy church, and the forgiveness of sins).[98] Rather, the metaphorical connection between the bread and Jesus' flesh is more closely linked to the symbols in their narrative context, establishing a correspondence between the multiplied loaves, the historical bread from heaven, and Jesus' own body. In *EpAp* 5.17–22, on the other hand, the spiritual meaning given to the number of five loaves exists outside of the coherence of the narrative, and thus it is more clearly allegorical. *EpAp* represents a distinguishable development in the written gospel tradition. It is not rewriting the gospel as the proto-canonical gospels did in succession; it is introducing allegorical interpretation to gospel texts that had attained a status worthy of such hermeneutical handling.

Additionally, *EpAp* has the vocabulary for condemning rival traditions about Jesus, explicitly censuring the teachings of Cerinthus and Simon. It is therefore significant that in 51 chapters it implies no literary invective against the Jesus books from which it draws. Far from treating the written gospel as a resource that lacks authoritative status, *EpAp* presupposes it, epitomizes it, defends it, interprets it allegorically, and builds its own argument upon it. Yes, the author of *EpAp* does freely rework narrative and dialogical elements from *GJohn* and *GMatthew*. But the author is not trying to rival or replace these written gospels; rather, he epitomizes them and reinterprets their contents in a proto-canonical context – a practice that is perfectly acceptable for Christian authors who uphold a gospel canon.

2.6.5 EpAp *as Gospel Compendium, Consensus Document, and Apologia for a Nascent Biblical Canon*

If the author of *EpAp* does not seek to rival or replace the gospels that later came to be the fourfold gospel, how does he envisage the function of *EpAp* vis-à-vis

---

[96] The first commentary on *GMark* was arguably as late as the seventh century; cf. Bockmuehl 2005: 289; Kealy 2007.

[97] For Clement's allegorical exegesis of *GMk* 10.17–31 see *Quis div.* 3–5; on Irenaeus' Valentinian interlocutors, see *Haer.* 1.2.3; 1.21.2.

[98] *EpAp* 5.20–22.

2.6 Textual Authority in the Epistula Apostolorum

these prior gospels? I suggest that *EpAp* 3.10–12.4 is a gospel compendium, a curated collection of excerpts from *GJohn*, *GMatthew*, *GLuke*, and possibly *GMark*, that gives the gist of the written gospel. This compendium includes *Sondergut* from *GJohn*, *GMatthew*, and *GLuke*, redactional material from *GJohn*, *GMatthew*, *GLuke*, and even *GMark*, *GMatthew*/*GLuke* agreement, *GMatthew*/*GMark* agreement, *GLuke*/*GMark* agreement, Triple Tradition, and material found in all four proto-canonical gospels. It summarizes the gospel narrative from birth to resurrection, and as a summary it constitutes a foundation upon which the author can discuss, through Jesus' mouth, matters of incarnation, eschatology, global mission, and church discipline in the post-resurrection dialogue in *EpAp* 13–50. Like the Acts of the Apostles, *EpAp* defines and defends orthodoxy as apostolic consensus – especially a consensus between Jesus' disciples and the apostle Paul.

The gospel compendium of *EpAp* 3.10–12.4 therefore has an insightful parallel in the gospel *précis* that Luke gives through the mouth of Peter in Acts 10.34–43. In this passage, the apostle Peter gives a gospel summary with a Markan outline and some Lukan details. By placing this summary in the mouth of Peter, Luke is not supplanting his first volume. Rather, he is epitomizing the gospel according to a Markan outline to fit the rhetorical thrust of his narrative – in this case, the emerging consensus of the early church (Judean, Antiochene, and Jerusalemite) to include Gentile Godfearers (Cornelius and his family) in the economy of salvation. In *EpAp*, the gospel compendium encapsulates the consensus account of the gospel emanating from the college of apostles, and it serves the rhetorical aim of anchoring *EpAp* in apostolic authority in its heresiological attack on the teachings of Simon and Cerinthus.

The gospel epitome of *EpAp* also fits into an *apologia* for a biblical canon in *EpAp* 31.10–12:

> As you have learnt from the scriptures that the prophets spoke about me and in me it is truly fulfilled, so you must provide guidance in them. And every word that I have spoken to you and that you have written about me,[99] that I am the Word of the Father and the Father is in me, you also must pass on to that man, as is fitting for you. Teach him and remind him [i.e. Paul] what is said in the scriptures about me and is now fulfilled, and then he will be the salvation of the Gentiles.[100]

Jesus refers to "the Scriptures that the prophets spoke," and the word that the apostles "have written" about him. Here we have a parallel between the Old Testament Scripture of the prophets and the gospel writing of the apostles, recalling the earlier parallel of "patriarchs, prophets, apostles, and disciples" in *EpAp* 3.9. *EpAp* 31.10–12 connects these scriptural foundations with the divinely authorized witness of the Apostle Paul to the Gentiles. *EpAp* is not a replacement for

---

[99] I have emended Watson's translation here by translating ደስፈሀሙ· as a simple perfect rather than a future perfect.

[100] Translation Watson 2020: 64, with my emendation.

76 *Chapter 2: The Epistula Apostolorum*

the Pauline corpus, nor it is completely ignorant of it. Rather, by situating Paul's witness within the same authoritative sphere as Old Testament Scripture and apostolic gospel writing, *EpAp* 31.10–12 is making an implicit *apologia* for an emerging biblical canon of Old and New Testaments. *EpAp* is a compendium of the gospel written by the apostles. This gospel is defended by *EpAp* and placed alongside the Old Testament and Paul's witness as the authoritative foundation of the church.

2.7 Summary and Conclusions

The *Epistula Apostolorum* is a testimony to the second-century propensity for *GMatthew*, *GLuke*, *GJohn*, and probably *GMark* to keep congenial company with one another. It also gives an example of how traditions that were eventually recognized as noncanonical could latch onto the canonical narrative and fill in certain gaps. The author of *EpAp* probably combined these gospels by the *mode* of excerpting, facilitating the memory of these Jesus traditions extracted almost entirely from the proto-canonical four. In *EpAp*, the insertion of noncanonical material does not detract from the extensive *interaction* shared by the proto-canonical gospels. A broad narrative integrity of birth, childhood, ministry, death, and resurrection is preserved in the form of a gospel epitome, but the *integrity* of each gospel combined into this epitome is flexible and is refashioned almost with a poetic touch. As a gospel compendium, *EpAp* does not challenge the authority of its gospel predecessors; it supplements them. As a consensus document, it implicitly brings together the collective *authority* of the gospels it combines.

Like *GThomas*, *EpAp* is an interpretive rewriting of the gospel, and Synoptic material forms a large portion of the material it reworks. Unlike *GThomas*, *EpAp* brings *GJohn* into conversation with the Synoptic tradition, and it affirms rather than undermines the collective authority that results from combining these diverse and early Jesus traditions. In our study, we will again encounter these same trends of weaving Synoptic material together with Johannine bookends, infusing it with Johannine theology, and sprinkling the occasional noncanonical tradition to fill gaps. If we date *EpAp* to the first half of the second century, it may be one of the earliest literary examples of the tendency of *GMatthew*, *GJohn*, *GLuke*, and *GMark* to congregate as a family – an outworking of the gospel-writing traditions preserved by Papias and his contemporaries (see Chapter 4) and a precursor to the comprehensive gospel-combining project of Tatian (see Chapter 3). If we date *EpAp* to the second half of the second century, it shows in literary form the habits of reading the four gospels in concert with an eclectic regard for other traditions as ancillary to the fourfold body of gospel literature, similar to Clement of Alexandria's reading habits (see Chapter 5).

Chapter 3

Orchestrating the Gospel: Tatian's *Diatessaron* as a Gospel Combination

In *GThomas* and *EpAp*, we have seen interpretive rewriting that combines gospel materials mostly from proto-canonical gospels, occasionally inserts noncanonical traditions, and contributes substantial, new, special material. If space permitted, we would also conduct an analysis of the *Gospel of Peter*, P. Egerton 2, and P.Oxy. 840 along these same lines. In each of these cases, we can see the tendency of Synoptic and Johannine traditions not only to come together in a new gospel text, but also to monopolize much of the creative space of the new composition.[1]

Enter Tatian the Syrian. Settling in Rome in the mid second century, he learned philosophy and theology from Justin Martyr.[2] He was exposed to all four proto-canonical gospels (Justin's ἀπομνημονεύματα), and sometime around 170 CE, combined at least these four gospels into one composition that would later be called the "Diatessaron." This is the gospel orchestration *par excellence*. It engages many of the dynamics we have already encountered, but in a comprehensive manner. This chapter will engage Tatian's *Diatessaron* based on the methodology proposed by the "New Perspective" on Diatessaronic studies.[3] In this method, Tatian's original inter-pericope sequence is established by the correspondences shared among the three major witnesses: Ephrem's fourth-century *Commentary on the Gospel* (extant in Syriac and Armenian recensions), the sixth-century Codex Fuldensis attributed to Victor of Capua, and the Arabic harmony translated from a ninth-century Syriac exemplar.[4] In the "New

---

[1] Cf. Foster 2013.

[2] Tatian's relationship to Justin Martyr is well known, and Petersen's case remains the strongest regarding Tatian's harmonizing strategy owing a lot to Justin Martyr's smaller-scale harmony (Petersen 1990: 512-34). Perrin 2019 has recently argued that Justin's gospel harmony – and therefore his hermeneutical influence on Tatian's project – was extensive; see Sections 3.3 and 3.4 below.

[3] For a helpful introduction to the "New Perspective" on Diatessaronic studies, see Schmid 2013.

[4] The Syriac recension for Ephrem's *Commentary* is found in Leloir 1963, 1990; all Syriac texts from Ephrem's *Commentary* cited in this chapter are from these volumes. The Armenian recension is in Leloir 1953, 1954. The text-critical relationship between the two recensions and their fidelity to Ephrem's original is a complex issue, summarized in Petersen 1989: 197–202,

78   *Chapter 3: Tatian's Diatessaron*

Perspective," the Western vernacular tradition is irrelevant for Diatessaronic reconstruction, and only Codex Fuldensis is legitimate for the enterprise. The most
reliable wording is reconstructed from the *lemmata* in Ephrem's *Commentary*
and citations from the fourth-century church father, Aphrahat of Persia.[5] We will
not enter into the debate regarding the original language of Tatian's composition
(whether Greek or Syriac) except in the limited cases where it has bearing on the
questions we are posing to Tatian's gospel combination.

3.1 Identities

Of first importance is the task of determining which gospels Tatian combined in
systematic fashion.

3.1.1 Proto-Canonical Gospels in Tatian's Diatessaron

It is beyond doubt that the *Diatessaron* systematically combined large portions
from the four proto-canonical gospels. This is immediately evident in the pericopes that it integrates from Matthean, Johannine, Lukan, and even Markan
Sondergut.

From *GJohn*, Tatian integrates the Johannine prologue (*GJn* 1.1–5),[6] the wedding at Cana in Galilee (*GJn* 2.1–11),[7] Jesus' meeting with Nicodemus (*GJn* 3.1–
21),[8] Jesus and the Samaritan woman at the well (*GJn* 4.1–42),[9] the Johannine
Sukkoth celebration (*GJn* 7.2–31),[10] the Johannine Hanukah celebration (*GJn*

Baarda 1983, McCarthy 1993: 23–38, and Leloir 1964: 303–31. In order to base my findings
on secure evidence, I will not base any of my arguments on sections of Ephrem's *Commentary*
that are deemed suspect by Diatessaronic scholars. The text of Fuldensis is found in Ranke
1868. The text of the Arabic harmony (henceforth AH) is found in Marmardji 1935. For the
ninth-century date of the Syriac exemplar, see Joosse 1999: 72–129.

[5] There is a debate about whether Ephrem is indeed the author of this commentary (see
discussion in Lange 2005). Space does not permit engagement with this issue. For convenience,
I will refer to the author as "Ephrem". For the text of Aphrahat's *Demonstrations*, see Parisot
1894–1907.

[6] Ephrem witnesses to the Johannine prologue as in incipit of the *Diatessaron*, *CGos.* 1.3–
5 (Leloir 1963: 3–4), as does Aphrahat, *Dem.* 1.10 (Parisot 1894: 22), bar Salibi (Vaschalde
1953: 173), and the Arabic Harmony §1.1–5 (Marmardji 1935: 3); cf. Baarda 2019: 1–24.
Fuldensis §1.1–8 (Ranke 1868: 29) switches the Johannine prologue with the Lukan prologue,
but the Johannine prologue is present, nonetheless.

[7] Ephrem, *CGos.* 5.1–5 (Leloir 1963: 38–41); AH §5.22–32 (Marmardji 1935: 42–45).

[8] Ephrem, *CGos.* 16.11–15 (Leloir 1963: 172–77); AH §32.27–47 (Marmardji 1935: 308–
11); Fuldensis §120 (Ranke 1868: 105–06).

[9] Ephrem, *CGos.* 12.16–20 (Leloir 1963: 88–95); AH §21.8–46 (Marmardji 1935: 202–09);
Fuldensis (§88).

[10] Ephrem, *CGos.* 14.28–29 (Leloir 1963: 138–39); AH §28.1–32 (Marmardji 1935: 266–
71); Fuldensis §106.

10.22–42),[11] the raising of Lazarus (*GJn* 11.1–46),[12] Peter's reinstatement and the question about John (*GJn* 21.15–23),[13] and the final Johannine colophon (*GJn* 21.24–25).[14]

From *GMatthew*, Tatian includes the coming of the Magi (*GMt* 2.1–12),[15] the massacre of the innocents and the flight to Egypt (*GMt* 2.13–21),[16] the Matthean antitheses (*GMt* 5.21–48),[17] the fish and the temple tax (*GMt* 17.24–27),[18] the parable of the two sons (*GMt* 21.28–32),[19] the parable of the ten virgins (*GMt* 25.1–13),[20] and the parable of the talents (*GMt* 25.14–30).[21]

From *GLuke*, Tatian integrates the annunciation and birth of John the Baptist *(GLk* 1.5–25),[22] Jesus the boy at the temple (*GLk* 2.41–50),[23] the Galileans killed

---

[11] AH §37.25–45 (Marmardji 1935: 354–57); Fuldensis §135. Ephrem noticeably skips over this feast in his commentary on the *Diatessaron*, quoting *GJn* 10.8 in *CGos.* 16.33 and transitioning straight to the Lazarus episode in *CGos.* 17.1. Barker 2020: 292–94 makes a good case that Ephrem intentionally suppressed Tatian's accounts of some Jewish feasts. It is therefore most probable that *GJn* 10.22–42 was in the original *Diatessaron*.

[12] Ephrem, *CGos.* 17.1–10 (Leloir 1963: 190–201); Arabic Harmony §37.46–38.30 (Marmardji 1935: 356–65); Fuldensis §136.

[13] Ephrem, *CGos.* 21.30 (Leloir 1963: 230–33); Arabic Harmony §53.25–48 (Marmardji 1935: 522–29); Fuldensis §180–81. The Arabic Harmony and Fuldensis have the entirety of *GJn* 21, but Ephrem includes only portions of *GJn* 21.19–23.

[14] *GJn* 21.24–25 is present in Fuldensis §181, and *GJohn* 21.24 is present in the Arabic Harmony §54.48. Neither of these verses, however, are cited or alluded to by Ephrem, and so there presence in the original *Diatessaron* are less plausible than the other Johannine examples given in this chapter.

[15] Ephrem, *CGos.* 2.18–3.5 (Leloir 1953: 32–39); AH §3.1–12 (Marmardji 1935: 22–25); Fuldensis §8.

[16] Ephrem, *CGos.* 3.6–9 (Leloir 1953: 39–42); AH §3.13–23 (Marmardji 1935: 24–27); Fuldensis §10.

[17] Ephrem, *CGos.* 6.4–15 (Leloir 1990: 60–71); AH §8.50–9.21 (Marmardji 1935: 76–85); Fuldensis §31–33.

[18] Ephrem, *CGos.* 14.16–17 (Leloir 1963: 126–29); AH §25.4–7 (Marmardji 1935: 238–41); Fuldensis §94.

[19] Ephrem, *CGos.* 16.18 (Leloir 1953: 232–33); AH §33.35–39 (Marmardji 1935: 318–19); Fuldensis §124.

[20] Ephrem, *CGos.* 18.19 (Leloir 1953: 266); AH §43.9–21 (Marmardji 1935: 410–11); Fuldensis §149.

[21] Ephrem, *CGos.* 18.20 (Leloir 1953: 266–67); AH §43.22–38 (Marmardji 1935: 410–15); Fuldensis §150.

[22] Ephrem, *CGos.* 1.9–24 (Leloir 1963: 8–23); AH §1.6–26 (Marmardji 1935: 4–7); Fuldensis §2–4.

[23] Ephrem, *CGos.* 3.16 (Leloir 1953: 45; 1990: 20–21); AH §3.24–36 (Marmardji 1935: 26–27); Fuldensis §12.

80 *Chapter 3: Tatian's Diatessaron*

by Pilate (*GLk* 13.1–5),[24] the lost coins, sheep, and son (*GLk* 15.1–32),[25] the rich man and Lazarus (*GLk* 16.19–31),[26] the Pharisee and the Publican (*GLk* 18.10–14),[27] and the Good Samaritan (*GLk* 10.25–37).[28]

Interestingly, it is nearly certain that Tatian also includes special material from *GMark*. There are twelve notable Markan redactional features preserved in Ephrem's commentary.

(1) Ephrem includes the Markan redaction from *GMark* 1.15, "the times they are fulfilled" (ܪܒܕ ܠܘܗ ܘܡܠܬܫܐܘ),[29] and it also appears in the Arabic Harmony (§5.43) and Fuldensis (§18, *impletum est tempus*).

(2) In *CGos.* 4.4 and 4.6, Ephrem cites the beginning of Jesus' temptation with the Spirit as the subject, actively leading Jesus into the desert. Only *GMark* has the Spirit as the active subject in this locution:

GMark 1.12 (NA28):	Καὶ εὐθὺς τὸ πνεῦμα αὐτὸν ἐκβάλλει εἰς τὴν ἔρημον
GMatthew 4.1 (NA28):	Τότε ὁ Ἰησοῦς ἀνήχθη εἰς τὴν ἔρημον ὑπὸ τοῦ πνεύματος
GLuke 4.1 (NA28):	Ἰησοῦς δὲ πλήρης πνεύματος ἁγίου ὑπέστρεψεν ἀπὸ τοῦ Ἰορδάνου καὶ ἤγετο ἐν τῷ πνεύματι ἐν τῇ ἐρήμῳ
CGos. 4.4:	*Spiritus sanctus traxit, evexit eum in desertum*[30]

(3) In the calling of the tax collector, Ephrem gives a version that resembles Markan redaction, calling the disciple "Jacob" rather than "Levi":

CGos. 5.17b:	ܠܝܥܩܘܒ܂ ܠܒܪ ܚܠܦܝ ܚܙܝܗܝ
GMatthew 9.9 (NA28):	καὶ παράγων... εἶδεν... Μαθθαῖον κτλ
GMark 2.14 (NA28):	καὶ παράγων εἶδεν Λευὶν τον τοῦ Ἁλφαίου κτλ
GMark 2.14 D Θ *f*[13] 565 it:	καὶ παράγων εἶδεν Ἰάκωβον τον τοῦ Ἁλφαίου κτλ

---

[24] Ephrem, *CGos.* 14.25 (Leloir 1963: 134–35); AH §27.31–35 (Marmardji 1935: 262–63); Fuldensis §104.

[25] Ephrem, *CGos.* 14.19–20 (Leloir 1963: 130–31); AH §26.1–33 (Marmardji 1935: 248–55); Fuldensis §97-98.

[26] Ephrem, *CGos.* 15.12–13 (Leloir 1963: 150–53); AH §29.14–26 (Marmardji 1935: 276–81; Fuldensis §107.

[27] Ephrem, *CGos.* 15.24 (Leloir 1963: 162–63); AH §32.16–21 (Marmardji 1935: 306–07); Fuldensis §119.

[28] Ephrem, *CGos.* 16.24 (Leloir 1963: 182–85); AH §34.26–45 (Marmardji 1935: 326–31); Fuldensis §129.

[29] *CGos.* 5.13; cf. Barker 2019: 137. Ephrem uses the third person plural verb (ܘܡܠܬܫܐ) and subject (ܪܒܕ ܠܘܗ), reflecting the Western text of Codex Bezae (πεπληρωνται οι καιροι) rather than NA28 (πεπλήρωται ὁ καιρὸς); *pace* Barker, the Siyame over ܪܒܕ indicates that it is plural and agrees with the verb.

[30] This passage is only preserved in the Armenian. The Latin is from Leloir's translation (1954: 35–36).

3.1 Identities

Not only does Ephrem's choice of "Jacob" here accord with a stream of Markan textual tradition, but it is easily explained as an interpretation of the *Ausgangstext* of *GMark* 2.14, which specifies the tax collector as the "son of Alphaeus" (named as "James" in *GMk* 3.18). Ephrem here appears to preserve a Markan tradition derived from the *Diatessaron*.[31]

(4) Ephrem in *CGos.* 10.5 cites the Markan redactional element, "he will be guilty of an eternal sin" (ܒܚܛܗܐ ܕܠܥܠܡ ܡܚܝܒ ܗܘܐ; cf. *GMk* 3.28), which both *GMatthew* (12.32) and *GLuke* (12.10) omit.

(5) In *CGos.* 11.12, Ephrem cites the Markan ascending order of magnitude of the seed's yield: "thirty, and sixty, and one hundredfold" (*GMk* 4.8 // *GMt* 13.8 // *GLk* 8.8).

(6) In the episode where Jesus heals the hemorrhaging woman (*CGos.* 7.1–6), Ephrem records both the Lukan redaction, "who touched me?" (*GLk* 8.45) and the Markan redaction, "who touched my garments?" (ܡܢ ܩܪܒ ܠܠܒܘܫܝ; *GMk* 5.30). Ephrem preserves another Markan redactional element in this episode, "she perceived within herself that she was healed of her afflictions" (*CGos.* 7.16). Ephrem also includes the detail that she had been spending her money on many doctors who could not heal her (*CGos.* 7.19; cf. *GMk* 5.26).

(7) Ephrem includes an episode of Jesus healing a blind man in *CGos.* 13.13 (it is also attested in the Arabic Harmony §23.26–30). The man is healed in stages, according to his increasing faith, resembling *GMark* 8.22–26 more strongly than the accounts of healing the blind in *GMatthew* 9.27–31, *GLuke* 18.35–43, and *GJohn* 9.1–34. That Ephrem's gospel text (i.e. the *Diatessaron*) includes Markan material is practically certain in that he cites the Markan phrase in *GMark* 8.25:

CGos. 13.13:	ܘܐܬܐ ܗܘܐ ܠܡ ܝܚܙܐ ܠܟܠ ܡܕܡ ܓܠܝܐܝܬ
GMark 8.25 (NA28):	ἐνέβλεπεν τηλαυγῶς ἅπαντα

Since Ephrem comments on this *Markan* episode, and since it also appears in the Arabic Harmony, it is virtually certain that Tatian included it in the *Diatessaron*.

(8) In the episode of the healing of the epileptic demoniac (*CGos.* 14.15), Ephrem preserves the Markan redactional element, "I command you, dumb spirit, come out from him and never come back again" (*GMk* 9.25).[32]

(9) Ephrem cites a Markan redactional detail from the Rich Young Ruler episode in *CGos* 15.6–8. Only Mark (*GMk* 10.21) relates the detail that Jesus *looked at* the rich man and *loved him* (ὁ δὲ Ἰησοῦς ἐμβλέψας αὐτῷ ἠγάπησεν αὐτὸν). Accordingly, Ephrem's commentary contains the Tatianic rendering, "he looked at him lovingly" (ܚܪ ܒܗ ܒܚܘܒܬܐ).

---

[31] Fuldensis §20 and the Arabic Harmony §6.46 (Marmardji 1935: 56–57) harmonize to Matthew's version, but Ephrem's wording is more likely to reflect Tatian's original.

[32] ܩܘܡ ܦܘܩ ܡܢܗ ܘܬܘܒ ܠܐ ܬܗܦܘܟ ܠܗ

82   *Chapter 3: Tatian's Diatessaron*

(10) The Markan redaction which includes the name of the blind man healed on the road to Jericho – Bartimaeus – is included in Ephrem's account in *CGos.* 15.22 (cf. *GMk* 10.46, 50). Ephrem also includes the detail that Bartimaeus "abandoned his cloak"[33] when he followed Jesus. Only Mark records this detail in the Triple Tradition.

(11) Ephrem includes a lemma from the Great Commission of the *Longer Ending of Mark* 16.15–16 (*CGos.* 8.1).[34] When we add to this evidence the fact that both the Arabic Harmony (§55.9–10) and Fuldensis (§182) include Jesus' promises to empower his disciples to heal the sick, drive out demons, handle serpents, withstand poison, and speak in tongues (*LEMark* 16.17–18), it is probable that Tatian's *Diatessaron* included the *Longer Ending of Mark.*

(12) Most convincingly, we even find a Markan intercalation preserved in Ephrem's *Commentary* (16.1–5). In *CGos.* 16.1, Ephrem comments on the cursing of the fig tree. In 16.2, he comments on the cleansing of the Temple (mostly in its Johannine form). Then, in 16.3–5 he returns to the discussion of the fig tree, and in 16.5 he even cites the Markan *lemma* that presupposes the Markan intercalation: "When they returned, they were saying to him, 'Look! This is the fig tree that you cursed!" (cf. *GMk* 11.20–21).[35] This is a clear instance in which Tatian actually fit other gospel parallels (i.e. the Johannine Temple incident) into a Markan schema of intercalation.[36]

Four more Markan redactional features appear across both Eastern and Western *Diatessaronic* witnesses, and although Ephrem does not comment on them, their presence in both Eastern and Western witnesses makes them likely to be in Tatian's original composition. (1) The Markan parable of seeds growing secretly (*GMk* 4.26–29) is found in the Arabic Harmony (§16.49–52) and Fuldensis (§77).[37] (2) The healing of deaf and mute man (*GMk* 7.31–37) is found in the Arabic Harmony (§21.1) and Fuldensis (§87), located in the same narrative spot in both Eastern and Western Diatessaronic witnesses (between the episodes of

---

[33] ܘܡܒܩ ܠܗ ܠܬܟܣܝܬܗ

[34] This *lemma* is not extant in the Armenian recension (cf. McCarthy 1993: 145), so its legitimacy is not certain. However, even without this fragment, the other phrases from *LEMark* that appear in both AH and Fuldensis still make a strong case for *LEMark* in the original *Diatessaron.*

[35] ܟܕ ܗܘܘ ܠܗ ܟܝ ܐܡܪܝܢ ܠܗ ܗܘ. ܘܗܐ ܗܝ ܬܬܐ ܗܘ, ܕܠܛܬ

[36] It must be said that we do not find any other Markan intercalations (*GMk* 3.20–35; 5.21–43; 6.7–32; 14.1–11; 14.53–72) in the *Diatessaron* as reconstructed by Ephrem's *Commentary,* the Arabic Harmony, or Codex Fuldensis. Presumably Tatian either found it unnecessary or impractical to include this Markan narrative technique. However, this does not negate the fact that so many Markan redactional features and even Markan *Sondergut* are so conspicuous in the earliest strata of the Diatessaronic witnesses. Moreover, as we shall see below, even while Tatian does not have an appetite for a Markan sandwich, he still goes to great lengths to preserve Markan sequence, sometimes even giving it precedence over Matthean sequence.

[37] Marmardji 1935: 158–61.

the Canaanite and Samaritan women).[38] (3) The Arabic Harmony (§48.45–47) and Fuldensis (§93) both include the man who fled the scene of Jesus' arrest naked (*GMk* 14.51–52).[39] (4) Of the four proto-canonical gospels, only *GMark* mentions Salome, and he does so at the crucifixion (*GMk* 15.40) and resurrection scene (*GMk* 16.1). The Arabic Harmony inserts her at the crucifixion (§52.23), and Fuldensis includes her as one of the witnesses at the crucifixion (§171) and the empty tomb (§174). In short, when we piece together the clear Markan redactional features and Markan *Sondergut*, it is virtually certain that Tatian made extensive use of *GMark* for the *Diatessaron*.[40]

We have sufficiently demonstrated that Tatian made extensive use of all four proto-canonical gospels. Our findings point in the same direction as George Foote Moore's 1890 study of the Arabic *Diatessaron*: that Tatian used the majority of each canonical gospel. According to Moore, 2,769 of the 3,780 verses of the four gospels were represented in the Arabic *Diatessaron*.[41] The Canon Tables on Codex Fuldensis tell a similar story. According to Charles Hill:

There are 83 places in the text of Fuldensis where one of the 62 unique sections of Matthew is accessed… there are 18 places where one of the 19 unique sections of Mark is accessed; 81 places where one of the 72 unique Lukan sections is accessed; and 109 places where one of the 96 unique sections of John is accessed.[42]

These data, together with the redactional and *Sondergut* features demonstrated above, make it difficult to avoid the conclusion that Tatian meticulously drew from each of the proto-canonical gospels, intentionally locating the special contributions from each of the four evangelists, and finding ways to weave them into one composition. This is especially telling in that *GMark* has so little material that *GMatthew* and *GLuke* did not absorb. Even with strict criteria – accepting only gospel materials found in Ephrem's *Commentary*, or in both the Arabic Harmony and Fuldensis – we have found 16 probable cases of Markan material in Tatian's *Diatessaron*. Tatian appears to have meticulously combined materials from each of the gospels that would later be declared canonical.

We will see in the following section how no other gospels even come close to the dominance of the proto-canonical four in the composition of the *Diatessaron*. In fact, it is questionable whether any of the noncanonical traditions in the *Diatessaron* were even in the original *Diatessaron*, and if they were, whether they came from written gospels. We will also see that all the narrative blocks in the *Diatessaron* are proto-canonical. There are no narrative episodes that can be proven conclusively to be derived from outside of the proto-canonical tradition.

---

[38] Marmardji 1935: 200–03.

[39] Marmardji 1935: 462–63.

[40] Barker 2019: 136–38 makes a similar but less detailed case for Tatian's use of *GMark*.

[41] Moore 1890: 203.

[42] Hill 2019: 30.

84   *Chapter 3: Tatian's Diatessaron*

3.1.2 Noncanonical Gospels in Tatian's Diatessaron

It has long been suspected that Tatian did not restrict himself to the proto-canonical gospels when collecting materials for his gospel orchestration. C. A. Phillips, in his classic 1931 study – endorsed enthusiastically by William Petersen's definitive 1994 monograph – identified six readings which led him to believe that "Tatian's Gospel sources were to some extent really five."[43] These were (1) that the man with a withered hand could not work with his hand, (2) inserting "Jerusalem" for "the holy city" in *GMatthew* 4.5, (3) combining *GMatthew* 18.21ff with *GLuke* 17.3ff and inserting "in one day" to Peter's question to Jesus about forgiveness, (4) calling Barachiah the "son of Joiade" in *GMatthew* 23.35, (5) the detail that the "lintel of the temple" split when Jesus was crucified, and (6) an alternate arrangement of gospel episodes regarding rich men.

Readings (1), (2), (4), and (5) are all based on a now obsolete "Old Perspective" on Diatessaronic studies which accepts readings that appear in the Western vernacular tradition but do not require attestation in Fuldensis.[44] These readings do not appear in Fuldensis, and they have no attestation in the Eastern witnesses (Ephrem, Aphrahat, or the Arabic *Diatessaron*). Rather, they appear across a variety of much later sources that are not directly traceable to the *Diatessaron*.[45] We can therefore exclude them from consideration. Readings (3) and (6) are much stronger cases, and we will consider them below alongside several other strong cases for Tatian integrating noncanonical traditions into his *Diatessaron*. Collectively, these cases have been marshalled to attest a lost Jewish-Christian gospel as a fifth source used by Tatian.

a. Tatian's Use of a Jewish Gospel – Redactional Elements?

Three eminent Diatessaronic scholars of the twentieth century, C. A. Phillips, Gilles Quispel, and William Petersen, argued that several fragments from the Tatianic tradition can be traced back to a Jewish gospel of the early second century.[46] We will analyze four in this section. Before we do, it is helpful to note that the identities of "Jewish" gospels – e.g. the *Gospel of the Ebionites* and the

---

[43] Phillips 1931: 8; cf. Petersen 1994: 259.

[44] As noted above, alleged Diatessaronic readings that appear in the Western vernacular tradition but are absent in Fuldensis have now been deemed irrelevant by the "New Perspective" for reconstructing the original *Diatessaron*; cf. Schmid 2013.

[45] These are the Liège Harmony (CE13), the Stuttgart Harmony (CE14), marginal glosses in Greek manuscript 566 (CE9) of *GMatthew* attributed to τὸ Ἰουδαϊκόν, and the *capitularia* in some manuscripts of Zacharias Chrysopolitanus' commentary on a gospel harmony known as *In unum ex quattor*. Alleged Jewish-Christian fragments in these witnesses find occasional parallels in the writings of Jerome and Origen, and this has caused certain scholars to suspect that these fragments originate in an earlier, Jewish-Christian gospel of some sort. For an appraisal of Phillips' six readings, see Hill 2019: 32–38.

[46] Phillips 1931; Quispel 1958/1959; Petersen 1994: 272–300.

Gospel according to the Hebrews – were unstable in the late second and third centuries.[47] These gospels had a close relationship to *GMatthew*,[48] and several ancient Christians appear to refer to them merely as an altered or confused version of *GMatthew*.[49] The close relationship between these gospels and *GMatthew*, and the corresponding textual variants in the New Testament manuscript tradition allow the possibility that fragments resembling a "Jewish" gospel in Tatian's composition were already present in Tatian's copy of *GMatthew*. To complicate things even further, Epiphanius – one of our main sources for readings from "Jewish-Christian" gospels – mentions those who think that *GHebrews* and the *Diatessaron* were identical.[50] The direction of influence between Diatessaronic fragments and an alleged "Hebrew" gospel is blurry. With this in mind, we proceed now to the fragments.

(1) First, the fire and/or light at Jesus' baptism.[51] In Ephrem's commentary (*CGos.* 4.5), Satan is said to have seen "the splendor of the light which appeared on the water, and the voice which came from heaven."[52] This tradition was popular in early Christianity:

Justin Martyr (*Dial.* 88.3):[53]	καὶ πῦρ ἀνήφθη ἐν τῷ Ἰορδάνῃ
Codex Vercellensis (at *GMt* 3.16):[54]	*et cum baptizaretur, lumen ingens circumfulsit de aqua*
Codex Sangermanensis (at *GMt* 3.16):[55]	*et cum baptizaretur Iesus lumen magnem fulgebat de aqua*
Gospel of the Ebionites §4:[56]	καὶ εὐθὺς περιέλαμψε τὸν τόπον φῶς μέγα

The two Old Latin manuscripts demonstrate that this tradition at some time entered the canonical gospel textual tradition. It is at least possible that Tatian was

---

[47] The textual instability of "Jewish" gospels is reflected in the fact that scholars – ancient and modern – have been unable to determine whether there were one, two, or of such gospels; Klijn 1992 favors three (distinguishing *GNazoraeans* as the third), Luomanen 2012 and Gregory 2017 favor two, and Edwards 2009 favors one.

[48] This is exemplified in the paratextual relationship between τὸ Ἰουδαϊκόν and *GMatthew* in Greek manuscript 566.

[49] See Jerome, *Comm. Matt.* 12.13.

[50] *Pan.* 46.1

[51] Cf. Hill 2019: 43–48.

[52] This part of Ephrem's commentary is only extant in Armenian (cf. McCarthy 1993: 84–85); translation from McCarthy 1993: 85.

[53] Greek text from Marcovich 2005.

[54] Codex Vercellensis is a fourth-century codex in the Old Latin manuscript family; cf. Houghton 2016: 26, 211; Latin text from Belsheim 1894: 3.

[55] Codex Sangermanensis is a tenth-century codex in the Old Latin manuscript family; cf. Houghton 2016: 213–14; Latin text from Houghton 2016: 158.

[56] Numbering and Greek text from Gregory 2017: 226; *Pan.* 30.13.7–8.

86   *Chapter 3: Tatian's Diatessaron*

consulting a text of *GMatthew* that contained this additional element, rather than a separate, "fifth" gospel. Since Codex Vercellensis dates to the fourth century, it is also possible that Ephrem inherited this additional element from traditions already attached to a canonical gospel manuscript. Interestingly, the "light at the baptism" detail is not a lemma located at the point in Ephrem's commentary where he is dealing with Jesus' baptism, but rather it is referred to retrospectively during Jesus' temptation. The *Gospel of the Ebionites* is the only identifiable noncanonical gospel in which this tradition appears. By itself, this brief non-canonical element adds little to the case for a fifth, Jewish gospel in Tatian's usage. Tatian could have easily inherited it from Justin, who had access both to written gospels and *agrapha* traditions. Alternatively, the Latin textual variant tradition might maintain vestiges of a second-century version of *GMatthew* that contained this "*agraphon*" (in which case, "*agraphon*" would be a misnomer), and both Justin and Tatian could have drawn from this textual tradition.

(2) Second, in the episode where Peter asks Jesus how many times one should forgive a brother, the Eastern Diatessaronic witnesses appear to correspond to a reading from the *Gospel according to the Hebrews*:

GMatthew 18.22 (NA28):	οὐ λέγω σοι ἕως ἑπτάκις ἀλλ᾽ ἕως ἑβδομηκοντάκις ἑπτά.
GLuke 17.4 (NA28):	καὶ ἐὰν ἑπτάκις τῆς ἡμέρας ἁμαρτήσῃ εἰς σὲ καὶ ἑπτάκις ἐπιστρέψῃ πρὸς σὲ λέγων· μετανοῶ, ἀφήσεις αὐτῷ.
GHebrews:	*si peccauerit, inquit, frater tuus in uerbo, et satis tibi fecerit, septies in die suscipe eum. Dixit illi Simon discipulus eius: Septies in die? Respondit Dominus et dixit ei: Etiam ego dico tibi usque septuagies septies.*[57]
Ephrem (*CGos.* 14.22):	English Translation[58]: "How many times, if he sins against me, shall I forgive him? Seven times?" He said, "over seventy-seven times seven... in one day."

ܐ ܟܢܦ ܐܬ ܠܡ ܗܟܚ
ܠܡ ܐܟܚܡ ܟܪ ܠܚܒܚ
ܢܦܬ ܐܬܚܒ
...ܒܚܒ ܒܚܒ ܠܚ ܒܚܒܝ ܐܪܝ ܡܝ ܢܓ ܘܗ
ܒ ܚܝܒ ܒܩܝܕ

---

[57] Latin text from Gregory 2017: 125; Jerome, *Pelag.* 3.2. Jerome (*Pelag.* 3.2) attributes this passage to "the Gospel according to the Hebrews, which was written in Chaldaic and Syriac language, but in Hebrew letters, which the Nazarenes use even today..." (translation Gregory 2017: 120).

[58] Translation my own.

Aphrahat (*Dem.* 14.44):	English Translation:[59] And our Lord says, "If a wrong-doer does wrong against you over seventy times seven times, forgive him in one day."

The most reliable Diatessaronic source here, Ephrem's commentary, gives no clear indication that it is based on *GHebrews*. Against the Lukan and the Hebrew evangelists, Ephrem's *lemma* here sides with *GMatthew*, omitting the "in one day" element in Jesus' direct speech. The Syriac phrase ܒܚܕ ܝܘܡܐ appears in the subsequent commentary, but it is probably not part of the Tatianic *lemma*. Even if it is, it can just as easily be explained by Synoptic, clausal-level harmonization that Tatian executes throughout his gospel.[60] The same can be said of the *lemma* embedded in the exposition by Aphrahat. Aphrahat preserves the saying "forgive him in one day" (ܫܒܘܩ ܠܗ ܒܚܕ ܝܘܡܐ) after a nearly direct quote from *GMatthew* 18.15–17 (*Dem.* 14.44). Thus, he is handling the Synoptic versions of this story somewhat systematically. The phrase "forgive him in one day" resembles *GHebrews* more than *GLuke*, but it could also be a harmonization of *GLuke* 17.4 with *GMatthew* 18.22, following a comment on *GMatthew* 18.15–17. The phrase "seventy times seven" parallels both *GMatthew* and *GHebrews*. The convoluted resemblances show that the earliest versions of this saying – *GMatthew* and *GLuke* – were easily confused, conflated, or harmonized. This undermines any confident assertion that Tatian borrowed from *GHebrews* here.

(3) Third, the Arabic *Diatessaron* places the pericope of the Rich Young Ruler (*GMt* 19.16–22 // *GMk* 10.17–22 // *GLk* 18.18–23) as the second of three "Rich Men" episodes, sandwiched by the Rich Fool (*GLk* 12.13–21) preceding it and Lazarus and the Rich Man (*GLk* 16.19–31) following it.[61] A fourth- or fifth-century Latin interpolation of Origen's *Commentary on Matthew* (15.14) says that, to introduce this episode, a "Hebrew Gospel" says "And another rich man…" Some have argued that this mention of "another rich man" coheres with the Diatessaronic sequence as preserved in the Arabic *Diatessaron*, and therefore the *Diatessaron* borrowed from this Hebrew Gospel. But the evidence allows for the relationship to be the other way around: this "Hebrew Gospel" mentioned in a late-antique Latin interpolation plausibly borrowed from the *Diatessaron*. The phrase "another rich man" does not appear in the citations of this passage by Clement of Alexandria, Tertullian, Origen, Ephrem, Aphrahat, nor is it in the

---

[59] Translation my own.

[60] Baarda 1994 makes the case that, oftentimes, Tatian's apparent insertion of noncanonical materials into the *Diatessaron* might be Tatian's own editorial touch rather than the use of a distinct noncanonical text.

[61] AH §28-29; Ephrem's *Commentary* only has two "rich man" episodes in sequence: the rich young ruler (*CGos.* 15.1–11) → the rich man and Lazarus (*CGos.* 15.12–13).

88   *Chapter 3: Tatian's Diatessaron*

Arabic *Diatessaron*.[62] If the Arabic *Diatessaron* preserves a Tatianic threefold sequence of Rich Fool → Rich Young Ruler → Lazarus and Rich Man, and if this Tatianic sequence introduces the second episode without the phrase "*another Rich Man*," then the mysterious "Hebrew Gospel" is plausibly dependent on and developing the Tatianic sequence by adding the phrase "another rich man".[63] This example should caution us from immediately concluding that a correspondence between a fragment from *GHebrews* and a Tatianic *lemma* means that the latter borrowed from the former, rather than the other way around.

There is another piece to the argument in favor of Diatessaronic dependence on a Hebrew Gospel: the phrasing of the Rich man's question, "what good thing must I do to have life?"[64]

GMark 10.17 (NA28):	τί ποιήσω ἵνα ζωὴν αἰώνιον κληρονομήσω
GMatthew 19.16 (NA28):	τί ἀγαθὸν ποιήσω ἵνα σχῶ ζωὴν αἰώνιον
GLuke 18.18 (NA28):	τί ποιήσας ζωὴν αἰώνιον κληρονομήσω
Ephrem, *CGos.* 15.1:	ܟܡܐ ܐܚܐ ܐܝܟ ܐܡܪ ܕܐܢܐ
GHeb (Origen, *Comm. Matt.* 15.14):[65]	*Magister, quid bonum faciens vivam*

Ephrem's *lemma* omits the phrase "eternal life" and replaces it with the first-person verb with the dolath affix ܕܐܚܐ ("that I may live"). This seems to correspond with the Hebrew Gospel fragment preserved in Origen, *vivam* ("that I may live"). If we presuppose that this Hebrew Gospel predated the *Diatessaron*, then this would be a strong case for Tatian using this Hebrew Gospel as one of his sources. Equally plausible, however, is that this Hebrew Gospel borrowed from Tatian's *Diatessaron*. Since there was confusion in antiquity about the identity of an alleged "Hebrew Gospel," we need to analyze each fragment on case-by-case basis.

(4) Fourth, the woes at the crucifixion. They feature in the following sources:

Ephrem, *CGos.* 20.28:[66]	*Vae erat, vae erat nobis, aiunt, Filius erat hic Dei... Ecce venerunt, advenerunt, ait, iudicia dirutionis Ierusalem*

---

[62] Cf. Clement, *Quis div.* 4–5; Tertullian, *Mon.* 14; *Ux.* 8; Origen, *Cels.* 6.16; Ephrem, *CGos.* 15.1–11; Aphrahat, *Dem.* 20.18.

[63] Cf. Phillips 1931: 8; Luomanen 2003: 255; Hill 2019: 41–43; Gregory 2017: 140 remains skeptical about placing this tradition as postdating the *Diatessaron*.

[64] Cf. Joosten 2019.

[65] Latin text from Gregory 2017: 130. Origen attributes this saying to "a certain gospel, which is called According to the Hebrews" (trans. Gregory 2017: 131).

[66] Latin translation from Leloir 1954: 215. The Latin is Leloir's translation of the Armenian.

Syr[sc]: *GLuke* 23.48:[67]

English Translation: And they were saying, "Woe to us! What has happened to us? Woe to us from our sins!"

ܘܐܡܪܝܢ ܘܝ ܠܢ ܡܢܐ ܗܘܢ ܘܝ ܠܢ ܡܢ ܚܛܗܝܢ

Aphrahat, *Dem.* 14.26:[68]

English Translation: "Woe to us! What has happened to us who have forsaken the Law and those of us who glory in wickedness?"

ܘܝ ܠܢ ܡܢܐ ܗܘܢ ܕܫܒܩܢ ܢܡܘܣܐ ܘܡܫܬܒܗܪܝܢ
ܐܢܫܝܢ ܡܢܢ ܒܥܘܠܐ

Doctrine of Addai:

English Translation[69]: "For if those who crucified him did not know that he was the Son of God, they would not have been announcing the destruction of their city. Also, they would not have been letting woes rain down upon their souls."

ܗܐ ܓܝܪ ܐܠܘ ܠܐ ܝܕܥܘ ܗܘܢ ܕܙܩܦܘܗܝ
ܕܒܪܗ ܗܘ ܕܐܠܗܐ. ܠܐ ܗܘܐ
ܕܡܕܝܢܬܗܘܢ ܡܟܪܙܝܢ ܗܘܘ. ܐܦ ܠܐ
ܚܘܪܒܐ ܗܘܐ ܥܠ ܢܦܫܗܘܢ ܘܝܐ ܡܠܩܛܝܢ
ܗܘܘ

Codex Sangermanensis:

... percutientes pectora sua reuertebantur dicentes, uae uobis quae facta sunt hodiae propter peccata nostra, adpropinquauit enim desolatio hierusalem.[70]

GPeter 7.25:[71]

τότε οἱ Ἰουδαῖοι καὶ οἱ πρεσβύτεροι καὶ οἱ ἱερεῖς γνόντες οἷον κακὸν ἑαυτοῖς ἐποίησαν ἤρξαντο κόπτεσθαι καὶ λέγειν· Οὐαὶ ταῖς ἁμαρτίαις ἡμῶν· ἤγγισεν ἡ κρίσις καὶ τὸ τέλος Ἰερουσαλήμ.

The fact that this saying appears in Ephrem, Aphrahat, and the *Doctrine of Addai*, makes it probable that it was present in Tatian's original composition. At the very least, we can say that this tradition about the crucifixion dates to the second century, and that *GPeter* also preserves this tradition. The question is whether there is a genealogical relationship between the use of this tradition in *GPeter*, the Eastern Diatessaronic witnesses, the Lukan *Vetus Syrus*, and the Lukan *Vetus Latina*. There are several equally plausible scenarios, and the evidence does not favor any one scenario more than another. It needs to be recognized, however,

---

[67] Syriac text from Burkitt 1904: 412; translation my own.

[68] Syriac text from Parisot 1894: 640; translation my own.

[69] Translation my own (Syriac text from Phillips 1876: folio 18). Petersen 1994: 415 transposes the wrong Syriac text alongside the English translation from Phillips 1876.

[70] Text from Petersen 1994: 415.

[71] Greek from Foster 2010: 183–85.

90   *Chapter 3: Tatian's Diatessaron*

that this fragment is relatively small, and its inclusion by Tatian does not amount to the use of a "fifth gospel" as one of his sources. It seems more likely that Tatian was reflecting the same scribal practices that led to the inclusion of *GJohn* 5.4, *GLuke* 22.43–44, and "Western" interpolations at *GMatthew* 20.28 and *GLuke* 6.4–10.[72]

b. Other Possibilities

Three more possibilities will be considered here.

(1) Ephrem comments on Zechariah the father of John the Baptizer as follows:

> This is why, [it is said], they killed Zechariah because he accepted Mary as a virgin, for the virgins used to gather together into one place. Or, when the infants were being killed and his son, [who] was at hand, was being demanded from him. Because he made [John] flee to the desert, they killed him on the altar, as our Lord had said.[73]

This account of Zechariah resembles the *Protevangelium of James* (22.1–24.4), which portrays Zechariah as dying a noble death for refusing to tell the officials where his son John was when they came to massacre the innocents.[74] There is a possible intertextual relationship between the harmonizing tendencies of *PJames* and Justin Martyr,[75] and since Tatian is related to Justin his mentor, we may have good reason to suppose that Tatian is indeed drawing from *PJames*. However, it is just as plausible that the relationship is rearranged, and that both Tatian and *PJames* derive their noncanonical traditions from Justin. Given that the date of *PJames* cannot be placed confidently in a particular decade within the second century,[76] this second option is at least as likely as the first. Therefore, we cannot say that the *Protevangelium of James* was one of Tatian's sources.

(2) The most extraordinary of the plausible noncanonical elements in the Tatianic tradition, discernible from the Eastern Diatessaronic witnesses, is the

---

[72] Several notable manuscripts preserve *GLk* 22.43–44 (א, D, 0171, L, Δ) while it is absent in several others (P75, A, B). Likewise, *GJn* 5.4 can be found in several notable manuscripts (A, L, Δ) but not in others (absent in P66, P75, א, B, C, D). In *GMt* 20.28, there is a substantial interpolation present in various "Western" manuscripts: it, vg^{mss}, syr^{c,hmg}, and Codex Φ (043). After *GLk* 6.4, there is an otherwise unknown *logion* preserved in Codex Bezae. None of these interpolations amount to a "fifth" gospel being appended to the canonical gospel codices in which the interpolations are found. For a concise discussion of *agrapha* in the manuscript tradition, see Knust and Wasserman 2019: 88–93.

[73] *CGos.* 2.5; translation McCarthy 1993: 62–63.

[74] Watson 2016: 95–112 hypothesizes on the basis of this parallel that Tatian drew inspiration from the editorial tendencies of *PJas*.

[75] Watson 2016: 95–112 documents the similarities in harmonizing tendencies between Justin and *PJas*, but he does not come down firmly on an intertextual relationship between the two.

[76] Scholars generally agree that *PJas* can be dated to anywhere between 140 and 230 CE, with many scholars favoring the earlier end of the spectrum (e.g. Foster 2013: 284–85; Zervos 1994).

3.1 Identities

91

"flying Jesus" who eludes death by levitating. Tatian probably inserted this peculiar tradition into the narrative of *GLuke* 4.16–31. Tjitze Baarda reconstructs the fragment from Ephrem's *Commentary* (11.24, 27) as follows:

They stood up and they led him out [from the town] and brought him by the side of the hill [on which their town was built,] in order to cast him down from the height into the depth [and?] he did not fall and was not hurt/harmed. ...through their midst he passed [and?] he flew [in the air?] and he descended [from above?] to Kapharnahum.[77]

The phrase "through their midst he passed" (ܒܚܝܠܗܘܢ ܥܒܪ) is a faithful rendering of *GLuke* 4.30 (αὐτὸς δὲ διελθὼν διὰ μέσου αὐτῶν). The phrase in question is "he flew in the air and he descended to Kapharnahum" (ܘܦܪܚ ܒܐܐܪ ܘܢܚܬ ܠܟܦܪܢܚܘܡ). Ephrem alludes to this aeronautical feat of Jesus on seven other occasions in his writings,[78] and Aphrahat seems to presuppose it as well.[79] It is impossible to prove that Tatian inherited this reading from an earlier source, though one might be tempted to hypothesize a Greek textual corruption of the Lukan text.[80] However, just as plausible, and indeed more economical, is that this is an instance of Tatian's own ingenuity in solving a textual ambiguity – how indeed does Jesus escape from an angry crowd singlehandedly? What is certain is that Luke's gospel is providing the architecture for this episode, and what we have is a slight modification of the original Lukan text. There is no sign of a formidable "fifth source" here.

(3) A final possibility is found in Ephrem's commentary, at *CGos.* 14.24: "Where there is one, I am there... and when there are three... their angels in heaven see the face of my Father." Matthew Crawford suggests that this might derive from *GThomas* 30.[81] William Petersen argues instead that both Tatian and the Thomasine evangelist derived it from a Jewish gospel.[82] Charles Hill offers a more economical solution, namely, that the Diatessaronic text that Ephrem is commenting upon is simply a rearranged sequence of *GMatthew* 18.10–20.[83] At the very least, it must be acknowledged that the Tatianic fragment here does not meet the redactional criterion; it does not cohere with the Thomasine *logion* sufficiently enough to outweigh the possibility that Tatian is merely rewording and rearranging a Matthean saying.

---

[77] Baarda 1986:331–32; see also Crawford 2018.

[78] *Carm. Nisib.* 43.22; *Carm. Nisib.* 35.16; *Carm. Nisib.* 59.13; *Hymn. de Virg.* 14.12; *Hymn. de Azym.* 16.10–13; *Hymn. de Azym.* 16.29; *Sermo de Domino Nostro* 21; for original texts, translation, and analysis, see Baarda (1986: 313–41).

[79] Aphrahat, *Dem.* 2.20.

[80] Cf. Baarda 1986: 336.

[81] Crawford 2013: 383; *GThomas* 30: "Jesus said, 'where there are three gods, they are divine. Where there are two or one, I am with that one'." Translation from Ehrman and Pleše 2011: 319.

[82] Petersen 1994: 298.

[83] Hill 2019: 50-51.

92   *Chapter 3: Tatian's Diatessaron*

Whatever the case may be, the Tatianic fragment is anchored in a Matthean text. *CGos.* 14.1–23 is broadly guided by Matthean sequence, commenting on Matthean pericopes from *GMatthew* 16.13, through various sections in *GMatthew* 17, taking a detour in *GMatthew* 19, and settling in *GMatthew* 18.10–20 in *CGos.* 14.24. Here it is important to highlight the fact that, since *GThomas* had such a wide influence in the late second and the third centuries,[84] and since *GThomas* meshed so well with the Synoptic tradition, one might expect that Thomasine *logia* would frequently appear in harmonized gospel traditions. On the contrary, what we find is that it rarely does. Our Diatessaronic sources only give us one possible instance of Thomasine redaction in Tatian's text (*CGos.* 14.24), but even this is questionable.[85]

c. Summary of Tatian's Noncanonical Traditions

None of the noncanonical traditions in the *Diatessaron* come from Jewish-Christian *Sondergut* pericopes, as we might expect if the hypothesis of a fifth, Jewish gospel source were true. All the noncanonical *logia* and narrative details in the *Diatessaron* are embellishments from episodes that originated in the Synoptic tradition. Since Tatian can be intentional about including *Sondergut* from *GMatthew*, *GJohn*, *GLuke*, and even *GMark*, it is significant that he includes no *Sondergut* from any noncanonical gospels. Moreover, even with *GMark* – 90% of which is absorbed by *GMatthew* – Tatian makes the effort to preserve sixteen Markan redactional features in Synoptic episodes. The same cannot be said of any of the noncanonical gospels that share material with proto-canonical gospels. If Tatian wanted to include a fifth gospel with the same verve as the other four,

---

[84] See Gathercole 2014: 62–90 for data on the early reception of *GThomas*.

[85] In addition, one scholar has argued that Tatian's *Diatessaron* contained several "Western Aramaisms" that signal Tatian's dependence on a noncanonical "Hebrew" gospel as a fifth source (Joosten 2019). According to this argument, Tatian the Syrian would not have naturally spoken Western Aramaic, but rather an Eastern Syriac dialect. Since Tatian would not have composed his *Diatessaron* in Western Aramaic, the argument goes, any Western Aramaisms would potentially point to an earlier Palestinian source used by Tatian. This argument fails on two counts. First, in the second century, Syriac was not fully separated as a dialect from Western Aramaic, as became the case in the third and fourth centuries (cf. Butts 2018). Second, Tatian plausibly could have come from Palmyra or Apamea (both were part of the "Assyria" that Tatian claimed as his homeland in *Or.* 42). The inscriptions at Dura Europos show significant interaction between Jewish Aramaic, Palmyrene Aramaic, and Syriac (cf. Butts 2018). Thus, Tatian could plausibly have spoken a form of Syriac in contact with what would become Western Aramaic. Any Western Aramaisms uncovered from Tatian's original composition do not necessarily imply that Tatian drew these phrases from a fifth source. It is also worth mentioning that this theory is predicated on Tatian having composed the *Diatessaron* in Syriac – a point that is hotly contested. I am grateful to Jeremiah Coogan for bringing these insights to my attention.

he had the method to do so. The data gives us every indication to believe that he did not. The *Diatessaron* remains the dia-*tessaron*.

One might well ask, however, whether the four allegedly Jewish-Christian fragments and the three additional possible fragments, taken as a group, constitute enough collective evidence to confirm Tatian's use of a "fifth" gospel source. In response to this question, it is helpful to emphasize that these noncanonical elements find parallels in a variety of sources: *GPeter*, *GThomas*, *PJames*, *GEbionites*, *GHebrews*, as well as numerous canonical manuscript traditions. These parallels are more likely to suggest that Tatian absorbed a variety of disparate Jesus traditions rather than incorporating one, major "fifth" gospel into his fourfold recipe. Also, there is no unifying character that would merit a link between the seven fragments. The only reason the fragments are even grouped together in our discussion is because they do not appear in the canonical tradition. As noncanonical fragments, they could come from myriad sources, and there is nothing to suggest that they all come from the same source. Finally, there is no evidence that establishes any of these fragments as genealogically posterior to any known "Jewish" or "Hebrew" gospels. If we consider these noncanonical traditions as a group, it is probably best to consider them as a loose constellation of Jesus traditions that Tatian integrated into his *Diatessaron* that was constructed almost exclusively from proto-canonical gospels.

There are no instances of special material from any of the gospels labelled as Jewish-Christian. Therefore, even if Tatian was drawing from a continuous gospel text such as *GHebrews*, it was not guiding his hermeneutical process in the same way as *GMatthew*, *GJohn*, and *GLuke*. Furthermore, the fact that Tatian can meticulously integrate the few bits of special material stemming from *GMark* shows us just how little any Hebrew gospel must have featured in his composition. The most we can say, then, is that if Tatian consulted a "fifth," Jewish-Christian gospel alongside the proto-canonical four, he did so in a way that viewed this fifth source as an ancillary, epiphenomenal supplement rather than a foundational document for his *Diatessaron*. By way of analogy, Tatian's use of noncanonical versions of Synoptic and Johannine sayings no more commits Tatian to a "fifth" gospel than the insertions of *agrapha* in the canonical gospel manuscript tradition imply a parallel status of a fifth gospel.[86]

One might counter by applying similar logic to my assessment of Tatian's use of alleged Markan redaction. Could the sixteen instances of Markan redaction merely be free-floating traditions that latched onto Tatian's threefold composition consisting of the other three proto-canonical gospels? Alternatively, could they have seeped into Ephrem's gospel reading through his access to the separated gospels rather than through the *Diatessaron*? These are both possible scenarios, but neither of them is likely. As shown above in Section 3.1.1, Ephrem's *Commentary* reveals Markan redaction in Triple Tradition (e.g. *CGos.* 4.4, 6;

---

[86] See discussion of *agrapha* in 3.6.2.

94　　　　　　　　　　　　*Chapter 3: Tatian's Diatessaron*

GMk 1.12), Markan redaction in *GMark-GMatthew* agreement (*CGos.* 5.13; *GMk* 1.15), and even a Markan intercalation guiding a Johannine version of the Temple incident (*CGos.* 16.1–5). Ephrem's *Commentary* at one point even gives precedence to Markan sequence over Matthean sequence (*CGos.* 5.17–24; *GMk* 2.14–28 guiding the sequence of its Matthean parallels; see below, Section 3.2.1). These are not the result of disparate Mark-like traditions floating into Tatian's composition, nor do they bespeak Markan seepage into Ephrem's commenting on a text bereft of *GMark*. Rather, they are best explained by a gospel orchestration into which *GMark* was already embedded and which served as the base text for Ephrem's *Commentary* – in other words, Tatian's fourfold gospel orchestration.

In summary, it is clear that the proto-canonical gospels constituted nearly the entirety of the material that Tatian reworked in his *Diatessaron*. Tatian added very little, if any, noncanonical material. What is more, these four gospels were the exclusive sources for Tatian's choice of pericope episodes. All the noncanonical material that Tatian plausibly integrated into his *Diatessaron* is epiphenomenal. The noncanonical material in Tatian's *Diatessaron* depends on the structured sequence of purely proto-canonical material.

3.2 Integrity and Interactions

How did Tatian's gospel sources interact in their combination? Which gospel(s) guided the sequence, and which gospel(s) were treated as most malleable and most able to be restructured? We must answer these questions on both the macro and micro levels.

3.2.1 Macro-Level Sequencing

The macro-level integrity and interactions of the four proto-canonical gospels can be seen in the way Tatian coordinates the storylines of each gospel into his one, cohesive sequence. This macro sequence is laid out in Table A in Appendix 1.

Tatian gives *GJohn* 1.1–5 the pride of place as the incipit of his gospel orchestration.[87] The Lukan *Sondergut* regarding the annunciation of John the Baptist's birth (*GLk* 1.5–25) is inserted before the Matthean narrative begins.[88]

---

[87] This corresponds to the way that Johannine theology runs thick in the bloodstream of the *Diatessaron*; cf. Perrin 2010; Baarda 2019:13–24.

[88] See Cook 2006: 462–71 for a strong case for *GJohn* and *GLuke* functioning as bookends that to a large extent set the rhetorical emphases of the *Diatessaron*. See also Baarda 2019: 13–24 for an argument for John's pride of place in the incipit being indicative of its theological centrality in the composition of the *Diatessaron*.

3.2 Integrity and Interactions 95

Notably absent are both the Matthean and Lukan genealogies.[89] Thereafter, Tatian mostly follows the Matthean sequence until just before Jesus' final entrance into Jerusalem in Matthew's reckoning (*GMt* 20.34 // *GMk* 10.52 // *GLk* 18.34).

There is one significant portion of the macro sequence, however, where Tatian chooses to follow where *GMark* and *GLuke* agree in sequence against *GMatthew*: the sections covered in Ephrem's *Commentary* 5.17–24. Here Tatian favors *GMark*'s and *GLuke*'s placement of the calling of Matthew rather than *GMatthew*'s. The following episodes occur in a sequence where *GLuke* and *GMark* parallel neatly in contrast with *GMatthew*, presenting pericopes that appear *after* Matthew's Sermon on the Mount but *before* Luke's Sermon on the Plain: the miraculous catch (*GLk* 5.1–11) → Jesus heals/forgive the paralytic (*GMk* 2.1–12 // *GLk* 5.17–26 // *GMt* 9.1–8) → Jesus eating with tax collectors and sinners (*GMk* 2.13–17 // *GLk* 5.30–33 // *GMt* 9.9–13) → the question about fasting (*GMk* 2.18–22 // *GLk* 5.33–39 // *GMt* 9.14–17) → the Lord of the Sabbath (*GMk* 2.23–28 // *GLk* 6.1–5 // *GMt* 12.1–8). At *CGos.* 6.1, the Diatessaronic sequence reverts to Matthean guidance, until the end of *CGos.* 15.23, where Ephrem comments on *GMt* 20.29–34 // *GMk* 10.46–52 // *GLk* 18.35–45.

Tatian largely succeeds at preserving the overall sequences of *GMatthew* and *GMark* in parallel (to do so, Tatian handles Lukan chronology flexibly). Tatian's handling of Johannine sequence demonstrates both creativity and a commitment to maintain a large degree of John's narrative integrity. Jesus' multiple festal visits to Jerusalem in *GJohn* are hard to square with his one, climactic visit to Jerusalem in the Synoptics. *GJohn* records Jesus celebrating six specific feasts, traveling to Jerusalem for almost all of them: a first Passover (2.13; JFst1), an unnamed festival (5.1; JFst2), a second Passover (6.4; JFst3),[90] Sukkoth (7.2, 10; JFst4), Hanukkah (10.22–23; JFst5), and a third Passover (12.1; JFst6) – entitled here, for convenience, JFst1–JFst6. *GJohn* records Jesus' Temple cleansing as the first of these feasts. In contrast, the Synoptics only record one visit to Jerusalem, when Jesus cleanses the Temple during his Passover pilgrimage – an act that precipitates his crucifixion. Tatian appears to be aware of this aporia. His solution: to rearrange the Johannine feasts in *GJohn* 2.13–7.36, and to transpose the Temple Cleansing to a later position. According to the sequence preserved in Ephrem's *Commentary*, Tatian rearranges the festal sequence in *GJohn* as

---

[89] For a comprehensive analysis of evidence of the genealogies' absence in the *Diatessaron*, see Petersen 1994: 30, 39–40, 45, 54, 63–64, 98, 118, 136, 430. Pastorelli 2011: 216–30 argues that the genealogies were in the original *Diatessaron*, but his analysis is based upon the "Old Perspective" method that gives undue weight to the Western witnesses which ultimately contribute no independent witness outside of Fuldensis (cf. Schmid 1993: 176–99), and his uses of Ephrem's *Commentary* as a witness is undermined by the fact that *CGos.* 1.26 is a later interpolation (cf. Crawford 2015c: 20–25). Crawford 2015c views the echoes of the genealogies in Ephrem's commentary as evidence that Ephrem also had access to the four separated gospels.

[90] *GJn* 6.1–4 and 7.1–2 record Jesus as staying in Galilee for this Passover.

96 *Chapter 3: Tatian's Diatessaron*

follows: JFst3 (*CGos.* 12.1–5 = *GJn* 6.1–15) → JFst2 (*CGos.* 13.1–4 = *GJn* 5.1–18) → JFst4 (*CGos.* 14.28–29 = *GJn* 7.1–19) → JFst1 (*CGos.* 15.23 = *GJn* 2.13–20) → JFst6 (*CGos.* 17.11–13 = *GJn* 12.1–8). Ephrem does not mention JFst5 (*GJn* 10.22–23) in his *Commentary*, but the Arabic Harmony (§37) and Fuldensis (§135) both include it as the fifth of six Johannine feasts, most likely reflecting Tatian's original sequence of Johannine material.[91]

Tatian comes up with a creative solution to the discrepancy between the Synoptic and the Johannine placements of the Temple Cleansing. In a bold move, Tatian situates the Temple cleansing not in Jesus' final visit to Jerusalem, but as the fourth of six feasts that Jesus celebrates, an entire year before Jesus' crucifixion.[92] Tatian relocates the Synoptic Temple Cleansing (*GMt* 21.12–17 // *GMk* 1.15–19 // *GLk* 19.45–48) to a narrative position *before* the triumphal entry (*GMt* 21.1–11 // *GMk* 11.1–10 // *GLk* 19.28–44),[93] and he synchronizes the Synoptic Temple Cleansing with the Johannine Temple Cleansing (*GJn* 2.13–22), fitting it into the same visit to Jerusalem that climaxes in Jesus' saying "on the last day of the feast" in *GJohn* 7.37. In this reworked sequence, Tatian opens a one-year period between the Temple Cleansing and the Triumphal Entry, corresponding to a one-year period between *GJohn* 7.37 and 11.55. Thus, Tatian dismantles key sections in the Synoptic and Johannine chronologies and reassembles them into a coherent sequence. It is at this juncture that we see Tatian exercise the most creative license. But this is not a blatant disregard for the narrative integrity of *GMatthew*, *GMark*, or *GJohn*. In fact, Tatian's Synoptic solution is ingenious in that it allows him to maintain Johannine chronology mostly unabated from *GJohn* 7.37 to *GJohn* 21.25 (with minor transpositions from *GJn* 10 and *GJn* 7 into Jesus' dialogue in *GJn* 12; *CGos.* 18.5–7).

The triumphal entry, passion, burial, and resurrection scenes intricately interweave all four proto-canonical gospels. Tatian includes the Johannine reinstatement of Peter, and he concludes with a commissioning scene that mixes elements from the final verses of *GMatthew*, *GLuke*, and the *Longer Ending of Mark*.

It is worth noting that Tatian's creative coordination of the Synoptic and Johannine chronologies does not by itself indicate that he was composing a fresh gospel that would make its predecessors obsolete. Irenaeus had a no less novel way of squaring the Johannine and Synoptic discrepancies. Like Tatian, Irenaeus refused to take the allegorizing route that Clement and Origen would later take.

---

[91] This reconstruction is based on Barker 2020.

[92] For this reconstruction of the single location of the Temple Cleansing episode in the *Diatessaron*, see Barker 2020.

[93] Ephrem comments on the Temple Cleansing in *CGos.* 15.23, before the triumphal entry in *CGos.* 18.1. The Arabic Harmony places the Temple Cleansing in §32.1–11, before the triumphal entry in §39.18–45. Fuldensis places the Temple Cleansing (§118) immediately after the triumphal entry in §117, but Fuldensis also does not make the triumphal entry Jesus' final visit to Jerusalem (this comes later, in §136). Fuldensis therefore agrees with AH and Ephrem in placing the Temple Cleansing *before* Jesus' final visit to Jerusalem.

3.2 Integrity and Interactions

Irenaeus executes a similar maneuver as Tatian and extends the temporal period of Jesus' ministry between *GJohn* 6.1 and 8.57 to a period of nearly twenty years.[94] Tatian extends the period into one full year. No one would consider Irenaeus' novel interpretation a sign that he was creating his own gospel to rival the four. Thus, Tatian's chronology alone does not prove that he envisaged his own role as an evangelist on par with his apostolic predecessors. We will discuss the intended authority of his gospel combination below, in Section 3.5.

At the macro level, Tatian's *Diatessaron* is a major attempt at coordinating the sequences of *GMatthew*, *GMark*, and *GJohn*. Tatian avoids episodic redundancy on the one hand and excessive reordering of gospel sequences on the other hand. One strategy to harmonize the four gospels would be to repeat parallel episodes if they appear at different places in each gospel. For example, Jesus' anointing happens at different narrative locations in *GLuke*, *GMatthew/GMatthew*, and *GJohn*. In *GLuke* 7.36–50, Jesus' anointing happens before he leaves Galilee for his final journey to Jerusalem. In *GMatthew* 26.6–13 // *GMark* 14.3–9, it happens after the triumphal entry, and in *GJohn* 12.1–8 it happens just before the triumphal entry. By including all three locations as three separate episodes, one could preserve the narrative integrity of all four gospels – but the result is an overly redundant narrative. Another strategy for harmonizing the four gospels would be to treat the four gospels as completely malleable. With this method, one could completely rewrite the Jesus story, ransacking the four gospels merely as repositories of dialogue and episodic content, but leaving their narrative frames behind like empty chests. Tatian toes a line between these two extremes. His handling of Jesus' anointing is insightful: he transposes the Matthean/Markan anointing episode to harmonize with the Johannine location before the triumphal entry,[95] but he keeps the Lukan anointing episode as a separate episode in the Galilean ministry.[96] Tatian can repeat an episode to maintain the narrative integrity of a gospel, and he can transpose an episode to harmonize with another gospel's sequence.

By and large, Tatian chooses *GLuke* as the gospel he rearranges with the most liberality so that, to a large extent, he can maintain the sequences of *GMatthew*, *GMark*, and *GJohn* in parallel. He applies a measure of creativity to coordinate the Synoptic and Johannine Temple Cleansings, and this in turn affects his placement of Jesus' final visit to Jerusalem. But other than these modifications, Tatian

---

[94] *Haer.* 2.22.3–6.

[95] Cf. *CGos.* 17.11–13 (the triumphal entry comes in 18.1); AH §39.1–17 (the triumphal entry immediately follows in §39.18–45); Fuldensis §138–39 (however, in Fuldensis, the triumphal entry comes before, in §117).

[96] Cf. *CGos.* 10.8–10 – interestingly, the *lemma* here mentions Simon the Pharisee, and the *lemma* in *CGos.* 17.11–13 mentions Simon the Leper; cf. AH §14.45–38 – this section omits the reference to Simon the Pharisee.

98 *Chapter 3: Tatian's Diatessaron*

is remarkably successful at preserving the narrative integrity of *GMatthew*, *GMark*, and *GJohn* in parallel.

3.2.2 Micro-Level Sequencing

In this section, we will look at two passages where Tatian's hermeneutical decisions are most visible in his micro-level sequencing: the Beatitudes and the resurrection appearances.

Tatian's blending of Matthean and Lukan materials in his arrangement of the Beatitudes offers insights into the interactions between the Synoptics in the *Diatessaron*.[97] Tatian situates the beatitude section after a Markan/Lukan macro-sequence subsection, which occupies a brief hiatus in a predominantly Matthean-guided sequence. Accordingly, the Matthean-phrased Beatitudes are introduced by the Lukan narrative detail that Jesus "lifted his eyes" (ܡܘܪܝ ... ܠܥܠ) to his disciples (cf. *GLk* 6.20: καὶ αὐτὸς ἐπάρας τοὺς ὀφθαλμοὺς αὐτοῦ εἰς τοὺς μαθητὰς αὐτοῦ).[98] Tatian prefers Matthean redaction where it directly parallels Lukan phrasing.[99] Tatian also includes Lukan woes, which are not present in *GMatthew*. Tatian views the Matthean and Lukan beatitudes as a tenfold whole. Tatian's treatment of the Beatitudes shows an attempt at preserving the unique contributions of both *GMatthew* and *GLuke*, and interpreting them together as a cohesive, collective witness to the teaching of Jesus.

The resurrection and appearance scenes show in great detail Tatian's micro-level sequencing of his gospel sources.[100] The *Diatessaron*'s resurrection and appearance scenes, reconstructed from Ephrem's *Commentary*, the Arabic Harmony, and Codex Fuldensis, evince an intricate textual dance where each proto-canonical gospel is given its time to shine. Special material from *GMatthew*, *GLuke*, and *GJohn* are featured. The plot to fabricate the story that the disciples had stolen the body in the night (*GMt* 28.12–13), Jesus' appearance to Mary (*GJn* 20.11–18), Jesus' appearance to Cleopas and his companion on the road to Emmaus (*GLk* 24.13–32), Jesus' eating with the disciples (*GLk* 24.41–43), and Jesus' appearance to Thomas (*GJn* 20.24–29) all appear in Ephrem, the Arabic Harmony, and Fuldensis. In the Arabic Harmony and Fuldensis, these episodes appear in the same sequence; Ephrem differs only in placing the story of the plotted fabrication (*GMt* 28.12–13) before Jesus' appearance to Mary (*GJn* 20.11–18) rather than after it.

Things get more complicated when reconstructing how Tatian handled *GMatthew* 28.1–8, *GMark* 16.1–8, *GLuke* 24.1–8, and *GJohn* 20.1–10. Ephrem only

---

[97] The Beatitudes and woes are found in *CGos.* 6.1–2; AH §8.26–39; Fuldensis §23–24.

[98] Cf. *CGos.* 6.1.

[99] E.g. in *CGos.* 6.1 Ephrem cites Matthean redaction in *GMt* 5.3 instead of *GLk* 6.20b.

[100] Consult Table B and Table C in Appendix 1 for the following discussion. The resurrection and appearance scenes are found in *CGos.* 21.22–29; AH §52.45–54.5; Fuldensis §174–79.

comments on Johannine *lemmata* in this section (*CGos.* 21.22–25), but we can reconstruct key facets of Tatian's original composition of the resurrection scene from correspondences between the Arabic Harmony and Codex Fuldensis. The Arabic and Fuldensis both commence with *GMatthew* 28.1a, they include the detail from *GJohn* 20.1b that it was still dark, and then they follow *GMatthew* 28.1b in naming Mary Magdalene first and the "other Mary" second. Both the Arabic and Fuldensis then follow a broad sequence of *GLuke* 24.1 → *GMark* 16.3–4 → *GMatthew* 28.2 → *GLuke* 24.2. Thus, the harmonists behind the Arabic and Fuldensis synchronize the Synoptic sequences of the stone being rolled away and the women noticing it. Another key feature that the Arabic and Fuldensis share is that they both place the Lukan appearance of the *two* angels to the women (*GLk* 24.4–7) *after* the Matthean appearance of the *one* angelic figure (*GMt* 28.2–6), rather than conflating the two accounts. Both the Arabic and Fuldensis finish the angelic commissioning to the women with a sequence of *GMatthew* 28.7 → *GLuke* 24.8 → *GMatthew* 28.8. Immediately thereafter, both the Arabic and Fuldensis insert Mary's report to the disciples and Peter and the beloved disciple's visit to the empty tomb (*GJn* 20.2–10), and both include *LEMark* 16.9 after this Johannine insertion (the Arabic includes *LEMark* 16.9 after *GJn* 20.17, while Fuldensis includes it after *GJn* 20.10).

The *Longer Ending of Mark* features in the resurrection appearance montage. The Arabic Harmony and Fuldensis insert *LEMark* 16.9, 16.10, 16.11, and 16.13 at almost exactly the same points in a combination involving *GMatthew* 28.11–15, *GJohn* 20.18, *GMatthew* 28.8–10, *GLuke* 24.9–11, and *GLuke* 24.13–35. This suggests that Tatian integrated *LEMark* into his resurrection and appearance scenes in a sequence approximating the sequence preserved in both the Arabic and Fuldensis.

Two verses are conspicuously missing from Ephrem and Fuldensis: *GMark* 16.8 and *GLuke* 24.12 (*GLk* 24.12 is also missing in the Arabic). The most likely explanation is that Tatian omitted these verses because they posed an ostensibly insurmountable contradiction. In the former, how could it be possible for the women to say nothing in *GMark* 16.8 but say plenty in the other Synoptics and *GJohn*?[101] In *GLuke* 24.12, Peter appears to run to the tomb *after* Mary Magdalene reports to Peter that Jesus had risen from the dead, whereas in *GJohn* 20.3–10, Peter goes to the tomb presumably *before* Mary is made aware of Jesus' resurrection. While these contradictions are not insurmountable,[102] it is likely that

---

[101] None of the manuscripts that include the *LEMark* after *GMk* 16.8 see any contradiction between *GMk* 16.8 and 16.10 (e.g. A, C, D, W, Δ, Θ, f^{13}, syr$^{c.p.h}$). It is plausible that *GMk* 16.8 simply tells of the initial reaction of the women as they were deliberating after the angelic appearance.

[102] When considering the geography of Golgotha and its surrounding area, these are not insurmountable (cf. Schnabel 2018: 346–75). However, we cannot assume that Tatian could envisage such a three-dimensional scenario.

100   *Chapter 3: Tatian's Diatessaron*

Tatian removed them for apologetic purposes. Discrepancies in the resurrection accounts were chief among the criticisms raised by Celsus around the same time that Tatian composed the *Diatessaron*,[103] and it is therefore likely that Tatian sought to counter these charges by offering a version of the resurrection account free from apparent contradictions.[104] In the case of Tatian's omission of *GLuke* 24.12, Tatian gives precedence to the Johannine account over the Lukan one.

These data from Tatian's resurrection and appearance scenes show us five things regarding how the proto-canonical gospels interacted in his compositional process. First, the sequences of each individual gospel are preserved: *GJohn* 20.2 is placed after *GJohn* 20.1 (even with Synoptic verses intervening), *GLuke* 24.9 is placed after *GLuke* 24.8 (even with a large Johannine block intervening), and so on. Second, regarding sequence architecture, no gospel holds a monopoly, but each is given a turn to display its unique contribution. Tatian coordinates a four-fold sequence, integrates longer Matthean, Lukan, and Johannine chunks, and even intersperses Markan phrases (including from the *Longer Ending*). Third, great care is given to include redactional features of each gospel. Fourth, apparent contradictions are smoothened or eliminated (i.e. *GMk* 16.8; *GLk* 24.12). When faced with an apparently irreconcilable difference, *GJohn* is given slight privilege over *GLuke*. Fifth, Tatian held that there was an authoritative account of what happened on Eastern Sunday, and every detail in Tatian's reconstruction comes from the four proto-canonical gospels. Tatian's task was to arrange these sources in an orchestrated sequence that accounted for as many details as possible. These five features suggest that, at least in the resurrection and appearance scenes of the *Diatessaron*, the four proto-canonical gospels enjoyed a congenial relationship in which each was given a turn to contribute to the authoritative account of the resurrection of Jesus of Nazareth, the Lord.

3.2.3 Integrity and Interactions: Summary

Our analysis has shown that Tatian's composition involved a dynamic interplay in which each of the four proto-canonical gospels contributed narrative and dialogical content. Each gospel was highly valued for the special contribution it brought to the full, four-formed picture of Jesus of Nazareth. This is clear in the micro-level sequencing of passages like the resurrection and appearance scenes. No stone is left unturned, and key phrases feature in order to give each evangelist a voice in the chorus. That said, at the macro-level of sequencing, *GMatthew* exhibits a leading role in determining the narrative trajectory. When compared with the large narrative chunks where *GLuke* and *GJohn* feature uninterrupted in order to avoid omitting their material, we might say *GMatthew* guides the

---

[103] Cf. *Cels.* 2.55; 2.70; 5.52.

[104] Cf. Baarda 1989; such harmonization tendencies are also visible in Codex Bezae and the Old Latin manuscripts, which omit *GLk* 24.12 and other minor details in the resurrection accounts, perhaps to iron out some of these discrepancies.

narrative sequence *primus inter pares*. What Tatian achieved in his fourfold arrangement is remarkable: he found a way in which each of the four proto-canonical gospels could coexist in congenial interaction within the same narrative field.

3.3 Mode

In the present study, analyzing the mode of gospel combination has typically come before an analysis of integrity and interactions. In the present chapter, however, because the mode of textual combination can be inferred from the integrity and interactions of the source texts, we have placed the analysis of mode after integrity and interactions.

A preliminary observation is that Tatian accessed his gospel sources as *textual objects*. The following reasons suggest that Tatian was working with a technology of gospel synopsis that enabled him to accomplish such a sophisticated, comprehensive form of gospel combination.

First, Tatian accesses the minutiae of redactional features, even Markan ones (see Section 3.1.1 above). Second, Tatian maintains, in parallel, large swathes of the progression of narrative sequence in *GMatthew*, *GMark*, and even *GJohn*, and he has the ability to pause the sequence of one gospel temporarily and resume that same sequence later (see Section 3.2.1 and Table A in Appendix 1). Third, Tatian rarely duplicates pericopes.[105] Finally, even with the gospel most freely rearranged in the *Diatessaron – GLuke* – Tatian finds a way to coordinate Lukan redactional features of pericopes and consistently insert these features within a Matthean narrative (see Table A in Appendix 1).

For Tatian to have accomplished a gospel combination with such intricacy, he probably had some kind of bibliographic technology wherein he could keep track of the pericopes he already accessed and avoid duplication. Perhaps he annotated four gospel codices as he went along.[106] But this technology must also have mapped a textual geography by which he could locate Lukan and Markan parallels alongside a largely Matthean narrative sequence. Such a technology would probably resemble what Ammonius of Alexandria used some thirty years after Tatian – a synopsis "in which he placed alongside the [Gospel] according to Matthew the concordant sections from the other evangelists."[107] This technology of gospel scholarship antedates Ammonius of Alexandria, and it was arguably already a phenomenon in Rome in the last third of the second century.[108]

---

[105] This is corroborated by the sequences of all four proto-canonical gospels in Table A, in Appendix 1.

[106] This was Bruce Metzger's hypothesis (Metzger 1977:12).

[107] *Epistle to Carpianus*, trans. Crawford 2019: 63.

[108] Cf. Coogan and Rodriguez 2023.

102 Chapter 3: Tatian's Diatessaron

3.4 Situating Tatian's *Diatessaron* in Its Historical Context

Tatian's gospel combination did not emerge in a vacuum. Locating Tatian's project within its socio-religious milieu will clarify the intended purpose and function of the *Diatessaron*, especially as it relates to the four proto-canonical gospels as distinguishable texts.

Post-synoptic harmonizing tendencies can be identified as early as *2 Clement* and the writings of Justin Martyr.[109] It has long been noted that *2 Clement*, Justin Martyr, and the *Pseudo-Clementine Homilies* overlap in their habits of harmonizing gospel materials.[110] This suggests the possibility of a common harmonizing source used by Justin and the respective authors of *2 Clement* and the *Pseudo-Clementine Homilies*. As we shall see in Section 4.4 below, Justin's use of gospel material was not restricted to a gospel orchestration. Justin draws from harmonized Synoptic traditions, and he can cite things as "written in the [singular] gospel."[111] But Justin also refers to the *gospels* in the plural, and he draws, at several locations, from the individual, separated gospels, distinguishable by their apostolic source.[112] Justin therefore serves as an example of how second-century Christians could use gospel harmonies alongside the separated gospels. Justin indicates in *1 Apol.* 67 that his ecclesial community used the separated gospels for their liturgical readings, so it follows that gospel orchestration served an ancillary function.

Theophilus of Antioch is another second-century Christian who, although he probably composed a gospel orchestration, was comfortable using the separated gospels. Jerome preserves the following tradition: "Into one work [Theophilus] joined together the sayings of the four evangelists."[113] Since Theophilus used the formula "the gospel says,"[114] the concept of a single, harmonized version of multiple gospels would fit well into his concept of the gospel as a text. On the other hand, Theophilus also read the separated gospels as discrete, distinguishable books. In *Ad Autolycum* 2.22 he singles out John the evangelist as one of the

---

[109] Cf. Perrin 2019; Kloppenborg 2019.

[110] Cf. Kline 1975.

[111] *Dial.* 100.

[112] See how Justin draws from the "memoirs of Peter" in *Dial.* 106, and how he uses Markan redactional (*GMk* 3.17) material in this section.

[113] *Epistle* 121.6: *quattuor evangelistarum in unum opus dicta compingens* (citation from Hengel 2000: 245n229). Jerome also says that he read commentaries "on the gospel" written "under his name," which might be a commentary on the harmonized gospel Theophilus constructed (*Vir. ill.* 25). Jerome's wording might imply, however, that he doubted the authenticity of this work; cf. Hengel 2000: 245n229; Kruger 2013b: 164–67.

[114] *Autol.* 3.14: Τὸ δὲ εὐαγγέλιον Ἀγαπᾶτε, φησίν τοὺς ἐχθροὺς ὑμῶν – "the gospel says, 'love your enemies'." Cf. *GMt* 5.44–46; see also *Autol.* 3.13. Greek citations of Theophilus from SC 20.

3.4 Situating Tatian's Diatessaron in Its Historical Context 103

"spirit-bearing men" who penned "the holy writings."[115] Theophilus also refers to plural "gospels" in parallel with Spirit-inspired prophets.[116]

In the last two decades of the second century, Irenaeus and Clement of Alexandria, both of whom are renowned for their lemmatized and systematic exegesis of many portions of the separated gospels, also used harmonized episodes of the gospels.[117] A generation after Clement, Origen could even speak of the fourfold gospel as literally the "*dia-tessaron*," the "one gospel *through the four*" (τὸ... διὰ τεσσάρων ἕν... εὐαγγέλιον).[118]

The Dura Fragment, dating from the first half of the third century, is a well-structured, harmonized account of the burial, engaging redactional features from *GMatthew*, *GLuke*, *GJohn*, and even *GMark*.[119] And yet, the Dura Fragment is found in the same Christian provenance as a church building[120] that housed distinctly Johannine frescoes (the Good Shepherd, the paralytic picking up his own mat and walking, the Samaritan woman),[121] as well as a Matthean fresco (Jesus and Peter walking on water),[122] and even a fresco that is arguably Markan (three women visiting the empty tomb).[123] The scenes of the paralytic, Jesus walking on water with Peter, and the three women coming to the tomb are on the same fresco of the north wall in the baptistry. The Samaritan woman is on the south wall, and the Good Shepherd is on the west wall. Johannine *Sondergut* and Matthean and Markan redaction literally share the same interpretive space on the walls of the Christian baptistry. We cannot be sure whether the the Dura

---

[115] *Autol.* 2.22: ὅθεν διδάσκουσιν ἡμᾶς αἱ ἅγιαι γραφαὶ καὶ πάντες οἱ πνευματοφόροι, ἐξ ὧν Ἰωάννης λεγει κτλ.

[116] *Autol.* 3.12: ἀκόλουθα εὑρίσκεται καὶ τὰ τῶν προφητῶν καὶ τῶν εὐαγγελίων ἔχειν – "agreeable statements are found to be both in the prophets and the gospels" (translation my own).

[117] Cf. Irenaeus, *Haer.* 3.10.6 (combining *GMk* 1.2 and *GLk* 1.17), *Haer.* 3.19.2 (combining *GMt* 16.16 and *GJn* 1.13), and *Haer.* 3.16.2 (combining *GMt* 1.18 and *GJn* 1.13–14). Clement's exposition of *GMk* 10.17–31 in *Quis div.* harmonizes to the Matthean and Lukan versions (see Section 5.2.4 below).

[118] Origen, *Comm. Jo.* 5.7 (SC 120: 386–88).

[119] It is contested whether the Dura Fragment is a manuscript of Tatian's *Diatessaron*. For arguments favoring its Tatianic identity, see Crawford 2016. For a recent and compelling argument against its Diatessaronic identity, employing the methods of the "New Perspective," see Mills 2019; see also Parker, Taylor, and Goodacre 1999. Whether or not the Dura Fragment is Diatessaronic, it still provides evidence for the congenial coexistence of gospel harmonies with separated gospels.

[120] The images can be viewed here: http://media.artgallery.yale.edu/duraeuropos/dura.html; accessed 25 August 2020.

[121] *GJn* 10.14–16; 5.1–9; 4.1–26.

[122] Although there are accounts of Jesus walking on water in *GMatthew* (14.22–33), *GMark* (6.45–52), and *GJohn* (6.16–21), only the Matthean version records Peter walking on water towards Jesus (*GMt* 14.28–33).

[123] Only the Markan account of the empty tomb (*GMk* 16.1) explicitly mentions three women eyewitnesses (Mary Magdalene, Mary the mother of James, and Salome).

104   *Chapter 3: Tatian's Diatessaron*

Fragment bookroll was used for communal reading or personal study, and we cannot know whether the separated gospels were also read at Dura Europos. But the frescoes in the baptistry evince an awareness of traditions particular to individual gospels – both Synoptic and Johannine. That the Dura Fragment was found in the same Christian setting as these frescoes suggests that the logic of the Dura gospel orchestration sits comfortably alongside separate gospels giving their accounts of Jesus.[124]

There is at least one instance in early Christianity of a gospel orchestration being used in competition with the separated gospels. The *Gospel of the Ebionites* was a Synoptic orchestration without genealogies or *GJohn*, and with some noncanonical material. Epiphanius preserves seven fragments that suggest the following sequence: 1) a gospel incipit that conflates *GLuke* 1.5a with *GLuke* 3.1–3 // *GMark* 1.4–5 // *GMatthew* 3.1–5,[125] 2) a description of John the Baptist (cf. *GMt* 3.4–5 // *GMk* 1.5–6),[126] 3) Jesus' baptism in the Jordan River (cf. *GMt* 3.13–17 // *GMk* 1.9–11 // *GLk* 3.21–22),[127] 4) Jesus' Galilean ministry and calling of the disciples (cf. *GMt* 9.9 // *GMk* 2.14 // *GLk* 3.23 + 5.27; *GLk* 9.1–2 // *GMk* 3.14),[128] 5) Jesus' mother and brothers (cf. *GMt* 12.47–50 // *GMk* 3.32–35 // *GLk* 8.20–21),[129] 6) a noncanonical saying against the sacrificial system,[130] and 7) Jesus' preparations for the Passover (cf. *GMt* 26.17 // *GMk* 14.12 // *GLk* 22.15).[131]

Irenaeus and Epiphanius relate that the Ebionites only used one gospel while rejecting the others.[132] Since it is clear that this gospel was an amalgamation of two or more Synoptics and some noncanonical material, and since it appears to have been used at the exclusion of other gospels, it serves as an example of a gospel orchestration replacing rather than complementing the separated gospels.[133] Richard Bauckham and Andrew Gregory have both made strong cases that *GEb* was composed in an effort to subvert the Synoptics.[134] *GEb* was a

---

[124] It should also be noted that the Dura Parchment was part of a bookroll, rather than a codex. This perhaps indicates that it was not used in the same ways as the individual protocanonical gospels, which were predominantly copied in codex format.

[125] *Pan.* 30.13.6; 30.14.3.

[126] *Pan.* 30.13.6; 30.14.3.

[127] *Pan.* 30.13.7–8.

[128] *Pan.* 30.13.2–3.

[129] *Pan.* 30.14.5.

[130] *Pan.* 30.16.4–5.

[131] *Pan.* 30.22.4.

[132] Irenaeus and Epiphanius both alleged that the Ebionites only used Matthew's gospel (*Haer.* 1.26.2; 3.11.7; *Pan.* 30.3.7), but Epiphanius specifies that what the Ebionites called "the Gospel according to Matthew" was a different text (*Pan.* 30.13.1).

[133] Scholars typically call this a "harmony", but for the reasons laid out in Section 1.3, I have called it an "orchestration".

[134] Bauckham 2003; Gregory 2017: 184–89 offers qualifications based on ancient compositional processes.

gospel orchestration that resembled Tatian's *Diatessaron* in its exclusion of the genealogies and its conflation of Synoptic episodes in and out of sequence, and so we must consider the possibility that Tatian's orchestration functioned in the same exclusionary way as *GEb*. However, when compared with the harmonies and harmonizing tendencies seen in Justin, Theophilus, Irenaeus, Clement, Origen, and the Dura Fragment, it is evident that gospel orchestration was typically compatible with the use of the separated gospels. But would Tatian have more affinities with the community surrounding *GEb* or with the majority of early Christians who used gospel orchestrations in tandem with the separated gospels?

In the decades preceding and following Tatian's composition, most other authors and users of gospel orchestrations also read the separated gospels. Equally, users of the four separated gospels were sympathetic to the concept of a harmonious orchestration of the gospels.[135] Gospel harmonies and separated gospels should therefore not be viewed, by default, as mutually exclusive or in competition with one another. Based on this Christian milieu in the century surrounding Tatian and his close association with Justin Martyr, it is unlikely that Tatian composed his four-formed gospel as an attack on the authority of the four separated gospels. We will develop this argument further in the following section.

3.5 Authority

Recent scholarship has rejuvenated questions about the authoritative status of Tatian's *Diatessaron* in its inception and early reception.[136] Did Tatian write a gospel orchestration or a fresh gospel in the same vein as the four proto-canonical gospels? Did Tatian intend to supplant the four or supplement them? These questions are directly related to the central pursuit of the present monograph: does Tatian's *Diatessaron* represent a definitive example of the four proto-canonical gospels congregating together with no other guests (indicating the ascendancy of the four to a place of unparalleled authority), or does the *Diatessaron* constitute a rival gospel, a "frontal assault on the four-gospel canon"?[137] To answer this set of questions, we must address the original name of the *Diatessaron*, the anonymity of the *Diatessaron*, the compositional habits, the parallel trajectories of the Old Syriac Gospel translations and the *Diatessaron*, and the tendency of some

---

[135] To my mind, there are no instances in antiquity of proponents of the four separated gospels opposing gospel orchestrations on ideological grounds until Theodoret of Cyrus (*Haer. fab.* 1.20) and perhaps Rabbula of Edessa (cf. *Canon* 43) in the fifth century. It is plausible that gospel orchestrations and the separated gospels coexisted amicably prior to the fifth century; cf. Hill 2019: 29; Perrin 2019: 109; and Barker 2019: 133–35.

[136] Cf. Petersen 2004; Watson 2016; 2019; Crawford 2013; 2016; Mills 2021.

[137] The image of the "frontal assault" comes from Petersen 2004: 67.

106

Chapter 3: Tatian's Diatessaron

second-century Christians to be flexible in their use of both individual gospels and harmonies.

First, the title of Tatian's composition might give us clues into its intended function and authority. Matthew Crawford has made a convincing case that, based on Ephrem's *Commentary* and Aphrahat's expositions on Tatian's *Diatessaron*, the earliest readers of the *Diatessaron* knew it only as "the gospel" (ܐܘܢܓܠܝܘܢ or ܡܚܠܛܐ).[138] The early fifth-century translation of Eusebius' *Ecclesiastical History* modifies Eusebius' tradition about Tatian's *Diatessaron* and refers to Tatian's work as both "Diatessaron" (ܕܝܛܣܪܘܢ) and "gospel... of the connected" (ܐܘܢܓܠܝܘܢ ... ܕܡܚܠܛܐ) but the phrasing indicates that the latter appellation was the more common one in Syrian Christianity.[139]

Recently, several scholars have argued that Tatian's earliest readers simply regarded his work as "the gospel," and Tatian himself as an "evangelist."[140] These scholars surmise that Tatian must have written his four-gospel combination as a "super-gospel", either to parallel the four gospels in authority or outright challenge their authority.[141] It is true that, for Ephrem, the *Diatessaron* was simply the "gospel". As such, Tatian's text of the *Diatessaron* served as authoritative, "canonical" Scripture for Ephrem. However, even if Tatian was an "evangelist" by Ephrem's reckoning, he was not an *apostolic* evangelist, for he did not derive his gospel directly from the Lord or directly from one of the Twelve. For Ephrem, the apostles bore an authority that paralleled Moses and the Old Testament prophets.[142] It is the teaching of the *apostles*, in its written form, that constitutes the second Testament of the biblical canon.[143] Therefore, if the *Diatessaron* had authority in Ephrem's thinking, it did so *because it was grounded in apostolic tradition.* The authority of the Diatessaronic text, then, must have been contingent upon its derivation from apostolic teaching, and this derivation could only have been mediated by Tatian's access to written records of earlier evangelists.

This account of the *Diatessaron*'s authority being contingent on apostolic authority is reflected in the late fourth-century Syriac document, the *Doctrine of Addai*. This text refers to the *Diatessaron* simply as "the New Testament."[144]

---

[138] Crawford 2013.

[139] Syriac text from Wright and McLean 1898: 243; see also Petersen 1994: 36; Watson 2019a: 72–73.

[140] See esp. Crawford 2013; Watson 2019a; Mills 2021.

[141] See esp. Watson 2016; 2019a.

[142] *Hymns of Paradise* 53.14; 65.1; *Reproof* 1.445–51; in *Reproof* 2.1965, Ephrem declares that "Messiah lives in his apostles," presupposing an authoritative position for the office of apostle.

[143] *Hymns of Paradise* 65.1; see esp. *Hymn* 22.1: "Give thanks to the Lord of all, who formed and fashioned for himself Two lyres – of the prophets and of the apostles – But one finger plays both: Distinct voices, two testaments" (trans. Wickes 2015: 160–61).

[144] Folio 23 (Phillips 1876); Petersen 1994: 38.

3.5 Authority   107

Elsewhere the singular "gospel" is juxtaposed to the law and the prophets as the set of books that are read in communal, liturgical settings.[145] Perhaps this indicates the canonical status of Tatian's composition as opposed to the separated gospels. However, the unqualified use of the lexeme ܐܘܢܓܠܝܘܢ ("Diatessaron") presupposes the foundational quality of the four gospels. In fact, as we saw above, Origen can speak of the four gospels as τὸ... διὰ τεσσάρων ἕν... εὐαγγέλιον. The name ܐܘܢܓܠܝܘܢ necessitates the four through which to proclaim the gospel. Simply calling the Tatian's composition "the gospel" would accord it more authority; referring to it as *Diatessaron* situates it in conversation with the four separate gospels.[146] It is likely, therefore, that the *Doctrine of Addai* reflects an understanding of the authority of Tatian's *Diatessaron* vis-à-vis its relation to the separate gospels authored by apostolic personas.[147] This is substantiated by the way the *Doctrine of Addai* upholds the authoritative office of apostle. Addai reminds the Christians of Edessa that Peter had sent to them a collection of Paul's epistles from Rome, and John had sent the book of the Acts of the Apostles from Ephesus, and Addai commands them to read these books along with the Law, the Prophets, and the Gospel. In fact, the *Doctrine of Addai* ends by linking Addai's successor, Palut, via Antioch, to Peter's bishopric in Rome, instituted by Christ himself. Textual authority in the *Doctrine of Addai* is predicated on apostolic agency. The fourth-century theology of Ephrem and the *Doctrine of Addai*, regarding the apostolic gospel, most likely reflects the late second- and early third-century Syrian Christian milieu of the earliest reception of Tatian's *Diatessaron*. Additionally, the *Epistle of Jesus to Abgar* and the *Didascalia Apostolorum* presuppose the unparalleled authority of the twelve apostles.[148] The *Didascalia Apostolorum* even speaks in the first-person voice of Matthew *as a gospel author*.[149]

By contrast, Tatian was never regarded in antiquity as having the same kind of authority as one of the apostles, and in our extant sources, his gospel-writing enterprise was never discussed as the same inspired act of the apostolic authors penning the four gospels. If Tatian's *Diatessaron* bore any authority in Syria

---

[145] Folio 29 (Phillips 1876).

[146] This is why the non-Syrian churches of antiquity preferred to identify Tatian's composition as the *Diatessaron*, since the four separate gospels were their frame of reference.

[147] It is worth mentioning that later in the fifth century, when Theodoret of Cyrus opines that orthodox Christians were using the *Diatessaron*, he says they were using it as an "abridgement for the [gospel] book" (συντόμῳ τῷ βιβλίῳ; *Haer. fab.* 1.20). He does not say that they were using it as a *replacement* for the four separated gospels, much less that these Christians were opposed to or ignorant of the four separated gospels. Their act of reading the *Diatessaron* as an "abridgement" presupposes an unabridged gospel of the four.

[148] For apostolic authority in the *Epistle of Jesus to Abgar*, see the final lines where Jesus promises to send one of his disciples to Abgar after his ascension (*apud.* Eusebius, *Hist. eccl.* 1.13).

[149] *Did. Apost.* chap. 10 (2.39).

108 *Chapter 3: Tatian's Diatessaron*

from the late second century to the late fourth century (and this is certainly plausible), it was not because of Tatian's agency as its author; rather, it was an authority contingent upon prior apostolic testimony. However, if the four separated gospels bore any authority in Syria during this same period (and the *Didascalia Apostolorum* and *Vetus Syrus* clearly indicate this), we can be reasonably certain that the agency of the apostolic gospel authors did play a role in the function of these gospels' textual authority. Judged side by side, the four separated gospels and Tatian's *Diatessaron* bear different kinds of authority. If textual authority of gospel literature is derivative of apostolic testimony, then Tatian's *Diatessaron* is at one remove farther than the proto-canonical gospels from the epicenter of authority.[150]

The nature of Tatian's composition also speaks to the question of textual authority. Tatian was doing a different kind of gospel writing than any other gospels, except perhaps that of Marcion. Tatian added almost no special material; his project was to orchestrate the gospel text through curation, omission, and rearrangement. This contrasts sharply with what the authors of *GMatthew*, *GLuke*, and *GJohn* do with *GMark*. Each of the post-Markan proto-canonical evangelists combine *GMark* with a considerable amount of their own material. Their respective *Sondergut* bespeaks their conscious authority as evangelists to introduce Jesus tradition unparalleled elsewhere. This self-conscious authority of gospel authors continues into later, second-century gospels, where the authors of *GPeter*, *GJudas*, *GThomas*, and the *Epistula Apostolorum* portray themselves as having exclusive access to Jesus tradition unparalleled in any other gospels. Tatian's *Diatessaron*, by contrast, was formally anonymous.[151] Tatian did not seek to fabricate the authority of his gospel based on pseudonymous appeals to personal eyewitness experience or special access to secret teachings of Jesus. Rather, Tatian's gospel was authoritative because it drew from gospels that already had currency in the Christian movement.

One might counter that the authors of *GMatthew* and *GLuke* might have been combining previously written sources without adding any of their own authoritative tradition. Perhaps there was an "L" or an "M" or a "signs" source to combine with "Q" and *GMark*. This may indeed be the case, but Christians of Tatian's time did not think in these terms. Tatian's contemporaries – Irenaeus, Theophilus of Antioch, and Clement of Alexandria – recognized redactional features as effects of the evangelists' own spirit-inspired pens.[152] Furthermore, in

---

[150] One might even subdivide this further and say that Tatian's *Diatessaron* stands at two removes, *GLuke* and *GMark* stand at one remove, and *GMatthew* and *GJohn* stand at the center. Early Christian reception of the gospels might indicate this dynamic.

[151] Tatian's composition was most likely known simply as the anonymous "gospel" until the time of Eusebius, and even after Eusebius, Ephrem and Aphrahat simply refer to it as "the gospel;" cf. Watson 2019a: 74–79; Crawford 2013.

[152] Cf. Irenaeus (e.g. *Haer.* 3.14.1–3; 3.16.2–3; 3.22.3–4); Theophilus of Antioch (*Autol.* 2.22); Clement of Alexandria mentions details special to *GMark* (*Quis div.* 5), *GJohn* (*Paed.*

the final quarter of the second century, the four proto-canonical gospels were distinguishable by formulaic titles under which they circulated.[153] Thus, Tatian, having been educated by Justin Martyr in Rome and having traveled through Christian centers in Asia Minor *en route* to Syria, would have encountered the four gospels as texts associated with apostolic names, and he is likely to have viewed the differences in the gospels as the authorial expression of each individual evangelist. His meticulous inclusion of nearly every bit of *Sondergut* from the four proto-canonical gospels suggests as much. Tatian therefore would probably not have viewed his own act of gospel combination as the same writing act as that of Matthew, Mark, Luke, and John, who, by their apostolic identity (or in the case of Mark and Luke, direct association with apostolic pillars) had the authority to insert whole swathes of *Sondergut* Jesus traditions.

However, it must be said that Tatian does, at times, "tweak" his base texts. Tatian gives additional phrases that have no parallel in gospel literature. He records Joseph saying that he does not want to be confused with the "father of her divine child."[154] In the account in *GLuke* 2.11, Tatian differs with the Lukan text and has the angels saying, "Today there is born to you a lawgiver."[155] Tatian adds the following statement to Jesus' discourse with John at the time of his baptism: "Do not be amazed, John, that you should baptize me, for I have yet to receive a baptism of anointing from a woman."[156] He also adds a statement of opposition from Jesus' detractors when he allowed the hemorrhaging woman to touch him (cf. *GMt* 9.20–34 // *GLk* 8.43–56 // *GMk* 5.25–34): "How can this [man] be one who keeps the Law, since a woman unclean according to the Law, has touched him and he did not shrink from her?"[157] When Jesus commissions his disciples for their mission to Israel (*GMt* 10.1–15 // *GLk* 10.1–13 // *GMk* 6.7–12), Tatian says that Jesus "sent them two by two in his likeness."[158] Just before the climax of the Johannine conflict narrative in *GJohn* 8.39, Tatian appears to insert a saying of Jesus elsewhere unattested.[159] These examples showcase the artistic

---

1.6), and *GLuke* (*Paed.* 2.1). Tertullian's awareness of the agency of the four canonical gospel authors is expressed in *Marc.* 4.2.2. Furthermore, Tertullian's redactional analysis of *GLuke* and *GMatthew*, in relation to *GMarcion*, is extensive (on which, see Roth 2008: 580–97).

153 For a discussion of gospel titles, see below, Sections 6.2.5c and 7.2.6b.

154 *CGos.* 2.5: ܕܕܝܢ ܣܟܠܘܬܐ ܗܝ ܠܝ ܕܐܬܩܪܐ ܐܒܐ ܕܝܠܕܗ ܐܠܗܝܐ; "Lest this be a sin for me that I be called father of her divine child."

155 *CGos.* 2.13: ܕܝܘܡܢܐ ܐܬܝܠܕ ܠܟܘܢ ܢܡܘܣܝܐ...ܕܐܬܝܗܘܗܝ, ܡܪܝܐ ܢܡܘܣܝܐ

156 *CGos.* 3.17:

ܠܐ ܬܬܕܡܪ ܝܘܚܢܢ ܕܡܥܡܕ ܐܢܬ ܠܝ. ܐܘܟܐ ܕܡܥܡܘܕܝܬܐ ܕܡܫܝܚܐ ܡܢ ܐܢܬܬܐ ܐܝܬ ܠܝ ܠܡܩܒܠܘ

157 *CGos.* 7.8: ܕܐܝܟܢܐ ܠܡ ܒܪ ܢܡܘܣܐ ܗܘ ܗܢܐ ܕܩܪܒܬ ܠܗ ܠܛܡܐܬܐ ܕܒܢܡܘܣܐ ܘܠܐ ܟܠܐ ܡܢܗ

158 *CGos.* 8.1: ܫܕܪ ܐܢܘܢ ܬܪܝܢ ܬܪܝܢ ܒܕܡܘܬܗ

159 *CGos.* 16.26: "Do not choose the name of one and the works of the other. Either do the works of the one in whose name you boast, or take the name of him concerning whose works you are earnestly engaged" (trans. McCarthy 1993: 256). The Syriac text is as follows:

ܠܐ ܬܓܒܘܢ ܫܡܗ ܕܚܕ. ܘܥܒ̈ܕܘܗܝ ܕܐܚܪܢܐ. ܐܘ ܥܒܕܘ ܥܒ̈ܕܘܗܝ ܕܗܘ ܕܡܫܬܒܗܪܝܢ ܐܢܬܘܢ
ܒܫܡܗ. ܐܘ ܫܩܘܠܘ ܫܡܗ ܕܗܘ ܕܝܢ ܕܡܬܚܦܛܝܢ ܒܗܘܢ ܒܥܒ̈ܕܘܗܝ

license that Tatian exercised when combining the four proto-canonical gospels. However, Tatian's artistic license is minimal in comparison with the numerous pericopes of *Sondergut* that Matthew, Luke, and John attach to their developments of *GMark*.

One final piece of evidence is the Old Syriac translation of the separated gospels. These translations probably emerged in the fifty-year window following Tatian's composition.[160] The Old Syriac gospels had a continued influence for the next three hundred years, as seen in the writings of Ephrem, Aphrahat, and the Curetonian and Sinaitic manuscripts.[161] Adding to this the tendency of some early Christians to use harmonies alongside separated gospels (e.g. Justin, Theophilus, Ephrem, and Aphrahat), and others to speak of the four gospels to be in essential harmony with one another (Irenaeus, Clement, Origen), and the tendency for gospels to proliferate rather than replace one another, the evidence weighs much in favor of Tatian's *Diatessaron* as a companion rather than a competitor to the four separate gospels. Tatian probably did not seek to replace the gospels he combined; rather, his was a précis of the fourfold gospel.[162]

3.6 Summary and Conclusions

In terms of gospel *identities*, Tatian's *Diatessaron* creatively integrated extensive portions of *GMatthew, GJohn, GLuke*, and even *GMark*. There is not enough evidence to suggest that a fifth gospel sat alongside the proto-canonical four in Tatian's compositional process. As for *mode*, Tatian accessed four proto-canonical gospels as complete *texts* set before him in some fashion. It is even plausible that Tatian employed a synoptic technology to facilitate the meticulous inclusion of Matthean, Markan, Lukan, and Johannine *Sondergut* and redactional features, and to avoid redundancy. Tatian mostly respects the narrative *integrity* of *GMatthew*, using it as his compositional architecture, but he also makes great effort to follow the sequence of *GMark* as well, even preferring Markan sequence when *GMark* and *GLuke* agree against *GMatthew*. Even with a more flexible handling of Johannine sequence, Tatian is far from blasé in the way he treats John's narrative when coordinating it with the Synoptic tradition. These factors indicate that the four gospels *interacted* amicably in the way Tatian combined them.

---

[160] The Old Syriac tradition is usually dated to sometime in the third century (cf. Williams 2012: 146), but Lyon makes a strong philological argument for an early third-century date (Lyon 1994).

[161] On the influence of the Old Syriac on Ephrem and Aphrahat, see Baarda 1975: 346–50; the Curetonian and Sinaitic gospel codices are fifth-century manuscripts that witness to the Old Syriac tradition, dated to the third century (cf. Williams 2012: 145).

[162] So Perrin 2019: 109. Another possibility is that the *Diatessaron* functioned as a gospel in the early Syriac church in a time when a four-gospel codex was hard to obtain.

In the gospel of Tatian, we see the blossoming of two important trends in second-century gospel writing and combining. First, we see the tendency of the proto-canonical four to dominate the literary imagination of second-century authors of Jesus books.[163] But unlike other second-century gospels, which add their own special material to a composition already dominated by proto-canonical influence, Tatian allows material from the proto-canonical four gospels to occupy nearly the entirety of his work, adding almost no special material of his own. Second, we see the congenial congregating of the Synoptic gospels and *GJohn* in second-century textual space. But rather than combining a handful of episodes from two or more gospels, Tatian causes the four proto-canonical gospels, nearly in their totalities, to inhabit the same textual space.

These two factors strongly indicate that Tatian's gospel is a culmination of the dynamics that would shortly lead Irenaeus to articulate his vision of the fourfold gospel canon – a canon that enabled Synoptic and Johannine gospels to keep company, and a canon within which the voice of Jesus spoke authoritatively only through the traditions written down by the apostolic personas of Matthew, Mark, Luke, and John. The *Diatessaron* was a successful companion volume to a preexisting fourfold gospel collection. Tatian's gospel combination was not a "frontal assault" on the emerging *authority* of the four proto-canonical gospels but rather a creative affirmation of it.

3.7 Excursus: The *Longer Ending of Mark*

The *Longer Ending of Mark* (*LEMark* 16.9–20) is a second-century gospel combination with important ramifications for the present study.[164] *LEMark* resides at the overlap between gospel orchestration and a pericope interpolation (see Figure 1.1 above). *LEMark* is presupposed in *EpAp* and attested in Tatian's *Diatessaron*, Irenaeus, and perhaps even as early as Justin Martyr.[165] It is therefore reasonable to date it to around the midpoint of the second century, if not earlier.[166] It also has attestation in nearly the entirety of the later manuscript tradition.[167] There are two levels of gospel combination in *LEMark*: 1) the combination of proto-canonical material in the composition of *LEMark*, and 2) the combination of *LEMark* with *GMark* as a second-

---

[163] On "literary imagination", see Mroczek 2016.

[164] The authoritative work on *LEMark* (especially regarding its sources, composition, and reception) is Kelhoffer 2000; Kelhoffer, building on the insights proffered by Rohrbach 1894 a century earlier, differs from the study by Hug 1978 by arguing that *LEMark* used all four proto-canonical gospels rather than sources anterior to these gospels.

[165] Kelhoffer 2000: 157–77.

[166] Kelhoffer 2000: 175 dates *LEMark* to after the four gospels were collected and before Justin Martyr wrote, namely, 120–50 CE; cf. Hengel 2000: 48–56. Gregory 2003: 86–87 finds the three-word parallel in Justin (*1 Apol.* 45: ἐξελθόντες πανταχοῦ ἐκήρυξαν) insufficient to establish Justin's knowledge and use of *LEMark*.

[167] E.g. A, C, D, L, W, Θ, most Old Latin witnesses, Syr[c, p], Cop[pt], and most minuscules.

112   Chapter 3: Tatian's Diatessaron

century pericope interpolation. We will apply our questions of identities, mode, integrity, interactions, and authority to the first level of gospel combination in *LEMark* below.

Regarding the second level, the several endings of *GMark* in the manuscript tradition demonstrate that *GMark* circulated in the first four centuries CE in a form that ended at 16.8 and a form that contained 16.9–20 (as well as other forms). These divergent textual traditions plausibly extend back into the second century.[168] The authorial touch of *LEMark* differs so vastly from that of *GMark* that most scholars have concluded that these two works were not authored by the same person.[169] When we piece together the fact that a second-century version of *GMark* circulated without *LEMark*, but that by the time of Tatian and Irenaeus (and, arguably as early as Justin Martyr) *LEMark* was considered to be part of *GMark*, we can conclude that *LEMark* was in fact a pericope interpolation that was inserted into *GMark* sometime in the first half of the second century.

Identities
The identities of *GMatthew*, *GMark*, *GLuke*, and *GJohn* make their imprint on the composition of *LEMark*. James Kelhoffer finds 37 parallels with the proto-canonical gospels and Acts in *LEMark* 16.9–20, accounting for "well over half of the 166 words in this passage."[170] Those who follow Koester's strict redactional criterion are correct to point out that *LEMark* contains only a few *redactional* features from the proto-canonical gospels.[171] However, *LEMark* also bears several features of Lukan, Johannine, and Matthean *Sondergut*, as well as a plethora of verbal parallels to all four proto-canonical gospels. The sheer number of parallels clustered together in the space of only 11 verses creates a cumulative case that outweighs the objection that, in its particulars, *LEMark* lacks the "smoking gun" of gospel redaction that Koester's method would require. I list the strongest parallels in Table D in Appendix 1.

Mode
The verbal parallels in *LEMark* with the proto-canonical gospels are so intricately intertwined, even clause by clause, that one might best describe its composition as an act of literary artistry. The author of *LEMark* is orchestrating material from each of the proto-canonical gospels in a way similar to what we have seen in Tatian's *Diatessaron*. To achieve such literary artistry, the author most likely had copies of each of the four proto-canonical gospels to hand.[172] Tatian's project certainly would have been impossible without physical access to gospel manuscripts, and the clause-by-clause orchestration apparent in *LEMark* legitimizes such a proposal for its mode of composition.

Integrity and *Interactions*
The author of *LEMark* shows artistic license in his or her creative reworking of proto-canonical material. The author "tweaks" the wording of the proto-canonical parallels in the process of composition, and the author does not follow a discernible sequence particular to one gospel. This artistic license is perceptible in the author's free use of synonyms for several of the

---

[168] Cf. Amphoux 1993; 1996.

[169] For a recent summary of this consensus, with bibliography, see Henderson 2012.

[170] Kelhoffer 2000: 122.

[171] E.g. Gregory 2003: 86–91.

[172] Kelhoffer 2000: 123–50.

3.7 Excursus: The Longer Ending of Mark

parallels as well as in the way that the author modifies the tenses and moods of the verbal forms of the parallels.[173]

While the integrities of each of the proto-canonical gospel appearance scenes are treated with flexibility, the gospels interact in a congenial, mutually interpretive way. The Johannine appearance scene with Mary Magdalene is correlated to a Lukan introduction to Mary,[174] the Matthean Great Commission is reworded in Markan fashion,[175] the Lukan account of apostolic failure to believe is put in counterpoint with the Johannine language of belief and signs,[176] and so on.

Authority

As a combination of all four proto-canonical gospels, *LEMark* summarizes and confirms the authority of the four-gospel collection. The Western order of the gospels – *GMatthew*, *GJohn*, *GLuke*, and *GMark* – lends itself to *LEMark* as a capstone of the fourfold gospel, and as a bridge between the fourfold gospel and the rest of the New Testament (as seen in the ordering of books in P45). In this sense, *LEMark* as a gospel combination upholds the fourfold authority of the proto-canonical gospels. It cannot be demonstrated that the author of *LEMark* intended to link the fourfold gospel with the *apostolikon*, but the intricate combination of elements of the four gospels certainly gives us reason to conclude that *LEMark* was summarizing and confirming the authoritative resurrection accounts of these gospels. The "capstone" function of *LEMark* is further substantiated by the fact that the second-century authors who show knowledge of *LEMark* also resemble the Western textual tradition in their gospel citations: Justin Martyr, Irenaeus, Tatian.[177] If *LEMark* appears in the gospel citations of second-century Christians who frequently used a textual tradition that resembled the Western text, then it is plausible that *LEMark* was associated with the Western ordering of the gospels as well. A number of later manuscripts with the Western order of the gospels contain *LEMark*, corroborating the correlation between *LEMark* as a capstone to the fourfold gospel and the Western order of the gospels. Indeed, C.-B. Amphoux has made a compelling case that this fourfold-capstone function of *LEMark* began sometime in the second century.[178]

Summary and Conclusions

With its bringing together of the four proto-canonical gospels through the *mode* of consulting manuscripts of each, *LEMark* operates in much the same way as *EpAp*'s gospel epitome and Tatian's *Diatessaron*, weaving together proto-canonical minutiae into an intricate, manifold tapestry. Even while the narrative integrities of the gospels are treated with flexibility, the nature of *LEMark* as an interpolation to an existing fourfold gospel collection reinforces both the *integrity* and the congenial *interactions* of the proto-canonical four, upholding them as the *authoritative* witness to Jesus. It is probably no coincidence that both *EpAp* and the *Diatessaron* draw from *LEMark*; *LEMark* perhaps set a precedent that these later gospel combinations

---

[173] The use of synonyms and the tense and mood modifications can be seen in Table D in Appendix 1.

[174] *LEMark* 16.9 = *GJn* 20.11–18 + *GLk* 8.2.

[175] *LEMark* 16.15 = *GMt* 28.19 + *GMk* 1.14.

[176] *LEMark* 16.11 = *GLk* 24.11 + *GJn* 20.24–29.

[177] Even though the Coherence-Based Genealogical Method has cast doubts on the legitimacy of strict text-types, one can clearly see a textual affinity among Justin, Tatian, Irenaeus, and numerous other Church Fathers; cf. Epp 2013: esp. 563–67. Epp uses the term "D-text Cluster" rather than "Western text" to avoid the mis-association with a Western provenance.

[178] Amphoux 1993.

114   *Chapter 3: Tatian's Diatessaron*

followed. As we shall see, *LEMark* also has the same canonical logic as Irenaeus' hermeneutics and the bibliographic intentions embedded in P45: the gospel is best understood as a pluriform (indeed, fourfold) witness, connected to the subsequent collective apostolic mission.

By positioning all four proto-canonical gospels alongside one another as equally authoritative, and by connecting them to the later ministry of the whole assembly of apostles, *LEMark* is an antipode to Marcion's project. Marcion's paradigm was at odds with an apostolic collective that included Petrine, Johannine, and Matthean testimony.[179] By orchestrating Johannine and Synoptic accounts of the resurrection, and by anchoring this orchestration as the completion of the whole Markan narrative, the author of *LEMark* constructed a robust apologia for a gospel of apostolic consensus. Since *LEMark* probably circulated in Rome around the midpoint of the second century (based on its attestation by Tatian, Irenaeus, and arguably Justin), it advances the case that, around the time Marcion was active in Rome, Christians were already engaged in Synoptic-Johannine hermeneutics that worked against the grain of Marcion's project.

In summary, *LEMark* confirms many of the patterns of gospel combinations that we encountered in *EpAp*, and Tatian's *Diatessaron*, and that in subsequent chapters we will see in Papias, Justin, Irenaeus, Clement, and P45, namely, that second- and third-century Christians read the Synoptics and *GJohn* in concert, and that even when they reworked the four gospels with artistic license, they did not undermine the authority of the four-gospel collection but rather confirmed and upheld it as the authoritative witness of the crucified and risen Christ. *LEMark*'s date at or before the midpoint of the second century testifies to the early and potent nature of this Christian reading *habitus*.

---

[179] On Marcion's incompatibility with an apostolic collective, see Lieu 2015: 242–48.

Chapter 4

Second-Order Discourse on Gospel Authors and Their Texts, Part 1: *GMark* to Justin Martyr

Thus far our study has focused on the dynamics of gospel combinations in interpretive rewriting and gospel orchestration. We have identified the presence of two or more gospels in the pages of three substantial early Jesus books: *GThomas*, *EpAp*, and the *Diatessaron*. *GMatthew* and *GLuke* have consistently interacted congenially when they are combined into a fresh composition, and as early as the *Epistula Apostolorum*, Synoptic gospels have been brought into constructive conversation with *GJohn*. With the *Diatessaron*, all four proto-canonical gospels have been brought to bear mutually upon another in the formation of a complete testimony of Jesus of Nazareth. No noncanonical gospels have been shown to keep company with the Synoptics or *GJohn* to the extent that these four gospels exhibit among one another.

In the present chapter, I will now explore a third kind of gospel combination: juxtaposing Jesus books in early Christian second-order discourse.[1] When early Christians begin second-order discourse on written gospels – in other words, when they begin to discuss gospel authors and the composition of their texts – how does this discourse illuminate the identities, mode, integrity, interactions, and authority of gospels in their various combinations? The development of early Christian discourse about gospel authors and their texts provides an angle into the process by which gospels began to cluster together. In what follows, we will see the identities of various Jesus books taking shape as they become embodied in the constructed personality of the author. The gospel-author persona serves to differentiate between Jesus books and facilitates their interactions within the same conceptual field of gospel writing.

Before tracing the development of second-order gospel-writing discourse, a brief word must be said about Matthew D. C. Larsen's recent work regarding gospel authorship in the first and second centuries CE. Larsen makes the claim that "there is no evidence of anyone using concepts of book, author, or publication to think about the gospel prior to Irenaeus."[2] Larsen's case rests on Greco-Roman usage of the lexemes (most often in the plural) ὑπομνήματα and *commentarii*, and he marshals Christian evidence from Luke, Papias, Irenaeus, and

---

[1] For a definition of second-order discourse, see above, note 45.

[2] Larsen 2018b: 150.

116 *Chapter 4: GMark to Justin Martyr*

Clement of Alexandria. Larsen has further substantiated his argument in subsequent articles and essays, and he has accumulated more early Christian data to support his hypothesis.[3] Larsen's hypothesis does not hold up to scrutiny, however, when we consider a broader set of evidence. Larsen has not engaged the Johannine corpus in his arguments,[4] nor has he examined the accounts of gospel writing in the *Gospel according to Thomas*, the *Apocryphon of James*, the *Infancy Gospel of Thomas*, the *Protevangelium of James*, the Muratorian Fragment, or the *Epistula Apostolorum*. Moreover, Larsen has not situated within the history of Christian origins the gospel-writing *testimonium* preserved by Eusebius in *Hist. eccl.* 3.24.5–8a. If any part of this fragment predates Irenaeus, then Larsen's hypothesis is falsified. Finally, Larsen's analysis of Justin, Irenaeus, and Clement is selective, and he does not fully appreciate the reading habits of these Christian authors as they engage gospel texts *qua* texts. Others have addressed these concerns,[5] and I will engage them when *apropos* to the argument in this chapter.

There is certainly data that, when individually compared with Greco-Roman parallels, might support Larsen's thesis that early Christians viewed *GMark* as authorless, rough notes of oral proclamation. Larsen has furthered the scholarly conversation by alerting us to these dynamics. However, we cannot construct with these data an all-encompassing paradigm of *the* early Christian view of gospel writing before Irenaeus. There was a diversity of ways gospel books interacted, expressed in various modes of written and oral tradition about gospel writers and their books. The origins of this discourse lie in the earliest gospels themselves.

4.1 The Beginnings of Multi-Author Discourse: Earliest Gospels

The four earliest extant gospels, *GMark*, *GMatthew*, *GLuke*, and *GJohn* demonstrate the development of the self-conscious gospel author and the awareness of other Jesus books. In *GMark* 13.14, we can see the first glimmers of authorial self-awareness in the comment, "let the reader understand" (ὁ ἀναγινώσκων νοείτω). It this short, parenthetical comment, the writer of *GMark*, by referring to the reader in the third person, signals a hermeneutical distance between the

---

[3] Larsen and Letteney 2019; Justin Martyr, *1 Apol.* 15–17; 66.3; Tertullian, *On Fasting* 10.3; Origen, *Cels.* 2.13, 27; *Gospel of Nicodemus* prologue. Larsen attributes *Hist. eccl.* 3.24.5–8a to Eusebius rather than to an earlier source.

[4] Larsen's case would be more convincing if he engaged the language of authorship in *GJn* 20.30–31 and 21.24–25.

[5] See especially the critiques by Margaret Mitchell 2020, Chris Keith 2020, and Timothy Mitchell 2020.

4.1 The Beginnings of Multi-Author Discourse: Earliest Gospels   117

reader and the text.[6] The reader's self is signaled by the otherness of the text. However, the author's agency is never made salient. In *GMatthew*, the agency of the gospel author gains more salience, and the possibility of multiple gospel authors is introduced. Some commentators suggest that πᾶς γραμματεύς in *GMatthew* 13.52 is a cryptic reference to Matthew's own identity as the "master of a house, who brings out from his treasure what is new and what is old."[7] Furthermore, the plural πᾶς γραμματεύς implies that there might be a collective of scribes writing treasures "old and new." By Matthew's reckoning, to belong to such a collective, a gospel author would need to be "discipled for the kingdom of heaven" (*GMt* 13.52). *GMatthew* 23.34 directly refers to this team of scribes, when Jesus predicts that he will send his own scribes to proclaim his prophetic message to the Jewish scribal elite.

GMatthew also takes the Markan usage of the lexeme εὐαγγέλιον and extends it to encompass his own narrative of Jesus' words and deeds.[8] In five instances, Matthew removes Mark's use of εὐαγγέλιον.[9] Unlike *GLuke*, *GMatthew* uses εὐαγγέλιον to summarize the content of Jesus' teaching (*GMt* 4.23; 9.35), and arguably to refer to an account of Jesus' actions (*GMt* 26.13). In two important instances, *GMatthew*'s redaction adds the near demonstrative pronoun to a Markan locution of εὐαγγέλιον. The first is *GMatthew* 24.14 (Matthean redaction in italics): *καὶ κηρυχθήσεται* τοῦτο τὸ εὐαγγέλιον *τῆς βασιλείας*. Matthew's omission of five Markan locutions makes Matthew's inclusion of the lexeme here more salient.[10] Matthew's insertion of the demonstrative pronoun and his distinctive appellation τῆς βασιλείας makes it probable that he is referring to his own writing. Interestingly, Matthew repositions the Markan locution ὁ ἀναγινώσκων νοείτω to follow closely after the phrase τὸ εὐαγγέλιον τῆς βασιλείας. Thus, at the moment of *GMatthew*'s closest authorial proximity to its

---

[6] Several commentators argue that this is Mark signaling his individual reader (e.g. Evans 2001: 320; Marcus 2009: 891; cf. Thiessen 1991: 128–29). Fowler 1991: 84–87 emphasizes that *GMark* was probably written for communal reading rather than private reading. Best 1989: 124–32 makes the case that Mark is giving a private note to the public reader, not to be read aloud (see also France 2002: 524; Wellhausen 1909: 103). Collins 2007: 597–98 points out that Josephus refers to his readers in the third-person plural but not in the singular: *Bell.* 7.11.5; *Ant.* 1.proem, 24; *Ant.* 11.3.10; 14.10.9; 14.10.26; *Vita* 6. Collins 2007: 598 summarizes: "the social setting of the expression 'Let the reader understand' was both oral and scribal. It is oral in the sense that the Gospel was publicly read aloud and probably interpreted and applied as well. It is scribal in the sense that the Gospel was a written text that the public reader had probably read privately and studied, but this private reading and study was most likely rooted in an oral context of teaching and handing on the tradition."

[7] Osborne 2010: 144; Allison 2004: 445; Gnilka 1988: 511.

[8] Stanton 1992: 1190–1196.

[9] *GMk* 1.1, 14, 15; 8.35; 10.29.

[10] Matthew omits εὐαγγέλιον in the passages parallel to *GMk* 1.1, 14, 15; 8.35; 10.29, and in the parallels to *GMk* 13.10 and 14.9 he expands the phrase to τοῦτο τὸ εὐαγγέλιον τῆς βασιλείας (*GMt* 24.14) and τὸ εὐαγγέλιον τοῦτο (*GMt* 26.13).

118 *Chapter 4: GMark to Justin Martyr*

reader, Matthew is referencing what could accurately summarize his entire Jesus book: τοῦτο τὸ εὐαγγέλιον τῆς βασιλείας. The second is *GMatthew* 26.13, which similarly adds the demonstrative pronoun to the Markan locution: ὅπου ἐὰν κηρυχθῇ τὸ εὐαγγέλιον τοῦτο. Again, the reference to "this gospel" plausibly signals to the reader that Matthew is providing a "capsule summary" of his own work.[11] In the transition from *GMark* to *GMatthew*, the gospel author emerges as an agent who can act in the company of other authors, and one gospel text becomes distinguishable from another. In short, Matthew opens a congenial space for multiple scribes of the kingdom to write about Jesus, and he subtly introduces the difference between "this" gospel and "that" gospel. The pieces are now on the table for the dialectic of unity and diversity in gospel writing.[12]

The author of *GLuke* furthers the discourse of distinguishable gospel authors and their texts (cf. 1.1–4). He explicitly refers to the "many" (πολλοί) who have "attempted to draw up an account" (ἐπεχείρησαν ἀνατάξασθαι διήγησιν) of Jesus. Luke does not name other gospels, but redaction criticism has made a convincing case that some form of *GMark* and at least one another discernable text (Q or *GMatthew*) are among these many διήγησεις anterior to *GLuke*.[13] It is probable that Luke is referring to *texts* rather than oral accounts, given the amount of *GMark* that he absorbs, and given that he parallels his *written* work (ἔδοξεν κἀμοὶ... καθεξῆς σοι γράψαι) with the previous attempts made.[14] Scholars are divided as to whether Luke implies any criticism of his forbears by using the verb ἐπιχειρέω. Some have argued that the verb signals a failed attempt, making Luke disparage prior Jesus books, or at the very least hint at their inadequacy.[15]

---

[11] Stanton 1992: 1195, citing Kingsbury 1975: 130, 163. Keith 2020: 120–21 remains unconvinced that Matthew uses the pronoun τοῦτο to refer to his own gospel book, but he concurs with Stanton that Matthew was the first to understand τὸ εὐαγγέλιον as a book.

[12] There is the possibility that *GMatthew*'s absorption of *GMark* implied an attempt to supplant the former gospel; cf. Sim 2011. However, *GMatthew*'s rewriting of *GMark* might indicate an understanding of *GMark* to have scriptural authority; cf. Goodacre 2020; Allen 2018.

[13] Keith 2020: 128: "Scholars are nearly unanimous that one of those books was Mark's Gospel in light of the amount of Markan material that Luke repeats."

[14] The most recent statistical analysis (Abakuks 2015: 119–39) has shown that *GLuke* absorbs 28% (3,057/11,078) of the *words* of *GMark* – and this 28% of overlap spans the entirety of Mark's gospel. In antiquity, a verbatim overlap of this extent would be nearly impossible without some kind of textual access. The percent of overlap is greater if one counts the episodes from *GMark* that *GLuke* absorbs. Presupposing the consensus of Markan priority, it is beyond reasonable doubt that the author of *GLuke* had access to *GMark*.

[15] Larsen 2018b: 84–86; Bovon 2002: 16–25; Franklin 1994; Klein 1964. Moessner 1992 argues that Luke offers both an affirmation of his predecessors intended goal, and a critique of their method and results. Moles 2011 argues on the basis of Greek decrees as *comparanda* that Luke is in fact showing the competitive superiority of his own work over against predecessors, but Dawson 2019 has demonstrated that Moles' *comparanda* are not precise enough to establish rhetorical parallels. Keith 2020: 127 offers a nuanced proposal: that Luke established his own work as a superior work without "a derogatory spirit or position contrary to his

4.1 The Beginnings of Multi-Author Discourse: Earliest Gospels   119

The verb itself is often used in self reference by authors as a token of modesty regarding their own work; used in the third person about other authors, the verb naturally becomes implicitly derogatory.[16] This seems to be confirmed by Luke's other two uses of the verb (Acts 9.29; 19.13). However, if Luke had wanted to mount criticism against his predecessors, he had ample tools to do so. But he is practically silent on this matter. By contrast, we can see explicit criticisms of rival accounts by Hippocrates, Thessalus of Tralles, Ps.-Isocrates, Diodorus Siculus, and Josephus.[17] Any criticism of Luke's is overshadowed by the commitment he shares with his forbears: to draw up an account according to the tradition of the original "eyewitnesses and servants of the word" (καθὼς παρέδοσαν ἡμῖν οἱ ἀπ' ἀρχῆς αὐτόπται καὶ ὑπηρέται γενόμενοι τοῦ λόγου).

Luke does, however, imply that he is improving upon the prior attempts to write the history of Jesus by introducing order to the gospel narrative.[18] What Luke means by an "orderly" account is a narrative that is well coordinated within the broader plot of salvation history.[19] Luke achieves this by connecting the narrative of Jesus from his birth to ascension in his first volume to the fulfillment of Israel's prophetic hopes in his second volume – every piece of this narrative arrangement is presented as part of the larger plan (βουλή) of God.[20] Luke implies no animus towards these previous attempts, even if he views his own work as a literary and theological development – or even improvement – of his forbears.

---

predecessors." Similarly, Watson 2013: 123 argues that in Luke "there is no overt criticism," but that Luke still viewed his predecessors as unsuccessful in their attempts at what Luke views himself to have achieved in writing a reliable account of Jesus.

[16] For modesty in self-reference, see Isocrates, *Philippus* 2; Strabo 1.2.1; Polybius 1.15.13; 2.37.4; 3.1.4; Aristoxenus, *El. Harm.* 2.32.19; 2 Macc 2.23; Dionysius of Halicarnassus, *Ant.* 1.7.1; 11.1; Wolter 2016: 41. Alexander 1999: 19–20; 1993: 76–77, 106–16 offers Hero of Alexandria (*Pneumatica* praef.; *De Automatis* praef.; *Dioptra* praef.) as a parallel of congenial interactions with predecessors.

[17] Josephus, *Apion.* 1.13; *Bell.* 1.1–3; Polybius 12.28.3; Diodorus Siculus 1.3.2; 4.1.2; Ps.-Thessalus, *De virtutibus herbarum* 1 praef.; cf. Wolter 2008: 42.

[18] Larsen 2018b: 86 argues that Luke anticipated Papias' later concern that *GMark* lacked τάξις, but such concern need not imply disdain, competition, or even literary supplanting. James Barker 2019 shows that the tendency in early Jewish and Christian literature was for similar works to proliferate and be read alongside one other rather than supplant or replace one another.

[19] Luke's term καθεξῆς is parallel to the well-known literary term τάξις, used by ancient historians to describe proper sequence of episodes in a historical narrative (διήγησις), carefully following (παρακολουθέω) the artistic arrangement (οἰκονομία) of the overall plot. These terms converge in Dionysius of Halicarnassus's critique of Thucydides' historiography, *On Thucydides* 9–12; cf. Moessner 1999; 2002. On τάξις in historiography, see Lucian, *How to Write History* 6, 48, 50; Porphyry *Life of Plotinus* 3.37–39; on τάξις in professional writing in general, see Galen *De ordine librorum suorum ad Eugenianum* 1.1–2 (Kühn 19.49–56); Larsen 2018b: 91–92. For Luke, the proper arrangement of the narrative is according to the plan of God in the history of Israel; Moessner 1992; 1999; 2002; see also Backhaus 2019.

[20] Cf. *GLk* 7.30; 23.51; Acts 2.23; 4.28; 5.38; 13.36; 20.27.

120 *Chapter 4: GMark to Justin Martyr*

His allusion to previous authors and their written narratives that circled within the orbit of the authoritative *paradosis* brings clarity to the congenial space within which multiple gospels can keep company – any διήγησις that was properly anchored in the testimony of the eyewitnesses and servants of the word would probably be in Luke's good books. We will see how many of the themes Luke introduces to the discourse become more developed in the second-century gospel *testimonia*.

In *GJohn*, the agency of the author and the aims of gospel writing are brought into sharper relief than in the Synoptics. In the "Johannine colophons" (*GJn* 20.30–31 and 21.24–25),[21] the agency of the Johannine evangelist is one of eyewitness testimony (whatever one makes of the historicity of the eyewitness claims), and in this way the author presents his written testimony as authoritative.[22] The author of *GJohn* perhaps has other Jesus books in mind when he distinguishes his own book as "this book" which leaves out the "many other signs" which Jesus did "in the presence of his disciples" (20.30). In the second colophon, the author considers the possibility of innumerable books written about Jesus (21.25). There is no explicit critique of other Jesus books, much less any animus against other gospel authors or their texts.[23] John is not criticizing or competing with other gospels; he is amplifying what he thinks should be the central thrust to a Jesus book – the call to believe in Jesus as the Christ, the Son of God (*GJn* 20:31). *GJohn* does not undermine the congenial space of gospel writing that the authors of *GMatthew* (13.52) and *GLuke* (1.1–4) presuppose.

Within the earliest Christian gospels, gospel authors and their texts can peacefully coexist and interact if they play by the right rules. Matthew's parameters are defined by scribal adherence to proper discipleship for Jesus' kingdom. Luke's are defined by proximity to the eyewitnesses from the beginning and conformity to the eschatological word. John's are defined by faithfulness to the witness of Jesus' soteriologically significant deeds and words. In theory, *GMatthew*,

---

[21] Smith 2001: 28–29 refers to *GJn* 20.30–31 and 21.24–25 as the "Johannine colophons," and Keith 2016; 2020:131–54 follows this terminology.

[22] An increasing number of scholars question the older consensus that *GJn* 21 was a later addition (see, e.g. Jackson 1999; Van Belle 2009; Porter 2015; Keith 2016; Bauckham 2017; Hill 2017). Hill 2017 makes a convincing case that the "we" in *GJn* 21.24–25, considered with regard to Johannine parlance, is the evangelist's own self-disclosure rather than a later addition by a Johannine collective.

[23] Keith 2016; 2020: 131–54 argues at length that the Johannine colophons "represent the most competitive instances of textualization in contemporary Jesus tradition," and that "John's Gospel asserts superiority to its competitors on the basis of continuing the scriptural textuality of Moses" (Keith 2020: 154). The evidence Keith marshals, however, at most demonstrates that the Johannine evangelist sought to improve upon his predecessors. Improving upon one's predecessors does not necessarily imply competition or supplanting of one's predecessors; more explicit intentions from the Johannine evangelist would be required to substantiate Keith's thesis. Furthermore, as Bauckham 1998 argues, *GJohn* presupposes *GMark* for its own narrative logic. Several essays address these issues in Becker *et al.* 2021.

4.2 Gospel Authorship in Papias and His Traditions 121

GJohn, and *GLuke* fall within one another's conceptual parameters, even as each engages in thoroughgoing, interpretive rewriting of *GMark*. Each of the latter three, through their rewriting of *GMark*, resemble *GMark* as the archetype. *GMark* serves as a middle term that creates and unites the conceptual space shared by a plurality of gospels. The second century fleshes out which gospels would keep company in this space (identity), how they would do so (mode, integrity, diversity), and what effect this would have on their perceived authority.

4.2 Gospel Authorship in Papias and His Traditions

Christian discourse on gospel authorship made an evolutionary leap in the period between the proem of *GLuke* and the writings of Papias. With Papias we have the first extant mention of named authors of Jesus books. Matthew D. C. Larsen observes that Papias does not call these books "gospels".[24] That said, Papias does introduce concrete human agents into the discussion of Jesus-tradition textualization in order to disambiguate multiple writings that occupied the same conceptual space.[25]

4.2.1 The Question of Papian Fragments

Before we can use Papias as a source for gospel origins, we need to establish which fragments are reliable for reconstructing genuine Papian traditions. Scholars are in general agreement about the authenticity of the Papian fragments preserved by Eusebius in *Hist. eccl.* 3.39.1–4 and 14–17, though even in 3.39, in several places it is difficult to decipher where Papias is speaking and where Eusebius is interpolating. More controversial is Charles Hill's proposal that *Hist. eccl.* 3.24.5–13 also draws from Papias' written record.[26] The first half of this passage (3.24.5–8a) is worth quoting in full, as well as the transition to the second half (3.24.8b etc.):

5. Yet nevertheless, of all those who had been with the Lord only Matthew and John have left us memoirs (ὑπομνήματα... καταλελοίπασιν); a record preserves (κατέχει λόγος) that they took to writing out of necessity (ἐπάναγκες ἐπὶ τὴν γραφὴν ἐλθεῖν). 6. For Matthew, after first

---

[24] Larsen 2018b: 87–93.

[25] It is often emphasized that Papias preferred the "living voice" over against written Jesus traditions (*Hist. eccl.* 3.39.4); e.g. Campenhausen 1972: 135; Hahneman 1992: 95–96. However, Papias' preference to the "living voice" is probably indebted to the value system of Greco-Roman philosophical schools, in which the living voice was an indispensable resource for the proper interpretation of classic texts (cf. Alexander 1990). Papias' traditions about the authorship of gospel books suggests that the "living voice" was utilized in the service of interpreting written Jesus traditions.

[26] Hill 1998 develops this argument, and he summarizes it in Hill 2004 and 2010b. He responds to criticisms by Bauckham in Hill 2010a.

122   *Chapter 4: GMark to Justin Martyr*

preaching to the Hebrews, when he was about to go to others, handed down in writing (γραφῇ παραδοὺς) the gospel according to himself, in his native tongue, thus in writing he fulfilled the lack of his presence among those from whom he was sent. 7. Now when Mark and Luke had already produced a published edition of the gospels according to themselves (τῶν κατ᾽ αὐτοὺς εὐαγγελίων τὴν ἔκδοσιν πεποιημένων), it is said (φασὶ) that John all the time was used to an unwritten proclamation, and at last he took to writing for the following reason. The three [gospels] that had already been written down were distributed to all, and also to him. It is said (φασὶ) that he welcomed them, bearing witness to their truth, but that the only lack in the writing was the account regarding the things done by Christ at first and at the beginning of the preaching. 8a. This record is certainly true (καὶ ἀληθής γε ὁ λόγος). 8b. For it is possible to see that the three evangelists (τοὺς τρεῖς γοῦν εὐαγγελιστὰς) had written down only the things done by the Savior during one year after John the Baptist had been shut in prison...[27]

Hill highlights that Eusebius uses the phrases "a record preserves" (κατέχει λόγος; *Hist. eccl.* 3.24.5), "the record is certainly true" (καὶ ἀληθής γε ὁ λόγος; *Hist. eccl.* 3.24.8), and "they say" / "it is said" (φασι; 3.24.7,11) to refer to an early, written tradition.[28] Hill argues that this written testimony is the major basis for Eusebius' entire account of Johannine Gospel origins in 3.24.5–13 (Hill argues that this is one unified account, rather than two accounts separated by καὶ ἀληθής γε ὁ λόγος at 3.24.8a). Hill makes the case that Papias is the source behind this written tradition of gospel origins. Hill builds his case on the following premises: 1) there are parallels between *Hist. eccl.* 3.24.8–13 and Papias' traditions about the origins of *GMatthew* and *GMark* elsewhere (*Hist. eccl.* 2.15.1–2; 3.39.15–16), 2) there are parallels between *Hist. eccl.* 3.24.5–13 and other early Christian authors who had contact with Papias' writings (e.g. Irenaeus, Clement of Alexandria, the *Muratorian Fragment*, Origen, and Victorinus of Pettau),[29] and 3) the other possible sources from which Eusebius could be drawing in 3.24.5–13 are not as convincing as Papias.[30]

Richard Bauckham and Enrico Norelli have offered critiques of Hill's arguments, most notably, that Hill does not fully appreciate the function of the logical marker γοῦν in *Hist. Eccl.* 3.24.8b.[31] This marker signals that Eusebius has finished citing his traditional source and has begun to comment on it (τοὺς τρεῖς γοῦν εὐαγγελιστὰς κτλ.). Bauckham also argues that the account of Matthew's gospel authorship in *Hist. eccl.* 3.39.16 differs considerably from that in *Hist. eccl.* 3.24.5–6, and that the solution to the problem of *GMark*'s lack of τάξις is

---

[27] Translation my own; Greek citations from *Hist. eccl.* from LCL 153.

[28] Hill 1998: 588–92, building on Hort 1894: 170–73, Lawlor 1973: 22–26, and Sellew 1992: 119.

[29] These parallels are 1) writing by request, 2) concern for order in the gospels, 3) the evangelists as "publishers", 4) the number and order of the gospels, and 5) "inspiration".

[30] Hill 1998: 606–11 considers the possibilities of Hippolytus, Clement of Alexandria, or Origen as Eusebius' source.

[31] Norelli 2005: 505–21; 521–31 (on Papias and the Muratorian Fragment); Bauckham 2017: 433–37.

different in *Hist. eccl.* 3.39.15 than in *Hist. eccl.* 3.24.11–13.[32] For Bauckham and Norelli, then, Hill's thesis is not convincing enough to include *Hist. eccl.* 3.24.5–13 in one's analysis of Papian gospel traditions. Several other scholars join Bauckham and Norelli in their criticisms of Hill's case, but without sustained engagement, and others fail to mention it entirely.[33]

T. Scott Manor develops these critiques, but still offers a defense of a genuinely Papian influence on *Hist. eccl.* 3.24.5–8a.[34] Manor argues that *Hist. eccl.* 3.24.5–8a can indeed be traced back to Papias' written account, but 3.24.8b–13 is Eusebius' own composition in response to Origen's supposition that the gospels, because of their discrepancies, "are not accurate records of history."[35] By arguing that *Hist. eccl.* 3.24.11–13 is Eusebius' constructive response to Origen, Manor has answered Bauckham's query regarding the discrepancy between Papias' account of τάξις in 3.39.15–16 and the narrative order of gospels in 3.24.5–13, and he has strengthened the similarities between 3.39.15–16 and 3.24.5–8a. The alleged differences between Papias' account of Matthean gospel authorship in *Hist. eccl.* 3.39.16 and 3.24.5 are also not incompatible.[36] The

---

[32] Bauckham 2017: 435–37 highlights the fact that Papias in 3.39.15–16 confronts the alleged problem of Mark's lack of τάξις, whereas the author of the tradition in 3.24.5–13 shows no awareness of differences in τάξις between any of the Synoptics. Bauckham 2017: 436 further infers that the Papias of 3.39.15 would have offered "that John's Gospel does follow a correct chronological order, while the other Gospels (at least Mark and Matthew) do not" and contrasts this with the solution in 3.24.5–13 that John wrote about Jesus' ministry before John the Baptist's incarceration. Bauckham's Papian inference is from silence and is not sufficiently load-bearing, and the discrepancy disappears if, like Manor, we allow that 3.24.8b–13 is a Eusebian response to Origen rather than a genuine Papian tradition. As for the absence of any mention of Synoptic deficiencies in τάξις, this could easily be explained by the fact that 3.24.5–8a seems to be moving towards a focus on Johannine gospel origins after summarizing Synoptic gospel origins, and the said issues in τάξις could have been mentioned earlier in the tradition lying behind 3.24.5–8a.

[33] Watson 2013: 445–46 dismisses Hill's argument in an extended footnote dealing with *Hist. eccl.* 3.24.5–13. Watson voices similar concerns as Bauckham, but he does not appreciate that the apparent discrepancies are not insurmountable. Watson cautiously states that the source is unnamed by Eusebius, but he does not offer an alternative source to Papias, and he does not deal with the date of this unnamed source, which I address in this section. Larsen 2018b makes no mention of Hill's scholarship. Moessner 2019: 488, 490 mentions Hill's 1998 article, but without reference to the specific arguments regarding *Hist. eccl.* 3.24.5–13.

[34] Manor 2013: 1–21.

[35] Manor 2013: 6.

[36] Bauckham's (2017: 433–37) main concern is that Papias in *Hist. eccl.* 3.39 portrays Matthew's gospel writing with τάξις (addressing the lack of τάξις in *GMark*), whereas the fragment in *Hist. eccl.* 3.24.5 says nothing to this effect. However, Papias could have given a cursory note about Synoptic gospel writing to introduce John's gospel writing, and in another place given a more in-depth exposition of Matthew's concern with τάξις. A point of strong similarity is that both the fragment in *Hist. eccl.* 3.39.15 and the fragment in *Hist. eccl.* 3.24.5 mention that Matthew wrote in Hebrew.

124 *Chapter 4: GMark to Justin Martyr*

criticisms of Hill's arguments meet a satisfactory explanation in Manor's modification of Hill's proposal.[37] Furthermore, even if we exclude *Hist. eccl.* 3.24.5–13 from the genuine Papian material, we would still have to reckon with the strongly Johannine naming of apostles that we see in *Hist. eccl.* 3.39.4.[38] The evidence weighs in favor of Papias' knowledge of *GJohn*.

There is, however, further evidence to support the Papian origin of *Hist. eccl.* 3.24.5–8a. This tradition on gospel origins found in *Hist. eccl.* 3.24.5–13 is the second of six such traditions in Eusebius' *Ecclesiastical History*. Eusebius' six major accounts of gospel origins appear in *Hist. eccl.* as shown in Table 12.

Table 12: Traditions of Gospel Origins Preserved by Eusebius in *Hist. eccl.*

Tradition	Reference	Alleged Tradent
1	2.15.1–2	Anonymous report shared by Clement of Alexandria and Papias
2	3.24.5–13	Anonymous
3	3.39.1–7, 15–17	Papias
4	5.8.1–4	Irenaeus
5	6.14.5–7	Clement of Alexandria
6	6.25.3–14	Origen

When placed in the order in which these traditions occur in *Hist. eccl.*, a pattern emerges. In Tradition 1 (*Hist. eccl.* 2.15.1–2), Eusebius presents an anonymous tradition that predates Clement of Alexandria and Papias. Scholars frequently claim that Eusebius attributes this tradition to Clement.[39] Eusebius says this tradition is "provided" (παρατέθειται) by Clement, and confirmed (συνεπιμαρτυρεῖ) by Papias, indicating that the source originates neither in Clement nor Papias, but predates them both. In Tradition 3 (*Hist. eccl.* 3.39.1–7 and 15–17), Eusebius cites a tradition that has been preserved in Papias' written work, but that itself is prior to Papias but also bears more of Papias' own

---

[37] Furlong 2016: 209–29 offers additional confirmation of Hill's thesis from a passage in Theodore of Mopsuestia's *Commentary on John*, praef (Greek text from Devreesse 1948: 305–07). The passage from Theodore discusses the origins of John's gospel with language parallel to Papias' fragment in *Hist. eccl.* 3.39.15 (τάξις, παραλείπω, the passive aorist of λέγω, ἀκολουθέω, the collocation of χρεία and διδασκαλία, and the collocation of ἀκριβῶς and μνημονεύω), as well as to the fragment in *Hist. eccl.* 3.24.5–8a (ἔκδοσις, διαδίδωμι, διήγησις, ἀρχὴ, and the roots ἀληθ- and λειπ-). Since Theodore does not include Eusebius' editorial remarks, Furlong concludes that Papias was the common source used by Theodore rather than Eusebius. Furlong differs from Hill, however, in that he understands *Hist. eccl.* 3.24.7–8a to be from Papias citing a tradition from a certain John who is both the Elder and the Evangelist.

[38] O'Connell 2010: 793–94 has argued that the statistical probability of Papias naming the apostles in exactly the same order as *GJohn*, without being influenced at all by *GJohn*, is highly unlikely. However, see the critique by Climenhaga 2020.

[39] E.g. Larsen 2018b: 96–98; Keith 2020: 51–52.

compositional marks. In Tradition 4 (*Hist. eccl.* 5.8.1–4), Eusebius preserves Irenaeus' account of Gospel origins. In Tradition 5 (*Hist. eccl.* 6.14.5–7), Eusebius names Clement's *Hypotyposeis* as the written source preserving a tradition of the early elders. Eusebius also says that this is Clement's own account. In Tradition 6 (*Hist. eccl.* 6.25.3–14), Eusebius names Origen's commentary on *GMatthew* as the written source of this testimony, but he also says that Origen himself learned this from an earlier tradition. Tradition 1 is pre-Papian. Tradition 3 is pre-Papian with Papias' own tweaking. Tradition 4, corroborated by *Haer.* 3.1.1, is Irenaean. Tradition 5 is pre-Clementine with Clement's own influence added. Tradition 6 is pre-Origenic with a touch of Origen's own development. Of course, Eusebius' fingerprints lie on every one of these traditions, but there is a clear progression of traditional material that Eusebius presents in Books 2–6, beginning from the time of the elders and extending to Origen. According to this pattern, then, in Eusebius' reckoning the tradition preserved in 3.24 is either contemporaneous with or predates Papias.

Therefore, with due caution, we may infer key elements of *Hist. eccl.* 3.24.5–8a as Papian tradition on the origins of the gospels. If 3.24 is not from Papias, then it is likely contemporaneous with Papias or prior to him. As such, it is a valuable source of early Christian discourse on the authorship of the gospels, and how these discrete authors, in the minds of early-second century Christians, represented Jesus books that occupied the same conceptual field while remaining distinct.

4.2.2 Analyzing the Papian Fragments

We may now analyze Papias' understanding of the texts that came to be known as the gospels. In terms of identity, we can be certain that Papias was aware of written texts that were associated with the historical figures of Mark and Matthew. If we consider *Hist. eccl.* 3.24.5–8a to be Papian, then we can conclude that Papias also had access to *GJohn*. A more conclusive piece of evidence for Papias' knowledge of *GJohn*, however, is the fact that in *Hist. eccl.* 3.39.4 Papias names Andrew, Peter, Philip, Thomas, James, and John in the same order as they appear in *GJohn*, combining the lists from *GJohn* 1 and *GJohn* 21.[40] Papias also has much shared vocabulary with *GLuke*'s preface.[41] Furthermore, the written tradition in *Hist. eccl.* 3.24.7 indicates that its author says that John was aware of *GLuke*; if this tradition comes from Papias as well, then Papias had access at least to the concept of a fourfold collection of Jesus books.

---

[40] Bauckham 2017: 417–19 develops this argument. The case for Papias' knowledge of *GJohn* is bolstered by his association with the Johannine circle in *Haer.* 5.33.4 and their interpretation of *GJn* 14.2 in *Haer.* 5.36.2.

[41] E.g. Luke's use of the words ἀνατάξασθαι (cf. Papias' τάξις and σύνταξις in *Hist. eccl.* 3.39.15–16), πραγμάτων (cf. Papias' πραχθέντα in *Hist. eccl.* 3.39.15), ἀκριβῶς (cf. *Hist. eccl.* 3.39.15), παρακολουθέω (cf. *Hist. eccl.* 3.39.4, 15); cf. Hill 1998: 625.

126 *Chapter 4: GMark to Justin Martyr*

In what follows, I will take this as my working hypothesis. Even if *Hist. eccl.* 3.24.5–8a cannot be used to reconstruct Papias' discourse on gospel origins, it is still a valuable, early testimony to Christian gospel-writing discourse. In either case, *Hist. eccl.* 3.24.5–8a demonstrates the emergence of a conceptual field occupied by all four of the proto-canonical gospels in the first half of the second century.

The following table lays out how Papias and proximate traditions discuss the authorship of the proto-canonical gospels.

Table 13: Gospel Traditions in *Hist. eccl.* 3.24.5–8a and 3.39.15–16

Reference		Aspects of Writing	Gospel
3.24.5	οὓς καὶ ἐπάναγκες ἐπὶ τὴν γραφὴν ἐλθεῖν	writing out of necessity	*GMt*; *GJn*
3.24.5	ὑπομνήματα... ἡμῖν... καταλελοίπασιν	leaving memoirs	*GMt*; *GJn*
3.39.15	ἐμνημόνευσεν ἀκριβῶς ἔγραψεν	writing accurately what he remembered	*GMk*
3.24.7	εὐαγγελίων τὴν ἔκδοσιν πεποιημένων	Making a published edition of their own work	*GMk*; *GLk*
3.24.5	οὓς καὶ ἐπάναγκες ἐπὶ τὴν γραφὴν ἐλθεῖν	put to writing	*GMt*; *GJn*
3.24.7	τῶν προαναγραφέντων τριῶν	previously written down	*GMt*; *GMk*; *GLk*
	ἔνια γράψας	writing down single points	*GMk*
3.24.7	εἰς πάντας ἤδη... διαδεδομένων	distributed to all	*GMt*; *GMk*; *GLk*
3.39.15	τῶν κυριακῶν... λογίων	The Dominical Logia	*GMk*
3.39.16	τὰ λόγια	The Logia	*GMt*
3.24.6	Ματθαῖος... πρότερον... κηρύξας...	From preaching to writing	*GMt*
3.24.7	γραφῇ παραδοὺς τὸ κατ' αὐτὸν εὐαγγέλιον	From unwritten kerygma to writing	*GJn*
3.39.15	Ἰωάννην... ἀγράφῳ κεχρημένον κηρύγματι... ἐπὶ τὴν γραφὴν ἐλθεῖν Πέτρῳ... ὃς... ἐποιεῖτο τὰς διδασκαλίας... Μάρκος... γράψας ὡς ἀπεμνημόνευσεν	From Peter's teaching to writing according to memory	*GMk*

4.2 Gospel Authorship in Papias and His Traditions

Reference			Apect of Writing	Gospel
3.39.15	τὰ ὑπὸ τοῦ κυρίου ἢ λεχθέντα ἢ πραχθέντα		what was said and done by the Lord	*GMk*
3.24.7	τὴν περὶ τῶν... ὑπὸ τοῦ Χριστοῦ πεπραγμένων διήγησιν		a narrative of what was done by Christ	*GJn*
3.39.15	οὐ μέντοι τάξει	παρηκολούθησαν... Πέτρῳ	not according to order following Peter	*GMk*
3.39.16	τὰ λόγια συνετάξατο		composing the oracles	*GMt*

It may first be observed that in *Hist. eccl.* 3.24.5–8a and 3.39.15–17, the names of the gospel authors play a key role in establishing the conceptual space in which multiple books coexist. This is a noticeable shift from prior discourse on gospel authorship (e.g. *GLk* 1.1–4). One might even say that the hermeneutical and exegetical interactions of the gospels as parallel accounts of Jesus are personified in the human interactions of the gospel authors as apostolic figures.

The names of human gospel authors yield a dizzying number of overlapping gospel combinations based on the descriptions of their composition. *GMatthew* and *GJohn* are both said to have been written "out of necessity" (ἐπάναγκες). Matthew and John are said to have left memoirs (ὑπομνήματα), and *GMark* fits this same description, having been written through a process of memory (ἐμνημόνευσεν ἀκριβῶς ἔγραψεν). Mark and Luke are both said to have made "final copies" of their gospels (εὐαγγελίων τὴν ἔκδοσιν πεποιημένων). Mark and Matthew are both said to have made a collection of Jesus' *logia*. Mark and John specifically record what Jesus did (πραχθέντα and πεπραγμένων). Matthew, John, and Mark take oral, apostolic preaching and textualize it in their gospels. *GMatthew, GMark*, and *GLuke* were all distributed (διαδεδομένων). Finally, all four proto-canonical gospels are written down in some manner.

GMatthew, GLuke, and *GJohn* occupy the same conceptual space by relating in some way to *GMark*: *GMark* and *GLuke* are described in similar terms, and the same goes for *GMark* and *GMatthew*, and *GMark* and *GJohn*. *GMark* occupies a central role in relating one gospel to another – it is a "middle term."[42]

---

[42] In scholarship on the Synoptic problem, *GMark* is commonly understood to be the "middle term" between *GMatthew* and *GLuke*, namely, the agreements between *GMatthew* and *GLuke* are typically mediated through *GMark* (Goodacre 2001: 54–76). In other words, in the Triple Tradition, *GMatthew* and *GLuke* agree with *GMark* more often than they agree with each other. *GMark* appears to be the gospel that initiated the gospel writing continued by *GMatthew, GLuke, GJohn*, and the Jesus books of the second century (Becker 2017: 117–40). *GMark* therefore functions as a yardstick by which to identify, characterize, and contrast later gospels, and we see this function in the collective witness of *Hist. eccl.* 3.24.5–8a and *Hist. eccl.* 3.39.15–16; for *GMark* as a "yardstick," see Breytenbach 2020.

128   *Chapter 4: GMark to Justin Martyr*

GMatthew and *GJohn* are described in similar terms, as written by apostles, and *GMark*, *GMatthew*, and *GJohn* are all products of apostolic memory. The Synoptics are categorized together as having chronological priority to *GJohn* and relating to different parts of Jesus' ministry than *GJohn*. In short, the compositional dynamics of the four proto-canonical gospels are deeply interrelated. The interrelations are characterized by complementary interactions among all four proto-canonical gospels. No other Jesus books feature in the testimonies preserved in 3.24.5–8a or 3.39.1–17, not even in an effort to discredit alternative Jesus accounts outside the proto-canonical four.

Of the traditions related in *Hist. eccl.* 3.24.5–8a and 3.39.1–17, those about *GMark* and *GMatthew* in 3.39.15–16 are attributed to the anonymous "Elder". This evidence indicates that the Christian discourse on the unity and diversity of various Jesus books, specifically on the relationship between *GMark* and *GMatthew*, predates Papias, going back to the "elders". It is even plausible that the traditions in *Hist. eccl.* 3.24.5–8a and 3.39.15–17 are indebted to the author of *GLuke* 1.1–4, whether directly or indirectly, consciously or unconsciously. The plausibility exists because of the overlap between vocabulary choices in *GLuke* 1.1–4 and the traditions preserved in the aforementioned passages. Luke's use of ἀνατάξασθαι is paralleled by Papias' use of both τάξις and σύνταξις. Luke's use of πραγμάτων is paralleled by Papias' use of πραχθέντα in *Hist. eccl.* 3.39.15, and by the use of πεπραγμένων in the tradition preserved in 3.24.7. Both Luke and the source in *Hist. eccl.* 3.24.7 use the term διήγησις; both use the verb παραδίδωμι. Both Luke and Papias use the adverb ἀκριβῶς and the verb παρακολουθέω (*Hist. eccl.* 3.39.15). The verbal overlap is unlikely to be a coincidence. The three most likely options are that (1) Papias is consciously shaping his account of gospel origins in Lukan vocabulary, (2) both Papias and Luke are using vocabulary commonly spoken at the turn of the century in Christian discourse on gospel origins, or (3) Papias is unconsciously using language that in the early second century was shaped by Luke's account. In each of these scenarios, what remains constant is that both Papias and Luke participate in the same Christian discourse but at different stages of development. Early Christians were concerned about how two or more books could tell the same story about Jesus; Papias develops Luke's discourse by introducing named authors and relating the historical situations and methods behind their compositional procedures.

How does Papias envisage the authority of these written texts? The title of Papias' five-volume work offers a clue: Λογίων Κυριακῶν Ἐξήγησις. There is a debate among scholars on whether to translate the word Ἐξήγησις as "account/report" or "interpretation". Based on this lexeme, some have posited that Papias wrote a commentary on the sayings of Jesus, while others have argued that Papias wrote historiography similar to the Gospel genre.[43] There is an important parallel

---

[43] Larsen 2018b: 87–93 and Watson 2013: 416–17 posit that Papias continued the same Jesus-book writing project in which the proto-canonical gospels participate. Bauckham 2014:

4.2 Gospel Authorship in Papias and His Traditions

in Clement of Alexandria's *Quis dives salvetur* that sheds some line on the meaning of this word.

> Therefore, it is necessary for those who are disposed to loving truth and loving the brethren… first of all, by means of the word (τῷ λόγῳ), to remove from the rich their newfound despair and to make clear, by the necessary exposition of the Lord's oracles (μετὰ τῆς δεούσης ἐξηγήσεως τῶν λογίων τοῦ κυρίου), that the inheritance of the kingdom of the heavens has not been completely cut off from them, if they obey the commandments.[44]

In this passage, Clement is introducing his extended discourse on *GMark* 10.17–31. After a quotation of this passage, Clement establishes this as an exposition of a gospel text: "These things are written in the gospel according to Mark, and everything shows the same harmony of meaning… in all the other accepted gospels." Clement's exegesis involves allegory, seeking "divine and mystical wisdom" (θεία σοφία καὶ μυστικῇ) in Jesus' words, not understanding them merely in "carnal" terms (σαρκίνως) but rather pursuing their "hidden meaning" (κεκρυμμένον νοῦν). Clement's collocation of ἐξηγήσεως τῶν λογίων τοῦ κυρίου offers a strong parallel with Papias' Λογίων Κυριακῶν Ἐξήγησις, and so we are justified in concluding that Papias' five-volume work involved exegesis of written gospel material.

Papias may not have written a commentary on the gospels, but the parallel with Clement confirms that he is offering an exegesis of textualized versions of the Jesus tradition. In *Hist. eccl.* 3.39.3, Papias says he has "put in ordered form" (συγκατατάξαι) the "interpretations" (ταῖς ἑρμηνείαις) that he learned from the elders. From this fragment, along with the fragments preserved in 3.39.15–17, we may deduce that the kind of interpretation that Papias is doing is different from the interpretive rewriting we see in the proto-canonical gospels. *GMatthew*, *GLuke*, and *GJohn* engage in interpretive rewriting of *GMark* without reference to Mark's role as an author. *Hist. eccl.* 3.39.15–17 shows that the authorship of *GMark* and *GMatthew* played some role in Papias' interpretation of the λογία κυριακῶν.

This is a major leap from the way *GMatthew*, *GLuke*, or *GJohn* interpret the Markan traditions they receive. The identity of the author of *GMark* has no bearing on these later gospels' interpretive processes of Jesus tradition preserved therein. On the contrary, Papias is interested enough in the apostolic authorship and historical background to the writing of Jesus books to preserve these traditions in writing, and these author-centric details must have played some role in his interpretation of the λογία κυριακῶν. Even if Papias' Ἐξήγησις is not commentary proper, it is a significant step toward the second-order discourse of

---

488 argues that Papias' work was historiography that was "something like a Gospel." Baum 1996 believes Papias' work to be commentary on Jesus' sayings drawn from canonical gospels, and Norelli 2005: 59–112 holds it to be commentary, but on oral sayings of Jesus rather than on authoritative texts.

[44] *Quis div.* 3; my translation. Greek text from LCL 92.274.

130   *Chapter 4: GMark to Justin Martyr*

Irenaeus and Clement of Alexandria, where the identities of the gospel authors bear on the interpretation of the gospel traditions preserved under their names, and toward the mature, lemmatized gospel commentary that we see in Origen and his scholarly predecessor, Heracleon.[45] In the later Christian commentary on the written gospel, the authority of the gospel text, inextricably linked with the apostolic authority of the authors, is presupposed. Papias' reflections on gospel tradition are not this developed, but his work can be placed on the same trajectory.

Christoph Markschies and Richard Bauckham are correct in arguing that Papias' ἐξήγησις is not a commentary on one or more Jesus books.[46] However, Papias' five-volume work does mark a shift in the reception of written Jesus tradition: by the time of Papias' writing, *GMark*, *GMatthew*, *GJohn*, and most likely *GLuke* were distinguishable entities within the same conceptual field, and they were already being interpreted in second-order discourse rather than merely rewritten. The way Papias reflected on *GMark*, *GMatthew*, *GJohn*, and *GLuke* differed with how the latter three Jesus books rewrote the first. Papias' discourse on gospel writing is more developed than Luke's, Matthew's, or John's. While he is arguably influenced by Luke, he introduces named gospel authors into the discussion, and he preserves in writing the first account of gospel interrelations. In these ways, Papias significantly develops the conceptual field of gospel writing by introducing author names as a mode by which to distinguish one Jesus book from another within its same genus. Finally, with Papias, the identity of Jesus-book authors first plays a role in the interpretation of the Jesus tradition and in the authorizing of that tradition.

4.3 Gospel Authors and Their Texts in New Testament Apocrypha

Numerous second-century books in the New Testament Apocrypha give data regarding how early Christians conceived of the role of the gospel author and his text, and the way in which one particular Jesus book interacted with others. Three tendencies emerge in these accounts: competitive textuality, solo performances, and apostolic collaboration.

4.3.1 Competitive Textuality

In the *Apocryphon of James* (*ApJas*), the *Gospel of Judas* (*GJudas*), and *GThomas*, secret revelation is given to a privileged pair of apostles or a single

---

[45] Origen's commentary presupposes and preserves an earlier commentary by Heracleon, who at least in one instance seems to reference John's role as author to aid the interpretation of the text of *GJohn* (*Comm. Jo.* fr. 3); cf. Gathercole 2018b: 468; Gunther 1980: 401; the fragment is documented in Brooke 1891: 55.

[46] Markschies 2015: 220; Bauckham 2014.

4.3 Gospel Authors and Their Texts in New Testament Apocrypha

apostle, and the other apostles are explicitly excluded from the sphere of textualized secret revelation. In *ApJas*, the apostle James recounts how the twelve disciples were gathered, writing down Jesus' teachings into books (both secretly and openly). Jesus pulls James and Peter aside from the other ten disciples and gives them secret revelation that they are to write down. This secret book is purported to have been written with the Hebrew alphabet, which is most likely an attempt to validate its originality over against competitors. *ApJas* constructs James and Peter as unique arbiters and "textualizers" of Jesus tradition, whose books have higher authority than others. In *ApJas* we see some of the earliest signs of a dynamic that says, "these books and not those." Through his written Jesus tradition, the apostolic author in these books claims superiority over other Jesus books. Essential to the message is the implication that "my Jesus book is better than the others."[47]

In *GJudas*, Jesus repeatedly takes Judas aside and gives him secret knowledge concealed from the rest of the twelve.[48] What Judas sees and declares about Jesus subverts much of the proto-orthodox Jesus tradition.[49] With *GJudas* we have another case of competitive textuality that establishes the boundaries of authority, and it excludes other Jesus books from the same conceptual category.[50]

In *GThomas* 13.6–8, Jesus picks Thomas out of the twelve and gives him exclusive access to secret revelations. More than a hint of animosity ensues when the other disciples question Thomas regarding what Jesus revealed to him in secret.[51] Earlier in this same *logion*, Thomas is placed alongside the testimony of Peter and Matthew in a setting with thick allusions to *GMatthew* 16:13–16 and its parallels. This *logion* is a possible reference to *GPeter* or *GMark* and a probable reference to *GMatthew*.[52] Thomas is elevated to a higher playing field than his fellow apostles, and by implication *GThomas* is exalted above its predecessors. When read in conjunction with the incipit of *GThomas*,[53] the portrait of Thomas as a gospel author with exclusive access to esoteric teaching of Jesus is

---

[47] Cf. Lindenlaub 2020.

[48] *GJudas* 35.14–36.10; 42.25–58.6.

[49] See, for example, Jesus' disparaging of the Eucharist (*GJudas* 33.22–35.14) and his mocking of the apostolate (*GJudas* 37.20–42.24).

[50] On the competitive impulses of *GJudas* against earlier gospels and other forms of Christianity, see Gathercole 2007: 161–71; Brankaer and van Os 2019: 30–41, 53–55.

[51] *GTh* 13.6–8: "And he took him [i.e. Thomas] and withdrew, and spoke three words to him. When Thomas returned to his companions, they asked him, 'What did Jesus say to you?' Thomas said to them, 'If I told you one of the words which he spoke to me, you would pick up stones and throw them at me. But fire would come forth from the stones, and burn you.'" Translation from Gathercole 2014: 259.

[52] Gathercole 2012a: 169–74.

[53] *GTh* incipit: "These are the [secret] sayings [which] the living Jesus [spo]ke [as Judas] Thomas w[rote them down] (Greek); "These are the secret sayings which the living Jesus spoke, and Didymus Judas Thomas wrote them down." Translation from Gathercole 2014: 189.

132 *Chapter 4: GMark to Justin Martyr*

clear. The author of *GThomas* is establishing his Jesus book as superior to the rest.[54] Competitive textuality is evident in *GThomas*.

4.3.2 Solo Performances

In the case of the *Infancy Gospel of Thomas*, the *Protevangelium of James*, and the *Gospel of Peter*, the author describes his own act of textualizing Jesus tradition, eliciting his own self-authentication as a Jesus-book author, but not necessarily at the exclusion of other Jesus-book authors or their books. *IGThomas*, *PJas*, and *GPeter*, though they show indebtedness to earlier gospels, lack explicit mention of other Jesus books or their authors. *IGThomas* begins: "I, Thomas, the Israelite, announce and make known to you all, brothers from among the Gentiles, the mighty childhood deeds of our Lord Jesus Christ..."[55] Similarly, *PJas* concludes: "Now I, James, wrote this history in Jerusalem when tumult arose on the death of Herod, and withdrew into the desert until the tumult in Jerusalem ceased."[56] The author of *GPeter* also speaks in the first person (plural and singular) in *GPeter* 14.59–60: "But we, the twelve disciples of the Lord, wept and were saddened, and each being sad because of the event withdrew to his house. But I, Simon Peter, and Andrew my brother, taking our nets went to the sea..."[57] Singular authorship in these Jesus books is characterized by silence about other Jesus books – even gospels to which they are indebted. The authors conspicuously name themselves in the body of their texts, in contrast with the proto-canonical four, which name their authors only in the superscriptions. Gospel authorship develops from formal anonymity in the proto-canonical gospels to self-identified authorship in several second-century gospels.[58]

4.3.3 Apostolic Collaboration

As we saw in Chapter 2, the author of *EpAp* gives evidence for another take on gospel writing in the second century: Jesus-book writing as a collective effort. The author describes the process of textualization as hearing, remembering, and writing (in that order), and it is the eleven apostles (twelve, minus Judas Iscariot,

---

[54] As shown in the incipit of *GThomas* (see above, Section 1.2.5); cf. Keith 2020: 154–60.

[55] Translation from Elliott 1993: 75.

[56] Translation from Elliott 1993: 66–67.

[57] Translation from Foster 2010: 205.

[58] Hurtado 2006b speaks of the emergence of "author-consciousness" in second-century Christianity, building on Barbara Aland's concept of "text-consciousness" in that same period (Barbara Aland 1989). The role of the gospel author was probably accentuated in second-century gospels because of competing claims of authority in diverse Christian sects (Hartenstein 2010). Lindenlaub 2020, building on the authorial categories set forth by King 2016, traces the transformation of the gospel authors as an agent in *GJohn* and developing further in the second century in *EpAp* and *ApJas*.

4.3 Gospel Authors and Their Texts in New Testament Apocrypha 133

Peter is named twice to bring the number to twelve), who are behind the first-person plurals:

What we have heard and remembered we have written for the whole world... We write to the churches of the East and West, to those in the North and South, announcing and making known to you the things concerning Jesus Christ. We have written about how we both heard him and touched him after he rose from the dead.[59]

What is striking is the difference between how the apostolic gospel authors interact in *ApJas* and in *EpAp*.[60] In the former, there is an implicitly competitive tenor between the pseudepigraphal James and the rest of the apostles (except for Peter, who partly shares in the special revelation given to James). The rest of the apostles write books according to what they remember Jesus saying, but James has an advantage in that Jesus revealed special knowledge to him. In the latter, however, the apostles display a firm catholicity, expressed in the first common plural verb ጸሐፍነ (we have written). Their teaching is neither secret nor esoteric, but it is public and intended "for the whole world" (ለኵሉ ፡ ዓለም). There is no competition between authors or special knowledge given to one over the other; rather, the apostles are portrayed as eleven authors of the one gospel (ቃለ ፡ ወንጌል – "the word of the gospel"). Interestingly, in *EpAp* 31.11 the gospel authors are even commanded by the risen Jesus to convey their written gospel to the Apostle Paul – an indication that *EpAp* is engaging in proto-canonical integration, if not canonical hermeneutics.[61] *EpAp* displays competitive textuality, but not against any of the eleven apostles – rather, it is directed against the heretics Simon and Cerinthus. Regarding the apostolic collective, *EpAp* shows the same dynamic we saw earlier – a congenial colloquium of apostolic voices that together write the story of Jesus.

The competitive textuality, solo authorship, and apostolic collaboration displayed in various New Testament Apocrypha demonstrate that second-century Christians had multiple strategies for relating one Jesus book to another. Some of these strategies enabled the process of gospel combination and collection, and some of these strategies worked against it. The movement toward gospel collections was not unilateral, but pluriform and dynamic, involving a dialectic between the one gospel message and multiple gospel authors. This dialectic continues in the writings of Justin Martyr.

---

[59] *EpAp* 1.3–5; 2.1–3; translation from Hills 2009: 21–22.

[60] Hill 2010b: 169–76 hypothesizes that *EpAp* was written in response to *ApJas*, which would make sense of the differences in how each book portrays apostolic interactions. On the plausibility of a relationship between these two texts, see Hartenstein 2000: 224–29.

[61] See Chapter 2.

134 *Chapter 4: GMark to Justin Martyr*

4.4 Justin Martyr

Justin Martyr, as a teacher and leader of a Christian community in Rome at the midpoint of the second century, illuminates the development of Christian discourse about gospel authors, their books, and how two or more written gospels could be grouped together. Justin's relationship to the gospels has been the subject of debate in recent years. After half a century of scholarship investigating the redactional features of gospels in Justin's writings, it seems probable that Justin had access to a written form of *GMatthew* and *GLuke*, and that he also used a harmonized version of these texts.[62] At present, the balance seems to be weighing in favor of Justin also having access to *GJohn*, though he uses this gospel much less frequently.[63] A single reference to Markan redactional material as belonging to a "memoir of Peter,"[64] as well as the extensive use of *GMark* by Justin's student Tatian,[65] make it more than likely that Justin also had some form of *GMark* at his disposal. Most citations from Justin's ἀπομνημονεύματα are paralleled in the Synoptic tradition. This includes Matthean *Sondergut* and redaction, Lukan *Sondergut* and redaction, Double Tradition, and Triple Tradition, covering Jesus' nativity, baptism, teaching, passion, crucifixion, resurrection, and ascension.[66] Verbal overlap with Johannine material outnumbers the overlap with noncanonical sources.[67]

---

[62] Kline 1975: 223–41; Bellinzoni 1967: 139–42, Koester 1990: 360–402, and Petersen 1990: 512–34 argue that Justin composed a gospel harmony with Synoptic material. Stanton 2004: 92–109 makes a strong case for Justin's access to *GMatthew*, *GLuke*, *GMark*, and even *GJohn.* Thornton 1993: 93–100 also makes a case for *GMark.* For a comprehensive list of gospel citations and allusions in Justin's *Dialogue*, see Allert 2002: 155–75.

[63] Stanton 2004: 92–109, Hill 2004: 316–42; 2007: 88–94, 191–93; 2010b: 233–300, Skarsaune 2007: 53–76, and Barker 2015b: 543–58 leave the *status quaestionis* in favor of Justin's use of *GJohn.*

[64] *Dial.* 106.3–4.

[65] See Chapter 3; on Tatian's use of *GMark* and how this dismantles the myth of Mark's disappearance in the second century, see Barker 2019: 127–28, 135–38.

[66] Koester 1990: 360–402 gives a meticulous analysis of the Synoptic quotations in Justin Martyr, and he concludes that Justin used a harmonized version if *GMatthew*, *GLuke*, and possibly *GMark*, as well as access to individual gospels including at least *GMatthew* and *GLuke*; cf. Bellinzoni 1967.

[67] Cf. Hill 2004: 312–42. Hill's cumulative case consists of strong verbal parallels with *GJn* 1.13 (*1 Apol.* 21.1; 23.2; 32.9; *Dial.* 54.2; 63.2); *GJn* 1.14 (*1 Apol.* 21.1; 22.2; 23.2; *Dial.* 61.1, 3; 76.2); *GJn* 1.20 // 3.28 (*Dial.* 88.7); *GJn* 3.3, 5 (*1 Apol.* 61.4); 19.13 (*1 Apol.* 35). Hill also includes parallels with how Justin cites Zech 12.10–14 (*Dial.* 14.8; 32.2; *1 Apol.* 52.12 // *GJn* 19.37); Isaiah 6.10 (*Dial.* 33.1 // *GJn* 12.40); Num 21.8–9 (*Dial.* 33.1 // *GJn* 3.14).

4.4 *Justin Martyr* 135

Justin identifies his Jesus books as "the memoirs composed by [the apostles], which are called gospels."[68] He also refers to these books as "the memoirs... drawn up by his [Christ's] apostles and those who followed them."[69] While εὐαγγέλιον is not Justin's preferred term, he accepts its usage. Justin is one of the earliest examples of the formula, "in the gospel it is written," using it to introduce Jesus' saying in *GMatthew* 11.27.[70] Justin's use of this formula is characteristic of the Christian milieu he inhabited, which, by the middle of the second century, had begun to reflect exegetically on the canonical gospels as books.[71] Justin's understanding of the apostolic memoirs as *gospels* is embedded within his biblical theology – a point not yet recognized in scholarship. Analysis of the verb εὐαγγελίζομαι in the writings of Justin demonstrates that his understanding of gospel writing is rooted in the prophetic tradition and the earthly preaching of Jesus himself. According to Justin's interpretation of the Jewish Scriptures, the pre-incarnate Jesus was the angel who "evangelized" Sarah, Abraham, Jacob, and Moses (*Dial.* 56). The prophets – David, Isaiah, and Jeremiah – evangelized about the coming of Christ (*Dial.* 29; 73; 74; 136). The content of their prophetic evangel was nothing other than "the mystery of salvation" accomplished through the suffering, death, resurrection, and enthronement of Jesus Christ (*Dial.* 74; 100). The ministry of John the Baptist is predicted in the prophets to be a ministry of evangelism (*Dial.* 50). Justin describes Jesus' entire public ministry after his baptism as one of evangelizing (*Dial.* 51). In short, Justin argues that the gospel message of salvation through Jesus was originally proclaimed by the pre-incarnate Christ, predicted through the ministry of the prophets, preached by John the Baptist, and finally preached, embodied, and fulfilled by Jesus of Nazareth.

The question remains: does Justin's use of the verb εὐαγγελίζομαι relate to his use of the noun εὐαγγέλιον to describe a written text? We can answer in the affirmative when we see how Justin traces a trajectory from prophetic "gospelizing", to Jesus' "gospelizing", to apostolic oral "gospelizing", to written gospel. We have already seen the lexical link between the prophetic evangel to Jesus' evangel, and Justin gives just as clear of a connection between the apostolic evangel and the written gospel. In *Dial.* 100–108, Justin gives extended proof of the

---

[68] *1 Apol.* 66.3; οἱ γὰρ ἀπόστολοι ἐν τοῖς γενομένοις ὑπ᾽αὐτῶν ἀπομνημονεύμασιν, ἃ καλεῖται εὐαγγέλια κτλ; all Greek text from *1 Apol.* cited in this chapter are from Minns and Parvis 2009.

[69] *Dial.* 103.8; Ἐν γὰρ τοῖς Ἀπομνημονεύμασιν, ἃ φημι ὑπὸ τῶν ἀποστόλων αὐτοῦ καὶ τῶν ἐκείνοις παρακολουτησάντων συντετάχθαι, κτλ; all Greek text from *Dial.* cited in this chapter are from Marcovich 2005.

[70] *Dial.* 100.1: καὶ ἐν τῷ εὐαγγελίῳ δὴ γέγραπται εἰπών κτλ. Justin only uses this formula once, and he anticipates the regular usage by Irenaeus, Clement of Alexandria, and Origen. The Valentinian *Treatise on the Resurrection* offers a possibly contemporary parallel phrase: "remember reading in the gospel" (NHC 1.4.48.8–9); cf. Watson 2013: 436n94.

[71] Ayres 2015 locates Justin in this milieu alongside the Valentinians that were conducting allegorical exegesis of *GMatthew* (Ptolemy) and *GJohn* (Heracleon).

136   *Chapter 4: GMark to Justin Martyr*

fulfillment of the prophetic evangel he establishes earlier in the *Dialogue* (e.g. *Dial.* 29; 50; 51; 56; 73; 74). His proof in *Dial.* 100–108 comes from a cluster of citations from the "memoirs (ἀπομνημονεύματα) of the apostles" (*Dial.* 100; 101; 102; 103; 104; 105 [2x]; 106 [3x]; 107). These memoirs are the written deposit of the oral proclamation of the apostles. *Dial.* 109–110 describes the apostles' ministry of proclamation extending outward from Jerusalem as a fulfillment of the *traditio legis* in Micah 4.2 (cf. Isaiah 2.3), that the λόγος and the νόμος would go forth from Zion/Jerusalem,[72] and *Dial.* 100–108 locates the content of this apostolic proclamation in the ἀπομνημονεύματα. This shows the link between the prophetic evangel, the apostolic evangel, and the ἀπομνημονεύματα.

We can go a step further and identify this chain of prophetic and apostolic tradition as the process that birthed the written gospel. In *Dial.* 100, Justin says:

> I have demonstrated that it is not only in the blessing of Joseph and Judah that the things about Him [i.e. Jesus] were proclaimed in a mystery, but also in the Gospel it is written (ἀλλὰ καὶ ἐν τῷ εὐαγγελίῳ δὴ γέγραπται) that He said: "All things are delivered unto me by my Father…"[73]

In this chapter, Justin refers to the angel Gabriel's role in this chain of tradition as "evangelizing" the Virgin Mary with the news that she should bear the son of God who would fulfill the hopes of the prophets. The intertextual links are so vivid, it is abundantly clear that, according to Justin, the written gospel, preserved in the apostolic memoirs, is the same evangel the apostles proclaimed, and it is an extension of the very message Jesus and the prophets before him proclaimed, indeed what the pre-incarnate Christ proclaimed long before his birth by Mary. Justin's definition of τὰ εὐαγγέλια, then, would be written deposits of the apostolic *kerygma* and the teachings of Jesus. Importantly, with Justin, we see the first mention of written gospels in the plural, as a finite collection of Jesus books (*1 Apol.* 66.3). Justin defines this collection as finite by identifying it as the memoirs of the apostles and those who followed them; it is delimited by the lifespan and finite number of the apostles and their followers.

Justin's language of a collection of gospels invites the dynamics of gospel combination we have already seen in our study: identities, mode, integrity, interactions, and authority. We mentioned above that Justin identifies his gospels as written by the apostles and those who followed them. This is likely to include *GMark*, since Justin cites Markan redaction,[74] and since Mark was regarded as

---

[72] Justin brings the lexeme διαθήκη into the same conceptual domain as λόγος and νόμος to describe the phenomenon that goes forth from Zion in the last days (*Dial.* 24.1; 109.2; 110.2; 122.5); Rodriguez 2020: 498–501.

[73] Translation my own.

[74] In *Dial.* 106.3–4, Justin recalls an event recorded in the ἀπομνημονεύματα of Peter that Jesus changed Peter's name, and the sons of Zebedee to "Boanerges." Given that *GMark* was closely associated with Peter since the tradition from Papias' elder, and that only *GMark* makes reference to the nickname "Boanerges" (*GMk* 3.17), it is all but certain that *GMark* was the gospel that Justin refers to as the "memoirs of him [i.e. Peter]" (καὶ γεγράφθαι ἐν τοῖς

one who followed Peter.[75] It is also likely to include *GMatthew*, since Justin draws frequently on Matthean material and since Matthew was considered by the mid second century to have been an apostolic gospel author.[76] If we take the tradition of *Hist. eccl.* 3.24.5–8a as a precursor to Justin, then we might also add *GLuke* and *GJohn* to the identities of gospels in Justin's collection, since he gives redactional features from each of these gospels.

There are four instances where Justin draws on details that are paralleled in noncanonical gospels: Jesus' birth in cave (*Dial.* 78.7–8; cf. *PJas* 18.1; 19.1),[77] the fire at Jesus' baptism (*Dial.* 88.3; cf. *GEb apud* Epiphanius *Pan.* 30.13.3–4),[78] the casting of lots for Jesus' clothes (*Dial.* 97.3; cf. *GPeter* 4.12),[79] and the nails in Jesus' hands (*1 Apol.* 35.7; cf. *GPeter* 6.21). In each of these cases, the noncanonical detail appears embedded within a canonically structured account. The cave as the location of Jesus' birth is mentioned in an account of Jesus' birth that is Matthean with some Lukan elements.[80] The fire at Jesus' baptism colors a Synoptic account of Jesus' baptism,[81] a pattern reflected in the Old Latin manuscript tradition of *GMatthew* 3.16.[82] The casting of lots and nails in Jesus' hands fit within Johannine-textured accounts of Jesus' passion.[83] In Justin's accounts

---

Ἀπομνημονεύμασιν αὐτοῦ); cf. Stanton 2004: 100–01; Hill 2010b: 132–35. Marcovich 2005: 252 supplies <τῶν ἀποστόλων> after ἀπομνημονεύμασιν, but it is not in the manuscript tradition.

[75] *Hist. eccl.* 2.15.1–2; 3.39.15.

[76] Justin's many citations and allusions to *GMatthew* are well known (see Massaux 1993: 10–44, 49–89); on Matthew as an apostolic author, see Papias' testimony in *Hist. eccl.* 3.39.16, and possibly *Hist. eccl.* 3.24.5; see also the portrayal of Matthew as a gospel author in *GTh* 13 (see Gathercole 2018b: 469–70).

[77] Jesus' birth in a cave was possibly a local tradition known to Justin as well as to the author of *PJas* (19.1–3; 21.3) and Origen (*Cels.* 1.51).

[78] Justin mentions the "fire" (πῦρ), but *GEb* mentions a "great light" (φῶς μέγα).

[79] *GPeter* and *GJohn*, against the Synoptics, use the phrase λαχμὸν βάλλω (*GPet* 4.12) or the cognate verb λαγχάνω (*GJn* 19.24) to describe the lots that were cast; Justin uses the expression λαχμὸν βάλλοντες as well as the phrase used in the Synoptics and in LXX Psalm 21 (22).19, κλῆρον βάλλω.

[80] *Dial.* 78.5; *Dial.* 78.1–8 is filled with *Sondergut* from *GMatthew* (e.g. the Magi's journey and gifts, the fulfilment of the prophecy from Micah 5.2, the angel warning Joseph in a dream not to divorce Mary, and the flight to Egypt) and *GLuke* (Joseph going to Bethlehem for the census, and the absence of available lodging).

[81] *Dial.* 88, parallels the accounts about John the Baptist's ministry in *GMt* 3.1–6, 11, *GMk* 1.2–8, and *GLk* 3.1–6, 15–16, and the accounts of Jesus' baptism in *GMt* 3.13–17, *GMk* 1.9–11, and *GLk* 3.21–23. *Dial.* 88.7 even includes a four-word exact parallel to Johannine redaction in the account of John the Baptist's preaching: οὐκ εἰμὶ ὁ Χριστός (*GJn* 1.20). *Dial.* 88 bears the marks of an account composed of harmonized Synoptic and Johannine materials.

[82] E.g. the fourth-century Codex Vercellensis and the ninth-century Codex Sangermanensis (which stems from a fifth-century pandect); Houghton 2016: 213–14; Hill 2019: 44.

[83] Justin's account of the passion and crucifixion in *1 Apol.* 35 contains the following Johannine elements: Pilate seating Jesus on the βῆμα (a plausible interpretation of *GJn* 19.13),

138 *Chapter 4: GMark to Justin Martyr*

from the ἀπομνημονεύματα, details that could later be identified as noncanonical are insertions in a body of gospel material that consists almost exclusively of the canonical four – a pattern we saw in *EpAp*, the *Diatessaron*, and in the gospel manuscript tradition.

Justin uses the verbs γράφω (8x), συντάσσω (1x), and γίνομαι (1x) to describe the compositional process of these apostolic memoirs.[84] In his teaching and writing, Justin brought the gospels into company with one another by grouping them into a collective body as εὐαγγέλια or ἀπομνημονεύματα. His *mode* of gospel combination was conceptual. If Justin's extensive knowledge of Matthean and Lukan redaction and *Sondergut* is indication of access to *GMatthew* and *GLuke* as physical realia, then we might deduce that his church community had a collection of two or more gospels. His weekly gathering, to which Christians journeyed every Sunday to hear the Scriptures read aloud, would have brought two or more gospels into physical company with one another as a physical collection of Scripture together with the Old Testament. In this sense, Justin engaged a physical mode of gospel collection as well as a conceptual one. Justin does not give much evidence regarding the integrity of each of the ἀπομνημονεύματα, but he does give us a clue about how one book of ἀπομνημονεύματα can be distinguished from another. Justin can speak of the "memoirs of Peter,"[85] presumably distinguishing this from the memoirs of other apostles. The fact that books of ἀπομνημονεύματα can be distinguished from one another by the apostolic persona to which they are connected presupposes the integrity of individual gospel books. On the other hand, Justin harmonizes citations of gospel material, particularly material paralleled in *GMatthew* and *GLuke*.[86] Justin has an ambidextrous handling of gospel books – he can harmonize them and treat them as discrete.[87] The gospels interact in diverse ways when Justin brings them into proximity with one another.

---

the nails in Jesus' hands (cf. *GJn* 20.25, 27), and the casting of lots (λάχμος) for Jesus' garment (cf. *GJn* 19.24). These elements have parallels in *GPeter*, but the case is stronger for dependence on *GJohn* than *GPeter* (e.g. *GPet* 3.7 uses καθέδρα κρίσεως instead of βῆμα); cf. Foster 2007: 104–12, 198–200; Greschat 2007: 197–214. *GPeter* likely drew from *GJohn*, which would explain the parallels (Hill 2004: 306–09).

[84] γράφω: *Dial.* 88.3; 100.4; 101.3; 103.5; 104.1; 105.6; 106.3, 4; 107.1. συντάσσω: *Dial.* 103.7. γίνομαι: *1 Apol.* 66.3.

[85] *Dial.* 106.

[86] There are clusters of Synoptic harmonization in *1 Apol.* 15–17 (various teaching material), *1 Apol.* 32–34 and *Dial.* 100 (birth narratives), *Dial.* 49 and *Dial.* 88 (John the Baptist's preaching), and *1 Apol.* 35, *1 Apol.* 38, *Dial.* 97, and *Dial.* 101 (Jesus' passion). These clusters lead Bellinzoni 1967: 139–42 and Koester 1990: 360–402 to conclude that Justin composed a gospel harmony.

[87] On Justin's (and later, Tatian's) parallel use of a gospel harmony and discrete gospel books, see Perrin 2019: 93–109.

4.4 Justin Martyr

Justin accords authority to his collection of apostolic ἀπομνημονεύματα.[88] In *1 Apol.* 67, Justin describes the communal reading practices of the church in Rome, which are centered in a weekly, liturgical, Sunday gathering.[89] Justin explains that the ἀπομνημονεύματα are read alongside the writings of the prophets, establishing a likely parallel with contemporary Jewish synagogue readings of Torah. Jewish communal reading in the first and second centuries embodied covenant praxis that echoed the textual events of Sinai that were foundational for Jewish identity in the ancient world.[90] In Exodus, Moses read the Book of the Covenant to Israel on Sinai, and from the Deuteronomist to Ezra, from Qumran to Philo, from Paul to the Mishnah, communal reading events mimicked the archetypal Sinai event with its covenantal texture.[91] The Torah functioned as a covenant document in these corporate acts of reading. Considering Justin's theology of the λόγος, νόμος, and διαθήκη going out from Zion to the nations in the last days,[92] one can deduce that the apostolic ἀπομνημονεύματα were for Justin the written form of this eschatological new covenant. The public reading of these texts embodied a covenant praxis analogous to contemporary Jewish Torah readings. The ἀπομνημονεύματα were likely to be covenant documents for Justin and his community. In short, Justin appears to treat this combination of gospels as authoritative Scripture.

Justin Martyr envisages the written gospel as a single and pluriform entity. One gospel can be distinguished from another based on the apostle authoring it or standing behind its composition, or the apostolic follower who authored it. On the other hand, two gospels can be blended when their parallels are conflated in citation. We can deduce Justin's use of *GMatthew, GLuke, GMark*, and *GJohn*. Noncanonical traditions occasionally latch onto the primary sources he accesses for authoritative Jesus tradition, but these traditions are in the minority, and we can say no more than that they contributed to the pool of Jesus tradition available. Justin demonstrates the requisite grammar for discourse about a fourfold gospel

---

[88] The following section is developed more fully in Rodriguez 2020: 496–515.

[89] Kloppenborg 2014b, Cirafesi and Fewster 2016, and Leonhard 2018 argue that Justin's reading habits resembled that of a philosophical association rather than Jewish synagogue readings, but these do not need to be mutually exclusive. At a time when Jewish covenantal language was suspect to Roman authorities after the Bar Kokhba revolt, Justin could be portraying his community to the Roman government in terms they would welcome while downplaying resemblances with Jewish covenantal practices.

[90] See Rodriguez 2017: 91–117.

[91] Exod 24.1–11; Deut 31.9–13; Josh 8.34–45; 2 Kgs 23.1–3; Neh 8.1–18. From Qumran: 1QSa 1.1–5; 1QS 5.20–23; 1QS 6.7–8. From Paul and other early Christian sources: 2 Cor 3.14–15; Acts 15.21. From the *Mishnah* and *Talmud*: *m.Meg.* 3.5; 4.1–5; *m.Yoma* 7.1; 7.8; *m.Ber.* 9.5; *y.Meg.* 4.1, 75a. See also *Epist. Arist.* 311, Josephus (*Ant.* 4.209–11; 16.43–44; *Apion.* 2.169), Philo (*Hypoth.* 7.9–14), and the Theodotus Inscription (*CIJ* 2.1404). For an explanation of these texts, see Rodriguez 2017: 91–117; Rodriguez 2020: 506–13.

[92] *Dial.* 24.1; 109.2; 110.2; 122.5; *1 Apol.* 39.1; 45.5; 49.5; see Rodriguez 2020.

140   *Chapter 4: GMark to Justin Martyr*

– a grammar for the pluriform, authoritative, delimited, written gospel. The broad picture that is now emerging is that the authentic Papian tradition in *Hist. eccl.* 3.39, as well as the anonymous tradition in *Hist. eccl.* 3.24.5–8a (arguably Papian), are not isolated anomalies. Nor is Justin reasoning in an unprecedented way. These were all paving the way for Irenaeus' fourfold gospel.

4.5 Summary and Conclusions

In this chapter we have surveyed Christian authors from Mark to Justin Martyr. We have highlighted the patterns that would come to fruition in the Christian discourse about several gospel books coexisting as written deposits of the words, deeds, and *kerygma* of Jesus of Nazareth. These patterns begin within the earliest gospels, with *GMark*, *GMatthew*, *GLuke*, and *GJohn* introducing and developing the concepts of gospel author(s) and their texts. In the first quarter of the second century, Papias develops this discourse by naming gospel authors, and using their names to differentiate the texts they represent. Herein the simultaneous unity and diversity of the written gospel begin to emerge with clarity. With Papias, the gospel texts also take on enough stability for them to be interpreted exegetically.

The concept of unity within diversity of the written gospel is continued in *EpAp*, which speaks of an apostolic collective that collaborates to author the gospel as a deposit of eyewitness testimony. However, this is not the only strategy for envisaging the textualization of Jesus tradition. *ApJas*, *GJudas*, and *GThomas* speak of competition among apostolic voices vying for the most authoritative account of Jesus. *IGThomas*, *PJas*, and *GPeter* make no mention either of collaboration or competition, but give a solo performance in their recollection of parts of Jesus' life. These NT apocrypha show a diversity in how gospel writing was envisaged in the second century. Interestingly, these NT Apocrypha do not find themselves in any standardized or consistent collection of Jesus books. No early Christians ever advocate for an alternative two-, three-, four-, or five-fold collection of noncanonical gospels.[93]

In the writings of Justin Martyr, we see further developments in Christian discourse on Jesus books. Justin can speak of multiple written versions of the one gospel. He can highlight a particular gospel author and he can also speak of the generic apostolic authorship of the gospels. He anchors the written gospel in the trajectory of prophetic revelation, fulfilled by Jesus and issued forth from Jerusalem by the apostles in the last days. Justin's gospels bear authority as covenant documents read in parallel with the OT Scriptures, and as such they have a textual integrity that enables exegetical reflection. Nevertheless, Justin's gospel texts are flexible enough to be harmonized. Justin's gospels – arguably all four proto-

---

[93] One might consider Marcion's and Tatian's one-gospel solutions as exceptions that confirm this general trend.

4.5 Summary and Conclusions 141

canonical gospels – are several, distinguishable memoirs of the apostolic kerygma that can be treated in fixed and flexible forms.

As early as the proto-canonical gospels, the conceptual space was expanding to allow more than one account into the congenial company of gospels. Through the personas of gospel authors, the *identities* of certain gospels distinguished themselves in a pool of written Jesus tradition. With distinct identities, gospel texts begin to exhibit textual *integrity* – an integrity that facilitated exegetical reflection. From at least the time of Papias, proto-canonical gospels often *interacted* congenially. Noncanonical gospels, on the other hand, often interacted in competition with other gospels. The *mode* by which proto-canonical gospels kept company was a conceptual one – in the discourse of early Christians. This discourse was transmitted and developed through oral traditions (as with Papias' Elder), but we only know it through the written record of early Christian authors. As early as *GLuke* and *GJohn*, the *authority* of the gospel text was envisaged as a collective authority in which an individual Jesus book could participate, based on its adherence to original apostolic tradition kept by the eyewitnesses and servants of the word. This authorization of gospel texts continued through Justin Martyr, and as we shall see in the next chapter, it became even more explicit in the writings of Irenaeus and his contemporaries.

Chapter 5

Second-Order Discourse on Gospel Authors and Their Texts, Part 2: Irenaeus, Clement, Heretics, and Celsus

In the previous chapter we located a trajectory from Mark to Justin Martyr in which gospel books gradually took shape, were differentiated from one another, and began to interact with one another. We noticed how the four proto-canonical gospels, from their inception, interacted without any antipathy toward one another, and as early as Papias, Synoptic and Johannine gospels were brought together to be read in concert. In contrast with the predominant pattern of second-century, noncanonical gospels, the proto-canonical Four gradually lent themselves to be considered as a diverse but united family in the period leading up to Justin Martyr. This trend crystallizes in the second half of the second century, in the writings of Irenaeus and Clement, and even in the writings of "heretics" and "pagans."[1]

5.1 Irenaeus

We have now arrived at Lyons in the last two decades of the second century. The bishop and migrant theologian, Irenaeus of Smyrna, writes concerning the four gospels:

It is not possible that the Gospels can be either more or fewer in number than they are. For, since there are four zones of the world in which we live, and four catholic winds, while the Church is scattered throughout all the world, and the pillar and ground of the Church is the gospel and the Spirit of life, it is fitting that she should have four pillars, breathing out

---

[1] I do not use these terms pejoratively. I use the terms "heretical" and "heretic" to describe Christian groups initiated by charismatic figures who intentionally founded sects (αἱρέσεις) either as a subgroup within the Great Church (e.g. Valentinus and his followers), or as an anti-movement in opposition to the Great Church (e.g. Marcion and his followers); cf. Behr 2013: 13–72. By the time of Marcion (ca. 144 CE), the "Great Church" was a recognizable yet diverse body of Christians that venerated Jesus of Nazareth, accepted the Jewish Scriptures as authoritative, and traced their lineage from the apostles and their successors; Ayres 2017: 106–21; Behr 2013: 1–12; Markschies 2015: 335–45; Lampe 2003. I use the term "pagan" to describe Greco-Roman society that rejected (intellectually or politically) the missionizing claims and impulses of early Christianity; cf. Kavin Rowe's definition of "pagan" as "the people in the ancient world who were neither Jewish nor Christian" (Rowe 2009: 14), building on the work of MacMullen 1981; 1984.

5.1 Irenaeus 143

immortality on every side, and vivifying men afresh. From which fact, it is evident that the Word, the Artificer of all, He that sits upon the cherubim, and contains all things, He who was manifested to men, has given us the Gospel under four aspects, but bound together by one Spirit... And, therefore, the Gospels are in accord with these things, among which Christ Jesus is seated.[2]

Many view this statement as the earliest explicit *testimonium* to the *tetraevangelium* as a collection of four distinct gospel texts. Some have argued that Irenaeus' articulation of the εὐαγγέλιον τετράμορφον indicates that the four-gospel collection was already well established in the last quarter of the second century. Others see Irenaeus' defense as tortured, special pleading, hardly a sign of a commonly accepted opinion at the time of Irenaeus' writing. In this section, we will see that the patterns of gospel combinations in the exegetical discourse of Irenaeus bear strong resemblance to the recurring patterns we uncovered in the period before Irenaeus.

5.1.1 Identities and Mode of Gospel Combinations in Irenaeus' Writings

The identities of Irenaeus' four apostolic gospels are unambiguous: *GMatthew*, *GMark*, *GLuke*, and *GJohn*. The mode by which he accesses these gospels and distinguishes them is textual. Irenaeus refers to the in-depth reading of *GMatthew*, *GMark*, *GLuke*, and *GJohn* as the "proof of the Scriptures of the gospel that was written by the apostles."[3] Irenaeus uses the literary term συγγράφω, signifying the composition of a literary work, rather than the simple putting down of words on paper (γράφω), and he uses this term to describe the writing process of each of the four evangelists.

In *Haer.* 3.1.1, Irenaeus refers to *GMatthew* as "the Scripture of the gospel" (γραφὴν... εὐαγγελίου) that "Matthew published" (Ματθαῖος... ἐξήνεγκεν). Irenaeus uses the technical term ἐκφέρω to describe Matthew's process of publication for a particular social network – "among the Hebrews" (ἐν τοῖς Ἑβραίοις). Irenaeus appears to be describing the normal ancient practices of the non-commercial, private book trade.[4] He then describes *GMark* as essentially the written form of the preaching of Peter (τὰ ὑπὸ Πέτρου κηρυσσόμενα ἐγγράφως). Larsen takes this to imply that, even by the time of Irenaeus, Mark's gospel was not viewed as a finished, published *book* in the fullest sense, but rather unpublished

---

[2] *Haer.* 3.11.8. In Chapter 5, all translations of ancient sources, unless otherwise indicated, are my own. All Greek and Latin citations from Irenaeus in this chapter are taken from Rousseau *et al.* 1965; 1969; Rousseau and Doutreleau 1974; 1979; 1982.

[3] *Haer.* 3.5.1: *eam quae est ex Scripturis ostensionem eorum qui Euangelium conscripserunt apostolorum*; Greek retroversion: τὴν ἐκ γραφῶν τῶν τὸ εὐαγγέλιον συγγεγραφότων ἀποστόλων ἀπόδειξιν.

[4] For the book trade in the Roman Empire, see Gamble 2012; for its relevance to the circulation of gospels, see Alexander 1998.

144   *Chapter 5: Irenaeus, Clement, Heretics, and Celsus*

notes on Petrine preaching.[5] Larsen has not appreciated, however, Irenaeus' description of the process of Mark's writing later in *Haer.* 3.10.6, when he speaks of how Mark "made the beginning of the gospel writing."[6] The fact that Irenaeus probably calls *GMark* a σύγγραμμα (a probable retroversion from *conscriptio*) elevates Mark's gospel to the level of literary work that Larsen claims *GMark* lacked in the second century. In *Haer.* 3.1.1, Irenaeus also considers *GLuke* to have the same status as a published piece of apostolic literature, since Luke "recorded in a book the gospel preached by [Paul]" (τὸ ὑπ'ἐκείνου κηρυσσόμενον εὐαγγέλιον ἐν βίβλῳ κατέθετο). Finally, Irenaeus says that John "published an edition of the gospel" (ἐξέδωκεν τὸ εὐαγγέλιον) while staying in Ephesus. Irenaeus gives unambiguous evidence that by the last quarter of the second century, some Christians were considering these four gospels to be published, written works that were distinguishable as discrete texts.[7]

The mode by which Irenaeus received the *concept* of a four-gospel collection was plausibly both a spoken and written tradition. Irenaeus received his tradition of Matthew's and Mark's process of writing from Papias. We know from Eusebius that Irenaeus was aware of Papias' five-volume written work,[8] and while Irenaeus probably came in contact with Papias' traditions by word of mouth,[9] Irenaeus confirmed this tradition by consulting Papias' work.[10] As we argued in the previous chapter, Eusebius preserves a tradition contemporaneous with Papias in *Hist. eccl.* 3.24.5–8a, in which the personas of Matthew, Mark, Luke, and John serve as identifiers of discrete gospel books that were circulating among several early Christian social networks. When Eusebius preserves this tradition, he is probably extracting it from a written source.

Another source for Irenaeus' conceptualization of the four-gospel collection is Polycarp of Smyrna. Irenaeus describes his early tutelage under Polycarp in *Hist. eccl.* 5.20.4–8. In Polycarp's *Epistle to the Philippians*, we can detect clear

---

[5] Larsen 2018b: 93–96. Margaret Mitchell 2020: 204–05 has shown the untenability of Larsen's hypothesis by a more careful reading of *Haer.* 3.1.1, appreciating the parallelism of Irenaeus' descriptions of each of the gospels in their compositional origins (on which, see below).

[6] *initium Euangelicae conscriptionis fecit*; Greek retroversion: τὴν ἀρχὴν τοῦ εὐαγγελικοῦ συγγράμματος ἐποιήσατο.

[7] Reed 2002 has the most comprehensive lexical analysis of Irenaeus' use of the term εὐαγγέλιον, and in her study she demonstrates conclusively that Irenaeus' use of this term is intentionally ambiguous and polysemic, covering both the connotations of "gospel" as an oral, proclaimed apostolic tradition and as a written text. She rightly argues that the data show that Irenaeus typically uses εὐαγγέλιον to refer to the former connotation, but relatively sparingly in the latter sense.

[8] *Hist. eccl.* 3.39.2

[9] Irenaeus spent at least some of his youth in the port city of Smyrna (*Hist. eccl.* 4.14; 5.20.4–8), located at the end of a major trade route that passed through Hierapolis, and he participated in the same Johannine circle as Polycarp and Papias (see Mutschler 2004; 2009).

[10] *Haer.* 5.33.4.

5.1 Irenaeus

usage of Synoptic tradition, which includes Double Tradition, Markan/Matthean agreements, and even Markan redaction, as well as a parallel to Johannine language.[11] Polycarp's defense of Quartodeciman practice is most likely based on a literal reading of *GJohn*.[12] In an anti-Marcionite fragment preserved by Irenaeus in *Haer.* 4.27–32, an anonymous "presbyter" who is most likely Polycarp repudiates Marcionite dualism by appealing to material shared by *GMatthew* and *GMark*, material shared by *GMatthew* and *GLuke*, and material from *GJohn*.[13] In all likelihood, Polycarp had a gospel collection that had at least one Synoptic gospel and *GJohn*. Irenaeus, who respected the work of his theological mentor, probably inherited a form of this gospel collection from him.

We can also add the Valentinians to our list of precursors to Irenaeus' fourfold gospel collection. According to citations preserved by Irenaeus, and Ptolemy's second-century *Epistle to Flora*, the Valentinians made ample use of *GJohn*, *GMatthew*, and *GLuke*. They even read portions of *GMark*. The Valentinians offered systematic, allegorical interpretations of, among others, *GMatthew* 11.25–27, *GMark* 5.22–43, *GMark* 15.34, *GLuke* 2.25–38, *GLuke* 3.23 + 4.19, *GLuke* 9.57–62, and *GJohn* 1.1–14.[14] The allegorical interpretations of the Valentinians strongly suggest that they treated all four of the proto-canonical gospels as Scripture. This Valentinian regard for the gospels as Scripture matured into a commentary on *GJohn* and probably a commentary *GLuke*, both produced by Heracleon in the last quarter of the second century.[15] We find no such high, exegetical regard among Valentinians for their own pieces of literature; the four gospels appear to have a special status among Valentinians. Valentinians therefore join the company of Papias and Polycarp as precursors to Irenaeus' predominant use of Synoptic and Johannine gospels as the authoritative body of Jesus material worthy of scriptural exegesis. In short, Irenaeus probably received the basic concept of a four-gospel collection from an earlier tradition that dated back to the

---

[11] For Synoptic parallels, see Pol. *Phil.* 2.3a // *GMt* 7.1–2 // *GLk* 6.36–38; Pol. *Phil.* 2.3b // *GMt* 5.10; Pol. *Phil.* 5.2 // *GMk* 9.35; Pol. *Phil.* 7.2b // *GMt* 6.13 // *GLk* 11.4; Pol. *Phil.* 7.2c // *GMt* 26.41 // *GMk* 14.38; Pol. *Phil.* 12.3 // *GMt* 5.44 // *GLk* 6.27. It is significant that Polycarp has access to Double Tradition, *GMark/GMatt* agreements, and even Markan redaction. For Johannine parallels, see Pol. *Phil.* 7.1, which shares language with *GJn* 1.1, 8.44, 1 John 4.2–3, and 2 John 7; see also the historical connection between Polycarp and John the "Disciple of the Lord" (*Hist. eccl.* 5.24.16; *Haer.* 3.4.4; 3.11.1).

[12] *apud* Eusebius, *Hist. eccl.* 5.24.6.

[13] Charles Hill (2006: 50–65) finds fragments of Polycarp's teaching that interpret Synoptic (*GMt* 7.26; 10.15, 24; 26.24; *GMk* 14.21; *GLk* 6.40, 49; 10.12) and Johannine (*GJn* 8.56) traditions in *Haer.* 4.28.1 and 4.31.1.

[14] *GMt* 5.17–18 (*Haer.* 1.3.2; *Ep. Flora* 33.5.1); *GMt* 19.6–8 (*Ep. Flora* 33.4.4–6); *GMk* 5.22–43 (*Haer.* 1.3.3); *GMk* 15.34 (*Haer.* 1.8.2 – the redaction has ὁ θεός μου in the nominative rather than vocative and is therefore Markan rather than Matthean; cf. SC 264.119); *GLk* 2.25–38 (*Haer.* 1.8.4); *GLk* 3.23 + 4.19 (*Haer.* 2.22.1, 5); *GLk* 9.57–62 (*Haer.* 1.8.3); *GJn* 1.1–14 (*Haer.* 1.8.5; *Ep. Flora* 33.3.6).

[15] On which, see Bockmuehl 2005 and Berglund 2020.

146   *Chapter 5: Irenaeus, Clement, Heretics, and Celsus*

first half of the second century, was preserved in writings like that of Papias, and was disseminated by word of mouth through Christian networks in Asia Minor, Italy, and Gaul.

Irenaeus' notion of a four-gospel collection might go back to the Papian traditions, but what about his seemingly fanciful interpretation of the four living creatures representing the four-formed gospel? There are two reasons to think that elements of Irenaeus' theology of the *tetraevangelium* drew from prior sources. First, in the context of his defense of the fourfold gospel, Irenaeus says that "the form of the gospel is well arranged and joined together."[16] Irenaeus also says elsewhere that "the entire Scriptures, the prophets, and the gospels, can be clearly, unambiguously, and similarly heard by all."[17] Irenaeus anchors the harmonious structure of the gospels in the ordered structure of creation, symbolized by the four living creatures: "the gospels, therefore, are in symphony with these things [the four living creatures], among which Christ is enthroned."[18] The harmony and symphony of the Scriptures, anchored in the ordering of reality by the One Creator, is a common theme in second-century Christian literature. Valentinus, Marcus, Athenagoras, and Tatian, all predating Irenaeus, speak of the universe as created according to the symphony and harmony of God's design.[19] Theophilus of Antioch uses this language of creational symphony to describe the unity of the prophetic witness of the Scriptures.[20] Shortly after Irenaeus, Clement of Alexandria develops the theology of the Divine Logos in terms of harmony and symphony of creation, Old Testament Scripture, and the written gospel.[21] In short, the second-century Christian theology of creational and scriptural harmony furnished Irenaeus with the raw materials and tools with which he constructed his theology of the one gospel in four forms.

Second, Irenaeus' creative contribution to a Christian theology of the four-gospel collection is to anchor the harmony of the gospels in the imagery of the four cherubim in Ezekiel 1, equated with the four living creatures of Ezekiel 10

---

[16] *Haer.* 3.11.9: *oportebat et speciem Euangelii bene compositam et bene compaginatam esse* (SC 211.174); Greek: ἔδει καὶ τὴν τοῦ εὐαγγελίου ἰδέαν εὔρυθμον εἶναι καὶ εὐάρμοστον (SC 211.175).

[17] *Haer.* 2.27.2: *uniuersae Scripturae et propheticae, et euangelicae in aperto et sine ambiguitate, et similiter ab omnibus audiri* (SC 294.266).

[18] *Haer.* 3.11.8: Καὶ τὰ εὐαγγέλια οὖν τούτοις σύμφωνα, ἐν οἷς ἐγκαθέζεται ὁ Χριστὸς (SC 211.165); on the cosmological signifiance of the fourfold gospel, see Coogan 2023.

[19] Valentinus: *Haer.* 2.14.1–5, 2.15.1–3; Marcus: *Haer.* 1.17.1–2, 2.14.6; Athenagoras: *Legatio pro Christianis* 16; Tatian: *Oratio ad Graecos* 12.1–3 (cf. Crawford 2015a). This makes sense within the framework of Pythagorean numerological aesthetics, which gained much traction in Jewish and Christian tradition through the theology of Philo of Alexandria; for a thorough history of this development of thought, see Kalvesmaki 2013.

[20] *Autol.* 2.9; 2.10; 2.25; 3.17; 3.29; esp. *Autol.* 3.17: διὸ σύμφωνα καὶ φίλα ἀλλήλοις οἱ πάντες προφῆται εἶπον.

[21] *Strom* 6.11.88.5; 6.15.125.3–4; *Ad Graecos* 1.

5.1 Irenaeus 147

and Revelation 4, and interpreted in conversation with Psalm 80.1. There is reason to believe that Irenaeus' synthetic theologizing on the four-formed gospel owes a lot to an Asian *Johannesschule*. Irenaeus, in *Haer.* 3.11.8, appears to be riffing in a Johannine style. Besides his obvious allusion to Revelation 4.6–8, Irenaeus probably derives his notion of the "four winds" from Revelation 7.1. The author of Revelation can show his own "tetraphilia," depicting four angels (7.1; 9.14–15), four directions (7.1; 20.8), the four occurrences of the formula "thunder, rumblings, and lightening" (4.5; 8.5; 11.19; 16.18), and the fourfold formula of "tribe, tongue, people, and nation" (5.9; 7.9; 14.6).[22] Irenaeus shows clear signs of inheriting interpretive traditions from the *Johannesschule*, via Papias and other "elders" who had known John personally.[23] In fact, Irenaeus' ideal model of reading the Scriptures of the Law and Gospel is to read "in the company of the elders," and his ideal elder is clearly a Johannine one.[24] John's Apocalypse frequently guides Irenaeus' typological biblical theology,[25] and its symbolic interpretation inspires Irenaeus' own exegetical and hermeneutical creativity. In the same context that he explicitly mentions John and cites from Revelation 6.2, Irenaeus exclaims: "with [God] there is nothing empty or without signification"[26] – an exegetical *habitus* inspired by John's creative, visionary pen. It is impossible to prove that Irenaeus' symbolic interpretation of the four living creatures as representing the four gospels originated in the pen of John or the elders who knew him. But Irenaeus' creative interpretation of the fourfold gospel follows a hermeneutical *Tendenz* already at work among the Asian elders who knew John.[27]

---

[22] Cf. Beale 1999: 58–64 and Kruger 2013b: 160–61.

[23] Irenaeus refers to these "elders" often in his exegesis: *Haer.* 4.26.5; 4.27.1; 4.30.1; 4.31.1; 4.32.1–2; 5.5.1; 5.33.3–4. That they are Johannine is made explicit in 5.33.3–4.

[24] Irenaeus' ideal reader of Scripture reads "in the company of those who are elders in the Church" (*apud eos qui in Ecclesia sunt presbyteri*); *Haer.* 4.32.1 (SC 100.798). Hill (2006: 7–31) has made a strong case that Polycarp is the anonymous "elder" from whose exegetical writings Irenaeus draws in *Haer.* 4.27–32. That this elder was influenced by an Asian John is clear from the reference to *GJohn* 1.1 as a *crux interpretum* in *Haer.* 4.32.1, the typological reading of the plagues in Exodus and Revelation 15–16 in *Haer.* 4.30.1, 4, and the allusion to *GJn* 8.58 in *Haer.* 4.31.1, not to mention the strong historic connection between Polycarp and John (*Haer.* 3.3.4; *Hist. eccl.* 5.20.6; 5.24.16); cf. Hill 2006: 57–65.

[25] Irenaeus brings together Isaiah 6.1–6, Ezekiel 1–2, *GJn* 1.14–18, and Revelation 4–5 as intertexts in *Haer.* 4.20.7–11. These are the same texts that form the bedrock of his theological interpretation of the fourfold gospel in *Haer.* 3.11.8, and John creativity stands at the center of Irenaeus' exegesis (see Irenaeus' mention of John in *Haer.* 4.20.11).

[26] *Haer.* 4.21.3: *nihil enim vacuum, neque sine signo apud eum* (SC 100.684).

[27] According to Farkasfalvy 2016, Irenaeus' testimony of the origins of gospel writing gives several indications that it is a combination of Eastern (Asian) and Western (Roman) traditions – a combination that dates to at least the mid-point of the second century as a result of a consensus reached by Anicetus (from Rome) and Polycarp (from Smyrna) around 153 CE (*Hist. eccl.* 5.24.14–18). Bingham 2016 takes issue with Farkasfalvy's exegesis of *Haer.* 3.1.1, but

148   *Chapter 5: Irenaeus, Clement, Heretics, and Celsus*

The above examples furnish us with proof that Irenaeus inherited the *concept* of a four-gospel collection from a previous generation of Christians – Asian or Roman, proto-orthodox or Valentinian. This mode of gospel combination involved the oral transmission of gospel-reading habits from one generation to the next, and from one continent to the next. But there was also a textual facet to Irenaeus' understanding of the gospels keeping company with one another. Irenaeus understood the discrete, bookish character of the individual gospels. Irenaeus portrays *GMatthew* as a circulated "writing of the gospel," *GMark* as a "written tradition" of the preaching of Peter, *GLuke* as the Pauline gospel "set down in a book", and *GJohn* as a "published edition" of the gospel. In these descriptions, Irenaeus sets forth the following parallelism: γραφὴν ἐκφέρειν (*GMatthew*) // ἐγγράφως παραδιδόναι (*GMark*) // ἐν βιβλίῳ κατατίθεσθαι (*GLuke*) // τὸ εὐαγγέλιον ἐκδιδόναι (*GJohn*).[28] This concentration of bookish terms in a tradition of gospel origins has led some scholars to believe that Irenaeus is drawing from an earlier "four-gospel library note," probably connected to an ecclesial library in Rome.[29] The fact that, by 172 CE, Tatian had full bibliographic access to the four gospels, and a decade earlier Justin probably had a similar access to all four gospels, corroborates that Irenaeus' bookish knowledge of each of the four gospels was in some way related to a Roman church library. Irenaeus' bibliographic and precise exegetical knowledge of vast portions of the gospels presupposes physical interaction with manuscripts of the four gospels. Suffice it to say that Irenaeus had both a *conceptual* understanding and a *physical* experience of the four gospels keeping company with one another.

We must not go so far as to say that the four-gospel collection was *the definitive* gospel collection in the decades preceding Irenaeus, but neither must we ignore the evidence that such a collection had currency in the Christian movement well before Irenaeus. The identities in this gospel collection are clear: *GMatthew*, *GMark*, *GLuke*, and *GJohn*. The mode by which they shared company in Irenaeus' theological discourse was through the oral traditions and the archival *realia* that preceded him.

5.1.2 Integrity of Gospels: The Persona of the Evangelist as the Means of Defining Unity and Difference

With Irenaeus, we see a sharp development in the *textual* handling of the four proto-canonical gospels *as books*. In this section, I will demonstrate how, in Irenaeus' exegesis, the discrete identities of the four gospels, distinguished by the

---

Mutschler 2019 sufficiently demonstrates that the *Vierevangeliennotiz* of *Haer.* 3.1.1 has enough early Roman elements, combined with early Asian and Syrian elements, to suggest that it was present in a Roman library at least two decades prior to when Irenaeus wrote Book 3 of *Adversus Haereses*.

[28] Margaret Mitchell 2020: 204–05.

[29] Farkasfalvy 2016; Mutschler 2019.

names of the evangelists associated with their authorship, emerge in an intricate, intertextual relationship one with another. Thus, their integrities are preserved even as they interact in an interpenetrating *perichoresis*.

Irenaeus' textual handling of the gospels is predicated on a dialectic of unity and difference – one gospel represented by four authors, each writing his own gospel. The persona of the *evangelist* plays the key role of differentiating one written gospel from another. Irenaeus' personification of the gospel authors enables him to read all four gospels in harmonious parallel. In *Haer.* 3.9.1–3, he focuses on passages from *GMatthew* 1.18–3.17; in *Haer.* 3.10.1–4, he focuses on *GLuke* 1.5–2.38; in *Haer.* 3.10.5, he focuses on *GMark* 1.1–4; and finally, Irenaeus devotes the following, lengthy section, *Haer.* 3.11.1–6, to *GJohn* 1.1– 53. Irenaeus distinguishes each of these gospel passages by assigning them to their respective authors: "Matthew the apostle" (3.9.1), "Luke, the follower and disciple of the apostles" (3.10.1), "Mark, the interpreter and follower of Peter" (3.10.5), and "John, the disciple of the Lord" (3.11.1). Irenaeus stays within the textual territory of the incipits to the baptism of John in the Synoptics, and he hovers around the incipit of *GJohn*, although he also extends to the narrative of Jesus' recognition of Nathanael. Irenaeus distinguishes these passages by attributing them to a particular evangelist, and he interprets them within an intertextual web in the major section of 3.9.1–3.11.6. This section is, in essence, a theological prelude to his main defense of the fourfold gospel in 3.11.7–9. In 3.9.1–3.11.6, Irenaeus uses the intertextual exegesis of the beginning chapters of each proto-canonical gospel to construct a counter-Christology in response to the elaborate Valentinian theological systems that preceded him. The numerous verbatim quotations from the first chapters of these four gospels, and the location of these quotations at roughly the same part of the textual geography from each gospel (i.e. the first three chapters), would be impossible without experiencing the four gospels as discrete, stable books.

5.1.3 Gospel Interactions: Bibliographic Reading of the Gospel on Two Axes – Vertical and Horizontal.

The fundamental mechanism by which Irenaeus brings the four, proto-canonical gospels into conversation with one another is to read the gospels on two axes: vertical (appreciating the narrative sequence of each separate gospel) and horizontal (comparing and contrasting parallels across the gospels). We saw this same kind of four-gospel reading *habitus* in Tatian, who preserved large swathes of narrative integrity for *GMatthew* and *GJohn* (reading along the vertical axis), and who weaved together details from parallels across all four gospels (reading along the horizontal axis). For Irenaeus to read the gospels across vertical and

150   *Chapter 5: Irenaeus, Clement, Heretics, and Celsus*

horizontal axes to such a large extent, he must first have a bibliographic conception of the four discrete gospel books.[30]

Irenaeus' bibliographic mapping of the gospels is evident in his handling of *GMark*. Although Irenaeus cites *GMark* much fewer times than the other three gospels,[31] Irenaeus does seem to have a firm grasp of its overall structure. Without chapters or verses, Irenaeus understands what constitutes the "beginning" and "end" of Mark's gospel. Irenaeus refers to Mark "forming the beginning of the gospel writing,"[32] and also Mark relating Jesus tradition "at the conclusion of the gospel."[33]

Irenaeus also shows bibliographic indexing of gospel parallels, redactional features, and *Sondergut*. Irenaeus appreciates the different emphases between the Matthean and Lukan genealogies without being troubled by their apparent discrepancies; he allows each to make its appropriate theological point.[34] In *Haer.* 4.5.6, Irenaeus points out that Matthew and Luke both "set down" the Johannine Thunderbolt saying in their gospels.[35] While he mistakenly says that Mark included the same saying, he correctly says that "John omits this passage." Even when Irenaeus mistakenly attributes this saying to *GMark*, he is showing that he reads the gospels across a horizontal axis on which he can identify parallels present in two or more gospels.

Irenaeus also has remarkable awareness of Lukan and Johannine *Sondergut*. Regarding *GLuke*, in *Haer.* 3.14.3–4, Irenaeus includes an extended discussion on passages "we have known through Luke alone."[36] These include unparalleled sayings, redactional influence on shared sayings, and unparalleled narrative episodes. Irenaeus lists 27 pericopes in total. The material that Irenaeus lists corresponds roughly to the following pericopes of Lukan *Sondergut*:

(1) 1.57–66, (2) 1.5–25, (3) 1.26–38, (4) 1.42, (5) 2.8–14, (6) 2.15–20, (7) 2.22–38, (8) 2.41–52, (9) 3.1–2, 3.23, (10) 6.24–26, (11) 5.1–11, (12) 13.10–17, (13) 14.1–6, (14) 14.7–11, (15)

---

[30] Bibliographic knowledge envisages texts as discrete, relatively stable, conceptual objects that can occupy space, often embodied in the form of a physical artifact. The following argument is developed more fully in Coogan and Rodriguez 2023: 85–92.

[31] On Irenaeus' high regard for *GMark* despite citing it much less than *GMatthew* and *GLuke*, see Verheyden 2017.

[32] *Haer.* 3.10.6: *Marcus... initium Euangelicae conscriptionis fecit sic* (SC 211.134). Greek retroversion: Μάρκος... τὴν ἀρχὴν τοῦ εὐαγγελικοῦ συγγράμματος ἐποιήσατο οὕτως (SC 211.135).

[33] *Haer.* 3.10.6: *In fine autem Euangelii ait Marcus* (SC 211.136); Greek retroversion: Ἐπὶ τέλει δὲ τοῦ εὐαγγελίου φησὶν ὁ Μάρκος (SC 211.137).

[34] He exegetes the Matthean genealogy in *Haer.* 3.16.2 and the Lukan genealogy in *Haer.* 3.22.3–4.

[35] *GMt* 11.27 and *GLk* 10.22.

[36] *Haer.* 3.14.3–4: *Et omnia huiusmodi per solum Lucam cognouimus* (SC 211.268); Greek retroversion: Πάντα τε τὰ τοιαῦτα διὰ μόνου τοῦ Λουκᾶ ἐγνώκαμεν (SC 211.269).

14.12–24, (16) 11.5–8, (17) 7.36–50, (18) 12.13–21, (19) 16.19–31, (20) 17.5–6, (21) 19.1–10, (22) 18.9–14, (23) 17.11–19, (24) 14.21, (25) 18.1–8, (26) 13.6–9, (27) 24.13–35.

15 of these pericopes match up precisely with the *kephalaia* of Codex Alexandrinus, and Irenaeus even approximates the corresponding *titloi* at several points, as shown in Table 14 below.

Table 14: Overlaps between Irenaeus' Lukan Section Titles and the *Kephalaia* and *Titloi* in Codex Alexandrinus

GLk	Irenaean Title	Kephalaia	Titloi
2.8–14	*angelorum ad pastores descensum*	(2)	Περι των αγραυλουντων ποιμαινων
2.22–38	*Annae et Simeonis de Christo testimonium*	(3)	Περι Συμεων + Περι Αννας της προφητειδος
3.1–2	*baptismum Iohannis*	(5)	Περι του γενομενου ρηματος προς Ιωαννην
5.1–11	*multitudinem piscium quam concluserunt hi qui cum Petro erant*	(11)	Περι της αγρας των ιχθυων
7.36–50	*peccatrix mulier osculabatur pedes eius et unguebat unguento*	(21)	Περι της αλιψασης τον κ̄ν̄ μυρω
12.13–21	*de parabola diuitis illius qui reclusit quae ei nata fuerant*	(45)	Περι του θελοντος μερισασθαι την ουσιαν
14.1–6	*de hydropico quem curauit Dominus die sabbatorum*	(52)	Περι του υδρωπικου
14.7–11	*quemadmodum docuit discipulos primos discubitos non appetere*	(53)	Περι του μη αγαπαν τας πρωτοκλησις
14.12–24	*quoniam pauperes et debiles oucare oportet*	(54)	Περι των καλουμενων εν τω δειπνω
16.19–31	*diuitis qui uestitur... et egenum Elazarum*	(59)	Περι πλουσιου και Λαζαρου
17.11–19	*de decem leprosis*	(60)	Περι των δεκα λεπρων
18.1–8	*parabolam iudicis qui Deum non timebat*	(61)	Περι του κριτου της αδικιας
18.9–14	*de Pharisaeo et de publicano*	(62)	Περι του φαρισαιου και του τελωνου
19.1–10	*eam quae ad Zachaeum publicanum facta est confabulationem*	(65)	Περι Ζαχχαιου
24.13–35	*super haec omnia post resurrectionem in uia ad discipulos suos quae locutus est*	(83)	Περι Κλεοπα

152   *Chapter 5: Irenaeus, Clement, Heretics, and Celsus*

The correspondences between the pericopes according to Irenaeus and Alexandrinus are striking.[37] Interestingly, Irenaeus can identify not only that these materials are special to *GLuke*, but also that an abbreviated form of these materials comprised the "mutilated" gospel of Marcion.[38] This indicates an even greater extent of Irenaeus' bibliographic knowledge of gospel books. On the one hand, Irenaeus has categories to describe and differentiate three gospel books that closely resemble each other – the gospels according to Matthew, Mark, and Luke. On the other hand, Irenaeus has a separate set of categories to differentiate between *GLuke* and Marcion's *euangelion*. For Irenaeus, there is a difference between redaction and mutilation.[39] Both of these categories of differentiation presuppose a robust understanding of gospel books as discrete conceptual entities that can interact congenially or competitively.

In *Haer.* 2.22.3–6, Irenaeus also shows awareness of Johannine *Sondergut* in its textual sequence. In this section, Irenaeus derides the Valentinians, who claim that Jesus' public ministry only lasted twelve months, for not reading the gospels carefully enough. He then gives a series of Johannine *Sondergut* episodes, each in reference to their proximity to Jesus' festal journeys to Jerusalem. Irenaeus gives these in their proper Johannine sequence: the Passover immediately following the miracle in Cana, the conversation with the Samaritan woman at the well, the curing of the official's son from a distance, Jesus' second festal journey to Jerusalem (in which he healed the paralytic at the pool), the healing of Lazarus, the Pharisees' plots, Jesus' withdrawal to Ephraim, his coming to Bethany, and his final journey to the Passover in Jerusalem from Bethany. Irenaeus explicitly says that he is following what "John the disciple of the Lord records."[40]

Not only does Irenaeus know *GJohn* in its textual sequence, but he also attempts to coordinate it with a Synoptic sequence – a task Tatian attempted a decade earlier. Irenaeus' implied solution is to posit that between the Johannine festal episodes, more time elapsed in Jesus' life, such that by *GJohn* 8.57 Jesus had nearly reached fifty years of age. Interestingly, Irenaeus chooses *not* to allegorize Johannine chronology to square it with Synoptic chronology. Rather, Irenaeus

---

[37] In Table 14, the Irenaean titles are extracted from Latin text in SC 211.266–73; *kephalaia* numbers and titles listed in W. Andrew Smith 2014: 167–76.

[38] Irenaeus speaks of Marcion's followers "mutilating" the gospel according to Luke in *Haer.* 3.14.3: *hoc enim quod est secundum Lucam… decurtantes* (SC 211.274).

[39] Space does not permit me to engage the current debate about whether Irenaeus' account of Marcion's revision of *GLuke* is accurate. Some scholars have recently resurrected the hypothesis that Marcion's gospel predated *GLuke* (Tyson 2006; Beduhn 2013; Vinzent 2014; Klinghardt 2015; cf. Knox 1942). Others have postulated that both Marcion's gospel and *GLuke* develop a proto-Luke gospel text (e.g. Lieu 2015). In the most detailed analysis to date, however, Dieter Roth has shown that a rigorously reconstructed text of Marcion's gospel shows, at several places, Lukan redaction and harmonization from *GMatthew* and *GMark* (Roth 2015: 437–40; 2017a; 2017b; cf. Hays 2008). This evidence weighs in favor of Lukan priority.

[40] *Haer.* 3.22.3.

takes *GLuke* 3.23 as factually correct on Jesus' ministry beginning at his thirtieth year of life,[41] and he accepts Luke's coordination of this date with Tiberius' emperorship.[42] But he also extends Jesus' ministry into the emperorship of Claudius, claiming that Pontius Pilate still ruled in Judea during the reign of Claudius.[43] By so doing, Irenaeus has expanded the historical "wiggle room" within which to coordinate all the events reported in the Synoptics and *GJohn*. Irenaeus is reading the Synoptics and *GJohn* in parallel, closely following at least the sequences of *GLuke* and *GJohn*. This is evidence that Irenaeus respects the sequential integrity of Synoptic and Johannine gospel alike, and he attempts to read them in harmony with one another.

Irenaeus can reason textually as if he were consulting a synopsis with each gospel laid out in parallel, such as Ammonius' early third-century technology.[44] This synoptic awareness respects the integrity of each gospel even while having them interact extensively and harmoniously. Irenaeus' habits of gospel reading can be described as reading along a vertical axis (following the sequence of each gospel on its own terms) and a horizontal axis (comparing and contrasting parallels). Across these two axes, all four canonical gospels coexist congenially.

5.1.4 Authority

Irenaeus is perhaps most famous for his artistic, theological defense of the fourfold gospel. In this defense, there is no room to doubt that Irenaeus accords a scriptural authority to the combination of *GMatthew*, *GMark*, *GLuke*, and *GJohn* into a *tetraevangelium*. In *Haer.* 3.11.8, Irenaeus combines these four gospels into one literary-theological icon – the four living creatures as the throne upon which the ascended Christ is seated as Lord. This iconographic gospel combination embodies a textual authority for the proto-canonical gospels *as a unity in diversity*. For Irenaeus, the fourfold gospel is more than the sum of its parts.

After a summary statement in *Haer.* 3.11.7, Irenaeus launches his defense of the fourfold gospel in *Haer.* 3.11.8. Irenaeus' well-known image of the four living creatures is an aesthetically powerful exposition of the same point he was making in 3.11.1–6, namely, that the invisible God was made known through the incarnate Word. Irenaeus' exposition of the fourfold gospel, therefore, is part of a larger theological discourse on the *visio dei invisibilis*. This is the same discourse that forms the intertextual links between Isaiah 6.1–16, Ezekiel 1–2, John

---

[41] *Haer.* 2.22.4–5. Irenaeus nowhere disparages Luke's historical factuality. In fact, in several places he applauds Luke's commitment to be faithful to the testimony of the original eyewitnesses (*Haer.* 3.14.1, 4; 3.15.1).

[42] *Haer.* 4.22.2.

[43] *Epid.* 74.

[44] For an in-depth description of Ammonius' synoptic technology – and whether this was a table with several gospels laid out in parallel or simply an edition of *GMatthew* with other gospel parallels in the margins – see Coogan and Rodriguez 2023.

154   *Chapter 5: Irenaeus, Clement, Heretics, and Celsus*

1.14–18, and Revelation 4–5, which Irenaeus certainly recognizes in *Haer.* 4.20.7–11. In *Haer.* 3.11.8, the four gospels enter the discourse by upholding the chariot-throne upon which Christ Jesus, the incarnate Word, the Artificer of all things, the Lord himself, is seated.

The imagery of the gospels as the four living creatures, upholding the chariot-throne of the Lord Jesus Christ, is Irenaeus' creative development of a Johannine theology of God's divine, Temple presence revealed in Christ the paschal Lamb.[45] John himself infused a high Christology into the Jewish *Merkavah* tradition that depicted in mystical terms the glory of the invisible God within the heavenly Temple-throne room. Irenaeus follows John's lead in interpreting the *Merkavah* tradition through the lens of a high Christology. The divine throne, upheld by the four living creatures, is located in the heavenly Temple, where the glory of God is beheld in the face of Christ. Given how tempting the *Merkavah* tradition might be for Gnosticizing Christians of the second century,[46] perhaps Irenaeus employs this imagery to show the antithesis to Gnostic dualism: the four-gospel *Merkavah* upholds the *incarnate* and glorified Word of God.

Irenaeus' other fourfold identifications – the four winds and the four pillars – are an expansion of the Temple imagery, constituting a gospel-centered ecclesiology constructed with Johannine building blocks. He calls the gospels the "four pillars" (τέσσαρας... στύλους) upon which the Church is built (*Haer.* 3.11.8). These pillars recall the instructions given to Moses for building the tabernacle, in which pillars are a central feature.[47] Irenaeus also envisages the church as scattered across the four winds but united by the same Spirit and around the tetramorph gospel. Irenaeus' "four-winds" ecclesiology in *Haer.* 3.11.8 recalls Revelation 7.1–4, where the four angels, holding the four winds, protect the 144,000 saints until they are sealed.[48] The numbering of the 144,000 is a strong allusion to the numbering of Israel in Numbers 2.1–34, where Israel encamps around the tabernacle, divided across the four cardinal directions.[49] Furthermore, in

---

[45] Di Luccio 2017 argues that Irenaeus refrains from mentioning the eschatological Temple, but Di Luccio does not integrate into this discussion Irenaeus' present, apocalyptic awareness of the heavenly Temple, and he underplays the significance of Irenaeus' hermeneutical correspondence between the tabernacle, the heavenly temple, and the New Jerusalem (see esp. *Haer.* 5.35.2).

[46] The fourth-century Nag Hammadi tractate, *On the Origin of the World* (104.35–105.19) speaks of an archon named "Saboath" who created a throne upon a four-faced chariot composed of cherubim. It appears that the Jewish *Merkavah* tradition was fertile ground for Gnostic speculation on transcendence and imminence; cf. Hannah, 2003.

[47] Cf. Exod 26.31–37.

[48] John himself might have been influenced by the Synoptic apocalyptic tradition here, since both *GMt* 24.31 and *GMk* 13.27 speak of the angels gathering the elect from the four winds. Koester 2014: 357–58 draws out several key parallels between the Synoptic apocalypse and John's Apocalypse.

[49] Cf. Bauckham 1993: 217–29; Beale 1999: 416–23; Koester 2014: 424–27.

Revelation 14.1–3, these 144,000 are singing on Mount Zion (the site of the heavenly temple) before the throne, in the presence of the four living creatures.

In the imagery created by the constellation of Revelation 4.6–11, 7.1–4, 11.19, 14.1–3, and 15.5–8, John envisages the church as the numbered congregation of Israel, gathered around the Ark of the Covenant. Irenaeus alludes to each of these passages as he reconstructs the heavenly tabernacle in various passages throughout Books 3–4 in *Adversus Haereses*,[50] and at several points he explicitly refers to John and the elders as his exegetical forbears.[51] According to Irenaeus, the heavenly tabernacle is the place where the sacrament of Christ's body and blood is communicated to humankind, lifting their bodies to "the hope of the resurrection to eternity."[52] Thus, in Irenaeus' theological framework, the fourfold gospel, depicted as the four living creatures upholding the incarnate Christ in the heavenly tabernacle, can also be said to communicate Christ sacramentally to humankind, "raising and bearing humanity upon its wings into the heavenly kingdom."[53]

Irenaeus is doing theological improvisation in a Johannine key when he interprets the *tetraevangelium* as the cherubim of the Ark of the Covenant, located at the center of the heavenly tabernacle, around which the Church is assembled even while scattered across the face of the earth. According to Irenaeus, the four gospels uphold the incarnate Word as the definitive, sacramental revelation of the invisible God, the Lamb seated on the throne, whose tabernacling presence fully reveals God's glory. The Church, though scattered, is still united by the Spirit around this fourfold, evangelic epicenter of divine glory. Irenaeus is hymning in a Johannine key the incarnate Christ proclaimed in the *tetraevangelium*. Here the four gospels are accorded the highest degree of authority as the exclusive, scriptural testimony of Jesus Christ the Incarnate Logos.

5.1.5 Summary of Gospel Combinations in Irenaeus

In the writings of Irenaeus, we find our earliest, extensive demonstration of fourfold gospel reading. The four proto-canonical gospels keep congenial company in Irenaeus' constructive theology. Irenaeus probably had physical experience of the gospels as four, discrete books, and his *mode* of bringing them together conceptually and exegetically probably involved both oral traditions and

---

[50] *Haer.* 3.11.8 (cf. Rev 4.6–11; 7.1–2; 14.1–3); *Haer.* 4.18.6 (cf. Rev 11.19); *Haer.* 4.30.4 (cf. Rev 15.5–8).

[51] Irenaeus refers to the elders as his exegetical forbears in *Haer.* 4.26.5; 4.27.1; 4.30.1; 4.31.1; 4.32.1–2; 5.5.1; 5.33.3–4. Irenaeus refers to John (for Irenaeus, the Evangelist and the Seer are the same person) over 60 times. For a full list, see Reynders 1954: 88, 92, 175, 185, 192–93, 237. For an analysis of Irenaeus' references to John, see Mutschler 2004: 695–742; 2006; 2009.

[52] *Haer.* 4.18.5–6. On Irenaeus' sacramental theology, see Pastor 2017.

[53] *Haer.* 3.11.8.

156   *Chapter 5: Irenaeus, Clement, Heretics, and Celsus*

manuscripts accessed in a Roman Christian library. The gospels as discrete books were able to maintain their *integrity* as stable entities in Irenaeus' exegesis, and as stable entities they *interacted* in a harmonious retelling of the story of Jesus. Irenaeus recognized the unique contributions of each gospel – not only in their *Sondergut*, but, to a certain extent, also in their narrative sequence. For Irenaeus, the bibliographic unity and diversity of the fourfold gospel was of a piece with the theophanic revelation of the God of Israel in the person of Jesus Christ, the incarnate Logos. The fourfold gospel held the highest, exclusive, scriptural authority. While Irenaeus trailblazes in his constructive theology of the fourfold gospel, he does so with the hermeneutical, exegetical, and bibliographic tools bequeathed to him by previous generations of gospel readers from Asia Minor and Rome.

5.2 Clement of Alexandria

Clement of Alexandria overlapped Irenaeus by two decades or so, and he ushered the discourse on the four-gospel collection into the third century. A polymath and bibliophile, Clement was a prodigious author with a firm grasp of a wide range of topics. Located in Alexandria, Clement probably had access to a well-stocked library that facilitated his eclectic reading habits that included both canonical and noncanonical gospels.

Table 15 (see below) shows the gospels Clement cites in his extant works and the number of times he cites each of them. This tally is based on the index by Otto Stählin,[54] cited in a recent study by Piotr Ashwin-Siejkowksi.[55] The first observation to be made here is that not one of the noncanonical gospels comes even close to approximating the volume of citations and allusions that Clement makes of the proto-canonical four. Taken as a corpus, the four proto-canonical gospels comprise the most frequently cited material in Clement's library. We have reason to classify these gospels as a corpus within Clement's reading habits because he marks them out as such (*Strom.* 3.13.93.1). Although Clement shows eclectic reading habits, they are chastened by Clement's own high regard for the authority of the four gospels that "have been handed down."

Table 15: Clement of Alexandria's Citations and Allusions

Ancient Text	References	Comments
GMatthew	742	
GLuke	407	
GJohn	335	78 of these references come from *GJohn* 1.1–18.

[54] Stählin and Treu 1980: 11–18.
[55] Ashwin-Siejkowski 2017.

5.2 Clement of Alexandria

Ancient Text	References	Comments
GMark	180	Clement's long citation of *GMark* 10.17–31 in *Quis div.* 4–5 does not match any known New Testament witnesses but is tightly harmonized with the Matthean and Lukan parallels.
Kerygma Petri	10	In 8 of these references, Clement mentions the title of this work.
GEgyptians	9	In 2 of these references, Clement mentions the title of this work.
GHebrews	4	In 2 of these references, Clement mentions the title of this work.
Traditions of Matthias	3	
Protevangelium of James	1	Clement never mentions the title of this work.
Pauline Epistles	1273	
Plato	618	
Homer	243	
Philo	279	

Notes: This table is based on Ashwin-Siejkowksi 2017, who draws from Stählin and Treu 1980: 11–18.

In the context of interpreting a noncanonical saying preserved in the *Gospel according to the Egyptians,* Clement differentiates "handed-down" gospels from those not handed down:

Πρῶτον μὲν οὖν ἐν τοῖς παραδεδομένοις ἡμῖν τέτταρσιν εὐαγγελίοις οὐκ ἔχομεν τὸ ῥητόν, ἀλλ᾿ ἐν τῷ κατ᾿ Αἰγυπτίους.

Firstly, therefore, we do not have this saying in the four gospels that have been handed down to us, but rather in the [gospel] according to [the] Egyptians.[56]

We find a similar statement by Clement in *Quis div.* 5:

Ταῦτα μὲν ἐν τῷ κατὰ Μάρκον εὐαγγελίῳ γέγραπται· καὶ ἐν τοῖς ἄλλοις δὲ πᾶσιν <τοῖς> ἀνωμολογημένοις ὀλίγον μὲν ἴσως ἑκασταχοῦ τῶν ῥημάτων ἐναλλάσσει, πάντα δὲ τὴν αὐτὴν τῆς γνώμης συμφωνίαν ἐπιδείκνυται.[57]

These things are written in the gospel according to Mark, and there is the same harmony of meaning in all the other accepted [gospels] – although perhaps, in various places, a little of the wording changes.

---

[56] *Strom.* 3.13.93.1; my translation. All Greek citations from *Paed.*, *Protr.*, and *Strom.*, in this chapter are from Stählin 1970–1985. Watson 2013: 420 calls this "the one and only occasion on which Clement speaks of a fourfold gospel" and Watson highlights that "[Clement] develops his point no further."

[57] Greek text from Butterworth 1919; LCL 92.

158   *Chapter 5: Irenaeus, Clement, Heretics, and Celsus*

Clement's comment here comes after a block quotation from *GMark* 10.17–31. These ruminations of Clement bring to the fore an important question we must address at the outset of our study of Clement's gospel combinations: what status did gospels that would later be deemed noncanonical have in Clement's interpretive framework? We will cover this in the following section.

5.2.1 Clement and Noncanonical Gospels

Some scholars have marshalled the witness of Clement in the case for a fixed, four-gospel canon in the final decades of the second century.[58] *Strom.* 3.13.93.1 and *Quis div.* 5 are the focus of such analyses. Others, however, have highlighted the diversity of Clement's citations and interpreted his reading practices as evidence for still-porous boundaries around authoritative gospel literature in the late second century. Francis Watson appreciates that by the third century, the fourfold gospel had much currency in certain parts of the Christian world (although he remarks that it "remained a work in progress until well into the fourth century"[59]), but he maintains that *before* Irenaeus and Clement, "the gospel" did not refer to "a fixed literary entity."[60] Watson locates Clement at the point of transition from "early proliferation [of gospel literature] to the construction of the canonical limit."[61] Watson argues:

> Clement's comment seems to represent a transitional moment in which a differentiation within the field of gospel literature is beginning to take shape, while excluded texts may still be valued insofar as they preserve authoritative utterances of the Lord himself.[62]

Watson continues:

> Clement's citational practice represents a moment of transition between the earlier nonspecific appeal to "the gospel" and the emergence of our "gospels" differentiated by the names of their purported authors.[63]

Watson minimizes the weight of Clement's comment regarding the "four gospels that have been handed down to us," reducing it to a mere passing comment "in a single passage that does not reflect his eclectic citational practice as a whole."[64]

Watson builds his case on three premises. First, Clement's typical practice is to cite "the gospel" in general and most of the time does not seem particularly interested in differentiating between his gospel sources. Second, Clement uses the same citation formula – "it is written in the gospel according to X" – to cite from proto-canonical gospels (*GMatthew*, *GMark*, *GLuke*, *GJohn*) as well as

---

[58] Hill 2010b: 70–75; Hengel 2000:15–19.
[59] Watson 2013: 453–54.
[60] Watson 2013: 414.
[61] Watson 2013: 416.
[62] Watson 2013: 427.
[63] Watson 2013: 435.
[64] Watson 2013: 436.

5.2 Clement of Alexandria 159

from noncanonical gospels (*GHeb* and *GEgy*). Third, in an extended exposition of a passage about Salome, preserved in *GEgy*, Clement appears to treat this noncanonical gospel material in the same manner as proto-canonical gospel material. Watson states this third premise as follows: "Nothing in the Salome passage implies that Clement regarded it as nonauthoritative or nonscriptural."[65] And again, "Clement does not assert the superiority of the 'canonical' passage over the 'apocryphal' one. No such distinction is mentioned here."[66]

The first and second premises are certainly true, but they need to be situated within the broader context of Clement's oeuvre and compositional practices, and his theology of scriptural revelation and historic, apostolic tradition. One needs to read Clement's eclectic citation habits in light of his *overall* gospel citations (see Table 15 above). Yes, Clement occasionally shows his eclectic knowledge of noncanonical gospel literature, but the much broader pattern is that the "handed-down gospels" directed his literary imagination regarding the Jesus tradition. One also needs to consider that *all* of Clement's noncanonical gospel citations occur in his *Stromateis*, which by definition is a miscellany.[67] Clement's intention in compiling this miscellany is to revive in his commentaries the memories that "are effaced, having faded away in the mind itself."[68] Otherwise, these memories might "escape" because they "remained unnoted."[69] Indeed, Clement notes remorsefully, "Many things, I well know, have escaped us, through length of time, that have dropped away unwritten."[70] Clement here is probably speaking of the "true tradition of the blessed teaching directly from the holy apostles."[71]

Clement's intention for writing his *Stromateis* gives us a framework for understanding his use and preservation of traditions found in noncanonical gospels. It shows that Clement's aim in excerpting material from *GEgyptians*, *GHebrews*, an unknown gospel, and other *agrapha* was to preserve words from the Lord that he deemed authentic. These noncanonical gospels share the same authoritative pool of tradition from which the proto-canonical gospels are derived. At the same time, Clement's supreme regard for that which has been handed down directly from the apostles places the four proto-canonical gospels on a higher plane of authority than other gospel books. In *Strom.* 7.17.106.4, Clement declares that "the teaching of the Lord, at his coming, beginning with Augustus and Tiberius

---

[65] Watson 2013: 421.

[66] Watson 2013: 422.

[67] On Clement's use of miscellany within the broader Greco-Roman culture of excerpting (e.g., Plutarch, Pliny, Aulus Gellius, and Athenaeus) see Heath 2020. Heath identifies Clement's miscellany as an act of Christian *paideia* in forming the soul toward knowledge of the hidden God.

[68] *Strom.* 1.1.14.3.

[69] *Strom.* 1.1.14.3.

[70] *Strom.* 1.1.14.2.

[71] *Strom.* 1.1.11.3: τὴν ἀληθῆ τῆς μακαρίας... διδασκαλίας παράδοσιν εὐθὺς ἀπὸ... τῶν ἁγίων ἀποστόλων.

160   *Chapter 5: Irenaeus, Clement, Heretics, and Celsus*

Caesar, was completed in the middle of the times of Tiberius,"[72] contrasted with the heretical teachings of Basilides, Valentinus, and Marcion, which took place under Hadrian and Antoninus. In theory, then, Clement would not think that a later gospel, composed of inauthentic Jesus tradition, would have the authority of the genuine gospels.[73] It was these gospel books that formed nearly the entirety of what Clement understood to be "the gospel," just as they did for Irenaeus' fourfold gospel, Tatian's *Diatessaron*, and Justin's gospel ἀπομνημονεύματα. This is evidenced in the fact that Clement uses material from every single chapter of the proto-canonical gospels except *GMark* 16.[74] According to Clement, "the gospel" is parallel to and in "ecclesiastical symphony" with the Law, Prophets, and Apostles.[75] Clement can call this four-part authoritative corpus – Law, Prophets, Gospel, and Apostles – "the Scriptures of the Lord."[76] These Scriptures are for Clement the Old and New Covenants,[77] delivered by Christ the Logos,[78] communicating the authentic voice of the Lord.[79] They are the "indemonstrable first principle" that is grasped by faith, upon which Clement builds his entire epistemology.[80] The written gospel is an integral part of the Scriptures of the Lord, and in Clement's reckoning, "the gospel" is most fully instantiated in the four gospels handed down.

Furthermore, Clement's sparse and relatively imprecise use of noncanonical gospels suggests that he did not have extensive access to them (or that these books themselves were not very extensive, but more like disparate collections of *logia* such as *GThomas*). If our most eclectic, most well-read Christian author of the late second century could only muster a handful of sayings from noncanonical gospels then it is unlikely that they captured the imagination of the broader Christian movement of that time. They probably did not enjoy the same extensive

---

[72] Clement's statement reads: ἡ μὲν γὰρ τοῦ κυρίου κατὰ τὴν παρουσίαν διδασκαλία ἀπὸ Αὐγούστου καὶ Τιβερίου καίσαρος ἀρξαμένη μεσούντων τῶν Αὐγούστου χρόνων τελειοῦται. In the final clause, Clement (or the scribe beyond the manuscript) probably misplaced Αὐγούστου for Τιβερίου, as a result of the mention of both figures in the previous clause.

[73] Cf. Tertullian's paradigmatic remark: *In tantum enim haeresis deputabitur quod postea inducitur, in quantum veritas habebitur quod retro et a primordio traditum est*; "For in as far as that which is introduced later will be considered heresy, in so far will that which has been delivered previously and from the very beginning be held as truth" (*Adv. Marc.* 1.1.6; text and trans. Moll 2010: 33); cf. Irenaeus' remarks in *Haer.* 3.1–3.

[74] Cf. the list of references in Stählin 1936: 14.

[75] *Strom* 6.11.88.5: λάβοις δ᾽ ἂν καὶ ἄλλως μουσικὴν συμφωνίαν τὴν ἐκκλησιαστικὴν νόμου καὶ προφητῶν ὁμοῦ καὶ ἀποστόλων σὺν καὶ τῷ εὐαγγελίῳ.

[76] *Strom.* 7.16.94.1: αἱ κυριακαὶ γραφαί; 7.16.95.4: τῇ κυριακῇ γραφῇ τε καὶ φωνῇ; cf. 7.1.1.4.

[77] *Strom.* 3.11.71.3; 3.18.108.2; 5.1.3.3; 5.13.85.1; cf. Gräbe 2006: 166–70.

[78] *Strom.* 5.13.85.1.

[79] *Strom.* 7.16.95.4: τῇ κυριακῇ γραφῇ τε καὶ φωνῇ.

[80] *Strom.* 7.16.95.6: πίστει περιλαβόντες ἀναπόδεικτον τὴν ἀρχήν ("by faith taking hold of the indemonstrable first principle").

5.2 Clement of Alexandria

distribution across the ancient Mediterranean as the proto-canonical four.[81] Even more, as we shall see below, Clement's extensive citations from the proto-canonical four demonstrate a thick, intertextual connection among these four gospels, even in the harmonization of the canonical sayings he recollects. In Clement's oeuvre, the proto-canonical four maintain their pride of place. This is no mere afterthought, but rather a thoroughgoing, fourfold approach to the gospels that Clement must have inherited from his predecessors who "handed down" these gospels to him.

Watson's third premise – that Clement appears to treat *GEgy* on the same playing field as the proto-canonical gospels – also needs to be queried. As Watson notes, Clement draws from *GEgy* in a larger discussion of marriage, chastity, and asceticism in Book 3 of the *Stromateis*. Clement responds to arguments made by Carpocrates, Marcion, Tatian, and Julius Cassianus (a former disciple of Valentinus). Clement frames this whole disquisition by the unity of the Law, the Prophets, and the Gospel – as he says in *Strom.* 3.10: "And at once the Law and the Prophets with also the Gospel in the name of Christ are gathered together into one knowledge."[82] Clement's citations from the gospel are saturated with excerpts from the Synoptic gospels, and he also makes copious use of the Pauline corpus. Clement interprets the portions from *GEgy* through the lens of the "Scriptures of the Lord" (Law, Prophets, Gospel, and Apostle).[83] Clement never appeals to noncanonical gospels to elucidate proto-canonical gospels, only the reverse.

More importantly, Clement only cites from *GEgy* reactively. He does so in response to Cassianus' allegorical exegesis of an episode from *GEgy* involving a discussion between Jesus and Salome. Clement appears to be beating the heretics at their own game by showing greater knowledge of their own cherished gospel to which they were appealing. Even so, Clement implies that *GEgy* does not bear the same authoritative weight as the canonical four. This is clear in Clement's rebuttal of Cassianus' exegesis of the following *logion* from *GEgy*: "When you trample on the garment of shame and when the two become one and the male with the female is neither male nor female."[84] Clement refutes Cassianus' ascetic interpretation of this statement in a twofold manner. He begins:

---

[81] The fact that Clement shows no antipathy towards these noncanonical gospels makes it unlikely his sparse quotation of them was the result of active suppression.

[82] νόμος τε ὁμοῦ καὶ προφῆται σὺν καὶ τῷ εὐαγγελίῳ ἐν ὀνόματι Χριστοῦ εἰς μίαν συνάγονται γνῶσιν.

[83] *Strom.* 3.6.45.2–46.1, where Clement cites from *GEgy*, contains a cluster of citations from the proto-canonical gospels: e.g. *GMt* 5.17; *GMt* 19.3 // *GMk* 10.2; *GMt* 19.6 // *GMk* 10.9; *GMt* 19.16 // *GMk* 10.17 // *GLk* 18.18; *GMt* 22.20 // *GMk* 12.23 // *GLk* 20.35; *GMk* 10.9; 13.17; *GLk* 17.28; 18.8; 21.23.

[84] *Strom.* 3.13.92.2: ὅταν τὸ τῆς αἰσχύνης ἔνδυμα πατήσητε καὶ ὅταν γένηται τὰ δύο ἓν καὶ τὸ ἄρρεν μετὰ τῆς θηλείας οὔτε ἄρρεν οὔτε θῆλυ; translation from Ehrman and Pleše 2011: 227–29.

162   *Chapter 5: Irenaeus, Clement, Heretics, and Celsus*

"Firstly, therefore, we do not have this saying in the four gospels that have been handed down to us, but rather in the [gospel] according to [the] Egyptians."[85] That is to say, the status of this *logion* as *outside* the proto-canonical four works *against* its gravity as a conduit of Jesus tradition. Clement continues his critique with a more substantial second point: "And next, it appears to me that they do not understand that 'male drive' signifies, by a riddle, the soul, and 'female' signifies desire."[86] Clement thus begins an allegorical exposition of the terms "male drive" (ἄρρην ὁρμή) and "female" (θήλεια) as used in the passage from *GEgy*, and he is guided by the broader council of acknowledged Scripture.[87] One could paraphrase Clement as saying, "I have my suspicions about this gospel because it does not have the same apostolic pedigree as the Four. But I grant that it may contain authoritative Jesus tradition. Even so, when we interpret the relevant passage in its broader context, guided by the rest of Scripture, it does not confirm Cassianus' disdain for marital sexual intercourse." Clement viewed *GEgy* as valuable insofar as it contained genuine Jesus tradition, but because of the tenuous nature of its transmission, Clement only engaged its material epiphenomenally, as tradition ancillary to the fourfold gospel.

In conclusion, Clement's use of noncanonical gospels does not undermine the status of the fourfold gospel in Alexandria at the end of the second century. Rather, it confirms that Clement participated in the common *habitus* of reading the four gospels as the authoritative body of Jesus tradition to which minor, regional traditions might be added in an ancillary way.

5.2.2 Identities and Mode of Gospel Combinations in Clement

We have just established that the four proto-canonical gospels are identities of the gospels that Clement upholds in a class of their own. Clement's mode of bringing these gospels (and other Jesus tradition as well) into company with one another is closely related to his access to physical manuscripts. Clement describes his eight-volume work, the *Stromateis*, as "notes stored up for my old age, a remedy against forgetfulness... a sketch of those clear and vital words

---

[85] *Strom.* 3.13.93.1: Πρῶτον μὲν οὖν ἐν τοῖς παραδεδομένοις ἡμῖν τέτταρσιν εὐαγγελίοις οὐκ ἔχομεν τὸ ῥητόν, ἀλλ᾿ ἐν τῷ κατ᾿ Αἰγυπτίους.

[86] *Strom.* 3.13.93.1: ἔπειτα δὲ ἀγνοεῖν μοι δοκεῖ ὅτι θυμὸν μὲν ἄρρενα ὁρμήν, θήλειαν δὲ τὴν ἐπιθυμίαν αἰνίττεται.

[87] In the following section (*Strom.* 3.13.93.2–3.14.95.3), Clement explicitly cites Paul (Gal 3.28; 2 Cor 11.3; Eph 4.24; Phil 3.20), and he also draws from canonical *GMatthew* (18.11–12; 5.28) and Genesis 3.21. These are his primary and highest sources of scriptural authority. In the next few sections (3.15.96.1–3.16.101.5), Clement draws on even more canonical Scripture from *GMatthew, GLuke, GJohn*, 1 Corinthians, Exodus, Isaiah, etc. Canonical Scripture forms the bedrock upon which Clement adjudicates the value of the *logia* in *GEgy* and the compass by which his interpretation of these *logia* is guided.

which I was privileged to hear, and of blessed and truly notable men."[88] This is the kind of description we find in Aulus Gellius regarding his own practice of excerpting from classic books for the sake of memory.[89] The *Stromateis* give ample evidence that Clement was in the habit of excerpting from the proto-canonical gospels.[90] The extended quotation of *GMark* 10.17–31 in *Quis div.* 4 is one such excerpt. Since Clement inhabited the intellectual milieu of late second-century Alexandria, it is likely that Clement made copious excerpts of the proto-canonical gospels, collected them, and interpreted these excerpts in hermeneutical juxtaposition. The mode of gospel combination was careful consultation of manuscripts, quite plausibly stored in the Alexandrian catechetical school that Clement oversaw.[91] To a lesser extent, the same can be said of Clement's mode of accessing and interpreting *GEgy*.

5.2.3 Integrity of Gospels in Clement's Writings

The vast majority of Clement's gospel citations are from Jesus' teachings, and one might even say that Clement shows relatively little interest in the narrative sequence of each individual gospel. However, a few examples demonstrate that Clement does respect the narrative integrity and sequences of gospels. Clement's gospels have structural integrity sufficient to facilitate comparison and disambiguation of gospels in exegesis. In *Strom.* 1.21.147.4–6, Clement highlights the specifics of Matthew's genealogy and directly cites *GMatthew* 1.17. Clement identifies this as the genealogy "in the gospel according to Matthew."[92] Given that Clement also knows the Lukan genealogy,[93] it is likely that Clement is disambiguating by identifying the gospel to which he is referring. In *Strom.* 1.21.145.1–2, Clement locates Jesus' ministry in history by quoting the introduction of John the Baptist's public ministry in *GLuke* 3.1–2: "And in the fifteenth year, in the reign of Tiberius Caesar, the word of the Lord came to John, the son of Zacharias." Clement then moves to Jesus' ministry in *Strom.* 1.21.145.2–3 as follows:

---

[88] *apud* Eusebius, *Hist. eccl.* 5.11.2–3. Clement downplays the written nature of his *Stromateis* in favor of the memory that it facilities, tapping into the Platonic trope that memory is better than writing; for the same dynamic in Aulus Gellius, see Howley 2018.

[89] See above, Section 1.2.1c; cf. Heath's (2020: 69–75, 82–104) erudite discussion on Clement's excerpting practices.

[90] The high concentration of citations from *GMatthew*, *GLuke*, and *GJohn* in *Strom.* 3.6 and 3.13–17, as well as the handful of citations from the single section of *GEgy* demonstrate Clement's habit of excerpting from gospel books.

[91] On the Alexandrian school of Pantaenus, Clement, and Origen, see van den Hoek 1997.

[92] ἐν δὲ τῷ κατὰ Ματθαῖον εὐαγγελίῳ κτλ.

[93] See Eusebius, *Hist. eccl.* 6.14.5–7.

164   *Chapter 5: Irenaeus, Clement, Heretics, and Celsus*

And again in the same [gospel]: "And Jesus was coming to his baptism, being about thirty years old." And that it was necessary for him to preach only one year, even so this is also written: "He has sent me to proclaim the acceptable year of the Lord."

Clement has followed the sequence from *GLuke* 3.1–2, to 3.23, to 4.18, reading the narrative progression of Jesus' ministry in "the same [gospel]."[94] Clement here presupposes the narrative integrity of *GLuke*, in the same section where he shows a similar regard for the narrative structure of *GMatthew* and the point of its genealogy.

In *Paed.* 2.1.15.2–3 Clement shows awareness of the narrative location of *GLuke* 24.41–44, placing it "after the resurrection". In *Paed.* 1.5.12.2–3 and 2.1.13.2, Clement shows that he is conscious of the narrative context surrounding the miraculous catch of fish in *GJohn* 21. These all demonstrate that Clement has at least a general awareness of the narrative location of his gospel citations. On the other hand, in *Paed.* 2.8.61.1–3, Clement conflates Matthean, Johannine, and Lukan versions of the episode of the woman anointing Jesus, and he seems to locate it close to Jesus' passion (with *GMatthew*, *GMark*, and *GJohn*, and against *GLuke*). If Clement has regard for the narrative integrity of the gospels, he can treat this flexibly. While Clement treats the gospels not merely as repositories of sayings traditions, he does not read along the vertical axis of narrative sequence as consistently as Irenaeus.

5.2.4 Gospel Interactions

We can see how gospel books interact in Clement's reading habits by analyzing how Clement's gospel citations harmonize parallel versions from separate gospels. In an extended quotation from *GMark* 10.17–31 (*Quis div.* 4), Clement's text of *GMark* shows harmonization with both *GMatthew* 19.16–30 and *GLuke* 18.18–30. In Table 16a–c (see below), I lay out the text, according to NA28, and the variation units that correspond with the text of *GMatthew* and/or *GLuke*. In this extended citation, Clement's Markan text harmonizes to *GMatthew* 3 times, *GLuke* 6 times, and to both *GMatthew* and *GLuke* 4 times. Clement's citation of *GMark* 10.17–31 differs so extensively from any known manuscript, that some have posited that it must have been Clement's own citation from memory rather than an extract copied from a manuscript of *GMark*.[95] However, Clement's own words strongly indicate that he was indeed referring to a manuscript.[96]

---

[94] *Strom.* 1.21.145.2: καὶ πάλιν ἐν τῷ αὐτῷ. We can reasonably supply εὐαγγελίῳ as the nearest referent, based on the prior phrase, ἐν τῷ εὐαγγελίῳ τῷ κατὰ Λουκᾶν γέγραπται οὕτως.

[95] Cf. Cosaert 2008: 120n63; Barbara Aland 2004: 119–20.

[96] This is evidenced by the fact that Clement quotes from the passage several times later in *Quis div.*, using the same textual variants in his citation in *Quis div.* 4; e.g. *Quis div.* 22 (*GMk* 10.29–30a), *Quis div.* 25 (*GMk* 10.30b), *Quis div.* 25 (*GMk* 10.30c), and *Quis div.* 26 (*GMk* 10.31). Furthermore, Clement plainly indicates that he is drawing from a written text: ταῦτα μὲν ἐν τῷ κατὰ Μάρκον εὐαγγελίῳ γέγραπται (*Quis div.* 5); cf. Clement's comment on the

5.2 Clement of Alexandria

There are at least 3 other instances where Clement harmonizes to a parallel in another Synoptic gospel,[97] and 2 instances where Clement conflates Synoptic material with Johannine material.[98] There are 11 instances where Clement appears to harmonize Synoptic material, but because the manuscript tradition also tends to harmonize, it is less certain that Clement is the one harmonizing the material.[99] What these harmonizations demonstrate is that, for Clement, the four proto-canonical gospels occupied the same conceptual, exegetical space. This is especially true of the Synoptic gospels, which makes it all the more salient that *GThomas* does not function as a fourth Synoptic gospel for Clement. In spite of the extensive literary overlap between *GThomas* and the Synoptics, Clement does not slip any Thomasine redaction into his citation of Synoptic material; even in the passages where he seems happy to conflate two or more Synoptic parallels into the same citation, he never inserts a parallel from a noncanonical gospel.[100] What is more, even though *GJohn*, in literary terms and by Clement's own admission, is a different kind of gospel (a πνευματικὸν εὐαγγέλιον versus the Synoptics as σωματικά; *Hist. eccl.* 6.14), Clement is happy to harmonize and conflate Johannine and Synoptic material.

It is also important to note how Clement refers to gospels with respect to their authors and original readership. In the note preserved by Eusebius in *Hist. eccl.* 6.14.5–7, Clement characterizes *GMatthew* and *GLuke* as those "which include the genealogies" (τὰ περιέχοντα τὰς γενεαλογίας). He then distinguishes *GMark* as the gospel connected to Peter's memory. Finally, Clement relates that John

---

value of regularly hearing the reading of the gospel text (*Quis div.* 4). I am grateful to Peter Head for these insights into Clement's quotation of *GMk* 10.17–31.

[97] *Strom.* 4.34.4 (*GMt* 16.26 + *GLk* 9.25); *Quis div.* 33.4 (*GLk* 6.37 + *GMt* 7.1); *Paed.* 2.102.4 (*GLk* 12.24 + *GMt* 6.26); this analysis was enabled by Charles Cosaert's comprehensive study of Clement's gospel citations; Cosaert 2008.

[98] *Protr.* 82.3 (*GMt* 18.3 + *GJn* 3.5), notably does not harmonize with parallels in *GTh* 22 or *GTh* 46; *Strom.* 6.94.2 (cf. *Strom.* 5.33.4) draws together material from Synoptic and Johannine accounts of the feeding of the five thousand (*GMt* 14.13–21 // *GMk* 6.32–44 // *GLk* 9.10–17 // *GJn* 6.1–15).

[99] (1) *Strom.* 4.6.26.1 (*GMt* 5.4 // *GLk* 6.21 + *GMt* 5.10); (2) *Ecl.* 12.2 (*GMt* 6.32 // *GLk* 12.30); (3) *Ecl.* 12.2 (*GMt* 6.33 // *GLk* 12.31); (4) *Strom.* 7.104.4 (*GMt* 7.21, 12.50, 21.31 // *GLk* 6.46); (5) *Strom.* 4.161.2 (*GMt* 9.22 // *GMk* 5.34 // *GLk* 8.48); (6) *Exc. Theod.* 14.3 (*GMt* 10.28 // *GLk* 12.5 + *GMt* 10.32 // *GLk* 12.38); (7) *Quis div.* 31.3 (*GMt* 11.11 // *GLk* 7.28); (8) *Strom.* 5.80.6 (*GMt* 13.11 // *GMk* 4.11); (9) *Strom.* 3.47.2 (*GMt* 19.8 // *GMk* 10.5); (10) *Strom.* 2.146.2 (*GMt* 5.32 + *GMt* 19.9 // *GMk* 10.11); (11) *Paed.* 1.73.1 (*GMt* 6.9 + *GLk* 11.2); cf. Cosaert 2008: 311–35.

[100] See especially the lack of Thomasine parallel in *Protr.* 82.3, which conflates *GMt* 18.3 with *GJn* 3.5, but not with *GTh* 22 or *GTh* 46, or the lack of Thomasine parallel in *Quis div.* 4, which harmonizes all three Synoptic accounts of the Rich Young Ruler, but it does not include the parallel from *GTh* 4. Also, *Strom.* 4.6.26.1 harmonizes *GMt* 5.4 + *GMt* 5.10 + *GLk* 6.21 but not the parallel in *GTh* 69; *Strom.* 5.80.6 harmonizes *GMt* 13.11 with *GMk* 4.11, but not with any of the language of kingdom secrecy found in *GThomas*.

166   *Chapter 5: Irenaeus, Clement, Heretics, and Celsus*

wrote the last gospel "conscious that the outward facts had been set forth in the gospels, was urged by his disciples, and, divinely moved by the Spirit, composed a spiritual gospel." Clement's account here corresponds at several points to the tradition of gospels origins in *Hist. eccl.* 3.24.5–8a.[101] Like the earlier tradition in 3.24.5–8a, Clement's tradition in 6.14.5–7 uses the persona of the gospel author – Mark and John – to create a space in which gospels can coexist in unity amid difference. We have seen in our study that early Christians had a variety of strategies for handling the discrepancies between John and the Synoptics. Clement's strategy is to treat *GJohn* as a "spiritual" gospel (πνευματικὸν εὐαγγέλιον) – a capstone to the Synoptic gospels that set forth the "outward realities" (σωματικά) of Jesus' ministry. Clement elsewhere demonstrates his commitment to finding the spiritual, allegorical meaning behind gospel texts.[102] In broad strokes, *GJohn* functions as a guide to spiritual exegesis of the four gospels handed down – a hermeneutical move that Origen later develops in his *Commentary* on John's gospel.[103] In this way, Clement contributes a distinctly Alexandrian flavor to the multi-author discourse on gospels and their authors that began with Papias' Elder.

---

[101] See above, Section 4.2.
[102] E.g. *Quis div.* 5.
[103] Cf. Dawson 2002: 127–37.

Table 16a: Synoptic Harmonization in *Quis div.* 4 – *GMark* // *GMatthew*

GMk NA28	GMk *Quis div.* 4	GMt Parallel	Verbal Parallels
10.20 ὁ δὲ ἔφη αὐτῷ· διδάσκαλε, ταῦτα πάντα ἐφυλαξάμην ἐκ νεότητός μου	ὁ δὲ ἀποκριθεὶς λέγει αὐτῷ· πάντα ταῦτα ἐφύλαξα	**19.20** λέγει αὐτῷ ὁ νεανίσκος· πάντα ταῦτα ἐφύλαξα	πάντα ταῦτα // *GMt* 19.20 omit ἐκ νεότητός μου // *GMt* 19.20
10.21 ἕν σε ὑστερεῖ· ὕπαγε, ὅσα ἔχεις πώλησον καὶ δὸς [τοῖς] πτωχοῖς	ἕν σοι ὑστερεῖ· εἰ θέλεις τέλειος εἶναι, πώλησον ὅσα ἔχεις καὶ διάδος πτωχοῖς	**19.21** εἰ θέλεις τέλειος εἶναι, ὕπαγε πώλησόν σου τὰ ὑπάρχοντα καὶ δὸς [τοῖς] πτωχοῖς	add εἰ θέλεις τέλειος εἶναι // *GMt* 19.21 word order πώλησόν σου τὰ ἔχεις // *GMt* 19.21 (πώλησόν σου τὰ ὑπάρχοντα)
10.24 ὁ δὲ Ἰησοῦς πάλιν ἀποκριθεὶς λέγει αὐτοῖς	πάλιν δὲ ὁ Ἰησοῦς ἀποκριθεὶς λέγει αὐτοῖς	**19.24** πάλιν δὲ λέγω ὑμῖν	πάλιν δὲ // *GMt* 19.24

Table 16b: Synoptic Harmonization in *Quis div.* 4 – *GMark* // *GLuke*

GMk NA28	GMk *Quis div.* 4	GLk Parallel	Verbal Parallels
10.17 εἷς καὶ γονυπετήσας αὐτὸν ἐπηρώτα αὐτόν	τις ἐγονυπέτει λέγων·	**18.18** Καὶ ἐπηρώτησέν τις αὐτὸν ἄρχων λέγων·	τις // *GLk* 18.18 λέγων // *GLk* 18.18
10.19 μὴ φονεύσῃς, μὴ μοιχεύσῃς, μὴ κλέψῃς, μὴ ψευδομαρτυρήσῃς	μὴ μοιχεύσῃς, μὴ φονεύσῃς, μὴ κλέψῃς, μὴ ψευδομαρτυρήσῃς	**18.20** μὴ μοιχεύσῃς, μὴ φονεύσῃς, μὴ κλέψῃς, μὴ ψευδομαρτυρήσῃς	word order μὴ μοιχεύσῃς, μὴ φονεύσῃς // *GLk* 18.20 μὴ κλέψῃς // *GLk* 18.20
10.21a ἕν σε ὑστερεῖ	ἕν σοι ὑστερεῖ	**18.22** ἔτι ἕν σοι λείπει	σοι // *GLk* 18.22

10.21b ὕπαγε, ὅσα ἔχεις πώλησον καὶ δὸς [τοῖς] πτωχοῖς	εἰ θέλεις τέλειος εἶναι, πώλησον ὅσα ἔχεις καὶ διάδος πτωχοῖς	18.22 πάντα ὅσα ἔχεις πώλησον καὶ διάδος πτωχοῖς	omit ὕπαγε // GLk 18.22 διάδος // GLk 18.22
10.25 τρυμαλιᾶς [τῆς] ῥαφίδος	τρυμαλιᾶς βελόνης	18.25 τρήματος βελόνης	βελόνης // GLk 18.25
10.29 οἰκίαν ἢ ἀδελφοὺς ἢ ἀδελφὰς ἢ μητέρα ἢ πατέρα ἢ τέκνα ἢ ἀγροὺς	τὰ ἴδια καὶ γονεῖς καὶ ἀδελφοὺς καὶ χρήματα	18.29 οἰκίαν ἢ γυναῖκα ἢ ἀδελφοὺς ἢ γονεῖς ἢ τέκνα	γονεῖς // GLk 18.29

Table 16c: Synoptic Harmonization in *Quis div.* 4 – GMark // GMatthew // GLuke

GMk NA28	GMk Quis div.	GMt Parallel	GLk Parallel	Verbal Parallels
10.20 διδάσκαλε, ταῦτα πάντα ἐφυλαξάμην	πάντα ταῦτα ἐφύλαξα	19.20 πάντα ταῦτα ἐφύλαξα· τί ἔτι ὑστερῶ;	18.21 ταῦτα πάντα ἐφύλαξα ἐκ νεότητος.	omit διδάσκαλε // GMt 19.20 // GLk 18.21 ἐφύλαξα // GMt 19.20 // GLk 18.21
10.26 οἱ δὲ περισσῶς ἐξεπλήσσοντο λέγοντες πρὸς ἑαυτούς	οἱ δὲ περισσῶς ἐξεπλήσσοντο καὶ ἔλεγον	19.25 ἀκούσαντες δὲ οἱ μαθηταὶ ἐξεπλήσσοντο σφόδρα λέγοντες	18.26 εἶπαν δὲ οἱ ἀκούσαντες·	omit πρὸς ἑαυτούς // GMt 19.25 // GLk 18.26
10.27 ἐμβλέψας αὐτοῖς ὁ Ἰησοῦς λέγει	ὁ δὲ ἐμβλέψας αὐτοῖς εἶπεν	19.26 ἐμβλέψας δὲ ὁ Ἰησοῦς εἶπεν αὐτοῖς	18.27 ὁ δὲ εἶπεν	add δὲ // GMt 19.26 // GLk 18.27 εἶπεν // GMt 19.26 // GLk 18.27
10.28 ἠκολουθήκαμέν	ἠκολουθήσαμέν	19.27 ἠκολουθήσαμέν	18.27 ἠκολουθήσαμέν	ἠκολουθήσαμέν // GMt 19.27 // GLk 18.28

5.2.5 Authority of Gospels in Combination

We have already encountered Clement's notion of scriptural authority in the gospels in our comparison of his use of *GEgy* and proto-canonical gospels (see section 5.2.1). For Clement, the authority of the gospel lies in its position within the covenantal revelation of God in the text of Scripture – the Law, the Prophets, the Gospel, and the Apostles. This fourfold Scripture – subdivided into the Old and New Covenants – is the foundation of the one, true, ancient church:

Therefore, with regard to essence and thought, according to its origin and pre-eminence, we say that the ancient and catholic church is alone, gathering together into the unity of the one faith – the faith that comes from the proper Testaments (τῆς κατὰ τὰς οἰκείας διαθήκας), or rather the one Testament in different times by the will of the one God (τὴν διαθήκην τὴν μίαν διαφόροις τοῖς χρόνοις ἑνὸς τοῦ θεοῦ τῷ βουλήματι), through one Lord – those whom God has already ordained.[104]

The authoritative gospel is part of this ancient foundation, and it consists of the words and deeds which Jesus taught and accomplished before the end of Tiberius' reign (*Strom.* 7.17.106.4). As we observed above, Clement contrasted the antiquity of Jesus' teaching – under the reign of Tiberius – with the relatively recent teachings of the heretics under the reigns of Hadrian to Commodus (*Strom.* 7.17.106.4–107.1).[105] For Clement, then, the gospel, at least conceptually, was not a phenomenon that was rewritten to his present day.[106] Rather, it was an ancient deposit that was the capstone of God's covenantal revelation (as we saw above in *Strom.* 1.1.11.3). Clement held that this ancient deposit was handed town in the form of four gospels to Clement's generation. For Clement, the diverse yet harmonious corpus of four gospels is the fullest expression of *the* gospel that is positioned as the capstone of divine, covenantal revelation.

Clement shows a degree of liberality in his "transposing" and conflation of gospel *logia*,[107] and he shows a qualified reverence for material outside the proto-canonical gospels, and in these respects, he differs from the more conservative Irenaeus. However, in Clement's ideology and exegetical practice, the four

---

[104] *Strom.* 7.17.107.5.

[105] Tertullian makes a similar argument regarding Marcion appearing on the scene much later than apostolic Christianity, in the reign of Antoninus (*Adv. Marc.* 1.19.2); cf. Moll 2010: 31–41.

[106] Of course, the proto-canonical gospels inspired rewriting of the Jesus tradition well into Late Antiquity, but in the discourse of Irenaeus, Tertullian, Clement, Origen, and others, there remained the *concept* of the pristine, unadulterated, apostolic gospel preserved in certain gospels and not in others.

[107] On Clement's transposing and conflation of gospel *logia*, see Watson 2013: 423, who highlights Clement's free reworking of the Beatitudes in *Strom.* 4.6.41.1–3 and his explicit mention of the practice of "transposing": ὡς τινες τῶν μεταθέντων τὰ εὐαγγέλια.

170   *Chapter 5: Irenaeus, Clement, Heretics, and Celsus*

proto-canonical gospels – as the only Jesus books to participate in the unity of the Old and New Covenants – simply have no rivals.[108]

5.2.6 Summary of Gospel Combinations in Clement of Alexandria

Clement of Alexandria had an intimate knowledge of many classical texts – pagan, Jewish, and Christian. His Platonic notion of the unity of Truth in the eternal Logos influenced his respect for ancient texts through which the Divine Logos could speak, even if only in a whisper. Clement's writings are a repository not only for proto-canonical gospels but also a scattering of noncanonical gospel traditions, some of which he ascribes to gospels outside of the Four. However, for Clement, the identities of the gospels that are part of the "Scriptures of the Lord" are none other than *GMatthew, GMark, GLuke*, and *GJohn*. Clement brings these gospels into company with one another by mode of excerpting, and we can conclude that his vast number of citations from almost every chapter of the proto-canonical gospels – as well as some of the ways in which he cites them – presupposes consultation of gospel manuscripts. While Clement is not usually concerned about the narrative sequence of gospels, there are several points at which narrative integrity plays a role in his exegesis. Furthermore, Clement's ability to disambiguate one gospel from another while reading in parallel presupposes at least a modest level of integrity for the gospels. In Clement's citations and exegesis, the four proto-canonical gospels interact extensively and congenially, most saliently in the way he harmonizes parallel passages. No noncanonical traditions join in this inter-gospel symphony. For Clement, the four proto-canonical gospels, in their rich diversity, are the culmination of God's authoritative revelation in history, through which the Divine Logos speaks most clearly.

5.3 "Heretics" and "Pagans" and the Emergence of the Fourfold Gospel

In this chapter I have focused on Irenaeus and Clement of Alexandria and found in their writings strong evidence that the gospel-combining patterns of the first half of the second century gained considerable momentum in the second half. Elsewhere, I argue, along with Jeremiah Coogan, that the same *habitus* of fourfold gospel reading is strongly confirmed in Ammonius of Alexandria's dual-

---

[108] Irenaeus also displays a covenantal understanding of the gospels as Scripture, as does Justin Martyr before him. Like Justin Martyr before him, Irenaeus develops the *traditio legis* as the driving force from the Law through the prophets to the new covenant (*Haer.* 4.34.4; 4.35.2). The new covenant is equated with the "gospel" that raises humanity to new life (*Haer.* 3.11.8), and this gospel is both a spoken and a written phenomenon (*Haer.* 3.11.8; 5.9.4). On Justin Martyr's covenantal reading of the gospels, see Section 4.4 above and Rodriguez 2020.

5.3 "Heretics" and "Pagans" and the Emergence of the Fourfold Gospel   171

axis gospel reading at the turn of the third century.[109] Papias, the author of *GThomas*, the author of the *Epistula Apostolorum*, Justin Martyr, Tatian, and Ammonius constitute a recognizable trend towards the fourfold reading of the gospels as the gospel combination *par excellence.*

It is not only the proto-orthodox among whom this fourfold gospel-combining pattern gains traction in the second century (indeed, our analysis thus far has engaged several writings on the outskirts or even beyond the pale of proto-ortho-doxy). The gospel reading patterns of "heretical" groups such as the followers of Valentinus and Marcus, as well as the reading habits of Celsus the "pagan" also confirm our suspicions.

As mentioned above (Section 5.1.1), the followers of Valentinus evidently read *GMatthew* alongside *GJohn*. Ptolemy's *Epistle to Flora* and the fragments of Valentinian exegesis preserved in Irenaeus' *Adversus Haereses* paint a picture of a Valentinian reading community that interpreted all three Synoptic gospels alongside *GJohn* – and read all four of these gospels as Scripture – suggested by their allegorical interpretation of these texts. The Valentinian *Epistle to Flora* interprets *GMatthew* and *GJohn* intertextually and treats both as Scripture.[110] The *Epistle* is not rewriting *GMatthew* and *GJohn* into a new gospel text to rival, supplant, or even supplement these authoritative gospels. Rather, the *Epistle* pre-supposes both *GMatthew* and *GJohn* as authoritative texts that, together with the Old Testament Law, form the basis of theological discourse.[111] The fragments of Valentinian exegesis preserved by Irenaeus in *Adversus Haereses* confirm the intertextual, allegorical exegesis of all four proto-canonical gospels.[112]

A certain "Marcus" – probably a contemporary of Irenaeus – and his followers also appear to read the Synoptic gospels in an intertextual web. However, the Marcosians also integrate material not found in the proto-canonical Four into their gospel reading. In *Haer.* 1.20.1–21.2, Irenaeus describes the scriptural prac-tices of the Marcosians, and relates a string of Marcosian interpretations with citations from *GLuke* 2.49, *GMark* 10.17, *GLuke* 18.18, *GMatthew* 21.23, *GLuke* 19.42, *GMatthew* 11.28, *GMatthew* 11.25–27, *GLuke* 12.50, and *GMark* 10.38. These are the sectarians who, in Irenaeus' words, make use of "an unspeakable number of apocryphal and spurious writings."[113] Among these writings is the alphabet lesson episode also found in *IGThomas* and *EpAp* discussed in Chapter

---

[109] Coogan and Rodriguez 2023.

[110] *Ep. Flora* 33.3.5–6.

[111] *Ep. Flora* 33.3.5–6 draws upon *GMt* 12.25 as an authoritative saying with the following introductory formula: "for our Savior says." It then combines this with a further citation from *GJn* 1.3 introduced with the formula, "the apostle states." Throughout the epistle, Ptolemy treats *GMatthew* as Scripture, evidenced by his parallel citations from the Torah and *GMat-thew*, introduced by "Moses" and "the Savior" respectively and with equal textual authority.

[112] See above Section 5.1.1; one could also mention Heracleon's allegorical exegesis of *GJohn*, on which see Berglund 2020.

[113] SC 264.288: ἀμύθητον πλῆθος ἀποκρύφων καὶ νόθων γραφῶν.

172   *Chapter 5: Irenaeus, Clement, Heretics, and Celsus*

2. Irenaeus' excerpts from their exegetical extracts show redactional features from all three Synoptic gospels, as well as an unidentified *agraphon*.[114] The Marcosians' text of *GLuke* appears to be flexible.[115] All of this Jesus material is given allegorical interpretation, indicating its status as authoritative Scripture. Even though the Marcosians are eclectic in their use of Jesus tradition (engaging what would later be deemed a noncanonical infancy tradition as well as *agrapha*), they still accord to the Synoptic tradition a central place of authority. According to Irenaeus (*Haer.* 1.20.3), the passage from *GMatthew* 11.25–27 (paralleled in *GLk* 10.21–22) is "the very crown of their hypothesis."[116] Even in their eclecticism, Marcosian habits of gospel reading suggest the hermeneutical centrality of Synoptic gospels in second-century exegetical discourse on the Jesus tradition.

Celsus leaves us clues regarding how at least one influential pagan philosopher viewed Christian gospel-reading habits. From the fragments of Celsus preserved in Origen's *Contra Celsum*, we can establish that Celsus had extensive knowledge of *Sondergut* from *GMatthew* and, to a lesser extent, *GJohn*.[117] It is also probable that Celsus knew of the Lukan genealogy. There are several narrative features of the Triple Tradition that Celsus mentions in his writings. It is harder to establish whether Celsus knew of traditions coming from *GMark* or *GPeter*. Celsus' most important statement about the gospels comes in *Cels.* 2.27:

> After this, [Celsus] says that some of the believers... have corrupted the gospel from its original writing by a threefold or fourfold or manifold measure (τριχῇ καὶ τετραχῇ καὶ πολλαχῇ) and have refashioned it in order to deny the objections.[118]

In his antagonistic account of the written gospel, Celsus alludes to four dynamics. First, Celsus not only disparages gospel narratives, but he alludes to multiple versions of the written gospel. Celsus mentions at least three instances of "corrupting" and "refashioning" the "original writing" of the gospel. This probably refers at least to the proto-canonical gospels as distinguishable (and, in Celsus' mind, distorted) versions of the gospel.[119] That Celsus has the proto-canonical

---

[114] *Haer.* 1.20.2: "Many times I have desired to hear one of these words, but I did not have the one who says them;" SC 264.291: Πολλάκις ἐπεθύμησαν ἀκοῦσαι ἕνα τῶν λόγων τούτων, καὶ οὐκ ἔσχον τὸν ἐροῦντα.

[115] See especially the free citations of *GLk* 19.42 and 12.50.

[116] SC 264.292: κορωνίδα τῆς ὑποθέσεως αὐτῶν. ὑπόθεσις here most likely refers to the overarching theme that forms the interpretive key through which each of the texts are interpreted.

[117] Cf. Alexander 2005; Alexander is less certain about Celsus' knowledge of *GLuke* and *GJohn*.

[118] Greek text from SC 132.

[119] Cf. Celsus' Jew's statement about Christian *books* (plural) in *Cels.* 2.74. Alternatively, Celsus could be referring to multiple instances of textual corruption of the original gospel. This would not necessarily preclude Celsus' understanding of the gospels as separate books; he could view later gospel books as full-bodied textual corruptions of the original gospel. That

5.3 "Heretics" and "Pagans" and the Emergence of the Fourfold Gospel 173

gospels in mind is corroborated by the redactional features he alludes to from *GMatthew*, *GLuke*, *GJohn*, and possibly even *GMark*.[120] Second, in Celsus' imagination, these books were at least threefold, perhaps even fourfold. Third, Celsus understands these books to exist in parallel. He mounts his critique of the account of Jesus' baptism by contrasting material from *GMatthew* and at least one other gospel.[121] In reading the gospels along a parallel, horizontal axis, Celsus finds fault in their conflicting accounts. In *CCels.* 5.52, Celsus alludes to the differences between the account that has one angel at the tomb (e.g. *GMark* and *GMatthew*), and the account that has two (e.g. *GLuke*). Fourth, as a pagan, Celsus does not have a vested interest in distinguishing between the proto-canonical four and the rest, and yet Celsus shows the strongest knowledge of proto-canonical gospels, and only possible, marginal knowledge of traditions found in noncanonical gospels.[122]

Whether Celsus had copies of multiple gospels to hand and read them in parallel to critique them, or whether he received these sundry gospel traditions second hand, Celsus shapes his critique by mimicking the early Christian habit of envisaging discrete gospels in parallel. Celsus uses the Christian concept of gospel-books-in-parallel to discredit the very gospel message these books promote. Whether he was writing in Alexandria or Rome, Celsus acts as an external witness of the emerging family of the proto-canonical gospels, between 160 and 180 CE.[123]

The indirect and direct *testimonia* of "heretics" and "pagans" confirm that by the time of Irenaeus and Clement, the four proto-canonical gospels were well established in an intertextual web of books that were treated as mutually-

---

Celsus has separate books in mind is supported by that fact that his gospel allusions closely resemble *GMatthew*, *GJohn*, and quite plausibly *GLuke* and *GMark*.

[120] Origen surmises that Celsus often quotes from *GMt* (*Cels.* 1.34; e.g. *Cels.* 1.40 // *GMt* 2.1–12; *Cels.* 1.41 // *GMt* 3.16–17). Celsus probably had contact with the genealogies from *GMatthew* and *GLuke* – mentioning Jesus' lineage from a king and from the first man (*Cels.* 2.32). Celsus gives "extracts from the gospel" (Origen's words) that resemble details from *GJn* 19.34–37 (*Cels.* 2.36), and Celsus appears to be aware of the account of Jesus and the Samaritan woman (*Cels.* 1.70 // *GJn* 4.6), the Johannine post-resurrection account of Mary Magdalene (*Cels.* 2.59 // *GJn* 20.1–18), and the demonstration of Jesus' pierced hands (*Cels.* 2.59 // *GJn* 20.25–27). Celsus even calls Jesus a "carpenter" (τέκτων; *Cels.* 6.36), which Jesus is called only in *GMk* 6.3 (although Origen takes issue with this appellation, claiming that it is in no copy of the gospels); cf. Hill 2010b: 155–57.

[121] *Cels.* 1.40.

[122] The strongest cases for Celsus' use of a noncanonical gospel are the instances where Celsus mentions that Jesus drank the vinegar and gall (τὸ ὄξος καὶ τὴν χολὴν) at the crucifixion (*Cels.* 2.37; 7.13) – a detail paralleled in *GPet* 5.16. But both ὄξος and χολή are mentioned in the Matthean crucifixion account (*GMt* 27.34 + 27.48) as well as the prophecy upon which this account is formed, LXX Psalm 68.22.

[123] On Celsus' dates, biography, and antagonism towards Christianity, see Chadwick 1953; Cook 2000.

174   *Chapter 5: Irenaeus, Clement, Heretics, and Celsus*

interpreting Scriptures. This was not merely the construction of the proto-orthodox, but rather it had a widespread currency among Christians of various sects. Even to outsiders, this commitment to treat certain gospels in a class of their own was recognizable.

5.4 Summary and Conclusions

Irenaeus and Clement did not invent new ways of reading the gospels. They developed patterns and habits inherited from previous generations. Several of the dynamics at work in the composition of *GThomas*, *EpAp*, and the *Diatessaron*, and developed in the discourse on gospel authorship from *GLuke* to Justin Martyr, come to fruition in the explicit exegetical reflections of Irenaeus and Clement. These dynamics are the predominance of canonical gospels as sources for Jesus tradition, their propensity to keep nearly exclusive company with one another, the confluence of Johannine and Synoptic accounts, the epiphenomenal use of noncanonical traditions, the intra-canonical harmonization of parallel passages, and the habit of reading along horizontal and vertical axes of two or more proto-canonical gospels. They are not only present in the ways Irenaeus and Clement conduct their gospel exegesis, but also in Irenaeus' and Clement's second-order reflections on the gospels as books to be interpreted. These dynamics relate to the *identity*, *integrity*, and *interactions* of gospels in the second century.

Irenaeus and Clement mark a significant development in the *mode* by which gospels came together. While excerpting and annotating was *plausible* in the composition of *EpAp*, it is *probable* in the exegesis of Irenaeus and Clement. Irenaeus' use of *titloi* and Clement's use of *hypomnemata* exhibit these sophisticated methods of reading gospel books as textual objects in parallel. The most significant development, however, is in the theology of the written gospel's *authority*. Irenaeus and Clement are the first to do explicit biblical theology in which they situate the authority of the fourfold, written gospel as the culmination of the New Covenant. Irenaeus does this by his depiction of Christ, seated on the tetramorph gospel throne as the climax of biblical revelation. We can infer it in Clement's writings when we consider his theology of divine revelation in the Old and New Covenants and his notion of the handing down of authoritative tradition from the time of Jesus.

Many studies have focused on whether second-century Christian authors were aware of one or more gospels, and whether these gospels influenced second-century Christian literature. Our study has taken the discussion further by analyzing the dynamics that emerge when two or more gospels are brought into proximity in Christian literature and literary discourse of the second century. What we have uncovered in our literary analysis – in interpretive rewriting, gospel orchestration, and second-order exegetical discourse – is that the proto-canonical Four become a familial group, interacting congenially and intertextually in the first half of the second century, and these family ties were only strengthened as we reach the latter decades of that century. In the following chapter we will query these findings with the material remains of ancient Christian gospel reading. If our findings are confirmed in these Christian *realia*, then we will indeed have a strong case for the tenacity and widespread popularity of the fourfold gospel corpus in the second century.

Chapter 6

Gospel Combinations in Early Christian Artifacts: Gregory Aland 0171 and P4+P64+67

Thus far we have journeyed through various kinds of gospel combinations: interpretive rewriting, gospel orchestration, and discrete juxtaposition of gospels in early Christian discourse. The pattern that has emerged is that *GMatthew* and *GLuke* frequently kept company in these textual venues, and as early as Papias, *GJohn* and *GMark* join in this company-keeping. Noncanonical gospels have mostly featured secondarily, and they have not shared in the same familial web of gospel writings. We now transition to a new subset of gospel combinations: discrete juxtaposition in multi-gospel codices. The pre-Constantinian gospel manuscript record is fragmentary, and these artifactual remains are exclusively from Egypt. Moreover, it is a precarious endeavor to date these manuscripts to a fifty-year window in the period from the late-second to early-fourth century. Thus, the extent to which our observations can identify patterns in early Christian gospel combinations is limited. However, even if the manuscript evidence by itself could not establish widespread patterns, it is valuable inasmuch as it corroborates, nuances, or problematizes the patterns already demonstrated in Chapters 1–5.

These early Christian artifacts demonstrate which gospels kept company within the same covers of a codex, the artifactual mode by which they were combined, how gospel titles and pericope sequencing preserved their textual integrity, and how these gospels interacted through scribal harmonization. We even find hints of textual authority in the physical features of these codices. In this chapter we will investigate two codices which arguably date to the turn of the third century, CE: Gregory Aland 0171 and P4+P64+67. After discussing matters of provenance, dating, and physical features, we will apply our methodological questions regarding the identities, mode, integrity, interactions, and authority of gospel combinations.

6.1 Gospel Combinations in Gregory Aland 0171

6.1.1 Provenance and Physical Features

Gregory Aland 0171 is the remains of a multi-gospel codex whose provenance is linked to Hermopolis Magna. It consists of two fragments: P.Berlin inv. 11863

6.1 Gospel Combinations in Gregory Aland 0171   177

(*GMt* 10.25–32) and PSI 1.2 + 2.124 (*GLk* 22.44–64).[1] The Florence fragments (PSI 1.2 + 2.124) were found in Hermopolis Magna and first published in 1912 and 1913, but the Berlin fragment (P.Berlin inv. 11863) was purchased in 1910 and first published in 1966.[2] The reconstructed page dimensions of the Florence and Berlin fragments (approx. 11–12 cm x 15 cm), column height (approx. 12.5 cm), the identical hands, the relatively rare two-column format used in both, and the use of parchment make it probable that these fragments came from the same codex.[3]

These fragments comprise portions of two leaves of a vellum codex, with each leaf presenting the text in a two-column format. Leaf 1 contains portions of *GMatthew* 10.17–32, and the continuity of the text from the front (hair side) to the back (flesh side) gives us a window into the composition of the codex. The front (hair side) contains 10.17–24.[4] The back (flesh side) contains 10.25–32, with 10.33 inserted by another hand in the top margin.[5] The top margin and the intercolumnar space are visible on both the hair and the flesh side. Since Greek text moves from left to right, this requires that the hair side appear on the right side of the codex when it lay opened, and that the continuous text of 10.17–32 was part of the same sheet, folded into a bifolium. The two Florentine fragments come from one leaf, and they together comprise portions of *GLuke* 22.44–64. The front (hair side) of Florentine Fragment 1 (PSI 1.2) contains 22.45–47 and the back (flesh side) contains 22.50, 52–53. The front (hair side) of Florentine Fragment 2 (PSI 2.124) contains 22.44, 48–50 and the back (flesh side) contains 22.54–56, 61, 63–64. The portion that would contain 22.57–60 is missing, but we can infer from the spacing that these verses were present. *GLuke* 22.51 and

---

[1] For P. Berlin inv. 11863, see Treu 1966: 25-28 and Plate 1; Aland 1987: 37–61. For PSI 1.2 + 2.124, see Pistelli 1912: 2–4; Pistelli 1913: 22–25; Wessely 1924: 452–54; Bover 1925: 293–305; Lagrange 1935: 71–76; Birdsall 1993: 212–27. For an analysis of both as part of the same codex, see van Haelst 1976: 131–32; Charlesworth 2016: 75–78.

[2] Pistelli 1912; 1913; Treu 1966; the provenance of the Berlin fragment can only be located in Hermopolis Magna by virtue of its association with the Florentine fragments.

[3] For a detailed description of the dimensions, see Charlesworth 2016: 75–76. The unity of these fragments is the consensus view, reflected in their single Gregory Aland number (0171). Alternatively, these fragments could come from two separate codices of the same manufacturer. This remains a possibility and must chasten the reader from putting too much weight on the evidence found in this codex. The strong possibility of these fragments consisting of the same codex, however, legitimate a cautious comparison of its data to the second-century, gospel-combining patterns discovered earlier in this study.

[4] 10.24 is lacunose, but the reconstructed space between where the fragment cuts off in verse 23 ([φευγε]τε) and where it picks up in verse 25 ([αυτο]υ και ὁ δουλος) on the flesh side allows us to consider that verse 24 filled this space.

[5] 10.33 was probably omitted by Scribe A, due to *homoioteleuton*; the final words of 10.32 and 10.33 correspond (εμπροσθεν του πατρος μου του εν ουρανοις → εμπροσθεν του πατρος μου του εν ουρανοις). Scribe B subsequently emended the text by adding 10.33 in the upper margin.

178   *Chapter 6: Gospel Combinations in Early Christian Artifacts*

22.62 are notable omissions in the text, but these are explainable by *homoiote-leuton* (22.51) and *homoioarcton* (22.62).[6] Intercolumnar space and portions of both the upper and lower margins are visible in the combination of the two Florentine fragments.

To reconstruct the codex, we would have to discern whether Leaf 1 (*GMt* 10.17–24 on the hair and 10.25–32 on the flesh) occupied the left or the right side of the bifolium. If it was on the left side of the bifolium (Option 1), then the leaf would be located within the first half of the quire; if on the right side (Option 2), then the second half (see Figure 7.1). This is significant because the approximate midpoint of *GMatthew* is somewhere around *GMatthew* 16.7. If the leaf containing 10.17–32 (hair to flesh) was on the second half of the quire, then the midpoint of the quire would be somewhere before 10.17–32 (well before the midpoint of *GMatthew* at 16.7), and the quire would end well before *GMatthew* 28.20. In this case, the only conceivable way for GA 0171 to fit a gospel text that extended as far as *GLuke* 22.64 would be through the technology of a multi-quire codex combining *GLuke* and *GMatthew*. The probability of GA 0171 being a multi-quire codex is further strengthened by the fact that there are currently no known examples of single-quire parchment codices in antiquity.[7] The fact that the Berlin fragment contains sayings material from *GMatthew* while the Florence fragment contains a portion of the Lukan passion account suggests that this codex contained both gospels in their entireties. A codex containing a Sayings Collection joined together with only a Passion account would be an anomaly in the history of gospel writing, at least insofar as the extant manuscript and literary record allows.

---

[6] Charlesworth 2016: 76–77. The last words in 22.50 and 22.51 correspond (δεξιον → αυτόν), and the first words of 22.62 and 22.63 correspond (και → και), leading to *homoiote-leuton* and *homoioarcton* respectively.

[7] Turner 1977: 58; Kruger 2012: 269.

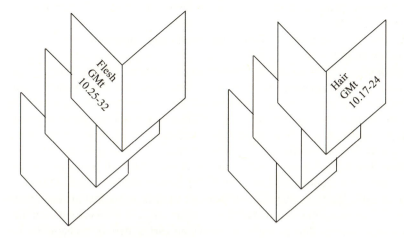

Option 1: *GMt* 10.17-32 on first half of quire

Option 2: *GMt* 10.17-32 on second half of quire

Figure 2: Possible Quire Constructions for P.Berlin inv. 11863

6.1.2 Paleography and Date

Until the landmark 2012 study by Pasquale Orsini and Willy Clarysse,[8] the consensus was that this codex was from the late third or early fourth century CE.[9] In the 1912 *editio princeps* of PSI 1.2, E. Pistelli dated the first fragment to the first half of the fourth century, based on a fourth-century *comparandum* from the 1911 Papyri Berolinensis collection compiled by G. Schubart.[10] Interestingly, Pistelli also mentions a second-century *comparandum* from Schubart's collection (Plate 31), as well as the third-century P.Oxy. 412, the third-century, P.Oxy. 1007, and the fourth-century P.Oxy. 1010, but he argues that the fragment most resembles the fourth-century *comparanda*. K. Treu, in the 1962 *editio princeps* of P.Berlin inv. 11863, dates the Matthew fragment to the fourth century based on its identification with PSI 1.2 + 2.124. Comfort and Barrett date GA 0171 by identifying the hand as a "biblical uncial" close to the fourth-century period when this script became standardized.[11] Orsini and Clarysse, however, have recently made a strong case for identifying the hand of 0171 as a "round majuscule influenced by

---

[8] Orsini and Clarysse 2012.

[9] Pistelli 1912; Treu 1966; van Haelst 1976; Aland 1987.

[10] Schubart 1911: plate 43.

[11] Comfort and Barrett 2001: 685; Naldini 1964: 16 also refers to the hand as "bella scrittura di tipo onciale," although Cavallo 1967: 66 refers to it as "di fuori della maiuscola biblica."

180 *Chapter 6: Gospel Combinations in Early Christian Artifacts*

contemporary chancery scripts."[12] They challenge the consensus and assign a date range of 175–225 CE.[13]

We must add the caveat, however, that most early Christian parchment codices are dated to the turn of the fourth century or later, with only a handful of exceptions from the third century. Indeed, since the work of E. G. Turner, it has been the consensus that papyrus preceded parchment in the development of codex technology. Thus, there are no known Christian parchment codices dating from the second century, and only a handful of Greco-Roman parchment codices from this period.[14] GA 0171, measuring 11–12 cm x 15 cm, also resembles the size of GA 059 (P.Vindob. G 39779) + GA 0215 (P.Vindob. G 36112),[15] GA 0162 (P.Oxy. 847),[16] P.Oxy. 1621,[17] and P. Amh. ii 24,[18] all which date to the fourth century. On codicological grounds, then, one has a stronger case for a late third- or early fourth-century date. Either GA 0171 is an anomalous parchment codex from around the turn of the third century, or it is a third/fourth-century codex with a script that strongly resembles an earlier period. Perhaps P.Oxy. 1007 – a parchment codex dated to the second half of the third century, containing a portion of Genesis, in two columns – lessens the anomalous character of a CE2–3, dual-column, parchment codex. Due do the uncertainty of dating GA 0171, we must consider what the implications would be for our study if GA 0171 is a late second-, third-, or early fourth-century codex.

Even if our codex dates to the fourth century, the dynamics of gospel combinations that it exhibits still inform our history of the four-gospel canon. For the sake of argument, let us suppose that all the codices considered in Chapter 6 and Chapter 7 – GA 0171, P4+P64+67, P45, and P75 – are fourth-century codices. If this were the case, mid fourth-century patterns of artifactual gospel combinations might still reflect reading habits that extend back to the latter decades of the second century. Our four codices in question would be added to an already substantial list of fourth-century codices that package together sequentially two or more

---

[12] Orsini and Clarysse 2012: 455n47. For a lengthy description of Alexandrian stylistic class, with its evolution into the Alexandrian Majuscule, see Cavallo 2005: 175–202.

[13] See Appendix 2A below.

[14] See Turner 1977: 39.

[15] These fragments are from a fourth-century parchment codex containing portions of *GMk* 15.20–38; Jongkind 2014.

[16] This is a page from a fourth-century parchment codex containing portions of *GJn* 2.11–22; cf. Schmid *et al.* 2007: 131–32.

[17] These fragments are from fourth-century parchment codex containing portions of Thucydides.

[18] LDAB 746; these are fragments of a fourth-century parchment codex containing portions of Demosthenes.

canonical gospels.[19] This would only highlight more prominently the contrast with the contemporaneous Nag Hammadi codices, *none of which contains any canonical writings*. In reality, the fourth century was a heyday for copying apocryphal gospels.[20] If, within this milieu of noncanonical codex construction, we only find canonical gospels packaged together with other canonical gospels – even at the outskirts of Christian Egypt in the Fayyum, Koptos, and Oxyrhynchus, where noncanonical gospels perhaps enjoyed a considerable level of popularity – then we are still looking at a durable pattern of canonical gospel combinations whose origins are anchored in the second-century theological program of Irenaeus and his forebears.[21] For heuristic purposes, we will begin our analysis with a cautious acceptance of Orsini and Clarysse's date of 175–225 CE for GA 0171, based on a paleographical analysis given in Appendix 2A (developed from the analysis of Orsini and Clarysse).

6.1.3 Scribal Collaboration

There are three distinct scribal hands behind the text preserved in 0171.[22] Scribe A wrote the main body of text in both the Matthean and Lukan fragments. This is the hand that Orsini and Clarysse characterize as in the transitional period between round chancery and Alexandrian stylistic class. Scribe B inserted the addition of *GMatthew* 10.33 on leaf 1v. This hand is smaller, much narrower, and appears cramped – which is to be expected when filling in an entire verse in the upper margin of a page. Even so, this hand is not fully documentary; it preserves some of the features of the informal round hand shared by Scribe A. Scribe C, on the other hand, corrected the text at *GLuke* 22.45 with a documentary hand that differs greatly from both Scribes A and B in its quick, nearly cursive, execution. The two-letter correction above *GLuke* 22.45 appears to have been made with less ink than the main body; the hue of the ink appears thin, suggesting that the ink did not penetrate the parchment as deeply. Scribe A and Scribe B, both with informal round hands, can be described as contemporaries. Scribe C has

---

[19] Codex Sinaiticus; Codex Vaticanus; 0242; Syriac Sinaiticus (Old Syriac); Codex Vercellensis (Old Latin); Codex Washingtonianus (CE4–5); 0214 (CE4–5). If we extend this list to include fifth-century gospel codices, the evidence mounts even further.

[20] Many of the extant noncanonical gospel fragments date to the fourth century or later: P.Oxy. 840 (CE4–5); P.Oxy. 1224 (CE4); P. Cair. Cat. 10735 (CE6–7); Codex Tchacos (CE4); and the many apocryphal gospel codices in the Nag Hammadi Library (CE4); for a summary of the dates of these artifacts, see Frey 2015; Kraus, Kruger, and Nicklas 2009; Brankaer and Bethge 2007. While many of these texts might have been composed as early as the second century, the point remains that these artifacts date to the fourth century. If P4+P64+67 dates to the same period as these artifacts, then it is notable that we do not see canonical gospels packaged together with any of the plethora of noncanonical gospel texts available at that time.

[21] We must factor into this discussion the fifth-century Vienna Palimpsest, which combines *GMatthew* with the *Acts of Pilate* and the *Infancy Gospel of Thomas*. See below, Section 6.3.

[22] Charlesworth 2016: 77.

182 *Chapter 6: Gospel Combinations in Early Christian Artifacts*

only left us two letters, and therefore we cannot come to any firm conclusions regarding his or her date.

As a contemporary of Scribe A, Scribe B probably served as a διορθωτής, correcting the text by including an entire verse that Scribe A had omitted. With these data we can reconstruct a scenario in which *GMatthew* and *GLuke* were copied by a group of scribes. Scholars have understandably avoided using the term "scriptorium" to describe a small enclave of scribes copying in the second and third centuries.[23] However, in the case of GA 0171, we can envisage a group of scribes who had concern for preserving an ἔκδοσις of both *GMatthew* and *GLuke*. If Scribe C was a contemporary of the other two scribes, this group would total three. If Scribe C was correcting the text at a later period, this would indicate a continued readership of this codex with an interest in the stability of the ἔκδοσις. In either scenario, GA 0171 constitutes the literary remains of a social network of readers, rather than merely the eccentricities of an individual reader. Based on the fine hand of Scribe A, and the standards of correction exhibited by Scribe B, the scribal collective behind GA 0171 bears the marks of formal competence.

Presupposing Orsini and Clarysse's date of 175–225 CE, we have in GA 0171 the remains of a codex that dates to the same fifty-year window as P4 and P64+47 (175–225 CE), and that overlaps considerably with the fifty-year window of P45 (200–250 CE). It is a multi-quire codex whose pages contain *GMatthew* and *GLuke* in two-column pages, perhaps in their entireties. The intertextual dynamics – the identities, mode, integrity, interactions, and authority of these gospels – displayed between *GMatthew* and *GLuke* in this codex thus serve as valuable data to be compared to the dynamics we have already demonstrated from the literary remains of second-century Christianity.

6.1.4 Identities and Mode

Containing in its canonical sequence the text of *GMatthew* 10.17–20, 21–23, 25–27, 28–32, Leaf 1 of GA 0171 is indisputably two pages from *GMatthew*. Containing in its canonical sequence the text of *GLuke* 22.44–56, 61–64, Leaf 2 is indisputably two pages from *GLuke*.

The text of *GMatthew* in 0171 has distinct but not exclusive affinities to D (i.e. the "Western" text).[24] The text of *GLuke* also has distinct but not exclusive affinities to D.[25] As I shall demonstrate below, the Matthean and Lukan textual

---

[23] Kruger 2013a: 39 argues that while the term "scriptorium" might be anachronistic for second century and third century Christianity, it is still abundantly clear that "in the second and third centuries there was a substantially developed system for copying, publishing, and distributing early Christian literature." Hurtado 2006a: 186–87 and Gamble 1995: 121–26 make similar observations.

[24] See Min 2005: 253–70; Wasserman 2012: 102–03.

[25] See Charlesworth 2016: 183–85; Elliott 1996: 165–67.

6.1 Gospel Combinations in Gregory Aland 0171

portions are also similar in that they both harmonize to the remaining two Synoptic gospels. This suggests that the scribes' exemplars for *GMatthew* and *GLuke* have the same textual character. This raises the possibility that the scribe was copying both *GMatthew* and *GLuke* from a single exemplar: a codex that already contained *GMatthew* and *GLuke*. Alternatively, the scribe could be copying from a Matthean exemplar and a Lukan exemplar, both of which came from the same provenance and textual affinity. It is impossible to be certain about whether the scribe of 0171 was the gospel-combiner, or whether it was the scribe of his or her exemplar(s), but the coherence of textual affinities between his Matthean and Lukan texts is more naturally explained by an exemplar that contained both texts. At any rate, the mode of this gospel combination was artifactual, and there is the possibility that such a combination had a codicological precedent.

6.1.5 Integrity

The technology of a multi-quire codex facilitates the discrete juxtaposition of *GMatthew* next to *GLuke* between two covers. Insofar as we can infer from a mere four pages remaining in GA 0171, the integrity of pericope sequences in *GMatthew* and *GLuke* is intact. The fragmentary nature of GA 0171, however, prohibits us from making a confident claim about the entire codex.

The *GMatthew* fragment in GA 0171 ranges from *GMatthew* 10.17 to 10.32, with 10.33 inserted in the upper margin by Scribe B. This section comprises the following dialogue units: Jesus' prediction of persecution (10.17–22 // *GMk* 13.9–13; *GLk* 21.12–19), "a disciple is not above his teacher…" (10.24–25 // *GLk* 6.40 // *GJn* 13.16), "there is nothing hidden…" (10.26–33 // *GLk* 12.2–9), and "whoever acknowledges me…" (10.32–33; cf. *GMk* 8.38; *GLk* 9.26). Sayings from the Double Tradition and Triple Tradition are particularly prone to rearrangement, as seen in the vast difference between the Matthean sequencing of these saying units (*GMt* 10.17–33) and the Lukan/Markan sequencing of the same material (*GLk* 21.12–19 // *GMk* 13.9–13, *GLk* 6.40, 12.2–9, and 9.26).[26] This makes it all the more striking that GA 0171 keeps the Matthean sequence intact, in the same codex that preserves the narrative sequence of *GLk* 22.44–64. Moreover, as we shall see below in Section 6.1.6 (and Tables 17 and 18 below), the Matthean text in 0171 harmonizes both to the Lukan and the Markan parallels. Thus, while the *text* exhibits harmonizing tendencies, the *sequence* displays remarkable Matthean integrity.

GA 0171 contains a portion of the narrative of Jesus' agony in Gethsemane (*GLk* 22.44–46), Jesus' arrest (22.47–53), a portion of Peter's first denial (22.54–56), a portion of Peter's second denial (22.61–62), and a portion of the episode

---

[26] In a famous passage, B. H. Streeter noted that "subsequent to the Temptation story, there is not a single case in which Matthew and Luke agree in inserting the same saying at the same point in the Marcan outline" (Streeter 1936: 183).

184 *Chapter 6: Gospel Combinations in Early Christian Artifacts*

of the guards mocking Jesus (22.63–64). This is the same inter-pericope sequence that appears in the major fourth-century codices, as well as in the third-century codex P75. What might be recovered from the extant fragments of P69 suggests the same inter-pericope sequence as well. While P75 and P69 have significant textual variants, Michael Holmes' hypothesis that the early text of the New Testament exhibited "macro-level stability" is true of the inter-pericope sequence unanimity among 0171, P75, and P69.[27] This bolsters the case that GA 0171 contains an intact narrative of *GLuke* with undisturbed integrity of sequence.[28]

While the evidence is indeed limited, we can tentatively suggest that the extant evidence does paint a picture of two Synoptic gospels maintaining their literary integrity within the same codex. More substantial remains of this codex would be needed to extrapolate whether this integrity persisted throughout *GMatthew* and *GLuke*.

6.1.6 Interactions: Scribal Harmonization

The interactions between the texts of *GMatthew* and *GLuke* in GA 0171 are fascinating. Most notably, the intra-Synoptic scribal harmonization at work in the text of GA 0171 gives evidence for a thick intertextual relationship among *GMatthew*, *GLuke*, and even *GMark*. As shown in Table 17 and Table 18, *GMatthew* 10.18 harmonizes to *GMark* 13.9, *GMatthew* 10.19 harmonizes to *GMark* 13.11, and *GMatthew* 10.30 harmonizes to *GLuke* 12.6–7. *GLuke* 22.51 harmonizes to *GMark* 14.47 // *GMatthew* 26.51, and *GLuke* 22.53 harmonizes to *GMatthew* 26.55. This harmonizing web leads Cambry Pardee to conclude:

> The very fact that the text of Matthew contains variants harmonizing to Mark and Luke and that the text of Luke contains variants harmonizing to Matthew and Mark shows that the scribe did not deliberately favor one Gospel over another. It is clear, however, that all three Gospels were read and copied in his community and that occasionally the parallel version of material being copied affected the scribe's transcription of the text at hand.[29]

---

[27] See Holmes 2013: 674–77 and 2020: 18–20.

[28] However, the omission of *GMt* 10.33 and *GLk* 22.51, 62, if not caused by *homoioteleuton* and *homoioarcton*, would downgrade the integrity of the canonical sequence.

[29] Pardee 2019: 108.

Table 17: Scribal Harmonization in GA 0171, *GMatthew* to Parallels

Reference	NA 28	0171	GMk parallel	GLk parallel
GMt 10.17	παραδώσουσιν γὰρ ὑμᾶς εἰς συνέδρια καὶ ἐν ταῖς συναγωγαῖς	πα[ραδωσουσιν] γαρ υμας [εις συνεδρι]α και εις [τας συναγ]ωγας	παραδώσουσιν ὑμᾶς εἰς συνέδρια καὶ εἰς συναγωηὰς (13.9)	Παραδιδόντες εἰς τὰς συναγωγὰς καὶ φυλακάς (21.12)
GMt 10.18	καὶ ἐπὶ ἡγεμόνας δὲ καὶ βασιλεῖς ἀχθήσεσθε ἕνεκεν ἐμοῦ...	[και επι η]γεμονων και [βασιλεω]ν σταθησεσθε [ενεκεν] εμου...	καὶ ἐπὶ ἡγεμόνων καὶ βασιλέων σταθήσεσθε ἕνεκεν ἐμοῦ... (13.9)	ἐπὶ βασιλεῖς καὶ ἡγεμόνας ἕνεκεν τοῦ ὀνόματος μου (21.12)
GMt 10.19	μὴ μεριμνήσητε πῶς ἢ τί λαλήσητε·	μη μεριμνη[σητε τι] λαλησητ[ε]	μὴ προμεριμνᾶτε τί λαλήσητε, (13.11)	
GMt 10.29	οὐχὶ δύο στρουθία ἀσσαρίου πωλεῖται;	[ουχι δυο] στρουθια [ασσαριου πω]λουνται		οὐχὶ πέντε στρουθία πωλοῦνται ἀσσαρίων δύο; (12.6)
GMt 10.30	ὑμῶν δὲ καὶ αἱ τρίχες τῆς κεφαλῆς πᾶσαι ἠριθμημέναι εἰσίν	αλλα κα[ι αι τριχες] της κεφαλης [υμων] πασαι ηριθμημ[εναι ει]σιν		ἀλλὰ καὶ αἱ τρίχες τῆς κεφαλῆς ὑμῶν πᾶσαι ἠρίθμηνται (12.7)

Notes: Adapted from Pardee 2019.

Table 18: Scribal Harmonization in GA 0171, *GLuke* to Parallels

Reference	NA 28	0171	*GMk* parallel	*GMt* parallel
GLk 22.50	καὶ ἐπάταξεν εἷς τις ἐξ αὐτῶν τοῦ ἀρχιερέως τὸν δοῦλον	και επαταξε εις τις εξ αυτων τον δουλον του αρχιερεως	ἔπαισεν τὸν δοῦλον τοῦ ἀρχιερέως (14.47)	καὶ πατάξας τὸν δοῦλον τοῦ ἀρχιερέως (26.51)
GLk 22.51	ἀποκριθεὶς δὲ ὁ Ἰησοῦς εἶπεν· ἐᾶτε ἕως τούτου· καὶ ἀψάμενος τοῦ ὠτίου ἰάσατο αὐτόν	omit	omit	omit
GLk 22.53	καθ᾽ ἡμέραν ὄντος μου μεθ᾽ ὑμῶν ἐν τῷ ἱερῷ οὐκ ἐξετείνατε τὰς χεῖρας ἐπ᾽ ἐμέ, ἀλλ᾽ αὕτη ἐστὶν ὑμῶν ἡ ὥρα καὶ ἡ ἐξουσία τοῦ σκότους.	καθ η[με]ραν οντος μου εν [τω ι]ερω ουκ εξετεινα[τε τας] χειρας επ εμε		καθ᾽ ἡμέραν ἐν τῷ ἱερῷ ἐκαθεζόμην διδάσκων καὶ οὐκ ἐκρατήσατέ με (26.55)
GLk 22.54	ὁ δὲ Πέτρος ἠκολούθει μακρόθεν	ο δε [πετρος ηκο]λουθει απ[ο μακροθεν]	καὶ ὁ Πέτρος ἀπὸ μακρόθεν ἠκολούθησεν (14.54)	ὁ δὲ Πέτρος ἠκολούθει αὐτῷ ἀπὸ μακρόθεν (26.58)
GLk 22.61	καὶ στραφεὶς ὁ κύριος ἐνέβλεψεν τῷ Πέτρῳ	omit	omit	omit

Notes: Adapted from Pardee 2019.

6.1 Gospel Combinations in Gregory Aland 0171

187

The horizon of expectation for the scribes behind 0171 brings together *GMatthew*, *GLuke*, and *GMark*.[30] For the present study, it is particularly salient that the Matthean text extant in this codex *does not* harmonize to the Thomasine parallel (*GMt* 10.26 // *GTh* 5). Thus, *GThomas* does not participate in the intertextual web formed by the three Synoptics.

Since 0171 is a multi-quire codex, it is tempting to imagine that it was a codex that included all three Synoptic gospels, based on the way that *GMatthew*, *GLuke*, and *GMark* interact in scribal harmonization. This, however, remains speculation. At the very least, we can conclude that in the provenance of 0171 – arguably late second-century or early third-century upper Egypt – *GMatthew*, *GLuke*, and *GMark* occupied the same conceptual space in the minds of certain scribes. In 0171, the interactions between *GMatthew*, *GLuke*, and by textual grounds *GMark*, can be characterized as a congenial web of intertextuality.[31]

6.1.7 Authority

It is impossible to determine with certainty whether a sense of textual authority was embedded in ancient Christian manuscripts, but a few details are suggestive. As noted above, GA 0171 resembles a round uncial with the influence of chancery scripts. While chancery scripts were workaday, round uncial was typically used for literary texts. One might surmise that whoever commissioned this codex regarded it as a literary product rather than a utilitarian document.[32] The two-column format of this codex, when opened, would have resembled an open scroll with four columns.[33] This columnar format was commonplace for works of Greek literature and Jewish Scripture. The elegant scribal hand and the competence involved in producing this codex corroborate that *GMatthew* and *GLuke* were treated as works of literature. A similar phenomenon is found in P. Baden iv 56 (Exodus; CE2) and Chester Beatty VI (Numbers and Deuteronomy; 2–3 CE).[34] These are Greek codices containing books from Torah, and their

---

[30] The term "horizon of expectation" describes the external influences at work upon the scribe, whether consciously or unconsciously, to prompt a harmonizing reading of Text B (e.g. *GMark*) to conform to Text A (e.g. *GMatthew*). Oftentimes Text A – read, heard, and deeply internalized by the scribe – constitutes the external influence that prompts the scribe toward "reflexive" harmonization of Text B. See discussion in Pardee 2019: 16–18.

[31] This intertextual web in an Egyptian context is confirmed by Clement of Alexandria in *Quis div.* 4–5. See Chapter 5.

[32] Stanton 2001 corrects Roberts 1979: 19–20 and Gamble 1995: 79 in pointing out that a substantial number of early Christian gospel papyri resemble literary books rather than workaday or utilitarian notebooks.

[33] There is also the possibility that when GA 0171 was opened to the first two pages, like P4+P64+67, *GMt* 1.1 was on the left-hand side, reinforcing its resemblance to the beginning of an opened Torah scroll. See Section 6.2.6 below.

[34] For a papyrological analysis of P.Baden iv 56, see Dorn, Rosenberger, and Trobisch 1985; 1986. For P. Ch. B. VI, see Kenyon 1935; 1958.

188   *Chapter 6: Gospel Combinations in Early Christian Artifacts*

resemblance of an open scroll is plausibly an effort to mimic a Torah scroll. Notably, Chester Beatty VI is a multi-book codex, containing two books of Torah, similar to GA 0171 housing two gospels. These parallels invite the conjecture that the scribes who manufactured GA 0171 accorded to *GMatthew* and *GLuke* a similar kind artifactual authority as the scribes who transmitted Jewish Torah to codex format in P. Baden iv 56 and Chester Beatty VI.[35]

6.1.8 Summary of Gospel Combinations in GA 0171.

If dated to the early third century, GA 0171 would be one of our earliest extant examples of two gospels combined within the same codex. In this codex we see *GMatthew* and *GLuke* in discrete juxtaposition by the technology of a multi-quire codex. The mode by which they were combined was manufactural, and it is entirely plausible that GA 0171 itself was copied from a single exemplar that combined *GMatthew* and *GLuke* physically. The stability of the pericope sequences in both the *GMatthew* and *GLuke* fragments testify to the integrity of these gospels in their combinations. This integrity coexists with an intertextual interaction involving not only *GMatthew* and *GLuke*, but also *GMark* (evidenced in the scribal harmonization). The physical features of this codex suggest that the manufacturers were constructing a codex that contained a work of literature, perhaps even intending it to function with a similar authority as contemporaneous Jewish Torah codices.

GA 0171 provides the first material corroboration of our conclusions thus far: proto-canonical gospels kept company with one another in a network of family resemblance and intertextual, congenial interaction. Its provenance at Hermopolis Magna establishes our first material, geographical coordinate for these practices of gospel-combining. If these patterns correspond to other geographical coordinates, we can begin to speak more broadly of early Christian material habits of gospel combination. We therefore turn to our next artifact for consideration: P4+64+67.

6.2 Gospel Combinations in P4+P64+67

6.2.1 Description and Provenance

P4 and P64+67 are two collections of gospel fragments that were found at separate times in the vicinity of Koptos. P4 contains portions of the first six chapters of *GLuke* and P64+67 contains portions of *GMatthew*, chapters 3, 5, and 26. P4

---

[35] Hill 2011: 85–88 draws the parallel between a four-column Torah scroll to the four-column opened codices of P. Baden iv 56, Ch. B. VI, and P4+P64+67. I extend the parallel to include GA 0171.

also contains a flyleaf with a title of the *Gospel according to Matthew*. We will describe these portions in detail in Section 6.2.3.

The Lukan fragments of P4 were discovered within the pages of a Philo codex, purchased by the Dominican scholar Père Scheil in Luxor, Egypt.[36] They were most likely discovered in nearby Koptos (modern-day Quft), but Scheil probably obtained this information from the antiquities dealer from whom he bought the Philo codex rather than from his own discovery in Koptos.[37] A number of scholars in the twentieth century accepted the premise that the Lukan fragments formed a wad used for stuffing in the binding of the Philo codex,[38] but Brent Nongbri has demonstrated that the fragments could have been slipped into the pages of the Philo codex for safekeeping rather than stuffing for the binding.[39] The Matthean fragments of P64 were purchased in Luxor, a little later, in 1901 – an acquisition made by Charles B. Huleatt.[40] In a 1953 article, C. H. Roberts seems to imply that the fragments of P67 were also obtained by Huleatt at this same location.[41] Nongbri summarizes:

> [O]n the basis of the evidence presently available, all we can confidently say is that the possibility exists that all of the pieces may have originated from a single dealer in Luxor and perhaps from a single codex that contained Matthew and Luke. Pushing beyond this conclusion about provenance is simply speculation.[42]

The provenance of these manuscripts does indeed establish the possibility that they constitute a unified, multi-gospel codex. As we shall see in the following section, however, the evidence goes beyond Nongbri's minimalism, and it points strongly in the direction of a multi-gospel codex.

6.2.2 Paleography and Date

P4 and P64+67 are typically dated to a period between 175 and 250 CE.[43] However, in the past decade Don Barker has widened the possible dating of these

---

[36] Nongbri 2018: 247–60; Nongbri summarizes and offers helpful critiques on the earlier reports by Scheil 1893: i–iii, Merell 1938, and Roberts 1963: 11–14.

[37] Nongbri 2018: 262.

[38] Roberts 1963:11–14; 1979: 13; Skeat 1997: 24.

[39] Nongbri 2018: 260. Nongbri cites the original description by Scheil 1893: iii, as does Gathercole 2012b. Scheil did not actually say that these fragments were stuffing, but rather "in order to fill up the capacity of the cover, there were several fragments of leaves glued together" ("et pour remplir la capacité de la couverture, se trouvaient plusieurs fragments de feuillet collés ensemble"); translation my own; cf. Nongbri 2018: 347n25.

[40] Nongbri 2018: 262–63; Roberts 1953: 233.

[41] Roberts 1953: 233–37.

[42] Nongbri 2018: 263.

[43] Roberts 1979: 12–13; Aland 1994: 29; Comfort 1995; Gathercole 2012a.

190   *Chapter 6: Gospel Combinations in Early Christian Artifacts*

papyri to a period extending from the mid second to mid fourth century CE.[44] Barker's analysis is based on a comparison between P4+P64+67 and Sinaiticus.[45] Barker argues that P4+P64+67 is at least as similar to Sinaiticus as it is to the securely dated second-century *comparandum*, P.Oxy. 661. Barker's comparisons do not give due analysis to the similarities between P4+P64+67 and P.Oxy. 661 (late CE2 / early CE3) and P.Ryl. 16 (before 253–56 CE), and he does not mention other important *comparanda*: P.Oxy. 3227 (CE2/3), P.Oxy. 4327 (early CE3), and P.Oxy. 3509 (late CE3, early CE4).[46] His conclusions should be queried, considering this more extensive dataset.[47] This more extensive dataset, analyzed in Appendix 2B, allows us to proceed with the consensus dating of P4+P64+67 to around 175–250 CE.[48]

6.2.3 Physical Features and Compositional Unity

There has been a spirited debate on whether P4 and P64+67 come from the same codex.[49] The intensity of the debate has been fueled by the hypothesis that P4+P64+67 was part of an early, four-gospel codex.[50] It is important to distinguish between two hypotheses here: first, whether P4+P64+67 was a multi-gospel codex, and second, whether P4+P64+67 was a *four-gospel codex*. Regarding the latter hypothesis, it should be noted that even the most substantial arguments in favor of a four-gospel codex are at best speculation. There are no manuscripts of *GMark* or *GJohn* that can be identified as constitutive of a four-gospel codex together with P4 and P64+67. While the theological motivations and

---

[44] Barker 2011; cf. also Nongbri's general skepticism towards paleographical precision in Nongbri 2016a; 2018; 2019; 2020.

[45] Images of Sinaiticus are available at https://codexsinaiticus.org/en/manuscript.aspx. Accessed 1 March 2021.

[46] P.Oxy. 3227 has a document written across the fibers "in a cursive style of the third century" (Orsini 2019: 72). On the other side of the fragments, along the fibers, is a portion of Hesiod's *Works and Days*. The document side forms the *terminus ante quem* as it reused the earlier Hesiod scroll. The literary hand of P.Oxy. 3227 can therefore be dated to CE2/3. The same method brings the date of P.Oxy. 4327 to CE2/3: along the fibers is a portion of Demosthenes' *Chersoneso*, and across the fibers is document written with a third-century cursive hand (Orsini 2019: 70). With P.Oxy. 3509, the document written across the fibers dates to the first half of the fourth century, so the portion of Plato's *Republic* written along the fibers probably dates to the latter part of the third century (Orsini 2019: 71).

[47] Orsini 2019: 57–72 responds to the criticisms of Cavallo's 1967 monograph and offers this wider dataset, based on securely datable manuscripts, for establishing the early development of the biblical majuscule hand.

[48] This conclusion is based on the analysis that the overall ductus and individual letter formations resemble P.Oxy. 661, P.Ryl. 16, P.Oxy. 3227, and P.Oxy. 4327, more than they do P.Oxy. 3509 or Sinaiticus.

[49] Roberts 1979: 13; Skeat 1997; Stanton: 1997; Head 2005; Head 2011; Charlesworth 2007; Hill 2011; Nongbri 2018.

[50] Cf. Skeat 1997 and Stanton 1997.

codicological technology necessary for manufacturing a four-gospel codex at the end of the second century might be plausibly reconstructed, the fact remains that P45 is the only codex with extant leaves from *GMatthew*, *GMark*, *GLuke*, and *GJohn* before the fourth century CE.[51] If one is going to argue from the early Christian hermeneutics of the fourfold gospel that P4+P64+67 is a four-gospel codex, then one cannot also argue the reverse – that P4+P64+67 confirms early Christian fourfold gospel hermeneutics. This would be circular reasoning. For the present study, then, I will not base any arguments on the imaginative premise that P4+P64+67 is a four-gospel codex.

It is a different matter, however, when one considers whether P4 and P64+67 inhabited the same codex. Perhaps the strongest argument against the compositional unity of P4 with P64+67 is that of Scott Charlesworth, who reconstructs the codicological layout of P4 and P64+67 based on fiber orientation and concludes that the fragments of P64+67 and P4 must have originated in different quires.[52] Charlesworth overstates his case, however, when he adds that P4 and P64+67 "are not from the same single- or indeed multiple-quire codex."[53] Charles Hill has offered a response.[54] Hill highlights the fact that Fragment A of P67 (*GMt* 3.9, 15) is a folio with a fiber orientation wherein vertical precedes horizontal ($\downarrow\rightarrow$), whereas Fragment B of P67 (*GMt* 5.20–22, 25–28) is a folio with a fiber orientation wherein horizontal precedes vertical ($\rightarrow\downarrow$).[55] The most plausible explanation of this change of fiber orientation, based on the most common form of quire construction in the period in question, is that Fragment A was located on the first half of the quire while Fragment B was on the second half. In such a construction, this quire would end well before the halfway point of *GMatthew* (by Stephanus' versification, the halfway point of *GMatthew* is at 16.7). The three fragments from P64 come from a single leaf that contained at least *GMatthew* 26.7–33. In this leaf, vertical fibers precede horizontal ($\downarrow\rightarrow$), indicating that this leaf was located at the first half of a separate quire to the fragments in P67. Given the consensus that P64 and P67 belong to the same codex, the evidence is clear: P64 and P67 were part of a multi-quire codex containing at least *GMatthew*.

P4 preserves four separate leaves from *GLuke* (various portions from chapters 1–6). These leaves follow the same pattern as P64+67. In Fragment A (portions of *GLk* 1.58–2.7), vertical precedes horizontal ($\downarrow\rightarrow$), and therefore it was part of the first half of a quire. In Fragment B (portions of *GLk* 3.8–4.2), horizontal precedes vertical ($\rightarrow\downarrow$), indicating the second half of a quire. Fragment C (portions of *GLk* 4.29–5.8) returns to the vertical-horizontal ($\downarrow\rightarrow$) fiber orientation of the

---

[51] For an exhaustive list of ancient multi-gospel codices, see Dormandy 2018.

[52] Charlesworth 2007.

[53] Charlesworth 2007: 604.

[54] Hill 2011: 75–91.

[55] Hill 2011: 82–84.

192   *Chapter 6: Gospel Combinations in Early Christian Artifacts*

first half of another quire. Charles Hill concludes that "[t]his shows P4 also to be a multiple quire codex put together in the same way as P64+67, with an alternating fiber pattern, beginning with vertical ↓ preceding horizontal →."[56] Hill here follows the same rigorous codicological analysis of Charlesworth. Hill notes that, while Charlesworth has demonstrated that Skeat was mistaken in arguing that P4+P64+67 was a *single-quire* codex containing *GMatthew* and *GLuke*, Charlesworth's analysis works in favor of P4+P64+67 being part of the same *multi-quire* codex.

Other factors must also be taken into consideration regarding the unity of P4 with P64+67. These are provenance, page color, the use of *ekthesis*, orthography, column format, column and page size, paragraph division, *nomina sacra*, scribal habits. We will engage these phenomena each in turn.

Several scholars have raised objections to the compositional unity based on an alleged discrepancy between the provenance of P4 and P64+67.[57] Both P4 and P64 were purchased in Luxor (the former in 1890, the latter in 1901),[58] and so technically both fragments can be considered to hail from the same provenance (probably the nearby ancient city of Koptos). The issue therefore lies in how P4 and P64+67 could have been separated between their composition in antiquity and their acquisition at the turn of the 20th century. The Lukan fragments of P4 were dismembered from a codex before they were inserted into the Philo codex in which they were discovered in the modern period, and it is probable that the same can be said of the Matthean flyleaf. Whatever caused the leaves of P4 to be dismembered from their original codex could also explain why P4 was separated from P64 and P67. Provenance is therefore no defeater to the compositional unity of P4 and P64+67.

Scholars skeptical of the unity of these fragments have also pointed to a difference in coloring between P4 and P64+67. P64 has been reported to have a lighter color than P4.[59] Differences in physical appearance between disparate fragments of the same artifacts are, however, well known. Hélène Cuvigny has noted that "[e]ven if [fragments] have spent the intervening years a few centimeters apart, they have been subjected to very different conditions of preservation."[60] Roger Bagnall confirms that this includes changes in color.[61] Furthermore, it is entirely possible that sections of papyri from more than one bookroll could be used to construct a single codex. Different bookrolls could therefore

---

[56] Hill 2011: 84.

[57] Charlesworth 2007: 599n98, summarizing the issue of provenance, expresses that "it is difficult to see how the latter [i.e P64] could have been separated from the former [i.e. P4]" in antiquity. Head 2005: 451–52 and Roberts 1953: 234 raise similar concerns.

[58] Skeat 1997: 24–25; Roberts 1953: 233.

[59] Charlesworth 2007: 596; Aland 1965/1966: 193.

[60] Cuvigny 2009: 50–51.

[61] Bagnall 2009: 34.

6.2 Gospel Combinations in P4+P64+67 193

account for differences in coloring within a single codex.[62] Finally, Charles Hill reports that a glue-like substance spread across various parts of the P4 fragments accounts for the uneven, darker coloration of P4.[63] Differences in color have little to no bearing on whether P4 and P64+67 were part of the same codex.

The patterns of *ekthesis* – the projection of letters into the margins to indicate sense-unit divisions – in P4 an P64+67 are within the range of consistency for a scribe producing a single codex. Charlesworth argues that the two extant examples of *ekthesis* in P64+67 (at *GMatthew* 5.25 and 26.31) are solidly one-letter projections into the margins, whereas the thirteen cases of clearly discernible *ekthesis* in P4 range from one to two letters (two were 2 letters, eight were 1.75 letters, two were 1.5 letters, and one was 1 letter). Charlesworth interprets this data to mean that "the scribe seems to have used different amounts of projection" in P4 and P64+67 respectively.[64] However, even within P4, we can see a range from one-letter to two-letter *ekthesis*, and this level of variation in a single codex was not uncommon.[65] The presence of regular *ekthesis* at paragraph breaks corresponding to the divisions in NA28, in both P4 and P64+67, even with the slight variation of letters-per-*ekthesis*, is an indication that these manuscripts came from the same codex rather than disparate codices.

The textual affinities and scribal habits of P4 and P64+67 also bear striking resemblance. Tommy Wasserman, in a detailed study of every variation unit in both of these manuscripts, concludes that P4 has a 19.4% ratio of deviation from NA27 and P64+67 has a 15% ratio of deviation, and thus, "both papyri… reflect a 'strict' transmission character."[66] Coupled together with paleographical evidence, Wasserman concludes that both manuscripts were copied by the same scribe, even if not in the same codex (Wasserman remains open to the possibility of a single codex). As we shall see below, both P4 and P64+67 share close textual affinities with Vaticanus and can be categorized as belonging to the same textual family, yet another piece of evidence contributing to their scribal proximity.

The scholarly consensus is that the same scribe copied P4 and P64+67. When all the common features are considered together, the cumulative evidence weighs heavily in favor of codicological unity. The strongest counterarguments are sufficiently answered by the fact that both P4 and P64+67 have the same multi-quire construction, and therefore are plausibly parts of the same multi-quire codex.[67]

---

[62] Hill 2011: 80.

[63] Hill 2011: 79, citing Scheil 1893, who noted that the fragments were previously glued together.

[64] Charlesworth 2007: 597.

[65] Bagnall 2009: 34.

[66] Wasserman 2010: 26.

[67] In a provocatively titled chapter ("Fabricating a Second-Century Codex") that dismantles several false assumptions undergirding the theory of P4+P64+67 as a four-gospel codex, Nongbri only mentions Hill's argument (Hill 2011) in a passing endnote (Nongbri 2018: 347n23).

194 *Chapter 6: Gospel Combinations in Early Christian Artifacts*

We will therefore proceed with the established premise that P4+P64+67 was indeed a multi-quire codex containing both *GMatthew* and *GLuke*.

6.2.4 Identities, Mode, and Integrity

The fragments of P64+67 contain, in canonical sequence, the following verses: *GMatthew* 3.9, 15; 5.20–22, 25–28; 26.7–8, 10, 14–15, 22–23, 31–33. The fact that these few fragments preserve text near the beginning and end of *GMatthew*, including both dialogue and narrative, makes it highly likely that P64+67 contained the whole gospel of *GMatthew*. The fragments of P4 contain, in canonical sequence, the following verses: *GLuke* 1.58–59; 1.62–2.1; 2.6–7; 3.8–4.2; 4.29–32, 34–35; 5.3–8; 5.30–6.16. This is a substantial portion of the first six chapters of *GLuke*. It is impossible to determine with absolute certainty whether P4 contained all of *GLuke*, but the extant narrative progression from *GLuke* 1.58 to 6.16 in P4 suggests that if the technology and financial means were available, this probably would have contained the entire gospel of Luke. A multi-quire codex could easily accommodate all of *GLuke*, and the high-quality production evident in the physical and paratextual features of P4 suggest that the financial means were available. Furthermore, there is a diverse array of Matthean gospel material extant in P64+67: John the Baptist's ministry, Jesus' baptism, the Sermon on the Mount, the Last Supper, the Mount of Olives. Likewise, there is a vast array of Lukan gospel material extant in P4: Jesus' birth, John the Baptist's ministry, Jesus' baptism, Jesus' genealogy, the wilderness temptation, Jesus' rejection at Nazareth, and the calling of the disciples. The diversity of episodes preserved in their canonical sequence across P64+67 and P4 give every indication that this codex contained the entireties of *GMatthew* and *GLuke*.

The mode of combination is artifactual, facilitated by the technology of a multi-quire codex. As noted above, the Matthean fragments (P64+67) and Lukan fragments (P4) both have a textual affinity to B and other Alexandrian witnesses. Since the Matthean and Lukan portions have the same textual character, this might imply that the scribe(s) were copying from an exemplar that itself was a multi-gospel codex containing *GMatthew* and *GLuke*. Alternatively, it might simply be the result of the scribe(s) copying from exemplars that could be traced back to a common geographical locus of the Alexandrian textual tradition. Since parallel readings of *GMatthew* and *GLuke* were widespread by the time of Tatian (ca. 170 CE), it is possible that a multi-gospel codex of *GMatthew* and *GLuke* existed as an exemplar antedating P4+P64+67, but this remains a conjecture.

Regarding integrity, all the extant fragments of P4+P64+67 keep the canonical sequence of pericopes, so it is likely that the integrities of *GMatthew* and *GLuke* are preserved throughout this codex.

6.2.5 Interactions

a. Scribal Harmonization

Within the pages of P4+P64+67, we can see a level of interaction between gospel texts in the ways that the scribe(s) behind this codex harmonized parallel Synoptic passages (for this section, the reader should consult Tables 19 and 20). This kind of harmonization can be seen between *GMatthew* and *GMark*, *GLuke* and *GMark*, and possibly between *GLuke* and *GMatthew*. Even though the extant portion of *GMatthew* in P64+67 is small, one assimilating variant stands out: *GMatthew* 26.31 // *GMark* 14.27. In the Matthean version, Jesus includes the personal pronoun ὑμεῖς, emphasizing the nature of the disciples deserting Jesus ("*you* all will stumble because of me this night"). The Markan evangelist does not include the pronoun. Although the papyrus is lacunose where we might expect to see the ὑμεῖς from *GMatthew* 26.31, we can infer from spacing that ὑμεῖς would not have fit on this line (the following line continues with σκανδαλισθήσεσθε κτλ.). We can agree with Skeat, Min, and Pardee that the scribe of P4 omitted the pronoun.[68] Perhaps the scribe omitted the pronoun out of carelessness, but this is unlikely, given how "strict" the scribe appears elsewhere. More plausibly, the scribe's horizon of expectation for the text of *GMatthew* might have overlapped with *GMark*, producing the harmonization, as shown in Table 19 (see below). We see similar overlap between *GLuke* and *GMark* in P4, displayed in Table 20 (see below).

The scribe of P4+P64+67 has a considerable regard for minimizing textual variation and preserving a "strict" form of the text.[69] Even so, the cross-pollination of *GMatthew*, *GLuke*, and *GMark* within his or her codex is evident. This cross-pollination is not shared with *GThomas*, which does indeed have parallel material; *GThomas* 47 parallels *GLuke* 5.36–39, which is extant in P4. There is no hint of harmonization with the Thomasine parallel here. Similarly, *GThomas* 104 parallels *GLuke* 5.33–35, but *GThomas* does not appear on our scribe's horizon of expectation.

Table 19: Scribal Harmonization in P64+67[a]

Reference	NA 28	P64+67	*GMk* parallel	*GLk* parallel
GMt 26.31	πάντες ὑμεῖς σκανδαλισθήσεσθ ε ἐν ἐμοὶ ἐν τῇ νυκτὶ ταύτῃ	παν[τες {υμεις?}] σκανδαλισθησεσθ ε εν εμοι εν τ[η νυκτι] ταυτη	πάντες σκανδαλισθήσεσ θε (14.27)	

Notes: [a] Adapted from Pardee 2019.

---

[68] Skeat 1997: 171; Min 2005: 169; Pardee 2019: 69; Head 1995: 260–61 remains undecided, suggesting that the letters per line can vary even within a small fragment like P67.

[69] This is argued in detail by Wasserman 2010.

196 Chapter 6: Gospel Combinations in Early Christian Artifacts

Table 20: Scribal Harmonization in P4[a]

Reference	NA 28	P4	*GMark* parallel	*GMatt* parallel
GLk 6.3	ὅτε ἐπείνασεν αὐτὸς καὶ οἱ μετ᾽ αὐτοῦ [ὄντες]	οτε επεινασεν αυτος και οι μετ αυτου	καὶ ἐπείνασεν αὐτὸς καὶ οἱ μετ᾽ αὐτοῦ (2.25)	ὅτε ἐπείνασεν καὶ οἱ μετ᾽ αὐτοῦ (12.3)
GLk 6.5	κύριός ἐστιν τοῦ σαββάτου ὁ υἱὸς τοῦ ἀνθρώπου	κς εστι ο υιος του ανθρωπου και του σαββατου[b]	κύριός ἐστιν ὁ υἱὸς τοῦ ἀνθρώπου καὶ τοῦ σαββάτου (2.28)	
GLk 6.7	παρετηροῦντο δὲ αὐτὸν οἱ γραμματεῖς καὶ οἱ Φαρισαῖοι εἰ ἐν τῷ σαββάτῳ θεραπεύει	παρετηρουντο δε [α]υτον οι γραμματεις και οι φαρεισαιοι ει εν τω σαββατω θεραπευσει	καὶ παρετήρουν αὐτὸν εἰ τοῖς σάββασιν θεραπεύσει αὐτόν (3.2)	

Notes: [a] Adapted from Pardee 2019. [b] Cf. Wasserman's reconstruction (2010: 8).

The scribal harmonizations of P4+P64+67 indicate that *GMatthew*, *GLuke*, and *GMark* occupied the same conceptual space for the scribe(s) who produced this codex. While Skeat and Stanton stretch the evidence too far in suggesting that P4+P64+67 is a four-gospel codex, the evidence does allow us to consider this codex to be part of an exegetical and hermeneutical space where all three Synoptics interact congenially.

b. Sense-Unit Divisions and Paragraphing

The sense-unit divisions and paragraphing in P4+P64+67 give insights into how *GMatthew* and *GLuke* interacted in this codex. The act of dividing the gospel texts into discernible units was a crucial step towards the intertextual reading of the gospels. Most of the text divisions in P4 and P64+67 correspond to those in NA28 (see Table 21 below).[70]

---

[70] Of course, NA28 is modern edition reconstructed from an eclectic textual base, but the paragraph markings do indicate sense-unit divisions that are natural to the narrative and dialogical structure of the text. The great New Testament codices of the fourth and fifth centuries reflect many of the same text divisions; further research is needed to demonstrate the extent of this correspondence.

Table 21: Text Divisions in P4+P64+67

Chapter breaks corresponding to NA28: *GLk* 2.1 (ek², pg); 4.1 (ek², pg); 6.1 (ek², pg)

Paragraph breaks corresponding to NA28: *GMt* 5.21 (ek², pg); 5.27 (ek¹; pg); 26.31 (ek¹·⁵, pg?); *GLk* 1.80 (ek², pg); 3.10 (ek?, pg?); 3.18 (ek²); 3.21 (ek¹·⁵, pg); 3.23 (ek², pg); 5.36 (ek², pg); 6.6 (ek², pg); 6.12 (ek¹, pg)

Verse breaks corresponding to NA28: raised central dot: *GMt* 3.9; *GLk* 1.63, 64, 66, 67, 79; 3.13, 16, 27, 28, 29, 30, 33; 5.7, 33, 38, 39; 6.2, 3, 4, 5, 8 (?), 9 (?), 11, 13, 15, 16; extra space: *GMt* 26.33; *GLk* 1.71; 3.11, 12, 20, 22 (?); 5.5, 31, 32; colon: *GMt* 5.22, 28; 26.23 (?)

Verse subdivisions corresponding to NA28 high points: raised central dot: *GMt* 26.22; *GLk* 3.9, 11; 16, 22; 5.7, 31, 33, 34, 36, 37, 39; 6.3, 6, 8, 10; extra space: *GLk* 6.5

Verse subdivisions corresponding to NA28 commas: extra space: *GMt* 26.14; raised central dot: *GLk* 3.22, 23; 6.1, 9

Paragraph breaks not corresponding to NA28: colon: *GLk* 1.76 (ek², pg); 3.14 (ek?, pg?), 19 (ek¹, pg); 6.8 (ek¹⁻², pg?)

Verse breaks not corresponding to NA28: raised central dot: *GLk* 1.68

Verse subdivisions not found in NA28: raised central dot: *GLk* 1.67, 71, 76; 3.17, (24, 25, 26, 27, 28, 29, 30, 31, 32, 33, 34, 35, 36, 37); 5.32, 36, 37; 6.2, 11 (14, 15, 16); extra space: *GLk* (3.26, 27, 31, 32, 34, 36, 37, 38)

Notes: This table is adapted from Charlesworth 2016: 41. ek¹ = *ekthesis* of one letter; ek² = *ekthesis* of two letters; pg = paragraphos. I have adapted it to the text of NA28.

The narrative units that are demarcated by *ekthesis* and *paragraphoi* are as follows: the Matthean antitheses (M; *GMt* 5.21); Jesus' predicts Peter's denial on the Mount of Olives (TT; *GMt* 26.31); Zechariah's prophecy (L; *GLk* 1.80); the account of Jesus' birth (L; *GLk* 2.1); John's preaching to the crowds (TT; *GLk* 3.18); Jesus' baptism (TT; *GLk* 3.21); Jesus' age and genealogy (L; *GLk* 3.23); the temptation of Jesus (TT; *GLk* 4.1); the parable of the new and old garments (TT; *GLk* 5.36); Jesus' disciples in the grainfields on the Sabbath (TT; *GLk* 6.1); Jesus healing the man with a shrivelled hand (TT; *GLk* 6.6); Jesus choosing the twelve apostles (TT; *GLk* 6.12). Of these units, eight are Triple Tradition (TT), one is Matthean *Sondergut* (M), and three are Lukan *Sondergut* (L) – although the Lukan genealogy (3.23ff) can also be described as parallel to *GMatthew* 1.1-18.

Dividing the text in this way is a prerequisite for constructing a topography upon which one can read the Synoptic gospels in parallel. That the scribe(s) of P4+P64+67 have Synoptic relations in their purview is plausible when we consider that *GLuke* 3.18 is marked off with a two-letter *ekthesis*. *GLuke* 3.17 //

198   *Chapter 6: Gospel Combinations in Early Christian Artifacts*

GMatthew 3.12 is quintessential Double Tradition, and both Luke and Matthew insert this material at the same place after Triple Tradition (*GLk* 3.16 // *GMt* 3.11 // *GMk* 1.7). The textual demarcation at *GLuke* 3.18 would plausibly have made the Synoptic parallels easier to access, compare, contrast, and preserve. As we have seen in previous chapters, reading the gospels in parallel could take the shape of orchestrating them into a super-gospel (Tatian), intertextual exegesis (Irenaeus), or constructing a Synoptic technology (Ammonius).[71] Tatian, Irenaeus, and Ammonius, in their various strategies of navigating the fourfold gospel, had an underlying notion of these sections existing in parallel, and the way they related to one another across Synoptic gospels. The scribal harmonizations of P4+P64+67 confirm the same dynamic of treating the Synoptic gospels as parallel texts within this codex.

One insightful example for how this plays out is the way that P4 marks off the Lukan version of Jesus' genealogy with a *paragraphos*, *ekthesis*, and raised central dots (P4 fragment B, at *GLk* 3.23–38). This is a major Lukan textual tradition later enshrined in Gregory Aland 01, 02, 03, 04, 032, and others. In a plausible reconstruction, P4+P64+67 also contained the Matthean genealogy near the beginning of the codex. If a single codex contained both genealogies, even with their differences, this would indicate an appreciation for *GMatthew* and *GLuke* as distinct yet compatible versions of the written gospel. Unlike Tatian's solution to the problem of discrepancy (to excise the genealogies), or the editors of Codex Bezae (to invent a new, harmonized version of the genealogy), P4 plausibly preserved the two distinct versions of Jesus' genealogy in the same codex.[72] Preserving both genealogies intact would indicate an appreciation of the interactive and diverse unity of the written gospel in its Matthean and Lukan versions, much like what we see in Irenaeus' reading of both genealogies in parallel.[73]

The sense-unit divisions and paragraphing in P4+P64+67 divide the gospel text into units that can be read in parallel – and indeed are read in parallel in Christian authors such as Tatian, Irenaeus, and Ammonius. These paratextual features are yet another sign of the dynamic, congenial interactions between *GMatthew* and *GLuke* in this codex.

c. Gospels Titles

One key facet to the interactions between P4 and P64+67 is the function of the ευαγγελιον κατα μαθ᾽θαιον title on the flyleaf in P4.[74] Matthew D. C. Larsen has

---

[71] For Tatian, see Chapter 3; for Irenaeus and Ammonius, see Chapter 5. See also Coogan and Rodriguez 2023.

[72] P1 confirms for us that the Matthean genealogy was circulating in upper Egypt during the period when P4+P64+67 was produced.

[73] *Haer.* 3.21.8–10; 3.22.4. For the development of the exegetical and textual tradition regarding the differing genealogies in *GMatthew* and *GLuke*, see Lorenz 2018.

[74] I follow the transcription by Gathercole 2012b: 214.

6.2 Gospel Combinations in P4+P64+67

highlighted the fact that no literary works in antiquity used the *kat' andra* formula to indicate authorship, prior to the Christian appropriation of this convention.[75] Rather, Larsen makes the case that the *kat' andra* formula was used in early gospel manuscripts to indicate not an author but "someone reworking [i.e. correcting] an already existing tradition, passing it from the past to the future in what the corrector believes to be a more amenable form."[76] Larsen's case is tenuous, however, because our earliest gospel manuscripts with the *kat' andra* formula come from a period when Christians unanimously used this formula to describe gospel authorship. Since Irenaeus, Clement of Alexandria, and Origen consistently use the *kat' andra* formula to describe gospel authorship, and they never use it to describe a "textual corrector", then it stands to reason that gospel manuscripts roughly contemporaneous with them (late CE2 and early CE3) would use the formula in the same way.[77] While early Christians inherited many of their cultural practices from Jewish and Greco-Roman influences, they were also known to introduce terminology and practices of their own that made sense from an emic perspective while remaining an enigma to outsiders.[78] In certain cases, Christians appropriated terms from either a Jewish or a Greco-Roman cultural lexicon and infused these terms with innovative meaning. It is well-documented that εὐαγγέλιον is one such term.[79] This term's meaning morphed in its Christian usage from Paul to Irenaeus,[80] but it is clear that by the first half the second century it had a distinct, Christian definition as a book about the life

---

[75] Larsen 2018a: 78.

[76] Larsen 2018a: 95.

[77] Larsen argues that Irenaeus does not refer to gospel authorship when he uses the *kat' andra* formula. Larsen dismisses the evidence of *Haer.* 1.26–27, but he gives no further justification for this dismissal beyond the fact that it only appears in Latin. In this section the agencies of Matthew and Luke in the production of their gospels are paralleled with the agency of Paul in the production of his letters; see also *Haer.* 3.12.12 for this same phenomenon. Furthermore, Irenaeus' discussion of the gospel author *qua* compositional agent saturates his discussion in Book 3 of *Adversus Haereses*, and he gives no positive evidence to the effect that he viewed the gospel authors as "correctors" or "revisers" of a received tradition. Larsen's contention is based entirely on parallels in Greco-Roman usage rather than any demonstrable instance in the Irenaean corpus. Clement uses the *kat' andra* formula to denote authorial intent for Matthew and Luke (*Strom.* 1.21.147.2–6; cf. Section 5.2.3 above). Origen uses the *kat' andra* formula (e.g. *Cels.* 1.34), but certainly understands Matthew to be an authorial agent (e.g. *Cels.* 1.1).

[78] On early Christian distinctiveness in the Greco-Roman world, see Hurtado 2017; Kinzig 1994a.

[79] On early Christian innovation for the term εὐαγγέλιον, see Hengel 2008:1–12. Hengel 2008: 5: "Im Vergleich mit den griechischen und jüdischen Parallelen erlangten der paulinische und der davon – zumindest anscheinend – verschiedene markinische Gebrauch von εὐαγγέλιον eine viel tieferegehende, ja *einzigartige* Bedeutung."

[80] For the transformation of this term, see Koester 1989a; Stanton 1992; Kelhoffer 2004.

200   *Chapter 6: Gospel Combinations in Early Christian Artifacts*

and/or teaching of Jesus of Nazareth.[81] If such in-house usage of the term εὐαγγέλιον was widespread among Christians by the mid second century, it would not at all be surprising if the extended terminology of εὐαγγέλιον + κατα + name (as found in second- and third-century Christian literature and gospel manuscripts) also owed its definition primarily to Christian traditions about the authorial origins of the gospels rather than to a Greco-Roman background of the formula.

Whether the *kat' andra* formula denotes authorship or something more like a "reviser" or a "corrector", this formula served the paratextual function of differentiating one version of the gospel from another. At a fundamental level, gospel titles create the space for multiple gospels to interact on the same plane with reference to one another as textual "others".[82] This is true conceptually, as in the discourse of Irenaeus and Clement, and it is also true artifactually, as we shall see is the case in P4+P64+67. The fragments that make up P4 contain a flyleaf with the title ευαγγελιον κατα μαθ'θαιον, though this flyleaf is seldom listed as part of P4.[83] This flyleaf was part of the same wad of papyrus as the Lukan fragments of P4 that were stuffed inside the Philo codex. When speaking of ancient codices, scholars use the term "flyleaf" to refer to a cover page, or, alternatively, a title page on the inside of a codex.[84] In the case of P4, it is worth noting that the title ευαγγελιον κατα μαθ'θαιον is written across the horizontal fibers. The flyleaf would have been inserted as a single page with horizontal fibers on the left side of the open codex, adjacent to vertical fibers on the right page. *GMatthew* 1.1 would have begun with the following page, with horizontal fibers. All of this would have been on the first half of a quire.

Furthermore, gospel titles enable a collection consciousness for those combining gospels.[85] As David Trobisch puts it: "The titles serve to group the individual writings into collection units."[86] Thus, the title ευαγγελιον κατα μαθ'θαιον in P4+64+67 serves not only to differentiate the Matthean version of the written gospel from the Lukan version, but also to group both *GMatthew* and *GLuke* as part of the same distinct collection within the broader body of early Christian literature. That the gospel title in P4+64+67 is an act of identifying this codex as a gospel collection in distinction from other corpora is likely when we consider that during that same period, scribes in Upper Egypt were also producing codices to house the Pauline corpus (e.g. P46).[87] In short, the gospel title in P4+P64+67

---

[81] Cf. Koester 1990: 46; Tuckett 2005: 241–44 (though with some reservations).

[82] Petersen 2006 argues that the gospel titles furnished the connection between the four gospels, even before they were part of a collection of codices.

[83] For a definitive discussion on this flyleaf title, see Gathercole 2012b.

[84] Skeat 1997: 18 and Gathercole 2012b: 209–12, 223.

[85] On collections, work combinations, and canon consciousness, see Dormandy 2018.

[86] Trobisch 2000: 41.

[87] Interestingly, P46 has titles for each of the epistles it holds (Romans, Hebrews, 1 Corinthians, 2 Corinthians, Ephesians, Galatians, Philippians, Colossians, and 1 Thessalonians – the

6.2 Gospel Combinations in P4+P64+67

facilitates intertextual, collection-conscious interactions between *GMatthew* and *GLuke*. Whether or not the proto-canonical gospels circulated with their titles in the period before Irenaeus, it is evident that by the end of the second century, gospel titles in manuscripts differentiated gospels as members of a corpus.[88]

6.2.6 Authority

As with GA 0171, the physical and scribal features of P4+P64+67 do not give explicit indication of the degree of authority accorded to *GMatthew* and *GLuke* in this codex. However, the two-column format bears close resemblance to P. Baden iv 56 and Ch. B. VI, as in GA 0171, and therefore it might imply a similar authority to the Torah texts inscribed in these *comparanda*. Several other factors increase the plausibility of this analogy for P4+P64+67. First, when the first quire of the Matthean portion of P64+67 is reconstructed, it is apparent that *GMatthew* began at the third column of the codex, that is, the left-hand column on the first left-hand page of the open codex. Two columns on the left-hand page and two columns on the right-hand page would have formed four columns across the opened codex, strongly resembling the first pages of an open scroll, with *GMatthew* beginning at the top left. The Matthean incipit (Βίβλος γενέσεως) would fit well in the physical context of a scroll of Jewish scripture.[89] The readers' aids also increase the similarities between P4+P64+67 and both P. Baden iv 56 and Ch. B. VI, and the combination of two works (*GMatthew* and *GLuke*) into a multi-book codex increase the similarities with Ch. B. VI. Combined with the elegant scribal hand in P4+P64+67 (a precursor to biblical majuscule), the physical and scribal features as a whole construct a picture of a collection of gospel texts that were revered by the producers and/or users of this codex.

---

manuscript breaks off here, but perhaps it contained more epistles), but it also has continuous pagination throughout. These paratexts simultaneously mark out each individual book and distinguish the entire book as a cohesive corpus. For provenance and date of P46, see Kenyon 1936a. Cavallo 2005: 184, 198 considers P46 to be Alexandrian stylistic class, and Orsini and Clarysse 2012: 462, 470 consider it to be chancery, dating it to 200–225 CE.

[88] Against the gospels circulating anonymously, see Gathercole 2018b; Hengel 2007: 527–67. Petersen 2006, on the other hand, building on Heckel 1999 and Trobisch 1996, argues that the proto-canonical did not have titles until they came together as a fourfold collection.

[89] The Jewish references to ἱεραὶ βίβλοι (Philo, *de Abr.* 117.4; 258.1; *de Vita Mos.* 2.11.1; 2.36.4; *de Dec.* 1.2; 155.1; *de Spec. Leg.* 2.151.1; *de Virt.* 201.2; *de Aet. Mund.* 19.3; Josephus, *Ant.* 1.26.3; 1.82.4; 3.81.3; 9.46.5), βίβλος Μωϋσέως (e.g. 1 Esdr. 5.48; 7.6, 9; Philo, *de. Cher.* 124.3; Josephus, *Ant.* 10.58.2) βίβλος τῶν προφητῶν (Acts 7.42), or other similar collocations are numerous (see also 2 Macc 8.23). In these collocations, the lexeme βίβλος denotes the physical realia of sacred Jewish books. While the lexeme βίβλος has a general sense that does not necessarily evoke a sacred writing, the specific collocation of Βίβλος γενέσεως, followed by a distinctly Jewish genealogy and a high concentration of citations from Jewish Scripture in *GMt* 1.1–4.25, all signal that Matthew is using Βίβλος γενέσεως as an analogue to Jewish books of Scripture; cf. Davies and Allison 1988–97: 1.149–55; Smith 2000: 7–8.

202 *Chapter 6: Gospel Combinations in Early Christian Artifacts*

6.2.7 Summary of Gospel Combinations in P4+P64+67

P4+P64+67 gives evidence strikingly similar to GA 0171. It arguably dates to the same period, combines *GMatthew* together with *GLuke* through the mode of a multi-quire codex, preserves the narrative and dialogical integrity of both *GMatthew* and *GLuke* through its stable pericope sequencing, demonstrates the same kind of Synoptic intertextual interactions through its scribal harmonization, and its elegant hand and two-column format resemble the same authoritative Torah manuscripts of that period.

One point of contrast is provenance. P4+P64+67 comes from the vicinity of Koptos, approximately 340 kilometers from the provenance of GA 0171 (Hermopolis Magna).[90] Given the differences between the textual affinities of GA 0171 and P4+64+67, we should probably envisage no small measure of diversity between the Christian communities behind both manuscripts. But this diversity – in geography and textual affinity – makes the correspondences between the two manuscripts even more salient. Taken together, GA 0171 and P4+P64+67 demonstrate that at least some Christians treated *GMatthew* and *GLuke* together physically (with *GMark* conceptually) as members of the same literary family.

6.3 Querying Canonical and Noncanonical Gospel Overlap in Manuscripts

Some scholars make the claim that we do not have extant any instances of canonical gospels being packaged together in the same manuscript as noncanonical gospels. Michael Dormandy, applying a rigorous methodology to Greek New Testament manuscripts, has concluded:

…there are no alternative gospel collections, containing, say, Matthew, Mark, Luke, and Thomas. There are no particular works that are not canonical today, yet that seem regularly to be combined with the (in modern terms) canonical ones, as a rival collection. There may be *other gospels*, but there is no *other gospel collection.* Although a variety of gospels circulated, work-combinations provide minimal evidence that any others had equal status with, or were interchangeable with, the canonical four.[91]

Dormandy's handling of the evidence is nearly comprehensive, and his table of data shows that there are no Greek manuscripts in the published record (as of 2018), that combine noncanonical and canonical gospels in the same codex.

Other scholars have attempted to minimize the significance of this claim by pointing to instances where a canonical gospel and a noncanonical gospel were found in the same vicinity and were possibly copied by the same scribe. Francis

---

[90] This distance was calculated on Google Maps as the distance between Al Ashmunin (Hermopolis Magna) and Qift (Koptos), accessed 4 March 2021.

[91] Dormandy 2018: 22.

6.3 Querying Canonical and Noncanonical Gospel Overlap in Manuscripts 203

Watson and Sarah Parkhouse, for example, highlight that P.Oxy. 1 (fragments of *GThomas*) and P.Oxy. 2 (fragments of *GMatthew*) were found in close proximity and have similar hands (perhaps from the same scribe).[92] Similarly, Geoffrey Smith and Brent Landau make the case for "fluid canonical boundaries" in the early fourth century based on the observation that P.Oxy. 209 (fragments of Rom 1.1–7) and P.Oxy. 210 (fragments from an apocryphal gospel-like text) were copied by the same scribe in the Christian circle of Aurelius Leonides.[93] It not surprising that the same Christian scribes could copy both canonical and non-canonical books. After all, Egyptian Christians like Clement of Alexandria, Origen, and Didymus the Blind had noncanonical books in their collections and made more than occasional reference to them. But this has little to no bearing on whether these scribes, their patrons, or the Christian intellectuals who used their manuscripts regarded all the books they copied as on the same authoritative plane. It does not follow that, just because we find fragments of *GThomas* and *GMatthew* in the same rubbish heap in Oxyrhynchus, Christians from Oxyrhynchus considered these gospels to belong to the same collection of authoritative writings. Nor does the fact that the same scribe copied the incipit of Romans and a portion of an apocryphal gospel justify the speculation that Irenaeus' treatise promoting a four-gospel canon was "read and rejected" in Oxyrhynchus, "finding its way into the town dump not long after its arrival."[94]

Another angle might be to argue that if a noncanonical gospel's redactional elements show up in canonical gospel manuscripts, this might indicate that the noncanonical gospel occupied the same intertextual horizon as the canonical gospels in the mind of the scribe. We have already demonstrated numerous cases where *GMatthew*, *GMark*, and *GLuke* overlap in scribes' horizon of expectation, and this overlap shows an intertextual web connecting these three gospels. If the same could be demonstrated of, for example, *GThomas* in a canonical gospel manuscript, might this show that *GThomas* shared in the canonical gospels' interpretive *koinonia*? In 1998, James M. Robinson and Christoph Heil, building on T. C. Skeat's papyrological reconstruction of P.Oxy. 655 and his UV-light recovery of text in Sinaiticus, argued that Scribe A of Sinaiticus was influenced by the text of *GThomas* 36 in his copying of *GMatthew* 6.28.[95] The parallels are laid out in Table 22 below.

---

[92] Watson and Parkhouse 2018: 11.
[93] Smith and Landau 2019: 143–60.
[94] Smith and Landau 2019: 155.
[95] Robinson and Heil 1998; cf. Skeat 1938.

204 Chapter 6: Gospel Combinations in Early Christian Artifacts

Table 22: Scribal Overlap between Sinaiticus and P.Oxy. 655

GMt 6.28 (NA28)	Sinaiticus (Scribe A)	Sinaiticus (Scribe D)	P.Oxy. 655 (GTh 36)	GLk (NA28)
πῶς αὐξάνουσιν· οὐ κοπιῶσιν οὐδὲ νήθουσιν	οὐ ξαίνουσιν οὐδὲ νήθουσιν οὐδὲ κοπιῶσιν κτλ.	πῶς αὐξάνουσιν· οὐ κοπιῶσιν οὐδὲ νήθουσιν	[ο]ὐ ξα[ί]νει οὐδὲ ν[ήθ]ει	πῶς αὐξάνει· οὐ κοπιᾷ οὐδὲ νήθει

The reconstruction of the lacunae in P.Oxy. 655, however, is not without its difficulties. Stanley Porter reminds us that, given the absent letters in the fragment and the continuous script, αὐξάνει is as plausible a reconstruction as οὐ ξαίνει.[96] Nevertheless, for the sake of argument, let us suppose with Robinson and Heil that the earliest layer of text in Sinaiticus at *GMatthew* 6.28 does read οὐ ξαίνουσιν, and that this reading came from the influence of *GThomas* 36 as preserved in P.Oxy. 655 (οὐ ξαίνει). Dirk Jongkind has shown that it was Scribe A (a scribe more prone to harmonization to parallels) that transcribed the reading οὐ ξαίνουσιν, but Scribe D (stricter in textual stability), corrected the text to accord with the now-canonical reading.[97] The harmonizing proclivities of Scribe A increase the probability that he or she did indeed assimilate an outside reading into the text of *GMatthew* 6.28. Does this single instance in Sinaiticus – which amounts to a change in only two letters – constitute the level of intertextual, scribal cross-pollination that is shared between the canonical Synoptics in the manuscript tradition?[98] Approximately 50% of *GThomas*' sayings (67 out of 114 sayings) have clear parallels with the Synoptic Tradition. If this is the only fragment of overlap that can be demonstrated between the scribal tradition of *GThomas* and the Synoptics, then it is most probable that *GThomas* was not indeed a member of the same intertextual network as the canonical gospels among the scribes of early Christianity.

Most recently, however, an unpublished gospel fragment from Oxyrhynchus has been uncovered that allegedly contains *Sondergut* from *GMatthew, GLuke,* and *GThomas* on the same page.[99] The entire fragment is a portion of the Sermon

---

[96] Porter 2001.

[97] Jongkind 2006.

[98] Jongkind 2006: 215 highlights how the difference between οὐ ξαίνουσιν and αὐξάνουσιν amounts to only two letters. The parallel between *GLk* 6.7 and *GMk* 3.2 in P4 was established in 7.3 (see above) on the basis of a single letter: θεραπεύει versus θεραπεύσει. However, the additional parallels of *GLk* 6.3 // *GMk* 2.25 and *GLk* 6.5 // *GMk* 2.28 strengthen the argument for scribal harmonization beyond what we have in Sinaiticus at *GMt* 6.28 // *GTh* 36.

[99] This manuscript is catalogued as P.Oxy. inv. 16 2B.48/C(a). I have not personally consulted this manuscript, but I base my general observations on conversations I have had with scholars who have seen the fragment but wish to remain anonymous. My comments here are therefore provisional and open to revision when this fragment is published. Further

6.3 *Querying Canonical and Noncanonical Gospel Overlap in Manuscripts* 205

on the Mount/Plain, in Matthean order. The fragment is not extensive enough to determine whether it is a Sayings Collection like *GThomas* (e.g. P.Oxy. 1, P.Oxy. 654, and P.Oxy. 655), or whether it has a narrative structure with dialogue sections interspersed throughout, such as *GMatthew* or P.Oxy. 840. It is important to say that this fragment is *not* an instance of an entire canonical gospel being juxtaposed with an entire noncanonical gospel. We do not have here a multi-quire codex consisting of *GMatthew*, *GLuke*, and *GThomas*. What we have is a small list of sayings with unique features from *GMatthew*, *GLuke*, and *GThomas*. If this comes from a larger collection, it amounts to nothing more than what we have already seen in *GThomas* – a compendious Sayings Collection drawing from an eclectic range of sources. A Sayings Collection, as such, does not constitute the same hermeneutical act of collection as a multi-gospel codex such as GA 0171 and P4+P64+67.

There is one further piece of evidence that must be addressed, one that might problematize Dormandy's assessment that, based on the artifactual record, there were no alternative gospel collections. There is a fifth-century Latin palimpsest known as Codex 563 that contains portions of *GMatthew* (fragments of chapters 26–28) together with the *Acts of Pilate* and the *Infancy Gospel of Thomas*.[100] It exists as an undertext to an 8th-century collection of patristic writings. Because the original codex was dismembered and rearranged before reuse, it is impossible to reconstruct the sequence of the three books packaged together, and there remains the possibility that there were other books in this codex. This codex provides the strongest evidence that some Christians not only read canonical gospels conjointly with noncanonical Jesus books, but that they also bound them together. But does it raise the possibility that some Christians in antiquity considered *GMatthew* to belong to a separate network of mutually interpreting texts, one that rivaled the fourfold gospel? Space does not permit a full-scale analysis of this codex, but a few general remarks are in order.

First, the earliest possible dating places this codex as a fifth-century production, and it represents a period in Christian reading outside the scope of the present study. The fifth-century patterns of gospel reading it represents cannot necessarily be traced back to second- or third-century habits.[101] The data simply does

---

confirmation is found on the Egyptian Exploration Society website (https://www.ees.ac.uk/news/professor-obbink-and-missing-ees-papyri; accessed 3 March 2021), which labels this fragment simply as "Sayings of Jesus."

[100] For an introductory study of this palimpsest, with special reference to its date and the texts it contains, see Philippart 1972; Baudoin 2020; for a general description of the original codex, see Houghton 2016: 230.

[101] One might mount the same criticism against the way that I use Ephrem's *Commentary*, Fuldensis, and the Arabic Harmony to reconstruct Tatian's *Diatessaron*, or the Coptic and Ethiopic translations (along with a Latin fragment) of the *Epistula Apostolorum* to reconstruct a Greek *Vorlage*. The presence of three witnesses for both the *Diatessaron* and *EpAp* give us the

206   *Chapter 6: Gospel Combinations in Early Christian Artifacts*

not allow us to make a firm decision as to whether the fifth-century manufacturer was the one who combined *GMatthew* with the *Acts of Pilate* and the *Infancy Gospel of Thomas*, or whether an earlier exemplar contained this combination. Both are viable options.

However, second, even though this codex's fifth-century date limits its value for reconstructing Christian reading habits of the second and third centuries, its combination of *GMatthew* with the *Infancy Gospel of Thomas* nevertheless corresponds to what we saw in *EpAp* and to a lesser extent Justin Martyr: infancy traditions that were later deemed noncanonical could occasionally come alongside proto-canonical gospels to form an exegetical nexus.[102]

Third, the text of the *Acts of Pilate* preserved in Latin Codex 563 is clearly an extrapolation based on *GMatthew*, and its juxtaposition with *GMatthew* probably evinces a creative reinterpretation of *GMatthew*. Our second and third points imply a fourth: *GMatthew* is the tree upon which the two noncanonical branches are grafted. Fifth, the juxtaposition of the *Acts of Pilate*, the *Infancy Gospel of Thomas*, and *GMatthew* is not paralleled in any other known gospel combinations. Furthermore, there are no extant canon lists or second-order discussions in Christianity antiquity that place these three texts within the same field of interpretation, much less describe them as an alternative collection of Jesus books. Their juxtaposition in Codex 563 can be accurately described as an anomaly.

These five observations demonstrate that there was a small degree of experimentation in ancient Christian gospel combinations that diverged from the tendency of proto-canonical gospels to keep company only with one another. This divergence, however, is an exception that confirms the prevailing trend: the *predominant* pattern of discrete, entire-gospel combinations was for proto-canonical gospels to keep company only with one another.

6.4 Summary and Conclusions

In this chapter we have identified the same gospel-combining patterns we discerned in early Christian interpretive rewriting, gospel orchestration, Christian discussions of gospel authorship, and intertextual gospel reading practices. Our

---

ability to triangulate a plausible second-century *Vorlage*, at least regarding sequence and gospel redaction. In contrast, there are no other witnesses to corroborate a *Vorlage* behind the gospel combination of *GMatthew* with the *Acts of Pilate* and the *Infancy Gospel of Thomas* in Latin Codex 563. One might also object that GA 0171 and P75 are plausibly fourth-century productions, and reading their gospel combinations back into the second century is therefore suspect. On this latter point, it must be noted that the plausible dating of GA 0171 and P75 extends as far back as the turn of the third century, whereas the earliest dating of Latin Codex 563 is fifth century. On the grounds of plausible dating alone, GA 0171 and P75 therefore have a stronger correspondence to second-century habits.

[102] See above, Sections 2.3 and 4.4.

analysis of two early, fragmentary, multi-quire codices provisionally suggests that by the end of the second century CE, Christians in Hermopolis Magna and Koptos began to put into scribal and codicological practice the same gospel-combining habits exhibited by Christians throughout the second century and across the Mediterranean Basin. Regarding *identities*, it was canonical gospels that kept company with one another through the *mode* of physical juxtaposition within the pages of these codices. The *integrity* of each of the gospels combined is demonstrated by the stability of pericope sequences. The gospels *interacted* congenially within an intertextual web, reflected in the scribal harmonizations (and in the case of P4, the gospel title) of these earliest multi-gospel codices. While we are limited in what we can deduce regarding the *authority* attributed to the gospels combined in these codices, a degree of literary gravitas is evident in the scribal hands and two-column format used in both (features that resemble scriptural artifacts of Jewish antiquity).

Chapter 7

Gospel Combinations in Early Christian Artifacts: P45 and P75

In the previous chapter, we uncovered the remains of two multi-gospel codices, whose modern discovery can be traced to Hermopolis Magna and Koptos. These two codices – GA 0171 and P4+P64+67 – are fragmentary, and so our conclusions are necessarily provisional. In the present chapter, however, we will analyze two other gospel codices whose remains are much more substantial: the third-century P45 and P75.[1] As we will argue below, these two codices add a third and a fourth locale to our geographical coordinates for Christian, multi-gospel, book production: the Fayyum and the vicinity between Nag Hammadi and ancient Tentyra. If these codices give evidence that corresponds to our findings in GA 0171 and P4+P64+67, then we are one step closer to identifying an early Christian *habitus* of codicological and scribal gospel combinations that corroborates the same patterns we uncovered in Chapters 1–5, namely, that the four proto-canonical gospels were read within a web of intertextual, mutually interpretive relationships. Furthermore, as we shall see, these later material remains reflect the earlier, second-century ascendancy of the proto-canonical gospels into the status of an authoritative collection of Christian Scripture.

7.1 Gospel Combinations in P45

P45 (P.Chester Beatty I) is a third-century codex of immense importance for the history of early Christianity. It contains portions of *GMatthew*, *GJohn*, *GLuke*, *GMark*, and Acts (in that order), in an eccentric codicological construction. In the following sections, I will analyze its physical and scribal features to uncover data relevant to our questions of the identities, mode, integrity, interactions, and authority in gospel combinations.

---

[1] We will discuss the dates of these codices below in Sections 7.1.2 and 7.2.2

7.1.1 Provenance

The provenance of the Chester Beatty Papyri has been notoriously difficult to establish, but there is a general consensus that it was somewhere around the Fayyum.[2] F. G. Kenyon initially suspected, based on the character of the papyri, that they originated from the Fayyum.[3] The Coptologist Carl Schmidt agreed that the findings came from the general vicinity of the Fayyum, but his investigations in the Nile valley led him to conclude that the papyri originated in 'Alalme, just east of the Fayyum (on the eastern bank of the Nile).[4] Kenyon later accepted much of Schmidt's account, but he remained convinced that the character of the papyri was still Fayyumic, based on Fayyumic Coptic glosses present in the papyri.[5] For the purposes of our present study, we will work with the general consensus of the Fayyum.[6] Importantly, this gives us a *different* provenance for P45 than for the other codices we have examined so far (Hermopolis Magna and Koptos).

7.1.2 Paleography and Date

F. G. Kenyon, in the *editio princeps*, initially dated this codex to "the third century... the first half of it rather than the second."[7] Kenyon also said that two other experts, H. I. Bell and W. Schubart, dated it to the same range independently of his analysis.[8] A. S. Hunt, however, around the same time, dated it to the second half of the third century.[9] Most New Testament scholars of the past few decades have followed Kenyon's dating,[10] and the consensus of this view is represented by Pasquale Orsini and Willy Clarysse, who date it to 200–250 CE.[11] Brent Nongbri, however, has offered a broad critique of dating codices based on their paleographic correspondence with rolls, and he uses this critique to destabilize

---

[2] In what follows, I summarize the brilliantly documented history of scholarship by Nongbri 2018: 122–30, 315–19.

[3] Kenyon 1933a: 5.

[4] Schmidt 1931: 285–93; 1933: 225–32.

[5] Kenyon 1936b: 112–13.

[6] Nongbri's analysis appears to accept a general vicinity of a 50-km radius around the Fayyum, but with considerable caution (Nongbri: 2018: 130). Even this broad vicinity, however, is several hundred km removed from the other manuscripts we are analysing (e.g. Hermopolis Magna, Tentyra, and Koptos), thus broadening the geographical scope of our analysis in spite of the ambiguity of the exact provenance of P45.

[7] Kenyon 1933: x.

[8] Kenyon 1933: x.

[9] Kenyon 1933: x; Cavallo 1967: 118–19 follows Hunt in dating P45 to the end of the third century.

[10] E.g. Hurtado 2006a: 36–37, 141; Head 2012: 114; Cole 2017: 205.

[11] Orsini and Clarysse 2012: 470.

210   *Chapter 7: P45 and P75*

the certainty of P45's dating to the first half of the third century.[12] Nongbri also points to the disagreement among the early analyses of P45 with regard to its dating.[13] However, analyzing P45 within the graphic stream flowing from the severe style to the sloping ogival style legitimates the consensus dating to 200–250 CE. With the requisite caveats given in the previous chapter, we may proceed with the standard dating of 200–250 CE.

7.1.3 Physical Features

a. Dimensions

P45 has a page size of 20 x 25 cm. It has one column per page, and the average column size (written area) is 15.5 x 19.5 cm. The written area (302.25 cm^2) is therefore approximately 60% of the page size (500 cm^2). There is an average of 39/40 lines per page, with approximately 50 characters per line. Close examination of the manuscript gives the impression that this codex has small letters with small margins, perhaps suggesting that the scribe was attempting to cram as much text as possible on the page while still maintaining an aesthetic standard.

b. Binding

The binding method of P45 is "stabbing", with holes slightly removed from the center, usually used for notebooks. In the stabbing method, the constructor would "[sew] the spine through a series of hole punches through the fold quire from

---

[12] Nongbri's contention is that the pool of dateable severe style hands "comes exclusively from rolls" (Nongbri 2019: 92), which become scarce in the fourth century CE. Thus, according to Nongbri 2019: 94, "overreliance on the corpus of datable literary manuscripts (i.e. reused rolls) will cause the dates of the codices as a group to skew early." Nongbri 2018: 138 uses this reasoning to call into question the consensus dating of P45. It is crucial to note that Nongbri's critique does not provide any positive evidence for the late dating of severe hands, nor does it weaken the plausibility of early dating based on solidly dated *comparanda*; rather, it only broadens the range of dating to encompass a span of 200 years (e.g. 200–400 CE). Furthermore, Nongbri dismisses too easily the plausible hypotheses of Cavallo 1967: 121–23 and Orsini and Clarysse 2012: 453–55 that identify an evolution from the severe style in the second and third centuries to the sloping ogival majuscule of the fourth and subsequent centuries (see Nongbri 2018: 63–71). Nongbri's critique of the Italian school's classifications of the severe style does not actually engage the particulars of paleographical analysis (in contrast with his critique of the "Rounded Majuscule", which does offer such particulars), but rather it rests on his skepticism of using rolls as *comparanda*. If we include the sloping ogival hand in the same graphic stream as the severe hand, then we have fourth- and fifth-century manuscripts that represent the transitional period between severe style and sloping ogival (e.g. the fourth-century P.Herm. 4 and P.Herm. 5, and the fifth-century P.Oxy. 11.1373, PSI 2.126 + P.Schubart 22, and GA 032), and we can contrast these with the earlier severe hands; see Orisini and Clarysse 2012: 453–54.

[13] Nongbri 2018: 138.

front to back at a slight remove from the central fold itself."[14] Eccentrically for gospel manuscripts, P45 employs the stabbing method to a multi-quire construction, each quire only of a single sheet.[15] This method was typically used for documentary texts. The notebooks and documentary texts that used the stabbing method were usually very thin.[16] Quite the contrary, P45 is made up of 110 leaves (= 220 pages = 55 quires), individually folded, stabbed, and sewn together. This would have been impractical to use.

c. Reading Aids

P45 does not use *ekthesis*, *paragraphoi*, vacant line ends, or spaces.[17] Pericopes are not marked off in this manuscript. Scott Charlesworth concludes from this data that P45 was not produced for public liturgical use, but rather for private use. However, Jan Heilmann has rightly called into question whether we can infer from a manuscript's paratextual features whether it was used for communal liturgy or for a private readership.[18]

d. Scribal Collaboration

There are 2 corrections in P45 that probably belong to a second hand: at *GMatthew* 25.42 and at Acts 7.12.[19] Furthermore, there are diagonal markings that appear to have been written at a later stage in the life of this codex – markings that a later scribe used in *GMark* and Acts (see below, Section 7.1.4a). It is impossible to determine whether these markings came from a scribe or a reader, and in most cases in antiquity, scribes were indeed readers of the texts they copied. Thus, we will refer to the person behind these diacritical markings as a scribe-reader. It is possible that this scribe-reader is the same person as the corrector who changed the text at *GMatthew* 25.42 and Acts 7.12. The work of this second hand suggests a level of scribal collaboration, and the diagonal markings suggest an interactive reader within the orbit of this manuscript and its producers (whether contemporary or subsequent to the two scribes).

e. Codicological Composition

T. C. Skeat, in a meticulous codicological reconstruction of P45, concluded that manufacturers placed the gospels in the "Western" order (*GMatthew, GJohn, GLuke,* and *GMark*).[20] Skeat ingeniously followed a trail of clues, beginning with

---

[14] Nongbri 2018: 29–30.
[15] Nongbri 2018: 138–40.
[16] Cf. Nongbri 2018: 140, 329–30.
[17] Charlesworth 2016: 72.
[18] Heilmann 2020.
[19] Royse 2008: 114.
[20] Skeat 1993 (= 2004).

212 Chapter 7: P45 and P75

F. G. Kenyon's discovery of two successive bifolia from *GLuke*.[21] These two bifolia show that P45 was made up of quires consisting of only 1 sheet (that is, 2 leaves, or, 4 pages) per quire. Based on these two bifolia, Kenyon also determined that each quire had the construction $\downarrow \rightarrow \rightarrow \downarrow$. Therefore, the fiber orientation for the entire codex is most plausibly $\downarrow \rightarrow \rightarrow \downarrow + \downarrow \rightarrow \rightarrow \downarrow + \downarrow \rightarrow \rightarrow \downarrow$ etc. Two more pieces of evidence uncovered by Kenyon were the page numbers 193 (at Acts 14.15–23) and 199 (at Acts 17.9–17), each on the second page of a leaf.

Following Kenyon, Skeat took the New Testament text of Alexander Souter and calculated that the pages of P45 averaged 35.92 lines of Souter's Greek New Testament per page for the gospels. Skeat confirmed these measurements by counting the *stichoi* of Souter's Greek New Testament (1 stichos = 15 syllables), making allowances for *nomina sacra*. The ratios between Souter lines counted for each gospel, and the ratios between *stichoi* counted for each gospel, are remarkable consistent. Armed with this freshly confirmed Souter line count for each complete gospel and for each page of P45, Skeat was able to reconstruct the page count for each gospel (and similar counts for Acts) in P45: *GMatthew* = 49.33 pages, *GMark* = 30 pages, *GLuke* = 50.66 pages, and *GJohn* = 38 pages, Acts = 50 pages. The total page count for P45 was therefore 218 pages. Acts, with portions located at pages 193 and 199, must have followed the four gospels in this codex. Furthermore, based on these page counts, Skeat could accurately estimate that *GMatthew* would have ended at pages 48–49, with fibers at $\downarrow \rightarrow$. The next gospel would therefore have started at page 50, with fibers directed $\rightarrow$, at the middle of the quire. Skeat's reconstruction brought *GLuke* to start at the beginning of a quire, so *GLuke* could not have followed *GMatthew*. Furthermore, page 56 would have had $\downarrow$ fibers. The first extant *GMark* fragment (folio 3r, at *GMk* 4.46–50) would have been located at page 56, but this fragment has $\rightarrow$ fibers. Therefore, *GMark* is ruled out as the gospel following *GMatthew* in P45. Skeat concludes: "Since both Mark and Luke are excluded, we have no option but to accept Kenyon's suggestion that the Gospels were in the 'Western' order, and that the Gospel which followed Matthew was consequently that of John."[22] After Skeat's confirmation of Kenyon's analysis, it is the consensus that P45 indeed follows the Western gospel order, with Acts attached to the fourfold gospel.

f. Summary of Physical Features

P45 was in many ways an eccentric, codicological experiment. The scribes and codex-constructors appear to be *avant-garde* on several fronts, but their

---

[21] The first of these bifolia consists of leaves 11+12 (*GLk* 10.6–11.46), and the second consists of leaves 13+14 (*GLk* 11.50–13.24); Kenyon 1933: vi; Skeat 2004:152.

[22] Skeat 2004: 147.

7.1 Gospel Combinations in P45 213

experimentation facilitated the combination of all four proto-canonical gospels, placed in the Western order.

7.1.4 Identities and Mode

P45 is the remains of a codex consisting of *GMatthew, GJohn, GLuke, GMark,* and Acts. This much is clear. More legwork is required to determine the mode of composition – whether P45 was itself copied from a multi-gospel codex or whether the constructors of P45 copied each gospel from separate codices. We can reconstruct the compositional background by investigating the readers' aids and textual affinities.

a. Readers' Aids

There are several indications that the producers of P45 used two or more exemplars in their composition of this codex. First, as mentioned above, P45 does not use *ekthesis, paragraphoi,* vacant line ends, or spaces. There is, however, the curious case of the diacritical diagonal marker (probably from a second hand) that often corresponds to natural hiatuses in the reading of the text. Raised dots that correspond to modern verse breaks and verse subdivisions occur frequently in *GMatthew, GLuke,* and *GJohn,* but comparatively infrequently in *GMark,* and they are absent in Acts.[23] The diagonal marker, on the other hand, only appears in *GMark* and Acts. The scribe uses this diagonal marker until Acts 6.9, where the diagonal becomes a "small, dark, oval blob," and still later in the text of Acts it becomes a mere dot. It appears that the scribe reverted to the raised-dot system of text-division used in *GMatthew, GJohn,* and *GLuke.* A plausible explanation of these data is that the exemplars of *GMatthew, GLuke,* and *GJohn* had the raised dots in abundance, whereas the exemplar of *GMark* had them sparingly, and the exemplar of Acts did not have them. The primary scribe of P45 replicated this pattern across the four gospels and Acts. The secondary scribe, then, added the diagonal markers to *GMark* and Acts.[24] These data initially suggest that the exemplars of *GMatthew, GLuke,* and *GJohn* were of a different character than those of *GMark* and Acts, increasing the likelihood that they comprised different codices.

b. Textual Affinities

The hypothesis of separate codices is corroborated by the fact that textual affinities differ in each of the books included in P45 (for this section, the reader should consult Tables 23, 24, and 25 below).[25] The text of *GMark* is closely related to

---

[23] Charlesworth 2016: 73–34.

[24] This is the scenario that Charlesworth 2016: 73–74 proposes.

[25] Since the advent of the Coherence-Based Genealogical Method (CBGM), text-types as stable categories have been called into question (see Gurry 2017: 11–19). The jury is still out

Washingtonianus and other witnesses in this textual family. Larry Hurtado and, more recently, Tommy Wasserman have documented this clear family resemblance.[26] According to Wasserman's updated version of Hurtado's analysis, in a body of 150–56 variation units, the text of *GMark* in P45 and W relate to f13, Textus Receptus, D, Θ, B, A, and א in remarkably similar ways.[27] This is laid out in Table 23 below. Moreover, P45 and W share 11 special agreements, and the scribal habits exhibited in these agreements reveal a tendency toward producing a harmonized, readable, at times even paraphrased text.[28] It is therefore most probable that the text of *GMark* in P45 and W belong to the same textual family.

It is remarkable that the text of *GLuke* in P45 has distinctly different textual affinities than the text of *GMark*. Juan Hernandez collates the data as follows: out of 223 non-singular variation units, P45 agrees with "Alexandrian" readings 165 times (74%), Western readings 22 times (10%), and other readings 36 times (16%).[29] The breakdown of the Alexandrian witnesses (P75, א, and B) is laid out in Table 24, and the Western witnesses (Old Latin, D, and relevant minuscules) in Table 25, below.

Hernandez's analysis relies on 233 non-singular readings, differing from Kenyon's earlier count of 288, but the affinity to Alexandrian witnesses is evident in Kenyon's analysis as well.[30] Kenyon's layout of the data also implies that *GLuke* in P45 has affinities with Western and Byzantine witnesses – 136/273 (50%) in agreement with D and 153/285 (54%) in agreement with L.[31] A number of scholars have followed Kenyon's lead in assigning a secondary, Western textual affiliation to *GLuke* in P45. In order to query whether P45's text of *GLuke* has any affinities with Western witnesses, Hernandez collates the number of non-singular readings that P45 shares only with Western witnesses (D, Old Latin, and some minuscules). Hernandez differs sharply from Kenyon's count, numbering only

---

on this debate, but even within the CBGM, there is still the underlying principle of identifying coherence and family-relations among sets of manuscripts. I use the term "Alexandrian" as a shorthand to refer to one cluster of manuscripts that undoubtedly are related in their affinities: P75, א, and B (with regard to *GJohn*, we might also add P66); cf. Epp 2013: 559. I use the term "Western" as a shorthand to refer to another such cluster of manuscripts: D, Old Latin, and a few minuscules. In the text of the Gospels, we are on firm ground to accept the postulate that "Alexandrian" and "Western" texts are indeed distinguishable textual clusters (see Epp 2013). Due to Hurtado's famous deconstruction of the Caesarean text-type (Hurtado 1981), I refrain from using the term "Caesarean," but I also accept along with Hurtado that the text of *GMark* in P45 and W are related to each other, even if we cannot use the term "Caesarean" to label it.

[26] Hurtado 1981; Wasserman 2014; cf. Kenyon's (1933: ii–xviii) earlier observation.

[27] Wasserman 2014: 148–51.

[28] Wasserman 2014: 151–54.

[29] Hernandez 2012: 129–30.

[30] Kenyon 1933: xi–xvii.

[31] Kenyon 1933: xiii.

7.1 Gospel Combinations in P45 215

22 times when P45 agrees exclusively with Western witnesses.[32] While we may remain skeptical along with Hernandez regarding P45's Western affiliations in *GLuke*, we can safely conclude that P45 does have a strong affinity with the Alexandrian family consisting of P75, ℵ, and B. One plausible explanation of these data is that P45's exemplar of *GLuke* was separate from *GMark* and had a different origin.

The extant text of *GMatthew* in P45 is sparse, containing only portions of *GMatthew* 20.24–32; 21.13–19; 25.41–26.17; 26.18–39. However, we may still draw tentative conclusions from these remains. *GMatthew* in P45 has affinities with P37. P45 shares significant omissions with P37 at *GMatthew* 26.21, 22, and 29, 33, an addition at *GMatthew* 26.22, and a seven-word order transposition at *GMatthew* 26.23.[33] The provenance of P37 has been tentatively assigned to the Fayyum, the same as P45. It could be that in the text of *GMatthew*, P45 and P37 have a local as well as textual relation. In contrast to its affinity to P37, P45 in *GMatthew* does not show strong affinities with a particular textual cluster.[34] Like *GLuke* in P45, *GMatthew* does not show the same affinity with W and its relatives as *GMark*, but nor does *GMatthew* have the same gravitational pull towards Alexandrian witnesses as *GLuke* in P45.

The text of *GJohn* in P45 was originally characterized by Kenyon, and later by Comfort and Barrett, as having affinities somewhere between Alexandrian and Western.[35] This is concluded based on the number of times P45 agrees with ℵ, B, and D in its 80–83 variation units. However, if we look at the significance of these variants, and the number of variants P45 shared exclusively with ℵ and B, and the number of variants P45 shares exclusively with D, it is evident that P45 leans more heavily in the direction of the Western textual tradition.[36] However, as with *GMatthew*, *GJohn* in P45 cannot be pinned down to one of these textual affinities.

Finally, the text of Acts is generally consistent with Alexandrian witnesses but with some minor overlaps with Western witnesses.[37]

---

[32] The discrepancy between Kenyon's and Hernandez's counts of agreements with Western witnesses is due to Hernandez finding *exclusive* agreements with western witnesses (I am grateful to Prof. Hernandez for explaining this to me in an email correspondence, 11 June 2021). Hernandez 2012: 130n52 mentions that his data needs to be double-checked against extant MSS. Further research should follow Hernandez's recommendation.

[33] Cf. Wasserman 2012.

[34] To demonstrate: out of 63 variation units visible in the extant Matthean text, P45 agrees with B 24 times, ℵ 28 times, D 25 times, and W 20 times. These figures were counted based on the apparatus provided in Min 2005: 111–21.

[35] Kenyon 1934: xiii–xiv; Comfort and Barrett 2001: 162.

[36] Cf. Kenyon 1933: xiii–xiv; Chapa 2012: 151–52.

[37] Cf. Kenyon 1933: xviii; Tuckett 2012: 165–67.

216 *Chapter 7: P45 and P75*

Table 23: P45 Affinities to W in the text of *GMark*

	W	P45
P45	70.4% (107/152)	-
W	-	70.4% (107/152)
f13	55.3% (84/152)	53.2% (83/156)
TR	42.1% (64/152)	42.9% (67/156)
D	40.7% (61/150)	37.7% (58/154)
Θ	44.1% (67/152)	39.1% (61/156)
B	36.8% (56/152)	39.7% (62/156)
A	38.1% (58/152)	42.3% (66/156)
א	33.5% (51/152)	36.5% (57/156)

Notes: This table is adapted from Wasserman 2014: 150–51. It summarizes Wasserman's collation of his own findings with the earlier study by Hurtado (1981).

Table 24: P45 Affinities to Alexandrian Witnesses in the text of *GLuke*

Agrees with P45	
P75 + א + B	94
P75 + B	21
B	13
א	16
P75	12
א + B	7
P75 + א	2
Total	165

Notes: Adapted from Hernandez 2012

Table 25: P45 Affinities to Western Witnesses in the text of *GLuke*

Agrees with P45	
D	3
D + Old Latin	5
Old Latin	2
D + Latin + minuscules	13
D + minuscules	4

Notes: Adapted from Hernandez 2012

To summarize, P45 has three major clusters of textual affinities. First, *GMark* lines up strikingly well with the textual family of Washingtonianus and its relatives. Second, *GLuke* and Acts correspond predominantly to Alexandrian witnesses, with minor, though not insignificant overlaps with Western witnesses. Finally, *GMatthew* and *GJohn* have relatively fewer affinities with Alexandrian witnesses than *GLuke*, and *GJohn* at times resembles Western witnesses.

The differing textual affinities exhibited in each of the gospels in P45 suggest that this codex is eclectic in bringing together various textual traditions. With textual affinities wide-ranging enough to include Washingtonianus, Vaticanus, Sinaiticus, P37, P75, and even Bezae, P45 reflects in its textual eclecticism the interactive diversity of early Christianity. If textual affinities are indications of separate exemplars, then we might argue that the artifactual mode of gospel combination in P45 brought together all four gospels and Acts from at least three separate exemplars: *GMark* (W), Acts and *GLuke* (Alexandrian with some Western), *GMatthew* and *GJohn* (Western with some Alexandrian). Thus, P45 was probably not a reproduction of an earlier four-gospel codex, but rather an eclectic, codicological experiment. This might indicate that at the turn of the third century, codicological representation of a four-gospel corpus was still in an experimental stage.

7.1.5 Integrity

The scribe of P45 has been characterized as "an exegete and a paraphraser."[38] He or she copied in phrases and clauses rather than letter by letter.[39] This kind of scribal *habitus* is behind the extraordinary number of 226 singular readings (an average of 5.3 singulars per page) in this multi-gospel codex.[40] The scribe seems more interested in copying the gist of the gospel text, rather than preserving the textual tradition intact. The relatively scant number of corrections corroborates this.[41] The scribe's free, interpretive, phrase-by-phrase approach to copying makes it all the more significant that he or she keeps the inter-pericope sequencing so stable – yet another example of macro-level stability coexisting with micro-level fluidity.[42] Notably, the inter-pericope sequence in the gospel texts of

---

[38] Comfort and Barrett 2001: 160; Pardee 2019: 144.

[39] Colwell 1969: 116.

[40] The total number of singular readings in P45 is given in Royse 2008: 886, and the rate per page is given in Royse 2008: 900. For comparison, P66 has 128 singular readings, at 2.3/page, and P75 has 161 singular readings, at 1.8/page (Royse 2008: 900–01). For gospels manuscripts, P45 ranks high in its singular readings; however, it is comparable to the rate of singulars in P46 (632 singulars at 4.9/page) and P47 (76 singulars at 4.8/page), and it has relatively fewer singulars when contrasted with P72 (150 singulars at 7.9/page); Royse 2008: 900–01.

[41] Royse 2008: 114–15 counts 14 corrections in the 30 extant folios of P45.

[42] See Holmes 2013 and 2020.

218   *Chapter 7: P45 and P75*

P45 does not differ even once from NA28. The macro-level stability preserved
in P45 is one of the mechanisms by which the four proto-canonical gospels maintain their identity and integrity while physically juxtaposed as discrete texts in a
codex.

7.1.6 Interactions

a. Work-Combinations in P45

P45 is the earliest extant codex to contain the fourfold gospel and the Acts of the
Apostles.[43] It is significant that Acts is placed after the fourfold gospel in one
codex. Acts "resurfaced" in the late second century as an authoritative text, crucial to the formation of the New Testament as a collection. By the time Irenaeus
was writing in Gaul, the fourfold gospel collection and the Pauline letter collection were established among certain Christian groups in centers such as Rome.
Although hard evidence of Christian usage of Acts prior to Irenaeus is small,[44]
Acts appears to have been "rediscovered" sometime in the second half of the
second century as a sort of canonical glue to connect the Pauline letter collection
with the fourfold gospel.[45] Acts was instrumental in the formation of the New
Testament as a combination of gospel and Apostolos, perhaps in response to
Marcion's earlier attempt at this kind of project.[46] P45 appears to be a material
manifestation of this same canonical consciousness, a "New Testament in min-
iature."[47] In this way, P45 works against the grain of Marcionite constructions of
the New Testament – whether by design or unintentionally. By placing Acts as a
follow-up to the ending of *GMark*, the scribes of P45 connect the ministry of the
apostles to the fourfold witness of the ministry, death, and resurrection of Jesus.
In the words of Francois Bovon, this is the "canonical structure of gospel and
apostle."[48] The logic of the gospel → apostle sequence in P45 presupposes the
fourfold cohesion of *GMatthew*, *GJohn*, *GLuke*, and *GMark* as the first part of a
bipartite New Testament. Granted, Acts is not an *apostolikon* (a collection of

---

[43] P53 consists of fragments of a third-century codex that contained *GMatthew* and Acts.
Hurtado 2006a: 37n90 speculates that this might have been a gospels codex together with Acts,
but he maintains that a codicological reconstruction would make it unlikely to have held more
than *GMatthew* and Acts. However, even if it only contained *GMatthew* and Acts, it would
exhibit the same hermeneutical logic of Gospel + Apostolos.

[44] Cf. Gregory 2003.

[45] Cf. Schröter 2007: 297–329, developing and modifying Harnack 1914: 46. That Acts was
in use before Irenaeus is more likely than Gregory allows, when we consider how the narrative
in Acts 1.16-26 is presupposed by *GJudas* (cf. Head 2007; Wurst 2006: 132–33), and especially
when we triangulate the strong allusions to Acts in *GJudas*, *EpAp*, and *LEMark*.

[46] For Marcion's influence on the formation of the New Testament, and his alleged inven-
tion of the term, "New Testament", see Kinzig 1994b and Beduhn 2013.

[47] Cf. Bird 2014: 275; Barrett 1996.

[48] Bovon 2002.

7.1 Gospel Combinations in P45 219

apostolic epistles). However, we may still consider P45 as an expansion of the same logic as Luke's two-volume work, arguably the "first New Testament," consisting of Jesus' ministry followed by the apostolic exposition thereof.[49] In the pages of P45, then, the four gospels interact in the formation of a nascent New Testament collection.

b. Scribal Harmonizations

While the integrity of each proto-canonical gospel is maintained by the stability of pericope sequences in P45, there is also a clear sign of intertextual interactions when we look at the scribal harmonizations (for this section, the reader should consult Tables 26, 27, and 28 below). Cambry Pardee's study shows that in P45, the text of *GMatthew* harmonizes with *GLuke* and *GMark*, the text of *GLuke* with *GMatthew* and *GMark*, and the text of *GMark* with *GMatthew* and *GLuke*. Pardee's examples of harmonizations that are "likely" (symbolized as "L"), "very likely" (VL), and "very likely, all but certain" (VL AbC) are presented in Tables 26, 27, and 28 below.

Pardee's comprehensive analysis has shown that the scribe of P45 harmonized in clusters, or "bursts" in Pardee's words. Since *GLuke* and *GMark* harmonize to *GMatthew* far more often than *GMatthew* harmonizes to *GLuke* or *GMark*, Pardee argues convincingly that *GMatthew* was the primary text to form the horizon of expectation for the scribe. This coheres with the harmonizing patterns we uncovered in Irenaeus and Clement of Alexandria, as well as the primacy of *GMatthew* in the sequential architecture of Tatian's *Diatessaron*.[50] However, the harmonization also happens in other directions: for example, from *GMatthew* to *GMark* and *GLuke*, or from *GLuke* to *GMark*. In contrast with the scribal web that exists among the Synoptic gospels in P45, it is notable that the scribe does not harmonize to Thomasine parallels in sayings material. There are four instances where the text of *GLuke* harmonizes with *GMatthew* and not with *GThomas* in P45. Two are Double Tradition (DT), and two are Triple Tradition (TT). Unfortunately, P45 only has portions of *GJohn* 10.7–11.57, which do not allow us to determine whether its text of *GJohn* harmonized with Synoptic parallels, so we cannot speak of *GJohn*'s scribal interactions with the Synoptics in P45.

The pagination used in P45 has implications for how the scribe(s) envisaged the interaction of the texts they combined into a codex. The pagination, which is extant only in two places – page 193 (ρϙγ) at the top of Acts 14.15–23 and page 199 (ρϙθ) at the top of Acts 17.9–17 – could not have applied only to one of the books incorporated within the codex. According to Skeat, Acts would only constitute 55 pages in a codex the size of P45. Furthermore, the four gospels would

---

[49] Barrett 1996 provocatively called Luke-Acts the "first New Testament".

[50] See above, Chapter 3 (on Tatian) and Chapter 5 (on Irenaeus and Clement).

220   *Chapter 7: P45 and P75*

combine to fill 167 pages. The pagination was therefore continuous throughout
P45, rather than restarting at the beginning of each book. The continuous pagination in P45 suggests that these texts constitute a cohesive corpus. This is confirmed when we contrast the continuous pagination of P45 with the Bodmer Miscellaneous Codex, which restarts pagination at two points where a new book begins.[51]

The scribal harmonizations occurring among the three Synoptics in P45 bespeak their interplay in the producers' horizon of expectation. The choice of the
books to fit within this codex (four gospels + Acts) seems *not* to be haphazard or
miscellaneous, but rather an active outworking of a conceptual family of the four
proto-canonical gospels. The strong links that connect this conceptual family are
shown in the propensity of the scribe to harmonize to parallels in other proto-
canonical gospels coupled with the absence of harmonization with noncanonical
gospels. The macro-level stability of the pericope sequences in P45 assures us
that the intra-Synoptic harmonization does not indicate a fluid textual melange
of gospel books within P45. Rather, gospels in this codex are stable, textual objects placed in discrete juxtaposition.

Table 26: P45 *GMatthew* harmonizing with Synoptic parallels

Very Likely: *GMt* 20.31 // *GMk* 10.48 // *GLk* 18.39
Likely: *GMt* 26.27 // *GLk* 22.20

Notes: Adapted from Pardee 2019.

Table 27: P45 *GLuke* harmonizing with Synoptic parallels[a]

All but Certain:
(1) *GLk* 11.12 // *GMt* 7.9; (2) *GLk* 11.13a // *GMt* 7.11; (3) *GLk* 11.42a // *GMt* 23.23; (4) *GLk* 12.24a // *GMt* 6.26

Very Likely:
(1) *GLk* 9.49 // *GMk* 9.38; (2) *GLk* 11.13b // Matthean style; (3) *GLk* 11.13c // *GMt* 7.11; (4) *GLk* 11.42b // *GMt* 23.23
Likely:
(1) *GLk* 9.35 // *GMk* 9.7; (2) *GLk* 10.11 // *GMt* 10.14 // *GLk* 9.5; (3) *GLk* 11.17 // *GMt* 12.25; (4) *GLk* 11.18 // *GMk* 3.26 // *GMt* 12.26; (5) *GLk* 11.31 // *GMt* 12.42; (6) *GLk* 12.4 // *GLk* 21.9; (7) *GLk* 11.34b // *GMt* 6.22 [DT not harmonized with *GTh* 24]; (8) *GLk* 12.2 // *GMt* 10.26 [TT not harmonized with *GTh* 5]; (9) *GLk* 12.6 // *GMt* 10.29; (10) *GLk* 12.7 // *GMt* 10.30; (11) *GLk* 12.22 // *GMt* 6.25 [DT not harmonized with *GTh* 36]; (12) *GLk* 12.24b // *GMt* 6.26; (13) *GLk* 12.24c // *GMt* 6.26; (14) *GLk* 12.31 // *GMt* 6.33; (15) *GLk* 13.30 // *GMk* 10.31 // *GMt* 19.30 [TT not harmonized with *GTh* 4]; (16) *GLk* 14.3 // *GMt* 12.10; (17) 19.3 // *GMk* 10.2

Notes: Adapted from Pardee 2019.

---

[51] Cf. Nongbri 2016b: 207n2.

Table 28: P45 *GMark* harmonizing with Synoptic parallels

All but Certain:
(1) *GMk* 6.3 // *GMt* 13.55; (2) *GMk* 9.2 // *GLk* 9.29; (3) *GMk* 9.19c // *GMt* 17.17 // *GLk* 9.41; (4) *GMk* 12.15 // *GMt* 22.18
Very Likely:
(1) *GMk* 8.10 // *GMt* 15.39; (2) *GMk* 8.17 // *GMt* 16.8
Likely:
(1) *GMk* 5.22 // *GMt* 9.18 // *GLk* 8.41; (2) *GMk* 6.40 // *GMt* 14.19 // *GLk* 19.15; (3) *GMk* 7.6 // *GMt* 15.3; (4) *GMk* 8.16 // *GMt* 16.7; (5) *GMk* 8.36 // *GMt* 16.26; (6) *GMk* 8.37 // *GMt* 16.26; (7) *GMk* 8.38 // *GLk* 9.26; (8) *GMk* 9.5a // *GLk* 9.33; (9) *GMk* 9.5b // *GMt* 17.4; (10) *GMk* 9.7 // *GMt* 17.5 // *GLk* 9.34; (11) *GMk* 9.19a // *GMt* 17.17 // *GLk* 9.41; (12) *GMk* 9.19b // *GMt* 17.17 // *GLk* 9.41; (13) *GMk* 9.28a // *GMt* 17.19; (14) *GMk* 9.28b // *GMt* 17.19

Notes: Adapted from Pardee 2019.

7.1.7 Authority

The paucity of text divisions in P45 – especially sparse in *GMark*, almost completely absent in Acts – has led Charlesworth to conclude that it was not manufactured with a lector in mind. Jan Heilmann, on the other hand, has repudiated the suggestion that we can draw conclusions about public reading based on sense-unit divisions and alleged "reading aids" in the New Testament papyri.[52] Heilmann's analysis shows that it is tenuous at best to draw confident conclusions about whether a codex was used for "public" reading based on these physical features. It would be equally tenuous to argue for a certain level of textual authority accorded to the contents of a codex based on the premise that the codex was used for public reading.

Nevertheless, the combination of a fourfold gospel corpus with the Acts of the Apostles in P45 suggests that a concept of a Gospel + Apostle New Testament collection is not too far from the manufacturers' or users' aims. At the turn of the third century, not only Marcionites but also the "Great Church" was using the term καινὴ διαθήκη to designate a collection of Scripture consisting of Gospel and Apostle.[53] This period overlaps with the consensus dating for P45. It therefore not unreasonable to suggest that P45, as a fourfold gospel combination and a combination of Gospel and Apostle, was an experiment in building a physical, authoritative collection of New Testament Scripture.

---

[52] Heilmann 2020.

[53] Kinzig 1994b amasses data to this effect from Marcion (*apud* Tertullian, *Marc.* 4.1.1; 4.6.1), Clement of Alexandria (*Strom.* 1.44.3; 3.71.3; 4.134.4; 5.85.1; 7.100.5), Tertullian (*Praescr.* 30.8–10), and Origen (*Princ.* 4.1.1; *Comm. Jo.* 5.8).

222 Chapter 7: P45 and P75

7.1.8 Summary of Gospel Combinations in P45

P45 was an early third-century, experimental codex that bears the marks of certain gospel-combining habits and hermeneutical intentions. By artifactual means, it juxtaposes continuous texts of all four proto-canonical gospels that preserve the stable integrity of each of these gospels at the inter-pericope level. Its scribal habits demonstrate a web of gospel intertextuality that includes all three Synoptics, but, notably, no noncanonical gospels, even when parallels are available. Moreover, P45 combines the four proto-canonical gospels together with Acts, probably as a nascent, authoritative New Testament collection consisting of Gospel and Apostle. In the early third century, the sophisticated codicological technology of the pandect (as we see in the great fourth-century codices) was not yet available to the Christian movement, nor would such luxurious bookmaking be readily available to the majority of Christians until centuries after Gutenberg. Perhaps the experimental character of P45 is the result of its scribes and manufacturers stretching the limits of a primitive technology to create an authoritative, scriptural collection of the four gospels, combined with the subsequent apostolic exposition.

7.2 Gospel Combinations in P75

P75 (P.Bodmer XIV–XV) is another third-century, multi-gospel codex of enormous importance for our study. The following detailed investigation of its provenance, physical features, and scribal habits will further elucidate our enquiry into the dynamics of gospel-combining.

7.2.1 Provenance

Many scholars in the latter half of the twentieth century believed that the Bodmer papyri originated in Panopolis (Akhmim).[54] This was based on the presupposition that the collection came from a single find. Thus, the fact that P.Bodmer I contained on its back a document which mentions the Panopolite nome provided ample reason for scholars to conclude that the entire collection came from Panopolis. But there were a few significant voices that offered a contrary story. Rodolphe Kasser attributed the finds to the small village of Dabba, about 10 km east of Nag Hammadi.[55] Similarly, Odile Bongard, the assistant of Martin Bodmer, is said to have believed that the codices were found "in the ruins of a iv-cent [*sic*]

---

[54] Turner 1968: 52; Bagnall 1993: 103–04; Martin and Primavesi 1999: 43–51; summarized in Nongbri 2018:162–63, 326.

[55] Kasser 1988: 191–94; summarized in Nongbri 2018: 163.

7.2 Gospel Combinations in P75

church at Dishna," about 30 km east of Nag Hammadi.[56] James M. Robinson, through a series of interviews with local Egyptian residents and consultation of archival material related to the purchases of the Bodmer Papyri, gathered that the collection was found within walking distance of Dishna (between Nag Hammadi and Tentyra – modern-day Dandarah).[57]

Most recently, Brent Nongbri has uncovered two clues that point to the vicinity just east of Nag Hammadi. First, there is a certain manuscript in the Chester Beatty Library, registered under the acquisition number 1390 (LDAB 2743), and it is probably best identified as part of the Bodmer find.[58] The entry for Ac. 1390 identifies the find at "Small Village, DESHNA, just after NAGH HAMADI..."[59] Second, the recently published P.Bodmer LVI mentions a certain "Ptolemaios son of Trimores" (Πτο[λεμαιος] Τριμωρου), a name that is rare in antiquity.[60] This same name shows up in P.Ryl. 4.705, which connects this name to the city of Tentyra (i.e. Dandarah), which is a mere 25 km East of Dishna.[61] These two bits of evidence, combined with the testimonies collected by Robinson, Bongard, and Kasser, lead Nongbri to conclude that the finds of the Bodmer papyri originate in the "region between Nag Hammadi and Dendera."[62] Nongbri's rigorous spadework has recovered the most plausible provenance for the find, and we will build on this hypothesis. As with P45, P75 expands even further the geographical diversity for our material evidence of early Christian gospel combinations. The Fayyum, Hermopolis Magna, the region just east of Nag Hammadi, and Koptos represent a region of just over 500 kilometers from North to South on the Nile.[63] We will unpack the significance of this geographic expanse below.

7.2.2 Paleography and Date

P75 has traditionally been dated to a period within the range of 175–275 CE.[64] Recently, Brent Nongbri has suggested P.Herm. 4–5 as an early fourth-century

---

[56] This is based on the account of classicist William H. Willis, in a personal letter to James M. Robinson (25 February 1980), cited in Robinson 2011: 37 and Nongbri 2018: 161.

[57] Robinson 2011: 108–29, helpfully summarized in Nongbri 2018: 163–67.

[58] Nongbri 2018: 166.

[59] Cited by Nongbri 2018: 166.

[60] P.Bodmer LVI was published in Fournet and Gascou 2015: 34–37.

[61] This distance is given by Nongbri 2018: 168. For a transcription of P.Ryl. 4.705, see: https://papyri.info/ddbdp/p.ryl;4;705, accessed 4 March 2021.

[62] Nongbri 2018: 168. Nongbri's work on ancient Christian artifacts and their provenances is truly groundbreaking, and though I disagree with him in matters of dating manuscripts, I am nonetheless greatly indebted to many of his codicological, archeological, and artifactual insights.

[63] This distance was calculated by ORBIS: the Stanford Geospatial Network Model of the Roman World (https://orbis.stanford.edu/), accessed 22 June 2021.

[64] Martin and Kasser 1961: 13–14 date P75 to 175–225 CE; Turner 1977: 95 to 225–75 CE; Orsini and Clarysse 2012: 471 to 200–50 CE.

224   *Chapter 7: P45 and P75*

comparandum for P75.[65] However, analysis of the overall ductus of the main scribe in P75, and contrasting this hand with the later hands evident in the codex, suggests that P75 belongs squarely in the third century rather than in the fourth. E. G. Turner's instinct is probably best: a date-range of 225–275 CE (see Appendix 2D below for a more detailed argument).[66] In the final analysis, if Nongbri's skepticism of a third-century date is still warranted, we point the reader to our caveat in Section 6.1.2, namely, that the data gleaned from this codex would still be valuable for their corroborative function, even if this codex were an early fourth-century production. For heuristic reasons, we will proceed with Turner's date range.

7.2.3 Identities

This codex probably contained *GLuke* and *GJohn* in their entireties. It is unlikely that P75 contained any other texts within its covers. T. C. Skeat and Graham Stanton speculated that this codex might have been bound together with *GMatthew* and *GMark*.[67] While it would have been practically impossible to fit two more entire gospels in a single-quire codex together with *GLuke* and *GJohn*, both Skeat and Stanton entertained the possibility that P75 was attached to another single-quire codex containing *GMatthew* and *GMark*, or even that P75 was collected together with this other codex as "two single-quire codices bound separately."[68] Skeat and Stanton build this case on the surmise that *GLuke* and *GJohn* were unlikely to be bound together in antiquity. The codicological construction and late-antique preservation and use of P75 rule out the possibility of a large, two-quire codex. The damage at the beginning of *GLuke* and the end of *GJohn* strongly suggests that these two gospels alone formed a cohesive codex, without being bound to another large quire. Peter Head rightly points out that "there is no ancient Christian parallel to using such large quires in a multiple-quire codex – this is just not the way books were created in the period."[69] Furthermore, there are clear indications that after the beginning of *GLuke* and the end of *GJohn* were damaged in antiquity, a leather binding was created using these damaged outside pages. Head suggests that this indicates that P75 was considered in antiquity as a single item containing only *GLuke* and *GJohn*. The evidence does not give any

---

[65] Nongbri 2016a. Nongbri also argues for a fourth-century date on codicological grounds, based on the similar dimensions (e.g Turner Group 8; cf. Turner 1977: 20–21) with securely-dated, fourth-century Nag Hammadi codices (Nongbri 2016: 430). Third-century codicological *comparanda* also exist, however (e.g. P.Bodmer XXV+IV+XXVI [LDAB 2743]; P.Bodmer XXIV [LDAB 3098]). Nongbri has widened the plausible date range to include the fourth century, but he has not disproven the likelihood of a third-century date.

[66] Turner 1977: 95.

[67] Skeat 1994: 264 and Stanton 1997: 326–27.

[68] Stanton 1997: 327; cf. Skeat 1994: 264.

[69] Head 2011: 98.

indication that P75 contained anything more than *GLuke* and *GJohn*. In fact, the evidence pushes against such speculation. Artifactually, P75 must be considered as a two-gospel codex. As we shall see below, however, there is evidence – in the form of scribal harmonization – that P75 was read alongside *GMatthew* and *GMark*. This leaves open the possibility that P75 existed alongside other codices of *GMatthew* and *GMark*, or a single-quire codex with both gospels packaged together – but we have no material evidence to support these claims.

7.2.4 Mode: Scribal Habits and Textual Affiliations as Clues to the Gospel Codex Composition

Juan Chapa accurately characterizes P75 as having "a careful elegance,"[70] and the quality of its text in *GLuke* and *GJohn* is strict.[71] The texts of *GLuke* and *GJohn* both have strong affinities to Vaticanus. *GLuke* in P75 boasts a 90% agreement with B, and *GJohn* in P75 shares 92% agreement with B (and as much as 96% with B in *GJn* 12).[72] The orthographic scribal habits are broadly consistent throughout *GLuke* and *GJohn*, further strengthening the similarities between the textual character of their exemplars.[73] There are two notable exceptions: the spellings of "John" and "Bethsaida." In *GLuke*, "John" is consistently spelled with a single *nu* (Ιωανηc), and this spelling continues into *GJohn* (1.6, 15, 19) until 1.26, where it is spelled with the second *nu* (Ιωαννηc), and it continues to be spelled in the geminate form for the rest of *GJohn* except in 3.27. The scribe corrects his or her spelling at 1.26 to the geminate form, and almost exclusively sticks to this form of the spelling for the rest of *GJohn*.[74] Plausibly, the Lukan exemplar and the Johannine exemplar differed in their spelling of "John," and the scribe noticed this at *GJohn* 1.26 and changed his or her orthography accordingly. Marchant King argues that this implies that the scribe used a different exemplar for *GJohn* than for *GLuke*,[75] but Royse observes that "the individual Gospels have their separate textual histories, and divergent orthographies could have arisen at various points (including the autographs)."[76] We see a similar pattern with the spelling in P75 of Bethsaida: in *GLuke* 9.10 and 10.13, the scribe spells it as βηδcαιδα, but in *GJohn* 1.44, he or she corrects it to βηθcαιδα, and then continues this spelling in *GJohn* 5.2 and 12.21. As with the

---

[70] Chapa 2012: 137.

[71] Chapa 2012: 148.

[72] Chapa 2012: 148–50; Colwell and Tune's (1969: 60) table shows 92% agreement; Martini 1966: 84 argues for 90%; Fee 1974: 25 shows 94%. On the relationship between P75 and B, see Edwards 1976; Royse 2008: 616–19, and bibliography.

[73] For scribal orthography across *GLuke* and *GJohn* in P75, see Royse 2008: 634–40, 647–51.

[74] Cf. Royse 2008: 639; Metzger 1961: 202.

[75] King 1965.

[76] Royse 2008: 640.

226   *Chapter 7: P45 and P75*

spelling of "John," it appears that the exemplar in *GLuke* had a different spelling than at *GJohn*, but this need not imply that these were two separate exemplars/codices.

Overall, the continuity in textual affinities and scribal habits between *GLuke* and *GJohn* in P75, and the scribe's tendency towards preservation rather than innovation or experimentation, point towards a compositional coherence between the two gospel books in this codex. This suggests that P75 was copied from a single, earlier exemplar that contained at least *GLuke* and *GJohn*. The mode of gospel combination was artifactual, plausibly continuing an earlier tradition of discrete, artifactual juxtaposition of these two gospels within the same codex.

7.2.5 Integrity

The integrity of *GLuke* and *GJohn* in P75 is evident in its inter-pericope sequencing and its use of gospel titles. P75 contains most of *GLuke* 3.18 to 18.18, most of 22.4 to 24.51, and most of *GJohn* 1.1 to 15.8. In this large section, neither *GLuke* nor *GJohn* breaks the canonical sequence of pericopes even once.[77] For P75, this is a certain sign that *GLuke* and *GJohn* maintained their narrative integrity in an artifactual combination. The gospel titles in P75 confirm the bibliographic integrity of *GLuke* and *GJohn* within this codex – namely, that these are distinguishable versions of the same phenomenon.

7.2.6 Interactions

a. Scribal Harmonization

The scribal harmonizations – inter-Synoptic and even between *GLuke* and *GJohn* – tell us a lot about the interactions between the gospels packaged together in this codex (for this section, the reader should consult Tables 29, 30, and 31 below).

---

[77] One might consider the absence of the *Pericope Adulterae* in P75 as a notable exception, but this is not so much a change in sequence as the absence of one pericope in an otherwise stable Johannine narrative sequence. In many ways, the *Pericope Adulterae* is the exception that proves the rule of the macro-level stability of the text of *GJohn* in P75 and other early manuscripts (cf. Knust and Wasserman 2019: 65–70, 96–135). On textual stability in *GJohn* in early papyri, see Bell 2018.

7.2 Gospel Combinations in P75   227

Table 29: P75 *GLuke* Harmonizing with Matthean Parallels

All but Certain: (1) *GLk* 17.14 // *GMt* 8.3
Very Likely: (1) *GLk* 8.21 // *GMt* 12.48; (2) *GLk* 11.24b // *GMt* 12.44
Likely: (1) *GLk* 6.33 // *GMt* 5.46; (2) *GLk* 8.5 // *GMt* 13.4; (3) *GLk* 8.7 // *GMt* 13.7; (4) *GLk* 10.15 // *GMt* 11.23; (5) *GLk* 11.31 // *GMt* 12.42; (6) *GLk* 11.48 // *GMt* 23.31; (7) *GLk* 11.50 // *GMt* 23.35; (8) *GLk* 13.30 // *GMt* 20.16; (9) *GLk* 17.24 // *GMt* 24.27

Notes: Adapted from Pardee 2019.

Table 30: P75 *GLuke* Harmonizing with Parallels in GMatthew and GMark

Likely: (1) *GLk* 9.23 // *GMk* 8.34 // *GMt* 16.24; (2) *GLk* 22.41 // *GMt* 26.42, 44 // *GMk* 14.39; (3) *GLk* 24.26 // Matthean and Markan idiom; (4) *GLk* 24.47 // *GMk* 1.4 // *GMt* 26.28 // *GLk* 3.3 // Acts 5.31
Possible: (1) *GLk* 9.28a // *GMk* 9.2 // *GMt* 17.1; (2) *GLk* 9.28b // *GMk* 9.2 // *GMt* 17.1; (3) *GLk* 14.34 // *GMk* 9.50 // *GMt* 5.13

Notes: Adapted from Pardee 2019.

Table 31: P75 *GLuke* Harmonizing with Markan Parallels

Likely: (1) *GLk* 8.16 // *GMk* 4.21
Possible: (1) *GLk* 4.35a // *GMk* 1.25; (2) *GLk* 4.35b // *GMk* 1.26; (3) *GLk* 8.52 // *GMk* 5.39

Notes: Adapted from Pardee 2019.

First, there are 12 probable instances of *GLuke* harmonizing to Matthean parallels. According to Cambry Pardee's classifications, 9 of these are likely, 2 very likely, and 1 all but certain, as shown in Table 29.[78] Pardee concludes: "The influence of Matthew is undeniable."[79] Second, we have 4 likely cases and 3 possible cases where the text of *GLuke* harmonizes with Triple Tradition material in *GMark* and *GMatthew*, as shown in Table 30. Third, we have 1 likely case and 4 possible cases where the text of *GLuke* harmonizes with *GMark*, as shown in Table 31. Fourth, we have 1 possible case of *GLuke* harmonizing with parallels in both *GMark* and *GJohn*: *GLuke* 24.1 // *GMark* 16.2 // *GJohn* 20.1.

Fifth, we have 3 possible harmonizations of *GLuke* with *GJohn*, all of which are instances of the so-called "Western non-interpolations"[80]: (1) *GLuke* 24.12 //

---

[78] Pardee 2019: 113–19.

[79] Pardee 2019: 142.

[80] On Western non-interpolations, see Martin 2005 and bibliography.

228   *Chapter 7: P45 and P75*

GJohn 20.3ff; (2) *GLuke* 24.36 // *GJohn* 20.19; (3) *GLuke* 24.40 // *GJohn* 20.20. The direction of influence for the Western non-interpolations is a complex matter. Is the shorter, Western textual tradition the earlier version, with Johannine influence creeping into the Lukan textual tradition at some later period? Or did the Western textual tradition excise Johannine elements from the Lukan text? Or perhaps there were (at least) two early versions of *GLuke* that circulated in the first two centuries of the Christian movement, one with certain Johannine textual affinities and one without them? If we may consider Marcion's gospel to be an early version of the Lukan textual tradition, then we do indeed have proof for this kind of phenomenon. Whatever the case may be, it is clear that in the second century there were scribal editions of *GLuke* that showed more intertextual links with *GJohn* than others. P75 represents a scribal edition of *GLuke* with key links to the Johannine text. It is probably uncoincidental that this same codex juxtaposes a complete text of *GLuke* next to a complete text of *GJohn*, with only the titles in between to differentiate these texts paratextually.

Finally, there are three significant instances where the text of *GJohn* harmonizes to Synoptic parallels. According to a plausible reconstruction by Sarah Alexander Edwards, a phrase in *GJohn* 6.5 reads: π[ο]θε[ν εαυτοις αγορασ]ωσιν κτλ.[81] The εαυτοις is a conjectural reconstruction based on letter-spacing, but the αγορασωσιν is discernible by the extant letters [αγορασ]ωσιν in the manuscript. Both εαυτοις and αγορασωσιν harmonize to the parallels *GMatthew* 14.15 and *GMark* 6.36.[82] At *GJohn* 1.27, the primary scribe of P75 replaces ἄξιος with ικανος in the phrase ου ουκ ειμι ικανος ινα λυσω κτλ (NA28 reads: οὗ οὐκ εἰμὶ [ἐγὼ] ἄξιος ἵνα λύσω κτλ), a clear harmonization to the Synoptic parallels at *GMatthew* 3.11, *GMark* 1.7, and *GLuke* 3.11.[83] The fact that there is so little narrative overlap between the extant portions of *GJohn* in P75 and Synoptic material, and that the scribe of P75 typically avoids harmonizing to parallels, makes these harmonizations all the more salient. The texts of *GLuke* and *GJohn* were intersecting in the scribe's horizons of expectation.

In P75, we have a version of *GLuke* that shows significant scribal overlap with the text of *GMatthew*, and some minor overlap with the text of *GMark* and *GJohn*. We also have a version of *GJohn* that shows overlap with Matthean and Markan parallels. These data suggest that *GLuke* and *GJohn* did not merely share space in the same codex; they also were enmeshed into a broader web of gospel reading that included *GMatthew* and *GMark*.

b. Gospel Titles

It is serendipitous for our enquiry that the leaf containing the end of Luke's gospel and the beginning of John's gospel is preserved in P75. The artifactual and

---

[81] Edwards 1976: 200–03.
[82] See Royse 2008: 690–91.
[83] See Royse 2008: 690–91.

7.2 Gospel Combinations in P75

229

paratextual mechanisms at work on this leaf are illustrative of the inter-gospel dynamics working through the hands of the scribes behind this codex. This single leaf gives us our earliest material evidence for how early Christians physically differentiated two gospels while juxtaposing them. The titles appear as follows:

ΕΥΑΓΓΕΛΙΟΝ

ΚΑΤΑ

ΛΟΥΚΑΝ

ΕΥΑΓΓΕΛΙΟΝ

ΚΑΤΑΪΩΑΝΗΝ

There is a space of about two lines intervening both titles, and each title is boxed in by dashed superlinear and sublinear lines. These circumscribing lines are also present in P66, GA 01, 02, 03, 04, 05, and 032. We see the same phenomenon in the Nag Hammadi corpus. Indeed, one may say that these "text boxes" become a convention in fourth-century gospel codices. These move towards greater definition and become more ornate the later the manuscript.

There is a marked difference between these gospel titular paratexts and epistolary titular paratexts found in composite codices. In P46 (a collection of Pauline Epistles and Hebrews), at the end of each epistle, the scribe did not write the title. This contrasts with the ubiquitous custom for scribes copying gospels. Rather, the scribe marks the end of the epistle with an extended sublinear line, and then with the space of approximately two text lines intervening, the scribe begins the next epistle with the title encased in the dashed text box just discussed. In contrast with this pattern, in P75 (and in most multi-gospel codices), the genre and/or content of the texts – ΕΥΑΓΓΕΛΙΟΝ – is stated both at the end of the first text (ΚΑΤΑ ΛΟΥΚΑΝ) and the beginning of the next (ΚΑΤΑ ΪΩΑΝΗΝ).

In the so-called Bodmer Miscellaneous Codex,[84] there is no consistent pattern of titling. This is probably because the codex as a whole does not function as a unified corpus; it is most likely a codex that was compiled over an extended period of time. The succession of 1 and 2 Peter, however, does provide a helpful *comparandum*. Both 1 Peter and 2 Peter begin with a centered title: ΠΕΤΡΟΥ ΕΠΙΣΤΟΛΗ Α and ΠΕΤΡΟΥ ΕΠΙΣΤΟΛΗ Β respectively (the first text of this codex, the *Nativity of Mary*, places the title in the body of the text, unmarked). Both texts also present their conclusions with the same title, but here the titles

---

[84] This codex consists of P.Bodmer V (*Nativity of Mary*) + X (a correspondence of Paul to the Corinthians) + XI (*Odes of Solomon* 11) +VII (Jude) +XIII (Melito's *Peri Pascha*) +XII (an unknown hymn) +XX (*Apology of Phileas*) + IX (Psalms 33-34) +VIII (1-2 Peter). The order of contents is contested; cf. Turner 1977: 8, 79–80; Junack and Grunewald 1986: 16–25; Wasserman 2005. On the codicology, construction, pagination, and reception of P.Bodmer VIII, and whether it is a "composite" or a "miscellaneous" codex, see Nongbri 2016b; Wasserman 2005.

230   *Chapter 7: P45 and P75*

are boxed in with paratextual lines and ornamentations. 1 and 2 Peter are, obviously, similar texts – one might even say two versions of the same kind of text (Petrine Epistles with universal audiences). The A and the B connect the texts to another, such that each is unavoidably read with intertextual reference to the other. Their intertextual, corpus-forming identity within the Bodmer Miscellaneous Codex is corroborated by the fact that page numbers restart at page "1" (α) at the beginning of 1 Peter and continue through to page 36 (λϹ) at the end of 2 Peter.[85] The ΚΑΤΑ ΛΟΥΚΑΝ and ΚΑΤΑ ἸΩΑΝΗΝ titles function in a similar way as the titles of 1–2 Peter in P.Bodmer VIII. They speak of an intertextually connected corpus within the covers of a codex. There has been no small debate in recent years as to whether the physicality of the codex has any bearing on the concept of a canon or self-contained literary corpus.[86] The upshot of this section is that while the codex does not *always* signify a literary corpus, when combined with other factors, it certainly can be used in the service of demarcating a literary collection. The ΚΑΤΑ + evangelist titles transform P75 into a codex that embodies – at least partially – the emergent literary collection of proto-canonical gospels.[87]

c. Paragraphs and Other Sense-Unit Divisions

P75 has an extensive system of paragraphing and demarcating smaller sense-unit divisions. According to Scott Charlesworth's tabulation, P75 corresponds to the text of NA27 in many of its chapter breaks, paragraph breaks, verse breaks, and verse subdivisions.[88] While there are paragraph breaks and verse subdivisions that are not found in NA27, the vast majority of P75's sense-unit divisions correspond to divisions at the same places in NA27.[89] Chapter breaks, paragraph breaks, verse breaks, and verse subdivisions are generously distributed in the extant leaves of both *GLuke* and *GJohn* in P75. Where the leaves have margins, the use of *ekthesis* appears to be consistently distributed throughout *GLuke* and *GJohn*. Interestingly, the textual divisions in the Johannine portion of P75 correspond closely to Vaticanus, and they also have significant overlap with P66.[90] Similarly, we can see P75 corresponding to B and to P4 at significant text

---

[85] These codicological and paratextual features are visible online at the Bodmer Papyri website: https://bodmerlab.unige.ch/fr/constellations/papyri/barcode/1072205366; accessed 1 January to 5 March 2021.

[86] Skeat 1994 and Stanton 2004 draw a connection between the codex and the four-gospel canon. Elliott 1996 and Kruger 2012 more broadly draw a connection between codex construction and the formation of New Testament canon. Meade 2019, on the other hand, is skeptical, arguing that canon lists are much more reliable for establishing collections of Scripture.

[87] This corpus-conscious function of gospel titles may extend back into the second century; cf. Trobisch 1996; Heckel 1999; Petersen 2006.

[88] Charlesworth 2016: 54–57.

[89] Charlesworth 2016: 54–57.

[90] See Hill 2015.

7.2 Gospel Combinations in P75

231

divisions. The Lukan texts of P75 and P4 overlap only at various portions of chapters 3–6, and in this span of text there are considerable lacunae. However, we can discern the same kind of text division at *GLuke* 3.21, and nearly the same text divisions at *GLuke* 6.12–16. The images in Martin and Kasser's *editio principes* of P75 do not show the full text of *GLuke* 3.21 that is only visible in the more recent high-resolution photographs at the Vatican Digital Library.[91] These more recent images reveal that there is, at *GLuke* 3.21, a raised dot immediately following φυλακη, and then a two-letter blank space, followed by εγενετο κτλ. This is the same way that P4 divides the text, and it occurs later in Alexandrinus, Vaticanus, and Washingtonianus.[92]

At *GLuke* 6.12 in both P4 and P75, there is an *ekthesis*, protruding to the left of the margin, marking off εγενετο. Although there are various lacunae in the following verses, P4 and P75 both insert a diacritical marker after each of the names of the apostles extant in the fragments.[93] This kind of marking a separation between each of the names of the apostles in *GLuke* 6.12–16 occurs visibly in Alexandrinus, Washingtonianus, and to a lesser extent, in Sinaiticus, but it does not occur in Vaticanus. This common scribal habit might indicate that P75 and P4 participated in a gospel reading *paradosis* that was early and widespread. At the very least, we can say that the reading habits in P75 in *GLuke* correspond significantly with P4 in the fragments that overlap – the overlap is probably more than coincidental when we consider that the provenances of both P75 and P4+P64+67 were in the same general vicinity.[94]

The correspondences between the Johannine textual divisions in P75, P66, and Vaticanus, and the Lukan textual divisions in P75, P4, and several later codices, are significant. First, these correspondences suggest that there were consistent reading practices for *GJohn* and *GLuke* at the turn of the third century. The gospel-reading habits of second-century Christians explored in Chapters 1–5 suggest that text division of *GLuke* and *GJohn* was already taking place in the second century, perhaps as early as the midpoint of that century.[95] The text

---

[91] Martin and Kasser 1961; for high-resolution images, see Papyrus Hanna 1, fragment 1A.2r, available at the Digital Vatican Library: digi.vatlib.it, accessed 1 January to 5 March 2021.

[92] I am grateful to Andrew T. Cowan for bringing this to my attention.

[93] The extant fragments of P4 have the diacritical marker after all the names from ιωανην to ιουδαν ιακωβου in *GLk* 6.14–16. The extant fragments of P75 have the diacritical marker after ωνομασεν, after ανδρεαν του αδελφου αυτου, and after ιουδαν ισκαριωθ ος εγενετο προδοτης.

[94] The region between Nag Hammadi and Dendera (the likely provenance of P75) was less than 100 km from Koptos (the likely provenance of P4+P64+67). This would less than a four-day journey by foot, and much less by river. Distances based on scale of map in Nongbri 2018: xii.

[95] See especially Irenaeus, Heracleon, Valentinus and his followers, who exhibited an awareness of lemmatized commentary on multiple gospels (see above, Sections 5.1.1; 5.3), as

232   *Chapter 7: P45 and P75*

divisions we find in P66, P4, and P75 can therefore reasonably be associated with earlier practices of dividing the text of proto-canonical gospels for interpretive reflection. Second, they suggest that P75 combined not only two canonical gospels, but common reading practices associated with these Synoptic and Johannine gospels. The upshot for the present study is that, within the pages of P75, we see not only two canonical gospels interacting in codicological juxtaposition, but also in the reading habits associated with these codices. Considered alongside the scribal connections between all four canonical gospels, exhibited in the scribal harmonizations in P75, these paratextual realities give us clues into a third-century, Egyptian Christian *habitus* of reading the four proto-canonical gospels together in consistent patterns.

7.2.7 Authority

As with the other codices examined in Chapters 6 and 7, it is impossible to discern with great confidence what kind of authority the users or manufacturers of P75 accorded to the gospels contained within this codex. There are, however, a few clues that point in the direction of P75 constituting a collection of early Christian Scripture. The careful scribal hand and the use of sense-unit divisions bespeak a knowledge of the texts in the codex as works of literature rather than sub-literary documents such as *hypomnemata*, and the *nomina sacra* used in the codex identify it as a Christian manuscript produced for in-house use. So, at the very least, we can say that this codex portrays *GLuke* and *GJohn* as works of Christian literature. But these features could also be true of Christian literature not considered in antiquity to be Scripture in any normative sense. However, the thick interrelatedness of *GLuke* to the rest of the Synoptics, and the interaction between *GLuke* and *GJohn* (evidenced by the scribal harmonizations and the combination of early Christian Synoptic and Johannine readings habits) in the pages of P75 suggests a fourfold collection consciousness in the producers and/or users of this codex. Such a collection, by the middle of the third century, was considered to be as an authoritative body of Scripture by multiple sources across the ancient Mediterranean,[96] and P75 contributes material evidence to the consolidation of this collection.

7.2.8 Summary of Gospel Combinations in P75

P75 is invaluable for helping us discern several dynamics of gospel combinations in the third century. The strict nature of its textual transmission and the presence

---

well as Tatian and the author of *EpAp*, who read parallel sections from multiple gospels horizontally (see above, Sections 2.4–5; 3.2).

[96] E.g. Hippolytus of Rome, Tertullian of Carthage, Origen of Alexandria, Dionysius of Alexandria, Cyprian of Carthage, Marinus of Caesarea, and Euplus of Catania; cf. Hill 2010b: 42–51.

7.3 Summary and Conclusions on Artifactual Gospel Combinations 233

of the gospel titles enable us to identify two gospels in this codex: *GLuke* and *GJohn*. The common textual affinities and scribal habits hint toward an artifactual mode of discrete juxtaposition that P75 inherited from a predecessor. This mode of discrete juxtaposition was facilitated by the use of conventional gospel titles, marking off the end of one version of the written gospel and the beginning of another. These titles signal an intertextually connected corpus within the covers of this codex. Two members of this corpus, *GLuke* and *GJohn*, were shown through scribal harmonization and sense-unit divisions to interact intertextually not only with one another but also with *GMatthew* and *GMark* (and, significantly, with no other extant gospels). These interactions are made even more salient in the way that P75 brings together early Christian Synoptic and Johannine reading practices. All the above factors situate P75 within a consciousness of the fourfold gospel as the cohesive, authoritative collection that contemporary church fathers articulated across the third-century ancient Mediterranean.

7.3 Summary and Conclusions on Artifactual Gospel Combinations

P45 and P75 give generous evidence that corroborates and expands the conclusions we drew from GA 0171 and P4+P64+67 in the previous chapter. These two third-century codices show us that not only *GMatthew* and *GLuke*, but also Synoptics and *GJohn* can keep company through the *mode* of artifactual juxtaposition. The *integrity* of the gospels is demonstrated again by the stability of pericope sequences (and in P75, by the use of gospel titles). The proto-canonical gospels *interact* extensively and congenially in both P45 and P75 by scribal harmonizations. In P75, gospel titles and sense-unit also contribute to the intertextual dance. P45, in its juxtaposition of gospels and Acts, bespeaks the emerging sense of the proto-canonical four as part of an *authoritative* corpus of New Testament Scripture.

P45 and P75 expand our body of Egyptian material evidence from the Fayyum to Koptos, including Hermopolis Magna and the region between Nag Hammadi and Dandarah, and arguably from the late second century to the middle of the third century. This broad area encompasses the cities and villages where most of our extant manuscripts of noncanonical gospels also originate, and indeed where they were packaged together in fourth-century codices. If any of these gospels were included in the same collection, this would be the place where we would expect to find such an expanded gospel collection in artifactual form. We find no such evidence. On the contrary, where the Synoptics would have parallels with *GThomas*, we find no sign of scribal cross-pollination, but where the texts of *GMatthew*, *GMark*, and *GLuke* overlap with one another in these codices, scribal harmonization makes it abundantly clear that these gospels shared interpretive horizons. Even more significantly, texts as different as *GJohn* and Acts find themselves attached both artifactually and in scribal harmonization to the already-cohesive corpus of Synoptic gospels. Taken as a whole, these four early gospel codices corroborate the same trends that began to emerge in second-century interpretive gospel rewriting such as in *GThomas*, the *Epistula Apostolorum*, and the *Diatessaron*, as well as in the discourse of second-century Christian authors. Because it is sparse, the material evidence by itself cannot establish any patterns of gospel combinations, but it does corroborate, in a limited way, what we have already demonstrated in Chapters 1–5. The Synoptic gospels and *GJohn* joined together to form a center of gravity for the written Jesus tradition in the first half of the second century. In Chapters 6 and 7, we have discovered that this center of gravity is reflected in the codicological and scribal habits of artifactual gospel combinations.

Summary and Conclusions

Gospel writing and gospel reading of the first two centuries CE testify to the broad diversity of the remembered Jesus. Yet within this diversity, a center of gravity emerged as particular gospels began to keep regular company with one another. In the present study, I have traced the developing patterns of these gospel combinations from approximately 100 CE to 200 CE, with a modest foray into the gospel manuscripts of the early third century. I investigated five central facets of gospel combinations: the *identity* of the gospels combined, the *mode* by which they were combined, the *integrity* of their structure in the process of combination, the *interactions* between these gospels, and the relative *authority* of each gospel vis-à-vis the authority of the literary object created by combination. These patterns display themselves across a variety of receptions of the Jesus tradition: interpretive rewriting, pericope interpolation, gospel orchestration, discrete juxtaposition, and scribal harmonization.

In Chapter 1 we found that the author of *GThomas* drew heavily from *GMatthew* and *GLuke* and brought these textual traditions into creative interplay. Not only so, but the Thomasine evangelist at several points mimics the redactional practices and tendencies of both *GMatthew* and *GLuke*, giving evidence to the power of *GMatthew* and *GLuke* to captivate the literary imagination of early Christians. On the other hand, traditions known to be paralleled in extant non-canonical gospels feature only marginally in *GThomas*. We concluded that the author of *GThomas* brought *GMatthew* and *GLuke* into company with one another, plausibly by consulting manuscripts of each, or perhaps by compiling or accessing excerpts from each. The Thomasine evangelist does not show much regard for the narrative integrity of these gospels, but rather he rearranges the *logia* from each into new juxtapositions. Nonetheless, *GThomas* presupposes the narrative foundations of the Synoptic gospels by its use of names, places, and occasions behind the *chreiai* it relates, without explanation. A significant degree of the integrity of *GMatthew* and *GLuke* remains, then, as they are treated not merely as contextless repositories of Jesus *logia* but rather as repositories in narrative form. *GMatthew* and *GLuke* interact congenially, treated by the author of *GThomas* as of the same cloth; traditions later deemed apocryphal mostly tag along for the ride on a Synoptic literary caravan. The author of *GThomas* creates a paradoxical, yet not mutually exclusive, literary dialectic. On the one hand, his writing presupposes the unrivaled cultural currency of *GMatthew* and *GLuke* among gospels in circulation in the second century, and that they lend themselves

236 *Summary and Conclusions*

to be read and interpreted conjointly. On the other hand, *GThomas* also undercuts the authority of these gospels by claiming exclusive access to a higher level of revelation from the living Jesus. At any rate, as an interpretive rewriting of the gospel, *GThomas* gives us an example of *GMatthew* and *GLuke* guiding the literary imagination of second-century Jesus-followers, and the propensity of non-canonical traditions to "tag along for the ride". Wherever *GThomas* is dated in the reasonable range from 135 to 200 CE, it contributes to an overall picture in which *GMatthew* and *GLuke* form a textual center of gravity for gospel writing and gospel reading.

In Chapter 2, we examined another interpretive rewriting of the gospels – the *Epistula Apostolorum*. The author of this genre-bending epistle brings together all three Synoptic gospels with *GJohn* and weaves them together into a gospel epitome. The author fills in a narrative gap by an apocryphal childhood episode, and he offers a bit of his own embellishment, but for the most part the gospel epitome – and *EpAp* as a whole – is a thoroughly Synoptic and Johannine composition. Even more so than *GThomas*, the summary of Jesus' earthly deeds in the gospel epitome appears to have involved the mode of excerpting. Regarding integrity and interactions, the epitome in *EpAp* maintains the broad canonical narrative from birth to resurrection. However, one can easily discern *GJohn* as the guiding force for the narrative sequence and structure. Johannine bookends – incarnation and post-resurrection appearances – bracket the gospel epitome. One feature that is of value for our study is the congeniality with which the Synoptic gospels and *GJohn* interact, even while *GJohn* guides sequence and idiom. The implied authors of *EpAp* address their audience with self-conscious authority, but they also presuppose textual authority for the written gospel summarized in the form of an epitome, and the ensuing post-resurrection dialogue builds upon this presupposed textual authority of the written gospel. If *EpAp* is dated to the first half of the second century, it would be a significant, early movement toward recognizing the four proto-canonical gospels as occupying the same field of discourse. On the other hand, if it is a contemporary of Tatian or Irenaeus, it would corroborate the late second-century dynamics described in Chapters 3–5.

In Chapter 3, we transitioned to another form of gospel combination: gospel orchestration. We argued that gospel orchestration, while overlapping with interpretive rewriting, differs from the compositional processes of works such as *GThomas* and *EpAp* because it includes little to no *Sondergut* added by the composer. The main example of gospel orchestration we analyzed was Tatian's *Diatessaron*. The *Diatessaron* combines nearly the entirety of all four canonical gospels, with very few (if any) fragments of noncanonical traditions. The comprehensive nature of Tatian's project of combining four gospels, with minimal redundancies, almost necessitates that the mode of combination involved the manual use of at least one copy of each gospel book, read and annotated simultaneously (probably with the help of assistants). Tatian's handling of the narrative sequences of *GMatthew*, *GMark*, and *GJohn* show a commitment to respect the

Summary and Conclusions 237

integrity of each narrative structure as much as possible while simultaneously coordinating them into a creative composition. Even *GLuke*, which Tatian re-works most liberally, retains its inter-pericope sequence in the larger blocks of Lukan *Sondergut* that Tatian situates at various locations in his overall narrative sequence. To an even larger extent than *EpAp*, in the *Diatessaron* we see all three Synoptic gospels coming together with *GJohn* into a fruitful, congenial intertex-tual habitat. And just as in *EpAp*, *GJohn* takes on a theological role in guiding the composition. Scholars have debated whether the *Diatessaron* is a testimony to the ascendancy of the fourfold gospel, an all-out attack against it, or something in between. Our analysis suggests that, based on the milieu of gospel orchestra-tions and the first 200 years of Diatessaronic reception, it functioned as a com-panion volume to the fourfold gospel rather than a rival to its authority. Securely dated to the 170s CE, the *Diatessaron* is a pre-Irenaean testimony to the consol-idation of all four proto-canonical gospels as a self-interpreting center of gravity for the written Jesus tradition.

In Chapters 4–5, we shifted gears and explored early Christian second-order discourse about gospel authors and their texts. We identified how the persona of the gospel author emerged between the composition of *GMark* and the exegetical reflections of Papias. The persona of the gospel author became the means by which gospel books were differentiated and read in concert. While the authors of the four proto-canonical gospels each contributed to the literary and theological lexicon for describing gospel authorship, Papias and the anonymous author of the tradition in *Hist. eccl.* 3.24.5–8a (arguably Papias himself or a near contem-porary) are the earliest witnesses to the practice of differentiating the four gospels and reading them conjointly, dating to the first quarter of the second century. These early second-century witnesses testify to the strong bond between the Syn-optic gospels and *GJohn* – later exhibited literarily in *EpAp* and the *Diatessaron*. We discovered that this propensity for Synoptics and *GJohn* to interact congen-ially is also exhibited in the reading habits of various Christian intellectuals who flourished approximately between 125 and 175 CE: Valentinus, Justin, Ptolemy, Marcus, and Heracleon.

In view of this milieu, in Chapter 5 we observed that the habits of fourfold gospel reading practiced by Irenaeus and Clement were not the inventions of these later figures. Rather, Irenaeus and Clement *developed* habits and strategies that began to emerge as early as Papias. The development we see in Irenaeus and Clement is a bibliographic awareness of the proto-canonical gospels as discrete objects that can be juxtaposed and read in parallel. Within a bibliographic field, the identities and integrity of discrete gospel books interact on a level plane of textual authority. Irenaeus showcases this bibliographic knowledge by his dual-axis strategy of gospel reading, his use of *titloi* to demarcate a particular gospel's *Sondergut*, and his use of gospel author personas as metonymic figureheads by which to differentiate gospels. Clement exhibits this same epistemic frame in his account of gospel authorship in *Hist. eccl.* 6.14.5–7, his intra-Synoptic and even

238 *Summary and Conclusions*

Synoptic-Johannine harmonizing of gospel citations, and his explicit excerpting from gospel books. Importantly, even though Clement and Irenaeus had access to a wide variety of gospel literature (Clement more so than Irenaeus), the proto-canonical four maintained the center of gravity in their reading and citational habits. Moreover, Irenaeus and Clement creatively develop a second-century Christian *theology* of gospel writing in which the four proto-canonical gospels, participants in the covenantal economy of divine revelation, are *the* authoritative accounts of Jesus of Nazareth. Irenaeus articulates this within a thoroughly Johannine grammar, suggesting that such theological understanding of the fourfold gospel predated his prodigious pen.

In Chapters 6–7, we posed the same questions about the dynamics of gospel combinations to the earliest extant multi-gospel codices: GA 0171, P4+P64+67, P45, and P75. These manuscripts have a probable date range from ca. 175 to ca. 275 CE, and in many ways, they provide material evidence for the congenial interactions between *GMatthew* and *GLuke* (GA 0171 and P4+P64+67), Synoptics and *GJohn* (P75), and all four proto-canonical gospels (P45). Intra-Synoptic scribal harmonizations abound (which, notably, include harmonization to *GMark* even where *GMark* is not extant in the manuscript), and there are even some cases of Synoptic-Johannine scribal harmonization. Harmonization to Thomasine redaction, however, is conspicuously absent. The physical and paratextual features of these manuscripts (i.e. sense-unit divisions and, in P75, gospel titles) also elicit a bibliography of proto-canonical gospels. P45, with its combination of the fourfold gospel and Acts, even hints at a New Testament collection awareness. While the pool of pre-Constantinian, multi-gospel manuscripts is admittedly thin, it does cover a geographic range of over 500 kilometers, and it maps entirely onto a provenance where noncanonical gospels flourished. Thus, even though only a small sample of *realia* survive from antiquity, we may cautiously infer from this sample that, through the mode of artifactual juxtaposition, the identities and integrity of proto-canonical gospels interacted congenially, corresponding to the authoritative corpus of New Testament Scripture articulated in the late second century.

Throughout this study, we have encountered more than a few instances of Jesus tradition that did not eventually make it into the canonical fourfold gospel (except, in some cases, by entering the scribal tradition of the canonical gospels). We have seen apocryphal traditions in *GThomas*, an infancy tradition in *EpAp*, several noncanonical fragments in Diatessaronic witnesses, an extended discourse by Clement on a passage in *GEgy*, and a Thomasine harmonizing variant in Sinaiticus. These examples showed us that most second-century Christians valued these traditions for preserving the words and deeds of Jesus (even if erroneously by modern standards). Some of these noncanonical traditions even found their way into streams of the New Testament textual tradition, especially in the "Western" textual family. Others were inscribed in other Jesus books such as *PJames*, *GHebrews*, *GPeter*, or *IGThomas*. At the same time, these examples

Summary and Conclusions 239

showed us that second-century Christians did not treat these traditions as stable books located at the gravitational center together with the proto-canonical four. Rather, these traditions orbited at one or more removes from the center, in an ancillary, epiphenomenal fashion.

Space has not permitted me to engage extensively one important piece of evidence: Marcion's *euangelion*. Marcion either opposed the combination of a form of *GLuke* with other proto-canonical gospels, or he only had access to a Lukan text.[1] Whatever the case may be, the composition and reception of his gospel represent a major departure from the propensity of many second-century Christians to combine two or more proto-canonical gospels (especially Synoptics with *GJohn*). Marcion's gospel shows that the second-century habit of combining proto-canonical gospels was not the *only* way Christians read gospels in the second century. In fact, according to Irenaeus, a handful of other Christian groups read only one gospel.[2] On the other hand, the early evidence we have accumulated (e.g., Papias, Polycarp, *LEMark*, Valentinus, and plausibly *EpAp*) demonstrates that the Synoptic-Johannine gospel combination was earlier and more widespread than the Marcionite habit of reading only one gospel and rejecting the others. In particular, *LEMark* contributes strong evidence that by the time Marcion was advancing his cause in Rome, Christians were already engaged in Synoptic-Johannine hermeneutics that worked in the opposite direction as Marcion's project.

My study has been an exercise in *Wirkungsgeschichte* – that is, a history of the effects that ancient Christian gospels engendered in subsequent readers, redactors, gospel authors, and scribes of the second and early-third centuries.[3] I have read gospel literature in conversation with various early Christian traditions stemming from a panoply of ancient provenances – Upper Egypt, Alexandria, Syria, Asia Minor, Rome, and Gaul. But I have also read gospel literature within the cultural encyclopedia of Jewish and Greco-Roman book production.[4] In a

---

[1] For the former view, see Hill 2006: 91–94; for the latter view, see Schmid 2002 (who argues that Marcion encountered the fourfold gospel after he published his *Euangelion*); cf. Moll 2010: 89–90.

[2] *Haer.* 1.26.2 (on Ebionites and *GMatthew*); 3.11.7 (on Ebionites and *GMatthew*, Marcionites and *GLuke*).

[3] On the merits of *Wirkungsgeschichte* in the study of the New Testament and Christian origins, see Bockmuehl 2006; 2007. The strength of Bockmuehl's case lies in his coordination of the New Testament's implied reader(s) and implied range of meanings with the reception of the New Testament within living memory of its authors and composition (up to ca. 200 CE). Considering the hermeneutical intention embedded in the text vis-à-vis the effects that the text engendered in its earliest readers is a fruitful course for historical, exegetical, and theological reflection. In the present study, I have applied Bockmuehl's method by focusing on the second-century effects of early Christian gospels and identifying how these effects bespeak a collaborative intention already embedded in the earliest gospels (see Section 4.1).

[4] On the concept of a cultural encyclopedia, see Rowe 2009: 8–16.

240 *Summary and Conclusions*

recent monograph on the origins of gospel writing, Robyn Faith Walsh has suggested that interpreting ancient gospels through the lens of Christian tradition – be it ancient or modern – at best obfuscates the historical data, and at worst it scatters historical diamonds across a dunghill of religious dogma.[5] In lieu of religious categories such as evangelists, ecclesial communities, and universal Christian mission, Walsh proposes that we analyze gospel book production exclusively within the lexicon of elite, Greco-Roman literary habits.[6]

Walsh's historical rigor is to be commended, but the evidence I have assembled in this study invites the reading of gospel literature through the lens of Greco-Roman book culture *and* in conversation with ancient Christian voices. The evidence put forth in the present monograph suggests that the four protocanonical gospels, written in the pre-Trajanic era, when combined, orchestrated, and read in concert, captivated the literary *and* religious imagination of Christians across the second century. Such evidence not only informs us of the strategies of second-century Christian identity construction, but it also reveals something about the valence of these early Christian gospels themselves. That is to say, the composition of these archetypal gospels is of a piece with their early reception, and their early reception cannot be disentangled from Christian religious praxis.

In conclusion, gospel writing and gospel reading of the second century evince, from early on, a tendency for the canonical birds of a feather to flock together as a fourfold family. Certainly, by the time that Christians began to read *GJohn* conjointly with the Synoptics, these four gospel books forged a tight bond, and their stories, episodes, sayings, and even phrasings began a perichoretic, congenial interplay. If our analysis is correct, this was taking place as early as the first quarter of the second century in the writings of Papias and his contemporaries. During the relatively peaceful reign of the Antonine dynasty, the gospel compositions (e.g. *GTh* and *EpAp*), gospel orchestrations (e.g. *Diatessaron*), and Christian reflection (from Papias to Clement of Alexandria) bore out this seminal bond between the Synoptics and *GJohn*, with other gospels orbiting at several removes around this fourfold center of gravity. At the turn of the third century, this pattern was concretized in the construction of two-gospel and eventually four-gospel codices.

---

[5] Walsh 2021: 1–19. The image of diamonds buried in a dunghill is Walsh's appropriation of an illustrative metaphor used by Thomas Jefferson for the same matter.

[6] Walsh advocates this exclusive approach especially in 2021: 15–19, and the exegetical payoff for interpreting the process of gospel writing is shown in 2021: 134–94.

Appendix 1: Synoptic Sequencing

Table A: Diatessaronic Sequence in Ephrem's *Commentary*[1]

Key

No brackets	gospel that is guiding the sequence
[brackets]	parallels that are not explicitly in the lemma (i.e. lacking certain redactional elements of Synoptic parallel).
MkR	Markan Redaction
MkS	Markan Sondergut
JFst	Johannine Feast (feast numbers given in original Johannine order).
ql	questionable *lemmata* in Ephrem's *Commentary*
absA	absent from the Armenian recension.
absS	absent from Syriac manuscript Chester Beatty MS 709

CGos.	GMatthew	GMark	GLuke	GJohn
1.2–8				1.1–18
1.9–24			1.5–25	
1.25–26	1.21		1.26–34	
1.27–30			1.39–56	
1.31–32			1.57–79	
2.1–11	1.18–25			
2.12			2.3	
2.13–15			2.11–14	
2.16–17			2.25–35	
2.18–3.9	2.1–23			
3.10–15				1.19–23
3.16ql			2.48–49	
3.17	3.4–9		3.8	1.29
4.1–3	3.14–15		3.23	
4.4–16	4.1–11	1.12 MkR	4.1–13	
4.17–18				1.35–46
5.1–12				2.1–11
5.13–14		1.15 MkR		
5.15				4.2
5.17absA	9.9–11	2.14 MkR	[5.27–32]	
5.18			5.1–11	
5.19–20	9.1–8	[2.1–12]	[5.17–26]	
5.21	[9.9–13]	[2.13–17]	5.30–33	
5.22	[9.14–17]	[2.18–22]	[5.33–39]	

---

[1] This table is adapted from Coogan and Rodriguez 2023.

Appendix 1: Synoptic Sequencing

CGos	GMatthew	GMark	GLuke	GJohn
5.23–24	[12.1–8]	[2.23–28]	[6.1–5]	
6.1	5.1–16			
6.2			6.20–26	
6.3	5.17–20			
6.4–15	5.22–48		6.29–30	
6.16	6.1–18		[11.1–4]	
6.17	6.22–23		11.34–36	
	6.19–21		12.33–34	
6.18a	6.25–34		12.22–32	
6.18b	7.1–2		6.37–38	
6.19–20	13.12 [25.29]		8.18	
6.21a	7.6			
6.21b	7.28–29			
6.22	8.5–13		7.1–10	
6.23			7.11–17	
6.24	8.18–20		9.57–60	
6.25	8.23–27	[4.35–41]	8.22–25	
6.26	8.28–34	[5.1–20]	8.26–39	
7.1–12, 15–17	9.20–34	5.25–34 MkR	8.43–56	
7.18			7.36–50	
7.19–27	9.20–34	5.25–34 MkR	8.43–56	
8.1a–6	10.1–16		10.1–10	
[8.1b[absA]]		16.15		
8.7–9	10.7–25			
8.10–14	10.26–39			
8.15			10.38–42	
9.1–3	11.1–7		7.18–24	
9.4–16	11.7–15		7.24–28; 16.16	
9.17	18.1–4			
10.1–3	20.20–28	10.35–45		
10.4–6	12.31–32	3.28–30 MkR	[12.10]	
10.7	12.22–24	3.22	[11.14–15]	
10.8–10			7.36–50	
10.11	9.35–38			
10.12–13			10.17–20	
10.14–15	11.25–27		[10.21–22]	
10.15	11.25–30			
10.16			14.26–30	
11.1–4	12.38–42		[11.29–32]	
11.5–8	12.43–45		11.24–26	
11.9–10			11.27–28	
	12.46–50	[3.31–35]	[8.19–21]	
11.11	[13.1–9]	4.1–9	[8.4–8]	
11.11a[absA]	13.10–15	4.10–12	[8.9–10]	
11.12–15	13.3–8	4.3–8	8.5–8	
11.16[ql]	19.20–22	10.20–22	18.21–23	
11.17–18	[13.8]	4.8 MkR		
11.19	13.24–30			

Appendix 1: Synoptic Sequencing

243

CGos	GMatthew	GMark	GLuke	GJohn
11.20	13.31–32	[4.30–32]	[13.18–19]	
11.21	13.33		[13.20–21]	
11.22	13.47–50			
11.23–26	13.53–58	[6.1–6]	4.16–30	
11.27	N/A	N/A	N/A	
11.28	14.1–12	[6.14–29]		
12.1–5	[14.13–21]	[6.32–44]	[9.10b–17]	[2.1–11]; 6.1–15 JFst 3
12.7–9	14.22–33	[6.45–52]		6.16–21
12.10–11				6.26–59
12.12	15.1–13	7.1–17	[6.39]	
12.13–15	15.21–28	[7.24–30]		
12.16–20				4.4–42
12.21–24	8.1–4	[1.40–45]	5.12–16	
13.1–4				5.1–18 JFst2
13.5ql	[12.3–4]	[2.25–26]	[6.3–4]	
13.6–7				5.1–17
13.8–12				5.24–47
13.13		8.22–26 MkS		
14.1–3	16.13–23	[8.27–33]	[9.18–22]	
14.4	16.21–23 // 20.17–19	8.31–33 // 10.32–34	18.31–34	
14.5–12	16.28–17.9	9.1–10	9.27–36	
14.13			13.31–33	
14.14–15	17.14–21	9.14–29 MkR	[9.37–43]	
14.16–17	17.25–27			
14.18	19.3–12	[10.2–12]		
14.19–20			15.1–32	
14.21			16.1–12	
14.22–23	18.21–22		[17.4]	
14.24	18.10–20			
14.25			13.1–5	
14.26–27			13.6–9	
14.28–29				7.1–19 JFst4
15.1–11	19.16–30	10.17–31 MkR	18.18–30	
15.12–13			16.19–31	
15.14–17	20.1–16			
15.18–19	20.17–19 20.20–28	10.32–45 10.35–45	[18.31–34]	
15.20–21			19.1–10	
15.22	[20.29–34]	10.46–52 MkR	[18.35–43]	
15.23	[21.12–13]	[11.15–17]	[19.45–46]	2.13–20 JFst1
15.24			18.9–14	
16.1–10	[21.18–22]	11.12–14, 20–25 MkR		[2.19–20]
16.11–15				3.1–15

CGos	GMatthew	GMark	GLuke	GJohn
16.16			18.1–8	
16.17[AbsS]	21.23–27	11.27–33	20.1–8	
16.18	21.28–32			
16.19–20	21.33–46	12.1–12	20.9–19	
16.21	22.15–22	12.13–17	20.20–26	
16.22	22.23–33	12.18–27	20.27–40	
16.23	22.34–40	12.28–34	10.25–28	
16.24			10.39–37	
16.25				7.37–39
16.26–27				8.39–59
16.28–32				9.1–41
16.33				10.1–18
17.1–10				11.1–48
17.11–13	26.6–13	14.3–9		12.1–8 JFst6
18.1	21.1–9	11.1–10	19.28–38	12.12–15
			19.41–44	
18.2	21.14–16			
18.3–4				12.30–36
18.5–7			17.20–21	
				10.37
				7.27
				7.42
				7.26
	24.26–27		17.23–24	
18.8–10			11.52	
			17.21	
	23.35–37			
18.11				12.47–48
18.12–14	24.15–25	13.14–23	21.20–24	
18.15–17	24.29–42	13.24–37	21.25–28, 34–36	
18.18			17.34	
	24.45–51		12.42–46	
18.19–20	25.1–30			
18.21		12.35–40		
18.22				13.1–11
19.1–3	26.21–24	14.18–21	22.21–22	13.21–26
19.4–5	26.26–29	14.22–25	22.15–20	
19.6			22.31–32	
19.7–9				14.8–30
				16.33
19.10			22.35–38	
19.11–12	26.20–24	14.17–21	22.21–23	
19.13				15.12–17
19.14–16				16.7–11
19.17				17.1–5
20.1–4	26.36–46	14.32–42	22.40–46	
20.5	26.51–52			18.10–11

Appendix 1: Synoptic Sequencing

CGos	GMatthew	GMark	GLuke	GJohn
20.6–10	26.39	14.36	22.42	
20.11			22.44	
20.12–13	26.45–50		22.46–48	
				18.4–8
	26.51–52			18.10–11
				18.12–13
20.14	26.69–75	14.66–72	22.54–62	18.15–18, 25–27
20.15	26.64–65	14.62–63	22.67–70	
				18.28
20.16				19.12–16
20.17	27.29	15.16–17	23.2	19.2
20.18–19	27.3–10			
20.20	27.31–32	15.20–21	23.26	19.16–17
20.21			23.31	
20.22–26	[27.38, 40]	[15.27, 32]	23.32–43	
20.27	27.34, 48	15.23, 36		19.29
				19.23
20.28–29	[27.54]	[15.39]		
20.30–32	27.46–48	15.34–35		
20.33–34	27.42	15.31		
20.35–39	N/A	N/A	N/A	N/A
21.1			23.46	
21.1	27.51	15.38	23.45	
	27.52–53			
21.2	N/A	N/A	N/A	N/A
21.3			[23.34]	
21.4–7	27.51	15.38		
			23.45	
	27.52			
21.8–9			23.49	
21.10–12				19.34
21.13		[15.42]	[23.54]	[19.31]
21.14–19	N/A	N/A	N/A	N/A
21.20–21	27.58	15.43	23.52	19.38
	27.66			
	27.60	15.46		
21.22				20.1
21.23				20.5–7
21.24	28.11–15			
21.25	N/A	N/A	N/A	N/A
21.26–29				20.11–18
21.30				21.18–22
21.31–33	N/A	N/A	N/A	N/A
22.1			24.49	
22.2	N/A	N/A	N/A	N/A
22.3–6	N/A	N/A	N/A	N/A

246 *Appendix 1: Synoptic Sequencing*

Table B: Diatessaronic Synposis of Resurrection and Post-Resurrection Scenes

Key:
Verses are sectioned according to the synopsis in Table C below. The sections in this table are coordinated according to how the Arabic (AH) and Latin (Fuldensis) texts adhere to the Greek text in NA28. Three phrases are labeled "UF" for "unidentified fragment," because they do not appear in any of the canonical gospels.

	Ephrem (*CGos.* 21.22a–21.27b)	Arabic Harmony (§52.45–54.5)	Fuldensis (§174–79)
1		*GMatt* 28.1a	*GMatt* 28.1a
2		*GLuke* 24.1b	
3	*GJohn* 20.1b		
4		*GJohn* 20.1c	*GJohn* 20.1c
5		*GMatt* 28.1b	*GMatt* 28.1b
6		*GLuke* 24.10b	
7			*GMark* 16.1c
8			*GLuke* 24.1c
9		*GMatt* 28.1c	
10		*GLuke* 24.1d	*GLuke* 24.1d
11			*GMark* 16.2c
12		*GMark* 16.3a	*GMark* 16.3a
13		*GMark* 16.3b	*GMark* 16.3b
14		*GMark* 16.4b	*GMark* 16.4b
15		UF: "as they were saying these things"	
16		*GMatt* 28.2a–b	*GMatt* 28.2a–b
17		*GLuke* 24.2	*GLuke* 24.2
18		*GMatt* 28.2c	*GMatt* 28.2c
19		*GMatt* 28.3–4	*GMatt* 28.3–4
20		UF: "and when he [the angel] was gone"	
21		*GMark* 16.5a	
22		*GLuke* 24.3b	
23		*GMark* 16.5.b–d	
24		*GMatt* 28.5a–c,	*GMatt* 28.5a–c
25			*GMatt* 28.5d
26		*GMatt* 28.5e	*GMatt* 28.5e
27		*GMark* 16.6d	
28		*GMatt* 28.6a–b	*GMatt* 28.6a–b
29		UF: "Our Lord"	UF: "Our Lord"
30		*GLuke* 24.4a–7c	*GLuke* 24.4a–7c
31		*GMatt* 28.7a	*GMatt* 28.7a
32		*GMark* 16.7b	
33		*GMatt* 28.7b–c	*GMatt* 28.7b
34		*GMark* 16.7d	
35		*GMatt* 28.7d	
36		*GLuke* 24.8	*GLuke* 24.8

Appendix 1: Synoptic Sequencing 247

37		*GMatt* 28.8a–b	*GMatt* 28.8a–b
38			*GMatt* 28.8c
39		*GMark* 16.8b–d	
40	*GJohn* 20.5–8	*GJohn* 20.2a–10	*GJohn* 20.2a–10
41		*GJohn* 20.11–17	
42		*GMark* 16.9	*GMark* 16.9
43			*GJohn* 20.11–17
44		*GMatt* 28.11–15	*GMatt* 28.11–15
45		*GJohn* 20.18	*GJohn* 20.18
46		*GMatt* 28.8	
47		*GMatt* 28.9–10	*GMatt* 28.9–10
48			*GMatt* 28.11
49		*GLuke* 24.9a	
50		*GLuke* 24.9b	*GLuke* 24.9b
51		*GMark* 16.10b	
52		*GLuke* 24.10a, c	
53			*GMark* 16.10c
54			*GLuke* 24.9c
55			*GMark* 16.10b
56		*GMark* 16.11	*GMark* 16.11
57		*GLuke* 24.11	*GLuke* 24.11
58		*GMark* 16.12	*GMark* 16.12
59	*GLuke* 24.18, 30	*GLuke* 24.13–35	*GLuke* 24.13–35
60		*GMark* 16.13	*GMark* 16.13
61	*GLuke* 24.41–43	*GLuke* 24.36…	*GLuke* 24.36…

Table C: Synopsis of Resurrection Accounts

GMatthew 28	GMark 16	GLuke 24	GJohn 20
1a Ὀψὲ δὲ σαββάτων τῇ ἐπιφωσκούσῃ εἰς μίαν σαββάτων	1a Καὶ διαγενομένου τοῦ σαββάτου	1a Τῇ δὲ μιᾷ τῶν σαββάτων	1a Τῇ δὲ μιᾷ τῶν σαββάτων
1b ἦλθεν Μαριὰμ ἡ Μαγδαληνὴ καὶ ἡ ἄλλη Μαρία	1b Μαρία ἡ Μαγδαληνὴ καὶ Μαρία ἡ [τοῦ] Ἰακώβου	1b ὄρθρου βαθέος	1b Μαρία ἡ Μαγδαληνὴ ἔρχεται
1c θεωρῆσαι τὸν τάφον.	1c καὶ Σαλώμη	1c ἐπὶ τὸ μνῆμα ἦλθον	1c πρωῒ σκοτίας ἔτι οὔσης
2a καὶ ἰδοὺ σεισμὸς ἐγένετο μέγας·	1d ἠγόρασαν ἀρώματα ἵνα ἐλθοῦσαι ἀλείψωσιν αὐτόν.	1d φέρουσαι ἃ ἡτοίμασαν ἀρώματα.	1d εἰς τὸ μνημεῖον
2b ἄγγελος γὰρ κυρίου καταβὰς ἐξ οὐρανοῦ καὶ προσελθὼν ἀπεκύλισεν τὸν λίθον	2a καὶ λίαν πρωῒ τῇ μιᾷ τῶν σαββάτων	2 εὗρον δὲ τὸν λίθον ἀποκεκυλισμένον ἀπὸ τοῦ μνημείου,	1e καὶ βλέπει τὸν λίθον ἠρμένον ἐκ τοῦ μνημείου.
2c καὶ ἐκάθητο ἐπάνω αὐτοῦ.	2b ἔρχονται ἐπὶ τὸ μνημεῖον	3a εἰσελθοῦσαι δὲ	2a τρέχει οὖν καὶ ἔρχεται πρὸς Σίμωνα Πέτρον
3 ἦν δὲ ἡ εἰδέα αὐτοῦ ὡς ἀστραπὴ καὶ τὸ ἔνδυμα αὐτοῦ λευκὸν ὡς χιών.	2c ἀνατείλαντος τοῦ ἡλίου.	3b οὐχ εὗρον τὸ σῶμα τοῦ κυρίου Ἰησοῦ.	2b καὶ πρὸς τὸν ἄλλον μαθητὴν ὃν ἐφίλει ὁ Ἰησοῦς
4 ἀπὸ δὲ τοῦ φόβου αὐτοῦ ἐσείσθησαν οἱ τηροῦντες καὶ ἐγενήθησαν ὡς νεκροί.	3a καὶ ἔλεγον πρὸς ἑαυτάς·	4a καὶ ἐγένετο ἐν τῷ ἀπορεῖσθαι αὐτὰς περὶ τούτου	2c καὶ λέγει αὐτοῖς· ἦραν τὸν κύριον ἐκ τοῦ μνημείου καὶ οὐκ οἴδαμεν ποῦ ἔθηκαν αὐτόν.
5a Ἀποκριθεὶς δὲ ὁ ἄγγελος εἶπεν ταῖς γυναιξίν·	3b τίς ἀποκυλίσει ἡμῖν τὸν λίθον ἐκ τῆς θύρας τοῦ μνημείου;	4b καὶ ἰδοὺ ἄνδρες δύο ἐπέστησαν αὐταῖς ἐν ἐσθῆτι ἀστραπτούσῃ.	3a Ἐξῆλθεν οὖν ὁ Πέτρος καὶ ὁ ἄλλος μαθητὴς
5b μὴ φοβεῖσθε ὑμεῖς,	4 καὶ ἀναβλέψασαι θεωροῦσιν ὅτι ἀποκεκύλισται ὁ λίθος·	5a ἐμφόβων δὲ γενομένων αὐτῶν	3b καὶ ἤρχοντο εἰς τὸ μνημεῖον.
5c οἶδα γὰρ ὅτι Ἰησοῦν	4b ἦν γὰρ μέγας σφόδρα.	5b καὶ κλινουσῶν τὰ πρόσωπα εἰς τὴν γῆν	4a ἔτρεχον δὲ οἱ δύο ὁμοῦ·
5d τὸν ἐσταυρωμένον	5a Καὶ εἰσελθοῦσαι εἰς τὸ μνημεῖον	5c εἶπαν πρὸς αὐτάς· τί ζητεῖτε τὸν ζῶντα μετὰ τῶν νεκρῶν;	4b καὶ ὁ ἄλλος μαθητὴς προέδραμεν τάχιον τοῦ Πέτρου
5e ζητεῖτε·	5b εἶδον νεανίσκον καθήμενον ἐν τοῖς δεξιοῖς	6a οὐκ ἔστιν ὧδε, ἀλλ' ἠγέρθη.	4c καὶ ἦλθεν πρῶτος εἰς τὸ μνημεῖον,
6a οὐκ ἔστιν ὧδε, ἠγέρθη γὰρ καθὼς εἶπεν·	5c περιβεβλημένον στολὴν λευκήν,	6b μνήσθητε ὡς ἐλάλησεν ὑμῖν ἔτι ὢν ἐν τῇ Γαλιλαίᾳ	5 καὶ παρακύψας βλέπει κείμενα τὰ ὀθόνια, οὐ μέντοι εἰσῆλθεν.
	5d καὶ ἐξεθαμβήθησαν.	7a λέγων τὸν υἱὸν τοῦ ἀνθρώπου	6a ἔρχεται οὖν καὶ Σίμων Πέτρος ἀκολουθῶν αὐτῷ
	6a ὁ δὲ λέγει αὐταῖς·	7b ὅτι δεῖ παραδοθῆναι εἰς χεῖρας	6b καὶ εἰσῆλθεν εἰς τὸ μνημεῖον,
	6b μὴ ἐκθαμβεῖσθε·		
	6c Ἰησοῦν ζητεῖτε		

Appendix 1: Synoptic Sequencing

6b δεῦτε ἴδετε τὸν τόπον ὅπου ἔκειτο. 7a καὶ ταχὺ πορευθεῖσαι εἴπατε τοῖς μαθηταῖς αὐτοῦ 7b ὅτι ἠγέρθη ἀπὸ τῶν νεκρῶν, 7c καὶ ἰδοὺ προάγει ὑμᾶς εἰς τὴν Γαλιλαίαν, 7d ἐκεῖ αὐτὸν ὄψεσθε· 7e ἰδοὺ εἶπον ὑμῖν. 8a Καὶ ἀπελθοῦσαι ταχὺ ἀπὸ τοῦ μνημείου μετὰ φόβου καὶ χαρᾶς μεγάλης 8b ἔδραμον 8c ἀπαγγεῖλαι τοῖς μαθηταῖς αὐτοῦ. 9a καὶ ἰδοὺ Ἰησοῦς ὑπήντησεν αὐταῖς λέγων· χαίρετε. 9b αἱ δὲ προσελθοῦσαι ἐκράτησαν αὐτοῦ τοὺς πόδας καὶ προσεκύνησαν αὐτῷ. 10a τότε λέγει αὐταῖς ὁ Ἰησοῦς· μὴ φοβεῖσθε· 10b ὑπάγετε ἀπαγγείλατε τοῖς ἀδελφοῖς μου 10c ἵνα ἀπέλθωσιν εἰς τὴν Γαλιλαίαν, 10d κἀκεῖ με ὄψονται. 11 Πορευομένων δὲ αὐτῶν ἰδοὺ τινες τῆς κουστωδίας ἐλθόντες	6d τὸν Ναζαρηνὸν 6e τὸν ἐσταυρωμένον· 6f ἠγέρθη, οὐκ ἔστιν ὧδε· 6g ἴδε ὁ τόπος ὅπου ἔθηκαν αὐτόν. 7a ἀλλ᾽ ὑπάγετε εἴπατε τοῖς μαθηταῖς αὐτοῦ 7b καὶ τῷ Πέτρῳ 7c ὅτι προάγει ὑμᾶς εἰς τὴν Γαλιλαίαν· 7d ἐκεῖ αὐτὸν ὄψεσθε, καθὼς εἶπεν ὑμῖν. 8a Καὶ ἐξελθοῦσαι ἔφυγον ἀπὸ τοῦ μνημείου, 8b εἶχεν γὰρ αὐτὰς τρόμος καὶ ἔκστασις· 8c καὶ οὐδενὶ οὐδὲν εἶπαν· 8d ἐφοβοῦντο γάρ. 9 Ἀναστὰς δὲ πρωῒ πρώτῃ σαββάτου ἐφάνη πρῶτον Μαρίᾳ τῇ Μαγδαληνῇ, παρ᾽ ἧς ἐκβεβλήκει ἑπτὰ δαιμόνια. 10a ἐκείνη πορευθεῖσα ἀπήγγειλεν 10b τοῖς μετ᾽ αὐτοῦ γενομένοις πενθοῦσιν καὶ κλαίουσιν· 11 κἀκεῖνοι ἀκούσαντες ὅτι ζῇ καὶ ἐθεάθη ὑπ᾽ αὐτῆς ἠπίστησαν. 12 Μετὰ δὲ ταῦτα δυσὶν ἐξ αὐτῶν περιπατοῦσιν ἐφανερώθη ἐν ἑτέρᾳ μορφῇ πορευομένοις εἰς ἀγρόν·	ἀνθρώπων ἁμαρτωλῶν καὶ σταυρωθῆναι 7c καὶ τῇ τρίτῃ ἡμέρᾳ ἀναστῆναι. 8 καὶ ἐμνήσθησαν τῶν ῥημάτων αὐτοῦ. 9a Καὶ ὑποστρέψασαι ἀπὸ τοῦ μνημείου 9b ἀπήγγειλαν ταῦτα πάντα τοῖς ἕνδεκα 9c καὶ πᾶσιν τοῖς λοιποῖς. 10a ἦσαν δὲ ἡ Μαγδαληνὴ Μαρία καὶ Ἰωάννα καὶ Μαρία ἡ Ἰακώβου 10b καὶ αἱ λοιπαὶ σὺν αὐταῖς. 10c ἔλεγον πρὸς τοὺς ἀποστόλους ταῦτα, 11a καὶ ἐφάνησαν ἐνώπιον αὐτῶν ὡσεὶ λῆρος τὰ ῥήματα ταῦτα, 11b καὶ ἠπίστουν αὐταῖς. 12a Ὁ δὲ Πέτρος ἀναστὰς ἔδραμεν ἐπὶ τὸ μνημεῖον 12b καὶ παρακύψας βλέπει τὰ ὀθόνια μόνα, 12c καὶ ἀπῆλθεν πρὸς ἑαυτὸν θαυμάζων τὸ γεγονός.	6c καὶ θεωρεῖ τὰ ὀθόνια κείμενα, 7a καὶ τὸ σουδάριον, ὃ ἦν ἐπὶ τῆς κεφαλῆς αὐτοῦ, 7b οὐ μετὰ τῶν ὀθονίων κείμενον 7c ἀλλὰ χωρὶς ἐντετυλιγμένον εἰς ἕνα τόπον. 8 τότε οὖν εἰσῆλθεν καὶ ὁ ἄλλος μαθητὴς ὁ ἐλθὼν πρῶτος εἰς τὸ μνημεῖον καὶ εἶδεν καὶ ἐπίστευσεν· 9 οὐδέπω γὰρ ᾔδεισαν τὴν γραφὴν ὅτι δεῖ αὐτὸν ἐκ νεκρῶν ἀναστῆναι. 10 ἀπῆλθον οὖν πάλιν πρὸς αὐτοὺς οἱ μαθηταί. 11a Μαρία δὲ εἱστήκει πρὸς τῷ μνημείῳ ἔξω κλαίουσα. 11b ὡς οὖν ἔκλαιεν, παρέκυψεν εἰς τὸ μνημεῖον 12 καὶ θεωρεῖ δύο ἀγγέλους ἐν λευκοῖς καθεζομένους, ἕνα πρὸς τῇ κεφαλῇ καὶ ἕνα πρὸς τοῖς ποσίν, ὅπου ἔκειτο τὸ σῶμα τοῦ Ἰησοῦ. 13 καὶ λέγουσιν αὐτῇ ἐκεῖνοι· γύναι, τί κλαίεις; λέγει αὐτοῖς ὅτι ἦραν τὸν κύριόν μου, καὶ οὐκ οἶδα ποῦ ἔθηκαν αὐτόν. 14 Ταῦτα εἰποῦσα ἐστράφη εἰς τὰ ὀπίσω καὶ θεωρεῖ τὸν Ἰησοῦν

εἰς τὴν πόλιν ἀπήγγειλαν τοῖς ἀρχιερεῦσιν ἅπαντα τὰ γενόμενα. 12 καὶ συναχθέντες μετὰ τῶν πρεσβυτέρων συμβούλιόν τε λαβόντες ἀργύρια ἱκανὰ ἔδωκαν τοῖς στρατιώταις 13 λέγοντες· εἴπατε ὅτι οἱ μαθηταὶ αὐτοῦ νυκτὸς ἐλθόντες ἔκλεψαν αὐτὸν ἡμῶν κοιμωμένων. 14 καὶ ἐὰν ἀκουσθῇ τοῦτο ἐπὶ τοῦ ἡγεμόνος, ἡμεῖς πείσομεν [αὐτὸν] καὶ ὑμᾶς ἀμερίμνους ποιήσομεν. 15 οἱ δὲ λαβόντες τὰ ἀργύρια ἐποίησαν ὡς ἐδιδάχθησαν. καὶ διεφημίσθη ὁ λόγος οὗτος παρὰ Ἰουδαίοις μέχρι τῆς σήμερον [ἡμέρας].	13 κἀκεῖνοι ἀπελθόντες ἀπήγγειλαν τοῖς λοιποῖς· οὐδὲ ἐκείνοις ἐπίστευσαν.	ἑστῶτα καὶ οὐκ ᾔδει ὅτι Ἰησοῦς ἐστιν. 15 λέγει αὐτῇ Ἰησοῦς· γύναι, τί κλαίεις; τίνα ζητεῖς; ἐκείνη δοκοῦσα ὅτι ὁ κηπουρός ἐστιν λέγει αὐτῷ· κύριε, εἰ σὺ ἐβάστασας αὐτόν, εἰπέ μοι ποῦ ἔθηκας αὐτόν, κἀγὼ αὐτὸν ἀρῶ. 16 λέγει αὐτῇ Ἰησοῦς· Μαριάμ. στραφεῖσα ἐκείνη λέγει αὐτῷ Ἑβραϊστί· ραββουνι, ὃ λέγεται διδάσκαλε 17 λέγει αὐτῇ Ἰησοῦς· μή μου ἅπτου, οὔπω γὰρ ἀναβέβηκα πρὸς τὸν πατέρα· πορεύου δὲ πρὸς τοὺς ἀδελφούς μου καὶ εἰπὲ αὐτοῖς· ἀναβαίνω πρὸς τὸν πατέρα μου καὶ πατέρα ὑμῶν καὶ θεόν μου καὶ θεὸν ὑμῶν. 18 Ἔρχεται Μαριὰμ ἡ Μαγδαληνὴ ἀγγέλλουσα τοῖς μαθηταῖς ὅτι ἑόρακα τὸν κύριον, καὶ ταῦτα εἶπεν αὐτῇ.

Appendix 1: Synoptic Sequencing   251

Table D: Gospel Parallels in *LEMark*

LEMark		*Canonical Parallel*
16.9	πρωῒ πρώτῃ σαββάτου	*GMk* 16.2 καὶ λίαν πρωῒ τῇ μιᾷ τῶν σαββάτων
		GJn 20.1 τῇ δὲ μιᾷ τῶν σαββάτων
	ἐφάνη πρῶτον Μαρίᾳ τῇ Μαγδαληνῇ	*GJn* 20.11–18 …Ἔρχεται Μαριὰμ ἡ Μαγδαληνὴ ἀγγέλλουσα τοῖς μαθηταῖς ὅτι ἑώρακα τὸν κύριον, καὶ ταῦτα εἶπεν αὐτῇ
	παρ' ἧς ἐκβεβλήκει ἑπτὰ δαιμόνια	*GLk* 8.2 Μαρία ἡ καλουμένη Μαγδαληνή, ἀφ' ἧς δαιμόνια ἑπτὰ ἐξεληλύθει
16.12	Μετὰ δὲ ταῦτα δυσὶν ἐξ αὐτῶν περιπατοῦσιν ἐφανερώθη ἐν ἑτέρᾳ μορφῇ πορευομένοις εἰς ἀγρόν	*GLk* 24.13ff Καὶ ἰδοὺ δύο ἐξ αὐτῶν ἐν αὐτῇ τῇ ἡμέρᾳ ἦσαν πορευόμενοι εἰς κώμην…
16.11, 13, 14	ἠπίστησαν… οὐδὲ ἐκείνοις ἐπίστευσαν… τὴν ἀπιστίαν αὐτῶν… οὐκ ἐπίστευσαν	*GLk* 24.11 καὶ ἠπίστουν αὐταῖς *GJn* 20.25 οὐ μὴ πιστεύσω
16.15	πορευθέντες εἰς τὸν κόσμον ἅπαντα κηρύξατε τὸ εὐαγγέλιον πάσῃ τῇ κτίσει	*GMt* 28.19 πορευθέντες οὖν μαθητεύσατε πάντα τὰ ἔθνη *GMk* 13.10 καὶ εἰς πάντα τὰ ἔθνη πρῶτον δεῖ κηρυχθῆναι τὸ εὐαγγέλιον *GMk* 14.9 ἀμὴν δὲ λέγω ὑμῖν, ὅπου ἐὰν κηρυχθῇ τὸ εὐαγγέλιον εἰς ὅλον τὸν κόσμον
16.16	ὁ πιστεύσας καὶ βαπτισθεὶς σωθήσεται, ὁ δὲ ἀπιστήσας κατακριθήσεται	*GJn* 3.18 ὁ πιστεύων εἰς αὐτὸν οὐ κρίνεται· ὁ δὲ μὴ πιστεύων ἤδη κέκριται

252 Appendix 1: Synoptic Sequencing

16.17	σημεῖα δὲ τοῖς πιστεύσασιν ταῦτα παρακολουθήσει	*GJn* 20.30–31 …καὶ ἄλλα σημεῖα ἐποίησεν ὁ Ἰησοῦς… ταῦτα δὲ γέγραπται ἵνα πιστεύσητε…
	ἐν τῷ ὀνόματί μου δαιμόνια ἐκβαλοῦσιν	*GMk* 9.38 …εἴδομέν τινα ἐν τῷ ὀνόματί σου ἐκβάλλοντα δαιμόνια…
		GMt 7.22 καὶ τῷ σῷ ὀνόματι δαιμόνια ἐξεβάλομεν
	γλώσσαις λαλήσουσιν καιναῖς	Acts 2.4 καὶ ἤρξαντο λαλεῖν ἑτέραις γλώσσαις
		Acts 2.11 ἀκούομεν λαλούντων αὐτῶν ταῖς ἡμετέραις γλώσσαις
16.18	ἐπὶ ἀρρώστους χεῖρας ἐπιθήσουσιν	*GMk* 6.5 … εἰ μὴ ὀλίγοις ἀρρώστοις ἐπιθεὶς τὰς χεῖρας ἐθεράπευσεν.
		GMk 6.13 καὶ ἤλειφον ἐλαίῳ πολλοὺς ἀρρώστους καὶ ἐθεράπευον
16.19	ἀνελήμφθη εἰς τὸν οὐρανὸν	*GLk* 24.51 καὶ ἀνεφέρετο εἰς τὸν οὐρανόν
		Acts 1.2 ἄχρι ἧς ἡμέρας… ἀνελήμφθη
		Acts 1.11 οὗτος ὁ Ἰησοῦς ὁ ἀναλημφθεὶς ἀφ' ὑμῶν εἰς τὸν οὐρανὸν
		Acts 1.22 ἕως τῆς ἡμέρας ἧς ἀνελήμφθη ἀφ' ἡμῶν
16.20	ἐκεῖνοι δὲ ἐξελθόντες ἐκήρυξαν πανταχοῦ	*GMk* 6.12 Καὶ ἐξελθόντες ἐκήρυξαν ἵνα μετανοῶσιν *GLk* 9.6 ἐξερχόμενοι δὲ διήρχοντο κατὰ τὰς κώμας εὐαγγελιζόμενοι καὶ θεραπεύοντες πανταχοῦ.

Appendix 2: Paleographical Analyses

A. Paleographical Analysis of GA 0171

The main hand of GA 0171 (LDAB 2982) is an upright, round, unimodular script with a steady, consistent ductus. The hand is bilinear, and often verges on looped formations, though the loops are often nothing more than an increased thickness in ink. Hooks are often visible at the top of the formation of *alpha*, *delta*, and *lambda*. Letters are frequently, though not always, connected (especially in the cases of *alpha*, *iota*, *sigma*, and *tau*). In GA 0171, *mu* has "middle strokes forming a curve and lateral strokes folded," and *upsilon* does not descend below the baseline. According to Orsini and Clarysse, these features "are never found in biblical majuscule."[1] The vertical stroke of *kappa*, *nu*, and *phi* have sharp, outward hooks at the top and bottom. In all of these features, GA 0171 corresponds more closely to the round chancery and Alexandrian stylistic class than to biblical majuscule.

On the other hand, certain letter formations in GA 0171 correspond to the early stages of biblical majuscule, especially *theta*, *sigma*, *epsilon*, and *omicron*. These letters are formed in a broad and circular ductus. The central lines of *epsilon* and *theta* are noticeably thinner than the outside strokes. *Sigma* and *omicron* show the slightest touch of shading (thinning) on the upper and lower extremities. The circular, lightly shaded texture of these letter formations does not feature in the round chancery or Alexandrian stylistic class, and they are much more common in biblical majuscule. In the development of the biblical majuscule canon, light shading is more common in the earlier period, around the beginning of the third century. One more letter formation that resembles biblical majuscule in 0171 is the *omega*. It is formed in two strokes, the first of which descends to the baseline but ascend minimally, and the second if which descends and ascends fully. The shared affinities that GA 0171 has with round chancery, Alexandrian stylistic class, and early biblical majuscule, anchor its date to somewhere near the turn of the third century CE. Orsini and Clarysse's 50-year window of 175–225 CE is the most plausible.

This leads Orsini and Clarysse to challenge the consensus and assign a date range of 175–225 CE for GA 0171. On the one hand, when we juxtapose the

---

[1] Orsini and Clarysse 2012: 455.

254   *Appendix 2: Paleographical Analyses*

script of GA 0171 with P.Oxy. 661 (LDAB 474; CE2/3), P.Oxy. 3227 (LDAB 1233; CE2/3), P.Ryl. 1.16 (LDAB 2661; before 253–56 CE), P.Oxy. 4327 (LDAB 734; early CE3), and P.Oxy. 3509 (LDAB 3823; late CE3–early CE4), we can see broad similarities between GA 0171 and the biblical majuscule script from the late second to the late third centuries CE.[2] On the other hand, when we set the letters in GA 0171 in parallel with PSI V.446 (TM 19292; 133–37 CE), P.Fay. 87 (TM 10930; 156 CE), and P.Oxy. 3917 (TM 27301; early CE2), we can see the similarities with the round chancery script. There are clearly resemblances between GA 0171 and both the biblical majuscule and the round chancery scripts. A careful analysis would place GA 0171 between both poles, strongly suggesting a timeframe between those two poles. Thus, Orsini and Clarysse's date of 175–225 CE is justified.

α   Formed in two strokes: a downward oblique stroke that crosses an open loop. There is rarely a hint of a hook at the top of the oblique stroke.

β   Composed of two strokes. A right-angle stroke formed in two movements, and the upper and lower loops formed in a single stroke. The upper loop curves back and touches the upright line, but the lower loop only curves back enough to touch the bottom right-hand edge of the baseline.

γ   Formed in two strokes at a right angle, and upper stroke slightly longer than the lower.

δ   Broad, in two strokes: an acute angle followed by a descending stroke. The descending stroke begins with a hook at the top. Sometimes the top leg of the acute angle does not touch the descending stroke.

ε   Circular, formed in three strokes: a lower curve, an upper hasta, and a horizontal bar. The horizontal usually is situated higher than the midpoint of the entire letter formation.[3]

ζ   There are no extant examples of *zeta* in GA 0171.

η   Formed in three strokes: two parallel descenders and a horizontal bar. The horizontal never extends beyond the right or left verticals. The left vertical has outward hooks at the top and bottom, and the right vertical has an outward hook at the bottom.

---

[2] P.Oxy. 661, P.Oxy. 3227, P.Ryl. 1.16, P.Oxy. 4327, and P.Oxy. 3509 form a reliable dataset of datable biblical majuscule hands from the second and third centuries. These dates are all established by documentary texts written on the reverse sides of the papyri that form a secure *terminus ante quem* for the literary hands. The verso of P.Oxy. 1.16 indicates a date of 253–56 CE, and the other examples have documentary hands that are securely datable to certain ends of the third century. For justification of these dates, see Roberts 1955: 12–22; Barker 2011: 576; Orsini 2019: 68–72.

[3] The overall formation of *epsilon* in GA 0171 resembles biblical majuscule (see esp. P.Ryl. 16), but the raised horizontal bar is a feature of round chancery (see esp. PSI V.446; cf. P.Oxy. 3917) and Alexandrian stylistic class (P.Fay. 87).

Appendix 2: Paleographical Analyses   255

θ   Circular, of the same unimodular ductus as *omicron*. The middle bar is occasionally above the midpoint of the letter formation.

ι   Formed by a single, short, descending stroke with a leftward hook at the bottom and sometimes a hook at the top. This stroke does not descend below the notional line.

κ   Composed of three strokes: a vertical and two obliques. The vertical descender begins and ends with hooks.[4]

λ   Formed by two obliques: a long rightward and a short leftward (beginning halfway down the rightward stroke). There are hooks at the beginning of the rightward stroke and end of the leftward stroke.[5]

μ   Composed of three strokes, the middle stroke "forming a curve and lateral strokes folded."[6]

ν   Compact, formed in three strokes. The left vertical has a slight upper and lower outward hook. The right vertical sometimes has a slight inward hook at the top.

ξ   Composed of a single, "zig-zag" stroke (beginning on the left and ending on the right) that remains within the bimodular ductus. The bottom horizontal movement curves downward (to the right).

o   Usually formed in a single stroke, though sometimes formed in two lunate strokes. Consistently round and of the same width as the unimodular ductus of the rest of the alphabet.

π   Formed in three strokes: a horizontal bar followed by two descenders. The horizontal bar is wide, extending beyond the mostly unimodular ductus of this script (the bar overreaches both the left-hand and right-hand verticals). The verticals have outward hooks at the bottom.

ρ   Thin, composed of two strokes. The descender has a hook at the bottom.

σ   Circular, formed in the same ductus as *epsilon*, but without the middle bar.

τ   Formed in two strokes. The horizontal is wider than the usually unimodular ductus of this script, often with a slight wave. The descender has a hook at the bottom.

υ   A single stroke of two movements, downward then upward. The top edges are often curved, and the stroke is occasionally looped. The bottom of the stroke never dips below the baseline.

φ   Long, composed of two strokes. The vertical extends well above and below the notional lines, and it has a conspicuous hook at the top and a smaller hook at the bottom. The middle oval begins on the vertical and loops first to the

---

[4] These hooks are characteristic of round chancery, and feature prominently in PSI V.446 and P.Oxy. 3917.

[5] These hooks in *lambda* are a feature of round chancery: see PSI V.446 and P.Oxy. 3917.

[6] Orsini and Clarysse 2012: 445. This curve in *mu* and the lateral, folded strokes are absent in biblical majuscule.

256   *Appendix 2: Paleographical Analyses*

left, creating a "squashed" shape that leaves a small gap on the right-hand side of the vertical.[7]

χ   Composed of two perpendicular, descending obliques. The second, descending from right to left, is curved on both ends, forming the effect of a "wave".

ψ   Long, composed of two strokes. The vertical extends well above the notional line (the bottom half of the letter formation is not extant), and there is a conspicuous hook at the top of the vertical.

ω   Formed in two u-shaped strokes, descending then ascending. The first stroke descends to the baseline but ascends only minimally, while the second stroke descends and ascends fully. There is a slight hook at the tops of the strokes.

B. Paleographical Analysis of P4+P64+67

The hand of P4+P64+67 (LDAB 2936) has a round, unimodular, bilinear ductus. The deliberate, careful formation of each letter produces a script in which letters almost never overlap, even when closely spaced. One notable difference between P4+P64+67 and the later biblical majuscule hand of Sinaiticus is the index of anteriority that produces irregular shading with only a slight contrast.[8] By the time biblical majuscule settles into a canon (CE4), the angle of anteriority becomes standardized at 75 degrees and produces consistent shading with noticeable contrast.[9] P.Ryl. 1.16 (LDAB 2661) can be securely dated to no later than 253–56 CE, and it clearly shows a greater angle of anteriority than P4+P64+67, thus producing more shading.[10] Even more shading is evident in the late third century (or possible early fourth century) P.Oxy. 3509 (LDAB 3823). The shading if P4+P64+67 is closer to P.Oxy. 661 (LDAB 474) than P.Ryl. I.16 or especially P.Oxy. 3509. The strong implication is that P4+P64+67 dates to a period before P.Ryl. 1.16 and P.Oxy. 3509. P.Oxy. 3227 (LDAB 1233) and especially P.Oxy. 4327 (LDAB 734) are also much closer *comparanda* than Sinaiticus or P.Oxy. 3509 (LDAB 3823) in this regard. The relatively flat *epsilon*, the round (as opposed to angular) *phi*, the lack of a hook at the bottom of *rho*, and the "sagging" median vertex and overshooting obliques of *mu* strengthen the correspondence of P4+P64+67 with these earlier biblical majuscule *comparanda*.

---

[7] These features of *phi* are characteristic of the Alexandrian stylistic class (P.Fay. 87) and round chancery (P.Oxy. 3917); the same is true of the formation of *psi*.

[8] Orsini and Clarysse 2012: 461–62; Skeat 1997: 2–9, 30.

[9] Orsini and Clarysse 2012: 451–52.

[10] The date of P.Ryl. 1.16 is based on a document that was written across the fibers in either January 253 or January 256 CE (Roberts 1955: 22; Nongbri 2018: 51). The literary text of an unknown comedy written along the fibers therefore dates to sometime before the middle of the third century CE.

Appendix 2: Paleographical Analyses   257

When these factors are considered as a whole, the hand of P4+P64+67 is earlier than P.Ryl. 1.16, and it is much closer to P.Oxy. 661 than Sinaiticus.[11]

Barker's analysis does not take into consideration the scribal hand used to write the Matthean title on the flyleaf. Simon Gathercole has offered a careful paleographical comparison between the Matthean title and the Bankes Homer (LDAB 1623; CE2), P.Oxy. 661 (late CE2), and P.Berol. 7499 (LDAB 1891; CE3).[12] Gathercole's comparison is particular strong when viewing how the *mu* is formed in the Bankes Homer and P.Oxy. 661, with the central stroke curved rather than angular (the central stroke of the *mu* in P.Berol. 7499 is angular). The curved central stroke is earlier than the angular version. Another indication of the Matthean title predating P.Berol. 7499 is the angle of anteriority; P.Berol. 7499 has noticeably more shading than the Matthean title, especially in the *epsilon*, *upsilon*, and *alpha*. The Matthean title appears to have more shading than P.Oxy. 661, but with a more curved central stroke in *mu* than P.Oxy. 661. While a narrower date range is not determinable with great certainty, the comparable characteristics allow us to place the Matthean fragment roughly between P.Oxy. 661 and P.Berol. 7499. We are therefore probably looking at a period of 175–250 CE. If we presuppose the compositional unity of the flyleaf with the rest of P4, then this confirms the date range of P4+P64+67 to the same period.

α   Formed in two strokes: the first an acute angle and the second an oblique descender. The oblique descender extends above and below the acute angle.

β   Formed in three strokes: a descender followed by the upper and lower loops. The lower loop is usually slightly broader than the upper loop.

γ   Formed in two strokes at a perpendicular angle. The horizontal bar is slightly thinner than the descender, due to the angle of anteriority. The descender does not dip below the bottom notional line.

δ   Composed of three strokes: two obliques and a baseline, forming an equiangular triangle. The right oblique extends above the adjacent leg.

ε   Composed of three strokes: a bottom curve, an upper horizontal, and a middle bar. The upper horizontal creates a flat impression of the letter as whole. The middle bar occasionally extending beyond the upper and lower horizontals.[13]

---

[11] Head 1995: 273, dealing specifically with P64, cautiously concludes: "Comparison with datable material supports a date within fifty years of AD 200 and there seems little point in attempting any more precision than that in a document without detailed provenance." Head includes P.Oxy. 1620, P.Oxy. 2832, and P.Dura 2 to the datable *comparanda*, and arrives at the same conclusion for the date of P64 as I have argued in this chapter.

[12] Gathercole 2012b: 224–33.

[13] The flat epsilon with an extended middle bar is a marker of an earlier form of the biblical majuscule (see esp. P.Oxy. 661; P.Oxy. 3227), contrasted with the fourth-century biblical majuscule (e.g. Sinaiticus) that is perfectly lunate, with the middle bar never extending beyond the upper and lower curves (in fact, the middle bar usually is shorter than these curves).

258   *Appendix 2: Paleographical Analyses*

ζ   Wider and flatter than other letters. Formed in three strokes: an upper horizontal, a descending diagonal, and a lower horizontal. A slight degree of shading evident in that the horizontals are thinner than the diagonal. A slight upward hook is sometimes visible at the beginning of the upper horizontal and a slight downward hook at the end of the lower horizontal.

η   Composed of three strokes, two parallel verticals with a horizontal bar, within the width of the unimodular space. The horizontal is situated more than halfway up the horizontals, on a slight incline (moving downward from the left to the right). Horizontal slightly thinner than verticals.

θ   Circular, the same diameter as *omicron*, middle bar noticeably thinner than circular stroke.

ι   Formed by a single descender. Descender formed with the slightest curve to the left.

κ   Composed of three strokes: one vertical and two obliques. The descender curves ever so slightly to the left. The upper oblique is sometimes thinner than the lower.

λ   Formed by two descending, curved obliques that meet at the top. At times, neither stroke extends beyond the other at the top, though regularly the right stroke extends higher than the left.

μ   Formed in four strokes: a left vertical, two median obliques, and a right vertical. The left vertical curves slightly to the left, and the right oblique often does not meet the top of the right vertical. The vertex formed by the two median obliques often dips almost to the baseline.

ν   Formed in three strokes. The medial oblique often begins slightly above or below the top of the left vertical. Left vertical often curves slightly to the left.

ξ   Composed of a single, "zig-zag" stroke. The upper horizontal begins with a slight upward hook, and the lower horizontal ends with a slight downward hook.

ο   Circular, bilinear, full-sized, formed in a single stroke.

π   Formed in three strokes, the parallel verticals are thicker than the horizontal bar, which usually extends beyond the top of the right vertical.

ρ   Formed in two strokes, the loop rather narrow, and the vertical descending slightly below the bottom notional line. There is inconsistently a hook at the bottom of the descender.[14]

σ   Formed in two strokes: the upper stroke is flatter than the lower, curve-shaped stroke.

τ   Slightly broader than the overall unimodular ductus. Formed in two perpendicular strokes, the descender usually situated to the right of the centre of the horizontal bar.

---

[14] The ornamental hook at the bottom of the descender in *rho* is much more frequently in the later, fourth-century canon (e.g. Sinaiticus).

υ Composed of two descending strokes. The left-hand stroke spans the length of the entire letter formation, and the right-hand stroke attaches as an arm. The right-hand stroke is thinner than the left-hand stroke. The left-hand stroke often descends below the notional line, and occasionally curves leftward at the bottom.

φ Formed in two strokes: an oval shape intersected by a descender. The descender dips well below the notional line. The left curve of the oval is round, but the right curve tends more toward an angular execution. The overall ductus of the oval, however, is performed in a single stroke, more round than angular.[15]

χ Composed of two descending, perpendicular obliques. The top of each oblique occasionally has a slight hook. The obliques intersect squarely in the middle. Shading is imperceptible.

ψ Formed in two perpendicular strokes, the descender dipping below the notional line and curving slightly leftward at the top and bottom of the stroke. The horizontal bar has a slight "wave" in its execution.

ω Formed in two u-shaped strokes, descending then ascending. Sometimes the first stroke descends to the baseline but ascends only minimally, while the second stroke descends and ascends fully. At other times, the first and second strokes both descend and ascend fully.

C. Paleographical Analysis of P45

P45 has the first hints of the much-later canon of the sloping ogival style (e.g. GA 032, CE5), but it is still comfortably in the severe style that flourished in the second century. If we plot the graphic stream flowing from the severe style to the sloping ogival style, then P45 sits somewhere towards the end of the severe style. Securely dated hands of the severe style are P. Mich.inv. 3 (LDAB 801; pre-192/193 CE), P.Oxy. 223 (LDAB 2026; 210–225 CE), P.Oxy. 2341 (TM 22213; 208 CE), BKT V.1 (LDAB 1239; post late-CE2), and P.Oxy. 7.1012 (LDAB 5448; mid-CE3). Securely dated hands of the sloping ogival style are P.Herm. 4–5 (TM 21123; TM 21124; 317–325 CE), and GA 032 (LDAB 2985; CE5). The overall ductus of P45 corresponds very closely to P.Mich.inv. 3 – bimodular (noticeable difference between narrow and broad letters), but compressed horizontally and vertically, inclining slightly to the right. However, the individual letter formations overlap more consistently with the severe hands dated to the first half of the third century.

---

[15] There is barely a hint of an angle in the central oval of *phi* in P.Oxy. 3227, and only slightly more so in P.Ryl. 16. Contrast this with the angular *phi* in the slightly later P.Oxy. 3509 (late CE3 / early CE4) the consistently angular *phi* in Sinaiticus.

260   *Appendix 2: Paleographical Analyses*

The major feature that defines P45 in the severe style is the angle of anteriority, which produces a contrast between thick and thin lines. The strokes in the *alpha*, *delta*, *lambda*, and *chi* in P45 have considerably less shading than the same letters in the sloping ogival hand of P.Herm. 4–5, which stands closer to the shading found in the fifth-century sloping ogival of GA 032. This shows that P45 has a lesser angle of anteriority than P.Herm. 4–5 and in this regard is more accurately identified as severe than sloping ogival. The hand of P45 also corresponds more closely to the severe style than sloping ogival in the following letter formations: *theta, mu, nu, xi, omicron, sigma*, and *tau*. The hand of P45 does, however, show affinities to P.Herm. 4-5 in its formation of *upsilon* and *omega*. In light of these considerations, P45 is best placed at the beginning of the transition from severe style to the sloping ogival style: 200–250 CE.

α   Formed in two strokes, the left stroke forming an acute angle and the right stroke curved down, often extending past both legs of the left stroke. The right oblique stroke is sometimes given a small space before the following letter – even before a *lambda* or an *iota*.

β   Composed of four strokes. An upright followed by a baseline stroke that forms an angle of approximately 70°. The baseline stroke often protrudes to the left of the upright stroke, resembling an upside-down T. The third and fourth strokes form the upper and lower curves of the *beta*. The lower curve usually extends only as far as the baseline stroke, without curving back to the upright. The baseline stroke always extends farther than the lower curve.

γ   Formed in two strokes at right angle. The horizontal stroke often extends over a subsequent *omicron* or *alpha*.

δ   The same size as *alpha*, formed in two strokes. The left-hand stroke almost forms an acute angle, but there is usually a slight hint of a loop at the vertex. The oblique stroke is more curved, usually crossing over the left-hand stroke at the top.

ε   Mostly square-shaped. Three strokes: a bottom angle, a hasta on top, and an elongated middle strong that typically touches a subsequent vertical stroke.

ζ   Two strokes: an upper horizontal line and a lower acute angle, which has a light loop.

η   Formed in two strokes: a left-hand, vertical, slightly oblique stroke, and a horizontal and right vertical formed by one stroke (first ascending then descending, making the top of the stroke thicker than the bottom).

θ   Four strokes; first three strokes form a shape that is more thin and triangular than an stout and oval (bottom stroke is flat with only a slight curve).[16] Fourth

---

[16] These features correspond to the severe hands of BKT V 1, P.Oxy. 2.223, and P.Oxy. 22.2341. The *theta* in the sloping ogival hand of P.Herm. 4-5 is more rounded, anticipating the hand of GA 032. The hand of P45 corresponds more closely to the former than the latter class.

Appendix 2: Paleographical Analyses   261

stroke is a crossbar that extends beyond both the left and right legs of the triangular shape.

ι   Single descending stroke, rarely crossing the bottom notional line. The hand delays slightly at the top, leaving a slight blob.

κ   Composed of three strokes: one vertical and two obliques, the bottom of which typically curves more than the top.

λ   Formed in two strokes, an upward curve, and a downward oblique. The top of the oblique occasionally has a slight serif above the left-hand stroke.

μ   Wide, composed in a single sequence, the middle curve sagging to the base-line, with no hint of an angle.[17]

ν   Formed in three strokes: two vertical and one diagonal. Consistently broad in formation.[18]

ξ   Formed in three strokes: two horizontal strokes in parallel, and a middle "squiggle."[19]

ο   The smallest of the letters in this hand, usually raised above the bottom no-tional line, especially when followed by an upright stroke as in *iota* or *kappa*.[20]

π   Three strokes: two vertical and a horizontal head stroke. Thinner in formation than other letters with parallel vertical lines (e.g. *eta*, *mu*, and *nu*).

ρ   Formed in two strokes: a vertical and an upper loop. There is no hint of a hook at the bottom of the vertical stroke.[21]

σ   Mostly angular. Two strokes: a bottom sharp angle and a slightly curved hasta on top.[22]

---

[17] This formation of *mu* is typical of the severe style, exemplified in BKT V 1, P.Oxy. 2.223, and P.Oxy. 22.2341. The *mu* in P.Herm. 4-5 is much thinner and appears more upright and taller, with the central curve beginning to hint at an angle. P.Herm. 4-5 therefore approaches the angular *mu* we see in the fifth-century GA 032.

[18] The *nu* in the severe style is broader and flatter (see esp. P.Oxy. 2.223, and P.Oxy. 22.2341) than in the upright ogival. P45 adheres more closely to the severe style than ogival in this letter formation.

[19] This is one of the clearest features by which P45 is located comfortably in the severe style. BKT V 1 and P.Oxy. 2.223 have several clear examples of nearly this same formation. This is remarkably contrasted from the later upright ogival habit of forming in the *xi* in a single, descending, "zig-zag" stroke (as in P.Herm. 4-5 and GA 032).

[20] This formation of the *omicron* is ubiquitous in the severe style, becomes less prominent at the early stages of sloping ogival (e.g. P.Herm. 4-5) and completely drops out in fifth-century sloping ogival. P45's formation of the *omicron* is more accurately placed in the severe style of the turn of the third century.

[21] GA 032 frequently has a rather pronounced hook at the bottom of the vertical stroke in *rho*, a hook that P.Herm. 4-5 begins to show. On the one hand, BKT V 1 shows little signs of a hook in *rho*, but on the other hand a hook is clearly discernable in P.Oxy. 22.2341.

[22] The *sigma* becomes less angular and more circular the closer ones gets to the formal canon of upright ogival. The angular *sigma* of P45 bears more resemblance to the severe style

262 *Appendix 2: Paleographical Analyses*

τ Composed of two perpendicular strokes. The horizontal stroke often has a swooping effect with the slightest hint of a serif on the bottom left-hand and upper right-hand sides of the stroke, probably formed by a slight delay at the beginning and end of the stroke. The horizontal stroke extends almost entirely over an *omicron* that follows, and halfway over an *alpha*.[23]

υ Formed by two descending strokes, the left-hand stroke frequently showing a hook.[24]

φ Not excessively high (the vertical stroke ascends only slightly above the upper notional line, but well below the lower notional line), the central loop more of a circle than a compressed oval and not angular.

χ Formed by two diagonal strokes, both of which have a slight curve.

ψ Formed in two perpendicular strokes, the horizontal stroke intersecting slightly more than halfway up the vertical stroke.

ω Well-rounded, the centre point half the height of the outer points.[25]

D. Paleographical Analysis of P75

Brent Nongbri argues that P.Herm. 4–5 is a reliable, early fourth-century *comparandum* for P75. Certain letter formations certainly correspond between these two hands, especially with *alpha*, *delta*, *epsilon*, and *xi*. The number of these correspondences brings a likely dating to a slightly later period than P45. The angle of anteriority in the hand of P75 is also greater than is typical for severe style (shading is noticeable particularly in *alpha*, *delta*, *lambda*, *pi*, and *phi*). This might possibly bring our manuscript to somewhere in the second half of the third century. However, when we look at the overall ductus of P75, it cannot be said to be a contemporary of P.Herm. 4–5. The hand of P75 is bimodular, with at stark contrast between narrow letters (*epsilon*, *theta*, *omicron*, and *sigma*) and broad letters (*delta*, *mu*, *nu*, *pi*, and *omega*). These same bimodular contrasts are still present in P.Herm. 4–5, but far less pronounced. In terms of ductus, then, P75 is much closer to the features of the severe style than P.Herm. 4–5.[26] The *omicron*

---

in BKT V 1 and P.Oxy. 2.223. The circular *sigma* of P.Herm. 4-5 is much closer to that of GA 032.

[23] This feature is comparable to BKT V 1 and P.Oxy.22.2341, becomes less prominent in P.Herm. 4-5, and entirely disappears in GA 032. It is more characteristic of the severe style at the turn of the third century than the sloping ogival of the fourth and fifth centuries.

[24] The hooked left-hand stroke of *upsilon* becomes an established feature of the upright ogival style (as seen in P.Herm. 4–5 and GA 032), but it is relatively absent in the severe style.

[25] The high midpoint of the *omega* is much closer to the sloping ogival hand of P.Herm. 4–5 and GA 032 than the datable severe hands, which consistently have a shallow middle.

[26] One can identify an earlier form of these severe characteristics in the same *comparanda* mentioned above: P. Mich.inv. 3 (pre-192/193 CE), P.Oxy. 2.223 (210–225 CE), P.Oxy. 22.2341 (208 CE), BKT V.1 (post late-CE2), and P.Oxy. 7.1012 (mid-CE3).

Appendix 2: Paleographical Analyses 263

and *sigma* of P75's hand are much smaller than P.Herm. 4–5. The *mu* is wider, the central curve closely adhering to the oblique strokes. In these particular letter formations, P75 is closer in resemblance to P.Oxy. 1012 than P.Herm. 4–5. Therefore, P75 belongs squarely in the third century rather than in the fourth. E. G. Turner's instinct is probably best: a date-range of 225-275 CE.

This paleographical dating is even more likely when we contrast it with other scribal hands in this codex (there are six hands in total). The second hand (Scribe B) gives two corrections to the main text (at *GLuke* 17.14 and *GJohn* 5.5).[27] This second hand resembles a chancery script, especially in its looped *alpha* that connects by a ligature in an upward motion to the following *rho*, its ligature connecting *theta* to *eta*, and its rushed formation of *eta*.[28] Based on these letter formations, there is a strong correspondence to P.Oxy. 2612, dated to 288–290 CE.[29] The third hand (Scribe C) gives illegible corrections at *GLuke* 11.34 and *GJohn* 11.41, and it is impossible to determine the date of this hand. The fourth hand (Scribe D), inserting marginalia at *GLuke* 10.20 (right side up in upper margin), copies the following line from the main body of the text in *GLuke* 10:20: γραπται εν τοις ουρανοις (abbreviating it as γρα[π]τα εν τοι ουν). This phrase may have been copied for reasons of personal piety. The hand used for this line of marginalia resembles both biblical majuscule and informal round, but it leans more towards a poorly executed, underdeveloped form of biblical majuscule (especially in its formation of *alpha*, *rho*, and *gamma*). This underdeveloped biblical majuscule hand is plausibly late third century, and it cannot be too far into the fourth century. The fifth hand (Scribe E) inserts marginalia at *GJohn* 8.22, upside down in the lower margin.[30] This hand bears a great deal of shading, and it resembles a well-developed biblical majuscule of the fourth century or later. Finally, the sixth hand (Scribe F) inserts marginalia at *GJohn* 12.19, right side up in upper margin, in what appears to be Coptic. This hand is a Coptic biblical majuscule that Turner dates to the fourth or fifth century.[31]

---

[27] Martin and Kasser 1961: 23, and Royse 2008: 645–46 argue that the correction at *GLuke* 11.31 belongs to the same hand as the corrections in *GLuke* 17.14 and *GJohn* 5.5. Close inspection, however, reveals that the interlinear insertion of νοτου at *GLuke* 11.31 has much more spacing than the other corrections just mentioned. It could possibly even be from the main hand, just with a "cramped" feeling to it due to its interlinear insertion.

[28] For this description, I consulted high-resolution photos available at the Digital Vatican Library: digi.vatlib.it, accessed 5 March 2021.

[29] Images are available at Oxyrhynchus Online: www.papyrology.ox.ac.uk/POxy/; accessed 5 March 2021.

[30] This instance of marginalia is enigmatic but very suggestive. Martin and Kasser 1961b: 49 transcribe it as ΤΟΝ ΥΟΝ ΩΣ ΚΥΡΙΟΝ ΑΠΟ ΤΗΣ ΤΡΑΠΕΖΗΣ. The fact that it is upside perhaps indicates that this codex was read among a collective of readers and scribes, sitting around and studying the same manuscript simultaneously. Perhaps the mention of "son", "lord", and "table" might have eucharistic undertones.

[31] Turner 1968: 174n37. For an analysis of Coptic biblical majuscule, along with datable *comparanda*, see Orsini 2019: 98–132.

264   *Appendix 2: Paleographical Analyses*

Including the marginalia just discussed, there are six hands at work in P75: Scribe A (main body), Scribe B (interlinear corrections), Scribe C (illegible interlinear corrections), Scribe D (marginalia at *GLuke* 10.20), Scribe E (marginalia at *GJohn* 8.22), and Scribe F (marginalia at *GJohn* 12.19). One can map a progression in time from the styles represented by the scribes. Working backwards, Scribe F, writing in Coptic, worked in the fourth/fifth century, Scribe E in the late fourth century, Scribe D sometime in the latter half of the third century, and Scribe B in the last quarter of the third century (Scribe C's writing is illegible). This brings us to Scribe A, whose hand contrasts with the other scribes, whose fourth- and fifth-century hands are positioned at the margins. This would cohere with a scenario in which Scribe A worked before the last quarter of the third century. This would fit the date range given by Orsini and Clarysse: 200–250 CE, though perhaps moving it forward to 225–275 CE (cf. Turner). Furthermore, the passage of time evident between Scribe A and Scribe D indicate that P75 was in use for at least 200 years (ca. 225–450 CE). This timespan lessens the validity of dating P75 with relation to the other manuscripts found in the Bodmer collection, as Nongbri does.[32]

α   Formed in two strokes, the left stroke usually looped, though sometimes angular. The right-hand stroke elongated, contrasted with the rather thin loop.[33]

β   Composed of four strokes. An upright followed by a baseline stroke that forms an angle of approximately 90°. The third and fourth strokes form the upper and lower curves of the *beta*. The baseline stroke often extends farther to the right of the lower curve, and sometimes farther to the left of the horizontal stroke.

γ   Formed in two strokes at a right angle. The horizontal stroke always separated from following letters.

δ   Formed in three strokes, creating an equiangular triangle with legs extending outward from the apex and the left-hand vertex.[34]

ε   Three strokes: a bottom "L" shape (oftentimes with a hook),[35] a hasta on top, and a slightly elongated middle strong that almost never touches the subsequent letter.

ζ   Composed of two strokes: an upper horizontal line and a lower acute angle. A slight hook is often perceptible at the left edge of the top horizontal line and the right edge of the bottom leg of the acute angle

---

[32] Nongbri 2016: 433–34 cautiously avoids giving a confident date to the later hands. This caution is judicious, given how little remains of these scribal hands in P75. However, the span of several distinct letters, even words, in Scribes B, D, E, F, give us enough to discern a ductus for each hand. This enables us to deduce in broad terms a time span across these hands.

[33] This formation of the *alpha* is in common with P.Herm 4–5, especially with respect to the elongated loop of contrasted with the oblique descender.

[34] In common with P.Herm. 4–5.

[35] In common with P.Herm. 4–5.

Appendix 2: Paleographical Analyses 265

η Formed in three strokes: two parallel vertical strokes joined by a middle horizontal stroke often protruding slightly beyond the right-hand vertical stroke.

θ Two strokes: a smooth oval followed by a horizontal line through the middle, often protruding to the right.

ι Formed by a single, descending stroke, often with a hook to the left at the bottom of the stroke and occasionally with a hook to the left at the top.

κ Usually formed in three strokes: a descending vertical stroke, two arms extending outward from the vertical stroke, forming an angle. Sometimes the second and third strokes are combined into one stroke in two movements. There is often a slight hook on the top of the vertical stroke, occasionally a hook at the bottom.

λ Formed in two downward, slightly oblique diagonals, the first rightward, the second smaller and leftward, extending from the first. The oblique movements usually leave only a slight curve on the ends of the strokes.

μ Broad, formed in three strokes, the central curve smooth and touching the baseline, hugging the right and leg legs, creating an impression of "sagging."[36]

ν Broad, formed in three strokes, the left vertical stroke often with a slight outward curve on the bottom.[37]

ξ Formed in a single, descending, "zig-zag" stroke.[38]

ο The smallest of the letters in this hand, usually raised above the bottom notional line, especially when followed by an upright stroke as in *iota* or *kappa*.[39]

π Three strokes: two vertical and a horizontal head stroke the extends past the edges of the parallel vertical strokes. As broad as the other letters with parallel vertical lines (e.g. *eta*, *mu*, and *nu*).[40]

ρ Formed in two strokes: a vertical and an upper loop. There is a hook at the bottom of the vertical stroke that matches the similar vertical strokes in *phi*, *upsilon*, and *psi*.

σ Formed in two strokes: both are curved, the top stroke often extended farther than the bottom. Both strokes are occasionally hooked.

---

[36] The *mu* in P.Herm. 4–5 is compressed, more closely resembling the later sloping ogival hand (e.g. GA 032) than P75. The broad, sagging *mu* in P75, on the other hand, often resembles P.Oxy. 223, P.Oxy. 2321, and occasionally BKT V 1.

[37] Like the *mu*, the broad *nu* in P75 is closer to severe than P.Herm. 4–5.

[38] In common with P.Herm. 4–5.

[39] This formation of *omicron* is more pronounced in P75 than in P.Herm. 4–5, though it is still present in P.Herm. 4–5. P.Oxy. 223, P.Oxy. 2321, and BKT V 1 show that P75 adheres closer to the earlier formation than P.Herm. 4–5.

[40] The *pi* in P75 is broader than the *pi* in P.Herm. 4–5, and while its extended horizontals do not resemble the severe hand of P.Oxy. 223, P.Oxy. 2321, and BKT V 1, its broad ductus is closer to severe than P.Herm. 4–5.

266   *Appendix 2: Paleographical Analyses*

τ   Formed in two perpendicular strokes, the left-hand edge of the horizontal stroke occasionally forming a slight hook upward. The descender begins to the right of the centre of the horizontal stroke.

υ   Formed in three strokes: upper left, followed by upper right, followed by descender. Hooks included in main strokes.

φ   Composed of two strokes. The central oval is wide and compressed, and the vertical line curves outward to the left at the bottom. The vertical stroke extends far above and below the notional lines.

χ   Formed by two diagonal strokes.

ψ   Formed in two perpendicular strokes, the horizontal stroke intersecting halfway up the vertical stroke.

ω   Broad, formed in a single stroke. Well-rounded, the centre point half the height of the outer points. The outer points are usually curved in. *Omega* is usually elevated slightly above the notional line.

Bibliography

1. Primary Sources

1.1 Manuscripts

Bover, J. M. 1925. "Un fragmento de San Lucas (22, 44–63) en un papiro recientemente descubierto." *Estudios eclesiásticos* 4: 293–305.

Dorn, H.-J., V. Rosenberger, and D. Trobisch. 1985. "Zu dem Septuagintapapyrus VBP IV 56." *ZPE* 61: 115–121.

–. 1986. "Nachtrag zu dem Septuagintapapyrus VBP IV 56." *ZPE* 65: 106.

Fournet, J.-L. and J. Gascou. 2015. "Édition de *P.Bodm.* LIV–LVI." *Adamantius* 21: 34–37.

Grenfell, B. P. and A. S. Hunt eds. 1898. *The Oxyrhynchus Papyri: Part I*. London: Egypt Exploration Society.

–. 1904. *The Oxyrhynchus Papyri: Part IV*. London: Egypt Exploration Society.

Junack, K. and W. Grunewald. 1986. *Das Neue Testament auf Papyrus I. Die katholischen Briefe*. ANTF 6. Berlin: de Gruyter.

Kenyon, F. G. 1933. *The Chester Beatty Biblical Papyri. II: The Gospels and Acts. 1. Text*. London: E. Walker.

–. 1935. *The Chester Beatty Biblical Papyri. V: Numbers and Deuteronomy. 1: Text*. London: Emery Walker.

–. 1936. *The Chester Beatty Biblical Papyri. III: Pauline Epistles. 1: Text*. London: Emery Walker.

–. 1958. *The Chester Beatty Biblical Papyri V: Numbers and Deuteronomy. 2: Plates*. Dublin: Hodges Figgis.

Lagrange, M.-J. 1935. *Critique textuelle, vol.2: La critique rationnelle*. Paris: Gabalda.

Martin, A. and O. Primavesi. 1999. *L'Empédocle de Strasbourg (P. Strasb. gr. Inv. 1665–1666)*. Berlin: de Gruyter.

Martin, V. and R. Kasser. 1961. *Papyrus Bodmer XIV: Évangile de luc chap. 3–24*. Papyrus Bodmer. Geneva: Bibliotheca Bodmeriana.

–. 1961. *Papyrus Bodmer XV: Évangile de Jean chap. 1–15*. Papyrus Bodmer. Geneva: Bibliotheca Bodmeriana.

Merell, J. 1938. Nouveaux fragments du Papyrus 4. *Revue Biblique* 47: 5–22.

Naldini, M. 1964. *Documenti Dell'Antichita Cristiana: esposti nella Biblioteca Medicea Laurenziana*. Florence: Libreria editrice florentina.

Philippart, G. 1972. Fragments palimpsestes latins du Vindobonensis 563. Évangile selon s. Mathieu, Évangile de l'enfance selon Thomas, Évangile de Nicodème. *Analecta Bollandiana* 90: 391–441.

Pistelli, E. 1912. "Evangelium Lucae XXII 45 sqq." *Pubblicazioni della Società Italiana per la ricerca dei Papiri greci e latini in Egitto: Papiri Greci e Latini* 1: 2–4.

–. 1913. "Evangelium Lucae XXII 44 sqq." *Pubblicazioni della Societa Italiana per la ricerca dei Papiri greci e latini in Egitto: Papiri Greci e Latini* 2: 22–25.

268 Bibliography

Scheil, J.-V. 1893. "Deux traités de Philon." *Mémoires publiés par les membres de la Mission Archéologique Française au Caire* 9.2 : iii–viii.

Schmid, U. B., D. Parker, and W. J. Elliott eds. 2007. *The New Testament in Greek IV — The Gospel According to John. Edited by the American and British Committees of the International Greek New Testament Project. Volume Two: The Majuscules.* NovTSup 37. Leiden: Brill.

Schubart, W. S. ed. 1911. *Papyri Graecae Berolinenses.* Bonn: A. Marcus & E. Weber.

Treu, K. 1962. "Neue neutestamentliche Fragmente der Berliner Papyrussammlung." *Archiv für Papyrusforschung und verwandte Gebiete* 18: 25–28.

Wessely, C. 1924. "Les plus anciens monuments du Christianisme écrits sur papyrus: texts édités, traduits et annotés, II." *Patrologia Orientalis* 18: 452–454.

1.2 Editions and Translations

1.2.1 Ancient Gospel Translations

Belsheim, J. 1894. *Codex Vercellensis: Quatuor evangelia ante hieronymum latine translata ex reliquiis codicis vercellensis, saeculo ut videtur quatro scripti et ex editione iriciana principe.* Christiania: Libraria Mallingiana.

Burkitt, F. C. 1904. *Evangelion Da-Mepharreshe: Introduction and Notes, 2 vols.* Cambridge: Cambridge University Press.

1.2.3 Apostolic Fathers

Holmes, M. W. ed. tr. 2007. *The Apostolic Fathers: Greek Texts and English Translations, 3rd edition.* Grand Rapids: Baker Academic.

1.2.4 Clement of Alexandria

Butterworth, G. W. tr. 1919. *Clement of Alexandria.* LCL 92. Cambridge: Harvard University Press.

Stählin, O. ed. 1970. *Clemens Alexandrinus, III. Stromata VII und VIII, Excerpta ex Theodoto, Eclogae Propheticae, Quis dives salvetur, Fragmente.* 2nd ed. Edited by Ludwig Früchtel and Ursula Treu. GCS 17. Berlin: Akademie-Verlag.

–. 1972. *Clemens Alexandrinus, I. Protrepticus und Paedagogus.* 3rd ed. Edited by Ursula Treu. GCS 12. Berlin: Akademie-Verlag.

–. 1980. *Clemens Alexandrinus, IV. Register, Erster Teil: Zitatenregister, Testimonienregister, Initienregister für die Fragmente, Eigennamenregister.* 2nd ed. Edited by Ursula Treu. GCS 39. Berlin: Akademie-Verlag.

–. 1985. *Clemens Alexandrinus, II. Stromata Buch I–VI.* 4th ed. Edited by Ludwig Früchtel, and Ursula Treu. GCS 15. Berlin: Akademie-Verlag.

1.2.5 Diatessaron

Ephrem the Syrian. *Commentaire de l'Évangile concordant, version arménienne.* Edited by L. Leloir. CSCO 137, Scriptores Armeniaci 1. Louvain: Imprimerie Orientaliste L. Durbecq, 1953.

–. *Commentaire de l'Évangile concordant, version arménienne.* Edited by L. Leloir. CSCO 145, Scriptores Armeniaci 2. Louvain: Imprimerie Orientaliste L. Durbecq, 1954.

–. *Commentaire de l'Évangile concordant, texte syriaque (MS Chester Beatty 709).* Edited by L. Leloir. CBM 8. Hodges Figgis: Dublin, 1963.

Bibliography 269

–. *Commentaire de l'Évangile concordant, texte syriaque (MS Chester Beatty 709): Folios additionnels*. Edited by L. Leloir. CBM 8(b). Leuven: Peeters, 1990.

Marmardji, A.-S. 1935. *Diatessaron de Tatien: Texte arabe établi, traduit en français, collationné avec les anciennes versions syriaques*. 1935: Imprimerie Catholique.

McCarthy, C. 1993. *Saint Ephrem's Commentary on Tatian's Diatessaron: An English Translations of* Chester Beatty *Syriac MS 709 with Introduction and Notes*. Journal of Semitic Studies Supplement. Oxford: Oxford University Press.

Parisot, J. 1894. *Aphraatis Sapientis Persae Demonstrationes. 2 vols.* Patrologia Syriaca. Paris: Firmin-Didot.

Ranke, E. 1868. *Codex Fuldensis: Novum Testamentum Latine Interprete Hieronymo ex Manuscripto Victoris Capuani*. Marburg: N. G. Elwert.

Vaschalde, A. 1953. *Dionysii Bar Salibi, Commentarii in Evangelia*. CSCO. Louvain: Imprimerie Orientaliste L. Durbecq.

1.2.6 Didymus the Blind

Migne, J.-P. ed. 1863. *Didymi Alexandrini Opera Omnia*. PG 39. Paris: Brepols.

Mühlenburg, E. 1975. *Psalmenkommentare aus der Katenenüberlieferung*. Patristische Texte und Studien. Berlin: de Gruyter.

1.2.7 Doctrine of Addai

Phillips, G. 1876. *The Doctrine of Addai, the Apostle*. London: Trübner & Co.

1.2.8 Ephrem the Syrian

Egan, G. A. 1968. *Saint Ephrem: An Exposition of the Gospel*. CSCO. Leuven: Secretariat du CSCO.

Wickes, J. T. 2015. *St. Ephrem the Syrian: The Hymns of Faith*. The Fathers of the Church. Washington, DC: Catholic University of America Press.

1.2.9 Eusebius

Lake, K. tr. 1926. *Ecclesiastical History, Volume 1: Books 1–5*. LCL 153. Cambridge, MA: Harvard University Press.

Oulton, J. E. L. tr. 1932. *Ecclesiastical History, Volume 2: Books 6–10*. LCL 265. Cambridge, MA: Harvard University Press.

Wright, W. and N. Mclean eds. 1898. *The Ecclesiastical History of Eusebius in Syriac*. Cambridge: Cambridge University Press.

1.2.10 Epiphanius

Holl, K. ed. 1915. *Epiphanius I: Ancoratus und Panarion haer. 1–33*. GCS 25. Leipzig: J.C. Hinrichs.

Williams, F. tr. 2013. *The Panarion of Epiphanius of Salamis, Book I (Sects 1–46)*. 2nd ed. NHMS 35. Leiden: Brill.

1.2.11 Epistula Apostolorum

Guerrier, L. and S. Grébaut eds. 1913. *Le Testament en Galilée de Notre-Seigneur Jésus-Christ*. Patrologia Orientalis. Paris: Firmin-Didot.

270 *Bibliography*

Hills, J. V. 2009. *The Epistle of the Apostles*. Early Christian Apocrypha. Santa Rosa, CA: Polebridge Press.

Müller, C. D. G. 2012. "B.VI.2. *Die Epistula Apostolorum.*" Pages 1062–92 in *Antike christliche Apokryphen in deutscher Übersetzung, 1.1–2, Evangelien und Verwandtes*, ed. C. Markschies and J. Schröter. Tübingen: Mohr Siebeck.

Schmidt, C. and I. Wajnberg eds. 1919. *Gespräche Jesu mit seinen Jüngern nach der Auferstehung: Ein katholisch-apostolisches Sendschreiben des 2. Jahrhunderts.* Texte und Untersuchungen 43. Leipzig: J. C. Hinrichs.

1.2.12 Irenaeus

Rousseau, A., B. Hemmerdinger, C. Mercier, and L. Doutreleau eds. 1965. *Irénée du Lyon: Contre les Hérésies Livre IV,* ii. *Texte et traduction.* SC 100.2. Paris: Lés Éditions du Cerf.

Rousseau, A., C. Mercier, and L. Doutreleau eds. 1969. *Irénée du Lyon: Contre les Hérésies Livre V,* ii. *Texte et traduction.* SC 153. Paris: Lés Éditions du Cerf.

Rousseau, A. and L. Doutreleau eds. 1974. *Irénée du Lyon: Contre les Hérésies Livre III,* ii. *Texte et traduction.* SC 211. Paris: Lés Éditions du Cerf.

–. 1979. *Irénée du Lyon: Contre les Hérésies Livre I,* ii. *Texte et traduction.* SC 264. Paris: Lés Éditions du Cerf.

–. 1982. *Irénée du Lyon: Contre les Hérésies Livre II,* ii. *Texte et traduction.* SC 294. Paris: Lés Éditions du Cerf.

1.2.13 Jerome

Hurst, D. and M. Adriaen ed. 1969. *Commentariorum in Matheum libri IV.* CCSL 77. Turnhout: Brepols.

Moreschini, C. ed. 1990. *Dialogus adversus Pelagianos.* CCSL 88. Turnhout: Brepols.

1.2.14 Jewish and Greco-Roman Sources

Aulus Gellius. *Attic Nights, Volume I: Books 1–5.* tr. J. C. Rolfe. 1927. LCL 195. Cambridge, MA: Harvard University Press.

–. *Attic Nights, Volume II: Books 6–13.* tr. J. C. Rolfe. 1927. LCL 200. Cambridge, MA: Harvard University Press.

–. *Attic Nights, Volume III: Books 14–20.* tr. J. C. Rolfe. 1952. LCL 212. Cambridge, MA: Harvard University Press.

Dionysius of Halicarnassus. Usener, Hermann and Ludwig Rademacher eds. 1965. *Dionysii Halicarnasei quae exstant.* Stuttgart: Teubner.

Galen, *Claudii Galeni Opera Omnia.* vols. I, V, IX, XV, XIX ed. C. G. Kühn. 1821–1833. Leipzig: Car. Cnoblochii.

1.2.15 Justin Martyr

Marcovich, M. ed. 2005. *Iustini Martyris Apologiae pro Christianis, Dialogus cum Tryphone.* PTS 38/47. Berlin: de Gruyter, 2005.

Minns, D. and P. Parvis. 2009. *Justin, Philosopher and Martyr: Apologies. Edited with an Introduction, Translation, and Commentary on the Text.* Oxford Early Christian Texts. Oxford: Oxford University Press.

Bibliography 271

1.2.16 New Testament

Aland, K., B. Aland, J. Karavidopoulos, C. M. Martini, and B. M. Metzger eds. 2012. *Novum Testamentum Graece.* 28th ed. Stuttgart: Deutsche Bibelgesellschaft.

1.2.17 Noncanonical Gospels

Brankaer, J. and H.-G. Bethge eds. 2007. *Codex Tchacos: Texte und Analysen.* Texte und Untersuchungen 161. Berlin: De Gruyter.

Brankaer J. and B. van Os eds. 2019. *The Gospel of Judas.* Oxford Early Christian Gospel Texts. Oxford: Oxford University Press.

Ehrman, B. and Z. Pleše eds. 2011. *The Apocryphal Gospels: Texts and Translations.* Oxford: Oxford University Press.

Emmel, S. ed. 1984. *Nag Hammadi Codex III,5: The Dialogue of the Savior.* NHS 26. Leiden: Brill.

Foster, P. 2010. *The* Gospel of Peter*: Introduction, Critical Edition and Commentary.* TENTS 4. Leiden: Brill.

Frey, J. 2012. "B.V.1.1 Die Fragmente judenchristlicher Evangelien." Pages 560-92 in *Antike christliche Apokryphen in deutscher Übersetzung, 1.1–2, Evangelien und Verwandtes.* Edited by C. Markschies and J. Schröter. Tübingen: Mohr Siebeck.

Gregory, A. F. 2017. *The* Gospel according to the Hebrews *and the* Gospel of the Ebionites. Oxford Early Christian Gospel Texts. Oxford: Oxford University Press.

Guillaumont, A., H.-C. Puech, G. Quispel, W. Till, and Y. Abd al Masih. 1959. *The Gospel according to Thomas: Coptic Text Established and Translated.* Leiden: Brill.

Hedrick, C. W. and P. A. Mirecki eds. 1999. *The Gospel of the Savior: A New Ancient Gospel.* California Classical Library. Santa Rosa, CA: Polebridge Press.

Kaiser, U. 2012. "B.V.5.3 Die Kindheitserzählung des Thomas." Pages 930–59 in *Antike christliche Apokryphen in deutscher Übersetzung, 1.1–2, Evangelien und Verwandtes.* Edited by C. Markschies and J. Schröter. Tübingen: Mohr Siebeck.

Kruger, M. J. 2005. *The Gospel of the Savior: An Analysis of P.Oxy. 840 and Its Place in the Gospel Traditions of Early Christianity.* TENTS 1. Leiden: Brill.

–. 2009. "Papyrus Oxyrhynchus 840." Pages 123–215 in *Gospel Fragments.* Edited by T. J. Kraus, M. J. Kruger, and T. Nicklas. Oxford Early Christian Gospel Texts. Oxford: Oxford University Press.

Roth, D. T. 2015. *The Text of Marcion's Gospel.* NTTSD 49. Leiden: Brill.

1.2.18 Origen

Blanc, C. 1996. *Commentaire sur saint Jean, tome I, Livres I–V: Texte critique, avant-propos, traduction et notes.* SC 120. Paris: Lés Éditions du Cerf.

Borret, M. 1967. *Origène Contre Celse, tome I, Livres I et II: Introduction, texte critique, traduction et notes.* SC 132. Paris: Lés Éditions du Cerf.

–. 1969. *Origène Contre Celse, tome III, Livres V et VI: Introduction, texte critique, traduction et notes.* SC 147. Paris: Lés Éditions du Cerf.

–. 1969. *Origène Contre Celse, tome IV, Livres VII et VIII: Introduction, texte critique, traduction et notes.* SC 150. Paris: Lés Éditions du Cerf.

Chadwick, H. 1953. *Origen: Contra Celsum.* Cambridge: Cambridge University Press.

Girod, R. 1970. *Commentaire sur l'Évangile selon Mathieu, tome I, Livres X et XI.* SC 162. Paris: Lés Éditions du Cerf.

Nautin, P. and P. Husson. 1977. *Origène: Homélies sur Jérémie, tome II: Homélies XII–XX et Homélies latines*. SC 238. Paris: Lés Éditions du Cerf.

1.2.19 Septuagint

Rahlfs, A. 2007. *Septuaginta*. Edition altera, ed. R. Hanhart. Stuttgart: Deutsche Bibelgesellschaft.

1.2.20 Theodoret of Cyrus

Migne, J.-P. 1864. *Theodoreti Cyrensis Episcopi. Opera Omnia*. PG 83.

1.2.20 Theophilus of Antioch

Bardy, G. and J. Sender eds. 1948. *Trois livres à Autolycus*. SC 20. Paris: Lés Éditions du Cerf.

2. Secondary Sources

Abakuks, A. 2014. *The Synoptic Problem and Statistics*. Boca Raton: Chapman & Hall.

Adams, S. and S. M. Ehorn. 2016. "What is a Composite Citation? An Introduction." Pages 1–16 in *Composite Citations in Antiquity: Volume One: Jewish, Graeco-Roman, and Early Christian Uses*. Edited by S. Adams and S. M. Ehorn. LNTS 525. London: T & T Clark.

Aland, B. 2004. "The Significance of the Chester Beatty Papyri in Early Church History." Pages 108–21 in *The Earliest Gospels: The Origins and Transmission of the Earliest Christian Gospels - the Contribution of the Chester Beatty Gospel Codex P45*. Edited by C. Horton. London: T & T Clark.

Aland, K. 1987. "Alter und Entstehung des D-Textes im Neuen Testament: Betrachtungen zu P69 und 0171." Pages 37–61 in *Miscellània papirològica, Ramon Roca-Puig, en el seu vuitantè aniversari*. Edited by S. Janeras. Barcelona: Fundació Salvador Vives Casajuana.

–. 1994. *Kurzgefasste Liste der griechischen Handschriften des Neuen Testaments*. ANTF 1. Berlin: de Gruyter.

–. 2001. *Synopsis Quattuor Evangeliorum*. Stuttgart: Deutsche Bibelgesellschaft.

Alexander, L. 1990. "The Living Voice: Skepticism Towards the Written Word in Early Christian and in Greco-Roman Texts." Pages 221–47 in *The Bible in Three Dimensions*. Edited by S. E. Fowl, D. J. A. Clines, and S. E. Porter. Sheffield Academic Press: Sheffield.

–. 1993. *The Preface to Luke's Gospel: Literary Convention and Social Context in Luke 1.1–4 and Acts 1.1*. SNTSMS 78. Cambridge: Cambridge University Press.

–. 1998. "Ancient Book Production and the Circulation of the Gospels." Pages 71–112 in *The Gospels for All Christians: Rethinking the Gospel Audiences*. Edited by R. Bauckham. Grand Rapids: Eerdmans.

–. 1999. "Formal Elements and Genre: Which Greco-Roman Prologues Most Closely Parallel the Lukan Prologues?" Pages 9–26 in *Jesus and the Heritage of Israel: Luke's Narrative Claim upon Israel's Legacy*. Edited by D. P. Moessner. Harrisburg: Trinity Press International.

–. 2005. "The Four among Pagans." Pages 222–37 in *The Written Gospel*. Edited by M. Bockmuehl and D. A. Hagner. Cambridge: Cambridge University Press.

Allen, G. V. 2018. "Rewriting and the Gospels." *JSNT* 41.1: 58–69.

Allert, C. 2002. *Revelation, Truth, Canon and Interpretation: Studies in Justin Martyr's Dialogue with Trypho*. VCSup 64. Leiden: Brill.

Bibliography

Amphoux, C.-B. 1993. "La 'Finale longue de Marc': Un épilogue des quatre évangiles." Pages 548–55 in *Synoptic Gospels*. Edited by C. Focant. Leuven: Leuven University Press.

–. 1996. "Le texte." Pages 337–54 in *Codex Bezae: Studies from the Lunel Colloquium, June 1994*. Edited by D. C. Parker and C.-B. Amphoux. NTTSD 22. Leiden: Brill.

Arnal, W. E. 1995. "The Rhetoric of Marginality: Apocalypticism, Gnosticism, and Sayings Gospels." *HTR* 88: 471–94.

Ashwin-Siejkowski, P. 2017. "Clement of Alexandria's Reception of the Gospel of John: Context, Creative Exegesis and Purpose." Pages 259–76 in *Clement's Biblical Exegesis: Proceedings of the Second Colloquium on Clement of Alexandria (Olomouc, May 29-31, 2014)*. Edited by V. Černušková, J. L. Kovacs, and J. Plátová. VCSup 139. Leiden: Brill.

Aune, D. E. 2002. "Assessing the Historical Value of Apocryphal Jesus Traditions: A Critique of Conflicting Methodologies." Pages 243–72 in *Der historische Jesus: Tendenzen und Perspektiven der gegenwärtigen Forschung*. Edited by J. Schröter and R. Brucker. BZNW 114. Berlin: de Gruyter.

Ayres, L. 2015. "Irenaeus vs. the Valentinians: Towards a Rethinking of Patristic Exegetical Origins." *JECS* 23.2: 153–87.

–. 2017. "Continuity and Change in Second-Century Christianity: A Narrative against the Trend." Pages 106–21 in *Christianity in the Second Century: Themes and Developments*. Edited by J. Lieu and J. Carleton Paget. Cambridge: Cambridge University Press.

Baarda, T. 1975. *The Gospel Quotations of Aphrahat the Persian Sage: Aphrahat's Text of the Fourth Gospel*. Meppel: Krips Repro.

–. 1983. "Mar Ephrem's Commentary on the Diatessaron, Ch. XVII:10." Pages 289–311 in *Early Transmission of the Words of Jesus: Thomas, Tatian and the Text of the New Testament*. Edited by T. Baarda, J. Helderman, and S. J. Noorda. Amsterdam: VU Boekhandel.

–. 1986. "'The Flying Jesus': Luke 4:29–30 in the Syriac Diatessaron." *VC* 40: 313-41.

–. 1989. "ΔΙΑΦΩΝΙΑ — ΣΥΜΦΩΝΙΑ: Factors in the Harmonization of the Gospels, Especially in the Diatessaron of Tatian." Pages 133–54 in *Gospel Traditions in the Second Century: Origins, Recensions, Text, and Transmission*. Edited by W. L. Petersen. Notre Dame: University of Notre Dame Press.

–. 1994. "Matthew 18:14c. An 'Extra-Canonical Addition in the Arabic Diatessaron?" *Le Muséon* 107: 135–49.

–. 2003. "The Gospel of Thomas and the Old Testament." *Proceedings of the Irish Biblical Association* 26: 1–28.

–. 2019. "The Diatessaron and its Beginning: A Twofold Statement of Tatian." Pages 1–24 in *The Gospel of Tatian: Exploring the Nature and Text of the Diatessaron*. Edited by M. R. Crawford and N. J. Zola. RJT 3. London: T & T Clark.

Backhaus, K. 2019. *Die Entgrenzung des Heils: Gesammelte Studien zur Apostelgeschichte*. WUNT 422. Tübingen: Mohr Siebeck.

Bagnall, R. S. 1993. *Egypt in Late Antiquity*. Princeton, NJ: Princeton University Press.

–. 2009. *Early Christian Books in Egypt*. Princeton: Princeton University Press.

Barker, D. 2011. "The Dating of New Testament Papyri." *NTS* 57: 571–82.

Barker, J. W. 2015a. *John's Use of Matthew*. Fortress: Minneapolis.

–. 2015b. "Written Gospel or Oral Tradition? Patristic Parallels to John 3:3, 5." *Early Christianity* 6: 543–58.

–. 2016. "Ancient Compositional Practices and the Gospels: A Reassessment." *JBL* 135.1: 109–21.

–. 2019. "Tatian's Diatessaron and the Proliferation of Gospels." Pages 111–41 in *The Gospel of Tatian: Exploring the Nature and Text of the Diatessaron*. Edited by M. R. Crawford and N. J. Zola. RJT 3. London: T & T Clark.

–. 2020. "The Narrative Chronology of Tatian's Diatessaron." *NTS* 66: 288–98.

Barrett, C. K. 1996. "The First New Testament?" *NovT* 38: 94–104.

Bauckham, R. 1993. *The Climax of Prophecy: Studies on the Book of Revelation.* London: T & T Clark.

–. 1998. "John for Readers of Mark." Pages 147–71 in *The Gospels for All Christians: Rethinking the Gospel Audiences.* Edited by R. Bauckham. Grand Rapids: Eerdmans.

–. 2003. "The Origin of the Ebionites." Pages 162–81 in *The Image of the Judaeo-Christians in Ancient Jewish and Christian Literature.* Edited by P. J. Tomson and D. Lambers-Petry. WUNT 2003. Tübingen: Mohr Siebeck.

–. 2014. "Did Papias Write History or Exegesis?" *JTS* 65.2: 463–88.

–. 2017. *Jesus and the Eyewitnesses: The Gospels as Eyewitness Testimony.* Grand Rapids: Eerdmans.

Baudoin, A.-C. 2020. "Latin Codex 563 of the Austrian National Library and Its Biblical Texts." Pages 125–48 in *At One Remove: The Text of the New Testament in Early Translations and Quotations. Papers from the Eleventh Birmingham Colloquium on the Textual Criticism of the New Testament.* Edited by H. A. G. Houghton and P. Montoro. Texts and Studies 24. Piscataway, NJ: Georgias Press.

Baum, A. 1996. "Papias als Kommentator evangelischer Aussprüche Jesu: Erwägungen zur Art seines Werkes." *NovT* 38.3: 257–76.

Beale, G. K. 1999. *The Book of Revelation.* NIGTC. Grand Rapids: Eerdmans.

Becker, E.-M. 2017. *Der früheste Evangelist: Studien zum Markusevangelium.* WUNT 380. Tübingen: Mohr Siebeck.

Becker, E.-M., H. K. Bond, and C. H. Williams, eds. 2021. *John's Transformation of Mark.* London: T & T Clark.

Becker, J. 2012. *Mündliche und schriftliche Autorität im frühen Christentum.* Tübingen: Mohr Siebeck.

Beduhn, J. 2013. *The First New Testament: Marcion's Scriptural Canon.* Salem, OR: Polebridge Press.

Behr, J. 2013. *Irenaeus of Lyons: Identifying Christianity.* Oxford: Oxford University Press.

Bell, L. D. 2018. *The Early Textual Transmission of John: Stability and Fluidity in Its Second and Third Century Greek Manuscripts.* NTTSD 54. Leiden: Brill.

Bellinzoni, A. 1967. *The Sayings of Jesus in the Writings of Justin Martyr.* NovTSup 17. Leiden: Brill.

Berglund, C. J. 2020. *Origen's References to Heracleon: A Quotation-Analytical Study of the Earliest Known Commentary on the Gospel of John.* WUNT 450. Tübingen: Mohr Siebeck.

Berthelot, K. 2012. "Philo and the Allegorical Interpretation of Homer in the Platonic Tradition (with an Emphasis on Porphyry's De antro nympharum)." Pages 155–74 in *Homer and the Bible in the Eyes of Ancient Interpreters.* Edited by M. Niehoff. Leiden: Brill.

Best, E. 1989. "The Gospel of Mark: Who Was the Reader?" *Irish Biblical Studies* 11.3: 124–32.

Bingham, D. J. 1998. *Irenaeus' Use of Matthew's Gospel in Adversus Haereses.* Traditio Exegetica Graeca. Leuven: Peeters.

–. 2016. "A Reading of Irenaeus in Response to Father Denis Farkasfalvy." *PRSt* 43.4: 429–36.

Bird, M. F. 2006. *Jesus and the Origins of the Gentile Mission.* LNTS 331. London: T & T Clark.

–. 2014. *The Gospel of the Lord: How the Early Church Wrote the Story of Jesus.* Grand Rapids: Eerdmans.

Birdsall, J. N. 1993. "A Fresh Examination of the Fragments of the Gospel of St. Luke in MS. 0171 and an Attempted Reconstruction with Special Reference to the Recto." Pages 212–27 in *Philologia Sacra: Biblische und Patristiche Studien für Hermann J. Frede und Walter Thiele zu ihrem siebzigsten Geburtstag, vol. 1: Altes und Neues Testament.* Edited by R. Gryson. Freiberg: Herder.

Black, C. C. 1994. *Mark: Images of an Apostolic Interpreter.* Columbia: University of South Carolina Press.

Blumenthal, H. J. 1981. "Plotinus in Later Platonism." Pages 212–22 in *Neoplatonism and Early Christian Thought: Essays in Honour of A. H. Armstrong.* Edited by H. J. Blumenthal and R. A. Markus. London: Variorum.

Bockmuehl, M. 2005. "The Making of Gospel Commentaries." Pages 274–95 in *The Written Gospel.* Edited by M. Bockmuehl and D. A. Hagner. Cambridge: Cambridge University Press.

–. 2006. *Seeing the Word: Refocusing New Testament Study.* Studies in Theological Interpretation. Grand Rapids: Baker Academic.

–. 2007. "New Testament *Wirkungsgeschichte* and the Early Christian Appeal to Living Memory." Pages 341–68 in *Memory in the Bible and Antiquity: The Fifth Durham-Tübingen Research Symposium (Durham, September 2004).* Edited by S. C. Barton, L. T. Stuckenbruck, and B. G. Wold. WUNT 212. Tübingen: Mohr Siebeck.

–. 2011. "The Son of David and His Mother." *JTS* 62.2: 476–93.

–. 2017. *Ancient Apocryphal Gospels.* Interpretation: Resources for the Use of Scripture in the Church. Louisville, KY: Westminster John Knox.

–. 2019. "Fourfold Gospel Writing." Pages 40–60 in *Writing the Gospels: A Dialogue with Francis Watson.* Edited by C. S. Hamilton. LNTS 606. London: T & T Clark.

Bovon, F. 2002. "The Canonical Structure of Gospel and Apostle." Pages 516–27 in *The Canon Debate.* Edited by L. M. McDonald and J. A. Sanders. Peabody, MA: Hendrickson.

Brankaer, J. 2005. "L'ironie de Jésus dans l'Evangile de Thomas: le logion 114." *Apocrypha* 16: 149–62.

Brant, J.-A. 2011. *John.* Paideia. Grand Rapids: Baker Academic.

Breytenbach, C. 2020. "The Gospel according to Mark: The Yardstick for Comparing the Gospels with Ancient Texts." Pages 179–200 in *Modern and Ancient Literary Criticism of the Gospels: Continuing the Debate on Gospel Genre(s).* Edited by R. M. Calhoun, D. P. Moessner, and T. Nicklas. WUNT 451. Tübingen: Mohr Siebeck.

Brooke, A. E., ed. 1891. *The Fragments of Heracleon.* Texts and Studies. Cambridge: Cambridge University Press.

Burke, T. 2004. "The Greek Manuscript Tradition of the *Infancy Gospel of Thomas*." *Apocrypha* 14: 129–51.

–. 2008. "The Infancy Gospel of Thomas." Pages 126–38 in *The Non-Canonical Gospels.* Edited by P. Foster. London: T & T Clark.

Butticaz, S. 2020. "Early Christian Memories of Jesus: Trajectories and Models of Reception in Early Christianity." *Early Christianity* 11.3: 297–322.

Butts, A. M. 2018. "Old Syriac." In *Brill Encylopedia of Early Christianity Online.* Edited by D. G. Hunter, P. J. J. van Geest, and B. J. Lietaert Peerbolte. Leiden: Brill.

Byrskog, S. 2000. *Story as History — History as Story: the Gospel Tradition in the Context of Ancient Oral History.* WUNT 123. Tübingen: Mohr Siebeck.

Campenhausen, H. von. 1972. *The Formation of the Christian Bible.* Philadelphia: Augsburg Fortress.

276 *Bibliography*

Carlson, S. C. 2014. "Origen's Use of the *Gospel of Thomas*." Pages 137–51 in *Sacra Scriptura: How "Non-Canonical" Texts Functioned in Early Judaism and Early Christianity*. Edited by J. E. Charlesworth and L. M. McDonald. London: T & T Clark.

Cavallo, G. 1967. *Ricerche sulla maiuscola biblica*. Florence: Le Monnier.

–. 2005. *Il calamo e il papiro. La scrittura greca dall'età ellenistica ai primi secoli di Bisanzio*. Papyrologica Florentina. Firenze: Edizioni Gonnelli.

Chapa, J. 2012. "The Early Text of John." Pages 140–56 in *The Early Text of the New Testament*. Edited by C. E. Hill and M. J. Kruger. Oxford: Oxford University Press.

Charlesworth, S. D. 2007. "T. C. Skeat, P64+67 and P4, and the Problem of Fibre Orientation in Codicological Reconstruction." *NTS* 53: 582–604.

–. 2016. *Early Christian Gospels: Their Production and Transmission*. Papyrologica Florentina. Firenze: Edizioni Gonnelli.

Cirafesi, W. V. and G. P. Fewster 2016. "Justin's ἀπομνημονεύματα and Ancient Greco-Roman Memoirs." *Early Christianity* 7: 186–212.

Clarysse, W. and P. Orsini. 2018. "Christian Manuscripts from Egypt to the Times of Constantine." Pages 107–14 in *Das Neue Testament und sein Text im 2. Jahrhundert*. Eited by J. Heilmann and M. Klinghardt. TANZ 61. Tübingen: Narr Francke Attempto.

Climenhaga, N. 2020. "Papias's Prologue and the Probability of Parallels." *JBL* 139.3: 591–96.

Cole, Z. J. 2017. "P45 and the Problem of the 'Seventy(-two)': A Case for the Longer Reading in Luke 10.1 and 17." *NTS* 63: 203–21.

Colwell, E. C. 1969. *Studies in Methodology in Textual Criticism of the New Testament*. Grand Rapids: Eerdmans.

Colwell, E. C. and E. W. Tune. 1969. "Method in Establishing Quantitative Relationships between Text-Types of New Testament Manuscripts." Pages 56–62 in *Studies in Methodology in Textual Criticism of the New Testament*. Edited by E. C. Colwell. NTTS 9. Grand Rapids: Eerdmans.

Comfort, P. W. 1995. "Exploring the Common Identification of Three New Testament Manuscripts: P4, P64 and P67." *TynBul* 46: 43–54.

Comfort, P. W. and D. P. Barrett 2001. *The Text of the Earliest New Testament Greek Manuscripts: A Corrected, Enlarged Edition of the Complete Text of the Earliest New Testament Manuscripts*. Wheaton, IL: Tyndale House Publishers.

Coogan, J. T. 2023. "Reading (in) a Quadriform Cosmos: Gospel Books in the Early Christian Bibliographic Imagination." *JECS* 31.1: 85–103.

Coogan, J. T. and J. A. Rodriguez. 2023. "Ordering Gospel Textuality in the Second Century." *Journal of Theological Studies*: 57–102.

Cook, J. G. 2000. *The Interpretation of the New Testament in Greco-Roman Paganism*. STAC 3. Tübingen: Mohr Siebeck.

–. 2006. "A Note on Tatian's *Diatessaron*, Luke, and the Arabic Harmony." *ZAC* 10: 462–71.

Cosaert, C. P. 2008. *The Text of the Gospels in Clement of Alexandria*. The New Testament in the Greek Fathers. Atlanta: Society of Biblical Literature.

Crawford, M. R. 2013. "Diatessaron, a Misnomer? The Evidence from Ephrem's Commentary." *Early Christianity* 4: 362–85.

–. 2015a. "'Reordering the Confusion': Tatian, the Second Sophistic, and the So-Called *Diatessaron*." *ZAC* 19: 209–36.

–. 2015b. "Ammonius of Alexandria, Eusebius of Caesarea, and the Origins of Gospel Scholarship." *NTS* 61: 1–29.

–. 2015c. "The Fourfold Gospel in the Writings of Ephrem the Syrian." *Hugoye: Journal of Syriac Studies* 18.1: 9–51.

–. 2016. "The Diatessaron, Canonical or Non-canonical? Rereading the Dura Fragment." *NTS* 62: 253–77.

–. 2018. "Rejection at Nazareth in the *Gospels of Mark, Matthew, Luke* — and *Tatian*." Pages 97–124 in *Connecting Gospels: Beyond the Canonical/Non-Canonical Divide*. Edited by F. Watson and S. Parkhouse. Oxford: Oxford University Press.

Crawford, M. R. and N. J. Zola eds. 2019. *The Gospel of Tatian: Exploring the Nature and Text of the Diatessaron*. RJT 3. London: T & T Clark.

Crossan, J. D. 1991. *The Historical Jesus: The Life of a Mediterranean Jewish Peasant*. San Francisco: HarperCollins.

Cullmann, O. 1960. "Das Thomasevangelium und die Frage nach dem Alter der in ihm enthaltenen Tradition." *Theologische Literaturzeitung* 85: 320–34.

Cuvigny, H. 2009. "The Finds of Papyri: The Archaeology of Papyrology." Pages 30–58 in *The Oxford Handbook of Papyrology*. Edited by R. S. Bagnall. Oxford: Oxford University Press.

Davies, S. L. 2005. *The Gospel of Thomas and Christian Wisdom*. Oregon House, CA: Bardic Press.

Davies, W. D. and D. C. Allison. 1988. *A Critical and Exegetical Commentary on the Gospel According to Saint Matthew. 3 vols.* International Critical Commentary. Edinburgh: T & T Clark.

Dawson, J. D. 2002. *Christian Figural Reading and the Fashioning of Identity*. Berkeley: University of California Press.

Dawson, Z. K. 2019. "Does Luke's Preface Resemble a Greek Decree? Comparing the Epigraphical and Papyrological Evidence of Greek Decrees with Ancient Preface Formulae." *NTS* 65: 552–71.

DeConick, A. 2001. *Voices of the Mystics: Early Christian Discourse in the Gospels of John and Thomas and Other Ancient Christian Literature*. Sheffield: Sheffield Academic Press.

–. 2006. *The Original Gospel of Thomas in Translation: With a Commentary and New English Translation of the Complete Gospel*. LNTS 287. London: T & T Clark.

Devreesse, R. 1948. *Essai sur Théodore de Mopsueste*. Vatican City: Biblioteca Apostolica Vatican.

Di Luccio, P. 2017. "Dimore eterne e fine dei tempi nei Vangeli e nell' Apocalisse, e per sant'Ireneo." Pages 337–62 in *Irénée de Lyon et les Débuts de la Bible Chrétienne: Actes de la Journée du 1.VII.2014 À Lyon*. Edited by A. Bastit and J. Verheyden. Turnhout: Brepols.

Dormandy, M. 2018. "How the Books Became the Bible: The Evidence for Canon Formation from Work-Combinations in Manuscripts." *TC: A Journal of Biblical Textual Criticism* 23: 1–39.

Dungan, D. L., ed. 1990. *The Interrelations of the Gospels*. BETL 95. Leuven: Leuven University Press.

Edwards, J. R. 2009. *The Hebrew Gospel and the Development of the Synoptic Tradition*. Grand Rapids: Eerdmans.

Edwards, S. A. 1976. "P75 under the Magnifying Glass." *NovT* 18.3: 190–212.

Elliott, J. K. 1993. *The Apocryphal New Testament*. Oxford: Clarendon Press.

–. 1996. "Codex Bezae and the Earliest Greek Papyri." Pages 161–82 in *Codex Bezae: Studies from the Lunel Colloquium, June 1994*. Edited by D. C. Parker and C.-B. Amphoux. NTTSD 22. Leiden: Brill.

Epp, E. J. 2013. "Textual Clusters: Their Past and Future in New Testament Textual Criticism." Pages 519–78 in *The Text of the New Testament in Contemporary Research: Essays on the Status Quaestionis*. Edited by B. D. Ehrman and M. W. Holmes. NTTSD 42. Leiden: Brill.

Evans, C. A. 2001. *Mark 8:27–16:20*. Word Biblical Commentary. Nashville: Thomas Nelson.

Eve, E. 2016. *Writing the Gospels: Composition and Memory*. London: SPCK.

Fallon, F. T and R. Cameron. 1988. "The Gospel of Thomas: A Forschungsbericht and Analysis." *ANRW* 2.25.6: 4195–251.

Farkasfalvy, D. 2016. "Irenaeus's First Reference to the Four Gospels and the Formation of the Fourfold Gospel Canon." *PRSt* 43.4: 415–27.

Fee, G. D. 1974. "P75, P66, and Origen: The Myth of Early Textual Recension in Alexandria." Pages 19–45 in *New Dimensions in New Testament Study*. Edited by R. N. Longenecker and M. C. Tenney. Grand Rapids: Zondervan.

Foster, P. 2004. *Community, Law and Mission in Matthew's Gospel*. WUNT 2.177. Tübingen: Mohr Siebeck.

–. 2007. "Is there a Relationship between the Writings of Justin Martyr and the Gospel of Peter?" Pages 104–112, 198, in *Justin Martyr and His Worlds*. Edited by S. Parvis and P. Foster. Minneapolis: Fortress.

Foster, P., A. Gregory, J. Kloppenborg, and J. Verheyden eds. 2011. *New Studies in the Synoptic Problem: Oxford Conference, April 2008: Essays in Honour of Christopher M. Tuckett*. BETL 239. Leuven: Peeters.

Fowler, R. 1991. *Let the Reader Understand: Reader-Response Criticism and the Gospel of Mark*. Minneapolis: Fortress Press.

France, R. T. 2002. *The Gospel of Mark*. NIGTC. Grand Rapids: Eerdmans.

Franklin, E. 1994. *Luke: Interpreter of Paul, Critic of Matthew*. Journal for the Study of the New Testament Supplement Series 92. Sheffield: Sheffield Academic Press.

Frey, J. 2002. "Leidenskampf und Himmelreise. Das Berliner Evangelienfragment (Papyrus Berolinensis 22220) und die Gethsemane-Tradition." *BZ* 46: 71–96.

–. 2015. "Texts about Jesus: Non-canonical Gospels and Related Literature." Pages 13–47 in *The Oxford Handbook of Early Christian Apocrypha*. Edited by A. Gregory, T. Nicklas, C. M. Tuckett, and J. Verheyden. Oxford: Oxford University Press.

Furlong, D. 2016. "Theodore of Mopsuestia: New Evidence for the Proposed Papian Fragment in *Hist. eccl.* 3.24.5-13." *JSNT* 39.2: 209–29.

Gallagher, E. L. and J. D. Meade. 2017. *The Biblical Canon Lists from Early Christianity: Texts and Analysis*. Oxford: Oxford University Press.

Gamble, H. Y. 1995. *Books and Readers in thte Early Church: A History of Early Christian Texts*. New Haven: Yale University Press.

–. 2012. "The Book Trade in the Roman Empire." Pages 23–36 in *The Early Text of the New Testament*. Edited by C. E. Hill and M. J. Kruger. Oxford: Oxford University Press.

Gathercole, S. J. 2007. *The Gospel of Judas: Rewriting Early Christianity*. Oxford: Oxford University Press.

–. 2010. "Luke in the *Gospel of Thomas*." *NTS* 57: 114–44.

–. 2012a. *The Composition of the Gospel of Thomas: Original Languages and Influences*. SNTSMS 151. Cambridge: Cambridge University Press.

–. 2012b. "The Earliest Manuscript Title of Matthew's Gospel (Bnf Suppl. gr. 1120 ii 3 / P4)." *NovT* 54: 209–35.

–. 2013. "The Titles of the Gospels in the Earliest New Testament Manuscripts." *ZNW* 104: 33–76.

–. 2014. *The Gospel of Thomas: Introduction and Commentary*. TENTS 11. Leiden: Brill.

–. 2018a. *Praeparatio Evangelica* in Early Christian Gospels. Pages 15–40 in *Connecting Gospels: Beyond the Canonical/Non-Canonical Divide*. Edited by F. Watson and S. Parkhouse. Oxford: Oxford University Press.

–. 2018b. "The Alleged Anonymity of the Canonical Gospels." *JTS* 69.2: 447–76.

Bibliography

–. 2021. *The Apocryphal Gospels*. New York: Penguin Books.

Gnilka, J. 1986. *Das Matthäusevangelium. I. Teil: Kommentar zu Kap. 1,1 – 13,58.* Freiburg: Herder.

Goodacre, M. 2012. *Thomas and the Gospels: The Case for Thomas's Familiarity with the Synoptics*. Grand Rapids: Eerdmans.

–. "The *Protevangelium of James* and the Creative Rewriting of *Matthew* and *Luke*." Pages 57–76 in *Connecting Gospels: Beyond the Canonical/Non-Canonical Divide*. Edited by F. Watson and S. Parkhouse. Oxford: Oxford University Press.

–. 2020. "The Orthodox Redaction of Mark: How Matthew Rescued Mark's Reputation." Pages 319–36 in *'To Recover What Has Been Lost': Essays on Eschatology, Intertextuality, and Reception History in Honor of Dale C. Allison Jr.* Edited by T. Ferda, D. Frayer-Griggs, and N. C. Johnson. NovTSup 183. Leiden: Brill.

Grant, R. M. 1959. "Notes on the Gospel of Thomas." *VC* 13: 170–80.

Graves, M. 2007. *Jerome's Hebrew Philology*. VCSup 90; Leiden: Brill.

Gregory, A. F. 2003. *The Reception of Luke and Acts in the Period before Irenaeus: Looking for Luke in the Second Century*. WUNT 2.169. Tübingen: Mohr Siebeck.

–. 2014. "Jewish-Christian Gospel Traditions and the New Testament." Pages 41–59 in *Christian Apocrypha: Receptions of the New Testament in Ancient Christian Apocrypha*. Edited by T. Nicklas and J.-M. Rössli. Göttingen: Vandenhoeck & Ruprecht.

Gregory, A. F. and C. M. Tuckett. 2005. "Reflections on Method: What constitutes the Use of the Writings that later formed the New Testament in the Apostolic Fathers." Pages 61–82 in *The Reception of the New Testament in the Apostolic Fathers*. Edited by A. F. Gregory and C. M. Tuckett. Oxford: Oxford University Press.

Greschat, K. 2007. "Justins 'Denkwürdigkeiten der Apostel' und das Petrusevangelium." Pages 197–214 in *Das Evangelium nach Petrus: Text, Kontexte, Intertexte*. Edited by T. J. Kraus and T. Nicklas. TUGAL 158. Berlin: de Gruyter.

Gunther, J. J. 1980. "Early Identifications of Authorship of the Johannine Writings." *JEH* 31: 401–27.

Gurry, P. J. 2017. *A Critical Examination of the Coherence-Based Genealogical Method in New Testament Textual Criticism*. NTTSD 55. Leiden: Brill.

Hagen, J. L. 2010. "Ein anderer Kontext für die Berliner und Strassburger 'Evangelien-fragmente'. Das 'Evangelium der Erlösers' und andere 'Apostelevangelien' in der koptischen Literatur." Pages 339–71 in *Jesus in apokryphen Evangelienüberlieferungen. Beiträge zu außerkanonischen Jesusüberlieferungen aus verschiedenen Sprach- und Kulturtraditionen*. Edited by Jorg Frey and Jens Schröter. WUNT 254. Tübingen: Mohr Siebeck.

Hahneman, G. M. 1992. *The Muratorian Fragment and the Development of the Canon*. Oxford: Oxford University Press.

Hannah, D. D. 2003. "Of Cherubim and the Divine Throne: Rev 5.6 in Context." *NTS* 49: 528–42.

–. 2008. "The Four-Gospel 'Canon' in the *Epistula Apostolorum*." *JTS* 59: 598–633.

–. 2021. "The *Vorlage* of the Ethiopic Version of the *Epistula Apostolorum*: Greek or Arabic?" Pages 97–115 in *Beyond Canon: Early Christianity and the Ethiopic Textual Tradition*. Edited by M. T. Gebreananaye, L. Williams, and F. Watson. LNTS 643. London: T & T Clark.

Harnack, A. von. 1914. *Beiträge zur Einleitung in das Neue Testament VI: Die Entstehung des Neuen Testaments und die wichtigsten Folgen der neuen Schöpfung*. Leipzig: Hinrichs.

–. 1961. *The Mission and Expansion of Christianity in the First Three Centuries*. Translated by J. Moffatt. New York: Harper & Brothers.

Hartenstein, J. 2000. *Die zweite Lehre: Erscheinungen des Auferstandenen als Rahmenerzählungen frühchristlicher Dialoge.* TUGAL 146. Berlin: de Gruyter.

—. 2010. "Autoritätskonstellationen in apokryphen und kanonischen Evangelien." Pages 423–44 in *Jesus in apokryphen Evangelienüberlieferungen. Beiträge zu außerkanonischen Jesusüberlieferungen aus verschiedenen Sprach- und Kulturtraditionen.* Edited by J. Frey and J. Schröter. WUNT 254. Tübingen: Mohr Siebeck.

Hays, C. M. 2008. "Marcion vs. Luke: A Response to the *Plädoyer* of Matthias Klinghardt." *ZNW* 99: 213–32.

Head, P. M. 1995. "The Date of the Magdalen Papyrus of Matthew (*P. Magd. Gr.* 17 = P64): A Response to C.P. Thiede." *TynBul* 46.2: 251–85.

—. 2005. "Is P4, P64 and P67 the Oldest Manuscript of the Four Gospels? A Response to T. C. Skeat." *NTS* 51: 450–57.

—. 2011. "Graham Stanton and the Four-Gospel Codex: Reconsidering the Manuscript Evidence." Pages 93–101 in *Jesus, Matthew's Gospel and Early Christianity: Studies in Memory of Graham N. Stanton.* Edited by J. Willitts, D. Gurtner, and R. Burridge. LNTS 435. London: T&T Clark.

—. 2012. "The Early Text of Mark." Pages 108–20 in *The Early Text of the New Testament.* Edited by C. E. Hill and M. J. Kruger. Oxford: Oxford University.

Heath, J. M. F. 2020. *Clement of Alexandria and the Shaping of Christian Literary Practice: Miscellany and the Transformation of Greco-Roman Writing.* Cambridge: Cambridge University Press.

Heckel, T. K. 1999. *Von Evangelium des Markus zum viergestaltigen Evangelium.* WUNT 120. Tübingen: Mohr Siebeck.

Heilmann, J. 2020. "Reading Early New Testament Manuscripts: *Scriptio continua,* 'Reading Aids,' and Other Characteristic Features." Pages 177–96 in *Material Aspects of Reading in Ancient and Medieval Cultures: Materiality, Presence and Performance.* Edited by A. Krauß, J. Leipziger, and F. Schücking-Jungblut. Materiale Textkulteren 26. Berlin: de Gruyter.

Henderson, S. W. 2012. "Discipleship after the Resurrection: Scribal Hermeneutics in the Longer Ending of Mark." *JTS* 63.1: 106–24.

Hengel, M. 1989. *The Johannine Question.* Translated by J. Bowden. London: SCM.

—. 2000. *The Four Gospels and the One Gospel of Jesus Christ: An Investigation of the Collection and Origin of the Canonical Gospels.* Translated by J. Bowden. London: SCM.

—. 2008. *Die vier Evangelien und das eine Evangelium von Jesus Christus: Studien zu ihrer Sammlung und Entstehung.* WUNT 224. Tübingen: Mohr Siebeck.

Hernandez Jr., J. 2012. "The Early Text of Luke." Pages 121–39 in *The Early Text of the New Testament.* Edited by C. E. Hill and M. J. Kruger. Oxford: Oxford University Press.

Hill, C. E. 1998. "What Papias Said about John (and Luke): A 'New' Papian Fragment." *JTS* 49: 582–629.

—. 1999. "The *Epistula Apostolorum*: An Asian Tract from the Time of Polycarp." *JECS* 7.1: 1–53.

—. 2004. *The Johannine Corpus in the Early Church.* Oxford: Oxford University Press.

—. 2006. *From the Lost Teaching of Polycarp: Identifying Irenaeus' Apostolic Presbyter and the Author of* Ad Diognetum. WUNT 186. Tübingen: Mohr Siebeck.

—. 2007. "Was John's Gospel among Justin's *Apostolic Memoirs*?" Pages 88–94, 191 in *Justin Martyr and His Worlds.* Edited by S. Parvis and P. Foster. Minneapolis: Fortress.

—. 2010a. "'The Orthodox Gospel': The Reception of John in the Great Church Prior to Irenaeus." Pages 233–300 in *The Legacy of John: Second-Century Reception of the Fourth Gospel.* Edited by T. Rasimus. NovTSup 132. Leiden: Brill.

Bibliography

–. 2010b. *Whose Chose the Gospels? Probing the Great Gospel Conspiracy*. Oxford: Oxford University Press.

–. 2011. "Intersections of Jewish and Christian Scribal Culture: The Original Codex Containing P4, P64, and P67 and Its Implications." Pages 75–91 in *Among Jews, Gentile and Christians in Antiquity and the Middle Ages: Studies in Honour of Professor Oskar Skarsaune on His 65th Birthday*. Edited by R. Hvalvik and J. Kaufman. Trondheim: Tapir Academic Press.

–. 2012. "'In These Very Words': Methods and Standards of Literary Borrowing in the Second Century." Pages 261–81 in *The Early Text of the New Testament*. Edited by C. E. Hill and M. J. Kruger. Oxford: Oxford University Press.

–. 2013. "A Four-Gospel Canon in the Second Century? Artifact and Arti-fiction." *Early Christianity* 4: 310–34.

–. 2015. "Rightly Dividing the Word: Uncovering an Early Template for Textual Division in John's Gospel." Pages 221–42 in *Studies on the Text of the New Testament and Early Christianity: Essays in Honour of Michael W. Holmes*. Edited by J. Hernandez Jr., D. Gurtner, and P. Foster. NTTSD 50. Leiden: Brill.

–. 2016. "'The Truth above All Demonstration': Scripture in the Patristic Period to Augustine." Pages 43–88 in *The Enduring Authority of the Christian Scriptures*. Edited by D. A. Carson. Grand Rapids: Eerdmans.

–. 2017. "The Authentication of John: Self-Disclosure, Testimony, and Verification John 21:24." Pages 398–437 in *The Language and Literature of the New Testament: Essays in Honor of Stanley E. Porter's 60th Birthday*. Edited by C. A. Evans, L. K. Fuller Dow, and A. W. Pitts. Leiden: Brill.

–. 2019. "Diatessaron, Diapente, Diapollon? Exploring the Nature and Extent of Extracanonical Influence in Tatian's Diatessaron." Pages 25–53 in *The Gospel of Tatian: Exploring the Nature and Text of the Diatessaron*. Edited by M. R. Crawford and N. J. Zola. RJT 3. London: T & T Clark.

Hills, J. V. 2008. *Tradition and Composition in the* Epistula Apostolorum. HTS 57. Cambridge: Harvard University Press.

Holmes, M. W. 2013. "From 'Original Text' to 'Initial Text': The Traditional Goal of New Testament Textual Criticism in Contemporary Discussion." Pages 637–88 in *The Text of the New Testament in Contemporary Research: Essays on the Status Quaestionis*. Edited by B. D. Ehrman and M. W. Holmes. NTTSD 42. Leiden: Brill.

–. 2020. "New Testament Textual Criticism in 2020: A (Selective) Survey of the *Status Quaestionis*." *Early Christianity* 11.1: 3–20.

Hornschuh, M. 1965. *Studien zur Epistula Apostolorum*. PTS 5. Berlin: de Gruyter.

Hort, F. J. A. 1894. *Judaistic Christianity: A Course of Lectures*. London: MacMillan and Co.

Houghton, H. A. G. 2016. *The Latin New Testament: A Guide to its Early History, Texts, and Manuscripts*. Oxford: Oxford University Press.

Howley, J. A. 2018. *Aulus Gellius and Roman Reading Culture: Text, Presence, and Imperial Knowledge in the* Noctes Atticae. Cambridge: Cambridge University Press.

Huck, A. and H. Greeven. 1981. *Synopsis of the First Three Gospels*. Tübingen: Mohr Siebeck.

Hug, J. 1978. *La Finale de l'Évangile de Marc: Mc 16, 9–20*. Paris: J. Gabalda.

Hurtado, L. W. 1981. *Text-Critical Methodology and the Pre-Caesarean Text: Codex W in the Gospel of Mark*. Grand Rapids: Eerdmans.

–. 2006a. *The Earliest Christian Artifacts: Manuscripts and Christian Origins*. Grand Rapids: Eerdmans.

–. 2006b. "The New Testament in the Second Century: Text, Collections and Canon." Pages 3–27 in *Transmission and Reception: New Testament Text-Critical and Exegetical Studies*.

282 *Bibliography*

Edited by J. W. Childers and D. C. Parker. Texts and Studies. Piscataway, NJ: Gorgias Press.

–. 2008. "The Greek Fragments of the *Gospel of Thomas* as Artefacts: Papyrological Observations on Papyrus Oxyrhynchus 1, Papyrus Oxyrhynchus 654 and Papyrus Oxyrhynchus 655." Pages 19–32 in *Das Thomasevangelium: Entstehung — Rezeption — Theologie*. Edited by E. E. Popkes, J. Frey, and J. Schröter. BZNW 157. Berlin: de Gruyter.

–. 2017. *Destroyer of the Gods: Early Christian Distinctiveness in the Roman World*. Waco, TX: Baylor University Press.

Inowlocki, S. 2006. *Eusebius and the Jewish Authors: His Citation Technique in an Apologetic Context*. AJEC 64. Leiden: Brill.

Jackson, H. M. 1999. "Ancient Self-Referential Conventions and Their Implications for the Authorship and Integrity of the Gospel of John." *JTS* 50: 1–34.

Jastrow, M. 1950. *A Dictionary of the Targumim, the Talmud Babli and Yerushalmi, and the Midrashic Literature*. New York: Pardes.

Jeremias, J. 1971. *New Testament Theology, vol. 1: The Proclamation of Jesus*. New York: Scribner's Sons.

Johnson, W. A. 2010. *Readers and Reading Culture in the High Roman Empire: A Study of Elite Communities*. Classical Culture and Society. Oxford: Oxford University Press.

Jongkind, D. 2006. "'The Lilies of the Field' Reconsidered: *Codex Sinaiticus* and the Gospel of Thomas." *NovT* 48.3: 209–16.

–. 2014. "Short Note: 059 (0215) and Mark 15:28." *TC: A Journal of Biblical Textual Criticism*.

Joosse, N. P. 1999. "An Introduction to the Arabic Diatessaron." *Oriens Christianus* 83: 72–129.

Joosten, J. 2019. "Tatian's Sources and the Presentation of the Jewish Law in the Diatessaron." Pages 55–66 in *The Gospel of Tatian: Exploring the Nature and Text of the Diatessaron*. Edited by M. R. Crawford and N. J. Zola. RJT 3. London: T&T Clark.

Jorgensen, D. W. 2016. *Treasure Hidden in a Field: Early Christian Reception of the Gospel of Matthew*. SBR 6. Berlin: de Gruyter.

Kalvesmaki, J. 2013. *The Theology of Arithmetic: Number Symbolism in Platonism and Early Christianity*. Washington, DC: Center for Hellenic Studies.

Kealy, S. P. 2007. *A History of the Interpretation of the Gospel of Mark*. Lewiston: Edwin Mellen Press.

Kelber, W. H. 1983. *The Oral and the Written Gospel: The Hermeneutics of Speaking and Writing in the Synoptic Tradition, Mark, Paul, and Q* Bloomington: Indiana University Press, 1983

Keith, C. 2016. "The Competitive Textualization of the Jesus Tradition in John 20:30–31 and 21:24–25." *CBQ* 78.2: 321–37.

–. 2020. *The Gospel as Manuscript: An Early History of the Jesus Tradition as Material Artifact*. Oxford: Oxford University Press.

Kelhoffer, J. A. 2000. *Miracle and Mission: The Authentication of Missionaries and Their Message in the Longer Ending of Mark*. WUNT 2.112. Tübingen: Mohr Siebeck.

–. 2004. "'How Soon a Book' Revisited: ΕΥΑΓΓΕΛΙΟΝ as a Reference to 'Gospel' Materials in the First Half of the Second Century." *ZNW* 95: 1–34.

Kenyon, F. G. 1936. *The Story of the Bible: A Popular Account of How It Came to Us*. London: John Murray.

King, K. 1987. Kingdom in the Gospel of Thomas. *Forum* 3: 48–97.

–. 2016. "What Is an Author?: Ancient Author-Function in the *Apocryphon of John* and the *Apocalypse of John*." Pages 15–42 in *Scribal Practices and Social Structures among Jesus'*

Adherents: Essays in Honour of John S. Kloppenborg. Edited by W. E. Arnal, R. S. Ascough, R. A. Derrenbacker, and P. A. Harland. BETL 285. Leuven: Peeters.

King, M. 1965. "Notes on the Bodmer Manuscript of Luke." *Bibliotheca Sacra* 122: 234–40.

Kingsbury, J. D. 1975. *Matthew: Structure, Christology, Kingdom*. London: SPCK.

Kinzig, W. 1994a. *Novitas Christiana: Die Idee des Fortschritts in der Alten Kirche bis Eusebius*. Göttingen: Vandenhoeck & Ruprecht.

–. "Καινὴ διαθήκη: The Title of the New Testament in the Second and third Centuries." *JTS* 45.2: 519–544.

Kirk, A. 2007. "Tradition and Memory in the *Gospel of Peter*." Pages 135–58 in *Das Evangelium nach Petrus: Text, Kontexte, Intertexte*. Edited by T. J. Kraus and T. Nicklas. TUGAL 158. Berlin: de Gruyter.

Klein, G. 1964. "Lukas 1,1-4 Als Theologisches Programm." Pages 193–216 in *Zeit Und Ge schichte: Festschrift Rudolf Bultmann*. Edited by E. Dinkler. Tübingen: Mohr Siebeck.

Klijn, A. F. J. 1992. *Jewish-Christian Gospel Tradition*. VCSup 17. Leiden: Brill.

Kline, L. L. 1975. "Harmonized Sayings of Jesus is the Pseudo-Clementine Homilies and Justin Martyr." *ZNW* 66: 223–41.

Klinghardt, M. 2015. *Das älteste Evangelium und die Entstehung der kanonischen Evangelien*. TANZ 60. Tübingen: Francke.

Kloppenborg, J. S. 2014a. "A New Synoptic Problem: Mark Goodacre and Simon Gathercole on *Thomas*." *JSNT* 36.3: 199–239.

–. "Literate Media in Early Christ Groups: The Creation of a Christian Book Culture." *JECS* 22: 21–59.

–. 2019. "Conflated Citations of the Synoptic Gospels: The Beginnings of Christian Doxographic Tradition?" Pages 45–80 in *Gospels and Gospel Traditions in the Second Century: Experiments in Reception*. Edited by J. Schröter, T. Nicklas, and J. Verheyden. BZNW 235. Berlin: de Gruyter.

Knox, J. 1942. *Marcion and the New Testament: An Essay in the Early History of the Canon*. Chicago: University of Chicago Press.

Knust, J. and T. Wasserman. 2019. *To Cast the First Stone: The Transmission of a Gospel Story*. Princeton, NJ: Princeton University Press.

Koester, C. 2014. *Revelation: A New Translation with Introduction and Commentary*. Anchor Bible. New Haven: Yale University Press.

Koester, H. 1957. *Synoptische Überlieferung bei den apostolischen Vätern*. TUGAL 65. Berlin: Akademie-Verlag.

–. "GNOMAI DIAPHOROI: The Origin and Nature of Diversification in the History of Early Christianity." *HTR* 58: 279–318.

–. 1989a. "From the Kerygma-Gospel to Written Gospels." *NTS* 35.3: 361–81.

–. 1989b. "Introduction (to the *Gospel of Thomas*)." Pages 38–49 in *Nag Hammadi Codex II,2-7, together with XIII,2, Brit. Lib. Or.4926(1), and P. Oxy. 1, 654, 655, vol. I*. Edited by B. Layton. Leiden: Brill.

–. 1990. *Ancient Christian Gospels: Their History and Development*. London: SCM Press.

–. 2005. "Gospels and Gospel Traditions in the Second Century." Pages 27–44 in *Trajectories through the New Testament and the Apostolic Fathers*. Edited by A. F. Gregory and C. M. Tuckett. Oxford: Oxford University Press.

Köhler, W.-D. 1987. *Die Rezeption des Matthäusevangeliums in der Zeit vor Irenäus*. WUNT 2.24. Tübingen: Mohr Siebeck.

Kok, M. J. 2015. *The Gospel on the Margins: The Reception of Mark in the Second Century*. Minneapolis: Fortress Press.

Konstan, D. 2011. "Excerpting as a Reading Practice." Pages 9–22 in *Thinking through Excerpts: Studies on Stobaeus*. Edited by G. J. Reydams-Schils. Turnhout: Brepols.

Kraus, T. J., M. J. Kruger, and T. Nicklas eds. 2009. *Gospel Fragments*. Oxford Early Christian Gospel Texts. Oxford: Oxford University Press.

Kruger, M. J. 2012. "The Date and Content of P.Antinoopolis 12 (0232)." *NTS* 58.2: 254–71.

–. 2013a. "Manuscripts, Scribes, and Book Production within Early Christianity." Pages 15–40 in *Christian Origins and Greco-Roman Culture: Social and Literary Contexts for the New Testament*. Edited by S. E. Porter and A. W. Pitts. TENTS 9. Leiden: Brill.

–. 2013b. *The Question of Canon: Challenging the Status Quo in the New Testament Debate*. Downers Grove: Intervarsity Press.

Kvalbein, H. 2006. "The Kingdom of the Father in the Gospel of Thomas." Pages 203–30 in *The New Testament and Early Christian Literature in Greco-Roman Context: Studies in Honor of David E. Aune*. Edited by J. Fotopolous. NovTSup 122. Leiden: Brill.

Lagrand, J. 1999. *The Earliest Christian Mission to 'All Nations' in Light of Matthew's Gospel*. Grand Rapids: Eerdmans.

Lampe, P. 2003. *From Paul to Valentinus: Christians at Rome in the First Two Centuries*. Translated by M. Steinhauser. Minneapolis: Fortress Press.

Lange, C. 2005. *The Portrayal of Christ in the Syriac Commentary on the Diatessaron*. CSCO 616. Leuven: Peeters.

Larsen, M. D. C. 2017. "Accidental Publication, Unfinished Texts and the Traditional Goals of New Testament Textual Criticism." *JSNT* 39.4: 362–87.

–. 2018a. "Correcting the Gospel: Putting the Titles of the Gospels in Historical Context." Pages 78–103 in *Rethinking 'Authority' in Late Antiquity: Authorship, Law, and Transmission in Jewish and Christian Tradition*. Edited by A. J. Berkovitz and M. Letteney.

–. 2018b. *Gospels Before the Book*. Oxford: Oxford University Press.

Larsen, M. D. C. and M. Letteney. 2019. "Christians and the Codex: Generic Materiality and Early Gospel Traditions." *JECS* 27.3: 383–415.

Leloir, L. 1962. *Le témoignage d'Éphrem sur le Diatessaron*. Leuven: Secrétariat du CorpusSCO.

–. 1964. "Divergences entre l'orginal Syriaque et la version Arménienne du commentaire d'Éphrem sur le Diatessaron." *Mélanges Eugéne Tisserant* 2: 303–31.

Leonhard, C. 2018. "No Liturgical Need for a Gospel in the Second Century." Pages 89–106 in *Das Neue Testament und sein Text im 2. Jahrhundert*. Edited by J. Heilmann and M. Klinghardt. TANZ 61. Tübingen: Narr Francke Attempto.

Lieu, J. M. 2015. *Marcion and the Making of a Heretic: God and Scripture in the Second Century*. Cambridge: Cambridge University Press.

Lindenlaub, J. 2020. "The Gospel of John as Model for Literate Authors and their Texts in Epistula Apostolorum and Apocryphon of James (NHC 1,2)." *JSNT* 43.1: 3–27.

Löhr, W. A. 2003. "Valentinian Variations on Lk 12, 8-9/Mt 10,32." *VC* 57: 437–55.

Lorenz, P. E. 2018. "The Lukan Genealogy (Luke 3:23–38) as a Living Text: The Genealogy of Jesus in the Traditions of Codex Bezae and Aphrahat." Pages 71–120 in *Liturgy and the Living Text of the New Testament: Papers from the Tenth Birmingham Colloquium on the Textual Criticism of the New Testament*. Edited by H. A. G. Houghton. Texts and Studies: Third Series 16. Piscataway, NJ: Gorgias.

Luhmann, N. 2013. *Theory of Society, Vol. 2*. Stanford: Stanford University Press.

Lührmann, D. 2004. *Die apokryph gewordenen Evangelien: Studien zu neuen Texten und zu neuen Fragen*. NovTSup 112. Leiden: Brill.

Luijendijk, A. 2011. "Reading the Gospel of Thomas in the Third Century: Three Oxyrhynchus Papyri and Origen's Homilies." Pages 241–68 in *Reading the New Testament Papyri in Context*. Edited by C. Clivaz and Jean Zumstein. BETL 242. Leuven: Peeters.

Luomanen, P. 2003. "Where Did Another Rich Man Come From? The Jewish-Christian Profile of the Story about a Rich Man in the 'Gospel of the Hebrews' (Origen, *Comm. On Matth.* 15.14)." *VC* 57: 243–75.

–. 2012. *Recovering Jewish-Christian Sects and Gospels*. VCSup 110. Leiden: Brill.

Lyon, J. P. 1994. *Syriac Gospel Translations: A Comparison of the Language and Translation Method Used in the Old Syriac, the Diatessaron, and the Peshitto*. CSCO 548. Leuven: Peeters.

MacEwen, R. K. 2015. *Matthean Posteriority: An Exploration of Matthew's Use of Mark and Luke as a Solution to the Synoptic Problem*. LNTS 501. London: T & T Clark.

MacMullen, R. 1981. *Paganism in the Roman Empire*. New Haven: Yale University Press.

–. 1984. *Christianizing the Roman Empire A.D. 100-400*. New Haven: Yale University Press.

Manor, T. S. 2013. "Papias, Origen, and Eusebius." *VC* 67: 1–21.

–. 2016. *Epiphanius' Alogi and the Johannine Controversy: A Reassessment of Early Ecclesial Opposition to the Johannine Corpus*. VCSup 135. Leiden: Brill.

Marcovich, M. 1969. "Textual Criticism on the Gospel of Thomas." *JTS* 20: 53–74.

Marcus, J. 2009. *Mark 8–16: A New Translation with Introduction and Commentary*. The Anchor Yale Bible. New Haven: Yale University Press.

Markschies, C. 2007. *Kaiserzeitliche christliche Theologie und ihre Institutionen: Prolegomena zu einer Geschichte der antiken christlichen Theologie*. Tübingen: Mohr Siebeck.

–. 2012. "Haupteinleitung." In *Antike christliche Apokryphen in deutscher Übersetzung, 1.1– 2, Evangelien und Verwandtes*, ed. C. Markschies and J. Schröter, 1–183. Tübingen: Mohr Siebeck.

–. 2015. *Christian Theology and Its Institutions in the Early Roman Empire: Prolegomena to a History of Early Christian Theology*. Translated by W. Coppins. Waco: Baylor University Press.

Martens, P. W. 2008. "Revisiting the Allegory/Typology Distinction: The Case of Origen." *JECS* 16.3: 283–317.

Martin, M. W. 2005. "Defending the 'Western Non-Interpolations': The Case for an Anti-Separationist *Tendenz* in the Longer Alexandrian Readings." *JBL* 124.2: 269–94.

Martini, C. M. 1966. *Il problema della recensionalità del codice B alla luce del papiro Bodmer XIV*. Analecta Biblica. Rome: Pontifico Istituto Biblico.

Massaux, É. 1990. *The Influence of the Gospel of Saint Matthew on Christian Literature before Saint Irenaeus*. Translated by A. J. Bellinzoni and N. J. Beval. Macon, GA: Mercer University Press.

Mattila, S. L. 1995. "A Question Too Often Neglected." *NTS* 41: 199–217.

McArthur, H. K. 1960. "Dependence of the Gospel of Thomas on the Synoptics." *ExpTim* 71: 286–87.

McDonald, L. M. 2002. "Identifying Scripture and Canon in the Early Church: The Criteria Question." Pages 416–39 in *The Canon Debate*. Edited by L. M. McDonald and J. A. Sanders. Peabody, MA: Hendrickson.

–. 2017. *The Formation of the Biblical Canon: Volume 2. The New Testament: Its Origin and Canonicity*. London: T&T Clark.

Meade, J. D. 2019. "Myths about Canon: What the Codex Can and Can't Tell Us." Pages 253– 77 in *Myths and Mistakes in New Testament Textual Criticism*. Edited by E. Hixson and P. J. Gurry. Downers Grove: Intervarsity Press.

Meier, J. P. 1991. *A Marginal Jew, vol. 1: Rethinking the Historical Jesus: The Roots of the Problem and the Person*. New York: Doubleday.

Ménard, J.-É. 1975. *L'Évangile selon Thomas: Introduction, traduction, commentaire*. Nag Hammadi Studies. Leiden: Brill.

Merkel, H. 1990. "Die Überlieferung der Alten Kirche über das Verhältnis der Evangelien." Pages 566–90 in *The Interrelations of the Gospels*. Edited by D. L. Dungan. BETL 95. Leuven: Leuven University Press.

Metzger, B. 1961. "The Bodmer Papyrus of Luke and John." *ExpTim* 73: 201–03.

–. 1977. *The Early Versions of the New Testament: Their Origin, Transmission, and Limitations*. Oxford: Clarendon Press.

Mills, I. N. 2019. "The Wrong Harmony: Against the Diatessaronic Character of the Dura Parchment." Pages 145–70 in *The Gospel of Tatian: Exploring the Nature and Text of the Diatessaron*. Edited by M. R. Crawford and N. J. Zola. RJT 3. London: T&T Clark.

–. "Zacchaeus and the Unripe Figs: A New Argument for the Original Language of Tatian's Diatessaron." *NTS* 66: 208–27.

–. 2021. "Tatian's Diatessaron as 'Canonical' Gospel: Walter Bauer and the Reception of Christian 'Apocrypha.'" *StPatr*: Forthcoming.

Min, K. S. 2005. *Die früheste Überlieferung des Matthäusevangeliums (bis zum 3./4. Jh.): Edition und Untersuchung*. ANTF 34. Berlin: de Gruyter.

Mitchell, M. 2020. "Mark, the Long-Form Pauline εὐαγγέλιον." Pages 201–17 in *Modern and Ancient Literary Criticism of the Gospels: Continuing the Debate on Gospel Genre(s)*. Edited by R. M. Calhoun, D. P. Moessner, and Tobias Nicklas. WUNT 451. Tübingen: Mohr Siebeck.

Mitchell, T. 2020. "Exposing Textual Corruption: Community as a Stabilizing Aspect in the Circulation of the New Testament Writings during the Greco-Roman Era." *JSNT* 43.2: 266–98.

Moessner, D. P. 1992. "The Meaning of ΚΑΘΕΞΗΣ in the Lukan Prologue as a Key to the Distinctive Contribution of Luke's Narrative among the 'Many'." Pages 1513–28 in *The Four Gospels, 1992: Festschrift Frans Neirynck*. Edited by C. M. Tuckett, F. van Segbroeck, G. V. Belle, and J. Verheyden. BETL 100. Leuven: Peeters.

–. 1996. "'Eyewitnesses,' 'Informed Contemporaries,' and 'Unknowing Inquirers': Josephus' Criteria for Authentic Historiography and the Meaning of ΠΑΡΑΚΟΛΟΥΘΕΩ." *NovT* 38.2: 106–22.

–. 1999. "The Appeal and Power of Poetics (Luke 1:1–4): Luke's Superior Credentials (παρηκολουθηκότι), Narrative Sequence (καθεξῆς), and Firmness of Understanding (ἡ ἀσφάλεια) for the Reader." Pages 84–123 in *Formal Elements and Genre: Which Greco-Roman Prologues Most Closely Parallel the Lukan Prologues?* Edited by D. P. Moessner. Harrisburg: Trinity Press International.

–. 2002. "Dionysius's Narrative 'Arrangement' (οἰκονομία) as the Hermeneutical Key to Luke's Re-Vision of the 'Many'." Pages 149–64 in *Paul, Luke and the Graeco-Roman World: Essays in Honour of Alexander J. M. Wedderburn*. Edited by A. Christophersen, C. Claussen, J. Frey, and B. Longenecker. JSNTSup 217. Sheffield: Sheffield Academic Press.

–. 2008. "The Triadic Synergy of Hellenistic Poetics in the Narrative Epistemology of Dionysius of Halicarnassus and the Authorial Intent of the Evangelist Luke (Luke 1:1–14; Acts 1:1–8)." *Neot* 42.2: 289–303.

–. 2019. "'The Living and Enduring Voice': Papias as Guarantor of Early Apostolic Plotting of Incipient Synoptic Traditions." *Early Christianity* 10: 484–519.

Moles, J. 2011. "Luke's Preface: The Greek Decree, Classical Historiography and Christian Redefinitions." *NTS* 57: 461–82.

Bibliography

Moll, S. 2010. *The Arch-Heretic Marcion*. WUNT 250. Tübingen: Mohr Siebeck.

Montefiore, H. W. 1961. "Comparison of the Parables of the Gospel according to Thomas and of the Synoptic Gospels." *NTS* 7: 220–48.

Moore, G. F. 1890. "Tatian's Diatessaron and the Analysis of the Pentateuch." *JBL* 9: 201–15.

Most, G. W. ed. 1997. *Collecting Fragments = Fragmente Sammeln*. Aporemata: Kritische Studien zur Philologiegeschichte. Göttingen: Vandenhoeck & Ruprecht.

Mroczek, E. 2016. *The Literary Imagination in Jewish Antiquity*. Oxford: Oxford University Press.

Mutschler, B. 2004. *Irenäus als Johanneischer Theologe: Studien zur Schriftauslegung bei Irenäus von Lyon*. STAC 21. Tübingen: Mohr Siebeck.

–. *Das Corpus Johanneum bei Irenäus von Lyon: Studien und Kommentar zum dritten Buch von 'Adversus Haereses'*. WUNT 189. Tübingen: Mohr Siebeck.

–. 2009. "John and His Gospel in the Mirror of Irenaeus of Lyons: Perspectives of Recent Research." Pages 319–43 in *The Legacy of John: Second-Century Reception of the Fourth Gospel*. Edited by T. Rasimus. NovTSup 132. Leiden: Brill.

–. 2019. "Irenäus und die Evangelien: Literarische Rezeption „des Herrn" und Anschluss an eine Vieretradition." Pages 217–52 in *Gospels and Gospel Traditions in the Second Century: Experiments in Reception*. Edited by J. Schröter, T. Nicklas, and J. Verheyden. BZNW 235. Berlin: de Gruyter.

Nagel, P. 2003. "Gespräche Jesu mit seinen Jüngern vor der Auferstehung — zur Herkunft und Datierung des 'Unbekannten Berliner Evangeliums'." *ZNW* 94: 215–57.

Nagel, T. 2000. *Die Rezeption des Johannesevangeliums im 2. Jahrhundert: Studien zur vorirenäischen Auslegung des vierten Evangeliums in christlicher und christlich-gnostischer Literatur*. Arbeiten zur Bibel und ihrer Geschichte. Leipzig: Evangelische Verlagsanstalt.

Nicklas, T. 2014. "Christian Apocrypha and the Development of the Christian Canon." *Early Christianity* 5: 220–40.

Nicklas, T. and J. Schröter eds. 2020. *Authoritative Writings in Early Judaism and Early Christianity: Their Origin, Collection, and Meaning*. WUNT 441. Tübingen: Mohr Siebeck.

Niehoff, M. ed. 2012. *Homer and the Bible in the Eyes of Ancient Interpreters*. Jerusalem Studies in Religion and Culture. Leiden: Brill.

Niehoff, M. R. 2011. *Jewish Exegesis and Homeric Scholarship in Alexandria*. Cambridge: Cambridge University Press.

Nolland, J. 1979. "Sib. Or. III.265–94, an Early Maccabean Messianic Oracle." *JTS* 30.1: 158–66.

Nongbri, B. 2014. "The Limits of Palaeographic Dating of Literary Papyri: Some Observations on the Date and Provenance of P.Bodmer II (P66)." *Museum Helveticum* 71: 1–35.

–. 2016a. "Reconsidering the Place of Papyrus Bodmer XIV–XV (P75) in the Textual Criticism of the New Testament." *JBL* 135.2: 405–37.

–. 2016b. "The Construction of P.Bodmer VIII and the Bodmer 'Composite' or 'Miscellaneous' Codex." *NovT* 58: 394–410.

–. 2018. *God's Library: The Archaeology of the Earliest Christian Manuscripts*. New Haven: Yale University Press.

–. 2019. "Palaeographic Analysis of Codices from the Early Christian Period: A Point of Method." *JSNT* 42.1: 84–97.

–. 2020. "Palaeography, Precision and Publicity: Further Thoughts on *P.Ryl.* III.457 (P52)." *NTS* 66: 471–99.

Norelli, E. ed. 2005. *Papia di Hierapolis: Esposizione degli oracoli del signore. I frammenti. Introduzione, testo, traduzione e note*. Letture Cristiane del Primo Millennio. Milan: Paoline.

O'Connell, J. H. 2010. "A Note on Papias's Knowledge of the Fourth Gospel." *JBL* 129.4: 793–94.

Ong, W. J. 1982. *Orality and Literacy: The Technologizing of the Word.* London: Methuen.

Orsini, P. 2019. *Studies on Greek and Coptic Majuscule Scripts and Books.* Studies in Manuscript Cultures. Berlin: de Gruyter.

Orisini, P. and W. Clarysse. 2012. "Early New Testament Manuscripts and Their Dates: A Critique of Theological Palaeography." *ETL* 88.4: 443–74.

Osborne, G. 2010. *Matthew.* Zondervan Exegetical Commentary on the New Testament. Grand Rapids: Zondervan.

Pardee, C. G. 2019. *Scribal Harmonization in the Synoptic Gospels.* NTTSD 60. Leiden: Brill.

Parker, D. C., D. G. K. Taylor, and M. Goodacre. 1999. "The Dura-Europos Gospel Harmony." Pages 192–228 in *Studies in the Early Text of the Gospels and Acts.* Edited by D. G. K. Taylor. Birmingham: University of Birmingham Press.

Pastor, J. B. 2017. "*Rationalis Esca* (*AH* 4.16.3), Manger et connaître dans l'exégèse irénéenne de Dt 8, 3." Pages 285–96 in *Irénée de Lyon et les Débuts de la Bible Chrétienne: Actes de la Journée du 1.VII.2014 À Lyon.* Edited by A. Bastit and J. Verheyden. Turnhout: Brepols.

Pastorelli, D. 2011. "The Genealogies of Jesus in Tatian's *Diatessaron*: The Question of their Absence or Presence." Pages 216–30 in *Infancy Gospels: Stories and Identities.* Edited by C. Clivaz, A. Dettwiler, L. Devillers, and E. Norelli. WUNT 281. Tübingen: Mohr Siebeck.

Patterson, S. J. 1993. *The Gospel of Thomas and Jesus.* Sonoma, CA: Polebridge.

–. 2014. "Twice More – *Thomas* and the Synoptics: A Reply to Simon Gathercole, *The Composition of the Gospel of Thomas*, and Mark Goodacre, *Thomas and the Gospels.*" *JSNT* 36.3: 251–261.

Pennington, J. T. 2007. *Heaven and Earth in the Gospel of Matthew.* NovTSup 126. Leiden: Brill.

Perrin, N. 2003. "Hermeneutical Factors in the Harmonization of the Gospels and the Question of Textual Authority." Pages 599–605 in *The Biblical Canons.* Edited by J.-M. Auwers and H. J. de Jonge. BETL 163. Leuven: Peeters.

–. 2009. "The *Diatessaron* and the Second-Century Reception of the Gospel of John." Pages 301–18 in *The Legacy of John: Second-Century Reception of the Fourth Gospel.* Edited by T. Rasimus. NovTSup 132. Leiden: Brill.

–. 2019. "What Justin's Gospels Can Tell Us about Tatian's: Tracing the Trajectory of the Gospel Harmony in the Second Century and Beyond." Pages 93–109 in *The Gospel of Tatian: Exploring the Nature and Text of the Diatessaron.* Edited by M. R. Crawford and N. J. Zola. RJT 3. London: T & T Clark.

Petersen, Silke. 2006. "Die Evangelienüberschriften und die Entstehung des neutestamentlichen Kanons." *ZNW* 97: 250–74.

Petersen, W. L. 1986. "New Evidence for the Question of the Original Language of the Diatessaron." Pages 325–43 in *Studien zum Text und zur Ethik des Neuen Testaments: Festschrift zum 80. Geburtstag von Heinrich Greeven.* Edited by W. Schrage and J. Verheyden. BZNW 47. Berlin: de Gruyter.

–. 1989. "Some Remarks on the Integrity of Ephrem's Commentary on the Diatessaron." *StPatr* 20: 197–202.

–. 1990. "Textual Evidence of Tatian's Dependence upon Justin's ΑΠΟΜΝΗΜΟΝΕΥΜΑΤΑ." *NTS* 36: 512–34.

–. 1994. *Tatian's Diatessaron: Its Creation, Dissemination, Significance, and History in Scholarship.* VCSup 25. Leiden: Brill.

Bibliography 289

–. 2004. "The Diatessaron and the Fourfold Gospel." Pages 50-68 in *The Earliest Gospels: The Origins and Transmission of the Earliest Christian Gospels - the Contribution of the Chester Beatty Gospel Codex P45*. Edited by C. Horton. London: T & T Clark.

Phillips, C. A. 1931. "Diatessaron — Diapente." *Bulletin of the Bezan Club* 9: 6–8.

Piovanelli, P. 2012. "Thursday Night Fever: Dancing and Singing with Jesus in the *Gospel of the Savior* and the *Dance of the Savior around the Cross*." *Early Christianity* 3: 229–48.

Plisch, U.-K. 2005. "Zu einigen Einleitungsfragen des Unbekannten Berliner Evangeliums (UBE)." *ZAC* 9: 64–84.

Poirier, J. C. and J. Peterson eds. 2015. *Marcan Priority Without Q: Explorations in the Farrer Hypothesis*. LNTS 455. London: T & T Clark.

Popkes, E. E. 2006. "About the Differing Approach to a Theological Heritage: Comments on the Relationship between the Gospel of John, the Gospel of Thomas, and Qumran." Pages 281–318 in *The Bible and the Dead Sea Scrolls, vol. 3: The Scrolls and Christian Origins*. Edited by J. H. Charlesworth. Waco, TX: Baylor University Press.

Porter, S. E. 2001. "*P.Oxy* 655 and James Robinson's Proposals for Q: Brief Points of Clarification." *JTS* 52.1: 84–92.

–. 2015. *John, His Gospel, and Jesus: In Pursuit of the Johannine Voice*. Grand Rapids: Eerdmans.

Preuschen, E. 1918. *Untersuchungen zum Diatessaron Tatians*. Heidelberg: C. Winter.

Puig, A. 2008. *Un Jesús desconocido: las claves del evangelio gnóstico de Tomás*. Barcelona: Ariel.

Quispel, G. 1957. "The Gospel of Thomas and the New Testament." *VC* 11: 189–207.

–. 1958. "Some Remarks on the Gospel of Thomas." *NTS* 5: 276–90.

–. 1959. "L'Évangile selon Thomas et le Diatessaron." *VC* 13: 87–117.

–. 1960. "L'Évangile selon Thomas et le 'Texte Occidental' du Nouveau Testament." *VC* 14: 204–15.

–. 1966. "Gospel of Thomas and the Gospel of the Hebrews." *NTS* 12: 371–82.

Reed, A. Y. 2002. "ΕΥΑΓΓΕΛΙΟΝ: Orality, Textuality, and the Christian Truth in Irenaeus' *Adversus Haereses*." *VC* 56: 11–46.

Reynders, B. 1954. *Lexique compare du texte grec et des versions latine, arménienne et syriaque de l'«Adversus haereses» de Saint Irénée*. Leuven: Imprimerie Orientaliste Durbecq.

Roberts, C. H. 1953. "An Early Papyrus of the First Gospel." *HTR* 1953: 233–37.

–. 1955. *Greek Literary Hands: 350 B.C.–A.D. 400*. Oxford: Clarendon Press.

–. 1963. *Buried Books in Antiquity*. Letchworth: Garden City Press.

–. 1979. *Manuscript, Society and Belief in Early Christian Egypt*. Oxford: Oxford University Press.

Robinson, J. M. 2004. "The Nag Hammadi Gospels and the Fourfold Gospel." Pages 69–87 in *The Earliest Gospels: The Origins and Transmission of the Earliest Christian Gospels - the Contribution of the Chester Beatty Gospel Codex P45*. Edited by C. Horton. London: T & T Clark.

–. 2011. *The Story of the Bodmer Papyri: From the First Monastery's Library in Upper Egypt to Geneva and Dublin*. Eugene, OR: Cascade Books.

Robinson, J. M. and C. Heil. 1998. "Zeugnisse eines schriftlichen, griechischen vorkanonischen Textes: Mt 6,26 א*, *P.Oxy* 655 I,1–17 (EvTh 36) und Q 12,27." *ZNW* 89: 30–44.

Rodriguez, J. A. 2017. "All that Yahweh Has Commanded We Will Obey": The Public Reading of Torah as Covenant Praxis in Early Judaism." *Journal of the Jesus Movement in its Jewish Setting* 4: 91–117.

–. 2020. "Justin and the Apostolic Memoirs: Public Reading as Covenant Praxis." *Early Christianity* 11: 496–515.

290 *Bibliography*

Rohrbach, P. 1894. *Der Schluss des Markusevangeliums, der Vier-Evangelien-Kanon und die Kleinasiatischen Presbyter.* Berlin: Georg Nauck (Fritz Rühe).

Roth, D. T. 2008. "Matthean Texts and Tertullian's Accusations in *Adversus Marcionem.*" *JTS* 59.2: 580–97.

–. 2017a. "Marcion's Gospel and the Synoptic Problem in Recent Scholarship." Pages 265–80 in *Gospel Interpretation and the Q-Hypothesis.* Edited by M. Müller and H. Omerzu. LNTS 573. London: T & T Clark.

–. 2017b. "The Link between Luke and Marcion's Gospel: Prolegomena and Initial Considerations." Pages 59–82 in *Luke on Jesus, Paul, and Earliest Christianity.* Edited by J. S. Kloppenborg and J. Verheyden. Leuven: Peeters.

Rowe, C. K. 2009. *World Upside Down: Reading Acts in the Graeco-Roman Age.* Oxford: Oxford University Press.

Royse, J. 2008. *Scribal Habits in Early Greek New Testament Papyri.* NTTSD 36. Leiden: Brill.

Schmid, U. B. 2002. "Marcions Evangelium und die neutestamentlichen Evangelien: Rückfragen zu Geschichte und Kanonisierung der Evangelienüberlieferung." Pages 67–77 in *Marcion and His Impact on Church History.* Texte und Untersuchungen 150. Edited by G. May and K. Greschat. Berlin: De Gruyter.

–. 2003. "In Search of Tatian's Diatessaron in the West." *VC* 57: 176–99.

–. 2005. *Unum ex Quattuor: Eine Geschichte der lateinischen Tatianüberlieferung.* Aus der Geschichte der lateinischen Bibel. Freiburg im Breisgau: Herder.

–. 2013. "The Diatessaron of Tatian." Pages 115–42 in *The Text of the New Testament in Contemporary Research: Essays on the Status Quaestionis.* Edited by B. D. Ehrman and M. W. Holmes. NTTSD 42. Leiden: Brill.

Schmidt, C. 1931. "Die neuesten Bibelfunde aus Ägypten." *ZNW* 30: 285–293.

–. 1933. "Die Evangelienhandschrift der Chester Beatty-Sammlung." *ZNW* 32: 225–32.

Schnabel, E. J. 2018. *Jesus in Jerusalem: The Last Days.* Grand Rapids: Eerdmans.

Schrage, W. 1964. *Das Verhältnis des Thomas-Evangeliums zur synoptischen Tradition und zu den koptischen Evangelienübersetzungen: Zugleich ein Beitrag zur gnostischen Synoptikerdeutung.* BZNW 29. Berlin: de Gruyter.

Schramm, T. 1971. *Der Markus-Stoff bei Lukas.* SNTSMS 14. Cambridge: Cambridge University Press.

Schröter, J. 2007. *Von Jesus zum Neuen Testament: Studien zur urchristlichen Theologiegeschichte und zur Entstehung des neutestamentlichen Kanons.* WUNT 204. Tübingen: Mohr Siebeck.

–. 2018a. "Jesus and Early Christian Identity Formation: Reflections on the Signficance of the Jesus Figure in Early Christian Gospels." Pages 233–55 in *Connecting Gospels: Beyond the Canonical/Non-Canonical Divide.* Edited by F. Watson and S. Parkhouse. Oxford: Oxford University Press.

–. 2018b. "Memory and Memories in Early Christianity: The Remembered Jesus as a Test Case." Pages 79–96 in *Memory and Memories in Early Christianity. Proceedings of the International Conference held at the University of Geneva and Lausanne (June 2–3, 2016).* Edited by S. Butticaz and E. Norelli. WUNT 398. Tübingen: Mohr Siebeck.

–. 2019a. "Gospels in the First and Second Century and the Origin of the 'Fourfold Gospel': A Critical Appraisal of Francis Watson's *Gospel Writing.*" Pages 90–101 in *Writing the Gospels: A Dialogue with Francis Watson.* Edited by C. Sider Hamilton. LNTS 606. London: T & T Clark.

–. 2019b. "Thomas under den Evangelisten: Zum Ort des Thomasevangeliums in der frühchristlichen Literatur." Pages 193–216 in *Gospels and Gospel Traditions in the Second*

Century: Experiments in Reception. Edited by J. Schröter, T. Nicklas, and J. Verheyden. BZNW 235. Berlin: de Gruyter.

Schröter, J., T. Nicklas, and J. Verheyden eds. 2019. *Gospels and Gospel Traditions in the Second Century: Experiments in Reception.* BZNW 235. Berlin: de Gruyter

Schulthess, F. 1903. *Lexicon Syropalaestinum.* Berlin: Reimer.

Sieber, J. H. 1965. "A Redactional Analysis of the Synoptic Gospels with Regard to the Question of the Sources of the Gospel according to Thomas." Dissertation: Claremont Graduate School.

Sigel, D. and H. Cancik-Lindemaier. 2002. "Allegoresis." Pages 511–16 in *Brill's New Pauly, Antiquity, Volume 1 (A—Ari).* Edited by H. Cancik and H. Schneider. Leiden: Brill.

Sim, D. C. 2011. "Matthew's Use of Mark: Did Matthew Intend to Supplement or to Replace His Primary Source?" *NTS* 57: 176–92.

Skarsaune, O. 2007. "Justin and His Bible." Pages 53–76, 179 in *Justin Martyr and His Worlds.* Edited by S. Parvis and P. Foster. Minneapolis: Fortress.

Skeat, T. C. 1938. "The Lilies of the Field." *ZNW* 37: 211–14.

–. 1993. "A Codicological Analysis of the Chester Beatty Papyrus Codex of Gospels and Acts (P45)." *Hermathena* 155: 27–43.

–. 1994. "The Origin of the Christian Codex." *ZPE* 102: 263–68.

–. 1997. "The Oldest Manuscript of the Four Gospels?" *NTS* 43: 1–34.

–. 2004. *The Collected Biblical Writings of T. C. Skeat.* Edited by J. K. Elliott. NovTSup 113. Leiden: Brill.

Smith, D. M. 2000. "When Did the Gospels Become Scripture?" *JBL* 119.1: 3–20.

–. 2001. *John among the Gospels.* Columbia: University of South Carolina Press.

Smith, G. S. and B. C. Landau. 2019. "Canonical and Apocryphal Writings Copied by the Same Scribe: *P.Oxy.* II 209 (=P10), *P.Oxy.* II 210, and the Archive of Aurelius Leonides." *ETL* 95.1: 143–60.

Smith, W. A. 2014. *A Study of the Gospels in Codex Alexandrinus: Codicology, Palaeography, and Scribal Hands.* NTTSD 48. Leiden: Brill.

Snodgrass, K. 1989. "The Gospel of Thomas: A Secondary Gospel." *SecCent* 7: 19–38.

Stanton, G. 1992. "Matthew: βίβλιος, εὐαγγέλιον, or βίος?" Pages 1187–1202 in *The Four Gospels, 1992: Festschrift Frans Neirynck.* Edited by C. M. Tuckett, F. van Segbroeck, G. Van Belle, and J. Verheyden. BETL 100. Leuven: Peeters.

–. 1997. "The Fourfold Gospel." *NTS* 43: 317–46.

–. 2001. "The Early Reception of Matthew's Gospel: New Evidence from Papyri?" Pages 42–61 in *The Gospel of Matthew in Current Study: Studies in Memory of William G. Thompson, S.J.* Edited by D. E. Aune. Grand Rapids: Eerdmans.

–. 2004. *Jesus and Gospel.* Cambridge: Cambridge University Press.

Streeter, B. H. 1936. *The Four Gospels: Treating of the Manuscript Tradition, Sources, Authorship, & Dates.* London: MacMillan and Co.

Sundberg, A. C. 1968. "Towards A Revised History of the New Testament Canon." *Studia Evangelica* 4: 452–61.

Tellbe, M. 2009. *Christ-Believers in Ephesus: A Textual Analysis of Early Christian Identity Formation in a Local Perspective.* WUNT 242. Tübingen: Mohr Siebeck.

Theissen, G. 1991. *The Gospels in Context: Social and Political History in the Synoptic Tradition.* Translated by Linda M. Maloney. Philadelphia: Fortress Press.

Thompson, M. B. 1998. "The Holy Internet: Communication between Churches in the First Christian Generation." Pages 49–70 in *The Gospels for All Christians: Rethinking the Gospel Audiences.* Edited by R. Bauckham. Grand Rapids: Eerdmans.

Thornton, C.-J. 1993. "Justin und das Markusevangelium." *ZNW* 84: 93–110.

292 *Bibliography*

Thyen, H. 2005. *Das Johannesevangelium*. Handbuch zum Neuen Testament. Tübingen: Mohr Siebeck.

Torrey, C. C. 1941. *Documents of the Primitive Church*. New York: Harper & Brothers.

Trobisch, D. 1996. *Die Endredaktion des Neuen Testament. Eine Untersuchung zur Entstehung der christlichen Bibel*. Göttingen: Vandenhoeck & Ruprecht.

–. 2000. *The First Edition of the New Testament*. Oxford: Oxford University Press.

Tuckett, C. 1988. "Thomas and the Synoptics." *NovT* 30: 132–57.

–. 2005. "Forty Other Gospels." Pages 238–53 in *The Written Gospel*. Edited by M. Bockmuehl and D. A. Hagner. Cambridge: Cambridge University Press.

Turner, E. G. 1968. *Greek Papyri: An Introduction*. Oxford: Clarendon Press.

–. 1977. *The Typology of the Early Codex*. Philadelphia: University of Pennsylvania Press.

Tyson, J. B. 2006. *Marcion and Luke-Acts: A Defining Struggle*. Columbia, SC: University of South Carolina Press.

Van Belle, G. 2009. "L'unité littéraire et les deux finales du quatrième évangile." Pages 279–315 in *Studien zu Matthäus und Johannes / Études sur Matthieu et Jean. Festschrift für Jean Zumstein zu seinem 65. Geburstag / Mélanges offerts à Jean Zumstein pour son 65e anniversaire*. Edited by A. Dettwiler and U. Poplutz. Zürich: Theologischer Verlag Zürich.

van den Hoek, A. 1997. "The 'Catechetical' School of Early Christian Alexandria and Its Philonic Heritage." *HTR* 90.1: 59–87

van Haelst, J. 1976. *Catalogue des papyrus littéraires juifs et chrétiens*. Paris: Publications de la Sorbonne.

Van Rossum-Steenbeek, M. 1998. *Greek Readers' Digests? Studies on a Selection of Subliterary Papyri*. Mnemosyne: Bibliotheca Classica Batavia. Leiden: Brill.

Verheyden, J. 2017. Four Gospels *Indeed*, but Where is Mark? On Irenaeus' Use of the Gospel of Mark. Pages 169–204 in *Irénée de Lyon et les Débuts de la Bible Chrétienne: Actes de la Journée du 1.VII.2014 À Lyon*. Edited by A. Bastit and J. Verheyden. Turnhout: Brepols.

Vinzent, M. 2014. *Marcion and the Dating of the Synoptic Gospels*. Studia Patristica Supplements. Leuven: Peeters.

Walsh, R. F. 2021. *The Origins of Early Christian Literature: Contextualizing the New Testament within Greco-Roman Literary Culture*. Cambridge: Cambridge University Press.

Wasserman, T. 2005. "Papyrus 72 and the Bodmer Miscellaneous Codex." *NTS* 51: 137–54.

–. 2010. "A Comparative Textual Analysis of P4 and P64+67." *TC: A Journal of Biblical Textual Criticism* 15: 1–26.

–. 2012. "The Early Text of Matthew." Pages 83–107 in *The Early Text of the New Testament*. Edited by C. E. Hill and M. J. Kruger. Oxford: Oxford University Press.

–. 2014. "P45 and Codex W in Mark Revisited." Pages 130–56 in *Mark, Manuscripts, and Monotheism: Essays in Honor of Larry W. Hurtado*. Edited by C. Keith and D. Roth. LNTS 528. London: T & T Clark.

Watson, F. 2013. *Gospel Writing: A Canonical Perspective*. Grand Rapids: Eerdmans.

–. 2016. "Towards a Redaction-Critical Reading of the Diatessaron Gospel." *Early Christianity* 7: 95–112.

–. 2018. "A Gospel of the Eleven: The *Epistula Apostolorum* and the Johannine Tradition." Pages 189–215 in *Connecting Gospels: Beyond the Canonical/Non-Canonical Divide*. Edited by F. Watson and S. Parkhouse. Oxford: Oxford University Press.

–. 2019a. "Harmony or Gospel? On the Genre of the (So-called) Diatessaron." Page 69–92 in *The Gospel of Tatian: Exploring the Nature and Text of the Diatessaron*. Edited by M. R. Crawford and N. J. Zola. RJT 3. London: T & T Clark.

–. 2019b. "On the Miracle Catena in *Epistula Apostolorum* 4–5." Pages 107–27 in *Gospels and Gospel Traditions in the Second Century: Experiments in Reception*. Edited by J. Schröter, T. Nicklas, and J. Verheyden. BZNW 235. Berlin: de Gruyter.

–. 2020. *An Apostolic Gospel: The "Epistula Apostolorum" in Literary Context*. SNTSMS 179. Cambridge: Cambridge University Press.

Watson, F. and S. Parkhouse eds. 2018. *Connecting Gospels: Beyond the Canonical/Non-Canonical Divide*. Oxford: Oxford University Press.

Watson, F. and S. Parkhouse. 2018. Introduction. Pages 1–11 in *Connecting Gospels: Beyond the Canonical/Non-Canonical Divide*. Edited by F. Watson and S. Parkhouse. Cambridge: Cambridge University Press.

Wellhausen, J. 1909. *Das Evangelium Marci übersetzt und erklärt*. Berlin: G. Reimer.

Whittaker, J. 1989. "The Value of Indirect Tradition in the Establishment of Greek Philosophical Texts, or the Art of Misquotation." Pages 63–95 in *Editing Greek and Latin Texts*. Edited by J. Grant. New York: AMS Press.

Williams, P. J. 2012. "The Syriac Versions of the New Testament." Pages 143–66 in *The Text of the New Testament in Contemporary Research: Essays on the Status Quaestionis*. Edited by B. D. Ehrman and M. W. Holmes. NTTSD 42. Leiden: Brill.

Wilson, R. M. 1960. *Studies in the Gospel of Thomas*. London: Mowbray.

Windisch, H. 1926. *Johannes und die Synoptiker: Wollte der vierte Evangelist die älteren Evangelien ergänzen oder ersetzen?* Untersuchungen zum Neuen Testament. Leipzig: Hinrich.

Wolter, M. 2016. *The Gospel According to Luke: Volume 1 (Luke 1-9:50)*. Translated by W. Coppins and C. Heilig. Waco, TX: Baylor University Press.

Yarbo Collins, A. 2007. *Mark: A Commentary*. Hermeneia. Minneapolis: Fortress Press.

Young, F. M. 1997. *Biblical Exegesis and the Formation of Christian Culture*. Cambridge: Cambridge University Press.

Zahn, T. 1881. *Tatian's Diatessaron*. Forschungen zur Geschichte des neutestamentlichen Kanons und der altkirchlichen Literatur. Erlangen: Andreas Deichert.

Zelyck, L. R. 2013. *John among the Other Gospels: The Reception of the Fourth Gospel in the Extra-Canonical Gospels*. WUNT 2.347. Tübingen: Mohr Siebeck.

Zervos, G. T. 1994. "Dating the Protevangelium of James: The Justin Martyr Connection." *SBLSP* 33: 415–34.

Zola, N. J. 2016. "Evangelizing Tatian: The *Diatessaron*'s Place in the Emergence of the Fourfold Gospel Canon." *PRSt* 43: 399–414.

Index of References

Old Testament and Jewish Literature

Genesis
3.21 — 162

Exodus
24.1–11 — 139
26.31–37 — 154

Numbers
2.1–34 — 154
21.8–9 — 134

Deuteronomy
17.6 — 68
19.15 — 68
31.9–13 — 139

Joshua
8.34–45 — 139

2 Kings
23.1–3 — 139

Nehemiah
8.1–18 — 139

Psalms
21.19 (LXX) — 137
68.22 (LXX) — 173
80.1 — 147

Isaiah
2.3 — 136
6.1–6 — 147, 153
6.10 — 134

Ezekiel

1–2 — 147, 153
10 — 146

Micah
4.2 — 136
5.2 — 137

Zechariah
12.10–14 — 134

2 Maccabees
1.111 — 1
1.1–5 — 51
1.1–9 — 51
2.19–32 — 51
2.23 — 119
2.23–31 — 51
2.26 — 51
3–15 — 51
8.23 — 201

1 Esdras
5.48 — 201
7.6 — 201
7.9 — 201

Bel and the Dragon
19–20 — 58

Letter of Aristeas
311 — 139

Josephus

Against Apion
1.13 — 119

Bibliography

2.169 — 139

De Bello Judaico
1.1–3 — 119
7.11.5 — 117

Jewish Antiquities
1 — 117
1.24 — 117
1.26.3 — 201
1.82.4 — 201
3.81.3 — 201
4.209–11 — 139
9.46.5 — 201
10.58.2 — 201
11.3.10 — 117
14.10.26 — 117
14.10.9 — 117
16.43–44 — 139

Vita
6 — 117

Philo

De Abrahamo
117.4 — 201
258.1 — 201

De Aeternitate Mundi
19.3 — 201

De Cherubim
124.3 — 201

De Decalogo
1.2 — 201
155.1 — 201

De Specialibus Legibus
2.151.1 — 201

De Virtutibus
201.2 — 201

De Vita Mosis
2.11.1 — 201
2.36.4 — 201

Hypothetica (Philo)
7.9–14 — 139

Mishnah

m.Ber.
9.5 — 139

m.Meg.
3.5 — 139
4.1–5 — 139

m.Yoma
7.1 — 139
7.8 — 139

Qumran
1QS
5.20–23 — 139
6.7–8 — 139
1QSa
1.1–5 — 139

Talmud
y.Meg.
4.1, 75a — 139

New Testament

GMatthew
1.1 — 187
1.1–17 — 45
1.1–18 — 197
1.17 — 163
1.18 — 12, 103

2.1–12 — 79, 173
2.13–21 — 79
3.1–5 — 104
3.1–6 — 137
3.9 — 191, 194
3.11 — 137, 198, 228

Index of References

3.12	198	10.1–15	109
3.13–17	104, 137	10.5–6	70
3.15	191	10.15	145
3.15	194	10.17–22	183
3.16	85, 137	10.17–32	177, 182
3.16–17	173	10.18	184
4.1	80	10.19	184
4.23	117	10.24	145
5.3	38, 98	10.24–25	183
5.4	165	10.25–32	177
5.10	145, 165	10.26	22, 187
5.15	22	10.26–33	183
5.17	161	10.28	165
5.17–18	145	10.30	184
5.18	10	10.32	165
5.20–22	191, 194	10.32–33	183
5.21	197	10.37	38
5.21–48	9, 79	11.11	165
5.25	193	11.25–27	145, 171
5.25–28	191, 194	11.27	135, 150
5.28	162	11.28	171
5.32	165	12.1–8	95
5.44	145	12.6	43
5.44–46	102	12.9–14	55
6.9	165	12.13	55
6.13	145	12.25	171
6.25	27	12.32	81
6.25–26	11	12.47–50	35, 104
6.26	165	12.48	35
6.27	27	12.50	165
6.28	203, 204	13.11	165
6.32	165	13.24–30	21, 22
6.33	165	13.31–32	38
7.1	165	13.45–46	35
7.1–2	145	13.52	117
7.7–8	35	13.54–58	12
7.21	165	14.13–21	63, 165
7.22–23	11	14.15	228
7.26	145	14.28–33	103
8.28–34	63	16.7	178
9.1–8	95	16.13	92
9.9	80, 104	16.13–20	43
9.9–13	95	16.16	12, 103
9.14–17	34, 95	16.17	22
9.20–22	55	16.26	165
9.20–34	109	17.24–27	54, 79
9.22	165	18.3	39, 165
9.27–31	81	18.10–20	91
9.35	117	18.11–12	162

Index of References

18.15–17	54, 87		27.33	64
18.16	68		27.34	173
18.22	86		27.38	55, 64
19.3	161		27.48	173
19.6	161		27.60–61	64
19.6–8	145		28.1	64
19.8	165		28.1–8	98
19.9	165		28.12–13	98
19.16	88, 161		28.19	70, 113
19.16–22	87		28.19–20	9
19.16–30	164		28.20	178
20.24–32	215			
20.28	66, 90		*GMark*	
20.29–34	95		1.1	117
20.34	95		1.1–4	149
21.1–11	96		1.2	12, 103
21.12–17	96		1.2–8	137
21.13–19	215		1.4–5	104
21.23	171		1.5–6	104
21.28–32	79		1.7	198, 228
21.31	165		1.9–11	104, 137
22.32	43		1.12	80, 94
23.1–39	10		1.14	113, 117
23.8–9	55		1.15	80, 94, 117
23.8–12	70, 71		1.15–19	96
23.34	117		2.1–12	95
23.35	84		2.13–17	95
24.14	117		2.14	80, 104
24.31	154		2.14–28	94
24.40	39		2.18–20	33
25.1–12	55		2.18–22	95
25.14–30	79		2.23–28	95
25.41–26.17	215		2.25	204
25.42	211		2.28	204
26.6–13	97		3.1–6	55
26.7–8	194		3.2	204
26.7–33	191		3.5	55
26.10	194		3.14	104
26.13	117		3.17	102, 136
26.14–15	194		3.18	81
26.17	104		3.20–35	82
26.18–39	215		3.28	81
26.22–23	194		3.32–35	35, 104
26.24	145		3.33	35
26.31	193, 195, 197		4.8	81
26.31–33	194		4.11	165
26.41	145		4.21	22
26.51	184		4.22	22
26.55	184		4.26–29	21, 82

4.31–32	38	13.11	184
4.46–50	212	13.14	116
5.21–34	55	13.17	161
5.21–43	82	13.27	154
5.22–43	145	14.1–11	82
5.25–34	109	14.3–9	97
5.26	81	14.12	104
5.30	81	14.21	145
5.31	55	14.27	195
5.34	165	14.38	145
6.2–6	12	14.47	184
6.3	173	14.51–52	83
6.7–12	109	14.53–72	82
6.7–32	82	15.22	64
6.32–44	63, 165	15.27	55, 64
6.36	228	15.34	145
6.45–52	103	15.40	83
7.1–23	10	15.46–47	64
7.31–37	82	16.1	56, 64, 83, 103
8.22–26	81	16.1–8	98
8.25	81	16.2	227
8.27–30	43	16.8	99
8.35	117		
8.38	183	*LEMark*	
9.25	81	16.9	99, 113
9.35	145	16.9–13	99
10.2	161	16.9–20	111, 112
10.5	165	16.10	64
10.9	161	16.11	113
10.11	165	16.15	64
10.15	39	16.15–16	82
10.17	88, 161, 171	16.17–18	82
10.17–22	87		
10.17–31	74, 103, 129, 158,	*GLuke*	
	164, 165	1.1–4	118, 127, 128
10.21	81	1.5	104
10.29	117	1.5–25	12, 79, 94, 150
10.38	171	1.17	12, 103
10.46	82	1.26–38	55, 150
10.46–52	95	1.42	150
10.50	82	1.57–66	150
10.52	95	1.58–2.7	191
11.1–10	96	1.58–59	194
11.20–21	82	1.62–2.1	194
12.13–17	33	1.80	197
12.23	161	2.1	197
12.27	43	2.6–7	194
13.9	184	2.7	55
13.9–13	183	2.8–14	150

2.11	109	6.12	197
2.15–20	150	6.12–16	231
2.22–38	150	6.20	20, 38, 98
2.25–38	145	6.21	165
2.41–50	79	6.24–26	150
2.41–52	150	6.27	145
2.49	171	6.28	204
3.1–2	150, 163	6.36–38	145
3.1–3	104	6.37	165
3.1–6	137	6.40	145, 183
3.8–4.2	191, 194	6.46	165
3.11	228	6.49	145
3.15–16	137	7.28	165
3.16	198	7.30	119
3.17	197	7.36–50	97, 151
3.18	197, 198, 226	8.2	113
3.21	197, 231	8.8	81
3.21–22	104	8.16	22
3.23	104, 145, 150, 153, 197	8.17	22
		8.20–21	35, 104
3.23–38	198	8.26–39	63
4.1, 80	197	8.43–48	55
4.16–31	91	8.43–56	109
4.19	145	8.45	55, 81
4.23–27	12	8.46	55
4.29–32	194	8.48	165
4.29–5.8	191	9.1–2	104
4.30	91	9.10–17	63, 165
4.34–35	194	9.18–21	43
5.1–11	95, 150	9.25	165
5.3–8	194	9.26	183
5.17–26	95	9.57–62	145
5.27	104	10.1–13	109
5.30–33	95	10.6	212
5.30–6.16	194	10.12	145
5.33–35	22, 33, 39, 195	10.22	150
5.33–39	95	10.25–37	80
5.36	197	11.2	165
5.36–39	22, 195	11.4	145
6.1	197	11.5–8	151
6.1–5	95	11.9–10	35
6.3	204	11.27–28	21
6.4	66	11.33	22
6.4–10	90	11.37–52	10
6.5	204	11.46	212
6.6	197	11.50	212
6.6–11	55	12.2–9	183
6.7	204	12.5	165
6.10	55	12.6–7	184

12.10	81	21.12–19	183
12.13–14	21, 22	21.23	161
12.13–21	87, 151	22.4	226
12.15–21	21, 22	22.15	104
12.22	27	22.43–44	90
12.22–24	11	22.44–64	177, 182, 183
12.24	165	22.51	184
12.25	27	22.53	184
12.30	165	23.27–31	21
12.31	165	23.32–33	55
12.38	165	23.33	64
12.50	171, 172	23.51	119
13.1–5	80	23.54–55	64
13.6–9	151	24.1	56, 64, 227
13.10–17	150	24.1–8	98
13.18–19	20	24.3	55, 64
13.24	212	24.11	113
13.26–27	11	24.12	64, 99, 227
14.1–6	150	24.13–32	98
14.7–11	150	24.13–35	99, 151
14.12–24	151	24.36	228
14.21	151	24.40	228
14.26	38	24.41–43	98
15.1–32	80	24.47–48	9
16.19–31	80, 87, 151	24.51	226
17.4	86, 87		
17.5–6	151	*GJohn*	
17.11–19	151	1.1	145, 147, 226
17.18–19	38	1.1–5	12, 78, 94
17.28	161	1.1–14	145
17.34	39	1.1–53	149
18.1–8	151	1.3	171
18.8	161	1.6	225
18.9–14	151	1.13	12, 103, 134
18.10–14	80	1.13–14	12, 103
18.17	39	1.14	54, 134
18.18	88, 161, 171, 226	1.14–18	147, 154
18.18–23	87	1.15	225
18.18–30	164	1.19	225
18.34	95	1.20	134, 137
18.35–43	81	1.23	44
18.35–45	95	1.26	225
19.1–10	151	1.27	228
19.28–44	96	1.37–41	35
19.42	171, 172	1.41	44
19.45–48	96	1.44	225
20.9–16	22	2.1–11	54, 60, 78
20.35	161	2.11–22	180
20.38	43	2.12	60

2.13	95	10.7–11.57	219
2.13–20	96	10.8	79
2.13–22	96	10.13	225
2.13–7.36	95	10.14–16	103
3.1–21	78	10.22–23	95, 96
3.3	134	10.22–42	79
3.5	134, 165	10.31–39	68
3.14	44, 134	11.1–12.11	67
3.27	225	11.1–46	79
3.28	134	11.5–12.2	68
4.1	69	11.55	96
4.1–26	103	12.1	69, 95
4.1–42	78	12.1–8	96, 97
4.6	173	12.4	69
4.8	69	12.21	225
5.1	95	12.38–41	44
5.1–18	96	12.40	134
5.1–47	68	12.49	54
5.1–9	103	13.1–30	10
5.2	225	13.16	183
5.4	66, 90	14.2	125
5.39	8, 43, 44	16.23–24	35
5.40–44	8	16.33	79
5.45	8	17.1	79
6.1	69, 97	18.37	44
6.1–13	63	19.3	44
6.1–15	96, 165	19.13	134, 137
6.3	69	19.17–18	64
6.4	95	19.18	55
6.5	228	19.24	44, 137
6.16–21	103	19.34–37	173
6.17	69	19.35–37	44
6.22	69	19.37	134
6.48–58	74	19.40–41	64
7.1–2	95	20.1	64, 227
7.1–19	96	20.1–10	98
7.1–52	10	20.1–18	173
7.2	95	20.2	68
7.2–31	78	20.3	228
7.10	69, 95	20.3–8	44
7.21–30	68	20.3–10	99
7.37	96	20.5	64
8.20–59	68	20.9	44
8.44	145	20.11	68
8.56	145	20.11–18	98, 113
8.57	97, 152	20.19	228
8.58	147	20.19–29	54
9.1–34	81	20.20	228
9.10	225	20.21	9

20.24–29	68, 98, 113
20.25	138
20.25–27	173
20.27	138
20.30–31	44, 120
21.14	69
21.15–19	44
21.15–23	79
21.19–23	79
21.24–25	44, 79, 120
21.25	96

Acts of the Apostles

1.16–26	218
2.23	119
4.28	119
5.38	119
7.12	211
7.42	201
9.29	119
10.34–43	75
13.36	119
14.15–23	212, 219
15.21	139
17.9–17	212, 219
19.13	119
20.27	119

Romans

1.1–7	203

1 Corinthians

4.14–15	71
12.28	71

2 Corinthians

3.14–15	139
11.3	162
13.1	68

Galatians

3.28	162

Ephesians

4.11	71

4.24	162

Philippians

3.20	162

Hebrews

10.28–29	68

1 John

1.1	69
2.1	71
2.12–14	71
2.18	71
2.28	71
3.7	71
4.2–3	145
5.21	71

2 John

1	71
4	71
7	145

Revelation

4	147
4.5	147
4.6–8	147
4.6–11	155
4–5	147, 154
5.9	147
6.2	147
7.1	147
7.1–4	154
7.9	147
8.5	147
9.14–15	147
11.19	147, 155
14.1–3	155
14.6	147
15.5–8	155
15–16	147
16.18	147
20.8	147

Noncanonical Gospel Literature

Diatessaronic Witnesses

Arabic Harmony

1.1–5	78
1.6–26	79
3.1–12	79
3.13–23	79
3.24–36	79
5.22–32	78
5.43	80
8.26–39	98
8.50–9.21	79
14.45–48	97
16.49–52	82
21.1	82
21.8–46	78
23.26–30	81
25.4–7	79
26.1–33	80
27.31–35	80
28.1–32	78
29.14–26	80
32.1–11	96
32.16–21	80
32.27–47	78
33.35–39	79
34.26–45	80
37	96
37.25–45	79
37.46–38.30	79
39.1–17	97
39.18–45	96, 97
43.9–38	79
48.45–47	83
52.23	83
52.45–54.5	98
53.25–48	79
54.48	79
55.9–10	82

Codex Fuldensis

1.1–8	78
2–4	79
8	79
10	79

12	79
18	80
23–24	98
31–33	79
77	82
78	12
87	82
88	78
93	83
94	79
97–98	80
104	80
106	78
107	80
117	96, 97
118	96
119	80
120	78
124	79
129	80
135	79, 96
136	79, 96
138–39	97
149	79
150	79
171	83
174	83
174–79	98
180–81	79
182	82

Commentary on the Gospel (Ephrem)

1.1–27	12
1.3–5	78
1.9–24	79
1.26	95
2.5	90, 109
2.13	109
2.18–3.5	79
3.6–9	79
3.16	79
3.17	109
4.4	80, 93
4.5	85
4.6	80, 93
5.1–5	78

Index of References

5.13	80, 94	27	91
5.17	80		
5.17–24	94, 95	*Epistula Apostolorum*	
6.1	95	1.1–4	72
6.1–2	98	1.1–5	71
6.4–15	79	1.3–5	133
7.1–6	81	1.4	59
7.8	109	1.1–12.4	50
7.16	81	1.1–2.4	51
7.19	81	2.1–3	133
8.1	82, 109	2.2	72
10.5	81	2.3	72
10.8–10	97	3.1–2	65
11.12	81	3.1–8	60
11.23–25	12	3.4–5	65
11.24	91	3.9	60
12.1–5	96	3.10	54
12.16–20	78	3.10–12.4	50, 56, 59, 60, 65, 75
13.1–4	96	3.13	72
13.13	81	4.1–4	56, 65, 66
14.15	81	4.1–5.22	65
14.16–17	79	4.2–4	48
14.19–20	80	5.1	8, 54
14.22	86	5.1–20	63
14.24	91	5.3–7	61
14.25	80	5.10–12	63
14.28–29	78, 96	5.14–16	8
15.1	88	5.15–16	54
15.1–11	88	5.17–22	61, 73
15.6–8	81	5.21–34	61
15.12–13	80	6.1–8.2	60
15.23	95, 96	8.43–48	61
15.24	80	9.1	55
16.1–5	82, 94	9.3–10.2	67
16.11–15	78	9.4	56, 64
16.18	79	9.5	55
16.24	80	9.20–22	61
16.26	109	10.1–3	68
17.1–10	79	11.7	54
17.11–13	96, 97	12.3	68
18.1	96, 97	13.1–50.10	50
18.5–7	96	14.1	55
18.19	79	14.3	59
18.20	79	17.4	54
20.28	88	17.8	54
21.22–25	99	18.5	54
21.22–29	98	20.3	59
21.30	79	21.5	72
23.48	89	26	54

306 Index of References

30.1	70	17	43
30.2	72	18–19	43
30.3	64, 72	20	20, 21, 38
31.10–12	75	21	38
31.11	72, 133	22	33, 39, 43, 165
34–37	49	26	21, 27
36.4	59	30	91
39.12	54	31	20, 21, 26
41.3–7	70	33	20–22, 26
41.4–5	55, 70	36	27, 203, 204
41.6	70, 71	38	35, 43
41.7	71	39	21
42.2–4	70	44–45	20, 21, 26
43	55	46	165
43.16–17	73	46–47	38
48.1–3	54	47	20–22, 26, 195
51.1–4	50, 55	52	43
		54	20, 21
GEbionites		55	38
4	85	57	20, 21
		61	33, 38, 39
GJudas		63	21, 22
33.22–35.14	131	65	20, 21, 22, 26
35.14–36.10	131	66	20, 21, 26
37.20–42.24	131	69	165
42.25–58.6	131	72	21
		73	21
GPeter		79	21
3.7	138	82	35
4.10	55	86	21
4.12	137	92	35
5.16	173	94	35
6.21	137	99	20, 21, 26, 35, 43
7.25	89	100	33, 38
14.59–60	132	104	20, 21, 22, 26, 33, 39, 195
		113–114	43
GPhilip		114	20, 38, 39
69	39		
		Infancy Gospel of Thomas	
GThomas		6.9	48
2	35		
3	21, 43	*PJames*	
4	21, 27, 165	18.1	137
5	20, 21, 26, 187	19.1	137
10	27	21.3	137
12	38	22.1–24.4	90
13	20, 21, 22, 26, 38, 43		
14	20, 21, 26		

Index of References

Early Christian Literature

Early Christian Literature

2 Clement
1.2	10
5.5	35
9.11	35
12.2	33, 39
13.3–4	10

Aphrahat of Persia

Demonstrations
1.10	78
2.20	91
14.26	89
14.44	87
20.18	88

Acts of John
93	58

Acts of Peter
38	39

Acts of Philip
140	39

Acts of Thomas
136	35
147	39

Ad Diognetum
11.6	10
12.1	10

Athenagoras

Legatio pro Christianis
16	146

Clement of Alexandria

Ad Graecos (Clement)
1	146

Eclogae Propheticae
12.2	165

Excerpta ex Theodoto
14.3	165

Paedagogus
1.5.12.2–3	164
1.6	109
1.73.1	165
2.1	109
2.1.13.2	164
2.1.15.2–3	164
2.8.61.1–3	164
2.102.4	16

Protrepticus
82.3	165

Quis dives salvetur
3	129
3–5	74
4–5	88, 187
5	108, 157, 158
22	164
25	164
26	164
31.3	165
33.4	165

Stromateis
1.1.11.3	159, 169
1.1.14.2	159
1.1.14.3	159
1.21.145.2	164
1.21.145.2–3	163
1.21.147.2–6	199
1.21.147.4–6	163
1.44.3	221
2.9.45.5	34
2.146.2	165
3.6.45.2–46.1	161
3.6–13	33
3.9.64.1	67
3.10	161
3.11.71.3	160
3.13.92	39
3.13.92.2	161

308 Index of References

3.13.93.1	156, 157, 158
3.13.93.2–95.3	162
3.15.96.1	162
3.18.108.2	160
3.47.2	165
3.71.3	221
4.6.26.1	165
4.6.41.1–3	169
4.134.4	221
4.161.2	165
4.34.4	165
5.1.3.3	160
5.13.85.1	160
5.14.96.3	34
5.33.4	165
5.80.6	165
5.85.1	221
6.11.88.5	146, 160
6.15.125.3–4	146
6.94.2	165
7.1.1.4	160
7.16.94.1	160
7.16.95.4	160
7.16.95.6	160
7.17.106.4	159, 169
7.100.5	221
7.104.4	165

Cyprian

Testimonia ad Quirinium

1.18	9

Didascalia Apostolorum

10 (2.39)	107

Didymus the Blind

Commentary on the Psalms (Didymus)

88.8	36

Doctrine of Addai

folio 18	89
folio 23	106
folio 29	107

Epiphanius

Panarion

30.3.7	104
30.13.1–8	104
30.13.3–4	137
30.13.7–8	85
30.14.5	35, 104
30.16.4–5	104
30.22.4	104
46.1	85
51.20.3–4	66
51.21.4	66

Epistle to Flora

33.3.5–6	171
33.3.6	145
33.4.4–6	145
33.5.1	145

Ephrem the Syrian

Carmina Nisibena

35.16	91
43.22	91
59.13	91

Exposition of the Gospel (Ps.-Ephrem)

83	36

Hymni de Azymis

16.10–13	91

Hymni de Virginitate

14.12	91

Hymns of Paradise

22.1	106
53.14	106
65.1	106

Reproof (Ephrem)

1.445–51	106
2.1965	106

Sermo de Domino Nostro

21	91

Sermones de fide

2.39–40	67

Index of References

Eusebius

Ecclesiastical History

1.13	107
2.15.1–2	122–24, 137
3.24.5–13	121–23
3.24.5–8	116, 125–28, 137, 144, 166, 237
3.25	36
3.39.1–4	121
3.39.1–7	124
3.39.15–16	122–29, 137
3.39.2	144
3.39.3	129
3.39.4	125
4.14	144
5.8.1–4	125
5.11.2–3	163
5.20.4–8	144
5.20.6	147
5.24.6	145
5.24.16	145, 147
6.14.5–7	125, 163, 165, 237
6.25.3–14	125

Epistula ad Carpianum

3–14	59

Irenaeus

Adversus Haereses

1.2.3	74
1.3.2	145
1.3.3	73, 145
1.5–2.38	149
1.8.2–5	145
1.17.1–2	146
1.18–3.17	149
1.20.1,	57
1.20.1–21.2	171
1.20.2	73, 172
1.20.3	172
1.21.2	73
1.26.1	67
1.26.2	104, 239
1.26–27	199
2.14.1–5	146
2.14.6	146

2.15.1–3	146
2.22.1	145
2.22.3–6	97, 152
2.22.5	145
2.27.2	146
3.1–3	160
3.1.1	125, 143, 144, 147
3.3.4	147
3.4.4	145
3.5.1	143
3.9.1	149
3.9.1–3	149
3.10.1	149
3.10.1–4	149
3.10.5	149
3.10.6	12, 103, 144, 150
3.11.1	145, 149
3.11.1–6	149, 153
3.11.7	104, 153, 239
3.11.8	143, 147, 153, 155, 170
3.11.9	146
3.12.12	199
3.14.1	153
3.14.1–3	108
3.14.3–4	150
3.14.4	153
3.15.1	153
3.16.2	12, 103
3.16.2–3	108
3.19.2	12, 103
3.21.8–10	198
3.22.3	152
3.22.3–4	108
3.22.4	198
4.5.6	150
4.10.1	9
4.18.6	155
4.20.11	147
4.20.7–11	147, 154
4.21.3	147
4.22.2	153
4.26.5	147, 155
4.27.1	147, 155
4.27–32	145, 147
4.28.1	145
4.30.1	147, 155
4.30.4	147, 155
4.31.1	145, 147, 155

310 Index of References

4.32.1	147
4.32.1–2	147, 155
4.34.4	170
4.35.2	170
5.5.1	147, 155
5.9.4	170
5.33.3–4	147, 155
5.33.4	125, 144
5.35.2	154
5.36.2	125

Epideixis

74	153

Jerome

Commentary on Matthew

12.13	34, 85

De Viris Illustribus

25	102

Dialogus adversus Pelagianos

3.2	33, 34, 86

Epistles

121.6	102

Justin Martyr

Apologia I

15.14	11
15–17	116, 138
21.1	134
22.2	134
23.2	134
32.9	134
32–34	138
35	134, 137
35.7	137
38	138
39.1	139
45	111
45.5	139
49.5	139
52.12	134
61.4	134
66.3	11, 116, 135–38
67	10, 139

Dialogus cum Tryphone

14.8	134
24.1	136, 139
29	135
32.2	134
33.1	134
49	138
50	135
51	135
54.2	134
56	135
61.1	134
61.3	134
63.2	134
73	135
74	135
76.2	134
78.1–2	8
78.7–8	137
88.3	85, 137, 138
88.7	134
97	138
97.3	137
100	135, 138
100.1	135
100.4	138
100–108	136
101.3	138
103.5	138
103.7	138
103.8	11, 135
104.1	138
105.6	138
106	102
106.3	138
106.3–4	134, 136
106.4	138
107.1	138
109.2	136, 139
109–110	136
110.2	136, 139
122.5	136, 139
136	135

On the Origin of the World (Nag Hammadi)

104.35–105.19	154

Index of References

Origen

Commentary on John
5.7   103
5.8   221
6.109   9

Commentary on Matthew
15.14   87

Contra Celsum
1.1   199
1.34   173, 199
1.40   173
1.41   173
1.51   137
1.70   173
2.13   116
2.27   172
2.32   173
2.36   173
2.37   173
2.55   100
2.59   173
2.70   100
2.74   172
5.52   100, 173
6.16   88
6.36   173
7.13   173

Homilies on Jeremiah
27.3.7   36

Homilies on Joshua
4.3   36

Homilies on Luke
1.2   36

De Principiis
4.1.1   221

Polycarp

Philippians
2.3   145
5.2   145
7.1   145

7.2   145
12.3   145

Tatin

Oratio ad Graecos (Tatian)
12.1–3   146
42   92

Tertullian

Adversus Marcionem
1.1.6   160
1.19.2   169
4.1.1   221
4.2.2   109
4.6.1   221

De Monogamia
14   88

De Praescriptione Haereticorum
8.1–2   35

On Fasting (Tertullian)
10.3   116

Theodoret of Cyrus

Haereticarum fabularum compendium
1.20   107

Theophilus of Antioch

Ad Autolycum
2.9   146
2.10   146
2.22   102, 108
2.25   146
3.12   103
3.13   102
3.14   102
3.17   146
3.29   146

Thomas the Contender
140.41–43   35
145.10–16   35

Greco-Roman Sources

Aristoxenus

Elements of Harmony
2.32.19   119

Aulus Gellius

Attic Nights
17.2.1–2   28

Diodorus Siculus

Library of History
1.3.2   119
4.1.2   119

Dionysius of Halicarnassus

Antiquities
1.7.1   119
11.1   119

On Thucydides
9–12   119

Galen

Ars. Medica (Galen)
1.410.8   51

De placitis Hippocratis et Platonis
5.466.12   51
30.8–10   221

In Hippocratis de natura hominis librum commentaria
15.25.10–17   51

Isocrates
Philippus
2   119

Lucian

How to Write History
48   119
50   119
6   119

Polybius

Histories
1.15.13   119
2.37.4   119
3.1.4   119
12.28.3   119

Pliny

Epistulae
6.20   28

Ps.-Thessalus
De virtutibus herbarum
1   119

Strabo

Geographica
1.2.1   119
1   28
9.431   51

Papyri

BKT V.1	259, 262, 265		PSI 2.124	177
Chester Beatty VI	187, 201		PSI 2.126	210
GA 0242	181		PSI V.446	254
PSI 1.2	177		P.Amh. ii 24	180

Index of References

P.Baden iv 56	188, 201	P.Oxy. 210	203
P.Dura 2	257	P.Oxy. 2192	28
P.Dura 10		P.Oxy. 223	259, 262, 265
(Dura Fragment)	103	P.Oxy. 2256	28
P.Egerton 2	68	P.Oxy. 2321	265
P.Mich.inv. 3	259, 262	P.Oxy. 2341	259, 262
P.Berlin inv. 11863	176	P.Oxy. 2457	28
P.Berol. 7499	257	P.Oxy. 2612	263
P.Bodmer I	222	P.Oxy. 2832	257
P.Bodmer LVI	223	P.Oxy. 3227	190, 254, 256
P.Bodmer V	229	P.Oxy. 3509	190, 254, 256
P.Bodmer VIII	230	P.Oxy. 3829	28
P.Bodmer XXIV	224	P.Oxy. 3830	28
P.Bodmer		P.Oxy. 3917	254
XXV+IV+XXVI	224	P.Oxy. 4327	190, 254, 256
P.Egerton 2	8	P.Oxy. 655	21, 27, 45, 203, 205
P.Fay. 87	254	P.Oxy. 661	190, 254
P.Haun. 1.7	28	P.Oxy. 840	10, 205
P.Herm. 4	210, 223, 259, 262	P.Ryl. 1.16	254, 256
P.Herm. 5	210, 223, 259, 262	P.Ryl. 16	190
P.Mil.Vogl. 1.18	28	P.Ryl. 4.705	223
P.Oxy. 1	21, 45, 203, 205	P.Schubart 22	210
P.Oxy. 412	179	P.Vindob. G 36112	
P.Oxy. 654	21–27, 34, 40, 45,	(GA 0215)	180
	205	P.Vindob. G 39779	
P.Oxy. 1007	179, 180	(GA 059)	180
P.Oxy. 1010	179	P1	198
P.Oxy. 1012	259, 263	P37	217
P.Oxy. 1373	210	P46	200, 229
P.Oxy. 1620	257	P47	217
P.Oxy. 1621	180	P66	214, 229, 230
P.Oxy. 2	45, 203	P72	217
P.Oxy. 209	203		

Index of Modern Authors

Abakuks, A. 118
Aland, B. 132
Aland, K. 177, 179, 189
Alexander, L. 119, 143, 172
Allen, G. V. 118
Allert, C. 134
Allison, D. C. 201
Amphoux, C.-B. 112, 113
Arnal, W. E. 26
Ashwin-Siejkowksi, P. 156
Aune, D. E. 19
Ayres, L. 135, 142

Baarda, T. 87, 91, 94, 100, 110
Backhaus, K. 119
Bagnall, R. S. 192
Barker, D. 189, 254
Barker, J. W. 10, 17, 18, 79, 80, 83, 96,
    119, 134
Barrett, C. K. 219
Bauckham, R. 104, 120, 122, 123, 125,
    128, 130, 154
Baudoin, A.-C. 205
Baum, A. 129
Beale, G. K. 147, 154
Becker, E.-M. 127
Becker, J. 9
Beduhn, J. 152, 218
Behr, J. 142
Bell, H. I. 209
Bell, L. D. 226
Bellinzoni, A. 134, 138
Berglund, C. J. 73, 145, 171
Berthelot, K. 73
Best, E. 117
Bingham, D. J. 147
Bird, M. F. 1, 18, 70
Birdsall, J. N. 177
Bockmuehl, M. 73, 145, 239

Bodmer, M. 222
Bongard, O. 222
Bover, J. M. 177
Bovon, F. 118, 218
Braenker, J. 39, 131
Breytenbach, C. 127
Burke, T. 57
Butticaz, S. 3

Cameron, R. 20
Carlson, S. C. 36
Cavallo, G. 179 190, 201, 209
Chadwick, H. 173
Chapa, J. 2, 225
Charlesworth, S. D. 45, 177, 178, 181,
    182, 190–93, 197, 211, 213, 221, 230
Cirafesi, W. V. 139
Clarysse, W. 179, 180, 201, 209, 210,
    223, 253, 256
Climenhaga, N. 124
Collins, A. Y. 117
Colwell, E. C. 225
Comfort, P. W. 179, 189
Coogan, J. T. 4, 59, 92, 101, 153, 171,
    198, 241
Cook, J. G. 94, 173
Cosaert, C. P. 164
Cowan, A. T. 231
Crawford, M. R. 59, 67, 91, 95, 103,
    105, 108, 146
Crossan, J. D. 26
Cullmann, O. 20
Cuvigny, H. 192

Davies, S. L. 39
Davies, W. D. 201
Dawson, J. D. 166
Dawson, Z. K. 118
DeConick, A. 26

Index of Modern Authors

Di Luccio, P. 154
Dormandy, M. 191, 200, 202
Dorn, H.-J. 187

Edwards, J. R. 85
Edwards, S. A. 225, 228
Elliott, J. K. 182, 230
Epp, E. J. 113
Evans, C. A. 117

Fallon, F. T. 20
Farkasfalvy, D. 147
Fee, G. D. 225
Fewster, G. P. 139
Foster, P. 77, 90, 138
Fournet, J.-L. 223
Fowler, R. 117
Furlong, D. 124

Gamble, H. Y. 143, 182, 187
Gascou, J. 223
Gathercole, S. J. 8, 19–27, 39, 43, 92, 131, 189, 198–201, 257
Goodacre, M. 8, 9, 19–27, 103, 118, 127
Grant, R. M. 19
Graves, M. 34
Gregory, A. F. 8, 85, 88, 104, 111, 112, 218
Greschat, K. 138
Grunewald, W. 229

Haelst, van, J. 177, 179
Hannah, D. D. 48, 56, 65, 66, 72, 154
Harnack, A. von 218
Hartenstein, J. 48, 49, 132, 133
Hays, C. M. 152
Head, P. M. 190, 195, 224, 257
Heckel, T. 1
Heckel, T. K. 18, 201
Heil, C. 203
Heilmann, J. 211, 221
Henderson, S. W. 112
Hengel, M. 1, 6, 102, 111, 158, 199, 201
Hill, C. E. 1, 8, 44, 48, 49, 65, 66, 71, 83, 85, 88, 91, 120–25, 133, 134, 138, 145, 147, 158, 173, 188, 191–93, 232, 239
Hills, J. V. 49, 58, 72
Holmes, M. W. 184, 217

Hornschuh, M. 48, 49, 58
Houghton, H. A. G. 85, 205
Hug, J. 111
Hunt, A. S. 209
Hurtado, L. W. 45, 132, 182, 199, 214

Johnson, W. A. 28
Jongkind, D. 180, 204
Joosse, N. P. 78
Jorgensen, D. W. 73
Junack, K. 229

Kaiser, U. 57
Kalvesmaki, J. 146
Kasser, R. 222, 223, 231, 263
Keith, C. 1, 44, 116, 118, 120, 124
Kelber, W. H. 9
Kelhoffer, J. A. 8, 49, 111, 112, 199
Kenyon, F. G. 187, 201, 209, 212, 214, 215
King, K. 43, 132
King, M. 225
Kingsbury, J. D. 118
Kinzig, W. 199, 218, 221
Klijn, A. F. J. 85
Kline, L. L. 102, 134
Klinghardt, M. 152
Kloppenborg, J. S. 8, 20–29, 102, 139
Knox, J. 152
Knust, J. 3, 90
Koester, H. 8, 9, 19, 20, 134, 138, 154, 199
Köhler, W.-D. 8
Konstan, D. 28
Kruger, M. J. 10, 102, 147, 178, 182, 230

Lagrange, M.-J. 177
Lampe, P. 142
Landau, B. C. 203
Lange, C. 78
Larsen, M. D. C. 1, 4, 11, 115–19, 121–24, 128, 144, 198
Leloir, L. 77
Leonhard, C. 139
Lieu, J. M. 114, 152
Lightfoot, R. H. 11
Lindenlaub, J. 131, 132
Lorenz, P. E. 198

Luijendijk, A. 36, 45
Luomanen, P. 85, 88
Lyon, J. P. 110

MacMullen, R. 142
Manor, T. S. 66, 123, 124
Marcovich, M. 137
Marcus, J. 117
Markschies, C. 130, 142
Marmardji, A.-S. 78
Martens, P. W. 73
Martin, M. W. 227
Martin, V. 223, 231, *263*
Martini, C. M. 225
Mattila, S. L. 10, 18
McArthur, H. K. 20
Meier, J. P. 19
Ménard, J.-É. 20
Merell, J. 189
Metzger, B. 10, 101, 225
Mills, I. N. 103, 105
Min, K. S. 182, 195
Mitchell, M. 116, 144, 148
Mitchell, T. 116
Moessner, D. P. 118, 119, 123
Moles, J. 118
Moll, S. 169, 239
Montefiore, H. W. 20
Moore, G. F. 83
Mroczek, E. 4, 111
Müller, C. D. G. 49
Mutschler, B. 144, 148, 155

Nongbri, B. 189, 190, 193, 209, 210,
    223, 229, 231, 256, 264
Norelli, E. 122, 129

O'Connell, J. H. 124
Ong, W. J. 9
Orsini, P. 179, 180, 190, 201, 209, 210,
    223, 253–56, 263
Osborne, G. 117

Pardee, C. G. 184, 187, 195, 219, 227
Parisot, J. 78
Parker, D. C. 103
Parkhouse, S. 15, 203
Pastor, J. B. 155
Patterson, S. J. 20

Perrin, N. 77, 102, 110, 138
Petersen, S. 200, 201
Petersen, W. L. 77, 84, 91, 95, 105, 134
Philippart, G. 205
Phillips, C. A. 84, 88
Pistelli, E. 177, 179
Porter, S. E. 44, 204
Puig, A. 26

Quispel, G. 19, 84

Ranke, E. 78
Reed, A. Y. 144
Reynders, B. 155
Ricoeur, P. 4
Roberts, C. H. 187, 189, 190, 254, 256
Robinson, J. M. 203, 223
Rodriguez, J. A. 4, 59, 101, 136, 139,
    153, 170, 171, 198, 241
Rohrbach, P. 111
Rosenberger, V. 187
Roth, D. T. 109, 152
Rowe, C. K. 142, 239
Royse, J. 217, 225, 228, 263

Scheil, J.-V. 189, 193
Schmid, U. B. 77, 95, 239
Schmidt, C. 48, 49, 209
Schnabel, E. J. 99
Schrage, W. 20
Schramm, T. 20
Schröter, J. 3, 218
Schubart, W. 209
Sieber, J. H. 20
Sim, D. C. 118
Skarsaune, O. 134
Skeat, T. C. 189, 190, 195, 200, 203,
    211, 212, 219, 224, 230, 256
Smith, D. M. 120, 201
Smith, G. S. 203
Smith, W. A. 152
Snodgrass, K. 20
Souter, A. 212
Stählin, O. 156
Stanton, G. 1, 117, 118, 134, 190, 199,
    224, 230
Streeter, B. H. 183

Taylor, D. G. K. 103

Index of Modern Authors

Thompson, M. B. 9
Treu, K. 177, 179
Trobisch, D. 187, 200, 201
Tuckett, C. 8, 20, 200
Tune, E. W. 225
Turner, E. G. 178, 180, 224, 229, 263
Tyson, J. B. 152

Vinzent, M. 152

Walsh, R. F. 240

Wasserman, T. 3, 90, 182, 193, 195, 214, 229
Watson, F. 1–3, 15–18, 38, 48, 49, 56, 58, 60, 64–73, 90, 105, 108, 119, 123, 128, 135, 157, 158, 169, 203
Wessely, C. 177
Williams, P. J. 110

Zelyck, L. R. 8
Zervos, G. T. 90

Index of Subjects

2 Maccabees 51

Acts of Pilate 181, 206
Acts, and fourfold gospel 218
agrapha 56, 58, 66, 86, 159
Akhmim 222
Alexandria 173, 239
Alexandrian stylistic class (scribal hand) 253–56
Alexandrian textual tradition 194, 214, 215
allegorical interpretation 73, 145, 171
Ammonius of Alexandria 59, 101, 153, 171, 198
Andrew (disciple) 68
anonymity 108
Antioch 107
Antonine dynasty 240
Aphrahat of Persia 78, 87, 91
apocrypha, apocryphal 6, 16
Apocryphon of James 116, 130
ἀπομνημονεύματα, 77 134, 136
apostolic collaboration, in gospel authorship 132
apostolic personas, of gospel authors 111
Arabic Harmony (of Diatessaron) 77, 78, 82, 98
Aristophanes 51
artifact, artifactual 15
Asia Minor 9, 146, 148, 239
Aulus Gellius 28, 59, 163
Aurelius Leonides 203
Ausgangstext 81
author-consciousness, in second century Christianity 132
authorial self-awareness 116

B (see Codex Vaticanus)

Basilides 160
Beatitudes 98, 169
bibliographic knowledge 148, 149
bibliographic technology 101
Bodmer Miscellaneous Codex 220, 229
book trade, in Roman Empire 143
book, gospel as 115, 120, 148

Cana in Galilee, miracle in 78
canon, canonical 3, 36, 75
– noncanonical 3, 16
– proto-canonical 15
canonical/non-canonical divide 15
Carpocrates 161
Celsus 172
– knowledge of noncanonical gospels 173
– knowledge of proto-canonical gospels 172
Cerinthus 67, 74
cleansing of the Temple, episode 82, 95
Clement of Alexandria 76, 87, 108, 146, 156–75, 199, 203, 219
– and allegorical interpretation 166
– and handed-down gospels 157
– and noncanonical gospels 158
– exegesis of *GMark* 129
– reading habits 156
– *Stromateis* as miscellany 159, 162
– use of noncanonical traditions 67
Codex Alexandrinus 151, 231
Codex Bezae (D) 66, 90, 198, 214, 217
Codex Fuldensis 77, 78, 82, 98
Codex Sangermanensis, 85 89, 137
Codex Sinaiticus 181, 217, 256
Codex Vaticanus (B) 181, 193, 214, 217, 225, 231
Codex Vercellensis 85, 137, 181
Codex Washingtonianus (W) 181, 214, 217, 231

Index of Subjects

codices, four-gospel 240
Coherence-Based Genealogical Method 213
commentarii 115
Commentary on Matthew (Origen) 87
Commentary on Matthew (Jerome) 34
Commentary on the Gospel (Ephrem) 77, 83, 85, 95, 98
– Armenian recension 77
– Syriac recension 77
communal reading 139
competitive textuality 44, 120, 130
conflation 11, 12
congenial interactions 64, 76, 100, 113, 153, 237
covenant, old and new 160, 169

D (see Codex Bezae)
Demonstrations (of Aphrahat) 78
Diatessaron 77–111
– and canonical status 107
– and fourfold gospel 83, 110
– and harmonization 87
– and separated gospels 107, 108
– as gospel 106
– as New Testament 106
– dependence on fifth gospel 90
– dependence upon fifth gospel 92
– parallels with *GThomas* 91
– use of *GHebrews* 87, 88
– use of *GJohn* 78
– use of *GLuke* 79
– use of *GMark* 80
– use of *GMatthew* 79
– use of Jewish gospels 85
– use of Johannine sequence 95
– use of Markan sequence 94
– use of Matthean sequence 95
– use of noncanonical gospels 84
– use of *PJames* 90
Didascalia Apostolorum 107
Didymus the Blind 36, 67, 203
διήγησις 120, 128
Diodorus Siculus 119
Dionysius of Halicarnassus 119
discrepancies between gospels 96, 100
Dishna 223
Docetic Christology 58
Doctrine of Addai 89, 106, 107

Double Tradition 19, 145, 183, 198
Dura Europos 104

ἔκδοσις 182
Egypt 176, 181, 189, 239
elders, and early Christian tradition 128, 147
Ἐξήγησις 128
Ephesus 9, 107
Ephrem the Syrian 77, 87, 91, 106, 107
– as author of *Commentary* 78
– use of noncanonical traditions 67
Epiphanius 66, 104
epiphenomena, epiphenomenal 11, 58
Epistle to Flora 171
Epistula Apostolorum 48–76, 108, 116
– and fourfold gospel 48, 69
– and gospel epitome 51, 59, 60, 64
– and noncanonical traditions 56
– as consensus document 70, 75
– as gospel compendium 75
– correcting previous gospels 67
– date of composition 49
– dependence on *GJohn* 54
– dependence on *GLuke* 55
– dependence on *GMark* 55
– dependence on *GMatthew* 54
– Ethiopic translation 71, 72
– presupposing written gospel 74
epitomes 28, 51
εὐαγγελίζομαι 135
εὐαγγέλιον 103, 107, 135, 143, 199
Eusebian canons 61
Eusebius 124, 144
excerpting 28, 29, 59

f13, family 13 (textual tradition) 214
Farrer hypothesis 39
Farrer theory 18
Fayyum 181, 209
feeding of the five thousand 73
Form Criticism 8, 20
four living creatures 146, 147, 154

Galen 28, 51, 119
Gaul 146, 239
GEbionites 35, 84, 86, 104
GEgyptians 30, 33, 67, 159, 161
genealogy, Lukan 150, 163, 197

320 *Index of Subjects*

genealogy, Matthean 150, 163
GHebrews 85, 87, 159
– parallels in GThomas 33, 34, 35
– Thomasine dependence on 34, 35
GJohn (see Johannine)
– use of prior gospels 44
GJudas 108, 130–31
GLuke (see Lukan)
– criticism of prior gospels 119
– relationship to prior gospels 3, 108,
   118
GMark (see Markan)
– as a source for later gospels 17
– as middle term 127
– as published book 144
GMatthew (see Matthean)
– use of prior gospels 6, 108
GNazoraeans 85
Gnostic, Gnosticism 40
gospel authors
– and gospel titles 199
– concept of 116, 127
– congenial interactions 120, 149
– in New Testament Apocrypha 130
– in Papias 129
– in proto-canonical gospels 117
gospel combinations 2, 14
– dynamics 18, 19
– of canonical and noncanonical
   material 39
– of *GJohn* and Synoptics 64, 76, 96,
   222, 233, 236
– patterns and strategies 6
Gospel of the Savior 35
gospel orchestration 4, 104–05
gospel origins 14
gospel précis 75
gospel proliferation 17, 119
gospel titles 198, 228
– and collection consciousness 200
gospel writing 1, 6
– before Irenaeus 116, 126
gospel, fourfold 1–3, 13, 17
– in *EpAp* 65
– in P45 218
– in second century 65
– theology of 146, 153
GPeter 108, 131
– parallels in *Diatessaron* 89

Great Church 142
Gregory Aland 0171 176–88
– affinities to D 182
– codicology 177
– paleography 253
– paleography and date 179
– scribal collaboration 181
– scribal hands 181
Gregory Aland 032 210, 259
GThomas 17–47
– and Synoptic tradition 19, 40, 41
– as a layered text 26
– as gnomological anthology 23, 29, 41
– as sayings collection 41, 44
– Coptic translation 22, 27, 34
– date 19
– dependence on Synoptics 8, 21
– noncanonical parallels 29, 36
– subverting Synoptic tradition 45
– use of *GLuke* 20
– use of *GMatthew* 20

harmonization 18, 71
– in *2 Clement* 102
– in Clement of Alexandria 103, 164,
   165
– in *GEbionites* 104
– in Irenaeus 103
– in Justin Martyr 102, 138
– in *Pseudo-Clementine Homilies* 102
Heracleon 73, 130, 145
heretic, definition of 142
Hermopolis Magna 176, 188, 202, 209
heterodoxy 14
Hippocrates 119
horizon of expectation (scribal habits)
   187
horizontal reading 59
hypomnemata 29, 232

imagination, literary 43
Infancy Gospel of Thomas 116, 181, 206
– date 57
– parallels in *EpAp* 56, 65
inspiration, of scripture 108
interpolations in manuscript tradition 90
interpretive rewriting 1, 3, 6, 17, 18, 76
intertextuality 2, 3, 208
Irenaeus 12, 108, 142–56, 198, 199, 219

Index of Subjects

- and allegorical interpretation 73
- and fourfold gospel 1, 144
- and noncanonical traditions 57, 66
- biblical interpretation 146, 147
- coordinating Synoptics with *GJohn* 152
- Johannine influence 147
- knowledge of *Sondergut* 150
- theology of fourfold gospel 153
Italy 146

James the Just 38
Jerome 34, 102
Jesus tradition 23, 39, 108, 109, 129, 139
- and secondary orality 9
- and social memory 3
- noncanonical 37, 39
Jesus' baptism, episode 85
Jesus' temptation 80
Jewish gospel, relationship to *GMatthew* 84
Jewish gospels 86, 93
Jewish Scriptures 135, 142
Jewish Scriptures, authority of 73
Johannesschule 147
Johannine anomalies 68
Johannine colophon 79, 120
Johannine evangelist 68, 69, 120
Johannine feasts, in *Diatessaron* 96
Johannine idiom 54, 60, 113, 147
Johannine prologue 78
Johannine Thunderbolt 150
John the Baptist 38, 90
John, as gospel author 127, 144, 147
Josephus 119
Julius Cassianus 161
Justin Martyr 10, 134–40, 171
- and gospel authorship 135
- and gospel writing 138
- and noncanonical gospels 137
- and Valentinians 135
- influence on Tatian 86, 90, 105, 109
- redactional features in 134
- use of *GJohn* 134

καθεξῆς 119
kephalaia 151
kerygma 136

Koester's method 8
Koptos 181, 188, 202, 209

Latin Codex 563 205
Lazarus 79
LEMark 11, 66, 111–14
- and four-gospel collection 113
- and other endings of *GMark* 112
- and Western textual tradition 113
- as gospel orchestration 111
- as pericope interpolation 111
- date of composition 111
- in *Diatessaron* 82, 99
- in *EpAp* 64
- in Justin Martyr 112
- parallels with proto-canonical gospels 112
lemmata, in Ephrem's Commentary 78, 87, 88, 99
lemmatized commentary 231
Liège Harmony 84
logia 30, 41, 129
logia, noncanonical 29, 58
Logos 146
Lucian 119
Lukan evangelist 118
Lukan genealogy 95
Lukan prologue 118, 128
Lukan redaction, in *GThomas* 26, 29
Lukan style 39
Lukan terminology, in *GThomas* 20
Luke, as gospel author 75, 127, 144
Luxor 189
Lyons 142

macro-level stability, in textual tradition 184
manuscript combinations, of gospels 202
manuscripts, as artifacts 10
Marcion 2, 108, 114, 142, 152, 160, 161, 218, 239
Marcosians 57, 73, 171
Marcus (heretic) 171
Mark, as gospel author 127, 144
Markan intercalation 82
Markan outline 75
Markan priority 17, 20, 118
Markan redaction 145
- in *Diatessaron* 80

322

Index of Subjects

– in *EpAp* 55
Mary, Magdalene 38, 40, 67–69, 113
Mary, of Bethany 69
Matthean evangelist 71, 117
Matthean genealogy 95
Matthean redaction, in *GThomas* 26, 29
Matthean style 39
Matthean terminology, in *GThomas* 20
Matthew, as gospel author 38, 107, 127, 143
memoirs, apostolic 135
Menander 51
Merkavah tradition 154
methodology 7
– in Diatessaronic studies 77
– in Thomasine studies 20
miracle catena 60
mode, of combinations 10
– in Clement of Alexandria 163
– in *Diatessaron* 101
– in *EpAp* 58
– in GA 0171 182
– in *GThomas* 28
– in Justin Martyr 138
– in *LEMark* 112
– in P4+P64+67 194
– in P45 213
– in P75 225
– in Irenaeus 148
Muratorian Fragment 116, 122

Nag Hammadi 181
Nag Hammadi Codex II 21, 26
New Perspective (Diatessaronic studies) 77
New Philology 15
New Testament, as gospel and apostle 218
New Testament, as Scripture 221

Old Latin manuscript tradition 137
Old Syriac gospels 89, 105, 110
Origen 36, 87, 130, 163, 199, 203
– and fourfold gospel 107
– use of noncanonical traditions 67, 88
orthodoxy 14
Oxyrhynchus 181

P4 230

P4+P64+67 188–202
– and compositional unity 190
– and *ekthesis* 197
– and gospels titles 198
– and paragraphing 196
– and *paragraphoi* 197, 198
– and sense-unit divisions 196
– codicology 191
– date 189
– fiber orientation 191
– paleography 189, 256
– provenance 189
– textual affinity to B 194
P45 113, 208–22
– codicology 211
– date 209
– pagination 219
– paleography 209, 259
– physical features 210
– provenance 209
– textual affinities 213, 217
– use of readers' aids 213
P75 10, 214, 217, 222–34
– date 223
– Paleography 223, 262
– paragraphs 230
– provenance 222
– sense-unit divisions 230
– textual affinities 225, 226
Panopolis 222
Pantaenus 163
Papias of Hierapolis 76, 121–30, 171
– access to *GJohn* 125
– and four-gospel collection 125, 128
– fragments 121
– genre of work 128
– influence on Irenaeus 144, 146
– knowledge of *GJohn* 124
Parthenius 28
Paul (apostle) 75
Pauline corpus 76
Pericope Adulterae 11, 66, 226
pericope interpolation 4
Peter (disciple) 38, 40, 43, 68, 75
Philo of Alexandria 73, 146
Pliny the Younger 28
Plutarch 51
Polycarp of Smyrna 144–47
– and *GJohn* 145

Index of Subjects

– and Synoptic tradition 145
– as Irenaeus' anonymous elder 145
– influence on Irenaeus 144
Porphyry 119
post-resurrection appearance 60
post-resurrection dialogue 75
praeparatio evangelica 43
pre-Johannine forms 60, 69
Protevangelium of James 116, 132
proto-canonical gospels, as center of gravity 236
Ps.-Isocrates 119
Pseudo-Apollodorus 51
Pseudo-Ephrem 36
Ptolemy 171
publication of gospels 115
Pythagorean numerology 146

Q (gospel source) 6, 17, 20, 118

redactional criterion 8, 20
re-oralization 9, 10
resurrection, episode
– in *Diatessaron* 98
– in *EpAp* 64
Rich Young Ruler, episode 81, 87
Roman church library 148, 156
Rome 9, 77, 101, 107, 109, 114, 134, 148, 173, 239
round chancery (scribal hand) 253, 254

Salome 33, 38
scribal habits 2, 214
scribal harmonization 5, 11
– in GA 0171 184
– in P4+P64+67 195
– in P45 219
– in P75 226
scribal practices 90
scriptorium 182
Scripture 12
– as law, prophets, gospel, and apostles 160, 169
– gospels as 76, 145
second century
– authors 12
– Christian reading habitus 114
– gospel reception 8, 9
– reading practices 28, 101, 139

secondary orality 9, 10, 33
second-order discourse 14, 115, 129
sequence
– harmonization in *Diatessaron* 96
– in Clement's gospel reading 163
– in *Diatessaron* 88–98
– in *EpAp* 60
– in GA 0171 182
– in *GThomas* 37, 41
– in Irenaeus' gospel reading 152
– in P4+P64+67 194
– Matthean 92
severe style (scribal hand) 259
Simon (early heretic) 74
Smyrna 142
social memory 3, 15
solo performance, in gospel authorship 132
Sondergut 6, 19, 54, 57, 75, 78, 83, 92, 94, 108, 109, 112, 134, 150, 152, 172, 197
source identity 8
– in Clement of Alexandria 162–63
– in *Diatessaron* 78–94
– in *EpAp* 54–59
– in GA 0171 182–83
– in *GThomas* 19–37
– in Irenaeus 143–48
– in *LEMark* 112
– in P4+P64+67 194
– in P45 213–17
– in P75 224–26
source integrity 11
– in Clement of Alexandria 163–64
– in *Diatessaron* 94–101
– in *EpAp* 60–65
– in *GThomas* 37–43
– in Irenaeus 148–49
– in Justin Martyr 138
– in *LEMark* 112
– in P4+P64+67 194
– in P45 217–18
– in P75 226
source interactions 11
– in Clement of Alexandria 164
– in *Diatessaron* 94–101
– in *EpAp* 60–65
– in GA 0171 184–87
– in *GThomas* 37–43

324   *Index of Subjects*

– in *LEMark* 112
– in P45 218–21
– in P75 226–32
– in Papias 126–30
Stuttgart Harmony 84
symphony 146
synopsis 101
Synoptic tradition 19
Syria 109, 239
Syriac Sinaiticus 181

Tacitus 28
τάξις 119, 123, 128
Tatian 2, 10, 12, 76, 77, 109, 146, 149,
   161, 171, 198, 219
– and composition of *Diatessaron* 58
– compositional technique 83, 87, 91,
   108, 110
Tentyra 223
Tertullian 87, 160
tetraevangelium 143, 146, 155
textual authority 12
– in Clement of Alexandria 169–70
– in *Diatessaron* 105–10
– in *EpAp* 65–76
– in GA 0171 187
– in *GThomas* 43–45
– in Irenaeus 153–55
– in Justin Martyr 139
– in *LEMark* 113
– in P4+P64+67 201
– in P45 221
– in P75 232
– in Papias 128
textual distinctiveness 8
textual objects, gospels as 101

Textus Receptus 214
Theodore of Mopsuestia 124
Theodoret of Cyrus 107
Theophilus of Antioch 102, 108, 146
Thessalus of Tralles 119
Thomas (disciple) 43, 68
Thomasine independence 20
Thucydides 119
titloi 151
traditio legis 136
trans-local 9
Triple Tradition 19, 43, 75, 82, 172, 183,
   197

ὑπομνήματα 115, 127
Valentinians 73
– and allegorical interpretation 145
– and four-gospel collection 145
Valentinus 142, 146, 160–61, 171
verbatim agreement 36
verbatim agreement in *GThomas* 21, 22
vertical reading 59
Victor of Capua 77
Victorinus of Pettau 122
Vienna Palimpsest 181

W (see Codex Washingtonianus)
Western Aramaisms, in Diatessaron 92
Western interpolations 90
Western manuscript tradition 90, 113
Western non-interpolations 227
Western textual tradition 182, 214, 215
Wirkungsgeschichte 239

Zacharias Chrysopolitanus 84

Wissenschaftliche Untersuchungen zum Neuen Testament

Edited by Jörg Frey (Zürich)

Associate Editors:
Markus Bockmuehl (Oxford) · James A. Kelhoffer (Uppsala)
Tobias Nicklas (Regensburg) · Janet Spittler (Charlottesville, VA)
J. Ross Wagner (Durham, NC)

WUNT I is an international series dealing with the entire field of early Christianity and its Jewish and Graeco-Roman environment. Its historical-philological profile and interdisciplinary outlook, which its long-term editor Martin Hengel was instrumental in establishing, is maintained by an international team of editors representing a wide range of the traditions and themes of New Testament scholarship. The sole criteria for acceptance to the series are the scholarly quality and lasting merit of the work being submitted. Apart from the specialist monographs of experienced researchers, some of which may be habilitations, *WUNT I* features collections of essays by renowned scholars, source material collections and editions as well as conference proceedings in the form of a handbook on themes central to the discipline.

WUNT II complements the first series by offering a publishing platform in paperback for outstanding writing by up-and-coming young researchers. Dissertations and monographs are presented alongside innovative conference volumes on fundamental themes of New Testament research. Like Series I, it is marked by a historical-philological character and an international orientation that transcends exegetical schools and subject boundaries. The academic quality of Series II is overseen by the same team of editors.

WUNT I:
ISSN: 0512-1604
Suggested citation: WUNT I
All available volumes can be found at
www.mohrsiebeck.com/wunt1

WUNT II:
ISSN: 0340-9570
Suggested citation: WUNT II
All available volumes can be found
at *www.mohrsiebeck.com/wunt2*

Mohr Siebeck
www.mohrsiebeck.com